INTRODUCTION TO

CULTURAL ANTHROPOLOGY

Essays in the Scope and Methods

of the Science of Man

Introduction to

CULTURAL

ANTHROPOLOGY

Essays in the Scope and Methods
of the Science of Man

EDITED BY
JAMES A. CLIFTON
University of Kansas, Lawrence

HOUGHTON MIFFLIN COMPANY · BOSTON
NEW YORK · ATLANTA · GENEVA, ILL. · DALLAS · PALO ALTO

Acknowledgments

We thank the following publishers, copyright holders, and owners for permission to quote from, reproduce, or otherwise employ their materials in this volume:

The Peabody Museum of Harvard University, for permission to reproduce the Poro Society mask in several sections of this volume.

The Taylor Museum of the Colorado Springs Fine Arts Center and the Seattle Art Museum for the map of the northwest coast of North America adapted from Erna Gunther's *Indians of the Northwest Coast.*

The Thomas Burke Memorial Washington State Museum for the photograph of a Chilcat blanket.

The Archives of the Provincial Museum of British Columbia for the photographs of the Haida village and the Kwakiutl mask.

Columbia University Press for the map of African Negro sculpture adapted from Paul S. Wingert's *The Sculpture of Negro Africa.*

The Chicago Natural History Museum for the photograph of the Benin plaque.

McGraw-Hill Book Company and Faber and Faber Ltd. for quotations from Paolo Graziosi, *Paleolithic Art,* 1960, pp. 16, 17, and 46.

Mr. Robert Campbell for the photograph of the Fang figure from his private collection.

E. P. Dutton Company for the photograph of the Jabbaren Site frescoe from Henri Lhote's *The Search for the Tassili Frescoes.*

The University of Chicago Press for quotations and figures from Fred Eggan's *Social Anthropology of the North American Tribes.*

Macmillan Company for quotations and figures from G. P. Murdock's *Social Structure.*

The Society for Applied Anthropology and *Human Organization* for quotations and other materials from Gerald Berreman's *Behind Many Masks.*

The American Anthropology Association and *American Anthropologist* for use of J. L. Fischer's "Totemism on Truk and Ponape" in its entirety.

The University of Illinois Press for quotations from Julian Steward, *Theory of Culture Change,* 1955.

Indiana University Publications in Anthropology and Linguistics and *International Journal of American Linguistics,* for permission to quote extensively from Harold E. Driver, "An Integration of Functional, Evolutionary, and Historical Theory by Means of Correlations."

TO THE MEMORY OF

STUART CLEVELAND

Foreword

This book is intended to provide a basis for one semester college and university courses in cultural anthropology. It is also aimed at the general reader who wishes an introduction to the very large subject of what cultural anthropology, and cultural anthropologists, are about. It is therefore a textbook, and because all textbooks are to some extent pieces of legislation, based partially on tradition and precedent but departing sufficiently to justify their existence and acceptance, we must mention the logic of the book's plan.

We begin by assuming that it is extremely difficult for any one person to write a text which covers the full range of the scope and subject matter of the science. Not that this has not been done — nor that it is not being done, and often well — but sooner or later the author comes to a topic which is not near and dear to him, and so he loses the sense of excitement and authority he commands in his own areas of special knowledge. Briefly, cultural anthropology has in recent years expanded so much and become so diversified that its teaching demands an assembly of specialists who can speak and write from personal involvement in their own subject. We have here tried to present such an assembly.

There is nothing in itself novel about a book composed of chapters prepared by specialists; there are in cultural anthropology several precedents for this, so we add another ingredient. Most texts in cultural anthropology tend to emphasize fact and substance, in an effort to summarize what is known about *man,* the varieties of his behaviors, and the types of his cultures. As the reader will shortly become aware, cultural anthropology has facts enough to keep the collective memories of many readers well occupied for a good long while. The difficulty with any body of facts or summaries of substance and findings is that they too quickly go out of date, if they are not even more quickly forgotten. Moreover, too frequently missed is the critical point that any body of information has meaning and relevance only in terms of some principles of interpretation. Therefore, the contributors to this book were asked to pay as much attention to the *why* and *how* issues of cultural anthropology as to the question, *"What* do we know?" We hope the reader will shortly understand that cultural anthropology is like all sciences in that it is a set of processes and techniques for knowing. If he reads well, and develops any enthusiasm at all, he may even come to decide that he can do *this* kind of observation at least as well as the writer of one chapter, or find a better means of thinking about or an improved method of engaging *that* problem or issue discussed by the author of another. And so we will have satisfied our wish to encourage the introductory student to use his anthropology rather than to forget it.

Because of the growth in the subject matter of cultural anthropology, the increase in the number of specialties, and the variety of its methods and approaches, we have had to exercise more than a little selectivity in choosing topics for the chapters of this book. Chapters 2 through 10 are essentially subject matter or topical essays. Here questions of anthropological fact loom the largest, yet are caught up in questions of method and theory. After

Chapter 2 (which introduces the reader to the complex and partially independent subject of Language), Chapters 3 through 5 cover illustrative topics in the narrowly defined domain of cultural content or expressive culture. Space permitting, we might have added or substituted here essays on the comparative study of music, drama, or other similar topics.

Chapter 6, in contrast, introduces the subject of social organization and social structure, and Chapters 7 through 10 carry through with more specific treatments of issues which are sometimes clearly within the area of social organization or which, as with religion and values, unavoidably spill over into various dimensions of the total way of life of a people.

Chapter 11 deals with the issue of the study of processes of cultural change, both on a minute or micro-temporal scale, and in terms of the evolution of types of cultural systems. Chapters 12 and 13 next turn to an area in which cultural anthropology and psychology overlap, the issue of the comparative study of various dimensions of the human psyche. Chapters 14 through 17, on the other hand, are oriented to explicit discussions of the major methods and techniques employed by cultural anthropologists as they go about studying one aspect or another of the human condition. Chapter 18 brings us full circle to an examination of anthropological ideas about the relationships between types of cultural systems and the geographic-ecological settings in which they occur.

Each author was encouraged to be just as forthright and provocative in his presentations as he saw fit. This was intended to counter another problem with introductory texts, which tend to sweep the loose ends of doubt and controversy under the rug of "References Cited." Because the mood of cultural anthropology is largely, if not entirely, that of science, and because the dominant attitude of science is that of inquiring scepticism, we believed that every author should state, critically examine, and defend or reject whatever points of view he wished. Thus we may anticipate the comments of a reviewer of this book and frankly admit that the net result is a somewhat disjointed presentation of the whole of cultural anthropology. But it happens that this is precisely one of the features of the science we are here examining. It happens to be the case that what one anthropologist says and does is not always received blankly and automatically by others. It is part of the nature of science for scientists to question and appraise other scientists. The presentation of controversy is little more than evidence for the fact that cultural anthropology is a set of processes, and that it is growing. And we wanted the reader to view contemporary cultural anthropology not as the conveniently summarized remains of past efforts, but as the edge of improved future understanding.

In this volume we use the word "culture," and see the scope of cultural anthropology, in the broadest fashion. What we mean by the scope of cultural anthropology is all that is left over after we deduct the commonly shared biological substratum of humankind. In this sense, there are several near synonyms for this title. "Ethnology" (in a different sense than we intend in Chapters 15 and 16), is roughly synonymous except that it generally excludes archaeological studies of the prehistoric development of cultures. Moreover, as the word is used in Britain and the United States, ethnology is sometimes identified with only *one* mode of interpreting and accounting for cultural differences, the ideas of the historicist school of thought. We see historical interpretations as only one of several modes of thought in cultural anthropology. Similarly, "social anthropology" comes close to the status of a synonym, except that social anthropologists tend to stress the primacy of sociological facts and to distinguish and set aside a narrowly defined cultural domain. Again, we see this as just one of several alternative approaches in cultural anthropology.

We have omitted a chapter on archaeology in the interests of economy, and because, as the subject is usually taught in the United States, the topic is placed largely in a separate semester where it is offered in conjunction with an introduction to the ideas and subject matter of physical anthropology. The other obvious omissions we will not defend, except to note that it is impossible to prepare one work containing a chapter each on all topical specialities in cultural anthropology and come up with less than an encyclopedia. There is one important exception to this, the omission of a chapter on the vital subject of cultural evolution, written and defended by a staunch advocate of the point of view. We admit that no one writes better about this subject than an evolutionist himself, and that the several too brief discussions of this important topic spotted throughout various chapters of this book are not necessarily satisfactory, but unfortunately no evolutionist was available for this volume. Perhaps another time and another edition.

Finally, the editor wishes to express his appreciation to the many unnamed persons and friends who contributed advice and suggestions over the several years during which this book was being prepared. He is especially grateful to his wife, Faye Clifton, who read manuscript with the readers' welfare in mind. And to each contributor he expresses thanks which are difficult to put into words, since each voluntarily took time away from the many tasks which occupy the lives of anthropologists to prepare a presentation of their ideas about a subject important to them. This is, of course, their book. And then, to Robert C. Rooney and Nancy G. Bergman of Houghton Mifflin Company many inadequate thanks for having assumed an unusually large share of what should, in the normal course of things, have been this editor's responsibility. But the normal course of things for an anthropologist, of course, is to be gone elsewhere and sometimes out of touch in critical final moments. Such defects as this book exhibits are, nonetheless, the full responsibility of the editor.

The idea for this text, and much of the form of its organization, was developed in company with the late Stuart Cleveland, College Editor of Houghton Mifflin. Stuart offered not only encouragement and advice, but the wise counsel of a truly scholarly man. His very sudden and quite unexpected death deleted a good friend to many, and a true humanist. If this book has any merit, it is thus rightfully offered in his memory.

JAMES A. CLIFTON

Santiago de Chile

Contents

xi

INTRODUCTION TO

CULTURAL ANTHROPOLOGY

Essays in the Scope and Methods

of the Science of Man

CHAPTER **I** is intended as a very brief introduction to cultural anthropology, hence to the remaining chapters of the book, which do the same job in a more extended, more detailed fashion. Here, some of the characteristics of the science, the scope of its subject matter, some assumptions on which it proceeds, and its relationships to other disciplines are discussed. Since one major objective of cultural anthropology has been to gather, interpret, and systematize comprehensive knowledge about the varieties of human behavior, some of the major intellectual tools used are discussed. Such technical ideas as custom, tradition, trait, pattern, and symbol, for example, are thus seen as anthropological means of imposing order on the many observable differences which mark communities and societies. Similarly, the deployment of cultural anthropologists, sometimes as natural historians who try to remain true to the task of accurate description and assessment of the exotic custom or the unique configuration, sometimes as comparativists who seek ordered general knowledge, is recognized as the anthropological expression of two modes of scientific procedure, the "ideographic" and the "nomethetic." Finally, some definitions of culture are discussed and viewed as a continuing effort to formulate a complex idea which, in the most general way possible, summarizes all we know about man's dependency upon other than biologically conditioned modes of adaptation to his environments.

THE AUTHOR AND EDITOR is from Chicago, and after finishing his undergraduate work at the University of Chicago, studied at San Francisco State College. He then took his Ph.D. in anthropology at the University of Oregon. He has taught at the Universities of Oregon and Colorado, and is now Associate Professor of Anthropology at the University of Kansas, where he supervises the training program in applied anthropology. His research interests have included studies of community organization and cultural change, social conflict and factionalism, and religion in three contemporary North American Indian groups, the Klamath, Ute, and Potawatomi. He has recently returned to the United States after studying some processes of economic and social development in rural and urban parts of modern Chile.

I

Cultural Anthropology:

Aspirations and Approaches

JAMES A. CLIFTON

University of Kansas

INTRODUCTION

Cultural anthropology is an area of inquiry concerned with the varieties of human behavior. As a field of study, it describes, interprets, accounts for, or explains human behavior, thus generating valid general knowledge. Its dominant mood is that of science, and as scientists, cultural anthropologists are intently involved in the continuing process of creating and testing technical ideas, fashioning methods for objective description of observed facts, deriving firmly demonstrated generalizations, and building general schemes of ideas, or theory.

In addition, cultural anthropology has always been characterized by a minor theme of humanistic inquiry, which encourages speculation about the nature, meaning, and future of man. Thus some cultural anthropologists reach for a kind of understanding that (to some minds) overreaches the strictly scientific sense. Moreover, some practitioners have given serious attention to the issue of the use of anthropological knowledge for other than purely scholarly purposes, for example, within public affairs, in deciding questions of policy and development for dependent or colonial peoples.

The fact that cultural anthropology is only one of many disciplines which attempt to confront and comprehend the nature of human behavior immediately raises several questions. And the fact that it is simultaneously one major branch of its parent science — anthropology — points the way to other issues for discussion. For example, what does cultural anthropology hope to accomplish, and what does it promise that other social science disciplines do not? How can a separate science of man be justified when there are so many alternative specialized approaches, each closely focused on this or

3

that fragment of the human condition? What is the scope of interests expressed by cultural anthropologists? What is the subject matter of the field? The key ideas? And the types of questions it asks about the nature of man?

Unfortunately, the label "cultural anthropology" does not provide even a partially satisfactory answer. The qualifying word "cultural" has long since departed from its original meaning, that which is most civilized, improved, or refined. And in much of his working life, the cultural anthropologist deals with aspects of human behavior which by no stretch of the imagination could be considered refined, even though he does not (in his professional capacity at least) use the attitude and value judgment which ranks men or their works in terms of "civilized" attainments.

However, nearly every adult with a secondary school education in the English-speaking world can make some such statement as "That's the way they do things in their culture," which reflects some grasp of the core anthropological meaning of a learned pattern of thinking, believing, and acting, and some understanding of the existence and variability of human behavioral patterns. But this recognition of cultural differences is not usually accompanied by systematic appreciation of the complete reality and force of such differences, much less by an understanding of their causes and consequences. As "culture" has re-entered the popular English vocabulary as a folk idea shared by educated Europeans and Americans, it has lost much of its scientific weight. Cultural anthropologists must share some blame for this, because rather than coin new and more specific words for newly invented or discovered bits of meaning, they have preferred to retain the one term, defined in many different, generally overlapping senses. In fact, John W. Bennett once commented to the effect that "Culture has become nothing

more than an expressive symbol standing for the solidarity of anthropologists." [1]

If there are a number of different senses of the word "culture," it follows that "cultural anthropology" is likely to mean several different things. Occasionally one hears someone (usually a nonanthropologist) speak of the "anthropology" or the "cultural anthropology" of a people or a community, but the area of reference is usually too inspecific and fluctuating to mean much to the listener. This is partly due to the great range of topics — the vast territory of content — which is cultural anthropology's subject matter. This subject matter is not one, or even several neatly bounded topical subdivisions of the total way of life of a few societies or types of societies; ideally, it is many (if not all) aspects of the cultures of most (if not yet all) societies. The science is thus broadly inclusive in its content, and today it is also largely nonrestrictive as to the kinds of societies it elects to study. A cultural anthropologist is now as apt to be found researching in metropolitan Tokyo, or with the Systems Development Corporation, or in a mental hospital in Lima (Ohio *or* Peru), or in a peasant community in Switzerland, as among a technologically primitive band of Australian hunters.[2]

SUBJECT MATTER AND SCOPE

Thus cultural anthropology is something like the philosopher's elephant; it has a

[1] For those interested in the subtleties of the matter, Bennett's judgment uses the definition of culture advanced by two sociologists, T. Parsons and Edward Shils, which makes the word refer mainly to the great expressive symbols characteristic of a social institution or a system of social action (see Kroeber and Kluckhohn 1963: 226–269).

[2] Cultural anthropologists even appear in the pages of the less-than-great world literature, where, doubling as part-time secret agents, they attempt to confuse the opposition by claiming to be studying something called culture-shock among the wives of overseas American military men (Sheldon 1965).

fluctuating popular image which depends upon which portion of the creature has been touched. And in terms of the global inclusiveness of those aspects of human behavior it studies, cultural anthropology is sharply contrasted to all other social sciences and humanistic disciplines. Its holistic, inclusive approach to an understanding of man does not come to a full stop after language, or art, or technology, or social organization, or education; it incorporates each under one scientific roof.

This feature is as old as the science itself; it was proposed very early in the history of the discipline by Edward B. Tylor as one of the first technical definitions of the idea of culture. He wrote: "Culture, or civilization . . . is that complex whole which includes knowledge, belief, art, morals, custom and any other capabilities and habits acquired by man as a member of society" (1871: reprinted 1958). Here, in effect, he enumerated the kinds of things anthropologists *should* study — Tylor was, as Kroeber and Kluckhohn have commented, ". . . deliberately establishing a science by defining its subject matter" (1963: 295).

Tylor's proposal suggested the direction cultural anthropology might take, because any enumeration of the problems to be studied by a science is partly arbitrary, and, since it is limited by the state of knowledge at the time, necessarily incomplete. Such traditionally defined subject matter areas as social organization and art are continually being added to by the definition and inclusion of new areas as our knowledge of man increases.

Aspect-Centered Specialties

To say that cultural anthropology is concerned with all these matters is not to say that every individual anthropologist has equally catholic concerns of competencies. Like all scientists and scholars facing the enormous growth of knowledge during the twentieth century, they have had to specialize to achieve mastery. One obvious way to do so is to concentrate on one, or a few, subject-matter subdivisions, in an attempt to break the total range of human behavior into meaningful and manageable segments. Figure 1-1 gives a partial listing of topical, or aspect-centered, specialities in cultural anthropology. All such listings are of course tentative and incomplete, and there is no systematic consideration of the relative importance or functional connection of one to another. But the entries shown will suggest the range of interests.

This list sets and classifies the range of types of behaviors found widespread in many (if not all) human communities. There are two important points to remember about such a list. First, anthropology insists that each topical subdivision be understood as part of the whole; hence each subdivision refers an evaluation of an art, or the technology, of a people to other aspects of their way of life, social organization, value system, or even their attributes of basic personality.

Second, whatever the topical subdivision may be that engages his attention, the anthropologist as specialist maintains the essential comparative perspective. He compares and contrasts the family and kinship systems of a society with those of other peoples, so as to provide both improved understanding of the studied community and a contribution to an analytic classification, to a series of types, and to an approximation of more general knowledge of kinship *systems*.

An important problem connected with such specialization is that of defining the topic to start with. Definitions of areas such as religion or economics, which are part of the anthropologist's own culture, are generally too restricted to be of much value. Moreover, many such definitions are nonempirical and normative — they are the sort that do not involve deliberate and systematic

Fundamental Cultural Values and Orientations
Systems of Beliefs about Man and Natural Phenomena
Nature and Use of Exact and Pragmatic Knowledge
Language and Speech Behavior
Systems of Writing and Other Memory Aids
Content, Style, and Use of Literature — Oral and Otherwise
Visual Arts, Crafts, and Ornamentation
Drama and Ritual — Public and Private
Patterns of Recreation and Entertainment
Clothing and Decoration of the Body
Architectural Styles and Types of Buildings
Types and Consumption of Foods and Beverages
Tools and Technical Skills
Concepts and Customs Concerning Property
The Marketing and Exchange of Commodities and Gifts
Utilization of Land and Settlement Patterns
Demographic Characteristics of Population
Social Stratification — By Age, Sex, Economic Class, or Otherwise
Kinds of Informal Groups and Styles of Interpersonal Relations
Nature and Functioning of Formal Organizations
Marriage Customs and Family Types
Kinship Terms, Relationships, Groups, and Systems: Real and Fictive
Kinds and Functions of Communities and Territorial Organizations
The Organization of Government and Political Behavior
Ethical Beliefs, Norms, Social Control, and Law Ways
Military Organization and the Nature and Conduct of War
Techniques of Socialization and Nature of Education
Definition and Handling of the Stages of the Individual Life Career
Diagnosis, Treatment, and Response to Disease
Religion and the Supernatural

FIGURE 1-1

Topical Specialties in Cultural Anthropology

examination of observed facts, they state what *should* be the case, and are thus bound up with issues of personal philosophy and public policy. Further, such definitions are usually evaluative, that is, charged with a series of emotion-laden assumptions about what is better (hence worthy of scholarly attention) or worse (hence appropriately ignored).

An anthropologist may begin with an appreciation of the kinds of definitions and theories of, say, economics, current in his own society, and aim to extend their general utility and validity, or he may address himself to a quite fresh and unclarified topic. Most anthropologists have had many experiences similar to that of John Fischer, who reports in Chapter 15 how he had to be stung by a centipede on Truk before he became aware of the existence of special medicines owned by a few individuals in this culture, and thus of the pattern of individual curing associated with totemism. In this particular instance, Fischer began with an explicit technical definition of "clan," which turned on the presence of the special identification of a group with a particular species or natural phenomena (i.e., the totem). When it did not quite fit the facts, he had to extend and qualify the original definition.

Therefore anthropologists begin by recognizing that, in themselves, definitions do not accomplish very much, but they are a necessary tool for inquiry. They have a coercive force, useful insofar as it orients attention and promotes ordering and classification, but this force can lead to misperception and error. Definitions must therefore be accepted as fragile, changeable things, subject to a continuing cycle of preliminary statement and re-examination against cross-cultural evidence.

A number of obvious difficulties associated with this topical specialization suggest that this approach is not sufficient unto itself as a means of understanding the varieties of human behavior. It is essentially a descriptive tactic, and does not provide a framework of ideas or principles for interpreting and accounting for, say, the distribution of different types of economics or art forms among the societies of the world. It provides no way of understanding the articulation of one aspect of culture with others. And, perhaps more important, it assigns no scale of priorities to or means of understanding the relative importance of language as against technology as against social organization.

Problem-Centered Specialties

A second method of breaking down the whole of culture — the varieties of learned, socially transmitted, and patterned human behavior — into manageable subspecialities does partially resolve some of these problems. This breakdown is made in terms of problem areas, special fields with theoretical or methodological relevance. The result is a series of larger entities, the recognizable specialties of contemporary cultural anthropology. One possible listing is given in Figure 1-2.

This listing includes frequently mentioned problem-centered special fields in cultural anthropology. These illustrate the fact that cultural anthropology treats man and the varieties of his behavior in several dimensions: in terms of history, the sequence of particular cultural events and developments; in terms of recurrent and regular sequences of sociocultural processes; in terms of his capacity for symbolization and speech; in terms of the social and culturally expressive aspects of his life; and in terms of human psychological functioning, relationships to the physical environment, and the consequences of his own biological nature. Applied anthropology, in turn, represents the actual or potential uses of knowledge of these kinds.

Some brief comment is needed on this listing to clarify its organization and purposes. First, the fields listed frequently overlap, they are not mutually exclusive. For example, it is easier to draw a verbal distinction between archaeology and ethnohistory than it is to maintain one in practice. At times archaeologists work with historically documented sites, say, a frontier fort, and their activities overlap those of the ethnohistorian. And when an archaeologist attempts to describe a prehistoric community at one stage in its development, he is in effect

Archaeology / or Prehistory

Ethnohistory / or Culture History

Ethnography / or Descriptive Ethnology

Ethnology / or Comparative Ethnology

Cultural Dynamics / or Micro-temporal Evolution

Cultural Evolution / or Macro-temporal Cultural Processes

Anthropological Linguistics / or Linguistics

Ethnopsychology / or Psychological Anthropology

Social Anthropology / or Comparative Sociology

Cultural Anthropology / or the Ethnology of Expressive Culture

Cultural Ecology / or Human Geography

Ethological Anthropology / or Biosocial Anthropology

Applied Anthropology / or Action Anthropology

FIGURE 1-2

Problem-Centered Specialties in Cultural Anthropology

doing a piece of ethnography under special and more difficult conditions.

Second, as was the case with the aspect-centered specialties shown in Figure 1-1, the problem-centered specialties given in Figure 1-2 are by no means complete. They are only the names of special problem areas which cultural anthropologists frequently attach to their work. The list could be greatly extended. For instance, applied anthropology could easily be divided into medical anthropology, psychiatric anthropology, administrative anthropology, action anthropology, space anthropology, educational anthropology, and military anthropology.

But more important, this list is not drawn up according to any coherent overall plan or set of criteria. For instance, the first two specialties, archaeology and ethnohistory, study cultural phenomena along the dimension of time. Because archaeologists elect to deal with the ways of life of peoples in the more or less remote past, their data consists not of observations of behavior, but of the products and results of behavior, the sometimes exceedingly scanty traces of the more

tangible and least perishable material products of human ingenuity. Therefore they require special research techniques and conceptual tools which may have little application to other anthropological specialties. And the archaeologist must be also a part-time surveyor or geologist, occasional climatologist, and temporary botanist and zoologist.

Similarly, ethnography names a major methodological tactic in cultural anthropology, the cross-sectional case study approach to the study of (usually) living societies. While ethnography takes cultural units, tribes or nations, or communities, one at a time, ethnology (as understood in this context) is another important methodological tactic, consisting of formal and deliberate comparisons of aspects of the cultures of a sample of several or many cultural units, with the goal of testing hypotheses and establishing generalizations. Both ethnographer and ethnologist (who may of course be the same person on separate occasions) reflect their own special interests by commanding extensive knowledge in such fields as law, or sociology, or technology. In addition, they must play jack-of-all-trades if they set upon the full ethnographic task of preparing a complete description of the traditions and customary behaviors of a society. And these two methodological specialties require skills and conceptual tools which may be of little use to the archaeologist or linguist.

The division between the specialties of anthropological linguistics, psychological anthropology, social anthropology, and (recollect that the same words may have several different meanings) cultural anthropology is made in terms somewhat different from those which yield archaeology and cultural evolution. To some degree these are subject-matter specialties derived in a topical fashion like those discussed earlier, but they differ. Linguistics exists both within anthropology and without, as a well established science in its own right. This results from the somewhat autonomous status of language with respect to other aspects of culture, from the ease with which language can be studied quite separately from other matters, and from the special importance of language for the conduct, transmission, and stabilization of tradition and customary forms of behavior. Even more than for other fields of cultural anthropology, the scientific study of language behavior in man has required the development of highly formalized methods for the study of pattern and structure, methods which some cultural anthropologists feel can be usefully transferred and applied to the study of social life and systems of knowledge.

The distinction between social and cultural anthropology is made so as to align the former (as the comparative study of the sociology of peoples) with inquiry into the content and nature of social roles, social relationships and institutions, the nature of social structure, and the like. Shown next to social anthropology here, cultural anthropology has a much narrower and more specific

sense than used generally in this volume. Here it refers to the study of the learned and patterned *content* and *pattern* of beliefs, ideas, values, and traits, patterns which may possibly be specific to one society, or patterns which may be found distributed among many societies.

Cultural ecology, or perhaps as Professors Vayda and Rappaport suggest, noncultural ecology (see Chapter 18), studies the relationships between societies and the physical-biological environments in which they exist. It attempts to deal with several kinds of phenomena which need explanation — for example, the distribution of different types of subsistence economies, or the consequences of a particular type of such economy for other aspects of the culture.

These problem-centered specialties in effect state the grand variables of cultural anthropology. Man and the varieties of his behavior are thus treated in terms of language, culture, society, environment, human biology, and psychology. But only about four of the specialties listed in Figure 1-2 are traditionally mentioned as the accepted subdisciplines of the science: archaeology, linguistics, social anthropology, and cultural anthropology (in the special, restricted sense). The identification and acceptance of scientific specialties, and the consequent division of scholarly labor, seem to ebb and flow with the tides of convenience.

Although as Professor Price-Williams indicates in Chapter 12, ethnopsychology or psychological anthropology has a considerable history of contribution to anthropology, the field is just beginning to be acceptable to a more conservative generation of social anthropologists. Moreover, cultural evolution, long subject to serious doubts and, in fact, once nearly excluded from serious consideration, now seems once more to be coming into its own. And although they have their own professional organizations and regular publications, applied anthropology and ethnohistory rarely receive mention as identifiable subdisciplines.

The many different specialties reflect the range and complexity of the subject matter, whereas the fact that cultural anthropologists approach the study of human behavior in many ways guarantees that few important possibilities are excluded. In anthropology, as in all sciences, specialization is a necessary function of the rapid growth of knowledge. Few individuals can hope to assimilate, master, and then contribute to knowledge in more than a few of the several special branches of cultural anthropology. Still, no one is simply an ethnohistorian or an anthropological linguist. The ecologist addresses himself to social anthropologists and archaeologists and is heard. The specialist in art or technology draws from ethnopsychology and social anthropology. Further, all are trained basically as anthropologists, and each individual scientist during the course of his career may himself contribute to a number of particular problem areas. Too, at least in the United States and other parts of the Americas, there is the idea of and the basic structure for a single unitary science of man, which brings together anthropologists of many persuasions, and fosters continuing communication. It is quite well understood that many critical anthropological problems — such as the reconstruction of a sequence of cultural developments in one region — cannot be resolved without the cooperation of a number of specialists, each of whom can contribute ideas and methods not fully controlled by every other. All these factors prevent the tendency to and need for specialization from slipping into a situation in which a sprawling set of disconnected professional segments are separated and insulated from one another by barriers of scholarly silence. Cultural anthropology, with its multifaceted perspective on the nature of man, is by nature interdisciplinary.

As we look, then, at the inner characteristics of the field, we find that cultural anthropology is a scholarly discipline embracing all that is human, everywhere, throughout time (White 1965). With other social and behavioral science disciplines, cultural anthropology assumes — and then proceeds to demonstrate the validity of the assumption — that human behavior, and systems of value, belief, and custom built thereupon are part of nature, that they are determined by knowable causes, and that they are susceptible to objective study.[3] Cultural anthropology's distinctive bent is the cross-cultural approach, to concentrate attention on men who live in other societies and who are driven by different kinds of ideas and beliefs. This does not mean that cultural anthropologists are disinterested in the high civilizations of the Western world or of the East. They look outward because the little communities of the Pacific world or the complex traditional states of West Africa are (or at least once were) there, representing the universe of cultural experiments and various parts of the human condition, hence are worthy of study and understanding.

METHODS AND TECHNIQUES

Knowledge obtained and methods perfected via the comparative or cross-cultural approach can often enough be used in studies of the world's industrial nation-states. The so-called community study method in contemporary social science, for instance, developed with a large infusion of anthropological research techniques. Then,

[3] A good many cultural anthropologists reared in the humanistic tradition would object to this statement, while most would agree that to be objective and scientific about man means something quite different from the pointer-reading objectivity of the so-called hard sciences. Read Maquet's 1964 essay for some wise insights into this issue, and see Chapter 14 for an extended discussion of the nature of anthropological objectivity in ethnographic research.

too, it is sometimes possible to use a smaller and more easily studied society as a kind of model for the understanding of a larger and a more complex one. Studies of the sort of factional conflicts which develop in small societies subject to intensive outside influence might, for example, conceivably help illuminate some of the events of recent years in the Dominican Republic and South Viet Nam (French 1962; Clifton 1965b).

But these are indirect consequences, and considering the very extensive direct interest of many contemporary cultural anthropologists in the complex cultures of contemporary nations, it is neither sufficient nor accurate to say that cultural anthropology is exclusively or even largely preoccupied with the smaller, supposedly stable, culturally homogeneous communities which make up what is called the primitive or pre-literate world. Cultural anthropology got its start as a separate discipline by assuming responsibility for studying and recording the details of the life ways of such peoples. This was, and sometimes still is, seen as a kind of rescue operation, since the cultures of these technologically primitive peoples were undergoing massive changes and because sometimes the populations themselves were threatened with extinction by the rapid expansion of the nations of Europe (Mead and Bunzel 1960). This responsibility for the study of the simpler societies is one which anthropology has never much shared with other disciplines, and it is one which is not yet by any means fully discharged. The primitive world continues to belong to anthropology, but not anthropology to the primitive world.

Nevertheless, whether living in an isolated paleotechnic society of horticulturists in the Central Highlands of New Guinea, or in a commercial-industrial suburb of modern Mexico City, cultural anthropologists prefer relatively small units of study. Although as they began to expand their interests to include the study of complex modern culture, a few intrepid explorers attempted to grasp the whole that is Japan, or Brazil, or the United States, most cultural anthropologists working with modern societies continue to prefer a lesser, more manageable unit of study. They focus on a definable part of the whole society, an entire peasant community, for example, or an urban slum neighborhood, perhaps even a sample of families representative of a subculture, or a neatly bounded institution such as a hospital or a factory.

By and large this has involved transferring into the study of complex cultures certain study methods and forms of thought polished in the little primitive community (Mead and Metraux 1953). Some of these techniques are not easily transferred, of course. For instance, the method of participant observation, which involves assuming at least a few of the traditionally defined roles in the study community — one is adopted as a grandson or accepted as a fellow herder of reindeer — just does not work in some modern institutions in which statuses and roles are professionalized and strictly controlled.[4] But no one should expect any scientific technique to be good for all scientific purposes, hence anthropologists have long been moving to develop new ideas and methods applicable to problems of study encountered in complex societies (Banton, ed. 1966a; Eisenstadt 1961).

One additional important fact about the preference for the study of a smaller sociocultural whole should be mentioned. While thinking of the community as kind of natural unit to be studied and understood in its own

---

[4] I am indebted to Dr. Robert Bechtel, a social psychologist, for this insight. Dr. Bechtel's specific reference was to research in mental hospitals, where no outside scientist can hope to be accepted as a temporary psychiatrist, and where the assumption of such positions as ward attendant or patient, although perhaps temporarily tenable, imposes severe restrictions on the observer's work.

right, anthropologists also consider that each such community is also a special kind of *sample* of one or more larger universes (Arensberg 1961). Thus a report on a Quechua-speaking peasant community in the Peruvian Andes tells us a very great deal about that community at one point in its history, and it therefore helps in understanding that community's past and forecasting its future. But this same report tells us something about the larger universe of Quechua-speaking Indian communities, something more about peasant communities, something about communities that have adopted and transformed an alien religion, something about the adaptation of human groups to extremely harsh physical and social environments, something about modern Peru and Latin America, hence something about man. It may even tell us something about ourselves, since whereas cultural anthropologists once insisted upon and were successful in placing alien cultures in the same context as our own, as legitimate and worthy objects of study, they now put parts of our own culture into the same context as alien ones, and insist on making legitimate comparisons (Spindler, ed. 1963). Here, if there is an implicit directive which anthropologists follow, it may well be, as John Rowe suggests, this: to understand ourselves we need first to understand others (Rowe 1965: 1).

In concentrating their energies on the comparative and contrastive study of social life, cultural anthropologists are seldom concerned with the precise measurement and description of isolated, microscopic bits of human behavior. Whereas the psychologist or the sociologist, say, ordinarily attempts to assess fluctuations and co-variation among a very few pre-selected variables studied under experimental or quasi-experimental conditions, the cultural anthropologist most frequently observes and records rather larger segments of naturally occurring behavior directly in their native context. And quite often, as is particularly true of archaeology, the cultural anthropologist does not deal directly with behavior at all. Sometimes he records and analyzes the products of human activity, for example, sampling a collection of art works or folk tales, which can profitably be described and analyzed in their own right. Sometimes his observations are quite indirect, as when he listens to informants narrate the details or characteristic form of a ritual he himself may not witness. Throughout, whether obtained first hand or indirectly, his descriptions are loaded with details of content, meaning, style, and pattern — expressions of social life which are not readily treated in quantitative terms. The aim of such observation is to go beyond what is inconstant, widely variable, fleeting, or idiosyncratic in the life of a community to what is central, regularly recurrent, or typical. The anthropologist does this, in part, by using a number of fundamental summarizing concepts. These technical ideas are put to work in one or another of the several major research strategies used in cultural anthropology, of which we will discuss two, ethnography and ethnology, in this chapter.[5]

Ethnography approaches the study of man via an inductive building up of a series of well described cases. While ethnography is implicitly comparative, the methods of ethnology are explicitly, deliberately, and formally so, for here the cultural anthropologist draws together a number of cases from existing ethnographic reports, and seeks correlations or co-variation in several aspects of the cultures, to test pre-set hypotheses, perhaps to infer lines of causation, and, ultimately, to state general laws. But both the descriptive ethnographic strategy and the formal comparative work of ethnology are atemporal, that is, they lack (if not delib-

[5] A much more extended discussion of ethnography, several varieties of ethnology, and ethnohistory is given in Chapters 14 through 17.

erately ignore) the dimension of time. They do not deal with sequences of events along the continuum of history, or with long- or short-term processes of cultural change and evolution.

CULTURAL ANTHROPOLOGY AS NATURAL HISTORY

To obtain general knowledge of man's behavior requires, first, detailed information about the customs and habits of men in particular societies throughout the world. Tylor's definition of the scope of cultural anthropology, accepted and refined by several generations of anthropologists, has thus required adoption of the strategy of ethnography. While the methods of ethnography are more fully described by Professor Berreman in Chapter 14, we must now consider some of its assumptions and implications. What kind of science is this? What are the important technical ideas and schools of thought associated with it? And, what does it contribute to comparative knowledge of man?

As indicated earlier, ethnography is sometimes considered a special field of cultural anthropology, but it is probably more informative and precise to recognize it as one important set of methods, one perspective on the nature and variety of human behavior. As an ethnographer, the cultural anthropologist comports himself as a kind of natural historian, in a fashion somewhat similar to that of the field biologist or geologist. Here we must note, as was emphasized by Van Nieuwenhuijze, that the essential ingredient of the natural history approach in science is not *history* at all, but *comparison* (1962:7–37). As we will see, the kinds of comparisons made in ethnography are of a rather different order from those of ethnology, but some degree of comparison is inescapable. The ethnographer must contrast and compare what he observes with what is known; he puts his present observations into

the context of existing knowledge about man. Still, a major aim of the ethnographer is to discover what was not known before, to see clearly what might not have been suspected, to learn to raise questions about the major and minor concerns of the people among whom he resides, questions that could not be raised before confronting the community, and to find ways of getting sound answers. Because of this, ethnography involves a great deal of innovation in method and technique, field expedients developed *in situ,* designed to answer questions arising from fresh observation of the unexpected. The ethnographer sets out to discover and understand the idiosyncratic uniqueness of the community, as well as to detail its similarities with others.

This large, if by no means exclusive, emphasis on discovery, uniqueness, and detailed description of observed facts thus marks the natural history tactic of ethnography. The method therefore represents the anthropological use of one of two major ways of thinking about natural phenomena. This is the "idiographic" mode or activity of thought, in contrast to the "nomethetic" or generalizing type which predominates in ethnology (Eckhardt 1961:76–77).[6] In general, the idiographic style of thought requires the scientist to concentrate on the single happening or event, an individual organism, one personality, or (as in cultural anthropology) one community, society, culture, or subculture. In linguistics, as Professor Chafe describes in the next chapter, the analog is the linguist's effort to describe fully a single unknown language. Thus ethnographic research, and ethnographic reports, attempt to provide an accurate, valid depiction of the unique pattern or mixture of all the elements characteristic of a single human

[6] The reader must watch both the spelling and the sense of "idiographic," which is too easily misperceived as "ideographic." A related word is idiosyncratic, not ideological.

group. Ethnographic research is, in this way, largely qualitative and does not in itself permit generalization, although anthropologists have long favored the use of this approach as a base for stating tentative theories or hypotheses of wider applicability. As the intent examination and description of the complexities of a single personality does for psychology, an ethnography in anthropology results in a case study of another kind of a human whole.

Two important questions remain unanswered. First, what are the *elements* ethnographers report and describe? The answer to this question involves the kinds of human behavior cultural anthropologists deal with, and the technical ideas they use to deal with them. We set aside this question for the moment, since it cannot be fully answered until the concluding section of the chapter, and turn to the second.

The second question concerns the kind of human *wholes* whose elements and patterns the ethnographer observes and describes. What are the major kinds of culture-bearing units which concern cultural anthropologists?

To say simply that these wholes are peoples, or tribes, or ethnic groups, or cultures, or communities, or societies, is really begging the question, for these are not equivalent to one another, and they are words often used so loosely that they lack consistent meaning. Moreover, there is no anthropological consensus on how to go about setting boundaries around or identifying a single "tribe" or "culture." Raoul Naroll, whose special interest is the logic and methodology of formal comparative studies, recently prepared a scheme of definitions and classifications, in an attempt to establish a few generally useful, readily applied criteria which could, when put together, be used both to identify any one such "culture-bearing unit" and to establish a series of types of such units. Twenty-four anthropologists

read his report and submitted written critiques of it: few disputed the importance of the problem, but all disagreed with the criteria and definitions he presented. Their criticism was based primarily on the fact that most believed he had used neither sufficient nor the right criteria, and that he had consequently not provided enough specific niches in his taxonomy.

Naroll's criteria, and the additional ones suggested by his critics, are presented in condensed and collated form in Figure 1-3. Using just three, Naroll defined the culture-bearing unit as a group of persons who (1) speak a common distinct language in their homes, (2) inhabit a common territory, and (3) are either members of a political unit which transcends the local community, or who (because many peoples lack political institutions of this degree of complexity) live sufficiently close to one another to maintain frequent contacts. These criteria in effect define two kinds of boundaries around a cultural unit, one linguistic, the other a "communication-link," that is, a political unit or contact group boundary. Either of these boundaries (or both, if they happen to coincide) define one independent cultural group (Naroll 1964:287).

When put together, these criteria also yield a series or typology of different kinds of culture units. For example, the Ute Indians, who prior to the expansion of the United States foraged over large parts of what is now Colorado and Utah, constitute one kind of culture unit. They spoke a single common language, occupied and claimed a large territory, and the component family groups were in frequent — if seasonal — contact with one another, but the Ute lacked a complex unifying political apparatus. However, the descendants of these aboriginal Ute are now lodged on a few reservations, which are their present territorial bases, continue to speak their own language (in addition to Spanish and English), but

1. The unit should consist of one society, or one or more communities.
2. The unit should consist of a group of persons who speak one common language, or group of mutually intelligible dialects.
3. The unit should consist of a single, sovereign political-administrative entity.
4. The unit should consist of the largest and most inclusive social entity defined and recognized by the natives themselves.
5. The unit should consist of a group of persons who occupy a single contiguous territory.
6. The unit should express a common ecological adaptation to the landscape.
7. The unit should consist of a group of persons who share a common (usually named) identity and belief in common history and heritage.
8. The unit should consist of a group of persons exhibiting high frequencies of mutual interaction.
9. The unit should consist of a group with a distinctive social structure, one contrasting with all others.
10. The unit should be defined in demographic terms, i.e., minimal population size, presence of both sexes, and three generations.
11. The unit should consist of a group (or an area) with a large number of culture traits in common, the occurrence and patterning of which contrasts with that of other groups (or areas).

FIGURE 1-3

Criteria Used to Identify Single Culture-Bearing Units

This listing includes many of the frequently used criteria used to identify a single unit for ethnographic study or ethnological comparisons. Note that, with the exception of the last criteria, the reference here is always to some type of *social* entity, and the partitive idea of "culture" here is that of one whole, functioning way of life, a *total* culture. Again, these criteria are not mutually exclusive; and some even presume or include one or more others. Cultural anthropologists generally use two or more, but obviously not all, of these criteria. Usually, a single criteria in itself is not considered sufficient to define "a culture." (Modified from Naroll and Discussants 1964.)

are citizens and subject to the authority of the United States (Clifton 1965a). Thus they are now, according to Naroll's definition, a cultural unit of a different type. On the other hand, many of the populations which inhabited the smaller Pacific islands had well structured local political systems, spoke a common language, and occupied neatly bounded territories, and were therefore of yet a third, and different, cultural type. Further, according to Naroll's scheme, the contemporary population of Great Britain would be divided into a number of different cultural groups of two different types,

those who speak the Queen's English, the language of the state, and those who speak what he believes to be the mutually unintelligible dialects of Welsh, Scots, or Cockney (1964:309–310).

Many of the criticisms of Naroll's scheme come from ethnographers who complained that the scheme did not conveniently fit the facts of specific cases they cited. At one end of this line of criticism was the argument that all cultures are so fundamentally different and unique that no economical classification can ever be devised; indeed, it was argued that such attempts at classification are so improperly distorting that they are useless. This is a very extreme ethnographic opinion, and since it effectively denies the application of vital scientific methods to cultural anthropology we can set it aside (Naroll 1964:299 & 310). At the other end were the many expressions of agreement with the need for an overall scheme of classification and an improved definition of the nature of the culture-bearing unit, with suggestions for additional criteria. In these we have a convenient sampling of views on the different ways anthropologists go about defining cultural units.

The list of criteria in Figure 1-3 is thus a kind of summary of anthropological thought about the matter. The criteria overlap, are sometimes inconsistent, and on occasion may consist of different ways of expressing the same kind of idea. Moreover, no anthropologist proposes that any one of these by itself is adequate for defining and identifying a single culture. All anthropologists use several, and it is clear from the discussion following Naroll's article that most are frankly prepared to use different criteria in different circumstances. This results from the general opinion, quite characteristic of the ethnographic style of research but a little surprising in a discussion of a fundamental problem in comparative ethnology, that any definition and typology must in part be true to the ideas of the members of the culture units themselves. That is, it is generally agreed that the people's own way of characterizing their identity must be part of the scientific scheme of things. This opinion is reflected in those criteria which insist that the unit must be defined in terms of the largest social unit identified and recognized by the people, or in terms of a group which shares a belief in a common identity, perhaps even a named identity — "We the Tikopia" — and/or in a common history or social heritage. The inadequacy of any single criterion like expressed group identity or

the importance of language is shown by the strength of the frequently expressed opinion that there is a union of English-speaking peoples which crosses national, societal, and (in the anthropological sense) probably cultural boundaries. At the same time, language itself cannot be a single, universally applicable, paramount criterion because of the fact of bi- or even tri-linguality in many societies, and because the same language may be used ordinarily — in the domestic speech — of several societies or cultures.

Fundamental to Naroll's argument (also expressed in all the criticisms) and implicit in our discussion so far is the conviction that the culture-bearing unit must exhibit important *social* dimensions. This goes beyond particular criteria which emphasize political integration or frequency of contact between the membership to the idea of "community" and "society." In his critique, John W. M. Whiting made the point, also expressed by others, that whatever the larger nature of culture-bearing units may be, cultural anthropologists ordinarily study only one or a few communities in their ethnographic research. Thus the reference of his description of a culture may be to a larger whole, but the sample the anthropologist actually observes intensively constitutes the community. Now, in contrast to vague motions like "a people," words with widely varying definitions and applications like "tribe," and the partitive notion of "culture" which remains tantalizingly illusive, "community" and "society" are two quite well defined and generally accepted concepts. Let us look at them more closely.

"Community" has two generally accepted meanings, a narrower one frequently used in formal comparative research, and a larger, more specific and richer one which incorporates the former. In the lesser sense, "community" refers to a localized grouping of men bound together by social relationships, frequently interacting with one another, and occupying a common territory. This is about the sense of the term Naroll used when he spoke of political systems transcending the local community. Obviously, this does not tell us very much about the nature of the community. The larger definition has, perhaps, been best expressed in the joint work of Conrad M. Arensberg and Solon T. Kimball, anthropologist and sociologist respectively, two scholars who work directly and consciously within the empirical, qualitative, inductive tradition of the ethnographic style of research (Arensberg and Kimball 1965).

In this larger sense, "community" is understood as an organized population aggregate utilizing a resource base and occupying and modifying a portion of the landscape. Here the critical term is "organized population," for, just as a swarm of bees is not equivalent to the hive, communities are not simply places. They consist of human groups which always include both sexes and three generations and which are characterized by a more or less complex division of labor. Each community, occupying its geographic setting, has a settlement pattern which to some degree reflects the values and structure of the community proper, but each may successively occupy several or many places. This is as true of primitive hunting and gathering bands, whose ecological adjustment and dependence upon the availability of naturally available foodstuffs requires frequent moves of the entire population, as it is of those populations of the communities of modern industrial nations which constantly change in a series of internal exchange migrations. However, it is the *organization* which persists and which has a continuity which extends beyond the life span or the physical presence of any of the members. Part of the organization of the community, the presence of both sexes and three generations, probably reflects certain biological facts, for instance, the fetalization and dependency of the human child, and the need for biological replenishment of the membership, as well as the requisite subsistence adjustment which promotes mutual aid and assistance. Seen thus, communities are a universal, pan-human phenomena, and a very ancient one. Indeed, some features of prototype human communities may possibly be directly observed in the few remaining contemporary primitive foraging bands, and, by more indirect inference, in the community organizations of the higher primates.

Considered as a type of organization, communities are a complex system of both social forms and cultural traits or behaviors which exist together as sets of connected and mutually interdependent activities of different kinds. These activities — reproductive, subsistence, technological, economic, artistic, political, and religious — are, on the most rudimentary level of social evolution, little elaborated and separated. But on more complex levels of socio-political organization, they become sufficiently independent and specialized to be called "institutions." Because every community exists in the midst of and linked to other communities, these sociocultural activities or institutions have both internal and external points of reference. For example, some economic and political activities involve the maintenance of relationships with other communities, of resource-getting or exchange, subordination or war. Thus, although the community is a fundamental unit of sociocultural transmission and continuity in its own right, it may also be only one of many quite like itself, each with similar social forms and customs. In brief, the community is a basic minimal unit of population sufficiently organized and differentiated to insure both biological and cultural continuity.

Communities may be very small, the lower limit probably being something like a hundred persons, or very large, numbering in the thousands. Similarly, in terms of their distinctive institutions and cultural behaviors, they may be near unique, with few or no other similarly organized communities extant, or they may be duplicated many hundreds and thousands of times, as they are in some hugely populated national cultures.

Finally, communities are of many different types. The autonomous hunting and gathering band has been mentioned; other types include the linked line of beachfront homestead-garden plots characteristic of some Pacific islands, the neighborhood of scattered farmsteads in agricultural societies, the peasant hamlet and the village of craft specialists, and the part-independent ward or barrio of towns, or even towns themselves.

The idea of "society" overlaps somewhat with that of community, both in conception and in the range of its application. In situations in which we deal with one or a very few closely linked communities which have no cultural counterparts elsewhere, *the* community and *the* society may be one and the same human group. But more generally societies are larger units of sociocultural integration — societies include and consist of communities (and certainly other kinds of social groups) linked to one another in a more complex structure. Thus societies are like communities insofar as they are complexly organized population aggregates; they differ from communities by not being localized, co-residential units. Indeed, a large part of the organization and activity of the society may be given over to the control and regulation of component communities, drawing resources from them via taxation or levies, ordering local religious belief and practice, or marshalling personnel for public works and war. A larger, more complex society may state goals or objectives which differ from and even conflict with those of special concern to local communities, and they may have distinctive tests and requirements for membership which are not relevant to those expressed by communities or

other kinds of social units. In brief, however similar societies may be to communities in possessing systems of role differentiation, shared values, ideals and goals, and in controlling and regulating the means men use to attain their ends, communities and societies differ in the content and the complexity of their organization (Aberle *et al.* 1950). Moreover, a large society is in a sense dependent upon the component communities, hence is not as self-sufficient as the community, in which members are born and socialized, and in which the society's resources are produced, processed, and marshalled. Also, we must recognize that societies vary widely in size and in kind. A progressive series of types, one following a line of increasing complexity of sociopolitical economic organization, would begin with the hunting and gathering band and go on to include at least tribal level societies, primitive states and empires, more complex preindustrial nation states, and industrialized nations and empires.

If we remember that Naroll and his critics were concerned with defining the boundaries of single *total* cultures, full or complete sets of customs, values, skills, and ideas integrated into a distinctive way of life, then several other issues will become clear and fall into line. For example, we mentioned "ethnic-group" as one possible culture-bearing unit. This word came into social science usage as a reasonably scientific substitute for the older folk notion of race, but as it has entered popular usage it has lost what little value it once had. Literally, it signifies a group of people who are characterized by some common beliefs and customs, and very little more, except that the crude and quite incorrect notion of biological determination of human behavior is set aside and avoided. Ethnic group is thus used to designate quite a wide variety of different kinds of lesser contained groups. Sometimes these groups may constitute population aggregates which constitute local communities or parts of communities, such as rural religious enclaves like the Hutterites, Mennonites, or Dunkards, or urban neighborhoods composed of second- or third-generation immigrants, such as the Puerto Ricans and Italians of North American cities (Glazer and Moynihan 1963). Sometimes the term is used to indicate all of a dispersed set of persons (some of whom may congregate in local communities and neighborhoods) who have little more in common than a different complexion, or an accent, or a heritage of deprivation and denial, such as many contemporary North American Indians, all American Negroes, and some Jews. The notion of ethnic group thus includes too much and contributes little to understanding. What then are these groupings?

With the exception of a few religious cults which deliberately isolate themselves to maintain a special set of beliefs, most are at least potential recruits for full membership and participation in the larger society and culture. This of course is the whole sense of contemporary North American Negro protest; and it is certainly the position of the voluntary immigrants of many societies. That such groups are not accepted fully, either immediately or in the long run, may be the result of their temporary inability to master language, values, and skills; or it may be the result of outright rejection and status placement in less favored socioeconomic classes, or, in the special case of the rural south of the United States, into a caste-like grouping. One exception seems to be the very large group of United States citizens who are of American Indian descent, but have no Indian language skills, social customs, or cultural behaviors. These persons continue to cling to their Indian identity because of the considerable prestige, and sometimes the economic and social rewards it entails, while otherwise behaving exactly as the larger population does (Clif-

ton 1965a; Fischer 1965). So far as their *sociological* nature is concerned, ethnic-groups constitute communities, neighborhoods, dispersed descent groups, parts of socioeconomic classes, voluntary organizations, religious congregations, or political groups.

But in the content and form of their language, beliefs, material possessions, ideas, values, and behaviors, the members of ethnic-groups are largely, if not entirely, representative of a larger cultural whole. If they are parts of complex societies, then they have part-cultures, or, to introduce the standard word for this idea, "subcultures." Thus a full description of the complex culture of modern Japan must present not only the values and behaviors of the elite, the urban middle and working class elements, and the peasantry, but also the so-called Eta caste and the nonassimilated American military and the Korean immigrant population. The notion of subculture is useful both to designate and help describe variations *within* the total culture of a group, and to make it clear that anthropologists do not consider that all (or necessarily any) societies possess cultures which are entirely homogeneous. The term thus allows us to discuss and to characterize internal variation, and to study and speak of the culture of poverty, or the culture of the upper-middle class, or the culture of an institution (such as a prison) or the culture of a professional group (such as medical doctors). In all these instances, the inclusion of a lesser contained sociological point of reference (i.e., "social class") makes it clear that a "subcultural" description is intended, one which by either implication or specification includes the nature of the larger whole of which it is a part. Thus in studying the medical doctors of Chile one would anticipate and be interested in the fact that they carry on their professional discussions in a professional jargon or dialect, but not surprised that this jargon is expressed in Spanish phonemes, morphemes, and grammar (although initially intrigued with the fact that such physicians can usually carry on the same conversation in both French and English [and occasionally German] as well).

We can now complete our discussion of Naroll's attempt to define the boundaries of that unit which bears and sustains a total way of life. This idea of a lesser contained part may help resolve some of the difficulties in his exposition. For instance, his example of Great Britain might also be interpreted in a fashion similar to that we used for the United States and Japan, recognizing the obvious historical differences. Great Britain is only a fairly recent amalgamation of formerly autonomous tribes, states, and peoples, differing considerably in language and customs. Only after a long series of wars, rebellions, invasions, and conquests came the political, and then the beginnings of the social and cultural union of these separate parts. Certainly there are today many remnant traces of this earlier cultural and political autonomy — Welsh singers of songs, players of customary Scots games, and communities of Gaelic speakers — many of whom are proud of their ancestry, and who, while accepting the appellation British, resent being identified as English. Certainly, these local groupings must be now considered at least as subcultures; but are they reasonably considered independent total societies and cultures? The answer must be no, because all these formerly separate peoples have gone through several centuries of common history sharing a common identity. The consequences and impact of the Industrial Revolution and of colonial expansion and retreat do not discriminate Scot from Welshman, nor, for that matter, Norman from Saxon. National educational systems, health services, economic institutions, military service, and many other assimilative forces have had a leveling effect

which has eradicated too many earlier differences, notwithstanding the isolated Scots crofter, ignorant of many details of the national culture, and certainly notwithstanding the pleas of a Welsh politician calling forth the common historic identity of his constituents as a convenient and necessary means of encouraging potential supporters.

Let us examine very briefly one other case before underscoring the point of this discussion. In the past few years the emergent nation of Indonesia has laid claim to and successfully obtained possession of the western half of the large island of New Guinea. Now, at this point in the history of its development, it is quite difficult to see Indonesia as a single society. Although the socio-political elite has managed to state, establish, and defend a new set of national boundaries, these boundaries do not correspond to any single set of societal, linguistic, or cultural boundaries. In fact, they correspond to the limits of the former Netherlands East Indian Colonial Empire, which in turn were largely co-extensive with an earlier, more ancient Hindu empire. Herein lies Indonesia's sole claim to what was a very few years ago Netherlands New Guinea.

Only a very few of the many small societies and cultures of New Guinea have had even slight contact with the peoples of Indonesia, involving some trade, an occasional *hongi* or piratical raid, and perhaps rather more experience with Indonesian and Eurasian employees of the Dutch administration. The inhabitants of these two areas differ biologically in race, and are vastly different linguistically, socially, and culturally. The issue is, has the Indonesian culture (if we can assume there is just one) suddenly expanded to include the cultures of New Guinea? The answer is perhaps too obviously a firm no. But it prepares the way for more important questions. Will the various peoples of Indonesia and New Guinea *ever* constitute a single people, one society characterized by a distinctive way of life or total culture? Unfortunately, it must now be confessed that cultural anthropology is in no position to make firm forecasts of such historical magnitude, but for the sake of the argument we will hazard the prediction: "Probably not, but it will depend; and it is probably as likely that Indonesia will come apart at its cultural and linguistic seams as that the New Guinean inhabitants of the Vogelskopf will become culturally and linguistically identified with any of the cultures of Indonesia."

It will depend upon what? And here all anthropologists, and for that matter all social scientists, must hesitate, for no one quite understands in generally useful terms how large, complex cultures get built. If we had this kind of general knowledge we would be in an excellent position to set about helping such new nations as Indonesia, Nigeria, and British Guinea build themselves a little faster and somewhat more successfully.

A list of conditions can suggest the kinds of processes which might be necessary to, if not sufficient for, the cultural incorporation of Western New Guinea into what may one day be the culture of Indonesia. It may depend upon whether or not the Indonesian elite manage to develop sufficient contacts with the various peoples of New Guinea to provide them with an opportunity for learning, perhaps through two-way migration; upon whether an ideology of union is developed, presented, and accepted; upon whether the Indonesians generate a sufficiently large and effective apparatus for communication and education to promote the wholesale transfer of large elements of their culture; upon whether Indonesian legal, political, economic, and religious institutions are developed and expanded sufficiently to manage this considerable acculturative task; and upon whether the many existing linguistic, social, cultural, and political divisions which now divide New Guinea into a large number of identifiably separate cultural units can be broken down. New Guinea is famed as an area made up of many autonomous groupings frequently related to one another by bonds of suspicion, fear, war, and raiding, and it just might be that a sufficiently large and effective external influence aimed at pacification and development might result in the growth of larger and more inclusive entities, and ultimately cultural and social union. Meanwhile, Indonesian New Guinea will remain a complex, isolated, and as the Dutch learned, not very profitable colony.

Thus, the earlier rather negative prediction may be hedged. The qualification is required by the fact that hardly more than a century ago the Central Plains area of the United States was occupied by a number of autonomous cultural units, the great bison-hunting tribes such as the Cheyenne and Sioux, as different in language, culture, and social forms from the bands of Scots, Irish, Dutch, Germans, English, French, and Irish (all very recently calling themselves Americans) who came upon *them* as the several varieties of New Guineans are now come upon by the several kinds of Indonesians. Within a few years after these contacts many knowledgable observers predicted not only the cultural but the prompt biological extinction of the Indian tribes. But descendants of these tribes are today present in greater numbers than existed previously; the social structural descendants of the tribes persist, if in greatly altered form, as do many old and many new customs, while many descendants of the Cheyenne labor and live conjointly with descendants of the self-same Americans in the cities and towns of the expanded and changed American culture. Of course, it might be said that the historical and social situations differ in the Indonesian-New Guinea and American Indian-American white cases, but then, we are not sure how much or what kind of a difference makes a difference.

We know of course that larger and more complex cultures do develop, as historians, ethnohistorians, and current events constantly remind us. The world's history consists substantially of just this process, the growth of newer and more complex cultures incorporating and submerging the preceding autonomous social units and cultural variants. But this expansion and development of new and more complex cultures is not simply a matter of the conqueror making the conquered much like himself. Just as Rome never quite recovered from its incorporation of Greece, a fair part of the national social structure of Great Britain and much of its common cultural content represents diffusion from and adaption to the (forcible) incorporation of Scots and Welsh into one society and a unitary culture.

Too, the expansionists do not always elect to live and merge with those upon whom they intrude. Sometimes, as contemporary South Africa illustrates, the alternative of setting the variant cultures aside and isolating them on remote and undesirable parcels of land is taken, and a deliberate policy of apartness or cultural separation is followed. Sometimes, as was true of all of the native peoples of the island of Tasmania and many of the small American Indian societies of north-central California, the newly arrived elect the simpler course of extermination. But these policies of isolation or extermination also mark and blot the developing culture, if only in the need to develop new institutions to deal with the isolated tribal enclave, or to defend national honor from the scorn and attacks of unsympathetic neighbors, or perhaps in a pervasive and lasting theme of shame.

Now let us look at the point of this discussion, and consider its relevance to understanding the nature of ethnography, of the idiographic approach, and ethnology, or the nomethetic approach to the study of cultural behavior. We have here what seems to be a confrontation between these two styles of research and thought. An ethnologist, Naroll, sets out to resolve a problem of concern to those who seek generalizations about a number of separate cultures. He wishes to define, formally and carefully, the fundamental nature of a single case, the irreducible elements of the identity of a culture. This interesting venture then seems to run aground on the shoals of ethnographic particulars. The ethnographers counter Naroll's definition with exceptions, and demonstrate that the basic elements of cultural identity vary from society to society. So far, we have an interesting example of a confrontation between ethnographers with their knowledge about particular peoples and cultures and an ethnologist attempting to work out general principles, a confrontation in which the scientific generalizations are tested and found wanting. This should illustrate the fact that, although we discuss ethnography and ethnology separately, and contrast the idiographic and nomethetic approaches to the study of man, they are in fact inseparably linked. But what more is involved?

The bands of Ute Indians being transformed from one societal condition to another, losing their autonomy and becoming incorporated into a larger society, is one example of a historical process the general name of which is acculturation. It is a kind of situation which is duplicated in many parts of the world with many other societies. So too for those immigrant populations, fragments of old societies and cultures, which merge partially or wholly into a larger social, cultural, and linguistic fabric. This process is also repetitive. Similarly for the expansion of the British state and the growth of a new and changed culture thereunder, and for the case of the current cultural confrontation between the new nation of Indonesia and the old societies of New Guinea. The latter constitutes — possibly — a very young instance of the expansion of another set of social and cultural boundaries. All these examples represent instances of the development of cultures along the continuum of time, and it is this pattern of historical sequence which is ignored or set aside by both ethnography and ethnology.

What more is involved then is this: just as ethnography and ethnology question each other, *both* can be and are held up to those subdisciplines within cultural anthropology which do attempt to deal with the phenomena of history and with sequences of cultural processes — ethnohistory, cultural dynamics, and cultural evolution. If the social situations and the cultural boundaries of tribal peoples change as a result of contact with expanding dominant cultures, and if fragments of whole societies migrate and settle into new ones, and if these historical events are influential in interfering with or modifying social and cultural boundaries, then they must be considered in any definitions of cultural identity.

However, the ethnographic approach tends to ignore the dimension of time and concentrates on describing the way of life of a single community or culture at one point in its history. Ethnography takes a "cut" from the developmental arc of a culture and gives a portrait of the manners and customs of a people within brief time limits, as shown in Figure 1-4.

The picture has a static, synchronic (or time-stopping) quality to it which presents obvious difficulties. Ethnography tells us, in full, rich detail, what the content and form of a culture is, but it does not suggest much about how it got that way. Ethnography also pretends that all the peoples of the world can be conveniently divided into a large (if not infinite) number of separate, independent units, when actually many communities, cultures, and societies overlap and blend with others.

These overlappings and blendings result

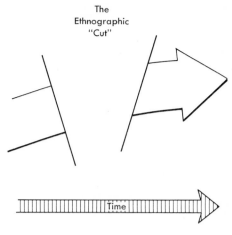

FIGURE 1-4

The Time-Stopping Perspective of Ethnography

The ethnographic approach takes a cross-section or "cut" out of the complete history of a community or a culture and develops a full-scale portrait of the way of life of the people within brief time limits. Compared to the perspective of other approaches, this *synchronic* or time-stopping model results in a quite static portrayal, one particularly emphasizing uniqueness and individuality of patterns of custom and belief.

from culture contacts and cultural changes, and the dynamic processes of development and evolution, which tend to be set aside and lost in the ethnographic model. These facts of historical sequence, particular events, and general processes introduce another order of phenomena into descriptions of culture. As Anthony F. C. Wallace has put it,

. . . anthropologists have only recently begun to realize that new ethnographic descriptions, like daily weather reporting, is an endless task. There is not a finite number of cultures which, once described, will stay fixed forever on some *scala culturae.* Culture change is constant, ubiquitous, and only moderately predictable. The ethnographic inventory will never be complete . . . (1961:2).

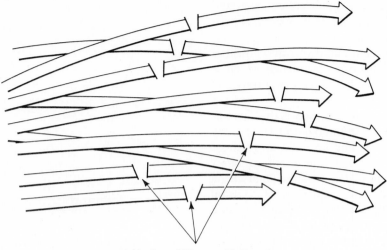

A Number of Ethnographic Portraits

FIGURE 1-5

The Comparative Perspective of Ethnology

This perspective involves comparison and correlation of parts or aspects of the cultures of several or a sample of many societies. Generally, so long as the societies in the sample satisfy the anthropologist's criteria for inclusion in his particular study, are well described, and have the required characteristics, he may ignore the historical period in which the culture was described.

The arrows above may be taken as representing (1) a smaller *sample* of *all* the world's societies, if the anthropologist is attempting to make generalizations about mankind; (2) a larger sample of a *set* of cultures of a similar *type* in various parts of the world; or (3) *all* those genetically related cultures of one region of the world, if the anthropologist is attempting to deduce and test ideas about the inner workings of one kind of cultural system, or perhaps, the sequence of cultural developments in one region. Note that here the rich descriptive detail of the ethnographic approach is lost, as the anthropologist stands farther back and looks for similarities in many cultures.

The prime contribution of ethnographic methods is a necessarily incomplete sample of well rounded descriptions of the cultural behaviors of the peoples of such social units as communities and societies. Ethnology in turn takes these descriptions as its data and seeks generalizations. However much both methods contribute to our knowledge of the varieties of human behavior, both have limitations, and they are not equally useful for studying all anthropological problems encountered.

CONCEPTS

The approaches used by cultural anthropologists for studying the varieties of human behavior have been examined and discussed. We may now look at some of the kinds of ideas anthropologists hold about the fundamental *parts* or *elements* of a whole system of customs, beliefs, and practices. This discussion will make it clear how anthropologists go about making summary statements, drawn from observations of and interviews with particular individuals, groups of individuals, and the products of human activity, about both the relatively constant and central and the changing and variant features of a culture.[7]

One critical term in Tylor's definition of culture was "custom." It is an idea that needs more attention. The idea of custom was taken directly from the standard English vocabulary very early in the history of the science. It is, as Edward Sapir pointed out, ". . . a variable common sense concept which has served as the matrix for the development of the more refined and technical anthropological concept of culture" (1931: 658). In its general sense, it refers to the complete set of behavior patterns characteristic of a community or society. In a more concrete sense it may designate a single set of behaviors of one type, a part of the whole. If the word "habit" is also accepted in its common sense usage, not in any technical modern psychological sense, then custom means something like the collective habits of a group.

In addition to the fact that the idea of custom is neither very specific nor very refined, it tends to center attention on those features of a group's behavior which are the most prominent, durable, and typical — it tends to highlight the striking and exotic, the static and unchanging, and the commonly shared. Meanwhile, cultural anthropologists have begun asking interesting and important questions about routine and perhaps unimpressive features, about the dynamics of change, about the variable and idiosyncratic aspects of cultural behavior. It is difficult to stretch

the meaning of custom to include such phenomena, and for this and other reasons it is no longer adequate as a working tool. As we will see, the same criticism applies to other, more sharply defined ideas which derive from the notion of custom or group habit.

Let us now see how the idea of custom might help in analysis and understanding of three specific illustrative cases, which can be used to show why other ideas are needed. Only the major outline of each case will be stated at first, and additional information will be worked into the discussion as needed.

The first case is that of the Man Who Scorched His Fingers, the second, that of the Unserved Housewife, and the last involves a Would-Be Witch. All three involve the kind of fundamental information which comes to the attention of the cultural anthropologist (especially the ethnographer) and which he must interpret and check out in the process of converting it to scientific data. But there is one exception. All these illustrations concern situations in which an individual operates in largely unfamiliar or threatening cultural surroundings. This selection is used to make a point. The response of all three individuals to their situation was ethnocentric or culture-bound, that is, they responded to the unfamiliar not with analysis and an attempt to understand the cause of their difficulty, but with confusion and complaint.

The man who scorched his fingers was a Chilean visitor to the United States. When asked how he was adjusting to life in Washington, he replied, "Everything's fine more or less except I keep burning my fingers with those little paper matches you use." He held up his right hand to show a blistered thumb and middle finger.

The housewife who went unserved was, on the other hand, a North American woman visiting Chile. When asked how she was adjusting to life in Chile, she replied, "Everything's all right *mas o menos* except I just can't get any service in the stores. Those

---

[7] Because in Chapter 6 Professor Gearing offers a full discussion of ideas about the elementary parts of social systems, here we review ideas about the parts of culture in the more general sense. To a considerable extent, such notions as "trait" are less useful, and less often used, when applied to social organization, than are such ideas as "social person" or "role," for reasons Professor Gearing makes clear.

clerks simply won't pay any attention to you."

The would-be witch volunteered his statement. He was a North American Indian and had for some hours been dictating the texts of a large number of songs that were part of a religious ritual. Somewhat tired, he sat back to rest, and then said quite spontaneously, "You know what people say about that man that killed Kennedy is not true. They say it was the Communists or those Birch people in Texas was the ones started that. That it was them put the idea in that man's head. That isn't so. It was us that did it. Two months before he got killed it was. At the winter ceremony we prayed to those divine powers, the spirits that protect us. We asked them to punish the President of the United States for all the wrong things he did to us. It was the divine spirits that put the idea in that man's head and made him do it. Not the Communists." This statement was offered unemotionally and matter-of-factly, in such a way as to indicate clearly that the informant had been present and had participated in the prayer willingly.

While the first two illustrations are essentially minor, perhaps trivial in their content, the last, coming as it did a few scant months after President Kennedy's assassination, had something of the quality of the centipede's sting. All three, of course, require interpretation and understanding, for each is as good as any example of one variety of human behavior.[8]

If we can safely assume that there is nothing in the heredity — the biological make-up — of these three individuals which caused their behavior in the described situations, we can ask: What is there about Chilean fire-making customs which causes a Chilean to

[8] For obvious reasons it is preferable to conceal the identity of this Indian informant and his reservation community. Therefore some of the cultural content of the following explication is twisted slightly for anonymity. This is necessary in spite of the fact that what he said was a lie.

have difficulty with North American matches? Similarly for North American shopping or marketing customs in the case of the housewife in Chile. And, at the other end, does this Indian community customarily arrange the murder of its enemies through collective prayer? The trouble with the notion of custom should now be apparent. This is an exceedingly pompous way to state the issue, and one which does not much focus attention on specifics. Moreover, the notion of custom here does not much discriminate the important differences between these three cases. Note that the first case involves a relationship between a person and a simple tool, while the second essentially seems to be a social matter of relationships between persons. The third is, on the face of it, a matter of relations between men and supernatural figures or forces, and then indirectly back to other men. But it is far more difficult to interpret because the Indian was obviously lying. Not in the sense that he or others could not have believed in this kind of supernatural power, because they do. He was lying about the prayer at the winter ceremony. Moreover, he knew it, and he knew the listening anthropologist knew it. And this makes understanding this bit of behavior difficult.

We can now look a little more closely at the match-lighting behavior of the man who burned his fingers. He would take one "of those little paper matches" from the booklet, hold the end of it between thumb and forefinger with his middle finger extending along the shank of the match, and then strike the match *downward* against the abrasive surface of the matchbook. Much too frequently, the force of the blow caused the match to bend backwards and the chemical to ignite against his finger tips. Part of his problem was that he was striking North American paper matches as Chileans strike their wooden ones, although North American book matches are not designed to be ignited in this fashion. Another part of his problem was the fact that he did not know that there are available in North America a number of different types of matches — thin paper book matches, stout paper book matches, small wooden safety matches, small wooden strike-any-where matches, large kitchen matches, wax impregnated Boy Scout matches, and very long matches for lighting fireplaces. Thus not only was he behaving in a fashion inappropriate to the structure of the type of tool he was using, but he was unaware of alternative possibilities. He translated *fósforos* as "matches" when requesting them in a store, and as is usual in North America, was given paper book matches.

The man who burned his fingers came from a nation where *fósforos* means one and only one kind of match, comparable only in form and appearance to the small North American box of wooden friction matches. And these matches are not designed to be struck as North Americans strike *their* "little paper matches," with a complicated *upward* blow and a twist of the fingers which allows the match to ignite safely in a cupped hand. If the Chilean *fósforo* is struck in the North American upward pattern, one of several things happens. The match fractures backwards against the fingers, causing an uncomfortable burn. Or the match breaks in half and the flaming end lands on thigh, lap, or floor. Or if the match lighter has been unusually forceful, the drop of blazing phosphorus, which is indifferently fixed to the wooden shank, flies up and catches him in the eye or lights in his hair. (Why there should be only one kind of match available in Chile, and why these should be of such quality, are separate and in themselves interesting questions. We can turn to them in a moment.) We can say simply that one element or part of the whole of Chilean culture consists of a quite specific learned skill (a particular combination of motor habits), a simple manufactured object associated with the skill, a name for and an idea about the object or tool,

a set of confident expectations about the workability or mutual "fit" of skill and tool, and an anticipation that skill applied to tool will make fire.

All this can be derived from quite objective observation, plus a little inquiry. Repeated observations in various parts of the country confirm that probably all Chileans use the downward strike technique with their matches. The mechanical properties of the match allow us to surmise why they do so. And the fact that there are, generally, no alternative types of matches available adds weight to the generalization. There are no other kinds of matches available because the industry is a government-supported monopoly. The borders of the culture are thus closed to importation of *any* matches, and matches are not the kind of thing smugglers customarily bother with. Moreover, the industry will produce only one kind of match, and that, as the Chileans themselves wryly admit, of poor quality. And the matches are — relative to the amount of time a man must work to earn the money to buy a box — extremely expensive. The Chilean pays something like fourteen to eighteen times as much for the same number of matches as does a North American, and he tends to be careful about breaking and wasting them. In brief, as regards a society made up of some eight million people, it is possible to make the kind of descriptive generalization about at least some of the parts of a whole way of life that cultural anthropologists make about the culture of tiny isolated human communities of hunters and gatherers.[9]

A technical anthropological idea useful in

---

[9] This Chilean culture trait is also related to the value system and has a place in the country's folklore. Chileans say about objects manufactured in the country: *¡Cuidado! Hecho en Chile.* "Be careful with it, it's made in Chile." That is, it will break, it won't work, it won't fit, it will wear out quickly, and so on. They thus consciously devalue the quality of their manufactured objects and have a whole series of public jokes and sayings detailing the specific failings of one or another type.

codifying and interpreting such observable phenomena as the case just discussed is that of a "culture trait." The notion of trait points to a fairly readily observable atomistic bit or piece of a whole way of life. But the trait is an abstraction about a regularly recurrent piece of behavior and perhaps a product or instrument. It may be one used by or characteristic of all members of the community, or only some — as the types of weapons adult male hunters use, or perhaps even only one — as the symbols and paraphernalia of office associated with *the* position of political leader. Thus the idea of trait embraces the standard way of accomplishing some end, the things generally employed (which may be as concrete as stone tools, as fleeting as a spell, or as abstract as an imagined spirit), the associated skills, and the categories of ideas and expectations directly connected to instrument and purpose.

A culture trait is thus seen as a kind of identifiable building block for a description of a whole way of life. If one complete culture can be thought of as a mosaic, made up of differently shaped and differently colored tiles or *tesserae*, then one culture trait is like one distinctively formed type of *tesserae* of a certain color (Seligman 1936:113). And just as a collection of tiles of one type will exhibit small variations within themselves, a number of distinctions can be observed within an abstracted trait. Thus it was not intended to say that each and every Chilean lights his matches in precisely the same way, nor that all Chilean matches are identical. There are variations, but variations within the characteristic form and within the range of quality. Moreover, once we can identify a series of traits, they can be put together in clusters of related ones or "trait-complexes," which consist of a set of different traits which fit together into some larger unity. For instance, the entire equipment of a hunter, including weapons, snares, lures, poisons, technical knowledge about animal behavior, and

so on, could be seen as one kind of trait-complex.

This notion of an atomistic unit has had considerable appeal and a history of useful service in modern cultural anthropology, but it has some limitations. It is quite possible to describe entire cultures in this way — indeed many of the American Indian cultures of the western United States have been studied in just this fashion. But the result is a long list of disconnected bits, wherein a sense of the inner organization and the dynamics of the workings of the culture is missing. Moreover, the isolation and depiction of the individual trait is not always so objective and certain a matter as might seem to be the case (Bennett 1944). Still, it is an idea with considerable utility, because as applied it does assist in understanding a number of things about cultural systems, including such problems as that faced by the man who burned his fingers.

Another idea omitted in a list of traits is that of their relationships to one another, or the characteristic form with which they are put together. The general idea of "pattern" as a fundamental element in cultural systems cuts across many levels of analysis. Cultural traits themselves exhibit patterned relationships between their parts, else we would find it difficult even to contrast so simple a thing as characteristic Chilean and North American match-striking behaviors. But here we must move to a somewhat different level and kind of analysis.

A few additional observations on the exact nature of the American housewife's difficulty in getting service in Chile are in order. First, we should mention that this is not a problem of just one individual: it is common to most (if not all) North American women in Chile. Second, it is not limited to women: their husbands suffer similar embarrassment, although perhaps not so frequently because they do not shop as often. Third, lest the reader go astray, it is not really a problem of language. Americans who arrive in Chile with a good command of Spanish have to face the same puzzle; and as those who do not at first control the language do begin to speak and understand it, the difficulty continues, although sometimes with diminished force. This is because as they learn the language they may learn also other things, among them what must be done to get served. The problem of getting service is a continuing one since there is nothing comparable to the simple instruction given the Chilean visitor to the United States, "Ask for *wooden* or *box* matches." And there is no simple alternative solution such as the North American employs in Chile to reduce the fire hazard from Chilean matches, which is to recognize the need for and to master a new and very simple motor skill (or else buy a mechanical lighter).

The housewife's problem is produced by the fact that she must go forth into unfamiliar cultural terrain to seek food, shelter, beverages, clothing, and so on. She begins by bringing to bear the skills she has mastered as a North American housewife and very quickly learns to make translations at the level of cultural traits from her past experience to her present situation. She soon discovers that salt comes in plastic bags rather than in round cardboard containers, that nutmeg is really a nut and not a powder, beef is available only two days a week, that houses are not well or conveniently heated, and that they come with at least five times as many locks and latches on them as she expects. These differences in cultural traits she quickly learns and adjusts to. This is not the root of her problem, for what she complains of is the difficulty of getting access to and possession of these goods and services. To do so she must at every juncture deal with individuals who control the approaches to and distribution of food and drink, shirts and shoes, medicines, houses, and what have you. She must deal with grocery clerks, butchers,

waiters, pharmacists, cashiers — Chilean salespersons — and she does not properly know how.

We could assess the cause of this problem with ideas like that of culture trait, but the result would be forced and mechanical. In Chapter 6 Professor Gearing introduces and explains several technical ideas which work well in this context, and we will simply use them here, with one additional idea about another elementary unit of culture. The notions are those of "social person," which refers to one of the many types of public identity a well socialized individual human must learn to control and to assume, and "role," a specific pattern of expected and appropriate behaviors associated with each and every type of public identity or kind of social person an individual must be to wend his way effectively through a social system. The additional idea we need is that of "theme," a concept which refers to a fundamental assumption or postulate that underlies many different kinds of behaviors, or which may recur influentially in the patterning of different roles (Opler 1945).

With these tools we can fashion a better statement of the housewife's problem: she is assuming the position of that kind of a social person called a *customer* and she thus conducts herself as North American customers properly should and effectively do to *buy* salt, meat, or tobacco. She further assumes that the Chilean she confronts in a place of business will behave and conduct himself as a man who assumes the stance of a *salesperson* properly should, so as to *sell* drugs, shoes, or a house rental. In both assumptions she is quite wrong, and she shortly gets slightly confused, perhaps rattled, somewhat frustrated, and occasionally mildly hostile. The Chilean does not behave, so far as she can see, as a salesman should; moreover, she does not, in his view, conduct herself as a customer.

Briefly, the content and style of behavior

of the *roles* of *customer* in North American and Chilean communities are quite different, as are the *roles* of *salesperson* in the two societies. To begin with, consider the simplest situation, in which the housewife enters a store in which she is the only customer, where she does not have to contend with the presence of other, Chilean customers and their strange conduct. Alone in the store, she waits, looking around at the merchandise, perhaps going to a counter or shelf and inspecting the displays. If she waits, she is waiting to be served, and she may wait quite a long while, which will eventually make her uncomfortable. If she begins to handle the merchandise (assuming it is accessible, which is not as frequently the case as she is used to), the salesman will rather quickly appear and stand uncomfortably close to her just so long as she has her hands on the goods, and he may then inquire if she wishes something.

If she finds what she wishes and makes her selection, she discovers that she must then carry a sales slip made out by the clerk to a cashier, since the salesman apparently does not handle money. Once at the cashier's she will once again wait, standing quietly and politely, anticipating that she will be quickly served. But the cashier will be auditing his books, or talking on the telephone, or perhaps just idly looking out the window; he may not notice her presence for an (uncomfortable) period of time. Once having successfully paid for her purchase the housewife is not yet through, for the cashier will probably only give her a paid receipt which must be taken back to the original salesman, who will then give her another certificate which must then be taken to a person who apparently does no more than wrap or bag purchases. At every point she will of course try, as a proper, polite customer should, to wait for service, although by the end her patient, expectant attitude and pleasant demeanor may be worn very thin. Apparently service

in Chile does not come to those customers who wait for it.

After a few experiences of this kind the housewife will start complaining that one simply cannot get served in these stores. Meanwhile, back at the store, the salesman will make amused comments to his companions about the peculiar behavior of the *gringa* who bought shoes from him earlier, the one he at first thought might be a shoplifter until he recognized from her dress and accent that she was only a *norteamericana,* hence somewhat unpredictable. And here we have a nice illustrative piece of intercultural misunderstanding.

There are many variants on this pattern, of course. Service is quicker in a one-person store where a single individual, the owner, acts out the separate and unfamiliar roles of salesman, cashier, and wrapper, for example. But here the owner, with a personal stake in the matter, may get quite abrupt and testy with anyone who presumes to handle *his* merchandise without *his* immediate presence and implicit permission. Then, some individual salesmen seem to need less time to become aware of the customer's presence. And there are numerous additional elements which add confusion for the housewife. For example, the salesman, as soon as he has handed over the sales slip, seems to end the interaction too abruptly and to turn away too quickly for the housewife's comfort. He says, in effect, the transaction is now ended, while she expects some small talk. Moreover, the salesman volunteers nothing: he does not actively sell, to suggest other purchases, except to say as he turns away, *"Otra cosita,"* in a tone which to the housewife seems to mean, "I hope you don't want any other little thing, as I have better things to do than be bothered with you."

Manifestly, shopping is more difficult and time consuming in Chile than in the United States, and this is partly due to the overall organization of the system of marketing goods and services. For example, there are many small specialty shops, each selling only one or a few kinds of goods, which obliges the housewife to go to many separate places to complete her list of purchases. Further, the fractionated and highly specialized division of labor within any one shop, office, or government bureau requires a number of steps before any item can be purchased or a service acquired. Thus part of the North American housewife's complaint is caused by this pattern and her unfamiliarity with the several or many special roles associated with the selling of goods or providing of services. She can take heart, if small comfort, when she realizes that the Chilean housewife also complains about the system. But the Chilean housewife copes, and she does not, at least not very effectively or comfortably.

If our housewife goes into a store in which there are many Chilean women attempting to make purchases and watches their shopping behavior she soon realizes that they do get served quickly and expeditiously. She can even see how they do so, but she cannot bring herself to imitate their example. Instead she says, "I can't act like one of those fishwives!" Let us now consider this more complex example, as it will clarify the elements of the roles of customer and salesperson in Chile, and several of the underlying themes which color these roles.

Our housewife enters, say, a meat market on a Friday morning, *the* day of the week when fresh beef is supposed to be available. She finds a great many women standing packed together in front of the counter, and she begins to look around. What does she look for? A line or queue, a place to wait, quietly and politely, her turn to be served. Now she must wait a very long time indeed, for there is no queue, and instead of the discipline and order she is accustomed to, she finds what to her looks very much like a mob

scene. It is not, however, a mob, but a group well organized and disciplined, if on different principles.

Each Chilean housewife approaches the salesperson directly and immediately, ignoring anyone else in the store (particularly other customers, who are her competitors), and quite intensely and vehemently forces the fact of her personal presence upon the quietly waiting salesman. She cites the existence of a remote kinship link between herself and him, or to the family of his employer, if possible; she narrates the facts of a long friendship or of a mutually rewarding relationship between herself, her husband, her family, and the clerk or his *dueño;* or she loudly recites the details of some special situation which requires that she receive immediate attention and service. Throughout, her manner is slightly imperious if not lordly, her tone forceful and insistent, and her attitude dominant and demanding. Meanwhile, she waves her shopping list in the clerk's face, elbows other customers out of her way, and forces herself to the center of the stage. Depending upon how well she does all this, and of course the facts of her case, she — sooner or only slightly later — makes her purchase and departs. Meanwhile, the *gringa* housewife, becoming more annoyed as the quarter-hours slip by, stands waiting on the outskirts of what she sees as a crowd of immature and tantrum-prone children. And the clerk of course does not even notice her presence. He is occupied with the task of sorting the persons who are very obviously customers into a line, not of those who arrived earlier or later, but one organized by differences in the manifest prestige and prominence of the competitors for his attention. The more successful customer is thus one who puts forward the better and more obvious claim for service.

The elements of the role associated with the public identity of customer in Chile differ considerably from those properly expected of a customer in North America. The same is true of the role of salesperson. The nearest analog of the Chilean salesperson in the United States and Canada is, perhaps, the librarian who protects the rare books and historical documents room in a large public or university library. He behaves as though his custodial responsibility of guarding and safekeeping is as important as that of allowing access to the goods in his care. He will not be bothered by just anyone who enters his place of business, and he does not comfortably watch people handle his merchandise. Moreover, he will relax his guard and provide service most readily to those individuals who approach him and state an appropriate case for their needs.

Some of the objectively differing elements of the roles of salesperson and customer in Chile and the United States are now clear. But there are more covert and implicit elements. The themes of Chilean culture relevant here are by no means restricted in their effect to relationships between customers and salespersons. They recur in other situations and are expressed in other kinds of public identities which Chileans assume. We may state these fundamental postulates as follows: (1) the supply of desirable things, goods, and services is limited and probably inadequate to supply existing demands. Rather than staying fixed or increasing, the supply will probably diminish. (2) No public identity or set of role behaviors can stand or be effective by itself. Each must be enhanced, given a personalized flair, or be publicly linked to other roles or relationships. (3) In role relationships involving representatives of the lower classes or employees generally, it is necessary to assert and maintain a position of dominance. (4) People, particularly if they are not close friends or close kin, will always take advantage of you whenever and wherever they can.

These statements are not simply inferences from behavior cast into anthropological language, they reflect a substantial body of sayings, words of wisdom, aphorisms, and maxims constantly and consciously expressed by Chileans in their everyday life. And they contradict the kinds of thematic principles held near and dear by the American housewife. For example, she assumes that there is a large, inexhaustible, and probably increasing supply of nearly everything. She wants to express a "democratic" attitude towards employees. And for her to make a public statement of her pedigree and social status is almost unthinkable. This is another reason why she has difficulty getting served, for the assumptions on which service is based are in her mind all wrong, and, moreover, morally suspect.

Such assessments are quite different from statements about culture traits like match-lighting behavior because much of social behavior is subject to a great deal more variability. More factors of different kinds are involved than in the earlier situation, and the absence or preponderance of one or more of these alters the way in which the public identity of customer is expressed. Some highly desirable things like beef or fresh bread are manifestly in much more limited supply than are others. This causes variation in the stridency of customer demand. Similarly, the owner-salesman of a small town market deals with regular and well known customers who do not have to emphasize their presence and personalize their needs on a daily basis, unless his attention lapses. Too, there are substantial immigrant populations in Chile, many of whom are engaged in commerce, and therefore the diffusion of different styles of salesmanship and merchandising has varied the pattern. Thus there are regional, socioeconomic class, and probably subcultural factors which cause variations in the acting out of the public identity of customer. The simple style of observation and assessment used for the problem of the man with the burned fingers will not do here.

In addition, because the elements of role behavior and the values expressed in the themes are aspects of culture which are thoroughly internalized as part of the structure of the individual character, personality, or ego, they are not so easy to modify. The North American housewife does not want to and cannot readily modify core elements of her social personality. She remains confused, frustrated, and affronted until she finds the butchershop owned by a German immigrant who refuses to serve customers unless they "queue up," or the *autoservicio* store managed by the enterprising Chilean who deliberately attempts to transplant the principle of self-service supermarkets to increase his sales. Otherwise, she continues to take her problem seriously and personally, which the man with the burned fingers never did. Therefore, the elements of a culture differ in the degree to which they have an impact on personality, the ease with which they may be learned or relearned, the degree to which they may be changed, and the amount and kind of connections they have with other aspects of the total way of life. Many culture traits do seem to stand largely alone. Themes such as described here, on the other hand, are expressed in many different ways.

In the instance of the would-be witch, the Indian who claimed that his people had arranged the assassination of President Kennedy through prayer to their spirits, as we shall see, one kind of theme in part provoked his deceit, and another helped the anthropologist understand that he was lying. We now have in hand most of the fundamental ideas about the elements of culture to allow us to dissect and understand this fragment of individual behavior; we need just one more, "mazeway," to complete the analysis.

The Indian's statement was of the kind that anthropologists actively engaged in ethnographic research must both record and eval-

uate. Coming unexpectedly, completely out of context of the work in hand, it was a striking, surprising claim. If true, it would have contradicted everything the anthropologist thought he knew about the religious ceremony mentioned, which would have required revision of many earlier conclusions. Therefore, in spite of the fact that he was initially certain that the Indian lied, the assertion needed careful checking and verification. How was it that the anthropologist was convinced that the statement was false, and how could he go about checking the story out?

A five-day ceremony was held in the month of October preceeding the president's death, as similar ceremonies are held every year. During this ceremony many people prayed. Although the anthropologist was not physically present all five days, he had access to many other people — members of the community — who were there. Moreover, when the informant said "prayer" he was referring to the style of praying characteristic of this religious ceremony, and the prayer here may easily enough be described as a trait. The elements of the trait of prayer in this context are these: (1) it is overt, public behavior, that is, it is spoken aloud. (2) It is individual, and never collective. (3) It is addressed by the one who prays to the members of the congregation and to the divine spirits, both of whom are present and listening. (4) It is generally a spontaneous thing, in response to a sudden private prompting, although an individual may confess beforehand to his need and plan for "giving a little talk." (5) The content of the prayer is always carefully recorded in the verbal "gossip column" of the community and is the subject of comment and evaluation in the days following. (6) The content and intent of the prayer is invariably morally good. The person who jumps up to pray asks the divine spirits and the community to come to the assistance of the sick, to remember and care for the souls of the departed, to comfort the bereaved, to protect the man leaving on a long journey, to give heart to the soldier in battle, and so on. The anthropologist, who had listened to many such prayers, had never heard or heard of an individual praying for harm to befall anyone. Much less could he believe that all or part of the community, assembled as a religious congregation, could have *jointly* requested the gods to intervene on their behalf by taking punitive action against anyone.

If any individual had made such a prayer during this ceremony, it would have been duly noted by the old women who remember such things best and who were conveniently available for later questioning. A hateful prayer would be so out of phase with the prevailing pattern it would have reinforced the memory. Moreover, the members of this congregation believe they enjoy the personal protection of the president, who as guardian of the Bill of Rights guarantees them the privilege of practicing their own native religion as they see fit. And most of the community were then strong Democrats and saw President Kennedy as their own political leader, while the great majority were completely taken by the vigor and promise of the Kennedy image. Thus an appeal to the spirits to harm President Kennedy could not have gone unmarked. In fact, had such a prayer occurred, it would have precipitated a battle, but only outside of the religious setting and ritual center. No such prayer in fact occurred.

The good prayer aimed at benefiting people is only one expression of a theme shown in many ways during the regularly scheduled rituals. This theme is one of peace and harmony, and the whole pattern of behaviors, ritual episodes, songs, prayers, and dramatic enactments emphasizes the need for living together peacefully, quietly, and in good spirits. Thus the listening anthropologist knew the informant's statements were false, just as an

experienced listener can recognize a sour note in a piano recital.

This is not to say that this Indian community does not harbor strong hostilities, angers, conflicts, and hates. Quite the opposite, for like many Indian communities, it is marked by powerful conflicts. But the community does not allow these to be expressed in their major religious celebrations. The ritual center is the one place where peace and harmony can and do prevail, and individuals who attempt to provoke even minor ill feelings therein are immediately sanctioned.

To state that the assertion of this Indian was a lie is, however, only a kind of judgment, and one which does not promote much understanding of the behavior itself. What was this informant doing? Now, the way he made the statement clearly seemed to imply that he had been the instigator of the prayer and that he was personally willing, if the anthropologist was willing to accept his words without too negative a judgment, to take credit for arranging the assassination. At the same time he attributed the prayer to the congregation as a whole, which would have shared the blame and given him an out in the event the anthropologist proved too ardent a Kennedy fan. Similarly, by suggesting that he had taken the lead in arranging the prayer, and the effective intervention of the spirits, he was laying the foundation for a claim both to community leadership and to a kind of magical power of a most potent variety.

The anthropologist knew very well that this man possessed little or no political power. For some years he had attempted to work himself into a position of effective leadership and had failed. In fact, he could not get anyone to follow him in any of the various programs and schemes he advocated. As to his tentative claim to magical power, this is the kind of thing which is difficult to dispute, particularly for an anthropologist who is trying to learn the nature of a culture, especially when the anthropologist is listening to a person who lays his bets after the race has been run. In brief, this Indian seemed to be flying a trial balloon. He was an ambitious and frustrated man, still desirous of gaining a position of power and repute, who seemed to be thinking out the foundation for a new attempt to elevate himself in the community. Why try out the story with an anthropologist? Because anthropologists listen patiently and (at least visibly) uncritically to almost anything, including some wild and unlikely tales.

Rather than saying that he was lying, it is more useful to say the Indian was engaged in the process of trying to invent or innovate something. Then, to carry our understanding of this case to the end, we must try something slightly more difficult than we have so far, which is to get inside the informant's skull and appreciate the details of the way this one man perceives the world he lives in. We must look closely at his own particular definitions of his situation or, to use the idea Anthony F. C. Wallace fashioned for us, his "mazeway." Wallace defines this concept as ". . . the entire set of cognitive maps of positive and negative goals, of self, others, and material objects, and of their dynamic interrelations in process, which an individual maintains at a given time" (1961:15–16). The mazeway thus is a complex mental image characteristic of an individual at one point in his personal history. Among other elements, it contains ideas about desirable goals and undesirable pitfalls, ideas about the self, other persons, and things, and ideas about instrumentalities or techniques which can be used to gain desirable ends. It encompasses much of what we have so far said about traits, roles, patterns, and so on, but now on the level of a specific individual. Fortunately, we do not need to attempt to map out this Indian's entire mazeway, only those parts related to this particular piece of inventiveness.

We have already indicated that one desirable end was implied by his behavior (and by other information available on his life history). He strongly wanted to gain increased prestige and power, a recognized position of leadership. Because of his history of failure, he was equally interested in avoiding an additional blunder and the blame that might result from taking a wrong course (claiming responsibility for the president's death). Further, he was obviously thinking in terms of somehow using both the president's death and the religious congregation to gain prestige. Here we must mention that he did in fact hold a very important position in this congregation where he acted as a priest. On this base, then, he wished to realize his greater ambition. But the cult grouping was not sufficient in itself to provide him with the means of advancing himself farther; he had gone quite as far as a man could in that social setting. He needed an issue and several additional instrumentalities. The issue he seems to have derived from the prevalent theme of great hostility and the intense sense of deprivation this Indian community expresses against the white world for all the community had lost in its history of contact with the United States. He seemed to want to expand on the theme of hostility and to link it to the death of the president, as something the community should be grateful for, and then, in the context of the ritual center, to lay claim to the power to control and punish the white world for its evil treatment of the Indian. To assert a claim to this kind of power, he needed to be able to assume the right kind of traditionally recognized social identity. That is, if he could make a legitimate claim to the ability to act out the public identity of one who could bid the gods kill for him, or one who might stimulate the congregation to pray to this end, then he might marshall the latent power of collective hostility and attain a new position of leadership.

We suggested earlier that the Indian wanted to work at being a witch. The role of witch was probably the final element needed for his scheme. But there was current in the community at the time of this incident no such clearly and fully recognized, well defined and respected role. There had been many years earlier, and this individual as a boy and young man had known, feared, and admired several of the old witches. He had also identified himself with them, and had probably played with the idea of taking up that career before entering community politics and religion. But all recognized and active practitioners of the arts of witchcraft, men who in this community would not only suggest but openly boast of their magical power to kill and maim, had long since been dead. There were, at this point in the community's history, a few very nasty old men and fewer old women whom some people would mention, because of their cantankerous habits, as being *like* witches. But none of these persons was feared for their magical powers as the true witches had been. The one among them who was specifically accused of sufficient evil intent to murder is supposed to have used nothing more esoteric than a tire iron to do the deed. Thus the position of witch as a conventionally defined social indentity was obsolete but still remembered. The Indian informant who inventively considered the possibility of claiming responsibility for destroying a community enemy by witchcraft knew as much of the details of the old role as anyone. The obsolete social identity of witch was thus one part of his mazeway. But another part was the knowledge that the few recent assertions of witchcraft were met with more skepticism and scoffing than frozen fear. Hence he understood that a public claim to this power could also be a pitfall and the source of another failure, which he could ill afford — therefore the need to try out the claim in private.

SCHOOLS OF THOUGHT

Cultural anthropologists do not simply approach the study of the varieties of human behavior with a list of ideas about the elementary parts of a way of life. They engage the study of variations and constants in man's behavior with one or another of several grand schemes of interpretation. In fact, the kinds of fundamental ideas we have just discussed may perhaps be seen as artifacts of these preferred modes of interpretation.

Metaphors on which these schools of thought are based are many. Man's way of cultural behavior has been seen as something like life itself, in the biological sense, as having phyla and species, subject to its own kind of grand laws and change and development. This analogy, fundamental to the evolutionary approach in cultural anthropology, is very old, but still current and persuasively effective. It is countered by a different perspective which holds that it is better for anthropologists to concentrate on single cultures or societies and to view them as being like organisms, with a durable structure of parts, each performing special functions and somehow systematically influencing the others. Or cultures are seen as a work of art or like a personality, with dominant motifs or moods, recurrent patterns or themes, and parts that fit or configurate into unique wholes. Cultures have also been understood as rather like rivers, moving down through and changing over time, yet retaining their identities despite widenings or narrowings and swirls or eddies here and there. Finally, culture is sometimes understood as having some properties like the weather, constantly changing, sometimes subject to gross fluctuations, if perhaps exhibiting constant elements and regular — perhaps seasonal — transformations. The latter was fundamental to Wallace's evaluation of the meteorological character of ethnographic research, quoted earlier. Let us now very briefly examine three basic frameworks for understanding used by cultural anthropologists.

Evolutionism

Evolutionism, although it has a discontinuous history of use, is the oldest, the most inclusive, and unmistakably the boldest. Of all the major theories, it is the most abstracted, for it quite ignores the kinds of small variations in cultural behavior we have just used as illustrations, and in many ways sets aside even consideration of the historical development or the nature of any *particular* whole culture. As defined by its contemporary proponents, evolutionism attempts to take a "birds-eye view" of *types* of sociocultural systems, where each type subsumes many variant forms (Service 1962: 11), or to cultivate the entire domain of human culture (White 1959a: x), so that local, regional, and historical diversity and particular cultural expressions become the subject of large abstraction and grand speculation. Thus the aim of the modern evolutionary school is to reduce the total sweep and content of human history to grand laws of universal applicability. In this context the word "history" may be misleading, since the object of evolutionism is to discover and expose long-term trends or sequences of stages of cultural and social growth from the earliest beginnings of a human style of existence to the present. In effect, contemporary evolutionists have not much interest in absolute time, the firmly fixed chronology and dating so critical to archaeology and ethnohistory, except as it may be relevant to deriving generalizations about the sequential occurrence of changes in the fundamental principles of organization of types of cultural systems. Thus evolutionists use the information provided by ethnographers, archaeologists, and ethnohistorians about the separate societies of the world as their data for constructing and testing very general propositions about the nature of man.

For this reason the ideas of evolutionists and the kinds of hypotheses they offer must be true to the materials offered by other approaches in cultural anthropology. Because an earlier version of evolutionary theory was tested against such data and found seriously wanting, the history of this approach is broken into two major periods. The earlier, or nineteenth-century unilinear evolution school was identified with such scholars as E. B. Tylor, Henry Maine, J. Frazer, and L. Morgan. It consisted mostly of armchair speculations based largely upon a quite inadequate body of fragmentary ethnographic data made available up to that point by, quite often, incautious amateur observers, together with some more systematically collected materials. The rallying point of this early brand of thought was in part the great success of Darwin's treatment of the development of variations in the forms of life. But other sources of theoretical stimulation entered, for example, from the positivist and rationalist philosophies of the era.

The early unilinear evolutionists were convinced that man was an increasingly rational creature, and that he had moved through a series of stages of cultural development. These stages were seen as progressing from lower to higher forms, from simpler to the more complex, and from worse to better. The contemporary peoples of the world exemplified these several stages, some being retarded, others having moved ahead. And, conveniently enough — given their own preconceptions about their own position and the child-like nature of the "primitive mentality" — they strongly emphasized the differences between the higher and the ruder cultures of the world. Still, all mankind was seen as fundamentally the same psychologically, and as capable of gradually and slowly evolving into a higher position no matter what its state; and these thinkers were firmly convinced that a cultural way of life was part of nature and subject to natural laws (Voget 1960).

Leslie A. White, who more than any other contemporary anthropologist has been responsible for keeping alive an interest in evolutionary theory, in introducing his own scheme of interpretation said, "The theory set forth in this work does not differ one whit in principle from that expressed in Tylor's *Anthropology* of 1881" (White 1959a: ix). However, it is difficult to credit this statement with complete validity. First, many of the basic positions of nineteenth-century evolutionism did not survive checking against later ethnographic and ethnohistorical data. Further, White himself, and particularly his associates such as Elman R. Service and Marshall D. Sahlins, have advanced new ideas and interpretations which reflect more recent findings and which counter the excesses of the earlier evolutionary scheme (cf. Sahlins and Service 1960; and Service 1962). But there are some continuities with the old as well as discontinuities and innovations in the trend of contemporary or neo-evolutionary thought.

A major contemporary distinction is that between "general" and "special" cultural evolution.[10] General evolution is the modern, modified rendition of the older unilinear evolution position. Here the aim is to arrange, in one sequence, major cultural types in the *order of their appearance* and to explain how one such revolutionary development is caused and how it gives way to the next. Thus there is a continuity in the concern with general unilinear trends; but contemporary evolutionists do not hold, as did their nineteenth-century predecessors, that all in-

dividual cultures have gone through or need to go through the recognized stages of cultural developments. These developmental stages, or major types of cultural forms, might include a progressive series of changes from a hunting and gathering to a horticultural to agricultural and industrial types of economies. Or, in terms of basic social structures, a general evolutionary progression might trace a development from very ancient primate social groups to primitive bands, to tribes and chiefdoms, thence to states and complex nations, in a series organized around increases in the level of complexity of socio-political integration.

Thus evolutionists attempt to reduce the observed differences among the world's cultures into a simplified, ordered series. They frankly admit the technologically primitive peoples in today's world are "contemporary ancestors," survivals from past epochs of human history (Service 1962:8–9), and they continue to express the "psychic unity of mankind" postulate. They prefer economic and technological variables as principles for explaining development, and they use as indices of evolutionary development such measures of growth as increases in the efficiency of control of energy resources or increases in the degree of complexity of social organization. Therefore, in some respects, modern evolutionism does not differ "one whit" from its predecessor, while in other respects it does.[11]

Historicism

As is generally the case in the humanities and the social sciences, cultural anthropology has many scholars who insist that the objects of study, man and culture, are fundamentally a *historical* phenomena, and that understanding and explanation of any social

---

[10] See Vayda and Rappaport's discussion of another contemporary version of this approach, Julian Steward's multilinear evolutionism, in Chapter 18.

[11] Dr. Lurie's discussion of "developmental" strategies in the study of cultural change in Chapter 11 contains a more complete assessment of the several evolutionary approaches.

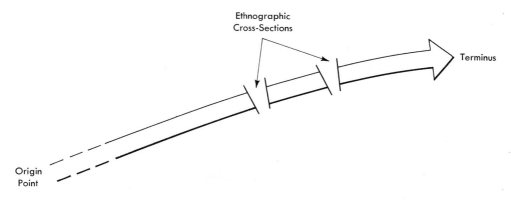

Ethnographic
Cross-Sections

Terminus

Origin
Point

FIGURE 1-6

The Historicist Perspective

In cultural anthropology the perspective of history focuses on specific detailed sequences of developments across the dimension of time. *What* is thus studied historically may be a single culture or society, or one particular institution, or a special aspect of culture such as a system of writing, or perhaps even a whole geographic area. In the absence of a rich body of documentation of the history of a particular culture, the data treated may be of many sorts — linguistic, archaeological, social structural, technological — or they may include other details indicating change, contact, and relationship. A special, if rarely used model is the *diachronic* study, which combines some aspects of both the historicist and ethnographic approaches. Here *before* and *after* (before and after some critical happening) ethnographic cross-sections of one community (or one institution) are compared and contrasted with each other to allow precise assessments of cultural change.

phenomena can only be sought through a chronologically ordered detailed recitation of a series of antecedent events (Van Nieuwen- huijze 1962: 7–37; Brown 1963: 47–57; White 1945; Lowie 1917). The American version of the historical approach, under the leadership of such men as Franz Boas, Al- fred Kroeber, Robert Lowie, and Clark Wiss- ler, developed partly in reaction to the nine- teenth-century evolutionary thinking which had attempted to order the growth and de- velopment of cultures into one long series, which as we have just seen had been dis- proved. Usually suspicious of any kind of broad abstracted generalizations, these schol- ars emphasized the need for very detailed de- scriptions of the unitary traits, trait-com- plexes, or patterns of single cultures. This emphasis on description of the parts and or-

ganization of a cultural system with the data obtained first-hand by a trained and objec- tive professional anthropologist was also partly a reaction to the use of data gleaned from the anecdotal accounts of travelers and explorers so important in an earlier decade. The major assumption of the historical ap- proach was and still is that an event occur- ring within a society, or a trait-complex char- acteristic of that society, or the whole cul- ture considered as one kind of thing, had to be viewed and interpreted as the result of specific historical happenings.

This point must be made clear; the his- toricist approach in cultural anthropology does not mean simply the study of history, what is past, for a great many anthropolo- gists operating within this frame of ideas have concentrated upon contemporary societies. Historicism emphasizes a preferred mode of accounting for or explaining the nature of a cultural system.

This historical viewpoint in its earlier years also had a strong geographic bias, partly the result of a preference for analysis of a culture in terms of its adaptation to a particular geographic setting, partly the result of the fact that many societies studied had little in the way of documented histories. In the latter instance, the operational device of studying the spatial or geographic distribution of cultural elements was adopted as a way to reconstruct in part the histories of societies.[12] However, the emphasis on spatial distribution and ecological adaptation is by no means either intrinsic or central to the historicist approach.[13] The central notion was that the culture of a society was something more than just a set of conveniently abstracted generalizations about the particular behaviors and beliefs of individual men and women. The early historicists were as opposed to reducing the comparative study of human behavior to psychological phenomena as they were to accounting for the nature of culture in terms of biological (racial), economic, or climatological determinism. They felt that social and cultural traits, complexes, and systems had an existence in their own right which transcended organic and psychological phenomena.

For historicism, the path to knowledge about man led through detailed particularizing reconstruction of the origin, development, diffusion, and growth of features of

[12] For a now classic example of the use of the historical point of view, one particularly stressing origins and diffusion of cultural elements as a means of explaining the content of American culture, see Linton 1937.

[13] See Chapter 18 on ecological studies for quite a different perspective, one emphasizing general theory rather than particularizing history. Moreover, in Chapter 17 Dr. Sturtevant discusses the role and activities of the cultural anthropologist as a kind of historian in much greater detail than is required here.

human social life, of men viewed collectively rather than individually. Moreover, to extreme exponents, the emphasis upon the uniqueness of cultural things and behaviors, the preference for explanation in terms of specific history, and the suspicion of taxonomies and generalizations seemed essentially anti-scientific. But this is so if we view science only in the nomothetic and not the idiographic sense discussed earlier.

Historicism emphasizes that human behavior and the products of behavior — individual and collective — exist in a time dimension. Accepting some definition of what constitutes a single culture or a unitary cultural trait in order to imagine an origin point and a terminus, the strategy seeks understanding of that abstracted cultural trait or intact society in terms of origins, growth and development, events and processes flowing along a temporal continuum which constitutes the unique career-arc of that society or bit of patterned behavior.

Structural-Functionalism

While the historical approach in cultural anthropology did and does produce ethnographic reports of the style of life of single societies and communities, its tendency to fragment the parts or elements of a way of life, and to account for the whole assemblage in terms of diffusion and historical contacts was to some anthropologists unsatisfactory. The third school of thought counters this tendency with some version or another of the organismic analogy. Called in its several varieties "functionalism," "structuralism," "structural-functionalism," or the "systems-theoretic approach," this framework is most nearly identified with the purely cross-sectional, ethnographic strategy discussed earlier. It is also well represented in many of the correlational studies of comparative ethnology, where cross-cultural studies of regularities in the association of customs or types of institutions are used to test propositions arising from structural-functional case studies.

Although this approach is best known for its comprehensive depictions of the social life of many of the world's societies, it is less well appreciated that the strategy has been profitably employed in areas other than the comparative sociology of hunting and gathering bands or a peasant community. Particularly in the study of the languages of the world, the structural approach has had a long and distinguished history, and it is being used with increasing frequency as a way to understand other aspects of cultural life, from religion to music.[14]

Working within the confines of the cut taken from the history of a people, the cultural anthropologist who adopts a structural-functional position in effect stops time and reports his findings in the present tense or in the "ethnographic present," to use a jargon phrase once fashionable. Sometimes this involves reconstruction of a now vanished way of life, as was the aim of many American cultural anthropologists concerned with reconstructing descriptions of American Indian societies. More often, as we have seen, the anthropologist depicts the customary ways of a people he has lived with and actually observed during his own lifetime.

These timeless, cross-sectional case studies are more than just anecdotal, subjective reports of collections of oddments of exotic customs. The structural-functional approach developed in reaction to one of the recognized difficulties of the historical strategy, which was relatively unsuccessful in tying together the bits and pieces of culture to make

a meaningful and recognizable whole.[15] In addition to analyzing the way of life of a people into discrete parts, structural-functionalists reconstitute the parts synthetically. Generally, this approach attempts to discover and describe the relatively permanent, normative or ideal, customarily valued aspects of a society's culture. While there is a good deal of philosophical dispute as to whether this skeletal "structure" is something that lies hidden, ready to be discovered in the doings and sayings of real people, or whether it is nothing more than a convenient abstraction or model applied by the observer to a mass of observations and sense impressions, the fact is that cultural anthropologists working with this approach do connect the separable parts of the way of life of a people and show how they are more or less integrated.

Thus, the structural-functional approach sees *a* culture, that is, one single tribe or community, as a unit, as a kind of a whole. The distinctive question of the approach is, what *kind* of a whole is this? The emphasis of the notion of "structure" is thereby upon depiction of the durable, normative features of the observed behavior of the members of society, whether observations concerned the kind of music enjoyed and played, the form and content of myth, or the preferred treatment of mothers-in-law. The central meaning of "function," in contrast, refers to the inner dynamics of the parts of the structure. Functionalism concerns the significant and perhaps causal ways in which, for example, features of belief and myth are related to ritual observance, or the ways in which child-rearing practices are connected to the train-

---

[14] See Chapter 2 for Dr. Chafe's extensive discussion of structuralism in linguistics, and Chapter 4 for Dr. Dundes' treatment of the structural approach to the study of oral literature. A general treatment of the structural perspective will be found in Claude Levi-Strauss' 1962 article, while his *Structural Anthropology* discusses this approach as applied to the study of language, social organization, religion, and art.

[15] Parallel to the development of structural-functionalism in British social anthropology, one offshoot of American historicism also responded to the tendency to fragment traditional behavior into disconnected pieces. For the best statement of this "configurational" development, see Ruth Benedict's 1932 paper, or any of the many editions of her *Patterns of Culture.*

ing of individuals for appropriate skills and motivations for adequate performance in adult roles. The idea of function can come into use only when at least several aspects of the way of life of a people are studied so as to discover the nature of their connectedness. For this reason, it is quite possible to adopt a structural approach without being concerned with functional relations, as is often done in linguistics when describing the grammar or phonemic system of a language. For certain limited purposes, it is very useful to study the structure of one aspect of a culture, say, the technology or art of a community, with very little reference, functional or otherwise, to other features. The notion of function comes into full play when the anthropologist attempts to view the social life of a society as a whole: then one major task involves determining how the different aspects fit together and influence one another.

With this discussion in mind, the sense of the term "systems," as sometimes used to describe this approach, will be appreciated. This idea, simply put, is that cultures or societies constitute some kind of a whole (e.g., a community or a chiefdom) consisting of various parts or subsystems (e.g., a social organization, a value-system or ideology, a world-view or belief system) arranged in orderly ways which exhibit some kind of a plan or scheme. Because it is so easy to become absorbed by and carried along with the impact of the narrative of a description of the total way of life of a people which follows this structural-functional strategy, the fact that each such report constitutes a kind of theory is obscured. To the extent that a social anthropologist working as an ethnographer observes and carefully records, analyzing out form or structure, then proceeds to form concepts about the nature of the whole system, he is constructing a theory. To be certain, it is a set of linked propositions of very limited reference and applicability, but so far as his synthesis accounts for

his observations, generates understanding, and facilitates prediction — which aims most such ethnographic reports accomplish — they constitute theoretical statements about the nature and workings of a single social or cultural system.

The structural-functional approach has obvious and well recognized limitations. In addition to the fact that the strategy produces sophisticated descriptions useful in understanding the joint activities or traditional behaviors of single societies, thus telling us little of the nature of any other culture, it is clear that such assessments are neither so complete, nor so objective, nor so reliable as is desirable.[16]

By concentrating upon that thin slice taken from the total career of a society, by ignoring history, the structural-functional approach creates an essentially static portrait of a way of life, lacking time-depth and comprehension of the dynamics of sociocultural change. The inability to deal with change characteristic of this strategy results from the concentration upon the typical, traditional, central, or dominant features of the way of life of a people, to the selective exclusion of the deviant, submodal, and transitory, which are often both clues to developments away from a past state of affairs and harbingers of the future.

This brief discussion of three major schools of thought in contemporary cultural anthropology will serve as an introduction to the more specific uses and mentions of each in the following chapters. We should emphasize that this discussion has centered on the core features of the major, traditional schools of thought, and that succeeding chapters will introduce a variety of others, including offshoots and more recent branchings

---

[16] See Gluckman and Eggan 1965 for a thorough discussion of these matters in the context of an introduction to a series of monographs reporting on recent trends in the structural-functional approach to the study of social organization.

and trends. Throughout, it should be appreciated that every approach and strategy used involves a series of choices, about what kinds of phenomena and data are relevant, about which issues and problems are critical, how data should be obtained and analyzed, and how all information and conclusions should be assembled, interpreted, and accounted for. Thus there are many frameworks employed by cultural anthropologists in their study of the nature of human social life and culture.

CONCLUSION: THE IDEA OF CULTURE

In concluding the chapter we do not propose to offer a formal definition of the word most frequently used in earlier pages. The idea of culture is perhaps too often defined and redefined, but the reason for such changes is less frequently discussed in the same context of a new formula. The many efforts to capture the immutable essence of the concept in a few words are, we believe, really an effort to provide an answer to one important question. That question is, "After all we have studied and observed of the varieties of human behavior, what can we say that is both general and true of the nature of man?" The motivation thus is to distill into capsule form the findings of more than a century of scholarly labor. The shape and content of the capsule have obviously had to be changed, as our knowledge has measurably expanded. Now we may consider some of the important components of understanding which, joined, have formed one or another of the definitions of culture.

First, let us say that Bennett's comment on the functioning of culture as a symbol for the solidarity of anthropologists is indisputably valid. Various definitions of the idea have been worked and overworked, treated as concrete things and given a tangible reality, and used as devices to explain almost anything that needed explanation in the realm of human social life. Through all this, and despite the differences of opinion which divide them, runs the conviction that somehow anthropologists appreciate the scope and understand the nature of the varieties of human behavior better than any others. Although this may be disputed, it is also probably true and valid, and it is captured by identification with the idea of culture.

There are two fundamental points of entry into an understanding of the nature of man which are critical to the anthropological perspective. Both came into full scholarly awareness only after the fourteenth century. One, as John Rowe has recently shown, was the gradually developing understanding that the past of mankind, indeed, the past of one's own society, was composed of different elements than the present (Rowe 1965). Thus certain Renaissance scholars during the fourteenth and fifteenth centuries demonstrated cultural and linguistic differences between the world of classical antiquity and what was then present; man began to be consciously aware of the phenomena of change in custom and belief through time. Hard on the heels of this understanding came the great explorations, as Europe began pushing its own cultural boundaries outside the limits of one continent. Then came the repeated discovery of vast differences in language and habit throughout the world. The issues of history and cultural change, and of geographic dispersion and cultural differences, are still with us, fundamental dimensions in the character structure of the discipline.

Historical change and regional differences in the varieties of human behavior required understanding and explanation, and biblical, astrological, climatological, and, finally, racial or biological explanations would not do. Then came anthropology, which attempts to face the manifest reality of observed behavioral differences among the peoples of the world and between the past and present and to master them with knowledge.

The first component of understanding is the firm conviction that mankind is one single biological species whose representatives share whatever important inborn propensities they have in common; the manifest important cultural differences which mark mankind could not and cannot be explained by the biologically given. Hence the further conviction that there was a certain arbitrariness or synthetic quality to all varieties of cultural behavior. This arbitrariness does not apply to the convictions and awareness of that group which shares a belief or expresses a value, but only across cultural boundaries. Early anthropology recognized that if man did have common needs or problems, he had invented diverse solutions to them.

Then there is the component of understanding which attempts to handle the obvious partial stability of individual lines of custom through time. Anthropologists have pointed to the social heritage, the separate bundles of tradition which are historically assembled and transmitted down through time, or, as the issue is always stated, from generation to generation. Thus "culture" was very early defined as that which was inherited from the past and which acts with deterministic force so as to mould the content and set the limits of individual and group behavior. While this has been an immensely important component, it creates serious problems when overly emphasized or used alone. It counters the idea of biological determinism with that of social or cultural inheritance, and thus is of critical value. But limiting anthropological attention to only that which is stable through time overly emphasizes continuity. As Jaques Maquet has shown, a whole generation of European anthropologists working in Africa, by concentrating their attentions on the stable customary elements of the tribal past, missed appreciation of the revolutionary developments, then

building, which have now swept Africa (1964).

Another component, as old or older than Edward Tylor's early definitions, is the idea that the customs or traditional behaviors of all peoples constitute some kind of a whole, a complex of parts, a system. This idea is still with us, finding particularly strong emphasis in the structural-functional school, in far more refined form.

If man's ways are not biologically given, but constitute a complexly organized system of beliefs and practices some of which are stable over time or traditional, then some mechanism of transmission must be inserted in our understanding. This adds another element, the idea that critical elements of a culture or a way of life consist of standardized rules or normative prescriptions and proscriptions. This is essentially a restatement of the idea of custom, with somewhat more specific emphasis on the means used by communities to train for and to secure conformity. Unfortunately, it is too easy to become convinced that normative regulation is equally important to and equally stressed by all societies, to fail to recognize that this is only one dimension of social life and that it is subject to variation. Anthropologists have in recent years begun to handle the variations between societies not only in terms of differences in the *content* of belief and custom, but also in terms of the degree to which norms are well stated, taught, stressed, and enforced.

The conviction that "culture" consists of a fixed pattern or set of norms is very much like that of the notion of heritage. It is defective and misleading considered by itself and when overly stressed. If man's ways are not rigidly fixed by his biological nature, neither are they immutably set by his cultural heritage or by the set of norms and standards which are part of his social environment. All men — some much more easily and frequently than others — to some extent recognize the arbitrariness of at least some features of their culture. All men can recognize that at least some elements of their way of life are manipulable and changeable, and all men sometimes create and innovate (Barnett 1953).

To the conviction that a cultural way of life consists of somewhat arbitrary traditional rules or means partially stable through time must be added an answer to the question, "Rules about what? And, means for what?" Thus the varieties of human behavior, or differences in culture, are seen as man's way of adjusting to his environment and his means of solving his problems and satisfying his needs. Thus "culture" is seen as a socially acquired problem-solving device. This may go so far as the assertion that, ultimately, culture developed in response to and as an improved means of reducing or satisfying physiological tensions or drive states of the organism. But at minimum it points to the understanding that different cultural traditions provide various and alternate solutions to at least some common human problems, nutritional needs, affectional needs, sexual needs, and so on.

However, this too can be overdone unless we remember that not only does tradition provide more or less reasonable levels of satisfaction for common needs, it also defines other, secondary or acquired needs, some of which may loom larger in consciousness than the press of basic drive states. Thus culture is a problem-*setting* and problem-*defining* as well as a problem-solving mechanism. In discussing the American woman unserved in Chile we mentioned that she had to learn to adjust to an unexpectedly large number of locks on her Chilean house. There is nothing innate in human or Chilean nature which requires several locks and latches on every exterior door, nor high fences, padlocked gates, fierce dogs, barred and locked windows, and locks on every interior door in the house, including the refrigerator and all closets. This emphasis on the security of self and possessions is a response to quite local fears among a socioeconomic elite for whom the class conflict is a very real and threatening thing. A great deal of culture is made up of such matters, which can only seem arbitrary and exaggerated to the outside observer.

A second part of the suggestion that cultural behavior consists of a set of more or less arbitrarily defined problems and traditional means of securing solutions is the expressed desire of many anthropologists to find a firm, objective lodgment for culture in human psychology. Sometimes this matter is put as the attempt to *reduce* culture to individual psychology, but this is not in itself an intrinsically important issue. However, if man's ways do consist, more or less, of socially acquired, traditionally defined problems and their socially acquired means of solution, then at minimum they are a learned phenomena, and anthropologists must give at least some attention to these dimensions of human psychological functioning. During the past fifty years, like anthropology, the science of psychology has grown and expanded. Consequently we find that at one time or another anthropologists have turned to a very large variety of psychological constructs and theories. The psychological concepts employed include those of conditioned stimuli and responses, cues, drives, rewards, punishments, conflicts, dreams, ego systems, id impulses, attitudes, values, cognitive orientations, ideas, and what have you. In our discussion of the Indian who toyed with the idea of playing witch, we indicated that one quite useful recently developed idea is that of the individual's own perception and understanding of his cultural situation, his cognitive map or mazeway. This represents only one end point of a long series of efforts to bring general assessments of the customs of groups into logical connection with the workings of the individual mind. It will probably not be the last such effort.

This discussion has not by any means covered all relevant dimensions of anthropological understanding of man's cultural forms, of the causes, character, and consequences of his distinctive styles of life. It has been an introduction only; more will come in the next seventeen chapters.

Suggested Readings

The reader beginning in cultural anthropology should turn first to the study of a few good ethnographic reports. He may start by selecting from among the Case Studies in Cultural Anthropology series (Holt, Rinehart and Winston), edited by George and Louise Spindler, a number of good, modern accounts. Because it is a fine description of a first-hand encounter with a hunting and gathering band, Hart and Pilling's 1960 report on the Tiwi of North Australia is a good point of entry. Then maybe to Hoebel's 1960 assessment of Cheyenne culture, an example of a reconstructed "memory" ethnography; perhaps next, John Beattie's small volume on Bunyoro, an African kingdom, which illustrates both the British social anthropological approach and a larger and more complex culture; and then Oscar Lewis' Tepoztlan, a Mexican peasant village. All these are available in the Spindler-edited paperback series. Now the reader should step up a level of difficulty and examine full-scale ethnographies, intended for professional audiences. Two valuable and now classic works here are Malinowski's Argonauts of the Western Pacific and Robert H. Lowie's The Crow Indians, which contrast British and North American approaches to the study of man, and which are also available in paperback format.

Having digested something of the content and style of anthropological data-reporting, the reader might now examine a few standard texts. Of these, one of the best is Melville Jacob's Pattern in Cultural Anthropology, which represents a mature end point in the long development of the American historicist school, and which contains quite valuable chapters on the expressive aspects of culture. A companion might be the relevant chapters of the 1948 edition of A. L. Kroeber's Anthropology, but here the reader must be cautioned that many of the conclusions reached therein have been superseded by later data and interpretations. In this volume Kroeber best expresses many aspects of the historicist position, and he discusses a number of classic problems in this light. Then, for the contrast of the British social anthropological approach, see Raymond Firth's Elements of Social Organization, or Evans-Pritchard, either 1954 or 1964. Claude Levi-Strauss' 1962 volume contains some thoughts of an exceedingly fertile mind and an exposition of the French "structural" position, but it cannot be considered an elementary book. Altogether, until quite recently, modern or neo-evolutionary thinkers have not produced much in the way of basic textbooks, but see Leslie White's book (1959a). Service (1962) attempts to present a coherent overview of the development of forms of primitive social organization, and is provocative, tightly reasoned, and valuable, while Wolf's 1964 essay offers a quick overview of the ideas of evolutionism. Moreover, just appearing is a new paperback series which seems to be dominated by the modern evolutionary perspective, and which will probably be further spiced by a dash of neo-Marxist economic determinism. Now available in this series is Eric R. Wolf's Peasants, the authoritative work on one of the types of communities between the primitive and the industrial orders. Other currently available texts which contain valuable reading are Herskovits (1950), Keesing (1958), Kluckhohn (1949a), and, edited by Sol Tax, *Horizons in Anthropology,* a volume containing many far too brief essays by a younger generation of anthropologists. And finally, see Hall (1959) for an elementary book using a linguistic framework for interpreting human behavior.

Next the reader might move to writings of a more general or theoretical nature. John W. Bennett's 1944, 1946, 1948, and 1964 articles contain a valuable running critique of many of the ideas and schemes used by cultural anthropologists of several persuasions. Spencer (1954) contains several useful essays on problems of method. Leach's 1961 book expresses the controversial position of the "Cambridge" school of social anthropology. Eggan (1955b) offers an overview of a position synthesizing elements of American historicism and the British structural-functional approach, while Tax (1955c) surveys the history of studies of social organization in a most illuminating fashion. The 1956b volume edited by Firth contains critical essays by various authors on the work and ideas of Bronislaw Malinowski. Steward (1955) and Sahlins and Service (1960) express two differing evolutionary positions. Finally, although reading it is like having one's teeth pulled, Marvin Harris' important 1964 *The Nature of Cultural Things,* an exercise in methodological puritanism, is recommended.

The distinction between theory and history is a difficult one, because cultural anthropologists often tend to write their history of the discipline in the form of critical surveys of what went before, prefaced to their own contributions. But see the now very obsolete 1937 volume by Lowie, which examines the history of theory up to that point. In addition, Mead and Bunzel's 1960 book covers salient episodes in the early history of American anthropology; while, although intended

as a critical review of definitions and concepts of the idea of culture, Kroeber and Kluckhohn's 1963 book contains much valuable commentary on the growth of other ideas in anthropology as well. The development of anthropology-like ideas in the period before there was such a profession is surveyed in Slotkin (1965), and Rowe's 1965 paper is quite valuable for this same period. Finally, although they should be approached critically and with the awareness that they are mostly long since superseded, the writings of some of the parental figures of modern anthropology might be examined. Here see, for example, Tylor (1958); Morgan (1963) (reprint of 1877 edition) or (1870); Boas (1940b); Dixon (1928); Maine (1963); Frazer (1922); or Goldenweiser (1933), which last contains a critical historical survey of earlier ideas.

Anthropological approaches to the study of complex societies or states are given in many writings. For an introduction, see Eisenstadt (1961) and Mandelbaum (1956) or Banton (1966a). The volume edited by Clifford Geertz, *Old Societies and New States,* contains several interesting chapters on the phenomena of the building of national level cultures in Africa and Asia. And for an appreciation of what anthropologists do in the way of applying their ideas and methods to practical problems, see Goodenough (1963b) or Foster's 1962 book, or the manual edited by Margaret Mead and published in paperback form in 1955.

Finally, for a look at technical papers reporting on various problems in the several sub-areas of cultural anthropology, see such journals as the *American Anthropologist,* the *Southwestern Journal of Anthropology, Current Anthropology, Man,* or, because its papers largely consist of rich, content-loaded reports in cultural anthropology, the journal *Ethnology.*

CHAPTER 2 introduces the reader to the nature of language and to the viewpoint and methods of linguistics. While the discovery and demonstration of pattern and order in the varieties of human speech has an intellectual fascination all its own, an understanding of the nature of language is fundamental for an appreciation of the foundations of human social life and for comprehension of the evolution and the creative (or destructive) manipulation of other cultural and natural systems. Yet our knowledge of language is largely the product of the efforts of linguistics, that discipline whose subject matter is the varieties of human speech behavior. The nature of this discipline must therefore receive more than passing attention, and also because linguistics enjoys a conceptual elegance and a methodological precision shared by few other branches of cultural anthropology. Thus many anthropologists regard its manifest successes and argue that linguistics might well afford a fruitful model for other areas of anthropological inquiry (cf. Jacobs 1964:393–402), but note should also be taken of a vocal dissent to this opinion in the form, perhaps, of a minority report (cf. Aberle 1960:1–15).

THE AUTHOR was born in Cambridge, Massachusetts, in 1927 and took both his B.A. and Ph.D degrees at Yale. He has taught at the University of Buffalo and worked as a specialist in American Indian languages at the Bureau of American Ethnology of the Smithsonian Institution. Since 1962 he has been with the Department of Linguistics of the University of California, Berkeley. His major research has been in American Indian linguistics, particularly with languages of the Iroquoian and Caddoan families. He has published several works, including *Seneca Morphology, Seneca Thanksgiving Rituals,* and *Handbook of the Seneca Language.* Professor Chafe is currently collecting materials for a description of the Caddo language, now spoken in Oklahoma.

THE LINGUISTIC SYMBOLS used in this chapter require a brief explanation. Vowels written with hooks under them (*ą* and *ų*) are nasalized. ʌ is like the vowel of *shut,* and ʃ is like the *sh* of the same word. *n̪* is a "dental" *n*, pronounced with the tip of the tongue touching the upper teeth; *t̪* is a dental *t* having the same characteristic. *th* is not the *th* of English spelling, but a strongly aspirated *t* such as we have at the beginning of *tea.* Similarly, *kh* is like the sound at the beginning of *key.* *čh* is similar to the sound written *ch* in *chew,* and *č* is the same sound without any aspiration. *x* is like the *ch* of German *machen,* and γ is the same sound accompanied by "voicing," or vibration of the vocal cords. ʔ is the so-called "glottal stop." The accent of certain syllables, a significant feature of Dakota and of other Siouan languages used here as examples, has been omitted to simplify the discussion of historical developments.

2

Language and Linguistics

WALLACE L. CHAFE

University of California, Berkeley

Linguistics is the science whose aim is the systematic accumulation of knowledge about language. This brief opening sentence raises three questions to which the chapter which follows will provide some possible answers. First, what is it that we call language? Second, how does one proceed in a systematic way to accumulate knowledge about it? Third, why should a chapter on this subject have a prominent place in a book concerned with cultural anthropology? The answers to none of these questions are obvious or simple, and it may be helpful to look for them within the context of some of the major trends of thought and investigation which have combined to produce linguistics as it exists today.

Unsystematic notions about language are widespread, just as are unsystematic notions about other things. Especially prevalent is the idea that language is inappropriate as an object of scientific study. All sciences have had to contend with opposition of this kind, but in the so-called physical sciences it is no longer taken very seriously. The social sciences, of which linguistics is one, are still confronted with deep-seated views that their

subject matter is too diversified, too unpredictable, or too ethereal to be amenable to study in any but unsystematic terms. The correctness or incorrectness of such views can be shown only by attempting to disprove them, and that in essence is what linguists and other social scientists are about.

There has also long existed an opinion that language is a more or less imperfect reflection of a kind of natural order in the universe, and, in fact, that different languages or different varieties of the same language can be rated as good or bad according to the closeness with which they approach this natural order. The ancestor of this opinion was the medieval notion that Latin was the perfect reflection of the way things really are. For example, the Latin cases — nominative, genitive, dative, and so on — were thought to reflect the fundamental relations to which all objects in the universe are subject. Other languages, to the extent that anyone paid attention to them at all, were therefore evaluated in terms of their approximation to Latin. One may occasionally still hear the argument that learning Latin "teaches you to think." But a more pervasive manifestation

49

of this normative approach to language in recent times is the opinion that change in a language always represents corruption. It is an attitude clearly evident, for example, in the reaction which followed the appearance of a new edition of Webster's unabridged dictionary in 1961 (Sledd and Ebbitt 1962). Many reviewers believed that all deviations from past stages of English were bad, and that a dictionary should either ignore them or clearly warn against them.

Related to the normative view is an attitude which might be characterized as glottocentrism, the linguistic analog of ethnocentrism. This is the opinion that some languages are superior to others in terms of their intricacy, subtlety, or expressive power. Nearly always, of course, it is the language closer to the person who holds the view that is superior to the languages of other people. Glottocentrism has appeared in numerous guises, but here we may note that it is common for a distinction to be made between languages which are civilized and those which are primitive. Because the civilization of ancient Greece has been held in high esteem among us, for example, we have thought of the Greek language of that period, the language of Euripides and Plato and the rest, as something of a totally different order from, say, the language of present-day African Bushmen. Of a piece is the notion that written languages are qualitatively different from those which are unwritten. There is, in fact, an extremely common confusion of language with writing, and languages which are not written are often thought to be necessarily inferior for that reason.

THE ROOTS OF LINGUISTICS

Such folk ideas about language are cultural phenomena which have developed and changed naturally among peoples everywhere, just as language itself has developed and changed. Systematic ideas on the same subject have developed less frequently and more self-consciously, and we are therefore able to trace them more easily. Modern linguistics has its principal roots in two disciplines, although many others have contributed to it from time to time. These two are philology, whose concern has been with the interpretation of the written records of language man has accidentally left behind at various times and places, and anthropology, whose concern has been with the total nature of man.

It was through philology that the first great impetus came. The earliest known efforts to scrutinize language objectively took place in ancient India, and the results, most notably Panini's description of the ancient liturgical language Sanskrit, were of extremely high quality. It may not be too much to say that the discovery of the worth of this material by Europeans toward the end of the eighteenth century started the chain reaction of linguistic investigation which has continued to the present day. Panini's work was purely descriptive, and based on an analysis of Sanskrit into its underlying patterns with a subsequent presentation of these patterns in terms of abstract formulas. The same general approach has continued as the basis of modern linguistic description. The most important single idea that reached Europe from India was that language is not an amorphous mass but has "structure" — that it contains regular patterns which can be systematically examined and described in exact terms. Europeans had tended to attribute structure to the universe rather than to language, which they saw as only an imperfect reflection of the universal order. Now, gradually, the view took hold that there is an objectively describable structure in language itself. Concomitantly, it began to appear that the kind of order which had been attributed to the universe, as reflected for example in the Latin cases, was illusory.

But nineteenth-century philologists were actually much less consciously concerned with the broad implications of the descriptive work of the ancient Indian grammarians than with the fascinating resemblances they found between Sanskrit and ancient languages like Latin and Greek which they already knew so well. The fact that a distant language in India was so much like the ancient, and indeed like most of the modern languages in Europe, seemed to rule out the earlier prevailing explanation that the resemblances already recognized among European languages were the result of their geographical proximity and of longstanding interinfluences. The alternative explanation, that all these languages had sprung from a single common ancestor, was quickly accepted. A prodigious amount of labor then went into the careful tabulation of the similarities among languages of the so-called Indo-European family, and valid ideas of the nature of language change emerged for the first time. By the end of the third quarter of the nineteenth century enough material had accumulated to justify a bold hypothesis: that there are important aspects of language change which are rigidly patterned. The formulation of this hypothesis has been called one of the great scientific achievements of that century. When coupled with the implications of Panini's work, it meant that language in both its descriptive and historical aspects is indeed amenable to scientific treatment. This realization was by all odds the single most important contribution philology had to make to modern linguistics, and in fact, by implication, to all of social science.

The other discipline most responsible for modern linguistics has been anthropology. A principal concern of anthropologists has been to learn the bases of human abilities, and certainly one of the most obvious examples of such abilities is language. In fact, language is often cited as the chief feature which distinguishes man from all other animals. An observer from a distant planet would notice that among all the animals on earth there is one which has the peculiar ability to communicate an unlimited range of messages by making noises with its mouth and respiratory tract. And anthropologists have realized that this one ability is so fundamental that most other distinctive aspects of human behavior could not exist without it. Social organization, law, economics, technology, education, folklore, or religion in anything like the forms known to us would be unimaginable. The whole unique development of man, with all his complex and varied ways of coping with his life and his environment, is closely tied to this one peculiar thing he has learned to do.

The anthropological approach to language which has had the greatest effect on modern linguistics developed strongly in the United States during the first half of the twentieth century. Undoubtedly the presence on this continent of an unusually large number of highly varied American Indian languages was a stimulating factor. These languages aroused a lively interest and curiosity, and a need was felt to formulate an approach to them which was consistent and adequate, and which remained consonant with, but not slavishly dependent upon, the knowledge already gained in dealing with the languages of Europe. The outstanding figures in this development were Franz Boas, Edward Sapir, and Leonard Bloomfield. Both Sapir and Bloomfield were thoroughly versed as well in the philological background of the linguistics of their time.

If we can summarize his contribution in a few sentences, we can say that it was Boas, followed by his students, who demonstrated most clearly the validity of a view which has been called linguistic relativity. It became clear from detailed studies of American Indian languages, languages which were unwritten and which popular opinion classed as primitive, that they were every bit as complex, as subtle in their means of expression, and as systematically patterned as Greek, Latin, Sanskrit, or any of the civilized languages of Europe. Through these studies of American Indian languages and through other studies of languages in parts of the world outside Europe and America, it became evident that there was no objective criterion for rating languages on a scale of superiority and inferiority. At the same time it was apparent that every language had to be studied on its own terms, that there was no justification for the long-standing practice of looking for features of Latin grammar in all the languages of the world, expecting them to have Latin-like cases, conjugations, and so on. But there also developed a realization that all languages are in certain ways alike, that there is, for example, no essential difference which distinguishes written languages from those which are unwritten. The most important implication here was that a universal theory of language might be developed which would apply with equal adequacy to all the languages of the world.

Sapir and his associates are thought of particularly as prime contributors to the idea that language is an integral part of culture, the total configuration of habits which results from man's interaction with his fellow men. Language came to be viewed as only one part of culture, but an unusually important part because it serves as a carrier of much of the rest. Linguistic study was shown not only to have its own intrinsic importance but to contribute significantly to other cultural study in at least three ways. First, language involves an organization of experience. People who speak different languages organize experience differently, and one student of Sapir, Benjamin Lee Whorf (Whorf

1956; see also Brown 1959:229–263), went so far as to suggest that a person's entire view of the world is determined by the language he speaks. In any case, it is now well established that learning a language does entail the learning of what has been called a cognitive mapping, and that there is a correlation between this mapping and the rest of the culture to which the language belongs. Second, different languages and varieties of languages have proved to be useful as identifiable characteristics of different cultures and cultural subdivisions. Fruitful discoveries have come from attempts to correlate linguistic differences with both large- and small-scale differences of other kinds. Third, language has in some ways proved easier to work with than other areas of culture, and advances in linguistic theory and methodology have suggested profitable approaches to other kinds of cultural material.

Bloomfield's approach to language exerted the greatest influence on the development of linguistics during roughly the second quarter of this century. From his work there developed a highly distinctive theory and methodology which is generally characterized as "Bloomfieldian," although it is as much the result of the particular direction in which Bloomfield's own ideas were elaborated and utilized by others.

BLOOMFIELDIAN LINGUISTICS

Bloomfield saw language as existing within a special framework which he adapted from behavioristic psychology. A stimulus acting on an organism may elicit a response. In human beings it is possible for the response to be either direct (obtaining food when hungry, for example) or indirect (asking someone else to obtain the food). This latter "substitute response," involving the production of sounds, Bloomfield called an "act of speech." From the point of view of the second person, the receiver of the sounds, the act of speech functions as a "substitute stimulus," for he procures the food, if he is cooperative, not because of his own hunger but because he hears some noises made by a person who is hungry. Bloomfield saw this combination of substitute response and substitute stimulus as the linguist's only proper focus of attention. A linguist should concern himself with the patterning found in the articulation of sounds and in their reception by the hearer. Anything else, particularly the nature of the original stimulus and the final response (hunger and obtaining food, for example), were believed to lie outside the linguist's concern and, in fact, to belong to areas far too vast and complex for anyone to deal with at the present stage of human knowledge. This attitude was not unrelated to the view, mentioned at the beginning of this chapter, that human habits are too diversified for systematic investigation. Bloomfield was unwilling to go further than to admit that the habits of sound production and reception associated with language can be systematically studied. His was a belief that came to be interpreted as an abrogation of linguistic concern for "meaning." And it is quite true that even up to the present time a major distinguishing characteristic of American linguistics has been an unwillingness to admit that language manifests itself in anything but sound in any way that a linguist can profitably handle.

Bloomfieldian innovations were centered chiefly within the area of descriptive linguistics. The goal was to develop rigorous methods which could be used in describing any and all of the languages of the world. Description was seen to involve, first, the observation of an adequate sample of the speech acts in a language; next, the subjection of this "corpus" of "raw data" to analysis; and finally, the systematic presentation of the results of the analysis.

The first task of a linguist was to sit down with a native speaker of the language he was interested in and to record as many acts of speech as possible. There arose a classic stereotype of the linguist sitting under an apple tree with a notebook and an old Indian. The linguist began by attempting to transcribe each utterance in the greatest possible detail. The ability to produce a good "phonetic transcription" came to be highly valued, and depended upon considerable training as well as some degree of talent. For every speech act the linguist recorded phonetically, he also wrote down a meaning. However, he had no special training in how to do this part of his job accurately, and he was taught to view whatever he wrote as a rough approximation which need only tell him whether the stimulus-response situation associated with the act of speech was the same as, or different from, that associated with other acts of speech.

We might catch a glimpse of a linguist as he works in these early stages with the Dakota language, spoken by the Dakota or Sioux Indians of the northern plains of the United States. At the outset the linguist asks the native speaker, usually referred to as the "informant," to say things which are relatively short in order to minimize his difficulties in transcribing the unfamiliar sounds. He might, for example, begin by asking for low numerals like "one," "two," "three," and so on, which more often than not turn out to be short words. Attempting to transcribe them in as much phonetic detail as possible, he would come out with a notation something like the following: *wǫ(ŋ)tsʌ* "one," *ŋ́u(m)pʌ* "two," *yamiŋi* "three," and so on. The precise significance of all the symbols need not concern us. We need only appreciate that the linguist uses them in an attempt to record the sounds as accurately and in as much detail as he can. He usually asks for a number of repetitions of the same word, expecting to find at least some perceptible variations, of which he also makes careful note. In this way he finds, for example, that the weakly articulated (η) in "one" and the (m) in "two" are sometimes there and sometimes not; for that reason they appear in his transcription in parentheses.

In recent years he has been aided by several electronic devices. The tape recorder has allowed him to preserve the actual sound itself, to be reheard at any time. And he has been able to make pictures of the utterances with a device called the acoustic spectrograph, which plots in detail the varying amplitude of the sounds on a vertical scale of frequency and a horizontal scale of time. The resulting picture, called a spectrogram, provides the linguist with precise acoustic data to supplement his phonetic transcription, which cannot help being in part subjective.

Once he has collected a small sample of the utterances of a language in this way, and as he continues to collect more, the linguist begins to subject the data to what has been termed a "phonemic analysis," the purpose of which is to "find the phonemes." To understand the significance of this activity we must broaden our scope momentarily beyond the strictly Bloomfieldian approach, and realize that all systematic thinking about language during the past half-century has in one way or another included the idea that language has both a concrete, externally observable substance — an outward manifestation — and an abstract, not directly observable form — an inner structure. Now for a Bloomfieldian linguist, the only relevant substance of language was sound, and it was his task to discover the structure which underlay the sounds he was able to observe. His theory was that this structure consisted of a series of levels, with units on the higher and more complex levels put together of units on the lower and more simple. The bottom level contained the smallest units, called "phonemes." One of the chief theoretical activities of Bloomfieldian linguists in the 1930's and 1940's was to look for a

rigorous method of characterizing phonemes so they could be readily identified in a consistent way for every language.

Phonemic analysis was accomplished by scanning the phonetic data for different sounds which were both "phonetically similar" and in "noncontrastive distribution." Thus, looking back at his Dakota data, our linguist would see that the final unaccented vowel of "one" and "two," transcribed as Λ, was a vowel quite similar in acoustic quality and articulation to the vowel transcribed as a in the first syllable of "three." As he examined an increasingly large sample of Dakota utterances he would find that Λ occurred only and always in the final unaccented syllable of a word, and a never in that position. The two would then be said to be in "complementary distribution." On this basis they would be regarded as variant manifestations of one and the same underlying phoneme. This particular phoneme might be symbolized as a in a subsequent phonemic (rather than phonetic) transcription, and it would be said to have the two "allophones" a and Λ. Which allophone actually occurred in the phonetic data would be predictable from the phoneme's environment. The other kind of noncontrastive distribution beside the complementary kind just illustrated was known as "free variation." Sound differences randomly distributed in the same environment were seen as nonsignificant differences insofar as the language was concerned, and thus ignorable in the phonemic analysis. The parenthesized (η) and (m) in the Dakota data are in free variation with their own absence, cropping up randomly between a nasalized vowel like a or u and a following t or p. The phonemicist would therefore feel justified in saying that insofar as the inner structure of the language was concerned, they were never there at all. Taking all these and other details of his phonemic analysis into account, he would eventually arrive at a new way of transcribing the language, not phonetically this time, but phonemically. Now the words for "one," "two," and "three" would be rewritten as *wą́ča, nųpa,* and *yamni.* These transcriptions would be said to specify the significant features of each word, and to omit everything nonsignificant.

Several justifications for a phonemic analysis were explicitly adduced by Bloomfieldian linguists. One was that it could be rigorously arrived at, that independent investigators working on the same language would arrive at the same results, whereas a purely phonetic transcription was always dependent upon the skill of the investigator and could in no case achieve the complete accuracy it aimed at, since the number of variations in sounds even within the same language was infinite. It proved to be the case that linguists did not arrive at the same phonemic analysis for the same language, but the argument was that any differences were relatively minor and mutually convertible, as phonetic transcriptions were not. Most important, however, was the point already made, that a phonemic analysis told something significant about the language, that it revealed an underlying coherent system which was back of all the seemingly infinite diversity that appeared on the surface. It is a truth about the structure of Dakota that it has some twenty-odd phonemes which combine with one another in certain specifiable ways, and it is the linguist's duty to ferret them out. "The phonetician who refuses to subject his material to phonemic analysis not only is not a linguist, but denies the very purpose of linguistic science" (Bloch and Trager 1942:39). The further inference that phonemes reflect a kind of psychological reality was made much of by Sapir (Sapir 1933), but it was characteristic of the Bloomfieldians that they rejected such considerations as outside the proper concern of linguistics: "The psychological correlates of [the facts of speech] are undoubtedly important; but

the linguist has no means — as a linguist — of analyzing them" (Bloch and Trager 1942:40).

After the linguist arrived at the phonemic analysis which more or less satisfied him, or, in actual practice, while he was in the process of doing so, he began to look for units on what he conceived of as the next higher level. These units were called "morphemes." They were thought to be made up of phonemes, but to differ fundamentally from phonemes by "having meaning." Thus *wą́ča* would be regarded as a morpheme made up of the particular phonemes which are indicated by the written symbols, and it would be said to have the meaning "one."

Morphemic analysis was thought to follow naturally on the heels of phonemic analysis, and to proceed in much the same way. As the search in phonemic analysis was for *phonetic* similarity and noncontrastive distribution, in morphemic analysis one looked for *semantic* similarity and noncontrastive distribution. Thus the phoneme sequence *wa* in Dakota has the meaning "I" in utterances like *wathi* "I dwell" and *wak?u* "I give it," and the phoneme *b* has the meaning "I" in utterances like *bduha* "I have it." Since *wa* meaning "I" never occurs with the verb meaning "have" and *b* meaning "I" never occurs with the verbs meaning "dwell" or "give," *wa* and *b* are in complementary distribution and would be said to be "allomorphs" of the same morpheme.

The minimal meaningful units of a language, then, were held to be morphemes, and they were thought to be made up of still more minimal, but not meaningful phonemes. The rest of a linguist's task was to discover the patterning by which morphemes were arranged together to form larger units: words, phrases, clauses, and sentences. This conception was based on the familiar schoolbook notion of "diagramming" or "parsing." Several of its characteristics which are especially associated with Bloomfieldian linguistics may be mentioned here. First, a difference was seen in the patterning of morphemes within words as opposed to the patterning of words within phrases or sentences. The structure of words was termed "morphology" and the structure of phrases or sentences was called "syntax." Second, the entire hierarchy from morpheme to sentence was seen as a series of successive inclusions, of boxes within boxes (Wells 1947). Thus the sentence *John loved Mary* would be said to have the "immediate constituents" *John* and *loved Mary*. The latter would have the immediate constituents *loved* and *Mary,* and *loved,* the immediate constituents *love* and *d* (past tense). All sentences were believed to be analyzable in this fashion, although further subtleties of various kinds had to be considered. Immediate constituents were said to belong to "constructions," which themselves have meaning, the meaning which relates the meanings of the several constituents. Thus, *John* and *loved Mary* are joined within a construction of "predication" or "actor-action," *loved* and *Mary* within a construction of "complementation" or "action-goal." Sometimes it was only this difference in constructional meaning which explained the ambiguity in phrases whose constituent structure seemed to be the same. Thus, *the love of women* may mean either that women love or that they are loved, and it was necessary to infer that two different constructions are involved in the relation of the prepositional phrase to what precedes it.

A Bloomfieldian description of a language was centered around a "grammar," which began with a list of the language's phonemes and a specification of their allophones. Then came a description of the morphology in terms of morphemes, their allomorphs, and their arrangements within words. Finally, although often omitted, there was a syntax, presented in terms of immediate constituents and constructions. In addition to the gram-

mar, an adequate description of a language was regarded as containing a dictionary or "lexicon," roughly, a list of all the morphemes with indications of their special peculiarities. Finally, there would be a series of representative texts, meant to illustrate the language in actual use. They generally consisted of folktales or narratives, and sometimes of conversational material.

Bloomfieldian linguistics held the center of the stage in the United States for several decades. Since a large number of widely varying languages were approached within a single, basically unified framework, both the methodology and its underlying theory had an unusually full opportunity to be defined, elaborated, and modified. By the 1950's it began to be realized that there were certain basic inadequacies which could not be overcome simply by making adjustments in the framework itself. More far-reaching changes seemed unavoidable. As this chapter is written, however, linguists are seriously divided as to what these revisions should be and it is impossible to set down any generally agreed upon theory which can be said to have replaced the Bloomfieldian. Two important, although by no means universally accepted revisions will be discussed below: the splitting of language into two parallel structures instead of one; and the splitting of phonemes and morphemes into still smaller units. But first, it will be useful to review briefly the fundamental how and why of what linguists do.

WAYS OF KNOWING ABOUT LANGUAGE

A linguist is like a person who has newly discovered the game of baseball and wants desperately to find out how it is played, but who has no one willing to tell him. He is reduced to attending as many games as possible and taking careful note of everything that happens. Since he is so ignorant, he will inevitably record many things which are superfluous; for example, let us say, the length of time of each inning. And he will inevitably miss many things which are significant; for example, perhaps, the factors which determine whether a pitch is judged a called strike or a ball. However, there is no limit to the degree of sophistication he may reach in recording what he observes.

But no matter how many games our baseball watcher attends and how great the detail in which he records them, he will never understand how baseball is played if he does nothing else. The underlying system will remain as obscure as it was at first. Apparently there is no way he can get at it except to guess what characteristics a system would have in order to produce what he has observed. The more observations he makes, the better his guesses will be, but the observations by themselves are never sufficient. They are but outward, and, in a sense, accidental manifestations of what he really wants to know. As he makes his guesses, he has to check them against further observations, modifying them when necessary, until he finally arrives at his goal: a collection of interrelated confirmed guesses which, in their entirety, constitute an understanding of baseball — guesses which explain everything he has observed, which allow him to predict that certain things will and will not happen in subsequent games, and which in general allow him to say he knows how the game is played.

The linguist works in just this way. Being able to observe only its outward manifestations, he must formulate a theory as to the underlying system of language — a theory which will explain everything he observes, which will enable him to predict that certain features will and will not be present in any subsequent observations, and which allow him to say he understands the nature of language. The Bloomfieldian linguist had a theory which was based on detailed observation of the sounds of many languages as

well as of certain phenomena which led him to characterize different utterances as having the same or different meanings. To explain what he found, he hypothesized the existence of certain underlying units such as phonemes and morphemes, and of certain kinds of patterns within which these units co-occurred. His total theory, a combination of all these hypotheses, did indeed enable him to explain and predict a number of things about language. Our objections today are that there were certain features of language which he accounted for inadequately, and that there were other, extremely important areas of language he did not account for at all.

Two ways of viewing the ultimate goal of linguistics have been characterized as the "hocus-pocus" school and the "God's truth" school. The former view amounts to saying that a variety of theories about language are equally acceptable, that any theory is all right so long as it works. The other view assumes that there is a single ultimate truth for which we are searching. In spite of their sometimes disconcerting lack of agreement, linguistic theories when viewed in perspective do in fact seem to be converging toward a common point, and this evidence may be taken to support the God's truth assumption. If there is any real difference among linguists in this area, it may ultimately boil down to nothing more than a difference in emphasis. Some linguists are predominantly concerned with the deductive aspects of theory formation; they tend to invent theories first and then to test them against observable facts. Other linguists emphasize induction. They work from a realization that the number of acceptable theories is inversely proportional to the extensiveness of the data collected, and they therefore devote a major portion of their efforts to the detailed recording of observations. However, it seems clear enough that the ultimate truth about language, if there is one, will be discovered only through a successful marriage of both induction and deduction, that the most detailed and wide-ranging observations must be combined with an imaginative exploration of all possible ways of explaining them.

One of the most noteworthy characteristics of recent theoretical developments in linguistics has been the attempt to achieve a high degree of explicitness, exactness, and conciseness. To some extent this trend can be attributed to the influence of electronic computers. Linguistic data has been overwhelming in its sheer quantity, and computers have offered a chance to cope with it in a way that was not possible earlier. Exploration of what computers can do for linguists is still in its initial stages, but it is already plain that the data and instructions presented to a computer must be stated with clarity and precision. At the same time there has been an influx into linguistics of scholars trained in mathematical logic, and their background has led them to seek a kind of rigorous formalism which was not a major part of the philological or anthropological traditions. One tangible result of these two separate, but not unrelated influences on linguistics can be seen in attempts to bring all statements about language within the format of "rules": quasi-mathematical formulas which aim at covering whatever needs to be said in as precise and concise a fashion as possible. Various kinds of rules have been suggested, and there are several rather different theoretical frameworks within which they have been applied. One of the most popular is known as "transformational grammar"; it is a movement which has stimulated considerable debate on the aims and methods of linguistics in general (Chomsky 1957).

TWO STRUCTURES FOR ONE

A contemporary of Franz Boas was a Swiss linguist named Ferdinand de Saussure, one of the group of Indo-European scholars responsible for the nineteenth-century theory of regularity in language change. He is remembered not only for his role in that area, but even more for the ideas on language in general which he set forth during the last years of his life and which were posthumously reconstructed from class notes and published by his students. Two of his ideas are especially pertinent here. One is the separation of the observable manifestation of language, which Saussure called "parole," from the underlying system, which he called "langue." This separation has, as we noted before, been accepted as valid by most modern linguists, but Saussure was the first to publicize it explicitly. The other idea is that language is a system of "signs," each sign being a two-sided coin with the "signifier" on one side and the "thing signified" on the other. Many others have made use of this concept, and it is implicit in Bloomfield's "substitute stimulus," which is in these terms a signifier of the original stimulus, the thing signified.

However, it remained for a Danish theoretician, Louis Hjelmslev, to disseminate a view which amounted to splitting the coin into two quite separate parts. Hjelmslev distinguished sharply between what, in the English translation of his work, are called the two "planes" of language. One plane is "expression," the realm of the signifier, and the other is "content," the realm of the thing signified. The two planes, said Hjelmslev, are structured in analogous fashion, and each has its own division into "form" and "substance." Thus there is an expression form, an expression substance, a content form, and a content substance. Hjelmslev emphasized that there are many other aspects of culture which show a division into two separate planes, and he envisioned linguistics as a model science whose results would eventually spread to all the humanities.

In contrast to the theory that language has two analogously structured but separate

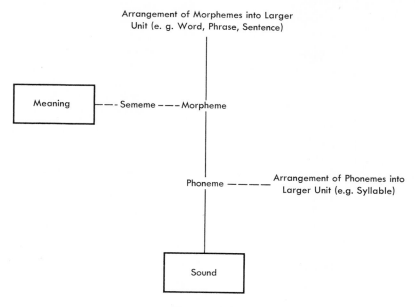

Arrangement of Morphemes into Larger
Unit (e. g. Word, Phrase, Sentence)

┌─────────────┐
│   Meaning   │ ── Sememe ─── Morpheme
└─────────────┘

Phoneme ─ ─ ─ ─ Arrangement of Phonemes into
Larger Unit (e.g. Syllable)

┌─────────────┐
│   Sound   │
└─────────────┘

FIGURE 2-1

planes of expression and content, the substance of one being sound, and of the other, meaning, the Bloomfieldian and predominantly American theory provided for only a single plane, whose substance was sound. The Bloomfieldian model of language might be diagrammed as in Figure 2-1. Linguists were held to be concerned only with the main vertical stem in this diagram. It was acknowledged that morphemes had meanings, and Bloomfield called the meaning of a morpheme a "sememe," but linguistic investigation of this area was thought to be impossible. It was also recognized that phonemes combined into larger units like syllables, and syllables into still larger units, in much the same way that morphemes combined into larger units like words, phrases, and sentences. But the conclusion that might have been drawn from the necessity to admit branches from the main stem remained obscure. In retrospect it appears that this conclusion might have been strengthened by another consideration, that the line between "phoneme" and "morpheme" in the diagram

was the area of language causing linguists by far the most trouble. Numerous articles during the 1940's and early 1950's tried to cope with it, and in fact illuminated many of the kinds of things which were found in this area. But the fact that the relation between morphemes and phonemes was of a completely different order than any other relation in language was never emphasized.

Suppose we perform several operations which will modify Figure 2-1. To indicate that the morpheme-phoneme relation is different from the others we can show it in a horizontal rather than a vertical line. And to indicate that the phoneme-syllable-etc. relation is like the others, we can show it in a vertical line. Furthermore, we can leave out the sememe category, since it would appear that Bloomfield's sememes and morphemes were in a wholly one-to-one relationship. These changes leave us with the diagram of Figure 2-2. The result is reminiscent of Hjelmslev's view of language, for we can identify the two planes of content and expression, represented here by the ver-

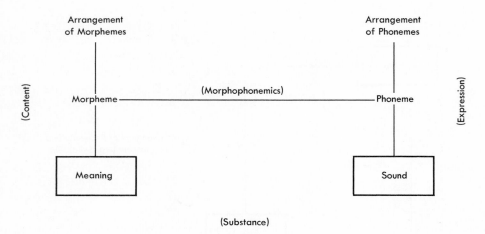

(Form)

Arrangement
of Morphemes

Arrangement
of Phonemes

(Content)

(Morphophonemics)

(Expression)

Morpheme ——————————————————— Phoneme

Meaning

Sound

(Substance)

FIGURE 2-2

tical stems on the left and on the right respectively, and we can also see that there is
a separation of substance, represented in the
two boxes at the bottom, from form, represented by everything above them.

The point of all this can be illustrated by
looking back to an item of Dakota, for example, *wǫ́ča* "one." To the Bloomfieldian
linguist this unit was simply *wǫ́ča,* a morpheme composed of the phonemes *w, ǫ,* and
so on. The meaning "one" was more or
less extraneous, tacked on to show the extralinguistic stimulus and response associated
with the linguistic form. The only "substance" was sound, the only "form" was that
associated with the sound. Adherents of
this view would point out that one pays a
telephone bill for the privilege of transmitting sound and nothing else. In one sense,
of course, this observation is correct. But it
would be curious to think that telephones
were invented only so that people could make
noises at each other across long distances.
Clearly, from another point of view, something beside sound is transmitted. Sound is
simply the "expression" of the "content,"

which is the only thing of interest to either
the sender or the receiver. In this light,
therefore, the Dakota item must be separated
into two quite different aspects. One we can
write as *wǫ́ča* and regard as a unit of expression composed of two syllables, each of
which is composed of certain phonemes. The
other we can write as "one," using this label
for a unit of content in the language, a formal
unit which is related to the substance, not of
sound, but of meaning. A unit of this kind
can still, if we like, be called a "morpheme,"
but it can no longer be thought of as *composed of* phonemes in any way. It is, rather,
symbolized by phonemes.

Language as illustrated in Figure 2-2 can
be thought of as a modified "*H*," with its
legs embedded in the two substances of
meaning and sound. The left-hand line is
content, the right-hand line, expression, and
the crossbar is the link between them. This
link is often referred to as "morphophonemics." It determines the way in which
units of content are symbolized by units of
expression. Thus, for example, the Dakota
morpheme "one" is symbolized by the

phoneme arrangement *wǎča*. As we saw earlier, the Dakota morpheme "I" is symbolized by the phonemes *wa* under some conditions, by the phoneme *b* under others. Frequently there is a great deal more complexity than this, and the adequate description of morphophonemics often calls for highly elaborate techniques.

When a person speaks, he begins with an experience he wishes to communicate. "Experience," in fact, might be a better label than "meaning" for the substance of content in Figure 2-2. He must first find an appropriate way to fit his experience into the content system of his language; he must in a sense "grope for words." In deciding to speak in the first place, and then in deciding which linguistic habits will serve best to communicate what he wants to say, the speaker has room for choice. That is, his language makes available to him a number of possible alternatives which may be more or less appropriate. But at this point, there follows a progression from the content structure through morphophonemics and the expression structure which is entirely determined for the speaker by his language and over which he exercises no control. He is able once again to make a choice at the very end of the process, when he can decide whether to translate the resulting expression form into the substance of sound, or to go no further than "talking to himself." If he goes on, he is speaking. If he stops at this point, he is thinking; at least a great deal of what is commonly called thinking is simply this. The hearer of the sound, provided he shares the language of the speaker, follows the same route in reverse. Hearing sound, he carries it through the structures of expression, morphophonemics, and content, and ultimately into his own experience. There is inevitable distortion in all these areas, so that the experience with which the hearer ends can never be precisely the same as that with which the speaker began. Often, of course,

there is serious misunderstanding. But, in the main, language functions as a remarkably effective mediator between the experiences of different individuals.

We have seen the advisability of transforming the Bloomfieldian framework, with its single structure rooted in sound, into a framework of two structures with a link between them and roots in both sound and experience. It is worth reflecting on why linguistics has been passing through a period in which it has been unwilling to build on other than chiefly phonetic observations. The reason seems to be, quite simply, that it is so comparatively easy to work with sound. The acoustic dimensions which combine in varying proportions in speech are fundamentally only three: the frequency of sound waves; their amplitude; and time. Electronic devices now permit accurate measurement of these dimensions, as well as the indefinite preservation of sounds and their facile manipulation for experiments. Studies in the physiology of speech sound production are well advanced, and there is hope for equal success in studies of hearing. Theories as to the nature of the structure of expression can therefore be built on a firm foundation of observable facts. Experience, on the contrary, has a formidable vastness. Part of it can be measured and manipulated with a great deal of sophistication, but other parts have remained inaccessible and there is no coherent method of attack on experience as a whole. It is nearly always difficult to know in particular instances whether all relevant dimensions are being taken into account. Incomplete approximations are accepted more often than not, in lieu of the kind of accurate and reasonably exhaustive coverage phonetics can provide. However, linguists, and particularly cultural anthropologists who are linguistically oriented, have made a start in coping with experience, observing it in a number of ways: through translation from an unfamiliar language to a familiar one;

through paraphrase within a single language; through introspection in those cases in which the investigator is himself a speaker of the language concerned; through careful observation of environmental factors correlated with features of language; and through experimentation. Some small indication of the approaches which are possible in this area will emerge from the following section.

FURTHER ANALYSIS OF PHONEMES AND MORPHEMES

Bloomfield illustrated the validity of the phonemic concept by pointing out that words like *pin* and *tin* differ from each other in that one begins with *p* and the other with *t*. The difference between *p* and *t* is thus shown to be significant in English and the two are identified as different phonemes. But in fact the difference which distinguishes *p* from *t* is exactly the same as that which distinguishes *b* from *d* or *m* from *n*. In each case the lips are closed for the first item, while for the second, the tongue touches the roof of the mouth just back of the upper teeth. Similarly, *pin* differs from *bin* (and *tin* from *din*) by virtue of the fact that, among other things, the vocal cords start vibrating only with the onset of the vowel in *pin* (and *tin*), while in *bin* (and *din*) they vibrate while the mouth is still closed. Furthermore, *pin* and *bin* both differ from *Min* in having the nasal passage closed at the beginning of the word. In *Min,* on the contrary, air is allowed to escape through the nose. All these facts have been well known for a long time, but until recently linguists continued to regard *p* as a minimal unit even though they described it as a "voiceless bilabial stop." It took some time to realize that "voicelessness" (lack of vibration in the vocal cords), "bilabialness" (involvement of the two lips), and "stopness" (complete closure of both the mouth and nose) were units themselves.

Thus it appears that the truly minimal

units of phonology are not those which have come to be thought of as phonemes, but something smaller. These smaller units have been called sometimes "distinctive features," sometimes "components." Other investigators have noticed that the same kind of further analysis is often possible in the case of morphemes. For example, it is evident that in English "father" is to "mother" as "uncle" is to "aunt," as "brother" is to "sister," and so on. Similarly, "father" is to "uncle" as "son" is to "nephew," and "father" is to "son" as "uncle" is to "nephew." Just as we identified three components of the phoneme *p* in English, therefore, we can also identify three components of the morpheme "father": "male," "lineal descent," and "one generation older than the reference point." These, it would seem, and not "father," are minimal units of content. "Componential analysis" of content units has been actively pursued in recent years. Analysis of kinship terms has proved especially successful (Lounsbury 1956; Goodenough 1956a), but similar work has been attempted in other areas too. Content units like personal pronouns have, for example, shown themselves equally amenable to "submorphemic" analysis. It might be instructive now to return to our Dakota informant to see how we might attack a small part of the content of his language from the point of view that it is a structure of units and combinations whose substance is meaning, not sound, and at the same time to see how certain submorphemic components might emerge.

Suppose we begin by asking our informant how he would say "I live" in his language. We might get one or both of two answers, transcribable phonemically as *wathi* and *niwaʔu*. Even though we have found that phonemes are analyzable into still smaller units, it is not necessary to give up the practice of transcribing speech in phonemic terms, for it is still true that morphophonemics (Figure 2-2) involves the symbolization of units which are comparable to traditional morphemes by units which are comparable to traditional phonemes, not of submorphemic components by subphonemic ones.

By looking for the words *wathi* and *niwaʔu̜* in more explicit contexts, perhaps just by asking the informant to use them in longer sentences, we would have little trouble in determining that the former could also be translated "I dwell" and the latter "I am alive." In fact, since in this case our informant speaks English, he might be quite willing to volunteer these alternative translations himself. Focusing on the word which means "I dwell," we might next decide to explore what would happen if we changed the person, gender, or number of the subject. We would find that the English stimuli given on the left below would elicit the Dakota responses on the right:

I live	*wathi*
you live	*yathi* or *yathipi*
he lives	*thi*
she lives	*thi*
it lives	*thi*
we live	*ʔu̜thi* or *ʔu̜thipi*
they live	*thipi*

It is obvious that Dakota does not divide up whatever experiences are involved here in the same way that English does. In some cases there are two Dakota responses for the same English, and in one case there are three English equivalents for only one Dakota word. Our task is to investigate precisely what makes up the Dakota pattern.

We might observe first of all that the phoneme sequence *thi* is consistently present. Apparently, therefore, it symbolizes a consistently present unit of content which we may take to involve an experience similar to that involved in English "live" or "dwell." We might also notice that this *thi* is preceded by other phonemes when "I," "you," or "we"

is present in the English, but not when the English contains "he," "she," "it," or "they." It appears, then, that first- and second-person subjects have some kind of overt phonological symbolization in Dakota, but that third-person subjects do not. The traditional interpretation of a situation like this is to say that Dakota simply lacks a third person. Another possible interpretation is that there is a third-person unit in the language, but that it is "unmarked"; it is symbolized by the absence of any other symbolization. Let us say that Dakota has a "third person" which is unmarked, a "second person" symbolized by *ya,* and, apparently, a "first person" which may be symbolized by either *wa* or *ʔu̜.* The difference between these last two is not yet clear.

We could observe further that a phoneme sequence *pi* sometimes follows the *thi,* and we might easily guess from the data that *pi* symbolizes plurality of the subject. We could ask the informant to use these words in larger contexts in which the number of the subject was explicit, and our guess would be confirmed. We would find that *yathi* symbolized "you (singular) live," whereas *yathipi* symbolizes "you (plural) live." But the difference between *ʔu̜thi* and *ʔu̜thipi* is still unexplained. For the meaning, "we live," we would actually be led by the rest of the patterning to expect a symbolization *wathipi,* but no such word seems to exist. We might ask the informant whether he would ever say such a word, and he would be unwilling to accept it as possible.

Further observation of the two words in larger contexts would show us that the singular *ʔu̜thi* is used when the subject can be paraphrased in translation as "you (singular) and I," while the plural *ʔu̜thipi* is used for all other senses of English "we," including "he, she, it, or they and I" as well as "you (plural) and I," or "you, I, and some other people." Evidently we have the unexpected situation that "you and I" is treated in Dakota as a singular meaning, even though two people are involved. Of course, "pair" and "couple" in English are singular also. Furthermore, the plural of "you and I" in Dakota is apparently any grouping of people at all that could be translated by English "we," except for a group consisting of the speaker and one hearer. It is impossible to translate the meaning of ʔų into English in any simple way.

We might summarize our findings as follows:

Singular (without *pi*)	Plural (with *pi*)
wa "speaker"	(doesn't occur)
ya "hearer"	"hearers"
ʔų "speaker plus one hearer"	"speaker plus several hearers, or plus one or more third parties, or plus one or more hearers and one or more third parties"
Unmarked "third party"	"third parties"

In contrast, the English way of dividing the same general area of experience could be shown in the following way:

I "speaker"
you "one or more hearers"
he "one male third party"
she "one female third party"
it "one nonhuman third party"
we "speaker plus one or more hearers and/or third parties (or, rarely, several speakers at once)"
they "third parties"

Looking a bit further, we would find that Dakota has another set of grammatical units which are quite parallel to those described above except that they involve the object rather than the subject of a verb. The contrast is similar to that between English "I" and "me," for example. Exploring the objects roughly corresponding to "me" and "you," we would find the following arrangement:

	Subject	Object
First person	*wa*	*ma*
Second person	*ya*	*ni*

From this it appears that the "morphemes" symbolized by *wa, ya, ma,* and *ni* are not minimal units of Dakota grammar. The meaning of *wa* is "first person subject," but we can analyze it further into "first person" and "subject." The truly minimal units here are "first person," "second person," "subject," and "object." These four, we can say, are some of the components of Dakota pronominal prefixes. They combine in the ways just illustrated, as well as in some other ways, the investigation of which would carry us deeper into the language than we can afford to go now.

COMPARATIVE LINGUISTICS

A linguist is faced initially with a bewildering variety of observations in the form of sounds, situations, translations, experimental results, and so on. Perhaps before long he will even have useful ways of more directly probing the brains of the speakers and the hearers of a language. He assumes that all these observed data are manifestations of an underlying system, which it is his principal task to uncover. He makes this assumption for no other reason than that he and other linguists have found it to be fruitful. While no one has yet discovered everything there is to be discovered about the system of any language or of language in general, linguists believe they have discovered more than enough to convince them of the validity of their basic assumption that a system is present.

Language can be regarded as in part a system of habits — habits learned by each individual from other individuals with whom he interacts, predominantly during his early childhood, but to some extent through his whole lifetime. No two people ever interact with exactly the same other people in all the same learning situations, and consequently there are never two individuals whose language habits are wholly identical. In the writer's own family, for example, such differences as the following abound. One member of the family pronounces the four words *merry, Mary, marry,* and *Murray* all differently. A second member pronounces *merry, Mary,* and *marry* differently but makes no distinction between *merry* and *Murray.* A third distinguishes between *merry* and *Murray,* but not between *Mary* and *marry.* Not only does one person's language differ from everyone else's, but no one speaks exactly the same way at different times in his own life. The most obvious differences are due to the learning and forgetting of vocabulary, but there are always other kinds of changes too. They are especially numerous during the earlier periods of a person's life, but they continue to some degree until he dies. The writer used no *r* in words like *park* until he was almost twenty years old, but in later years he has used it consistently.

The unique language of a single individual at a certain stage of his life is often called an "idiolect." Characteristically we find a collection of very similar idiolects existing within a group of people who are in close social interaction with each other. Such a collection may be called a "dialect." Moving outward, we eventually always come to linguistic differences which are so great that communication is impossible, and at this point we say we are dealing with separate "languages." A language, in this sense, can thus be regarded as a collection of dialects, and a dialect as a collection of idiolects. But the gamut from idiolect to language may not show categories so clearly differentiated as this statement suggests, and often the categories must be qualified or extended; it may be necessary to identify subidiolects or superdialects. The situation is not unlike that which confronts a taxonomist in botany or zoology.

In addition, most people have learned to speak differently in different situations. In English, for example, one may say *going to* in some situations, *gonna* in others. Differences of this kind seem to be extensive in all languages, and they often permit the identification of a number of distinct but overlapping "styles," as they are sometimes called. We might be able to identify a formal style, a colloquial style, a polite style, an obsequious style, or whatever styles there were. Everyone is to a degree multilingual, having mastered different varieties of his language which are appropriate to different occasions.

All this presents an obvious problem to descriptive linguists, for they must decide what kind of linguistic unit they want to describe and how they are going to cope with the differences which fall within the province of their description. One solution is to describe a single style of a single individual, and possibly afterwards to state the relationships of this variety of the language to other styles and other idiolects. Another solution is to describe the "common core" which styles, idiolects, or dialects possess, leaving differences outside this core for subsequent description as appropriate. A third possibility is to describe the "overall pattern" which includes everything present in any of the styles or idiolects investigated. All these solutions have a certain awkwardness, and no wholly satisfying way has been found to deal with this problem. The awkwardness is inherent in the situation itself.

Comparative linguistics has developed as a subscience concerned with the study of linguistic differences at any of the levels mentioned above. Differences are recorded, then examined for possible explanations. The explanation of linguistic differences always involves in some way changes over time; this aspect will remain for discussion below. Also of great interest, however, and particularly from an anthropological point of view, are correlations between linguistic differences and cultural differences of other kinds.

It has proved useful to think of linguistic differences as either "horizontally" or "vertically" distributed. Horizontal differences are those which are tied to geography — which can be indicated by lines on a map. Vertical differences are those which may exist within the same geographical area, and which are tied to stratifications of society or of situation.

The study of horizontal differences is the province of a specialized branch of comparative linguistics known as "dialectology" or "dialect geography." Large-scale work of this kind began in Europe in the nineteenth century and is now being carried on in several parts of the world. Work on a Linguistic Atlas of the United States and Canada was begun in 1930 and is continuing. The techniques of this American project are derived from those of the earlier European studies. Field workers are assigned a number of carefully chosen localities in which they interview representative informants, filling in a pre-arranged questionnaire. A great deal of advance planning goes into the selection of localities, informants, and questions, since it seems physically impossible to obtain a comparable amount of significant data by random investigation. Computers now offer greatly expanded possibilities in this area. Once the material has been collected, it is prepared for publication in the form of maps or tables. Figure 2-3 is a map of the eastern United States showing the boundary between the area in which *you-all* is used as a second

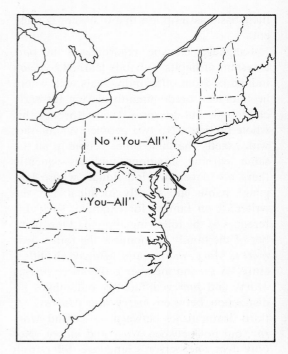

FIGURE 2-3 *

* Adapted from W. Nelson Francis — *The Structure of American English*. Copyright © 1958 The Ronald Press Company.

person plural and the area in which it is not. The line marking such a boundary is technically known as "isogloss." Separate isoglosses can be drawn for each of a number of linguistic differences, and subsequently compared and interpreted. The relationship of isoglosses to one another is frequently complex and calls for sophisticated explanation. One feature that is often found is a close coincidence of a number of isoglosses to form what is called a "bundle." A significant bundle of isoglosses can be said to mark the boundary between two "dialect areas." One can then search for nonlinguistic culture-historical factors which show a geographical correlation with these linguistic dialect areas, hoping thus to be able to explain the latter as the consequence of a specific barrier to communication. Often there is found to be a coincidence with political boundaries of some kind. In the United States and Canada dialect areas very often reflect the patterns of movement of the early settlers.

The study of vertical differences, sometimes identified as "sociolinguistics," is in many ways analogous to what has just been described. However, here the linguistic differences are correlated with extralinguistic factors that are not necessarily geographically separated, but that may coincide in a single area, even in a single individual. If isoglosses could be drawn, they would have to be drawn between different social statuses, roles, personalities, or situations. The use of the word *ain't,* for example, is common all over the United States, but only among certain people or in particular circumstances. The frequently encountered phenomenon of a codified linguistic norm or "standard language" is one object of such studies, as is the presence of class dialects and jargons. One investigation in this area concerned itself with extralinguistic factors correlated with the use of *–ing* or *–in'* as the present participle ending of verbs — the difference, for example, between *coming* and *comin'* (Fischer 1958b). In a group of New England school children it was found that *–ing* was used more often by girls, by children whose families were of higher socio-economic status, by children with cooperative rather than aggressive personalities, and in relatively formal situations, while *–in'* was used more often by the converse kinds of people or in the converse kinds of situations. Sociolinguistics promises to throw considerable light on previously obscure relationships between linguistic and nonlinguistic patterns of behavior.

The Dakota language provides abundant material for comparative linguistic investigation. The English word "Dakota" itself comes from *dakhota,* meaning "Indian," but the same word appears as *lakhota* and as *nakhota* in other parts of the Dakota speak-

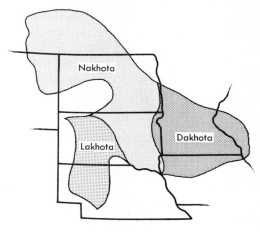

FIGURE 2-4

ing area. The extent of this area when these people were first contacted by white men is shown in Figure 2-4; the boundaries separating initial *d, l,* and *n* in the words just mentioned are marked by isoglosses. Many other isoglosses coincide exactly or almost exactly with these, forming heavy bundles which delimit three quite distinct dialect areas. Within each major area, however, a large number of other isoglosses could be drawn, some of them forming smaller bundles delimiting minor dialect areas.

A particularly interesting sociolinguistic phenomenon found in Dakota and in other languages of the same northern plains area is the existence of linguistic differences correlated entirely with differences in sex. Certain forms are restricted to use by men among themselves, although women recognize and understand them and may even use them in quoting what a man has said. Other forms are the ones which women use consistently, and which men also use in talking to women. The differences are not profound, but for the most part involve simply the use of distinct monosyllabic words at the end of a sentence or phrase. Men, for example, will say *nina wašte yo* "it's very good!" while women say *nina wašte ye.* A few differences between men's and women's speech may be found sporadically in English; only a woman would say "he's darling!" when confronted with a new baby, and certain kinds of profanity are pretty much restricted to use by men.

HISTORICAL LINGUISTICS

Languages change. We know this in the first instance because for a few languages we are lucky enough to have continuous written records extending over a long period of time in which the change is demonstrated, as it were, before our eyes. For the English language we have such records extending from the eighth century, and even a glance at writings from these earlier periods is enough to convince us that the language has not stood still. The differences between our English today and that of Chaucer or the King James Bible are easily seen. But even if writing had never been invented, we would still have good evidence in languages themselves that continuous change has been and is taking place. There are certain things within and between languages which are not readily explainable unless change is considered.

We have already seen, in the comparison of speech varieties of several kinds, that the language habits of different individuals may be more or less similar, even though not identical. Similarities can in fact be found not only between mutually intelligible idiolects and dialects, but also between many clearly separate languages. The English word *hound* and the German word *Hund,* for example, show both phonetic and semantic similarities, although in neither respect is there complete identity (*Hund* means "dog," not "hound"). Countless parallel examples can be found between these two languages, as between many others. Many such similarities are random and accidental; for example, there is a Burmese word for "far" that sounds almost like the English word *away*. But often a systematic relationship is found

among such similarities, a network of recurrent correspondences between linguistic units. For example, English *pound* and German *Pfund* show all the same phonological correspondences as *hound* and *Hund* except for the consonants at the beginning. English *pan* and German *Pfanne* show a recurrence of one of these initial consonant correspondences, *can* and *Kanne* repeat the noninitial correspondences in these words, and so on. The chain of correspondences extends in all directions.

When linguists find such a chain of recurrent correspondences, they assume it cannot be accidental, that the languages must have had some kind of historical connection. At some time in the past they must have (1) constituted one single language, (2) been in close enough contact that one left a mark on the other, or (3) been subject to similar influences from some third source. To decide among these three possible explanations is not always easy. The considerations involved would lead us far afield, so we will focus attention here on the ramifications of the first possibility: the explanation of linguistic similarities as the result of "common descent" or "genetic relationship."

Many similarities between languages can be explained by inferring the existence at an earlier time of a single relatively homogeneous language, among whose speakers there then arose, for whatever nonlinguistic reason — political division, for example, or migration — a communication barrier which split the community into two or more separate groups. Speakers within each group continued to interact among themselves, reinforcing one another's language habits in such a way that, as these habits inevitably changed through time, the same changes tended to be carried through the entire group. The changes which took place within the speech of each group, however, were independent of those which took place in the speech of any other. Whatever changes oc-

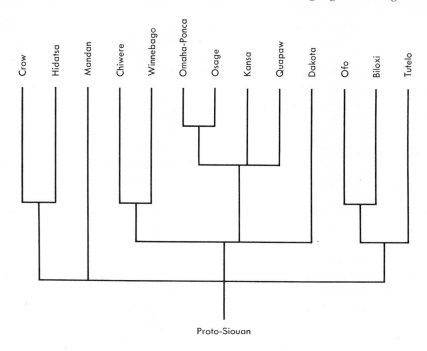

Proto-Siouan

FIGURE 2-5

curred could not cross the communication barrier which had arisen. Little by little, then, over generations and over centuries, the speech of each group became less and less like that of each other group. In this way, first separate dialects, then separate languages came into being. But within each newly formed group new communication barriers might again have arisen, resulting in new splits. The total historical picture thus inferred can be represented in the form of a family tree; Figure 2-5 is an illustration. All languages which, by this analogy, trace their descent from a common ancestor, are said to be "related." A group of related languages is a "family." The common ancestor is called a "proto-language"; in Figure 2-5 it is Proto-Siouan.

Usually it is only the languages as they exist at the top of the tree that we can observe and describe directly. This situation obtains for the great majority of the lan-

guage families which are represented by living languages in the world today. However, for a few families there are written records which provide us with evidence of earlier stages of some of the languages, and occasionally even with evidence of the proto-language. The Romance languages, French, Spanish, Italian, Rumanian, and so on, have as their common ancestor the colloquial form of Latin which spread outward from Rome through territorial conquest. This language, Proto-Romance, while not precisely the same as the literary Latin preserved for us in great abundance, was something very close to it.

But even in the majority of cases, where we do not have written records, it is still possible for us to know something, and sometimes a great deal, about earlier stages in a language family. This we do through a method of comparative reconstruction which amounts to an application of comparative linguistics for historical purposes. In essence, the method involves nothing more than the tabulation of recurrent correspondences in the later languages and their systematic assignment to single origins in the proto-language. The amount and quality of the reconstruction that can be accomplished is dependent upon the number and variety of attested languages available, as well as on the nature and extent of the correspondences to be found among them. In no case is it possible to reconstruct an entire proto-language in full detail, but often a surprisingly extensive picture can be gained, as has happened, most notably, with Proto-Indo-European.

A brief example will show the kind of procedure followed in comparative reconstruction, although necessarily with the omission of numerous fine points. The word for "heart" in Dakota is *čhǫte*. Four languages which are related to Dakota within the "Siouan" family are Hidatsa, Mandan, Biloxi, and Ofo. The word for "heart" in each of these four respectively is *rata, natka, yǫti,* and *čǫti.* Because these words are similar both phonetically and semantically, we hypothesize that they are all "cognate," that is, that they stem from a single common source. If we line them up one under the other, we can see that they fit together as follows:

Dakota	čh	ǫ	t	e
Hidatsa	r	a	t	a
Mandan	n	a	tk	a
Biloxi	y	ǫ	t	i
Ofo	č	ǫ	t	i

We infer that the initial consonant correspondence *čh/r/n/y/č* is traceable to a single consonant of the proto-language, which we might symbolize as **y.* An asterisk is traditionally used to show that something has been arrived at by reconstruction, or, more generally, that it has never been attested either directly or through written records.

The symbol **y* is chosen for this reconstruction because the phonetic nature of its attested descendants and the total picture of the proto-language's expression structure both suggest that this proto-phoneme was phonetically something like what the symbol *y* suggests. The attribution of phonetic values to reconstructed phonemes is admittedly more tenuous than the reconstruction itself, and some linguists have preferred to regard reconstructions as nothing more than abstract formulas.

The correspondence *ǫ/a/a/ǫ/ǫ* is inferred to have developed from a proto-phoneme **ǫ,* and the correspondence *t/t/tk/t/t* from the consonant cluster **tk.* Not only is it more probable that **k* was lost after **t* in several languages than that it developed spontaneously in Mandan, but a *k* is actually attested in this position in some other Siouan languages which have been omitted here for the sake of simplicity. The final vowel correspondence *e/a/a/i/i* leads us to reconstruct a phoneme to which, considering the total pattern of proto-vowels, we assign the symbol **e.* We can now put all these reconstructed phonemes together in the form **yǫtke,* which we describe as our reconstruction of the phonemic shape of the Proto-Siouan word for "heart."

We might note also the way in which the Proto-Siouan form for "lung" is reconstructed on the basis of the words for "lung" in these same five languages:

Dakota	čh	a	γ	u
Hidatsa	r	a	x	u
Mandan	r	e	x	
Biloxi	y	a	x	u
Ofo	č	a	s	u
Proto-Siouan	**y*	a	x	u

Here the initial consonant correspondence is *čh/r/r/y/č,* which is slightly different from the correspondence in which we based our first reconstruction of Proto-Siouan *y; we now have an r in Mandan instead of an n. Ordinarily two different correspondences, no matter how similar, will lead us to reconstruct two different proto-phonemes. They need not, however, if these similar correspondences can be attributed to tentative reconstructions that were in complementary distribution in the proto-language. In this case the complementary distribution is clear, and phonetically very plausible. The first *y, which led to Mandan n, a nasal consonant, occurred before Proto-Siouan *ą, a nasalized vowel. The second *y, which led to Mandan r, occurred before Proto-Siouan *a, an oral vowel. The two *y's can therefore be equated without difficulty.

On the basis of these two Proto-Siouan reconstructions, *yątke "heart" and *yaxu "lung," the following statements regarding the historical development of phonemes in the Siouan languages can be made:

(1) Proto-Siouan *y became Dakota čh, Hidatsa r, Mandan n before nasalized vowels and r before oral vowels, Biloxi y, and Ofo č.
(2) Proto-Siouan *ą became Dakota ą, Hidatsa a, Mandan a, Biloxi ą and Ofo ą.
(3) Proto-Siouan *t became Dakota t, Hidatsa t, Mandan t, Biloxi t, and Ofo t.
(4) Proto-Siouan *k when preceded by *t was lost in Dakota, Hidatsa, Biloxi, and Ofo, but retained as k in Mandan.
(5) Proto-Siouan *e became Dakota e, Hidatsa a, Mandan a, Biloxi i, and Ofo i.
(6) Proto-Siouan *a became Dakota a, Hidatsa a, Mandan e, Biloxi a, and Ofo a.
(7) Proto-Siouan *x became Dakota γ, Hidatsa x, Mandan x, Biloxi x, and Ofo s.

(8) Proto-Siouan *u became Dakota u, Hidatsa u, was lost in Mandan, became Biloxi u, and Ofo u.

Further evidence would produce certain modifications in these statements. For example, it would be seen that Proto-Siouan *u was not lost everywhere in Mandan, but only when it was the final phoneme in a word.

There has been considerable interest among anthropologically oriented linguists in what have been called "remote" relationships among languages. Such relationships have been hypothesized in cases in which the number of recurrent correspondences is extremely small, and even where systematically recurrent correspondences have been difficult to establish at all. Frequently, too, the meanings of the forms compared have been very divergent — not, as in the cases above, so close as to be translatable by the single English words "heart" or "lung." The probable validity of any relationship is a matter of degree, ranging from the satisfying extreme in which extensive reconstruction is possible to the frustrating opposite in which any reconstruction at all is scant and tenuous.

One remote relationship which has been suggested several times unites the Siouan and Iroquoian language families of North America into a larger superfamily or "stock," with Siouan and Iroquoian as its two branches (Chafe 1964a). The Iroquoian languages include those spoken by the Iroquois Indians of New York State as well as the Cherokee language and some others. Suggestive evidence of the relationship does in fact exist. The Proto-Siouan word *yątke "heart," for example, reconstructed as outlined above, is reminiscent of an Iroquoian form *-yęte- meaning "know." The meanings are quite different, but plausibly related (compare the English phrase "I know it in my heart"), and all the correspondences y/y, ą/ę, tk/t, and *e/e* can be found to recur and co-occur a number of times between the two families. For example, the first two of these correspondences recur together in Proto-Siouan **ya* "lie down, sleep" and Iroquoian **-yę-* "set down." The totality of such interlocking correspondences is reasonably convincing in this case. There are other sets of language families in which it is less so, but in which there is just enough to suggest tantalizingly that a relationship exists.

The forces which lie behind changes in language are not fully understood. It may be that the patterning of a language creates within itself certain pressures and tensions which tend to be resolved by modifications of one kind or another (Martinet 1955). It may be that languages have a built-in tendency to "drift" in a particular direction (Sapir 1921:147–170). And it may be that language is subject to mutations which are wholly accidental and unmotivated. Each of these theories has its advocates and partisans, and probably each has some validity. The causes of language change may be many and varied.

There is more agreement on what happens next. Most changes probably extend no further than a particular idiolect and are short-lived. But occasionally, a change, or an interrelated set of changes, may spread among a group of closely interacting people so that their speech becomes in some way distinguishable from the speech of those around them. Sometimes, perhaps in the total picture very rarely, the modifications may spread beyond the small group to affect a large segment of the language, perhaps even the entire language. The general process is thus one which begins with a motivated or unmotivated, gradual or abrupt modification in the language of perhaps just a single individual, and which then diffuses to cover a greater or lesser area of the population which shares the same language. It has often been

said that changes spread from "centers of prestige," that the habits of more prestigeful speakers are mimicked by the less prestigeful. Probably there is something to this notion, since it is known that changes spread more readily in some directions than in others, although it is also clear that "prestige" in this sense is a complicated and variable notion which is difficult to pin down; the popular idea of prestige is not always what is involved.

The concept of linguistic changes spreading outward from various centers in waves, like ripples on a pond, is an old one. It has sometimes been taken to be in contradiction to the family tree theory mentioned above. The contradiction would be real if there were nothing but a collection of randomly overlapping waves, each diffusing outward from a different center; but in fact a great many of them seem to share a common source and to spread approximately to the same limits. In this way a considerable homogeneity of language within a specific area is often maintained, and it is still possible to think of languages as dividing into dialects which may themselves become separate languages and divide again in turn, so long as it is remembered that the borders between dialects and often even between languages may be gradient rather than sharply drawn. The picture of a family tree oversimplifies the real situation to some degree, but it remains a useful model of language relationships and much reliance upon it continues.

Diffusion of linguistic features takes place not only within languages but between them as well. Linguists traditionally speak of these influences as "borrowing," or of "loans" from one language to another, although diffusion is a more appropriate concept. The kinds of influence one language may exert on another as a result of contact between their speakers may be quite varied; it seems to be that any part of the structure of a language may be modified in this way. In sheer quantity as well as easy identifiability the phenomena known as "loanwords" seem to predominate. The English words *tepee* and *Dakota,* for example, were taken from the Indian words *thipi* and *dakhota* cited above. A remarkably large proportion of the modern English vocabulary goes back to borrowings from French in the period following the Norman conquest. Not only words, however, but grammatical and phonological features of all kinds may be introduced into a language through contact with another language.

LINGUISTICS AND CULTURAL ANTHROPOLOGY

Language, as we have seen, can be regarded as an ability which underlies certain kinds of distinctively human behavior as well as certain internal processes which are also peculiarly human. The potential to acquire this ability may be regarded as inherent in the human biological organism. No other animal has been able to acquire anything like it. One may speculate that the universal features of linguistic systems — the presence in them all, for example, of discrete units and of certain universal ways in which these units are combined — may reflect inherent characteristics of the human brain. But on the other hand, it is clear enough that the specific features of specific languages — particular inventories of units and their particular manifestations, the particular patterns within which they co-occur, and so on — are learned by each person from other persons with whom he interacts, from other members of his own "culture."

What has been said of language could just as well be said of other aspects of culture, except that language is perhaps the most distinctively human aspect of all. It may be true also that language is less sus-ceptible to conscious manipulation. Religion or law are sometimes deliberately controlled or revolutionized, while language goes on for the most part unheeded. But the difference seems only a relative one. People are generally unaware or vaguely conscious, at best, of the influence any aspect of their culture exerts on their behavior. And there certainly are attempts to regulate language in a conscious way, as any school child knows.

We noted before that, aside from its own intrinsic interest, the study of language may be helpful to students of other areas of culture in several ways. The organization of experience associated with language may be correlated with the experiential properties of other parts of culture. Linguistic differences can be investigated as correlates of other cultural differences. And the theories and methods linguists develop can be, and to some extent have been profitably applied in other areas. Some linguists, in fact, have regarded the investigation of language as a model which would eventually spread and ramify to cover the entire field of culture.

To agree that there is some validity in this last idea is not to suggest that anthropologists should be looking for specific analogs of language structure in every cultural phenomenon. It is more fruitful to look for broader applications of those linguistic concepts which are not necessarily tied to the nature of language itself. There are of course the broadest concepts of all, those linguistics has borrowed in turn from other sciences: the mutually supportive roles of induction and deduction in the formation of theories which extend our knowledge beyond the observation of random facts. Linguistics was fortunate in finding that language had at least one manifestation, sound, which could be observed and recorded with great facility. Similarly complete and exact observation in other areas of culture is not so easy, and, in fact, it is not a simple matter in the experiential area of language either. But the success linguists have had with phonetic recording can serve as a stimulus to the development of adequate methods in the recording of folklore, music, religion — of cultural manifestations of all kinds.

The success linguists have had in distinguishing among descriptive, comparative, and historical studies suggests that the same distinctions could profitably be made elsewhere. Cultural anthropologists have been prone to confuse the dimensions of time and space, while linguists may have tried too hard to keep them apart. A language or any other part of culture is the product of its history and represents only one stage along a continuum of time. But linguistics has shown that it is very useful to study individual stages by themselves, as self-contained systems, and then to consider how these systems change and interrelate by comparing several which are temporally or spatially separated.

Surely the most important contribution linguistics has to make, however, is the extent to which it has validated the assumption that a great deal of human behavior is an outward manifestation of an underlying system. The distinction drawn by Saussure between an outward "parole" and an inward "langue" has proved so fruitful that linguists have no doubt as to its basic correctness. If it is further accepted that language is only one aspect of culture as a whole, then without a doubt there exist outside of language the same general relationships linguists find between the data they observe and the systems they posit to explain what they observe. The existence of discrete cultural units, for

example, and of distinctive patterns within which such units co-occur may be profitably taken as a starting point for a variety of nonlinguistic investigations.

The study of language sets in strong relief the finding that no individual is free to behave in anything approaching a random fashion. It is obvious that communication through language depends upon conventions which are unconsciously agreed to by all the parties concerned. We might compare the act of listening to someone speak English, or any other language familiar to us, with the act of listening to a language we have never heard before. Listening to English, we normally are aware only of the content of what is being said. Aside from possible distortions, the speaker has succeeded in transferring a part of his own experience into the experience of us the listeners. He could not do so unless we shared with him the habits of our language, for listening to an unknown language we are aware only of someone making unusual noises which it seems impossible for us to imitate. In neither situation, however, is there any direct awareness of how the language actually organizes sound and experience and links the one to the other. But these are the matters with which linguists are preoccupied. And it is these unconsciously agreed upon conventions in areas outside of language that concern other cultural anthropologists. If we understood the entire field, we might hope to understand everything about human behavior which is dependent upon all the unconscious conventions man learns through interaction with his fellow man. The extent and nature of the residue, once isolated, would be equally worth knowing.

Suggested Readings

A comprehensive survey of the development of linguistics in the nineteenth century is Pedersen 1962. Basic developments in this century can be traced in Boas 1911, Saussure 1959, Sapir 1921, Bloomfield 1933, Hjelmslev 1961, and Chomsky 1957. The school characterized as "Bloomfieldian" is represented in Bloch and Trager 1942 and Joos 1957. Sturtevant 1947 is an introduction oriented toward historical linguistics, while Hoenigswald 1960 is a more technical handling of this subject. The influences of languages on one another are surveyed in Weinreich 1963. There are several useful textbooks. Hockett 1958 covers the entire field of linguistics. Gleason 1961 presents a generally Bloomfieldian descriptive linguistics, while Bach 1964 provides a textbook on transformational grammar. Lehmann 1962 is a textbook on historical linguistics. Chomsky 1965 is an exploration of the present frontiers of descriptive linguistic theory. Fodor and Katz 1964 is a selection of articles on transformational linguistics.

CHAPTER **3** presents one major portion of the domain of expressive culture, or culture narrowly defined, the plastic and graphic arts (another segment, oral literature, will be covered in Chapter 4). Here Professor Gunther focuses sometimes on the form and content of the arts in their own right, pointing up the humanistic aspect of cultural anthropology, sometimes on the human meaning and social contexts of the art, an approach with links to questions of social structure and cultural change. The contrasts drawn between the arts of the primitive world and those of the so-called high civilizations highlight not only the special involvement of cultural anthropologists in the little communities of nonliterate peoples, but also the world-wide scope of the discipline's interests and the vital importance of systematic comparative study. The presentation rests, for obvious reasons, on a necessary selectivity. Four cultural settings are used: the American Indian arts of the Northwest Coast of the United States and Canada, to exemplify a single richly developed style and two techniques, sculpture and painting; and the grand and quite different traditions of sculpture and painting of three parts of Africa. Then, because at least one form of textile arts should be included, follows a discussion of the most widely distributed textile art of all — basketry. Finally, the "cave art" of Europe is discussed, despite the fact that the social meaning of this art has to speak for itself, for we have no direct ethnographic data to supplement it. Here the author follows the suggestions of Morton Levine (1957) and compares this very ancient set of styles and techniques with those of modern, ethnographically known cultures. Altogether, the point is made that, for the cultural anthropologist, the study of primitive art makes a quite distinct contribution to the history of culture, since studying the diffusion of art styles may often lead to clarification of cultural relationships between living and archaeological societies.

THE AUTHOR was born in Brooklyn, New York, and studied at Barnard College and Columbia University, where she received her Ph.D. She has been Chairman of the Department of Anthropology and Professor of Anthropology at the University of Washington, as well as Director of the Washington State Museum. She has recently joined the staff of the University of Alaska. Her field research experience has been primarily among the peoples of the Northwest Coast, and her many publications include ethnographies and monographs on Northwest Coast tribes. In addition to her scholarly productivity, she has arranged many exhibitions of Northwest Coast Indian art, the largest being the exhibition at the 1962 Seattle World's Fair, and has been generally prominent in bringing understanding and the beauty of these arts to public attention.

3

Art in the Life
of Primitive Peoples

Erna Gunther
University of Alaska

The Cultural Background
of Primitive Art

Why does anthropology discuss primitive art? Because it is a part of culture. The anthropologist places art in its cultural setting, while some art historians and critics prefer to admire only the aesthetic aspects of an art and disregard the function and history of the object in the culture in which it was created. In any serious study of art the culture of the people producing it cannot be ignored. This is not so apparent to us within the heritage of western Europe until we face, for instance, the arts of the Orient, where the cultural background is less well known to the Western world. Then we begin to realize the depth of the cultural background, an understanding of which is necessary to comprehend an art. For example, hundreds of years of European art could not be understood without a knowledge of Christianity. The further one moves from his own culture, the more necessary such background becomes. In studying the art of a primitive community the anthropologist must understand the attitude toward art, who produces it, and his position in the society. What is the artist's motivation and how is he trained? And finally, how are the objects he created used in the culture?

Studies made from this viewpoint are scarce in the anthropological literature, but their absence can be justified as a matter of theoretical approach. General ethnographies written in the late nineteenth and early twentieth centuries seldom were problem-oriented, and the interaction between persons was not recorded. If the arts in the community under study still flourished, the anthropologist was content to describe the techniques and take the finished product back to a museum; he seldom discussed the process of its creation with the artist or inquired about the position of the artist in the society. Occasionally these facts could be derived from casual information, but true studies of primitive art came later, after authors were no longer concerned with the "origin and development" of art and turned to the people and attitudes involved. In the late 1920's and early 1930's several studies using a new approach were published. Ruth Bunzel spent more than a year at the Pueblo of Zuñi in New Mexico where she lived with an outstanding potter and learned the technique of pottery-making from her. In the process she discussed the art with her teacher and from this experience brought the thoughts of the artist into the literature. Later Lila O'Neale took back to the northwestern California reservations whence they had come the Yurok and Karok baskets which had been in the Robert H. Lowie Museum of Anthropology at the University of California in Berkeley. She did this because she was afraid she would not be able to find enough specimens still in possession of the Indians to supply an adequate series for discussion. She asked the current basket-makers to criticize the baskets in workmanship and design. This project was one of the first attempts to discuss criticism of a body of primitive art with the people to whom it belonged. Basketry in these tribes is the primary visual art form and is made by all women in their communities. Fortunately they were cooperative and voluble in their discussions. Another anthropologist who tried the same approach elsewhere was greeted only by weeping, for the baskets had been made by women who were no longer living and the sight of these pieces aroused mournful memories. "The best laid schemes. . . ."

The title of this chapter immediately calls attention to the all-pervasive character of art in the primitive community, where it is generally impossible to discuss the round of life of any person without touching on his or her participation in some form of art. This includes not only the plastic and graphic arts

but also oral literature, music, and dancing. All these arts are more frequently brought together in primitive cultures than in our own. For the average individual in our society, art is gathered together in museums and art galleries and music is heard in concert halls, unless we go to ballet or opera, in which the plot draws on literature, the settings and costumes on the decorative arts, and the execution on singing and dancing. The great dramatic rituals and ceremonies which have a much wider cultural impact in primitive communities also unite these arts. But one also finds in many collections of primitive arts beautiful painted boxes, house posts, water jars, and even fish hooks, which indicate that people need daily aesthetic satisfaction. Not only do they use these objects, but more people make them, spreading participation in the arts throughout the community. More people know the techniques involved and the traditions of the designs, and thus have the experience necessary to render judgment on the quality of the workmanship, which is the basis of criticism.

In some more complex societies skilled workers were sometimes set apart and allowed to practice their art to such an extent that they did not take an active part in the daily community routine. These people may be regarded as professional artists, but they differ in many respects from their counterparts in the Western world. They may occasionally create something for their own aesthetic satisfaction, but their principal output is more often in response to the society's ceremonial, social, and economic needs. An artist might produce these objects as a member of a ceremonial group responsible for certain rituals performed for the welfare of the whole group. These objects are made with other members of the group, in fact, several people may contribute to the making of a single piece in this way. On the other hand, in an affluent society in which there are persons with more wealth than others, art patrons occur, just as in historical periods in western Europe. Then the artist makes what the patron needs for his lavish entertainments or for the ceremonies which go with his status. What the artist produces is not only controlled by these circumstances, but also by a tradition of design.

In spite of all these ramifications there is a freshness about primitive art which is amazing. Within long series of similar objects collected in museums one seldom finds an exact duplicate. There are several reasons for this happy situation. In the first place, the artist usually does not have a similar model at hand from which to copy, and patterns are seldom available. Furthermore, ceremonial objects are frequently used only once, then destroyed, so they cannot serve as patterns. The end result is that the artist works in an accepted line and never departs from it to such a degree that his output cannot be recognized as coming from a certain tribe or even a group within the tribe, but he does not copy.

The primitive artist has other difficulties in communicating in any but his accustomed media. As has been said, he follows a tradition closely and if the object is to have ceremonial use, it must be accurate so the supernatural spirits being addressed will recognize it and give it their magical powers. However, his mark may be left on minor details which give each piece the novelty that is so apparent when large series of objects are studied. Rather than thinking of creation in the terms of the modern artist, the primitive artist while carving a ritual piece thinks of the supernatural world with which he is communicating. This difference in cultural background makes any comparison between the primitive artist and his modern counterpart invalid. Thus some students of this situation argue that he is a craftsman, not an artist. This distinction between art and craft is an historical approach in the study of the arts of high civilization, but the same implications cannot be carried into the anthropological study of primitive arts. Basketry is regarded as a craft, and a very utilitarian one at that, but the baskets made by many Indian tribes of western America, where this is the major aesthetic expression, cannot be considered in any other category than as an art in these groups. If we accept the amphora of Greece among the arts, we cannot turn about and deny an equal place to the beautifully shaped and painted water jars of the Pueblo Indians of the southwest United States, or to the pottery of the Inca of Peru. In the field of primitive art, therefore, we must disregard the medium as we would ordinarily classify it by Western standards, and determine the attitude toward it in the society in which it occurs. It is not enough in anthropological data to indicate the presence of a custom, it must also be analyzed in its relation to the whole culture. This limits the appreciation of those who devote themselves only to the aesthetic pleasure which can be derived from objects of art, without knowing the cultural background in which they were created.

Art historians and aesthetic philosophers in our culture have long searched for an analysis of the process of creativity, usually with discouraging results. They forget that the artist speaks in his chosen medium and finds it difficult to change to another. If he can say what he thinks on a canvas, why should he be asked to express it again in words? It happens that our culture is verbally oriented and there is a tendency to reduce all other forms of communication to this form, like the titles of pictures and the program notes with music. In his discussion of Tiv art, Paul Bohannon (Smith, ed. 1961:87) brings out the point that in some cultures the object is important, not the man who made it. Often, in fact, among the Tiv, when a person is seen working at wood-carving or weaving, anyone passing by may take a hand at it to help since such techniques are known to everyone. Can the artist really be distinguished in such a community?

THE ART OF THE NORTHWEST COAST OF NORTH AMERICA

On the Northwest Coast of North America the Indians lived in scattered villages along a thousand miles of protected coves and inlets. The Pacific before them and the coniferous forest at their backs provided a constant food supply, fresh in season and capable of being dried and preserved for the remainder of the year. The villages consisted of wooden houses, many sheltering several families. These houses were built of red cedar planks on a huge framework of posts and crossbeams. The people lived in these houses through the winter months and carried on their feasts and ceremonial dancing. In the spring the communities broke up and scattered to their fishing sites, where for several months they harvested what nature had provided in the salmon runs, and native vegetable foods, such as roots, berries, bulbs, and sprouts.

This economy was the basis of life throughout the area, more elaborate among the Tsimshian, Tlingit, and Haida of the north, and simpler among the Salish-speaking tribes of the south. The men in the whole region were skilled carvers and their communities made many demands on them. They themselves needed fishhooks, floats, decoys, fish clubs, and decorated stakes for salmon weirs. The women wanted boxes for cooking and for storing food and clothing, spoons and dishes for feasts, spindle whorls for winding thread, and rattles for dances. The attitude in the community was that a man should be capable of supplying these items; but if a large canoe were needed, a specialist canoe-maker might be called in, while in the north, totem poles were also considered beyond the talents of the average carver. Extensive participation in carving

gave most men the experience necessary for art criticism, which in turn raised the standards for this technique.

All the objects mentioned so far were utilitarian, but they were made with consummate skill in craftsmanship and virtuosity in design. These Northwest Coast tribes lived with art in their daily lives; the ceremonial occasions broadened the needs for art, particularly in the activities of the secret societies and — in the north — the dramatic performances staged by clans and lineages. For some people, preparations for a ceremonial season consisted not only of assembling food and facilities for receiving guests, and arranging for costumes, but also of some contemplation of the reason for the occasion, in which man came closer to the supernatural spirits. As those who expected to dance carved the masks that were to help them represent these spirits, they felt their presence, for during the winter months they were supposed to come again into the region. Not every dancer could carve his own mask and on some occasions that was not required, for a man who had the privilege of putting on a certain dance often had the masks made for the performers, who were members of either his family or clan. Masks were often inherited or transferred in ownership.

On these occasions the plastic and graphic arts were employed and also music and dance, with the oral traditions furnishing the content of the dramatic presentations. These could be clan myths or the mere representations of characters from the group's general mythology.

Another kind of dramatic performance was that of the medicine man or shaman, who also combined all the arts. The shaman had much closer communion with spirits who gave him the power to cure the sick, bring souls back from the land of the dead, and compete with other medicine men to

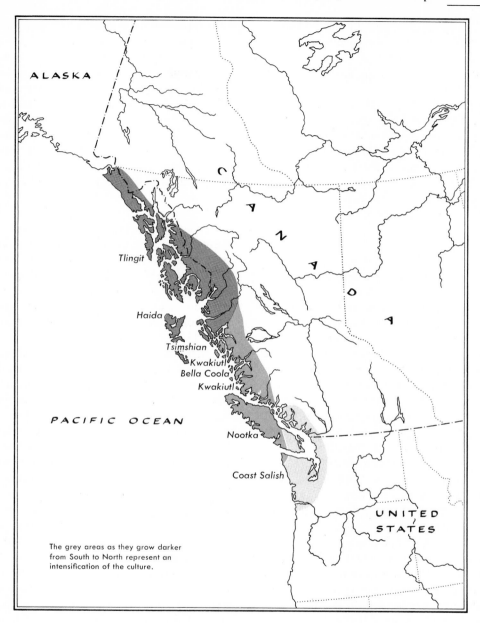

ALASKA

C
A
N
A
D
A

Tlingit

Haida

Tsimshian

Kwakiutl
Bella Coola
Kwakiutl

PACIFIC OCEAN

Nootka

Coast Salish

UNITED
STATES

The grey areas as they grow darker
from South to North represent an
intensification of the culture.

FIGURE 3-1 *

The Northwest Coast of North America, Showing the Major Tribes and Cultural Subdivisions

* Adapted from E. Gunther, *Indians of the Northwest Coast,* Taylor Museum of the Colorado Springs Fine Arts Center and the Seattle Art Museum, 1951.

show his power through his spirit helpers. The performances provided much of the dramatic entertainment in these tribes and the greater a showman the shaman was, the larger his following and the demand for his services. For these occasions he needed masks, and he wore suspended around his neck and sewn on his dance apron carved bone and ivory amulets representing his spirit powers. Among the Tlingit he kept all these things in a beautifully carved box. He usually made these objects for his own use and they were often buried in his grave with him.

History of the Art

The culture which produced this art is known to us since the last quarter of the eighteenth century. Some stone carving can be dated earlier but it is sporadic and often not clearly associated with other cultural elements that can be placed chronologically. A few pieces of the stone carving indicate some features of Northwest Coast style as being established to some degree in this medium. More consistent information on this art begins in the last quarter of the eighteenth century when its character was first brought to the attention of Europeans through the journals of explorers and fur traders, and when some objects were taken to Europe by the expeditions. This short history is due partly to the fact that the exploration of this region was contemporary with the beginnings of the United States as an independent nation, a century and a half after the settlement of the Atlantic seaboard. The other reason lies within the Indian culture itself: the majority of the objects made were of wood which does not last long in a moist climate. There was no long lasting pottery which is always such a good indicator of art styles and cultural change. The earliest objects collected in the eighteenth century showed the style associated with the

area later was well established and that the technique of wood carving was under good control. It is also clear that the introduction of commercial paints later in the nineteenth century did more to change the aspect of the art than did the increased use of metal tools. Commercial paints caused many details which were formerly carved to be painted instead, possibly because more and brighter colors were available or because it was found easier and quicker for the artist to accomplish.

The history of the art is closely linked with the fortunes of the Indians in other respects. The fur trade expanded their economy and gave those who already were regarded as wealthy more prestige objects and a greater hold on the economic activity of the community. The feasts became greater and more frequent and the display of wealth more lavish until the end of the fur trade and the increased settlement of the region terminated a short but intense era of cultural expansion. When this society collapsed there ceased to be a continuing demand for the art made by the Indians for themselves, and much of that made in the last fifty years was produced primarily to sell. Somehow this use does not bring forth the finest efforts of carvers, and because in the present economy they must devote much more time to making a living, the daily way of life does not include the exercise of their ability as carvers. Even though in the old culture carving did not take the exclusive attention of many, all the men thought about carving and designs for carving. When they were surrounded by a compatible culture better work naturally resulted. So today there is no hope of reviving Northwest Coast Indian art as it once was, but one can hope that the skill and aesthetic appreciation once common among these people may some day find sufficient stimulation in the newer society in which they find themselves to develop another great art.

Material and Tools

This brief resume leaves the figure of the artist rather nebulous. Since every man could carve as necessary for his daily needs, the artist was one who had greater skill, whose pieces were sometimes bartered. Among the northern tribes in which the totem poles were made, a carver could have this as a specialty and could partially live by his art. The canoe-maker, who needed more technical skill than the totem pole carver, seemed to rank below him, but perhaps that is our conception from the ethnographies and not the attitude within the culture. Even the dancers who carved their own masks were considered as simply fulfilling the requirements of their parts in the presentation. Everyone who carved or painted had to know the mythology, for many subjects from this body of oral tradition were used. They were presented in such highly conventionalized style that they cannot be regarded as illustrations, but rather as inspiration.

Just as the environment was rich in foods, so it supplied a great variety of materials which could be used for art. The monumental carvings were made of red cedar, as were the planks of their houses. This wood has a straight grain and cuts readily. Other woods used were yellow cedar, alder, maple, and yew. For spoons and small dishes the horns of the mountain goat and mountain sheep were used. Amulets and charms were made of the leg bone of deer, and the carver took advantage of the curve of the bone to give the piece greater volume. Small carvings and amulets were also made of bears' teeth and some teeth of the sperm whale. Many wood carvings were inlaid with the irridescent shell of the abalone or haliotis which was traded northward from Monterey Bay in California. These shells were also used alone for earrings and pendants. Another unusual shellfish sought out by the carver was the sea snail whose operculum (the hard shell closure of the animal) was often inlaid on the rim of a finely carved food box.

The carver used adzes and knives with blades of ground stone which usually are known today only from archaeological sites. The handles of the knives were of various lengths, tailored to fit the hand of the carver. Frequently they were also gently curved and tapered. The first European explorers in the area were surprised to find the Indians had a word for iron and recognized its advantages. It is possible that for perhaps the previous century they had been familiar with the metal through its arrival on the coast in the drift from shipwrecks on the Siberian coast. This previous knowledge led them to prefer strap iron or sheet metal to finished tools, for they could then fashion their tools to suit themselves. So in many instances the shape and function of the tool did not change, but the iron gave the carver greater efficiency and reduced the time necessary to execute the work. They used the stalks of scouring rush and the skin of dogfish as abrasives but were careful never to smooth away the texture created by the adze strokes, which gave the wood a quality that was one characteristic of Northwest Coast carving.

Analysis of the Art

The carver also drew many of the native animals in Northwest Coast designs. Many of these occur as characters in the mythology, and these myths in turn are the origin tales of the clans and lineages in the north, and of the villages in the south. From the land came the bear, the beaver, the wolf, the raven, the eagle, the hawk; and from the sea, the shark, the killer whale. To these were added some imaginary creatures like the thunderbird and the sea wolf or sea monster. From this bestiary the artist developed an iconography which shows them whole or in designs created from diagnostic parts. The animal is dissected and placed where he best fits the space, which, according to the principles of the art, must be completely covered. These figures are not found in equal use among all the tribes of the region and the same features are not always used to symbolize them; however, though they may be recognized generally by these characteristics, they cannot be "read."

Some of the more standard characterizations are:

Bear
Has a large mouth, often with jagged teeth, his long tongue protruding; his feet, with strong claws, are usually turned inward. He is often in a sitting position.

Beaver
Has his large incisors showing, holds a stick in his front paws, and has a cross-hatched tail turned up between his legs, covering his belly. He is usually sitting upright.

Wolf
Has a large face like the bear but his snout is more pointed and his ears are always erect. If his body shows, the ribs are defined and his long tail is often laid along his back.

Raven
Has a long straight beak of undetermined length, regulated by the needs of the design. By preference it stands out from the face, but if the design requires, it can be folded down on the breast.

Eagle
Has a much heavier and shorter beak than the raven, and it curves down slightly at the tip.

Hawk
Has a beak that recurves to the face.

Shark
Has a heavy face with a high forehead and a large mouth that turns down at the sides and is set

with jagged teeth. The sad looking eyes follow the downward trend of the mouth and on the sides of each cheek are three gill slits.

Killer Whale
Has a rounded body with a prominent dorsal fin, a large mouth, and a round eye.

Thunderbird
Has a combination of beaks of the raven and eagle. It is straight, heavy, and curved downward at the tip. Often the thunderbird also has some scroll-like decorations on the head which could be interpreted as feathers or horns.

Sea Wolf
Is a combination of the lithe figure and face of the wolf and the dorsal fin of the killer whale; in fact, sometimes he has two dorsal fins to distinguish him as the imaginary creature.

These figures were manipulated in many ways in carving and painting, two techniques in which the artist had to be equally competent, for they were used together or alone, as the work required. The style ranged from the realistic portrait masks carved by the Tlingit, Haida, and Tsimshian to the completely abstract design of the Chilcat blanket (Figure 3-2). But regardless of the mode of expression, the artist always subordinated his design to the requirements of the function of the piece, and a large part of Northwest Coast art is found on functional pieces.

Let us look at some specific problems in the variety of functional pieces made. The Salish carver was often asked by his wife to make a spindle whorl for spinning the heavy mountain goat wool she used in weaving blankets. This whorl was a platter of wood about eight inches in diameter, and it had to have a hole in the center for the spindle to go through. In one example from the Cowichan Indians of southern Vancouver

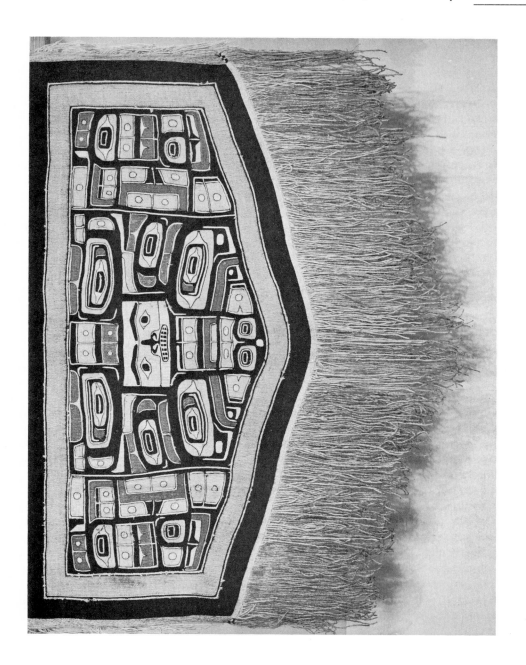

FIGURE 3-2 *

A Chilcat Blanket, Woven by the Tlingit Indians of Southeastern Alaska

* Reproduced by permission of the Thomas Burke Memorial Washington State Museum, University of Washington. Cat. No. 9511.

Island, the hole was cut as the mouth of a human figure whose round face incised in detail forms a second circle. The body of the man is disproportionately small compared to the head and has large arms bent at the elbows. Above his outspread fingers are figures of land otters, one on each side, with their heads facing each other over the man's head. It is a beautiful example of design, with the man's hands and the land otters forming a third concentric circle. The flow of the design and the variety are all related to the circular space necessary for the object.

Another example of the use of circular space is the crown and brim of a woven spruce root hat. The crown slopes gently into the brim without a break. The design is an eagle painted in red, black, and green, placed with the beak at the front and the tail at the back of the hat. The bird is split its full length and the crown rises through its body with the wings folded on each side. Splitting a figure in this way is a common convention in the art, often misinterpreted as representing two animals instead of one. The same manner of designing is also found in small dishes in which the beak and tail form the flat handles and the body is hollowed out to form the dish. In such cases the design is continued along the side of the body by incising or it is carved and forms a protruding edge around the cavity.

An example of splitting a figure to fill a space more adequately is seen in an appliquéd shirt. This specimen uses new materials introduced through trade with the whites. The shirt is sleeveless and is pulled over the head. It is made of blue broadcloth and the design of a thunderbird is appliquéd in red flannel. The bird is split down the back through the head and body so that the sides of the face are still joined at the beak, which is short, and at the tail, which is of one piece. If this design were folded down the center, the bird would be restored in profile. This restoration of the

split profile into a three-dimensional object raises an interesting question as to which is the older and more fundamental, the two- or three-dimensional form of this art.

The artist is often not content with showing only what is visible from one point of view; he adds what he knows is present but invisible. This is sometimes called "X-ray" art, and, again, is a reorganization of nature by enlarging minor features and showing them in great detail. Perhaps the most abstract design in this art is the Chilcat blanket, an excellent example of both devices. This design is also unusual in that it requires the cooperation of men and women in its creation. The men are regarded as the masters of this type of design, while the women create the geometric designs found in their baskets. In weaving the Chilcat blanket, the convention is that the men prepare the design for the women to copy. This is done by painting the pattern on a cedar board, from which the weaver is supposed to copy. When one weaver was asked if she needed to consult the pattern often, she smiled as a reply. The design generally relates to an incident in a family origin myth and sometimes two or three blankets are woven from the same pattern board for persons in the family who are entitled to wear them. Since the blankets have often been traded in modern times these principles do not always hold now. In the design, the principal animal is represented completely reorganized so that the natural features are lost; it may be shown from the front and both sides, as is the bear in Figure 3-2. The "X-ray" device is found on many old stone pieces and on petroglyphs where the ribs and vertebrae of an animal or human figure are used as decorative motifs. In the historic period this device is also found on bird rattles, showing the skeletal structure of the bird in a painted design on the surface.

The artist's desire to fill the space is not limited to a relationship of the design to the total area, but he also does not like to have blank spaces within the confines of the design itself. On some pieces delicate texturing of the wood with fine adze strokes are enough to satisfy. Elongated stippling is used on the argillite carvings of the Haida to indicate a bear's hair, and cross-hatching fills in the beaver's scaly tail. When the body of a bird or animal is used one often sees "eyes" in strange places. These indicate the joints in the creature's anatomical structure and are found principally where there is a ball and socket joint, as at the hips, shoulders, and ankles. The appliquéd thunderbird mentioned above is an excellent example of this device.

There is greater stress on the head of the animal than on the body. This is particularly true of the birds, except in the use of the whole body as a rattle, but there again the significant details are concentrated in the head, the body is used as the vehicle for further design. This same emphasis occurs in the costumes of dancers, who may wear an elaborate headdress and/or mask, but cover the body with a cedar bark blanket, one of the most commonplace garments in the days before white contact. Only in recent years has the Chilcat blanket been used by the Kwakiutl dancers, while the button blanket has also become a part of the dancing costume. Many of these items are loaned so often today that one wonders whether — except for this mask — this haphazard costuming is due to the cultural changes and disorganization or was always the case.

There are two examples of the wood carver's art which are distinctive of the Indian culture in the Northwest: the totem pole and the double mask. The totem pole is a red cedar tree, trimmed of branches and bark, then carved for some or all of its total length. These poles reach to seventy feet in height. It has been difficult to trace their origin and development because cedar which has been cut and exposed to the elements in the Northwest seldom has a life of more than sixty years. This means that the majority of poles known to ethnographers were made after 1850. However, it is also known that the form of the totem pole is not old for it is not mentioned in the journals of the eighteenth-century Europeans who came to the coast. They did mention inside house posts, and Webber, the artist with the Cook Expedition in 1778, sketched the inside of a Nootka house showing two large carved house posts. Such carved and painted house posts were widely distributed in the area, but the tall pole with many figures developed in the north and spread southward in the second half of the nineteenth century. The Kwakiutl of northern Vancouver Island and the mainland of British Columbia opposite were perhaps the last and most vigorous exponents of this expression of art and many of the poles made since 1900–1910 are the work of their artists. A praiseworthy project has been the efforts made in recent years by the Province of British Columbia to save the poles which still exist, especially those at deserted village sites.

There were several kinds of poles serving different functions in the society. Foremost was a pole erected by a wealthy man to enhance the social prestige of his family, often to commemorate an important event. For this a carver was engaged and given a down payment at a feast during which all the guests heard the announcement and thus became witnesses to the transaction. When the pole was finished it was erected in connection with another feast given by the owner. At this time the artist was paid the remainder of his fee. When all this had been accomplished the pole had served its major social function and it received little, if any, care. It is clear from the manner in which the poles were placed that their function was never considered to be decorative. The illustration showing the poles in the Haida village of Massett is typical (Figure 3-3).

FIGURE 3-3 *

The Haida Village of Masset on the Queen Charlotte Islands, Taken by A. H. Maynard in the 1880's

* Reproduced by permission of the Archives of the Provincial Museum of British Columbia.

Several other interesting features can also be seen here. The uncarved sections with circular bands at the tops of the poles, indicate the segments of a chief's hat which were added as he gave more potlatches. These are all poles set up for the sake of social prestige.

The pole in the left corner of the picture is a mortuary column which is always uncarved. On top it has an oblong box with a large face carved on the front. This is the burial box of an important member of a wealthy family. Such a memorial is often not set up for several years after the death of the individual, who is temporarily buried elsewhere until the box and pole can be prepared and a great feast arranged.

The designs carved on the pole are related to the legends telling the origin of the family or some important incident in their legendary history. The adaptation of the figures to the vertical space on the pole required a highly skilled carver. On the third tall pole from the right (Figure 3-3) the top carved figure is a raven whose beak is turned down on his breast instead of standing straight out. The latter would involve attaching an extra piece for the beak, and the carvers preferred to work on a single block of wood. This design also makes a better and more compact piece of sculpture.

The Northwest Coast masks are as famous as the totem poles and, within the culture, perhaps preferred. It is clear from what chronology can be derived for Northwest Coast art that masks were used in the late eighteenth century. Again, the subjects are the mythological characters and the spirits of the supernatural world. These are represented in many kinds of masks and headdresses, the distinction between them being the degree to which the face of the wearer is hidden from view. The simplest is the face mask, and these are often the realistic ones, representing spirits of the dead, but not specifically ancestors. There are many animal masks which also have a degree of realism. The supernatural character most popular with the Kwakiutl is Tsonoqwa, the Cannibal Woman who roams the woods looking for victims. Her face is always painted black with a red mouth, her cheeks are sunken, and she has concave areas at her temples. Her eyebrows are made of a strip of bear fur and, in spite of being a female character, she has a fur beard. The Nootka have a wolf mask which once had more realism, but it has been elaborated by combining it with the symbols of the thunderbird and adding scrolls on the top.

Most spectacular are the double masks which open to reveal a second face within. For instance, an eagle face is split down the center and opens to show the face of a man. In many myths such transformations took place, for the supernatural beings who lived in the world before the present people could change from animal to human at will. The most complicated masks were made by the Kwakiutl toward the end of the nineteenth century when their stagecraft had reached its height, before the ceremonies were banned by the authorities. The "Cannibal of the Mountains" and his servant "Hoxhok," a mythical crane, were represented in tremendous masks with two or three heads. One example is six feet two inches wide with two faces that have beaks which open and close on strings manipulated by the dancer (Figure 3-4). Long strands of shredded cedar bark hang down over the shoulders of the dancer, who wears the mask on a shoulder harness, because it is too heavy for the head alone. The dancer stays in a crouching position, turning and moving the beaks which clap with a loud noise. All this was seen in silhouette against the firelight.

One cannot leave the subject of Northwest Coast art without calling attention to the specialized carving of the Haida. On the Queen Charlotte Islands where they live there is a quarry of material called carbonaceous

FIGURE 3-4 *

A Mask Representing Raven and the Cannibal of the Mountains Used by the
Kwakiutl in the Winter Dances of the Secret Societies. Collected in 1941 by
Dr. G. E. Newcombe.

shale by geologists and known in the anthropological literature as argillite or black slate. Since the term "argillite" is preferred by the Canadians and this is their territory, an effort should be made to use it consistently to avoid constant explanations. This stone is very soft when first taken from its location, but it hardens quickly when exposed to the air and becomes brittle. This means that it must be kept moist while being carved and work on it cannot be delayed too long.

While the Haida used argillite for charms and amulets, it was never an important material in their culture until the early nineteenth century, when they found that European visitors liked carvings made of it, and a "tourist" art began which is still carried on today. C. Marius Barbeau, who has studied this art intensively, relates its beginning and encouragement to the seamen on whaling ships who were the famous scrimshaw carvers (Barbeau 1953). That there was such an outside influence is apparent, but in spite of it, the Haida kept an easily identifiable style of their own. They included rope, ships' wheels and cabin housing, men in seamen's clothing, floral designs, and other copies of decoration on the ships, but they also resorted to many interpretations of myths of their own, principally the story of the Bear Mother. During the years this art was practised the objects and subjects that were carved changed with the tastes of the visitors. Many early pieces were pipes which the seamen liked. Some were functional and others were so highly decorated that they were virtuoso productions. Later, plates and oval platters with figures in high relief on the face (which made them nonfunctional) were produced, as well as small boxes in imitation of the carved wooden chests. Finally, they made model totem poles, all souvenir items of a high class.

The carvers in this medium became known by name because of their extensive dealing with European purchasers who were accustomed in their culture to know artists by name. Barbeau brought many of these men to public attention in his writings and from internal evidence has identified pieces of their work as they have been found. Occasionally these Haida carvers did initial their work as they became acquainted with this custom from their European customers.

This brief summary of the art activity on the Northwest Coast shows a large culture area in which a number of diverse languages are spoken, with two major focal centers, the Salish-speaking tribes of the South, and the more elaborate cultures among the Tlingit, Haida, and Tsimshian of the north, with an intermediate central group of Wakashan-speakers who shared traits from both extremes. A single great art developed here from an archaeological base now only partially known, and from the likenesses in a cosmological outlook which in each region were revised to fit into a social pattern, especially in the highly developed northern area. These cultural differences are minor compared to the basic unity the graphic and plastic arts exemplify.

AFRICAN ART

Background of the Art

The vast continent of Africa can be divided culturally into a number of subareas for the study of its art. First, the discussion must be limited to Negro Africa, which can be defined as south of the Sahara. The Sudan can be eliminated because the people are mostly Mohammedans who are not allowed by their religion to represent any living form in their art. A further limit can be set by concentrating on the region in which the great sculptural styles have been developed, which forms a great diagonal band from the west coast south and eastward, including the drainages of the Niger and the Congo (see Figure 3-5). This area consisted of great populations representing many tribes joined

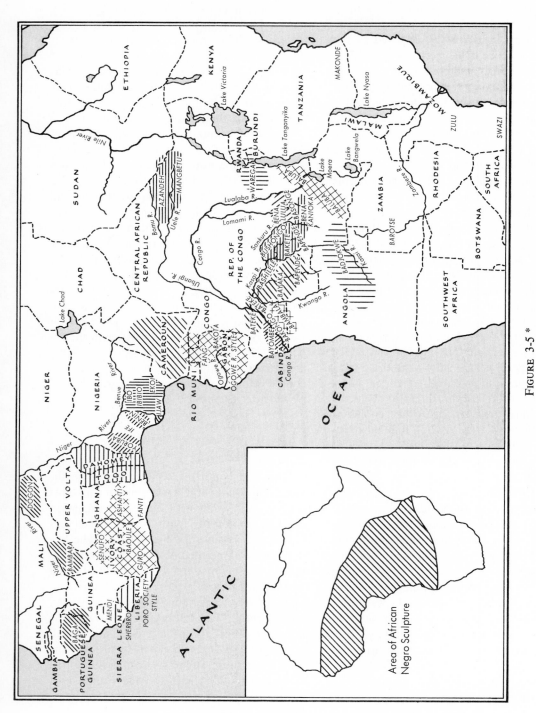

FIGURE 3-5 *

Map Showing Areas of African Negro Sculpture, Major Styles or Traditions
Indicated by Shading

* Adapted with permission from Paul S. Wingert, *The Sculpture of Negro Africa.*
New York: Columbia University Press, 1950, facing p. 1.

into states or kingdoms which have been compared to the kingdoms of feudal Europe. Their territorial boundaries, like their European counterparts, were often very unstable, but many royal families maintained considerable continuity even if their territory varied. Not every tribe in this area carves or produces a craft that can be so elevated as to be called an art, even though they share beliefs and other culture traits. Carvings are not always thought necessary, even for the same kind of ceremony. For example, Himmelheber describes the use of a piece of cloth with holes for the eyes and mouth cut in it to cover the face, instead of a wooden mask, and a crude symbol of clay substituted for the fine ancestor figures found among neighbors (Himmelheber 1963:80).

The people involved in the creation of the art now in the museums and described in the literature are sometimes called by their tribal names or by subgroup or even village names, so the literature is often difficult to follow. For instance, the Fang, who live on the border of the Cameroons and Gabun, are also called the Pahouin together with several other groups, but this may also be written Pangwe; and sometimes the southernmost of the group are called Ogowe from the river that flows through their territory. This type of confusion is common among primitive groups but seems too frequent for the peace of mind of the casual student of African art. To add to this confusion, many countries in this area have in recent years become independent nations under still other names, but since the most concise map of the area showing the art styles has the older territorial names, it will be used here, to be consistent with the ethnographic literature.

As can be seen, the great area of sculptural art is concentrated in the center of Africa, where the most typical Negro population is found and where influences from outside the African continent are least. There is great variation in the art styles but a few similarities are apparent that permit identification of an object as African. The art is carried out in two major media, wood and metal. The presence of the latter is extraordinary in a primitive society and is one of the unique features in Africa, where the metallurgical technique of casting by the lost wax (*cire perdue*) process was highly developed. Woods of many qualities were used, hard and soft. Many of the pieces seen in museums today are dark brown or black and thus give a false impression about the use of color. Many native pigments were used as paint on wood carvings, and polychrome objects were common in many parts of the area. Age has softened or wiped out these colors.

In style, the predominance of the human figure is obvious, even in the metal casting. Animal forms occur principally as decorative motifs. This is a great contrast to the Northwest Coast of America where animal forms are derived from some of the ancestor myths. In Africa, ancestor cults are very common but the ancestor is never nonhuman. While some local styles are easily recognized, there are many pieces which are baffling because of borrowing and actual trading of objects. Also, with the instability of territorial lines, the provenience of an object is sometimes uncertain. These matters are important because so much of the material to be studied was collected by travellers, missionaries, and government administrators who did not realize that identifying the piece as coming from Africa might interest guests after dinner, but was not sufficient for the scholar who later found it in a museum.

Liberian Sculpture: Art under the Control of the Secret Society

Since the area is so large and so many styles of carving exist, it would be an endless and monotonous task to review them all.

Consequently, a few cultures have been chosen for "case studies" in the hope that they will cover to some degree the status of the art in the life of these people and some visual concept of their output.

The first area to be discussed is Liberia, since there are two excellent studies from this region. The first is by Dr. Etta Becker-Donner, now of the Museum für Völkerkunde in Vienna, and is based on two field trips she took in 1934–1935 and 1936–1937. The second is by George W. Harley, whose paper, "Masks as Agents of Social Control in Northeastern Liberia," (1950) places the art in its awesome position in these tribes that share the Poro secret society. He concerns himself with the mask and its functions, while Dr. Becker-Donner describes all the art activities in the tribe she studied, and gives details of their manufacture in the best ethnographic style.

The people represented by these two authors include the Mano, Dan, and the subgroups associated with them by language and/or culture. Becker-Donner describes the whole range of the arts, including metallurgy, weaving, pottery, and wood-carving, but this latter art occupied a very special place in the society. Next to it was metallurgy, which also was carried on under the patronage of a local chief or a paramount chief of a tribe or region. The smith lived in the compound of his patron and limited his work to his command. He was further tied to his patron by the fact that the latter controlled the metal to be used. The smith worked with some secrecy, but was not as strictly confined as the wood-carver. He inherited his taboos, together with his technique, from his father. The metal was always poured into the mold at night. The smith's output consisted of realistic figures made by the lost wax (*cire perdue*) process. The function of these figures, which ranged from a few to 30 centimeters in size, was not revealed. He also made jewelry such as arm-

lets, with especially handsome ones designed for warriors, anklets with bells on them, and necklaces. These were all decorated with simple interlocking geometric designs. He also made knives and weapons. The metals used were iron and copper, the latter alloyed to form brass for the ornaments. The sources of these materials was also kept a secret.

The wood-carver could get his own materials, and he worked for others beside his patron because anyone who had inherited the right to use a mask could order one. There was also general demand for ancestor figures and household articles. The critical pieces were those that represented human faces, because this meant contact with the spirits, and the carver had to observe many regulations in his conduct while he was at work. Only his apprentice could see a piece while he worked on it. When a mask was finished it was put in a fiber sack and delivered during the night to the man who ordered it. Since unfinished pieces were kept in the house of the carver there was always the danger that they might be seen by a member of his family. If such an accident was known to have occurred the carver had to sacrifice a white chicken or a white goat and smear some of the blood on the unfinished piece, asking its forgiveness so the ghost to which the piece belonged would not make the carver's wife and children ill. The occupation of wood-carver was passed on in a family, if there was someone who showed any skill for it.

In Northeast Liberia figure carving is no longer restricted to representations of ancestors but rather tends to become memorials to remind the relatives of a deceased family member. Many represent women whose "portraits" are ordered by their husbands or widowers. Occasionally one is ordered by a woman herself, if she is childless, so her ghost will have a home. These memorial figures, because they are representations of the human face, have strong magical power and need careful handling. Becker-Donner describes in detail the ceremony at the delivery of a figure. The carver wrapped it in a mat and took it to the village elder or whoever was head of the village and told him that on the next day he would show him something extraordinary. To see it he would have to lay "something" under it, meaning a leopard skin or a cow hide. If it was a cow hide, the animal would be eaten at the feast which followed. At this time the owner of the figure paid the artist for his work and toward this sum he received contributions from all who were present at the ceremony and partook of the feast. Formerly, the head of the village asked all owners of such figures to contribute to a feast held for the figures during the new moon (but not every month), indicating their important religious significance.

These female figures are not exact portraits but are highly stylized. Some show individual characteristics, such as traces of tattooing. The body is elongated in relation to the short legs, which are slightly bent at the knees. The coiffure is carved in great detail. Necklaces of native or trade beads are put around the heavy columnar throat and around the waist as a support for a small cotton or leather apron. Some figures carry a child on the back. There are tribal differences throughout the area in these details.

Harley studied the same area with emphasis on the secret society, the Poro, and the masks used both within the rituals of the group and in effecting their control of the community (see Figure 3-6). Information of this kind is very difficult to elicit when the society is still functioning, for the members are sworn to secrecy and nonmembers can only offer guesses. The information was gathered by Harley during a period of governmental suppression of the society, but it has since been permitted to function again in a more restricted form. The society initiated boys at puberty in a "Bush" school where they lived in the forest in a sacred compound

for three or four years, learning not only the ritual but also the occupations of men, so that on completing the initiation they were ready to be accepted as adults by the community. They learned to carve the masks of the society while learning the rituals and the functions of the society in the affairs of the community. This study brings about a much larger conception of the functions of masks and their wearers, a form of social control completely unknown in other societies.

The Poro society worked in secrecy and presented its actions and findings as decrees from the spirit world, communicated through the masks. These judgments were passed on to the public by a masked figure whose identity was supposed to be unknown. There were four types of masks: (1) the small individual mask with a human face that fits into the person's hand and is never shown except in a high ritual, and is never seen by a woman. It is prayed to every morning and a chicken is sacrificed to it every new moon. At death the mask is put on the grave or given to a son or a nephew who will care for it. It can also be given back to the carver. (2) The great or oracle mask, which is considered a god spirit that makes the final judgment in cases brought before the high council. These masks have protuberant eyes faced with perforated china or metal discs, red felt lips, a long beard hung with calabar beads, palm nuts, or heavy glass beads. Masked officials were used by the "Great Mask" for all kinds of errands, to settle quarrels, and so on. (3) Masks with animal features superimposed on human faces by means of a grotesque mouth or protruding eyes. (4) Best known to the public were the masks of dancers, clowns, and minstrels who appeared on public occasions. Even for the public appearances of some of these masks women and children had to hide from sight.

The masks all have spirits living in them that can easily be offended, so all must have

FIGURE 3-6 *

An Initiation Ceremony Mask of the Poro Society, Mano, Liberia

careful handling as soon as they are finished. Through these spirits the mask exercises social control, for all its actions and judgments are attributed to the spirit, never to the unknown wearer. He is guided by the mask and is not responsible for his actions. This fundamental concept deeply affects the attitude toward art in these communities, for while the skill of the carver is recognized, his creative possibilities are very limited and his work is judged by its supernatural potency rather than by aesthetic appreciation. This is a far cry from the spirit in which the masks have been admired in our culture in the last half-century.

Art under the Aegis of the King's Court

The kingdom of Benin is a considerable contrast to the villages of northeastern Liberia because of its superstructure of a political organization functioning from a central capital. The ruler of Benin is a king or *Oba* who lives in a palace in Benin City. The people are Edo-speaking and are generally known as Bini.

The political structure makes Benin art a court art, not one of the people. The very organization of the capital points to this. Benin City is cut in two by a broad street which divides the town into the area in which the king lives in his palace with his court, and the other side in which the town chiefs live with all the professionals who serve the king. These include all the craftsmen like the blacksmiths, wood- and ivory-carvers, and bronze-casters. Each group lives in certain wards and the larger crafts are subdivided into further specialties. For instance, among the bronze-casters there are ten hereditary chiefs and each has a specialty.

Bini art can be understood only against the background of this complex state organization and ceremonial, together with the religious beliefs of the people. The universe of the Bini is divided into two parts: the actual visible world; and the invisible abode of the spirits of those who were once human, as well as deities who were never incarnated. The spirits of the dead are worshipped by their descendants. When a man dies his senior son or nephew sets up an altar and acts as priest to the deceased. The altars of past *Obas* are furnished with carved staffs, bronze bells, and bronze memorial heads with winged caps, inset on the top with carved ivory tusks which carry mythological scenes. A frieze of wood faced with chalk runs behind the altars and is carved with low relief figures of cow and ram heads, coiled mudfish, and a figure of the messenger of the god of death. The head is regarded as the seat of judgment and the *Oba* sacrifices to his head at one of the great rituals of the year, a ritual which demanded many forms of art.

In this culture the casting of metals takes precedence over wood carving, although this may be a false modern impression since many of the wooden figures were burned in the palace fire during the Punitive Expedition of 1897. It is therefore of considerable interest to find out something of its origin. There are theories about this and the chronology of its development. Fagg, of the British Museum, divides the development into three periods: (1) the 200 years up to the sixteenth century; (2) late sixteenth century to the middle of the eighteenth century; and (3) to the end of the fine art (which date he does not state, but presumably ending in the middle of the nineteenth century) (Forman and Dark 1960:18). This is one of the few places in Africa where it is possible to establish so long a chronology for an art. All theories concede that the art of bronze casting came from elsewhere, either from the Ife as early as the fifteenth century or from the village of Udo, only twenty miles from Benin City. Much more careful study is necessary before the problem can be solved so that we may be able to date Benin art with greater certainty. The art of bronze casting has been

FIGURE 3-7 *

A Bronze Plaque from Benin

This plaque represents three kings wearing tall bead caps and bead shirts. Hanging from the waists of the three figures are pendant plaques, of crocodiles on the two outer figures, and of three European heads on the central figures.

* Reproduced by permission of the Chicago Natural History Museum. Cat. No. 8258.

sufficiently preserved so that when it has been fully analyzed in the great study now under way by Philip J. C. Dark and R. E. Bradbury, the scholar will have an unequalled knowledge of the history of one of the world's great arts.

Benin bronze casting was done primarily in two forms, plaques (see Figure 3-7), which were attached to pillars in the palace and other important buildings, and heads. The plaques show assemblages of kings, warriors, and their attendants, and are done most frequently in high relief. The great detail shown in the costumes and accessories are very important in reconstructing the culture of their periods. The age of plaques seems to have ended at the beginning of the eighteenth century, when a civil war destroyed much of the splendor recorded by the early visitors to the kingdom. The Portuguese who arrived in 1485 not only described what they saw, but in turn were depicted in the processions carved spirally on the great elephant tusks. In their introductory chapter from which much of this material is taken, Forman and Dark end by saying: "Benin art does not generate in the Western observer an aesthetic reaction of a perceptual nature" (1960:24). They speak of the limited area in which the Bini artist could work, for this art is an interesting example of the static quality produced by the heavy hand of tradition and ceremonial background.

Sculpture and an Ancestor Cult

Still farther south in Africa there is another group of related tribes that produced some very interesting human figures. In addition to the individual tribal styles, this area adds to the mask and metal castings the third important vehicle of artistic expression in Africa — the human figure. All three forms are found in many groups, but in this brief résumé of the great arts of a large continent it seems best to stress one form in each of the few areas selected.

The Fang are included with the Beti and Boulou in a group known as the Pahouin or Pangwe on the borders of the Cameroon-Gabun region. The Fang have expanded southward to the Ogowe River and that name is also attached to them. Any of these terms may be found attached to their art. According to Wingert, the Fang do not use masks and do not have the variety in their art forms found elsewhere (Wingert 1950:46). The human figure, the half-figure, and the head dominate the art. As is so often true in Africa, the figures are connected with ancestral rites, for the Fang trace their ancestry to Nzame, supposedly the first man; however, he also had ancestors.

The best known works of the Fang are mortuary carvings, which once consisted only of a head carved on the side of a box containing the skull of the deceased. Then half-figures were made and, more recently, full figures (see Figure 3-8). Wingert comments on the demarcation of parts of the body and its disproportion (Wingert 1950:48). The cylindrical form of the neck continues into the body. The figures are painted a dull black, dark red, or gray monochrome, and some eyes are inlaid with metal. More exact details about the artists who make them are not easily found. A number of ethnographies of this group were consulted and, amazingly, nothing was said about the art except that objects were made in connection with ancestor cults. The authors were certainly not visually oriented!

Other Arts

The sculptural art of Africa is made either by people ritually prepared to handle it, like the artists initiated into the Poro secret society, or by the professional artists of Benin, but the wide production of more utilitarian objects that are also decorated has received little attention. Perhaps the best examples are the discussions by Rattray (1927) and Herskovits, who in his ethnography on Da-

FIGURE 3-8 *

Human Figure from the Fang

* From the collection of Mr. Robert Campbell, Portland, Oregon, with the owner's permission. Photograph by Mr. Campbell.

homey devotes a long section to a discussion on the principal forms of graphic art, appliquéd cloths, and incised calabashes. These are both media not familiar to Europeans, but must be considered in their context. The appliquéd cloths are made by a restricted family guild and can be acquired only by those of rank and power. The only exception is that a cloth-sewer can sell a piece he makes that is not ordered. Then anyone having the large amount of money necessary may acquire it. State umbrellas and caps worn by the chiefs, banners of associations, and decorated cloths used for worship of the gods are the primary uses for this material. It seems that this cloth has a long history and was probably a native weave since it is mentioned by Snelgrove in a book published in 1734 (Herskovits 1938b:329). The designs are appliquéd on the cloth by sewing, and the smoothness and flatness of the finished piece is a standard for judging its value. The designs are insignia of the royal house and important chiefs and may be represented in human or animal forms. Great artistry is shown in the combinations of colors, which are bright when new but fade rapidly in the strong sunlight. Relative natural sizes of the objects depicted are not in proportion; the most important figures are made larger, for instance, a chief would tower over his attendants. In the brass castings the patterns of the cloth skirts and umbrellas are often shown.

The cloth-sewers follow patterns kept in the compound where they work, each at an assigned place. The patterns consist of small pieces which the sewer combines to make the complex he wishes, this being his artistic contribution. The appreciation the Dahomeans have for these cloths stems from their narrative appeal and the validity and social importance of the incident depicted (Herskovits 1938b:331–341).

In every household, the undecorated calabash is used as a food container or drinking cup, but there is an incised calabash that is very sophisticated and, like the appliquéd cloths, is found only in the capital, Abomey. The design on these calabashes is taken from a proverb and they are sent as a message to a loved one, men usually sending them to women. This practice might best be described as Valentine's Day throughout the year. These calabashes are carved by cutting away the brown skin to show the white underneath, which forms a background for the brown of the outer skin as the design. Very few people carve these calabashes, the principal carver being a priest.

Another art medium used by the Dahomey and also by the Ashanti is brass-casting by the lost wax process. The Dahomey produce small scenes of several figures, such as a chief with several retainers who carry his umbrella or other insignia of status. These are carried out with a great deal of detail, and give the anthropologist another opportunity to study costumes as well as relations between people of different social rank. The Ashanti are famous for their gold weights, made by the same process and used to weigh the gold dust brought to the king. They are done both in small blocks with geometric designs and small figures of people and animals.

The fact that so much more has been written on the sculptural art of Africa may be due partially to the manner in which African art was introduced to the Western world by the avant-garde artists of Paris in the early part of this century. That its influence has been felt cannot be denied, though few agree on specific examples. However, when one sees a figure like that produced by the Fang or any similar ones from many other parts of the "sculptural belt" of the continent, its general influence is obvious in the art of the Western world in the twentieth century. As this new interest spread, curators of ethnological collections gradually brought out pieces which had always been displayed or stored, but as examples of ancestor worship,

and which had been written about in ethnographic terms without even illustrations. Then the art was returned again to the anthropologist, whose theoretical approach had been broadened so that he now realized the importance of studying the cultural setting of an art and the character of the artists or people involved in creating it. So a new literature is being developed which considers both points of view.

THE TEXTILE ARTS

Because it is truly an art of the primitive world, we will use basketry to represent and tell the story of the textile arts. While woven textiles are also found in many tribes, the extensive use of baskets in the economy is peculiarly distinctive of primitive life. Among some people basketry was developed with a virtuosity that put it into the field of art, especially among the tribes for whom it was the major aesthetic expression. Basketry is not exclusively women's work, but tends to be so when it reaches an artistic level and when it remains a home "industry," in contrast to the situation wherein men make coarse baskets to sell as containers, as in some of the markets in Africa. Women make baskets principally for household uses, but in many cultures, their production serves more abstruse purposes. How far into the history of man's culture this technique goes is hard to determine, because the remains of baskets are not often found in ancient sites. Occasionally, if the basket itself has disintegrated, its texture may have been imprinted in the soft clay soil surrounding it. There is reason to believe that the technique was probably the forerunner of weaving, which is generally dated as a product of the Neolithic period.

Making basketry requires a creative imagination. There is no obvious relationship between the finished product and the many materials that go into its manufacture. It is widely thought that baskets are made of grasses but that is a misconception since few grasses are strong enough for the structure, though many are used for the decorative elements. Baskets are generally made of some part of a shrub or tree, such as the inner bark, or the roots, and the strong vine-like limbs. A bundle of such material as it is gathered looks hopeless; and even after it has been prepared and trimmed, it is still far removed from the finished product. A basket-maker once commented that when the gathering and preparing of the elements was completed half the work of making a basket was done. Perhaps she felt this way because it seemed like unproductive labor, whereas the work ahead was creative and more stimulating.

Making a basket takes very careful planning and involves conceptual control beyond that basic to artistic production. An artist about to paint a picture has his space defined by stretching the canvas in a frame. When a potter paints a clay vessel, the area to be decorated is before him. But a basket-maker creates her space and her design at the same time. If she works in a twining technique she is faced by a mass of warps which are turned upwards from the bottom when that is completed. If the design is arranged in a large V-shape she must place the center stitch of the V in the proper color on the first row of the body of the basket. Then, as she works upward on the sides, the pattern develops with the space, and if the basket flares toward the top that must also be allowed for in the increase of stitches in the pattern. Horizontal bands of design are much easier to create, yet one finds fewer of them than of those more difficult to adjust. The basket-maker accepts the challenge.

One of the areas of the finest basketry in America centers around California, extending into some tribes of the Southwest and also northward along the Pacific Coast. At the peak of this development stand the Pomo of north-central California, whose exquisite work is found in every representative collection of Indian basketry. The Pomo have become so well known also because of the excellent publication on their work by S. A. Barrett who said: "With these people basketry in aboriginal times took the place of almost every sort of utensil for the gathering, transportation, storage, grinding of vegetable products, cooking and serving foods and for ceremonial and mortuary purpose" (Barrett 1908:135).

Basketry among the Pomo, as with almost all aboriginal populations, was essentially a woman's art, but men also knew some of the techniques needed for making fish traps, coarse, burden baskets, and quail traps. Only baskets made by the women had designs consciously applied to them. The technique in some of the men's baskets might create a self-pattern, but it could scarcely be classified as art. Basketry among the Pomo was, then, a series of techniques that were understood by every adult in the community and to some degree practiced by all. With such a broad base of participation, the appreciation of fine work was high and critical analysis was intelligent.

The designs, forms, and techniques were so varied as to give the baskets endless interest, all this with a minimum of range of color except for those ornamented with feathers and shells. The design elements are triangles, rectangles, rhomboids, and zigzags; from combinations of these, placed horizontally or diagonally on the basket, great variety of pattern is achieved. A sharp distinction is made between these individual design elements and the patterns formed by combinations thereof in giving them names. The simple design element has the name of a well-known natural or artificial object, geometric figure, or the like, but when worked into a composite pattern, the name becomes a descriptive sentence or phrase name. These are not the same with all basket-makers, due to difference in dialect and individual traditions.

The purposes for which baskets are used have close relationships to the choice of weave and ornamentation. The coarse baskets made by the men have no ornamentation and many are made in open-work technique of materials that are sturdy and not prepared with much precision. They serve as fish traps and heavy burden baskets. Many of the latter are shaped in a functional form which is characteristic of California. They are cone-shaped, with the wide mouth at the top so that the burden is carried at the level of the upper back, a very practical consideration. The cooking basket, made by the women, is twined in a close weave so that when the elements swell with moisture it will be watertight. The medicine man uses an elliptical basket to store his sacred objects, a shape that allows space for the feather wands too long for the average round basket. The choicest of all is the treasure basket, which is usually covered at least partially with feathers. These are woven into the basket by inserting the quill before the element in the weaving is pulled tight. The design is created with the feathers, which are gathered from a variety of birds. The green head of the mallard duck, the yellow breast of the meadow lark, the orange feathers of the oriole, the dark brown breast of the varied thrush, the red patches on the wings of the red-winged blackbird, and the red head of the woodpecker all contribute to these extraordinary baskets. The jet black topknot of the California quail decorates the rim of the fully feathered baskets as well as others. Some baskets have a woven design and are stippled with tiny red feathers from the woodpecker. Added to these ornaments are beads ground of clamshells and small arrow-shaped pendants of abalone shell. All these carefully chosen items create most imaginative objects of materials derived directly from a natural environment.

The Pomo women enjoy their basket-making to such an extent that they play with their skill in making miniature baskets, remarkable exhibitions of their technique. These are usually less than a half an inch in diameter, perfectly woven and with a well-placed design. While they are sometimes sold, a basket-maker can earn a reputation for her work by giving these as gifts on proper occasions, and this is worth more to her than the money she might earn from a sale. In a tribal group where everybody participates in a craft, the standards are high and so is the appreciation of excellent performance.

North of the Pomo, almost at the northern border of California, is a group of three tribes who, though speaking different languages, have much the same customs including great ability at basket-making. Two of these, the Yurok and Karok, were studied by Lila O'Neale, who published a monograph that is a delight to the anthropologist interested in the anthropological approach to art. She took back to these villages pictures of baskets or the baskets themselves that were made there, from the collections of the University of California. These were discussed with the contemporary basket-makers in these tribes, and a true understanding of the place of basket-making in these cultures in which it is the principal aesthetic expression resulted.

The Yurok and Karok live along the lower Klamath River, in one of the more isolated parts of the state. It was not unusual in former days for a person never to leave this river valley in his life, and even when this study was made about thirty years ago, Indians of these groups were not curious about other people and grouped them all together as "outsiders." These people lived on a simple economy of fishing, hunting, and gathering wild vegetable foods — especially acorns, which they leached and ground into flour. Baskets were used for every household purpose and were classified as food baskets,

Indian pans and plates, fish baskets, spoon baskets, cradles — all these were referred to as "stick" baskets and were done in an open weave. Close-twined baskets included dippers, cooking and serving baskets, water baskets, trays for meals, storage baskets, gift baskets, hats, Brush Dance and Jumping Dance baskets, and fancy baskets. With such a variety it is not surprising that women specialized in a few and traded with others for those they needed but did not make.

Everyone shared in basket-making, including the men, who were willing to help gather materials, for which they had to learn the standards for selection. Men often took part in interviews with O'Neale and volunteered information even after protesting that they knew very little. This interest may have been due partially to the fact that the men really had no visual aesthetic expression in this culture. They knew rituals and lead ceremonials and the Yurok men did a little wood carving. Men were proud of their wives' work and helped sell it when they could. But a sale to white people was important only economically, while a sale to other Indians built the reputation of the basket-maker.

The baskets under discussion were made of hazel, willow, and myrtle sticks, of the roots of redwood, alder, willow, and wild grape for the body and of white grass, the midribs of maiden hair fern, the stems of woodwardia fern, and porcupine quills for designs. Dyes were made of alder bark for red to brown, and Oregon grape and a lichen for mustard yellow. As mentioned before, all these materials needed much preparation and every woman preferred to do her own. The "sticks" were used for the openwork baskets and cradles and only the finest materials were put into women's hats. These were regarded as the most difficult to make and only an accomplished weaver would attempt them.

The design units are called "marks" and are very similar to those of the Pomo, but the combinations of units used by the Yurok bring a very different aspect to the finished product. The Yurok and Karok basketmaker does not aim to be original and ingenious, she wants to be correct, to work in a moulded tradition which includes not only the design and its placement, but also the size of the basket, the choice of materials, and colors. O'Neal gives as an example of this attitude:

Fern has its own place; it is the basic color for a cap to which smaller black and white areas give emphasis. This is not an inflexible rule. If a weaver wanted to render a small design element in red fern in her very nice cap, no Indian law is transgressed, or no bad luck follows, but she would thereby depreciate the value of weeks of work, and display what is to beholders an incongruous selection of colors and materials. Naturally, she follows custom in self-defense (O'Neale 1932:161).

There is also no play with technique, not even to the degree of displaying virtuosity in making baskets very small or very large. But as O'Neale says, "Far from being deadened by a craft in which so much is reduced to conformity the women of the two tribes have developed an appreciation of quality, design-to-space relationships and effective color dispositions which are discriminating and genuine" (O'Neale 1932:165).

This study of interviews with forty-three women of all ages from teens to octogenarians revealed the universal interest in this art and the great importance it has in the lives of the women. As with crafts everywhere in the primitive world, the young people do not carry this on. One mother explained that her girls were away in boarding school at the time they should have been learning basketry. It is even more unfortunate that nothing from the education they received has replaced this void in the Yurok and Karok women's world. Not only have these women lost an absorbing interest but those who have continued to weave have allowed themselves to deviate from this tradition in the use of color and execution of dubious designs for the sake of pleasing a white customer. The ray of light in this dismal picture is the fact that, for themselves and for each other, the traditions are still followed and it is hoped that the generation that worked with O'Neale will be successful in persuading some of their younger women to continue the art.

One of the oldest problems in the history of primitive art has been whether geometric designs preceded realistic ones or vice versa. It was argued that the geometric design was simpler and should have come first. These arguments took place largely before the discovery of the great Upper Paleolithic cave paintings with their realism. Also, by then it was realized that the geometric design may look simple but it can also be abstract and conceptually much more sophisticated. The cave paintings, furthermore, also revealed the presence of geometric design in the "grills" that often appear which have been interpreted as traps and are called tectiforms. It seems that any attempt at a world-wide chronology for the development of these two art forms is meaningless, but with the expansion of the textile arts in the Neolithic period, geometric designs had a better medium for expression.

PAINTED STONE WALLS, ANCIENT AND NOT SO OLD

Given the title of this chapter, it may seem strange to include the art of a people about whom we know only what archaeological remains reveal. Superficially this might mean that we know little about their philosophy or any other traits of a subjective nature, and therefore it would be impossible to relate the art to the remainder of their culture. In a very stimulating paper, "Prehistoric Art and Ideology," Morton Levine suggests that some reconstruction of Paleolithic man's thought, which he expressed in his art, can be made by comparing it with a known people who have been studied ethnographically and who live in similar circumstances (Levine 1957). Of all the contemporary primitive people it is generally agreed that the native Australians are probably the nearest in their way of life to Paleolithic man. They are hunters and gatherers, wresting a living from an inhospitable environment, and at the same time expressing themselves in an art comparable to that of ancient times. Because this study is based on extensive research in the field of Paleolithic art, and recent works on aboriginal Australian art, it is possible to deduce from cave man's art and the life of the Australians some possible clues as to the place of art in the Paleolithic period.

Before the conclusions of Levine's study can be discussed what is known about Paleolithic art must be reviewed. When ancient man in Europe (Upper Paleolithic, 40,000 years ago) wished to express himself in a two-dimensional form of art, he could not resort to canvas, for weaving had not yet been developed, but he might have painted on the inside of animal skins if he cleaned them sufficiently. Instead, he chose to use the great walls of stone in the caves of southern France and northern Spain where he lived. It is fortunate for posterity that this happened, for if he had painted outdoors, the art would have been lost; many of the pictographs on canyon walls in other parts of the world are difficult to trace and are much more recent. Rock painting and carving is found almost universally in caves, large and small, or on walls and cliffs sometimes difficult of access, more often than not away from sites of habitation, giving the impression that they may have been part of a secret ritual.

Europe in the Upper Paleolithic period was the scene of the late Würm glaciation and final retreat of the glaciers, which brought about great climatic changes. While a single generation of men did not live through much perceptible change, there was great uncertainty about the weather, which had a direct effect on the food supply. A hunting and gathering people are very closely related to the weather and in many environments even minor changes can determine whether they can remain where they are or must migrate again to find more favorable conditions. Technology protects modern man from his immediate environment and it is sometimes difficult to comprehend the intimate relationship primitive man had with these features of his existence.

In the Upper Paleolithic period there was an expansion and development in the technique of flaking and chipping stone implements and the use of bone and antler objects became extensive. This culture is referred to by archaeologists as Aurignacian, a term from the geological subperiod of the Quarternary. Typical implements of this period are the burin — a small stone flake with a strong point used for carving hard materials such as stone and ivory, the keeled scrapers and, later, the beautiful symmetrical "laurel leaf" blades of the Solutrean, the next cultural period. In weapons, barbed bone harpoon points were coming into use. This inventory sounds very meager and its importance does not lie in quantity, but in the proportion of the rate of development over previous periods when such progress was not made for thousands of years. Man's culture speeded up as it approached the beginning of recorded history.

The people who developed these new forms lived in the river valleys and plains of France, which were just recovering from the rigorous climate of the glacial period and which were also occupied by a group of fauna of cold-adapted species that now live in the Arctic, if they still exist. Many wandered northward, but the reindeer stayed behind and ran in herds on the plains of European countries. Other animals belonging to a more temperate climate stayed with man and became his major food supply — antelope, chamois, ibex, the small horse and a small donkey, the deer, and the mammoth. Man may have been a migratory hunter in an area only when the "temperate climate" animals were also there; the "cold" species may have come in when he had gone. If they ever met he may have been sufficiently impressed with them to use a few in his paintings. On the other hand, this selection of fauna may indicate that the painting may have been done years apart. The cave bear and cave lion probably harassed man, but were also eaten when they were killed. These creatures were at once man's food and his menace.

In this rough setting man struggled for existence and the flourishing of an art of such quality and in such quantity as has been found is one of the great wonders in his history. When anthropology began as a science in the middle of the nineteenth century, some of the first finds of Paleolithic art were being made. It is entirely possible that many things had been previously discovered and were disregarded because of ignorance or lack of anything with which to associate them. In the 1860's finds were made in France, and from then on, these pieces were recognized and brought to the attention of scholars. Today the tendency is to think first of the painting in the caves, but actually small sculptures were known before the paintings were authenticated. Graziosi tells the story of a find very dramatically and since many others are known today through similar chance circumstances it is worth repeating here as he gives it:

About ten years prior to the discovery a sportsman, while searching the thickets on the gentle slopes on which Santillana del Mar is built, noticed that his dog, who was pursuing a fox, had disappeared among the bushes, and that the sound of its barking seemed to be coming from a great way away. He immediately realized that the animal had crawled into a hole in the earth, and searched the scrub until he found a narrow opening. That was how the Altamira cave was discovered. It is a very large cave, burrowing for hundreds of metres into the bowels of the hill. Seventy years later a dog once more touched off a discovery of the same kind — equally sensational: the Lascaux in France.

Nothing of particular interest was found at the time in the Altamira cave, and it was forgotten until six years later when Marcelino de Sautuola, who used to spend the summer months on his property near Altamira, was told by a labourer of the discovery of the cave; he decided to excavate the deposits that had accumulated in several parts of it as he was interested in prehistory.

His research continued intermittently for four years, and finally one day in the summer of 1879, while rummaging in the blackish earth of a large trench the sensational discovery was made. On that day, as on many others, de Sautuola had taken his little daughter Maria with him; suddenly the child, who had wandered off into the cave to where light filtered in, raised her eyes to the ceiling and exclaimed: "Papa, mira toros pintados!" Her father rushed in, shone his lamp to where the child was pointing and in the uncertain glimmer saw the outline of a great bison, vigorously painted on the uneven rock surface; then he saw another, and yet another, all painted in vivid colour, fresh and clear as though they had been finished that very day (Graziosi 1960:16–17).

Work in this area has been carried on since by many famous archaeologists, and many theories regarding these paintings have developed. The finding of sculptural figures was less dramatic because they usually came together with other archaeological finds in known sites, or out of the treasures of an amateur collector when they were often more difficult to include in a study series because of lack of exact data regarding their origin. The sculptured objects Graziosi called "mobiliary art" have a wider distribution on the European continent than cave art and are also found in Siberia and a few in North Africa. Whether the exceptional number found in France are due to the intensive study the area has had, or to their frequency, we do not know, thus a true indication of France as the focal center of the art is not yet clear.

This mobiliary art consists of small figures and engraving on small objects, that is, pieces which could be carried with a migratory group. These figures are carved of stone, bone, antlers of deer and reindeer, and ivory from mammoth tusks. There is also some clay modelling which is done directly on the ground or against the wall of a cavern like the painting. If the sculptor of the Paleolithic era also used wood, there are no remains to prove it, but it is not unreasonable to assume that this might have been done in areas where suitable woods were available. This sculpture in the round belongs to the early Upper Paleolithic, a period called the Aurignacian-Perigordian. In the Magdalenian, the last of the cultural periods of the Upper Paleolithic, sculpture in the round was less frequent. The Magdalenians also were very skillful in engraving bone. The shape of the material had great influence on the early work, and this is also apparent in the choice of places for painting; when the artist exploited a swelling in the limestone to give greater volume to the form he painted on it. The decorative art of the Magdalenians was applied to a functional object which constitutes an added problem for the artist.

The statuettes made during the Upper Paleolithic have been called "Venuses" by their first discoverers; perhaps this was someone's sense of humor, or it could have been based on the thought that they represented the personification of feminine charms. They were usually feminine with enormous breasts and buttocks. The feet were not developed and the legs merged below the knees. The arms, when not missing, were underdeveloped. The head was small and the features were not defined, but much care was given to the hair, which may be braided or in circles around the head. Quoting again from Graziosi, who interprets thus:

The exuberant fleshiness, full of life and feeling; the sense of female fulfillment radiating from the little masterpieces, unequivocally reveals that the end sought by the artist was an expression of fertile femininity — maternity in its fullest, most absolute sense.

This is the period in which the female body in all its vibrant realism triumphs in Palaeolithic art: during the entire prehistoric period, only in the Aurignacian-Perigordian statuettes and in the bas-reliefs of the same period (of which we shall speak later) was the image of womanhood permeated with so potent a breath of life. Later, with the advent of the Solutrean period, the tradition of fine female representation was lost, and in the subsequent Magdalenian period the female form was treated in a crude, rudimentary fashion or else — as recent discoveries have disclosed — in a fashion which, while adhering to realistic traditions, approaches what we might call a kind of composite academism. The religious mentality of the new Palaeolithic generations turns toward other interests (Graziosi 1960:46).

These figures varied from 3.5 to 22 centimeters in height, the majority being in the lower part of this range. They were not all equally well made, but this differs in areas rather than in possible chronological succession.

As the statuettes lost importance the mobiliary engravings were developed which show animals in action and which distinguished details such as hide and hair. In the Upper Magdalenian the subject matter is almost exclusively from the animal world. The carver's skill is simple but forceful and expressive. Animals appear in many action positions. Many pieces have a hole in them for suspension and are of a size to be worn as pendants. Among many ancient and modern people such pendants have served magical purposes as well as sheer ornamentation.

Since the discovery of the cave paintings other forms of art have often been neglected, so in this study it seemed advisable to deal with the sculpture first and then present the finest in the paintings of the same epochs and areas. There are two great centers of painting in the Franco-Cantabrian region, the valley of the Dordogne of France and the north coast of Spain along the Bay of Biscay and inland to the south. Both these regions have many famous sites, but Lascaux, in the valley of the Dordogne, is probably the best known and represents the climax of its art style. The figures are large, none less than $\frac{1}{2}$ meter high, and so is the space in which they are set. The comparable site in the Spanish area is Altamira and its neighbor, El Castillo. Many other sites have choice figures and show slightly different combinations of animals. The site at Les Trois Frères shows a number of anthropomorphic figures, one of which has been called "The Sorcerer." It may be a man with an animal skin and head with antlers, but the reason for naming him so specifically does not seem to be without question. It is another example of using our cultural conventions for people who lived in a totally different world.

These paintings are deep in caves, usually in areas that have not yielded archaeological remains in the immediate vicinity, though some indications of occupation are sometimes found near the entrance. Thus it would seem that the paintings were done in secrecy by some members of the community, a feature they have in common with the ceremonial pattern of many primitive groups in which the uninitiated men, and the women and children, may not enter such an area and are not even supposed to know of its existence.

The paintings themselves represent in great realism the animals of the immediate surroundings which were hunted for food. Sometimes they are indicated in herds, as by a forest of antlers with only a few animals partially drawn in the foreground. Many animals are shown as pregnant females, repeating the theme of many of the small carved figures discussed earlier. Increase of the food supply was a constant necessity for hunting people who lived on a meager margin.

The techniques used were engraving and painting. Many forms were outlined with shallow engraved lines done with the burins found in the living sites. This outline was filled in with black. Then the body was painted, usually in red and a mustard yellow, and details such as the features of the face and the hair of the body and manes of horses were done in black. The realism of these paintings is not so complete that every detail is shown to create the resemblance, but details were selected so as to indicate that there was a purpose to the art beyond individual aesthetic expression. The horned animals were usually shown with the horns in twisted perspective (perspective tordue), which is explained by Levine as follows: "Perspective tordue in the Upper Palaeolithic art is not a manifestation of inept perspective rendering but evidence for the intense concern of the hunter with his inadequate armament, over the danger he faced from horned wild beasts" (Levine 1957:961). In this rendering, the horns of the animals, otherwise shown in profile, are turned around full face to the viewer. The hoofs are also often twisted. The art historian who regards this as ineptitude has in mind the Renaissance ideal of perspective and anything less is put at an early stage of art striving toward this goal.

These selections of details create an art style, and the philosophy on which the selections are based makes art an integral part of a culture. An artist can only portray the experiences his culture furnishes him. These may be presented in a form recognizable to everyone, or he may abstract from them forms which may be remote from the conventional reality familiar to the alien viewer.

Individually and collectively, the paintings themselves are difficult to describe for they are overwhelming, especially for those who have had the privilege of seeing them. A number of fine books on the paintings have been published and reference to them is made in the bibliography. Each tries to explain the purpose of the paintings: "totemism," sympathetic magic, and cults of fecundity. Leroi-Gourhan, in his introduction to Windels' book, answers these suggestions by saying they are of little value since they try to explain the motives in the mentality of the twentieth century (Windels 1950:11–12). In order to obtain greater and more valid understanding, we suggest that Levine's theory and approach is more sound, namely, to compare these paintings to similar artistic expressions of contemporary primitive people whose culture is known to some degree. For this, Levine selected the native Australians, a hunting and gathering people who live in meager ecological surroundings. What does their art share with the work of the Upper Paleolithic? Both people had an intimate and intense relationship to their natural surroundings, so they created spirits who could control or ameliorate unfavorable situations. These spirits were nonhuman, especially in the Paleolithic. A fundamental thought was that a work of art is identical with the thing it represents and in the Paleolithic art these figures were mainly nonhuman. That the art was a ritual production seems probable for several reasons: in both cultures the paintings are in remote places, caves, or other sacred areas. The importance of such places in Australian culture has often been recorded in ethnographies and can be seen there and elsewhere by the superimposition of painting or engravings at one spot when many other places were easily available. This pattern is found also in the locations of petroglyphs in many parts of the world. For instance, in the western United States, petroglyphs are found superimposed at remote sites, but also at points of vantage, lookouts for game, friends, or enemies. There the superimposition may be for another reason: the work may have been done to while away time when the watcher could not go beyond the area from which he could see, so he was forced to re-use space already covered with earlier work.

The paintings were probably done by selected people who may not have been primarily thought of as artists, but as men who knew the proper way to carry out the ritual. A parallel is the singer at a Navaho ceremony involving a sand painting. He knows the chants and the quality of his voice is not important. Learning to paint may have been part of the initiation of young men, just as mask carving belongs to the initiation training of the novices in the Poro society in Africa. However, it does seem strange to think that the art of painting could have been so widespread in the little hunting community that many men were capable of creating such excellent art. It is also of interest that there is no record of a formative period. While all the painting is not of equal quality, there is none that can be pointed out as the work of a novice or, because of lack of technique, interpreted as earlier than other examples. This type of painting extended over a longer period of time and covered a greater area in space than any school of painting developed in the history of European art.

Coming back to the Australian comparisons, Sir Herbert Read in his introduction to a beautiful book, titled *Australia — Aboriginal Paintings — Arnhem Land,* feels that there is a closer similarity between the Australians and the East Spanish or Levantine art style, which is also found in North Africa. Furthermore, this style — which is Neolithic (c. 5,000 B.C.) or New Stone Age in Africa — is continuous with that of the Bushman rock paintings of more recent times. Read classifies the painting of Lascaux and Alta-

mira as vitalistic, while he calls the East Spanish and their related ones, haptic. The Aurignacian-Magdalenian paintings developed through two environmental conditions: the retreating ice cap, and the use of deep caverns, conditions not familiar to the Australians. After hunting on the tundra, Paleolithic man came back to caves and brought with him the imagery of animals he could not presently observe. The conditions of the Levantine and Bushman art do not differ too much from the Australian chasing a kangaroo over the hot plains. However, regardless of the specific comparison, the objectives in the development of art in Australia and the Old World seem to have a common denominator. The ritualist is the artist, for the two activities go together and if it were possible to know any ancient vocabulary, it would not be surprising to find that they had a word for ritualist, but perhaps that there was no word for artist.

For comparison with the Paleolithic of Europe some more recent rock paintings have been selected from many to be found in both the eastern and western hemisphere. These two do not have a living culture to which they have been compared, in fact, nobody lives in one region because of the complete change in the landscape. This is the Tassili area in the Sahara where during Neolithic times active cultures existed in the midst of lush vegetation. The paintings there can be traced through four periods: early neolithic hunters; then cattle herdsmen; a protohistoric period with chariots and horses; and, finally, a historic period with the use of the camel, indicating the desiccation of the area. The earlier period shows very schematic figures of humans, wearing only loin cloths. They were round-headed, a human type that continues for a long time in these paintings. They carried bows and seemed to be hunting. The animals of the chase were principally mouflon and elephants (see Figure 3-9). The round-headed type continued

FIGURE 3-9 *

A Frescoe from the Jabbaren Site in the Tassili Region of the Sahara

These figures are in the style of the "Round-headed Men" showing the loin cloth and the use of the bow.

until the cattle herdsmen, a Hamitic type, took over, and finally, in the historic period, a European type of Caucasian was found with horses and chariots. As with culture sequences elsewhere, each successive period was shorter. Such changes in physical types give a clue to the shifting population in the area, and representations of their activities are an important asset in reconstructing their culture.

The discovery and study of this area has just begun and shows great promise. Since there are human figures in action, much more about the people and the culture can be deduced from them than from the fauna alone, as in the majority of the European paintings. The schematic figures and the hunting scenes are also found in the Bushman art of South Africa.

Another area, in the western hemisphere, is one of many such in western North America where the art itself is not extraordinary, but for which studies are excellent as regards the statement of anthropological problems and the methods of working toward a solution (Heizer and Baumhoff 1962). This particular study started with a survey of the petroglyphs of Nevada and eastern California, on the eastern slopes of the Sierra Nevada. Many sites were found and plotted on maps. The locations were then matched against maps showing the migrations of large game — deer, antelope, and mountain sheep. The distribution of petroglyphs and that of large game animals largely coincide, whereas the areas in which petroglyphs are found do not overlap areas where seed-gathering, fishing, and rabbit-hunting take place. The conclusion is drawn from this that there must be a magical or ritual connection between the petroglyphs and large game hunting. Moreover, certain design elements have a wide distribution and can be traced as having diffused from a few central sources. Six petroglyph styles have been identified and a relative chronology has been set up (Heizer

and Baumhoff 1962:239). This type of intensive work would probably yield similar results in many other areas in which petroglyphs exist. Many records have already been made in various parts of the country but either the area plotted was too small for such an analysis or else the interest was principally in an exotic form of art and the anthropological values were not considered.

There is one uniform aspect of the study of rock and cave paintings: the natives living near them today generally deny all knowledge of them and their origin. Up to the present this has usually been the mystery which fascinates both the amateur and the professional student.

CONCLUSION

Art goes beyond the demands of the so-called "necessities" of life, and primitive peoples have an intimacy with art that brings it into the position of being almost one of the "necessities." The arts are used to secure a relationship with the supernatural world, be they in plastic or graphic form, in dancing, or in music, and this participation is widespread in the community. Art is also a method of communicating in a preliterate society. To study these relationships is the duty of the anthropologist, who has developed methods of procedure and analysis in dealing with societies of all kinds. In the past, many formulations regarding primitive art have been made by scholars with no first-hand experience with the people who created it. These are aesthetic philosophers, psychologists, and art historians who do not have cross-cultural dimensions in their studies. This the anthropologist can give. Raymond Firth quotes an art critic at a London show in 1935 calling anthropomorphic masks evil in origin, but these Eskimo carvings were wholly innocent and healthy. This showed a total lack of understanding of cultural differences. What an object means to a person outside the culture in which it was created is secondary, the important matter is the attitude within the society. The concept of beauty differs with this attitude and therefore what is beautiful also differs from one society to another. Beauty can be expressed with fear as well as serenity.

In addition to these intracultural relationships, the anthropologist is also concerned with art as an index of the diffusion of culture and of historic contacts between cultural groups. The changes that take place in art through culture contacts are as important, and often related to, other areas of disorganization. For such studies the great ethnological collections in museums are important assets even though their lack of background data is often frustrating. Many such collections have historic depth and great spread as to origins, so that successive styles and their distribution can be studied. This is a more traditional approach to the study of art and both this and the more dynamic aspects obtained from study of the creators of art make of this segment of the field of anthropology an important way to understand man and his unique genius: the building of cultures.

Suggested Readings

Franz Boas' *Primitive Art* (1927) was the first comprehensive work in the field of primitive art by a modern anthropologist and remains a standard work in the field. Three thoughtful lectures by anthropologists who have worked extensively in this field will be found in Redfield, Herskovits and Ekholm (1959). Marian Smith (1961) has edited the record of a symposium on primitive art held in London, and this volume includes both the lectures delivered at the symposium and the ensuing discussion. A recent book

on primitive art, one which offers good descriptions of some regional arts including African and the South Pacific, if little new by the way of theory, is Wingert (1962).

Collections and Exhibitions of Primitive Art

Some of the greatest permanent collections of primitive art are still in the ethnological halls of the large museums and it is an adventure to go on a trip of discovery to find them. An effort is being made in some institutions to show their finest pieces in the manner of an art exhibition. The Chicago Natural History Museum has a Curator of Primitive Art and a section in which he exhibits pieces away from their ethnological context. From the point of view of the anthropologist that is very satisfactory because in the ethnological halls one can see similar pieces in their relation to the culture.

On the other hand, the art galleries and museums also have become interested in primitive art and in many exhibition schedules there is a show of primitive art at least once in every two-year cycle. Since many art museums do not have large enough collections to organize such exhibitions they must usually borrow and in this way many fine pieces come to light to be admired and studied. With such exhibitions a special catalogue is usually prepared and much of the current literature in this field consists of these writings. For examples there are two in the bibliography: Dark, *The Art of Benin,* and Gunther, *Northwest Coast Indian Art.* These catalogues are important not only because they list the pieces gathered for the exhibition but they also give a brief description of the culture of the people who created the art since for many visitors this is a new experience.

There are now a number of art historians and anthropologists who work in the field of primitive art, an area in which they can well combine their efforts and knowledge.

Some Permanent Collections
of Primitive Art

A list of the large permanent displays of collections from the areas discussed in this chapter:

American Museum of Natural History, New York City

Chicago Natural History Museum, Chicago

Museum of the American Indian, Heye Foundation, New York City

Museum of Primitive Art, New York City

National Museum of Canada, Ottawa

Portland Art Museum, Portland

Royal Ontario Museum, Toronto

University Museum, University of Pennsylvania, Philadelphia

CHAPTER 4 outlines cultural anthropology's approach to the traditionally transmitted, "authorless" verbal art forms of the peoples of the world. The study of oral literature, with the more inclusive field of folklore, is a branch of cultural anthropology in which theory and research methods seem to be approaching the degree of formal elegance true of linguistics; yet, as Professor Dundes (himself a major contributor to the structural analysis of cultural products) makes clear, the natural history task of collecting and recording folktales, myths, legends, riddles, and jokes has scarcely diminished the supply, and we are extensively ignorant of large areas and places. Moreover, human creativity, and the recognized relationship between the content and form of the expressive verbal arts and social structures and other areas of human culture, all subject to change in an increasingly interconnected world, ensure a seemingly unending supply of data and meaningful problems. The largely ethnographic task of description and close analysis of content, form, and style proceeds apace with the comparative ethnological task of creating meaningful typologies, schemes of classification, and schemes of ideas — or theory — aimed at generating firm understanding. As Professor Dundes suggests, one further vital area of study consists of the analysis of each society's own traditions of oral literary criticism; he thus makes a point analagous to that discussed by Dr. Sturtevant in his chapter on ethnohistory about the "ethnography of history." Here it is plain that cultural anthropologists no longer (if they ever really did) consider man the mute, passive, unresponsive bearer of cultural tradition handed down, in that misleading phrase, "from generation to generation." If there are traditions of narration, there are also traditions of criticism and creative modification. Here analysis of the interplay between cultural transmission (intergeneration, intercultural, or otherwise) and individual and group dynamics may some day yield greater understanding of how men make and remake cultural content and tradition.

THE AUTHOR is a native of New York State and has studied at Yale and Indiana Universities. He received his professional training in folklore and anthropology at Indiana and has taught at the University of Kansas. Currently on the staff of the Department of Anthropology of the University of California at Berkeley, he is author of *The Morphology of North American Indian Folktales,* numerous articles on the folklore of American Indian and other cultures, and editor of *The Study of Folklore.* His special continuing interest is in the formal or structural analysis of folktales, games, and myths.

4

Oral Literature

ALAN DUNDES

University of California, Berkeley

The term "oral literature" contains a paradox. Literature is usually thought of as *writings* in prose or verse, especially those of an imaginative character. If literature must be *written,* how then can one speak of oral (as opposed to written) literature? The answer is that, functionally, there are among primitive or nonliterate peoples numerous forms of verbal art which correspond in part to the written literature of literate societies. Myths, tales, and epic songs are clearly vehicles for the artistic expression of the life of a people. Moreover, if one looks at the analogy from an evolutionary perspective, one can see that it is the literate societies who have analogs for older and originally oral literary forms. Folktales were told the world over long, long before writing was ever invented. It is only the curious ethnocentric bias of members of Western societies in favor of writing which has substantially discouraged students of literature from seriously studying oral literary products. Many Western anthropologists continue to divide or classify the peoples of the world on the basis of one single culture trait: the presence of writing. Peoples without writing are commonly labelled pre- or nonliterate peoples.

Oral literature is part of the more inclusive term "folklore." Folklore includes both verbal and nonverbal forms (Dundes 1965). Oral literature, however, usually means verbal folklore only and does not include games and folk dances. Although oral literature broadly viewed could cover a wide variety of verbal forms from riddles, proverbs, curses, charms, to tonguetwisters and puns, it is most often used as an alternate term for folk narrative or folk literature. Different cultures have different categories of folk narrative. For example, some have two basic divisions: narratives which are true, and narratives which are fictional (Bascom 1965). In Euro-American culture, there is a tripartite division of oral literature into myth, folktale, and legend.

To the folklorist, myth is not a synonym for fallacy or error, but is a sacred narrative transmitted orally from one generation to another, a narrative which relates how earth and man came to be in their present form. Frequently in myths a social or universal necessity such as fire is obtained. Sometimes an initial state of luxury or surplus is lost. In contrast, a folktale is usually a secular story consisting of the adventures of in-

117

dividuals who work for their own ends, rather than for all mankind. In folktales, an animal trickster seeks food or a hero attempts to win a princess; in myths, a culture-hero struggles to acquire fire or daylight for the whole world. Legends are stories normally localized in time and place. Legends, unlike most myths and folktales, are set in the real world of today. They may tell of such supernatural creatures as fairies, ghosts, or witches; or they may explain how a mountain or village got its name. Bascom (1965) has surveyed these three forms and has summarized the characteristics of each. Perhaps one of the most useful means of differentiating the three is the criterion of time. Myths are set in a time of pre-creation before the world was in its present form. There is no time before myth. Thus myth runs from one end of an open-ended continuum up to the time of creation. Folktales are set in no particular time (or place), but the general time is post-creation. Certainly in the *Märchen* (the German term used by folklorists instead of fairy tale), the shape of the earth is not changed. Legends are set in the recent past and present. They may even extend into the future, into the other end of the open-ended time continuum. The wandering Jew is still wandering and will presumably continue to wander; haunted houses continue to be haunted. This time dimension of legends suggests that the actions of the characters of legendry may not end in the same way the actions of characters in myths and folktales end.

Whatever a given culture's categories of oral literature may be, the fact remains that its various forms of oral literature may be subjected to precisely the same kinds of analysis that are so often applied to such typical Western written forms as novels and short stories. Yet comparatively few structural, stylistic, aesthetic, philosophical, and psychological studies have been undertaken. Far too often the ethnographer in the field, if he bothers to record oral literary forms, does little more than append them to his ethnography. No attempt is made to relate the ten folktales or fifteen proverbs to the culture as a whole. What is sorely needed is a kind of "literary anthropology" or, to put it another way, a kind of "anthropological literary criticism."

There are some important differences between oral and written literature and these differences must be taken into account before methods of studying oral literature can be considered. For one thing, the matter of authorship provides a sharp contrast. In written literature, the author of a particular item is usually known; in oral literature, the author is rarely, if ever, known. Written literature is thus, by and large, an *individual* creation and the individual is known. Moreover, because of writing, or rather, printing, the work is transmitted to the reader *as the original writer created it*. The few middlemen are editors and printers who allow or in most cases require the original author to read galley proofs in order to correct any errors — errors being here defined as any inadvertent changes or deviations from the original versions created by the author. All this tends to make literary forms relatively fixed and unchanging.

In contrast, oral literary products are *collective* rather than individual creations. While it is true that there might be a particular individual who composed a tale, in accordance with his culturally defined compositional conventions, the tale, if it lives after the death of its creator, must be *related orally* by men other than the creator. Because of the oral-aural transmission process, the work is rarely transmitted to new audiences exactly as the original creator made it. Depending upon the particular culture and specifically upon its range of permissiveness with respect to variation (Edel 1944), each transmitter of the tale will alter it in some way, one more than another. Different locales or different characters would be small changes; different plot actions, for example, or a different ending, would be greater changes. Often these changes which occur in the process of a tale's diffusion can provide important insights into individual personality make-up and cultural biases. An unmarried girl may tell tales about heroines who are unmarried; American Negroes may recast a borrowed European folktale into a powerful statement of social protest against what is essentially European culture. Because oral literature *lives* in tradition, as opposed to "dead" written literature, the task of analysis is *never* completed. As long as a tale lives (is told), it must continue to be recorded and analyzed. If the tale does change, then the way in which it has changed may provide clues indicating the direction of general culture change. If the tale does not change, this also provides valuable data, suggesting perhaps something about the role of tradition and conservatism in a given culture.

This is quite different in the case of written literature. A novel by James Joyce or a play by Shakespeare may be analyzed many, many times, but presumably the text subjected to analysis rarely changes. This fixed nature of the text is a characteristic of written literature, but in oral literature, the text may be considered to be in a continual state of change. One version of a folktale is no more than one synchronic slice of a protean diachronic continuum. For this reason, it is incorrect to speak of "the" version of a folktale. One has only "a" version. Various members of the same culture or even of the same family may tell a given tale very differently. Sometimes even one informant may vary the same tale in the course of repeated tellings. This is why ethnographers should collect many versions of any one given tale.

Folklorists, trained in the study of oral literature, are well aware of the importance of collecting and analyzing variants, but some ethnographers are not. Such ethnog-raphers, probably influenced by their training in the study of written literature, are willing to stop collecting after they record one version of a tale. If another informant begins to offer what sounds like a tale which has already been collected, an unsophisticated ethnographer is likely to interrupt, saying that he has that one already. The professional student of oral literature depends upon the collection of variants, many variants. The mistake of regarding "a" version of a tale as "the" correct version also occurs in analyses of oral literature. Many scholars have attempted to make analyses on the basis of one version alone as if it were simply a bona fide edition of an unchanging specimen of written literature. In essence, then, one principal difference between oral and written literature is that oral creations enjoy multiple existence, usually with some variation, while written creations exist in fixed form, usually without much variation.

Another extremely important factor in the study of oral literature is that of the narration context. While the author of a written work may live and create in an isolated way, the teller of a folktale must be in immediate contact with his audience. The audience must be within the sound of his voice. While the author of a written work need never face any of his readers, the oral artist must face all his listeners. The distinction may be illustrated by stating it in terms of a rough communications model. The author of a written work is a transmitter and his reading public may be considered receivers. Note that there is no contact between transmitter and receiver. Specifically, there is no feedback. The transmitter operates in a vacuum, so to speak. The transmission is complete and finished *before* it reaches the receiver. In contrast, the oral model shows feedback. The receiver may even exert an influence over the transmitter. For example, the receiver may provide certain stimuli (grunts or traditional exclamations) to encourage or discourage the transmitter. In a culture in which excessive variation in oral narrative is inhibited, for example, the Eskimo, a narrator will be corrected if he strays too far from the traditional path. (How often is a contemporary novelist corrected by his readers?) Further, the transmission may be interrupted at any time. Because of the great importance of the receiver, that is, the audience, it must be taken into account in the study of oral literature.

Even in Western culture, a narrative, for instance, a joke, will vary in its content or delivery depending upon the audience or the relationship existing between narrator and audience. There may be alternative punchlines whose use depends upon whether the audience is all male, all female, or mixed — and also upon the sex of the raconteur. A male might tell a joke to a group of males; a female might tell the same joke to a group of females; but neither raconteur would tell the joke to a mixed group or a group made up of members of the opposite sex. In the analysis of written literature, the audience need not be considered in this way. While characters of novels published in serial episodic form may be removed if reader response is unfavorable, few authors have alternate forms of their written stories for different audiences. Unfortunately, the history of the study of oral literature reveals that the textual differences in versions of a given folktale have been recorded without taking the audience or narration context into account. In other words, there are plenty of recorded instances of alternate punchlines but there is almost no information regarding which punchline was used in which social situation.

The oral presentation also requires the narrator to be both creator and performer. He is essentially both playwright and actor. In the study of written dramatic literature, there is a useful distinction between a play as something first written, and theater, which

is the performance of the play. The distinction is somewhat blurred in oral literature. In many tales, a great deal of finesse in vocal delivery and in the use of accompanying gestures is required. In American Indian tales, for example, individual animal characters often have special idiosyncratic ways of speaking which involve unusual pitch levels, intonation patterns, and other linguistic oddities such as lisping (Reichard 1947:26–31). These special speech characteristics are as traditional as the story itself and the audience expects a given character to speak in a given way. The ability to tell tales well requires the same sort of linguistic versatility that a master of the dialect stories, a popular form of oral literature in our own culture, needs to possess. In African tales, hand movements are often very eloquent. The importance of the element of performance in the presentation of oral literature cannot be minimized.

One reason performance is so important is that the audience present at a tale-telling session *already knows the story which is to be narrated.* It is a story which has been told many times before. Part of the pleasure for the audience is the rediscovery of the familiar; but just imagine, from our ethnocentric perspective, what it would be like to tell a joke to a group when you knew every single member of the group had already heard the joke. The fact that traditional narratives are told again and again also provides a significant point of contrast with written literature. There are not many novels and short stories which an individual reads more than once or twice in his lifetime. To summarize, one could say that in written literature, a work is composed once, in isolation from the prospective audience, and the audience, although unfamiliar with the work, may read it only a few times. In oral literature, a work is composed and recomposed many times, in the presence of the audience, who although they may be thoroughly familiar with the work, will enjoy it many times during their lives.

One other salient distinction between oral and written literature concerns the presence or absence of originality. The authors of freshman composition primers and writer's handbooks frequently fail to distinguish between the oral and written traditions in our culture when they urge students not to use clichés, slang, folk similes ("as blind as a bat"), and folk metaphors ("to paint the town red"). They should realize that these forms of speech are acceptable in spoken or oral tradition. In oral tradition, originality is usually neither expected nor desired. Since a child learns to speak before he learns to write, he is bound to carry over into writing some of the conventions of oral tradition. Children should not be taught never to use clichés but rather never to confuse the conventions of oral tradition with the conventions of written tradition. Because of the marked differences between the two traditions, a child must not be told to write as he speaks or to judge written forms by what they "sound" like. It is rare to find a fine speech which reads well in print and it is equally rare to find a paper written for publication which is very effective when presented orally.

The problem of translation between oral and written traditions crops up when collectors of oral literature seek to publish their field-recorded tales. Many of the oral features such as expletives, the "ums," the "you know's" which *sound* all right to the ear do not *look* all right to the eye on the printed page. As a result, most of the published collections of oral literature have been edited to conform with the canons of written tradition and consequently the printed tale bears only a slight resemblance to the oral original. The inadequacy of our orthographic system means that most of the all-important oral stylistic intonational features — the emphasis on one word, the extended pause before

another — are lost in the process of translating from oral to written tradition. This is not to mention the equally important concomitant gestures. Hand movements and facial expressions, essential parts of oral literary performance, cannot easily be transcribed, and rarely survive the translation from speech to writing. One need only think of the difference between reading a joke in a book and hearing a master raconteur tell the same joke.

Oral literature is a universal. All peoples have oral literatures. This is in contrast to written literature, which is not a universal. Moreover, while oral literature is the only literature of the so-called nonliterate peoples, written literature is not the only literature of literate peoples. Both oral and written literature coexist among literate peoples with some interplay. An element of oral literature may provide the inspiration for a masterpiece of written literature. Many of Chaucer's Canterbury tales have folktale analogues. On the other hand, a specimen of written literature may enter the stream of oral tradition. Not only does oral literature thrive in literate societies, it is more widely known in these cultures than written literatures. In our own culture, there are many more people who tell or listen to jokes than who write or read poetry. There are far more individuals who know and sing folksongs than who know and sing opera. Oral literature belongs to everyone; written literature belongs to a cultural élite. Yet despite the fact that oral literature is a universal and that it is more widespread than written literature in cultures wherein both occur, one finds thousands of students of written literature and almost no students of oral literature.

The study of oral literature includes collection, classification, and analysis. Most effort has been devoted to collection, with the Grimms' work in the early nineteenth century providing an important impetus among European scholars. The romantic movement which glorified the common man and the noble savage fostered a growing interest in peasant and primitive artforms, including oral literature. The original motivation for collecting oral literature was partly a regressive desire to return to the past. It was widely held that oral literature was a product of the past and that it was gradually dying out. This interest in using folk-narrative materials to reconstruct the past has continued into the twentieth century. However, most contemporary anthropological students of oral literature tend to see folklore as a reflection of present culture rather than past. Accordingly, oral literature is collected to illuminate present realities rather than solely to attempt to reconstruct the historical past.

The notion that oral literature belonged to the past led to "object collection." Since oral literary forms were considered as being survivals in culture, survivals from hoary antiquity, these forms were not seen as functioning elements of the cultures in which they were found. No attempt was made to relate these forms to their cultural contexts. Texts or iterations of tales were removed from their contexts and placed in voluminous collections much as butterflies might be mounted for display. One looks in vain in most collections of oral literature for such data as who (sex, age, clan, occupation, and so on) told the tale to whom at what time of year or day for what purpose and to what end. It was not realized that *if a genre of oral literature is found in a culture there will also be a tradition of the use of that genre.* For example, if riddles are told by the members of a culture, there will inevitably be a riddling tradition. In fact, there will probably be several traditions (Hart 1964). Riddles may be used in courtship rituals or death rituals, or they may be used in competitions between villages, families, or individuals. In our culture, they are used by children in one-upsmanship contexts with peers and also

with parents as traditional means of reversing the parent-child educational relationship. With a riddle, the child may be able to ask a parent a question he cannot answer, thereby forcing the parent to come to the child for the answer. This provides some small measure of revenge for all the occasions on which parents withhold answers to children's questions.

Not only does a form of oral literature have diverse functions, but each individual proverb or folktale is used according to specific rules. The rules for the use of a particular proverb or folktale or what has been termed "the ethnography of speaking folklore" (Arewa and Dundes 1964) influence an individual's decision to employ that proverb or folktale. Typical crucial factors are the identity and relationship between addressor and addressee. A male could tell a particular joke to another male, but perhaps not to an elder or a member of his immediate family. Another critical factor in the ethnography of speaking folklore is the presence and identity of a third party. A male could tell the joke to another male of the same age, but he would not be likely to do so if there were a woman or a minister in the same room (even if this third party were not actually listening). These principles may be illustrated by linguistic examples.

Two standard greeting formulas in American culture are "How do you do?" and "How are you?" A foreigner learning these might be unable to use them properly unless he also learned the rules for their usage. Although we do not necessarily formally articulate the rules, they are nonetheless operative. "How do you do?" is used in formal greeting situations *on the occasion of a first meeting.* "How are you?" is a greeting used in formal and informal situations but almost always when the speaker and addressee have previously met. One would not normally say "How do you do?" to greet an old friend; one would probably not say "How are you?" to a person one was meeting in a formal situation and for the first time.

Another simple but striking illustration of the importance of context is provided by kinship reference terminology. My wife would be "mommy" if I were talking to my very young daughter; "grandma" if I were talking to my granddaughter; "Mrs. Dundes" if I were talking to a servant; "Carolyn" if I were talking to a close family friend; and "my wife" if I were talking to a senior colleague whom I had just met. Note that the determining factor is not so much the speaker's relationship to the addressee or to the referent, but the speaker's conception of the addressee's relationship to the referent. In each case, I would use the term I would expect the addressee to use in referring to (and in most cases also in addressing) my wife. Thus my "reference" term is what I think the person to whom I am speaking should use as a term of reference or "address." The point is that just as early students of kinship used to "object collect" out of context by listing terms of address and terms of reference without regard to the rules for the use of individual terms of various particular situations, so students of oral literature have recorded a multitude of contextless texts with no indication as to how any one specific text might be used in a particular concrete situation. Thus the volume upon volume of American Indian tales so assiduously garnered by Franz Boas and his students are in some ways like collections of primitive musical instruments lining the walls of a museum. We have the instruments plucked out of context, and while we can marvel at their material composition (from our own ethnocentric esthetic standards), we have no idea how they are tuned or played or, more important, when or why. It is precisely because oral literature has been so badly collected that the majority of professional anthropologists have difficulty in seeing value in oral literary materials for serious anthropological research.

A significant attempt to remedy the failure to collect oral literature in context was made by Melville Jacobs. In his book, *The Content and Style of an Oral Literature,* published in 1959, and in a sequel volume, *The People Are Coming Soon,* which appeared a year later, Jacobs sees the telling of a tale as a literary event and seeks to place this literary event in the native setting so that it may be intelligible to members of other cultures. The delineation of such a literary event includes both the text and the probable audience responses to it (Jacobs 1959:2). Unfortunately, much of Jacobs' reconstruction is highly subjective and speculative. For instance, in his interesting discussion of humor among the Clackamas Chinook, he lists examples in the oral literature to which *he thinks* an audience would have responded with smiles. The fact that Jacobs collected his tales from one somewhat acculturated informant who was one of the last several native speakers of Clackamas Chinook and who has since died makes it impossible to verify Jacobs' reconstructions and educated guesses. However, Jacobs' aims, if not his actual results, provide a useful model for future investigations of living oral traditions.

What is also needed besides the collection of oral literature in context is the collection of *oral literary criticism.* Oral literature is literature transmitted orally; oral literary criticism is the criticism and interpretation of that literature which are also transmitted orally. It is sad to report that almost no oral literary criticism has been recorded. Most collections of oral literature consist of unadorned texts. A few of the collectors have given *their* suggestions as to the meaning and significance of some of the tales. Rarely are the informant's own evaluations and interpretations of his oral literature solicited in any rigorous manner. The seriousness of this deficiency may be easily understood when one considers the subject of oral humor. Unless there are indications, perhaps parenthetical, in the recorded transcriptions of folktale texts, noting at which points in the tale the narrator or audience laughed, it may be extremely difficult to ascertain whether a particular tale was meant to be humorous or whether the audience regarded it as humorous. Consider the relativity of audience response to jokes in our own Euro-American culture. A joke which gets a laugh in a city is received in silence in a rural area. The question is: could one tell from the lines alone whether or not an audience laughed at them? One needs to know for certain precisely where laughter occurred, what kind of laugh, who laughed, and perhaps some information from the laughing audience as to just why they laughed. Since most oral literature is recorded in an artificial situation, that is, from an informant who is alone with an ethnographer (and his tape recorder, a third party whose presence definitely influences the content of the material elicited), it is difficult to obtain audience response data. However, few ethnographers even try to elicit details about the normal context of the tales. Obviously, an ideal occasion for recording oral literature is an actual tale-telling session. That there are almost no examples in the published literature of the kind of collection outlined above suggests the great opportunities for research in this area.

The classification of oral literature has perhaps been more successful than collection, although much more work is needed here also. The problem of classification is one which logically arises after collections have been made. In order to facilitate the identification of individual tales and to provide a way of organizing folklore archives in which huge numbers of unpublished tales are housed, a system of classifying folk narratives was devised. In 1910, a Finnish folklorist named Antti Aarne published his famous *Verzeichnis der Märchentypen*. This "Index of Tale Types" has twice been revised by the American folklorist Stith Thompson. In his second revision, *The Types of the Folktale: A Classification and Bibliography,* published in 1961, Thompson gives synopses of more than 2000 Indo-European tales. Each synopsis is given a number and professional students of oral literature usually refer to a given tale by its number in the Aarne-Thompson tale type index. Thus Cinderella is Tale Type 510 and Tom Thumb is Tale Type 700. Following each synopsis are references to versions of the tale, including both published and archive materials. For example, from the tale type index, one can see among the references to Tom Thumb that there are the following versions: Finnish, 90; French, 59; Irish, 66; Lithuanian, 42; Polish, 11; Slovenian, 25; Swedish, 41; Turkish, 11; and so on. This information enables a student to obtain other versions of a tale he may have collected. Without this help, a student would have to wade through hundreds of individual folktale collections searching for parallels, often in vain. Comparison with these other versions assists the student in determining how his version differs, if it does differ, from the one or more normal forms of the tale. It is precisely these differences which may illuminate some important characteristic of the culture or the individual informant from which the collector elicited his version. The tale type index also gives bibliographical references marked with a single asterisk. The asterisk indicates that the reference contains a listing of numerous other parallels to the tale. References marked with a double asterisk indicate a whole monograph or article devoted to that particular tale type.

The Aarne-Thompson index has been used to organize many of the European folklore archives. It has materially aided in the exchange of data between scholars and has made the publication of archive holdings much easier. It is too bad that the index is for Indo-European tales only. There are no comparable indexes for the tales of the rest of the world, for example, no published African tale type indexes or North and South American Indian tale type indexes. As a result, the state of American Indian, African, and Oceanic narrative classification is virtually the same as European narrative classification prior to 1910.

Happily, there is another classification scheme which does offer worldwide coverage. This is the monumental *Motif-Index of Folk-Literature: A Classification of Narrative Elements in Folktales, Ballads, Myths, Fables, Medieval Romances, Exampla, Fabliaux, Jest-Books and Local Legends,* compiled by Stith Thompson. First published in the years 1932–1936, the six-volume *Motif-Index* was issued in a revised and enlarged edition in 1955–1958. Generally speaking, the motif is a smaller unit of narrative content than the tale type (Thompson 1951:415). A motif may be an actor (e.g., an ogre), an item (e.g., a magic wand), or an incident (e.g., the obstacle flight in which fugitives throw objects behind them which magically become obstacles in their pursuer's path). Each motif has an identifying letter and number designation. For example, the obstacle flight is D 672, and following the synopsis of this worldwide motif, one finds the same sorts of reference and bibliographical information as that provided in the tale type index.

The motif is not a very satisfactory unit from a theoretical point of view (Dundes 1962b). An incident motif clearly includes actors or items or both. Moreover, the distinction between motif and tale type is not always clear. There are a number of single-incident tale types. Most of the animal tales in the Aarne-Thompson tale type index (that is, Types 1–299) consist of single incidents. This means that these tales have both tale type numbers and motif numbers and that the two classificatory schemes are confusingly overlapping. On the other hand, many complex folktales include a great many mo-

tifs, and in these instances the overlapping is not so glaring. The indispensability of the *Motif-Index* for students of oral literatures lies in the fact that it covers myth and legend, genres which are *not* included in the Aarne-Thompson tale type index, which abstracts folktales only. Secondly, the *Motif-Index* offers some coverage, albeit incomplete, of the whole world, whereas the tale type index treats Indo-European tales only. Thus the student of American Indian or African oral literature would consult the *Motif-Index* to identify his materials. The serious student of oral literature should certainly be acquainted with both these valuable classification tools.

The collection and classification of oral literature are not ends in themselves. They are only means to the end of analysis. The concern of analysts of oral literature may be with the origin, the function, or the form of a given item. For nineteenth-century scholars, the emphasis was upon the origins of oral literature. In the twentieth century, the interest has moved from questions of origins to questions of function and form. The study of origin may be further subdivided into (1) the study of historical origins, that is, *where* and *when* a myth came to be, and (2) the study of psychological origins, that is, *why* a myth came to be. Most studies have been concerned with historical rather than psychological origins. The two principal characteristics of oral literature to which advocates of the various origin theories have addressed themselves are (1) multiple existence, and (2) irrationality. How is it that essentially the same myth, for example, the myth of initial primeval waters (Motif A 810), can exist in a variety of cultures all over the world, and how can one explain the creation of earth or man from mud, clay, or dust (Motif A 812, Earth Diver; A 1241, Man made from clay [earth])?

The most common explanations of multiple existence are: (1) monogenesis and diffusion, or (2) polygenesis. Champions of monogenesis (one birth) argue that a myth originated in one place and then spread to other places by the process of diffusion. Advocates of polygenesis (many births) contend that the same myth or tale can arise independently among many peoples, perhaps because of an alleged basic similarity of the human psyche, or perhaps because of some constant universal features in the human experience. The explanations for the apparent irrational or magical elements in oral literature vary according to whether the analyst employs a literal or symbolic approach. For those favoring a literal approach (which is the one held by the majority of anthropologists), oral literature says what it means (Malinowski 1955:101). It is argued that the historical truth may be slightly distorted because of the unreliability of the oral transmission process and the fallibility of human memory. A literal interpretation of the deluge myth is that there was an actual flood. According to those adhering to one of many symbolic approaches to oral literature, myths and tales do not literally say what they mean. Instead, these oral literary forms must be interpreted by means of a symbolic code. The difficulty here is that each school of symbolism claims to have *the* key required to unlock the secrets contained in oral literature. One such school, the psychoanalytic, would interpret the flood myth as a cosmogonic projection of the amniotic fluid accompanying each human birth. Critics of the symbolic approach usually claim that such interpretations are *read into* rather than *read out of* the oral literature. (For a symbolic interpretation of the creation of earth and man from mud or dust, see Dundes 1962a.) The conclusions of neither literal nor symbolic approaches are easily verified. As a rule, those interested in historical origins favor monogenesis and a literal approach, while those seeking psychological origins lean towards polygenesis and a sym-

bolic approach. However, the approaches are not really mutually exclusive. For example, there could have been an actual flood, the story of which spread partly because of the imagined similarity to the features of human birth.

The functions of oral literature are manifold (Bascom 1954). Oral literature can educate, amuse, promote group solidarity, provide a sanctioned vehicle for social protest, or serve as a means of escape from reality. Malinowski was one of the first to direct attention to the functional significance of oral literature. For Malinowski's important notion of myth as a validating sociological charter for belief, a sort of sacred past precedent for present behavior, the student should refer to his "Myth in Primitive Psychology" (Malinowski, 1955:93–148). But Malinowski did not emphasize, as Bascom later did, that oral literature not only transmits, maintains, and strengthens acceptable social behavioral norms, it also provides an institutional outlet for escapes from these norms. In trickster tales, the hero frequently ignores or violates prescribed cultural amenities. For example, in a culture with mother-in-law avoidance taboos, the trickster may have intercourse with his mother-in-law. Similarly, in jokes, behavior frowned upon if not forbidden in "real" life is a common occurrence. At the very moment the audience is reminded of taboos and behavioral restrictions, the trickster or joke-cycle figure is flagrantly disregarding them. This suggests one of the most important of all the functions of oral literature. It provides an impersonal, guilt-free acceptable mode of communication capable of carrying discussions of anxiety-ridden topics. In jokes, for example, both the teller and the addressees can consider topics, often using lexical items not normally used in everyday conversation, which would be difficult to discuss outside this culturally defined frame. It is precisely this function of oral literature which should be of interest to ethnographers. From analyzing the content of the oral literature of a culture, one can obtain information about themes and topics which are of great concern to members of that culture, but which might not be easy to discuss using the more conventional question-and-answer techniques of normal discourse. Since oral literature is frequently considered to be a collective phenomenon, hence distinct from any one individual, an individual informant need accept no personal responsibility for the content of the tale or joke. He is merely reporting what "others" say. For this reason, it may be a relatively simple matter to elicit oral literature in a situation in which it would be almost impossible to obtain personal convictions and commentary.

The study of the structure or form of oral literary materials is a comparatively new line of investigation. The aim of this approach is to delineate the basic patterns of oral literature. Some of the most successful studies of this kind consist of analyses of hero patterns. For example, Lord Raglan and Otto Rank, among others, have analyzed a number of Indo-European hero biographies and have convincingly shown that there does appear to be a basic pattern. Raglan (1956), by showing that twenty-one traditional heroes, including Oedipus, Theseus, Perseus, King Arthur, and Moses, apparently led identical lives consisting of twenty-two standard incidents, hoped to demonstrate the lack of historicity of any of the lives. Raglan attempted to derive the basic pattern from ritual, specifically, from ritual regicide. Rank, in contrast, tried to derive the pattern from the supposedly typical child-parent relationship, using conventional Freudian analytic techniques. Other structural studies include Vladimir Propp's analysis of 100 Russian fairy tales into one formulaic sequence of thirty-one narrative plot slots which he termed "functions"; Claude Lévi-Strauss's analysis of myth structure into a

successive series of binary oppositions requiring mediation; and Alan Dundes' morphological analysis of North American Indian tales. In the same general intellectual trend, one finds the notion that singers of oral epics do not memorize the thousands of lines verbatim but rather recall the necessary sequence of plot frames which they can fill with traditional formulas and clichés. One of the pioneers of this "oral-formulaic" approach to oral literature is Albert Lord, whose book *The Singer of Tales* (1960) explains the approach in detail. The results of these and similar studies suggest that oral literature can be as highly patterned as sophisticated written literature.

Having discussed oral literature in terms of its differences from written literature and the way in which it may be studied, one might indicate just a few of the ways in which a knowledge of oral literature and the techniques used to study it may be of value to the professional anthropologist. First of all, one must remember that most of what an anthropological field worker "discovers" is in some sense already known by the members of the culture being investigated. What is less often realized is that much of this ethnographic information is already "recorded" as well. Boas pointed out that oral literature constituted a kind of autobiography of a people (1916:393), and his "Description of the Tsimshian, Based on Their Mythology" forcefully demonstrated just how much ethnographic data was contained in folk narratives (1916:393–564). Moreover, the recording is made by the natives themselves rather than by the visiting ethnographer. This makes the information even more valuable inasmuch as the ethnographer's own unavoidable ethnocentric bias which is bound to affect *his* recording of ethnographic data may be avoided — at least to the extent to which the oral literature is not "edited" by the informants to "protect" the ethnographer when they tell their tales for him. *Oral literature can provide a way of seeing the culture inside-out instead of outside-in,* which is the usual position of the ethnographer. Oral literature may reveal how a people views itself and this self-image, however distorted it may be, is of great importance for anyone who would describe and understand that people.

Oral literature is also invaluable source material for the discovery and identification of so-called native categories. "Native categories" is a term referring to the ways in which a people divide the world or slice reality. The categories may be color categories — many peoples of the world do not divide the spectrum the way we do — smell categories, disease categories, directional categories, and so on (Sturtevant 1964:117–119). An important part of seeing a culture inside-out entails knowing what that culture's native categories are, but it is often difficult to ascertain the nature of these categories. For one thing, because the observing ethnographer is so accustomed to his own native categories, it may not occur to him to question the "naturalness" of them. One of the most common human occurrences is the projection of one's own culturally relative native categories into "the nature of reality." Much of what each people believe is the nature of nature turns out to be the nature of culture instead. Another obstacle impeding the discovery of native categories is that they may be so different from any cognitive category in the category repertoire of the ethnographer's culture that even a well-trained investigator might never stumble upon them. In oral literature, native categories are commonly recorded. An illustration is afforded by a portion of a version of a Winnebago twin-brother cycle collected in 1963 by the author. My informant told how the powerful younger brother stamped his foot near a spring and called for a water spirit to appear. When the water spirit appeared, the boy told him he was going to

appropriate his "óoze-ah-luh." At that point the tale recitation stopped for twenty minutes while the informant tried to explain what this was. Apparently it refers to the "body system" or to the proper arrangement of the inner body organs. It does not refer to the organs themselves, but to the arrangement of the organs. It is not like a soul or spirit. When the tale-teller continued, he related that the brothers took the "óoze-ah-luh" and sprinkled it in a village. The next morning the brothers heard a kind of popping sound. The stomachs of the villagers had become bloated and had popped. Presumably the placement in the village of the water spirit's removed "óoze-ah-luh" had caused appropriate injury to the villagers' physical equilibrium through sympathetic magic. What is important for students of anthropology to realize here is that it is extremely unlikely that the author would ever have asked his informant if there were a native concept of the harmonious arrangement of the interior body organs! In one sense, the discovery of the curious native category was almost entirely fortuitous, but the methodological point is that whenever an ethnographer collects oral literature, he automatically increases his chances for such serendipity.

There are many other anthropological uses of oral literature. It may yield valuable ethnohistorical information (Vansina). Comparative studies or oral literatures may reveal historical relationships between peoples. The greater the number of tale types and motifs that two peoples have in common, the more likely it is that they are either genetically or culturally related (Boas 1940b:427). Thus the relationship between Asian peoples and the American Indians is attested by numerous folk narrative parallels (Hatt 1949). Some oral literary borrowings can provide an index of acculturation. For example, if a European tale borrowed by an American Indian group has been changed little, if at all, one might guess that the culture of the Indian group was waning. On the other hand, if the European tale were altered in such a way as to serve as a vehicle for attacking Euro-American culture, then one might assume that the Indian culture was still actively functioning, and perhaps resisting the onset of white influence. The nature of the kinship relationships between pairs of protagonists and antagonists in the oral literature can provide indications as to sensitive interpersonal relationships (Stern 1963). For example, in many of the matrilineal Northwest Coast Indian tales, the hero's antagonist is his mother's brother. Oral literature, considered as projection material, may be a "natural" T.A.T. (Thematic Apperception Test), natural in the sense that it is not an artificial, contrived device introduced from outside the culture by the ethnographer. Informants could be asked to draw pictures or give associations to oral literary themes and characters. In any case, the results of a content analysis of myths and tales could be compared with the results obtained with the standard projection tests used by psychologically oriented anthropologists (Kaplan 1962).

The problem and also part of the appeal of the study of oral literature is that it stands squarely between the humanities and the social sciences. Oral literature is art and it can be studied as art. Accordingly, it may be subjected to any of the techniques of literary analysis used in the study of written literature. On the other hand, oral literature, like all art, provides rich source material for the social sciences. From a scientific perspective, oral literature can be considered as an expression of human personality and culture. This means that it can and must be considered by students of anthropology. For this reason, new techniques and methods for the study of oral literature must be evolved by drawing from both the humanities and the social sciences. Only in this way will there ever be developed a "literary anthropology" or "anthropological literary criticism" adequate for the study of oral literature.

Suggested Readings

A comprehensive high-level survey of the anthropological approach to the study of oral literature will be found in J. L. Fischer (1963), while Dundes' *The Study of Folklore* (1965) is a college textbook anthology of readings illustrating theories and techniques of studying folklore. Goldstein (1964) is an excellent introduction to the problems involved in undertaking field work in this area, and Bascom (1955), Dorson (1963), and Utley (1961) each discuss various technical and theoretical aspects of the field. Chadwick and Chadwick (1940) contains a selected worldwide survey of various oral and written literary traditions. Herskovits and Herskovits (1958) consists of a collection of Dahomean myths and tales, preceded by an essay on a cross-cultural approach to the study of myths. Melville Jacobs' *The Content and Style of an Oral Literature* (1959) is a pioneering study in anthropological literary criticism. Radin (1954) and (1956) is one of several important literary analyses of Winnebago tale cycles written by a leading anthropologist. Róheim's *The Gates of the Dream* (1952) is a disorganized but insightful psychoanalytic study of primitive mythology. Finally, Stith Thompson's *The Folktale* (1951) remains a standard textbook, although it is literary-historical rather than anthropological in emphasis and treats primarily Indo-European materials.

CHAPTER 5 directs attention to technology, an aspect of human life with largely instrumental functions, if by no means lacking in meaning and symbolism. Through his spiraling technological skill and material culture man has achieved great (although as Professor Spier indicates) yet limited control of the natural environment, and in fact substantially recreates that environment to serve his own ends. As was the case in Chapter 4, this chapter discusses an episode in the history of contemporary cultural anthropology, for the writer points to the effort of anthropologists to place technology — skill and tool — into its total cultural, social, and human setting. One emphasis of this chapter contrasts with what has gone before, for in anthropology, scientific study of technology and the fundamental questions of variation in environmental adaptation have developed in close association with an interest in cultural evolution, a very large issue indeed, one to which Cohen, in his chapter on macroethnology, and Vayda and Rappaport, in theirs on ecology, will later return. Thus the comparative study of technologies is an old one; it antedates the discipline of anthropology as such. For in western Europe it was the accidental discovery and the growing understanding of the true nature of prehistoric artifacts which raised the question of the antiquity of man and which provided one impetus for the development of a science of man. The substance of this chapter provides a bridge between the interests of those cultural anthropologists — ethnographers and ethnologists — who deal with living peoples and their cultures, and of the archeologists — prehistoric and historic — who deal with what is past. Fundamental contrasts between a human and a less than human existence, cultural growth and evolution, environment, and, specifically, the technologies of subsistence, shelter, and transport, are some of the topics touched on here.

THE AUTHOR was born in Seattle and has studied at the Universities of California and New Mexico, and at Harvard, where he received his doctorate in anthropology. He has taught at the Universities of Minnesota, Wisconsin, Oregon, and California, and is presently Professor of Anthropology at the University of Missouri. His research interests have taken him to Northern California, for studies of the Chukchansi Yokuts and immigrant Chinese, and to Holland, for studies of European-American hand tools. Professor Spier has written numerous scholarly articles on technology, anthropometry, culture history and — craftsman and technician in his own right — on improved, ultrasonic means of preparing archeological artifacts and skeletal remains.

5

Technology and Material Culture*

ROBERT F. G. SPIER

University of Missouri at Columbia

INTRODUCTION

Technology embraces the means by which man controls or modifies his natural environment. Included within technology are a series of techniques. Man's material culture is the product of his technology. As with many anthropological terms and usages, the term "technology" may be used comprehensively to refer to all techniques and their products, either of all men in all times and places, or those of the men of a particular time and place. Alternatively, a specific type of material product may be the referent, as when we speak of the technology of glass or of hunting or of pottery.

By contrast with technology, which, whatever the reference, is a comparatively comprehensive term, the word "technique" refers to a specific mode of technical operation. Each major activity area, be it pottery, fur-dressing, or plant cultivation, involves a sequence of coordinated techniques through which the goals are attained. While the term may be broadly applied, for example, to "techniques of social manipulation," in this context we will deal only with techniques applied to items of a material nature.

While attention has long been directed to material culture, only recently has there been a serious effort to study technology broadly. Museums, once simply repositories, are now becoming centers for studies placing artifacts in their total cultural context.

The study of technology may address itself to a wide variety of problems. The development of a given technology may be traced as pure history — with regard to its state at any time, to its evolution, to the contributions of various sources, and to contributory techniques. Given this background one may study intertechnological relations or the relationship to nontechnical aspects of culture, for example, to economic and social developments. Or one may seek to gauge the effects of technological advances on the educative process. Finally, to name but another, studies to reconstruct probable techniques of prehistoric peoples are standard in the repertoire.

The sphere of discourse in this chapter will be primarily the cultures, prehistoric and historic, of the nonliterate peoples of the

* The sketches included in this chapter are by Dr. Spier, who has kindly granted permission for their use.

world. The prehistoric record comes to us through archeological investigation, while historic peoples are known from documents and ethnographic research. Because the advent of writing brought no sharp discontinuity throughout man's technology, the story is continuous to the present day. Only the nature and sources of our evidence are changed. The past of modern civilized peoples is not distinguishable in this regard from that of nonliterate peoples whom we consider primitives. Therefore we will range freely in both time and space, drawing examples from a wide variety of contexts.

MAN AND THE NATURAL ENVIRONMENT

As stated, technology embraces the means man uses to control or modify his natural environment. This control or modification can generally be viewed as exploitation; man seeks to serve his ends. Conservation for its own sake, if found at all, is a refinement well beyond the crass self-interest which usually governs man's actions. There are philosophies and cultures which eschew gross changes in the environment and stress the harmony of man and nature. Overtly stated or not, some harmonization must exist, for there are ultimate limits to exploitation. The rate of use of regenerating resources should not exceed the rate of replacement if an indefinite harvest is contemplated. To ignore this fact for long is to change the environment, its resources, and, eventually, the way of life.

Coordinately, one may ask if man controls nature or is its pawn. The ultimate answer must lie between these extremes. However, as cultural complexity increased, the balance swung toward control by man. Perhaps the degree of control is a proper measure of technological advancement. Vagaries of weather certainly interfere less today in human affairs than they did in the

past. However, one should not be led to believe that primitive man cowered powerlessly before the forces of nature. He knew rather well the relationship he bore to the rest of nature — the potentialities and limitations of his cultural equipment. When activity would be to no avail, he conserved his energies against a more favorable future.

Similarly, one should not equate modern arrogance with total mastery of nature. Occasionally it is borne home to us — perhaps as one's home is borne away on the flood — that we have not yet completed our projected conquest of nature.

TECHNOLOGICAL DETERMINISM

Some anthropologists view the cultural world through a technological lens (White 1949). They evaluate cultures in terms of technological advancement, especially the use of nonhuman power sources. For these theorists, technological development is the base on which rest, in turn, the social order and the ideological order of a culture. While a good case can be made for this point of view, the relationship is not strictly unidirectional.

Hunting-and-gathering peoples, to discuss a type case, are customarily limited in social complexity by the size of the group. This form of subsistence economy is commonly incapable of supporting large, dense populations. Though social complexity rarely characterizes small populations, we find an elaborate social system among the central Australian aborigines whose subsistence is almost the epitome of the meager food-collecting status.

In the same vein, modern industrial development is seen as linked to corporate ownership. Only a large number of investors can provide the capital sums needed to launch and sustain large technological industries. But one must remember that these may grow, through reinvestment of profits, from modest beginnings. Some twentieth-century industrial giants were basically family companies. Corporate ownership of production means occurs among nonliterates whose activities never reach this modern scale.

Whether a technological state determines the rest of culture or not, a close relationship certainly exists between technology and the rest of culture. This is best described as mutually supportive or mutually influencing. Changes in technology alter society, and societal changes are reflected back on the technology.

Technological states have been used as markers to establish a prehistoric chronology. While the theoretical base of lineal cultural evolution is no longer prevalent, the terminology is still with us. The Stone Ages — Paleolithic, Mesolithic, Neolithic — reflect the common use of edged stone tools. The succeeding Metal Ages — Copper, Bronze, Iron — show the gradual replacement of stone by metals. The contemporary view equates these ages, still retaining the classic names, with more than tools alone. Especially stressed is the succession of subsistence bases, with food-collecting (hunting, fishing, berrying, root-digging) giving way to food-producing (horticulture, agriculture, husbandry). We now understand that the nature of subsistence had more important consequences than did the difference between chipping or grinding stone tools.

Similar terminology, based on material culture, is still current. We may speak of the Age of Steam, of Electricity, of the Atom. More comparable evaluative terms would denote such entities as the Industrial Revolution or the Age of Automation. However chosen, terminology must not ignore the role technologies and their resulting artifacts have played in man's development. The proper perspective on this role must suit one's purposes in analysis, not some Procrustean scheme.

The making and using of tools is a feature which distinguishes man from nonhuman animals. The distinction of hominid forms from proto-hominid forms on this basis has brought forth considerable controversy about many early specimens, but there is general agreement to the basic proposition. But it should quickly be made clear that tool-using and tool-making are not the sole property of man. Other living forms do both, but the difference in degree is sufficient to produce a difference in kind. As an analogy, one might point to the distinction between a drug and a poison; dosage often makes the difference. In regard to tools, no animal's activities even remotely approach those of the most primitive men known to us ethnographically. The consistent and extensive use of tools, made according to patterns transmitted through overt learning, not instinctively, is an unique human ability.

Further, human association with tools has come to include symbolism and foresight. For example, the plow is to most men much more than a tool to turn or furrow the soil; it may symbolize a whole technology or even a way of life. The aspect of human foresight is shown in the retention of tools, once made for present use, against future need, and also in the making of tools, not immediately needed, for the foreseeable future. Neither of these behaviors characterizes the lower primates or other animals. We cannot know very much about these traits among the proto-hominids and the earliest men. The occurrence of utilized natural stones (eoliths) suggests that they did not possess foresight, but used any suitable stone at hand, then promptly discarded it. However, the objects of our principal concern, recent and modern man, do differ as stated above from other living creatures.

We must not place too great a stress on retention of tools as evidence of foresight. If a man is mobile and tool-making is easy, we can expect him to make tools as needed, to be abandoned on completion of the job. This pattern is reported for some Australian tribesmen who keep with them only items in frequent use; their limited transport capabilities (often only a shoulder bag) make this a sensible procedure. The most important point is that the tools, whether retained or discarded, are made to a learned pattern and need not be re-invented each time, nor is their design instinctive.

THE CONTENT OF TECHNOLOGIES

An artifact of technology which has aroused much interest is the tool. Tools are extenders and modifiers of the hand — increasing its force, its hardness, its precision, and its reach. They may protect the hand from heat, cold, abrasion, or radiation, for despite its marvellous dexterity and adaptability, many human activities carried on through the ages would have been barred had the hand not been assisted by the tool. In the following discussion no distinction will be made between tools for peaceful purposes and those for war or the chase, the latter commonly called weapons. The same general considerations apply to both and, in fact, many are used interchangeably. This interchangeability, or convertability, of tool and weapon has doubtless existed throughout the life of man, from the hand axes of the Lower Paleolithic to the modern atomic explosives.

Tools may be categorized on a number of different bases. Archeologists sometimes distinguish them by the materials of which they are made, separating wooden or bone tools from those of stone or of the several metals. Aside from the convenience afforded by such a preliminary sorting, this practice may be linked to the designation of prehistoric ages discussed above. Another basis for sorting tools may be their form. In its best, and most abstract, application, the categorization is usually in geometric or proportional terms, classifying together all discoidal items or all wedge-shaped tools.

Tools may also be categorized with terms derived from a modern inventory, an instrument shaped like a modern hammer being so called. This practice, despite its innocuous intent, can lead to pernicious results. No sooner is the tool called a "hammer" than someone takes the term in its functional sense and assumes that the tool was used for striking blows. This may not have been the classifier's intent, but can result from his unfortunate choice of word.

Finally, it is possible to categorize on a functional basis. To use this technique, one must know the function of the tool. In many prehistoric contexts, the true function may be unknowable, but it is possible in many instances to make an educated guess. Such suppositions are usually based on analogies drawn from artifacts and practices known ethnographically among recent or contemporary nonliterate peoples. Two avenues are open to a functional classification. One is to group together all tools employed in a particular activity, as tanning, hunting of seals, or canoe-building. The other is to classify tools according to their precise action — splitting, scraping, shaving, grinding, pressing, or what have you.

Before we quit a discussion of tools, it would be well to remark on a feature of conservation not too apparent nowadays. Design in the past was generally such as to conserve valuable materials, though not always to conserve labor. Many parts of a tool need not be of first-class materials; substances in greater abundance may be used at these points. One of the first evidences of this approach may be found in the microlithic tradition of stone-chipping which began in the Upper Paleolithic and continued through the Mesolithic and into the Neolithic Age. Microlithic tools often consist of a stone cutting edge, formed of many tiny pieces (the size of a postage stamp) mounted in a bone, wood, or antler body. It has been seriously suggested that the supply of first-quality flint was diminishing in Europe and the Mediterranean world; to use such valuable stone for tool bodies was wasteful. Hence this solution, which gave many more linear inches of cutting edge per pound of flint than had earlier designs.

Another illustration of this tendency toward material conservation may be found in medieval, and later, spades. We are accustomed to spades with steel blades and wooden handles. By contrast, the earlier spades (and most other digging tools) were basically of wood, including any top handle. To increase their service life and provide a

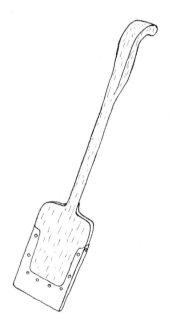

Medieval Iron-Shod Spade

sharper cutting edge these spades came increasingly to be metal shod. The iron shoe covered the edges of the blade and partially plated its front and back surfaces. The absence of all-iron blades was not a reflection of the incapacity of smiths of the time; it is clearly a product of the shortage, and value, of metals. Peasants, the principal users of such tools, could not afford or command the metals more needed for the weapons and armor of the upper classes. In fact, a large tool made entirely of iron, or any other metal, was something of a rarity until a century or two ago in our own culture.

The same circumstance is evident in the building construction and heavy machinery of medieval Europe. Insofar as possible buildings and bridges were made self-fastening through the fitting together of parts. Wooden pegs (treenails) were the rule, with an occasional piece of iron at some crucial point. Machinery, as in a mine or mill, was also largely nonmetallic. Here more use might be made of metal, but only when all else failed. The wooden shafts, bearings, and gears may have been cumbersome, inefficient, and noisy (they creaked and groaned most horribly) but they were cheap, wore well, and could be readily repaired or replaced with materials on hand. Today we still associate building construction and carpentry but forget that the millwright of the past was a first-rate carpenter, not a mechanic or machinist.

The materials used in tools, and material culture generally, have reflected human progress. As with tool types, the net effect of many technological innovations has been chiefly additive rather than substitutive. Only in the last few centuries have major changes appeared. Characteristic of earlier times was the use of natural materials comparatively unaltered. True, fibers were spun to increase their size and length, and stones were chipped or ground into desired shape, but, until the advent of metallurgy, the most radical alteration of a natural material was likely the conversion of suitable clays into ceramics. This act created a new material which possessed hardness, a permanent shape, fire-resistance, and insolubility.

As with the design of tools to take advantage of natural circumstances, so a material's use was governed by the same consideration. Use was often made of things in the form in which they came to hand. If a handle was needed, a stick of appropriate diameter was sought; the same was true of beams for buildings. Only among nonliterate peoples exceptionally well endowed with skill, tools, and materials were the latter radically altered to provide the desired items. Occasionally we find such peoples deliberately training growing plants to provide, ultimately, a particular curve or formation of material. Lumber, wood ready cut to standard dimensions and usable for a variety of purposes, taken for granted today, was almost unknown a few centuries ago. More common in a time when the materials-collector and the ultimate user were the same person was the selection of raw materials with a particular use in mind. One then cut his "canoe tree" or dug into a clay bank located several years previously.

The use of unaltered natural materials has been emphasized above, but some of these required extensive processing. An untanned hide would spoil and stiffen. Vegetable fibers, once cleaned, required spinning and weaving. Roots and withes had to be split and scraped before they were usable for basketry.

Materials were given forms not existing in nature, but comparatively few entirely new substances were produced in the prehistoric world. The ceramics mentioned above are the outstanding example of the latter. The production of metals in late prehistoric or proto-historic times had vast importance for man's cultural development.

In very recent times man's ingenuity has led to substantial changes in the inventory of available materials. The roster of metals has been augmented, enormous quantities of existing metals produced, and substantially better metallurgical technique introduced. Additionally, alterations have been made in the natural materials themselves, principally (from the viewpoint of present consideration) in uniformity, strength, and quantity. It is now possible to grow plants to specifications rather than having to rely on random variability to produce these desirable attributes in some few of the crop. Man has, so to speak, improved on nature.

Improvement on nature has proceeded in two other directions. First, many natural substances can now be synthesized in the laboratory and factory, without relying on their natural production. These artificial products have the same basic properties as those naturally produced, but may possess certain advantages. The time and place of production can be controlled: for example, one need not search tons of earth for gem stones made synthetically. These artificial stones may possess a regularity not characteristic of those occurring in nature. A further merit of this approach is that it is theoretically possible to produce substantial quantities of substances occurring only rarely in nature. Second, synthesis permits the production of materials which do not, or never did, exist in nature. These may, subject to conditions, be endowed with desirable properties not otherwise available.

Thus one may make a good case for man's increasing control of his environment through technological development. None of the foregoing is true solely of modern man: his forerunners achieved some of the same triumphs on a different scale by cultivating plants, domesticating animals, alloying bronze, and creating ceramics.

THE TECHNOLOGY OF SUBSISTENCE

Subsistence technologies are basic to the life of any people, for survival without adequate nourishment is a matter of a comparatively short time. But one is led to wonder if man's improvements in this realm have kept pace with those in other lines of endeavor. A strict comparison of progress or of efficiency is doubtless impossible. For example, has our raising of chickens increased in speed and ease in proportion to our evolved transportation facilities? This is probably a moot point, but may be kept in mind to illustrate differential progress within various parts of culture.

From analysis of dentition, of its wear, and of associated musculature, it is supposed that the proto-hominids were predominately vegetarian. The advent of weapons and of fire (through the technique of cooking) did much to convert early man to a part-time carnivore. A protein-rich diet in turn reduced the time necessary for the food quest, releasing time for other activities. Even so, the earliest and longest-lived of man's basic patterns of subsistence depended upon the collection of food. Such collection might be done with the hand, a digging stick, a seed-beater, a fish hook, a trap, or an arrow. The mode mattered less than did the relation to nature. It is obvious that one cannot collect food which does not exist, yet this truism lies at the heart of the relationship.

Food-collectors were dependent upon their habitat for the occurrence of food, its nature, its quantity, and its seasonal appearance. Even contemporary food-collecting bands can do little to increase the basic supply except to expand their diet. Bear in mind that few peoples customarily ate every edible thing within their grasp. Human hunger is converted by culture into appetite. Consequently, one means of augmenting the effective food supply was to become omnivorous, to eat everything within the capacity of the human digestive apparatus. Another way to increase the food supply was to exploit a larger territory. As populations increased, larger and larger food-collecting territories were needed. Because there is a limit to the area which can be exploited by members of one social group, a limit imposed by

facilities for travel and transport, either a population limit was reached or fission of the group occurred. Finally, a theoretical saturation point would be reached as the territories of contemporaneous groups met.

Much has been written about the food-collecting techniques of nonliterate peoples, especially their hunting. The taking of a sustained yield of game required skill, patience, organization, knowledge, and foresight. Conservation practices, some in the guise of religious beliefs and practices (e.g., taboos on the killing of certain animals), were not unknown. Hunting and trapping often called for substantial ingenuity and knowledge of animal psychology and we can admire its application, but we must not overrate the abilities of these primitive hunters.

Recent popular literature has generated a species of folklore about the infallible native hunter and tracker. One may be certain that such a man possessed no superhuman powers, he relied on clues not evident to the civilized observer. In the nature of things, he was operating in a territory with which he had a lifelong familiarity and among creatures, both animal and human, whose habits he knew well. Certainly failure was not unknown — wounded game escaped, traps froze, no game was found, bows broke, and so on. Though some peoples wrested a living from the most inhospitable environments, others lived rather miserably in the midst of reasonably abundant resources. As with men in all other human endeavors, the skills and fortunes of the nonliterate food-collector varied.

The tools for plant-collecting were few and simple. A digging stick often sufficed. Otherwise, the equipment was comparatively unspecialized and might have other uses as well.

Hunting called forth greater attention to artifacts. Most people had some form of projectile weapon. In point of time, a stone, thrown from the hand, may have been the

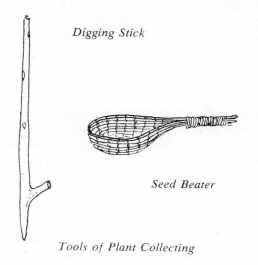

Digging Stick

Seed Beater

Tools of Plant Collecting

first such tool. The sling, to augment the force of the arm, was widely known. Bolas, consisting of two or three stones yoked on short lines to the end of a longer line, seem to have considerable antiquity. This device, used to entangle game for subsequent dispatch with a club or other means, is probably attested by sets of stones found in Paleolithic sites. In historic times it was known among Argentinian Indians, from whom the gauchos adopted it.

The use of the atlatl (sometimes known as a spear-thrower, throwing-stick or -board) is also traceable to the Paleolithic period. Older than the bow and arrow, the atlatl effectively lengthened the human arm and increased the velocity of the dart, hence its energy. (Remember $e = \frac{1}{2}mv^2$?) Its accuracy was somewhat less than that of the bow, but it was nonetheless a formidable weapon. The Aztecs, whose name for the item we have borrowed, and some other American Indians used the atlatl at the time of first white contact. The Eskimos used a variant form, as did peoples in Australia and Melanesia.

The bow and arrow is so well known as to require little comment. It was widely used in the Americas, Europe, and Asia, but was only occasionally found in Africa and Oceania. As a variant, the crossbow occurred in West Africa (probably as a recent introduction) and in Southeast Asia. The crossbow was highly developed in China, where a magazine-loading form was known, and in medieval Europe. The European crossbow was capable of piercing body armor with an arrow and came to be so feared as to be banned from "civilized" warfare, a distinction later achieved by poison gas and nuclear weapons!

Finally, among projectile weapons one should mention the blowgun. This was principally found in tropical regions, as in Southeast Asia and the adjacent island archipelago and in tropical South America, where suitable canes and bamboo are found. The efficacy of the blowgun's light dart against any but the smallest target was dependent upon the use of poisons, commonly those which quickly disable or kill through action on the nervous system.

The blowgun provides us with an example of the sophistication which sometimes characterized these "primitive" devices. In central Borneo, the tube was double — an inner tube of wood had the actual bore while an outer bamboo shell protected it from harm. The bore in the inner tube was curved in such a fashion that it was straightened out by the sagging which resulted from its own weight when the whole blowgun was held in the firing position by both hands at one end.

Clubs were common hunting weapons because they were readily made. In use they might be held in the hand or they might be thrown at the quarry. Clubs intended for the latter use are sometimes called "throwing sticks," thus leading to possible terminological confusion with the atlatl. Throwing clubs ranged in complexity from simple sticks to the boomerang, not all of which, we should note, were of the returning type.

Spears and harpoons complete the roster

of major hunting weapons. The former were either thrust or thrown, while the latter were generally thrown. The distinction between the two lies in the attachment of the point. A harpoon point is detachable and expected to come loose from the shaft after it has penetrated its target. The point was often fastened to a line which led to the shaft, to a drag or float, or to the hunter. The hindrance caused by the trailing shaft or drag helped to exhaust the wounded animal. If the line was held by the hunter or his companions, the animal was played until exhaustion or death. The line might also aid in retrieving a carcass which would otherwise be lost. Harpoons were common during the Upper Paleolithic cultural period in Europe, evidently used against land animals. More recently the harpoon was best known as an Eskimo weapon used to take marine mammals such as seal and walrus. The Nootka and Makah Indians of the Pacific Northwest Coast used the harpoon in their offshore whale fisheries.

Spear points, fixed to the shaft, ranged in complexity from a simple fire-hardened point formed on the wooden shaft itself to compound heads formed of many bone, tooth, or stone elements. Iron or mild steel spear points were native to Africa, to Indonesia, and to the later prehistoric periods in Europe. The leister, a type of spear, had a central point flanked by two inwardly curved lateral points equipped with barbs on their inner aspects and was widely used to spear and hold fish.

If one were to select one area of nonliterate technology to admire for its ingenuity and cleverness, it would probably be the making of traps. It was in this activity that most nonliterates produced their only mechanisms. As most of these peoples lacked the principle of wheel and axle, they made most effective use of levers, springs, weights, and pivots. Traps were important because through their use a hunter might considerably extend his effective presence. These devices were the hunter's surrogates lying in ambush for unwary creatures.

The use of traps requires even greater knowledge of the habits and nature of game than does active hunting, since the trap cannot adjust itself to unforeseen contingencies. It either works properly or fails totally. The trapper must know how to design, locate, build, bait, baffle, and camouflage his trap in order to catch the desired quarry. By contrast with modern steel traps, most traps of nonliterate peoples were fixed in location and built on the spot of local materials. Natural features such as growing trees, rocks, and declivities were often incorporated. Motive power for the trap might be provided by a suspended rock, a balanced log, a bent sapling, or the animal itself. On this latter point, if an animal was known to pull back and keep pulling when it felt a noose around its neck no further mechanism was necessary to choke or hold it.

Types of traps and their effects varied widely. Pit traps, deadfalls, nooses, and clamp-action traps were used by many nonliterates. A given culture might employ a number of trap types simultaneously because not every type will catch all kinds of game. Traps for larger game usually killed or seriously injured them so that they could not break up the trap and escape. Smaller game was often caught by confinement, alive and uninjured.

The lures which drew animals to be caught were based on the attractions of food, sex, pugnacity, or curiosity. The tendency for animals to follow habitual trails led to the placement of unbaited traps — such as set-bows and pits — along these trails.

The shift from food collection to food production has been hailed by some scholars as man's most important advance since he learned to use tools or to speak. The magnitude of this change and of its consequences may not be belittled. With the advent of food production a greater measure of control was gained over the environment. The food supply could be expanded to feed larger populations and even to provide surpluses which facilitated trade and occupational specialization. The consequences were felt far outside the economic sphere in religion, art, social organization, and virtually every other aspect of human life.

One of the many changes wrought was that which affected the food quest itself. The division of labor, while remaining primarily based on sex and age, was altered. Among food-collecting peoples, able-bodied men were the chief hunters; women, assisted in part by children, were responsible for the gathering of vegetable foods. The aged individuals of both sexes played a very minor role in either activity. Only in communal hunts or drives, where large numbers of beaters were needed, were all members of a group likely to be engaged in the same pursuit. The difference to be observed between men's and women's activities in the food-collecting economy have been attributed to differences in strength and the involvement with child care.

Food production, by contrast, was an activity in which almost everyone could take part. The gardens and fields were not far from the village, and the tasks were generally those requiring persistence rather than great strength. Most individuals were able to assist, in some way, in planting, weeding, or harvesting. Even children or the aged could guard fields against predators, either scaring them away or sounding the alarm when they approached. Only land clearing, the heaviest work of all, was performed by the men with little assistance from others. In some cases, once the land had been cleared all subsequent work was done by women. Consequently, proportionally more members of the group could contribute to their joint support.

While the so-called food-producing revolution probably took place more rapidly than did preceding major cultural changes, it was a gradual affair. Conservatism, or the disinclination to abandon proven food collection for untried food production, would slow the revolution. Food collection continued among some groups while other peoples had adopted a mixed economy and still others had turned entirely to food production. Even today in the United States there are some people who derive a substantial part of their subsistence from food collection, primarily by hunting and fishing, while living in an otherwise modern style. And, of course, commercial fishing and some hunting are a significant part of our national economy.

In anthropological terminology, horticulture refers to plant cultivation using means other than the plow. The tools used in the past were mainly the digging stick, the hoe, and the spade. Each society tended to specialize in the use of one tool. The bulk of nonliterate peoples were horticulturalists, as

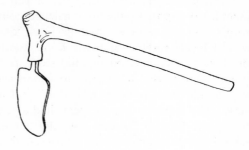

African Iron Hoe

the plow was unknown in the New World and in Oceania, and uncommon in sub-Saharan Africa and in Southeast Asia-Indonesia. The plow was most commonly used, prehistorically, in the zone from Europe to India, but was not universal in this region.

Because the possession of suitable draft animals and of the plow are prerequisite to agriculture, we believe horticulture to have historical priority. The earliest horticulture known is that in the Near East, perhaps as early as 8,000 B.C., but other centers of horticultural development are known. These include Southeast Asia, Meso-America, and possibly the Western Sudan. The crops of these regions differ greatly from those of the Eurasiatic complex. The contrast here is between the grains of Eurasia and the many root- and tree-crops of other areas. Rice may have been domesticated as a result of a stimulus from the Near East, but corn (maize) was clearly an independent, New World domesticate.

From these several centers horticulture spread to adjacent areas. At the times of first European contacts, plant cultivation was found generally through most of the Americas, excepting the southern portion of South America, the United States west of the Rockies, and that part of North America north of the present United States–Canadian border. In Africa most of the peoples had some cultivation, with the exception of those living in the desert regions. Virtually all of the Near East, southern and Southeast Asia, and the Far East had horticulture. Cultivation was marginal in Central Asia and lacking in most of Siberia. The native Australians had no cultivation, while most of the people who occupied the Pacific Islands did. The exception to this general picture occurred among smaller ethnic groups which were a bit atypical for their region, as the hunters of tropical South America or the Pygmies of the Congo, or among peoples who lived by animal husbandry (pastoralists).

We tend today to visualize cultivators as sedentary peoples and, compared to most food-collectors, they certainly were. However, many of the early horticulturalists practiced shifting cultivation (also known as slash-and-burn, milpa, or swidden cultivation). This practice involved clearing land

by girdling trees to kill them, then felling the trees and burning the debris. Crops were planted in the ash-fertilized spaces between the stumps. Lands treated in this fashion could be used only a short time, perhaps a decade at most, before they became unusable due to infertility and secondary growth of weeds and shrubs. Once this exhaustion occurred, the people cleared other patches and cultivated those. Sooner or later, as the fields in use were increasingly distant from the village, it became necessary to move the village to another area. Depending upon the context, exhausted lands would regenerate themselves in twenty to thirty years and the cycle could be repeated. This might mean that a village would be moved about within a general region and that shifting cultivators would require a total area approximately four times the size of that which they were cultivating at any given moment. Only as improved techniques such as fertilization and flood-plain cultivation came into use were villagers able to remain indefinitely in one place.

This does not mean that all nonliterate horticulturalists, or cultivators generally, engaged in shifting cultivation. Many were enabled by the nature of their habitat, of their crops, and of their techniques to remain for protracted periods in the same place, tilling substantially the same lands year after year.

Agriculture has been defined anthropologically as plant cultivation with the plow. Both logically and historically it followed horticulture. Subsequently agriculture became dominant in some formerly horticultural areas. The change involved not only the means of cultivation but also what was cultivated. Technological complexes involve materials, tools, and techniques. Accordingly, the plow brought with it certain food plants, especially the grains, and the inherent advantage of utilizing animal power.

The agricultural complex had its origin in the Near East, where substantial experience had already been gained with culti-vated plants and domesticated animals. Its spread, both by migration and diffusion, was influenced by the inability of crude, early plows to handle heavy soils. Areas unsuit-able for the plow remained either in the hands of hunters or horticulturalists. Some remaining traces of this circumstance were to be found recently in marginal areas of Europe.

Because all lands were not immediately serviceable for agriculture, land-clearing operations were often conducted in connec-tion with this subsistence mode. Slash-and-burn techniques might be employed, but the remaining stumps were an even greater problem for the agriculturalist than for the horticulturalist. Additionally, irrigation and land draining might be called for. These last-named needs often required massive and organized efforts. The archeological discov-ery of large irrigation works is usually con-sidered prima facie evidence for complex social organization.

Another major orientation of subsistence economics is that of animal husbandry, in this context primarily the exploitation of ani-mals as food sources. The domestication of animals occurred about as early as that of plants (excepting the dog which was do-mesticated earlier), but does not seem to have had important repercussions at an early date. Again the Near East and environs played a major role, with the horse, cattle, sheep, and goats all present. The camel came somewhat later but from the same area. Pigs may have had two origins as do-mesticates, in the European-Mediterranean area and in Southeast Asia. Our domestic fowl were chiefly of European origin, except-ing the chicken which came from Southeast Asia.

Animal husbandry may be practiced along with plant cultivation as has been the case for many parts of the world. Excepting the pastoralists and a few other special instances,

noted below, most of the peoples who kept domestic animals for food were sedentary, which makes horticulture or agriculture vir-tually mandatory. The interaction between these several sources of livelihood is well re-vealed in the development of agriculture when suitable traction animals were present.

One puzzling aspect of animal domestica-tion is why it occurred in the first instance. Today we find many of the domesticates' traits of obvious advantage, but most of these traits were present in only rudimen-tary form in the wild animals from which the domesticates were derived. It was in the domesticated state that cattle began to give substantial quantities of milk, that sheep be-came very woolly, that chickens laid eggs in large numbers. The inclusion of these ani-mals within man's cultural shield, in the man-made artificial environment, made pos-sible greater variability and subsequent se-lection for desired traits. Logically, the earli-est domestication must have been for a read-ily available meat supply, for the flesh was always present whatever else was present or lacking.

Though a great deal has been done through the ages, mostly by selective breed-ing, to enhance the characteristics for which certain animals were prized, one change has not been made. For all practical purposes the roster of modern domesticated forms is identical with that held by prehistoric man. We have not added one significant animal to this group. A study of this circumstance concluded that all the domesticable animals had been domesticated a long time ago and that, saving the discovery of hitherto un-known species, no additions are likely to be made in our time.

The contributions of domestic animals to the economy are manifold, with virtually every part or product having some use. Some products may be obtained from the living animal — milk, blood, eggs, horns, wool, hair, and manure. Other products usually require that the animal be slaughtered — flesh, bones, teeth, hides, and feathers. Animals have been kept specifically to provide any one or more of these materials. In modern times we have added to this list the keeping of animals for certain physiological byproducts, for example, the raising of horses for medical serum production, but this is a very sophisticated purpose.

Peoples whose mainstay is the raising of herd animals are usually referred to as pastoralists, but pastoralism as a way of life was not as widespread as the other economic modes. It was best known in Central Asia and in parts of the Near East. Other areas of pastoralism in the Old World included some parts of Africa, as along the Saharan fringes and from the Upper Nile and Somaliland to South Africa. There was no bona fide pastoralism in the New World; the closest approach was the raising of llamas and other cameloids by Andean peoples whose actual subsistence was horticulture.

There is some doubt as to whether or not pastoralism as it was commonly practiced was in fact a self-sufficient economy. Pastoralists maintained trading relationships with sedentary peoples from whom they received cultivated foods and craft products. The pastoral contribution to this barter consisted of animal products, live animals, and transport services. Marauding pastoralists were also known to have extorted what they wanted in exchange for protection, or simply to have helped themselves. Despite the foregoing it is likely that a pastoral economy could be self-sufficient at the expense of monotony.

The division of human labor in animal husbandry tended to fall along sexual lines. A difference was found between those peoples who raised animals as a sideline to plant cultivation and those who were pastoralists. In the former circumstance the animals might be tended by either men or women or even by children. The number of animals

was comparatively small and they were usually kept close to the village or farmlands. Among pastoralists there was a strong tendency for men to do the herding. The herds numbered in the hundreds or thousands and ranged far from home, if, indeed, any home base were maintained. Women and children often assisted in animal care, but were not primarily responsible.

The Technology of Shelter

As much as any other aspect of man's technology and material culture, his mode of shelter is coordinated with his physical environment. This coordination seems to have been more true in prehistoric times than recently, when considerations of style and fashion have been permitted to intervene at the expense of function. In the following discussion attention will be directed primarily to dwellings.

Man's technical solutions to the problem of shelter have used almost every conceivable material, but characteristically these materials have been local rather than imported. A moment's reflection will reveal that the following materials have played a major and visible role in dwelling construction: wood, stone, earth (rammed earth or *pisé de terre*), clay (adobe and puddled clay), ceramics (brick and tile), bone (Upper Paleolithic pit houses), whale ribs (among the central Eskimo), bark, vegetable fiber, animal entrails (gut windows among the Eskimo), paper (Japanese wall screening), water (in the snow and ice of an Eskimo igloo), animal hair (in felt tents), and animal skins. Few of these materials are synthetic and most of them could be put to use without extensive processing after they were collected.

The earliest known shelters of man were natural ones — caves — but it seems likely that artificial shelters were equally early. Nest-building is a habit of the modern lower primates. For all that man has diverged far from his primate relatives, it is possible that early man retained some of this nest-building proclivity. In the Upper Paleolithic period of Eurasia we find the first unequivocal evidence for man-made structures.

Permanence of residence and permanence of structure bear a high correlation. One may reasonably expect that peoples who remained for protracted periods in one place would build substantially in the first place and possibly add to their dwellings as time passed. This expectation was often realized among sedentary cultivators. Assuming that suitable materials were available, such peoples often occupied the same house for generations; some of the Indian pueblos of the American Southwest show centuries of continuous inhabitation. By contrast, food-collectors and pastoralists utilized more impermanent structures, sometimes using types which were especially designed for portability.

Shifting of residence, as a consequence of economic demands, brought with it improvement of communal hygiene. All communities produce refuse which need not be removed if the location itself is soon abandoned for another site. Most of the debris, excepting shells and potsherds which are both unobjectionable, was organic and soon disappeared. The site could then be reoccupied without hazard. Truly sedentary peoples, by contrast, came to live on top of their own growing garbage heaps or middens, which sometimes grew to enormous size, assuming the aspect of small hills.

While some migratory hunters lived in very rudimentary shelters, other migratory peoples, both hunters and horticulturalists, built substantial structures. Generally these were abandoned when a move was made. In tropical areas such houses deteriorated very rapidly or became infested with vermin or were accidentally set afire when the ma-

terials dried. By the time a group shifted to another site the houses were worn out. Sometimes, however, all or part of the house might be moved. In East Africa a house roof, which is separable from the walls, is removed and carried on the heads of men to a new location where it is set on new walls and supporting posts. The classic example of house-moving comes from central Borneo. Here the whole village lived in a single long apartment house which extended for several hundred feet. When exhaustion of arable land forced a move the house was dismantled and the timbers rafted along a river to be re-erected at the new location. A parallel case of house-moving was found among the Indians of Vancouver Island. These food-collectors (hunters and fishermen) moved seasonally from a winter village to a summer village. Their houses were heavy plank affairs built on a log frame. Each village had permanent frames erected and the wall and roof planks were carried on canoes from one settlement to the other. Therefore, each house had two identical frames, one in each location, and one set of planking.

Specialized structures, intended to be moved readily and often, were the exception rather than the rule. The best known of these was the tipi. The basic pattern of a weather-proof covering over a conical pole

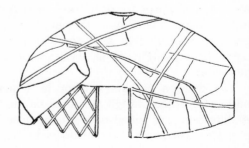

Mongolian Yurt, Cover Folded Back to Show Frame

frame was found from Lappland through Siberia into northern North America. The elaborated style which we associate with the Plains Indians in the United States represents the zenith of development made possible only after the introduction of the horse which could haul the heavy poles and assure a generous supply of buffalo hides for such a large model. Most tipis were much smaller. The yurt, developed by the Mongol pastoralists of Central Asia, was another specialized portable structure. The wall frame was a diagonal latticework supporting the roof, which was formed of poles springing from the eave-line and converging to a hoop at the apex of the roof. The covering of the yurt was of overlapping felt mats, held in place by narrow woven bands. Given the circular floor plan and the flexible domed roof, the proportions of the structure could be altered as desired. It could be of large diameter and low height, or the reverse, without a change in materials. The whole affair could readily be dismantled for transport by collapsing and rolling the wall lattice, rolling the felts, and bunching the roof poles while still fastened to their ring. Finally, a third specialized movable structure was the so-called black tent of the nomadic Arabs. The covering was a large rectangle of woven cloth composed of strips sewed edge to edge. Poles held the cloth off the ground and the sides were raised or held to the ground as the weather or desires of the resident dictated.

THE TECHNOLOGY OF TRANSPORTATION

Once, within the hearing of the writer, a National Park ranger commented that "the American Indian could carry everything he could pack on his wife's back." While perhaps open to question, this remark does make an important point. The basic means of transport of nonliterate peoples was, indeed, human porterage. Therefore, within any writing devoted to transport, consideration must be given to human burden carriers and any adjuncts to their task.

The manner in which loads are carried shows distinct cultural and sexual differences. Among American college students, books and notebooks, when not enclosed in a briefcase or other handled container, are carried in different fashions by men and women. The men carry their books at the side, resting on the bent hand and pinned between the forearm and the hip. The women more commonly carry their books in the crook of the arm, resting against the lower chest. This may also be said of the carrying habits in other cultures; the mode used will often differ by sex.

Burden-bearing on the head was quite common, for both sexes, in tropical Africa, but was found only among the women in the Southwestern Pueblos. It was similarly a feminine trait in Indonesia. Not infrequently those who carried loads on their heads used

Arabian Black Tent

a pad or ring to cushion and steady the load.

Other modes of carrying loads are linked with particular cultures. For instance, one finds the African habit (among women) of carrying loads on one hip; the load is steadied with one hand. Small children, especially, were carried, seated astride the hip. The most general carrying position, for loads of all kinds, was on the back. Because the load will usually not stay in place of its own accord, back-carrying involved a wide variety of auxiliary devices. Carrying baskets were found in peasant Europe, in the hill regions of Southeast Asia and Indonesia, and in western North America. They might be supported on the back by shoulder straps, by a tumpline (a strap passing across the upper forehead), or by both of these.

The shoulder bag, used as a catchall, was found in central Australia. Its use freed the hands to carry weapons or for other purposes along the route. Generally one does not find loads carried great distances in the hands. The shoulders, though, were used for carrying. In northern Europe, for example, burdens were carried on shoulder yokes. These wooden devices lay across both shoulders, passing behind the neck, and had a burden suspended from each end. One shoulder supported the balance pole of the Far East.

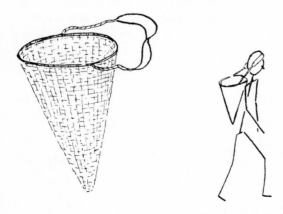

Pack Basket with Tumpline

This pole, a simple long stick, was carried in line with the direction of travel with a load suspended from each end. When the load became too great for one man, the positions of load and man were exchanged; each end of the pole rested on the shoulder of one man with the load suspended between.

The litter, or the elaborated sedan chair, was probably southern Asiatic in origin. Except for the litter, and the carrying of infants and small children (either free or on a cradle board), there was very little carrying of human loads. In most nonliterate societies the incapacitated either travelled by animal or by vehicle (or its equivalent), or they did not travel at all. One can readily understand why the feeble aged or those seriously ill or wounded were frequently abandoned to their fate.

In speaking of foot travel, one may not overlook another important class of auxiliaries. Many nonliterate people did not wear footgear at all times, but donned foot coverings only for travel. Even the most toughened foot welcomes some protection when on the trail and there were very few people who did not have some sort of footgear for travel. Skis, to permit travel over deep snow, were known aboriginally in the Old World in the arctic zone from Lappland to eastern Siberia. They were unknown in the New World until recently introduced by Europeans. Snowshoes were found in the northern reaches of both hemispheres. Travel on snowshoes was not as fast as on skis but the former gave better traction when pulling a load and were generally more useful in brush or around camp.

We may turn from circumstances in which human beings supported all the weight of a burden to those in which they provided motive power but little or no support. Sleds or toboggans, in both Old and New Worlds, were not infrequently pulled by man; it is most probable that this form of traction antedated the harnessing of reindeer or dogs.

With the sled a man could haul a greater load than he could carry. One exception to this generality may exist. It is reported that some porters in southwestern China were able to carry loads of 700 pounds a distance of ten miles in a day. A remarkable performance for one man, if true.

Quite different in many respects, yet within the same general category, was the Chinese wheelbarrow. This was used on the coastal plain to transport both goods and people. The wheelbarrow differed from our own in that the load was poised over a central wheel. When a favoring wind was blowing a helping sail might be hoisted. This did not relieve the pusher from plodding along behind, but did lessen the force he had to exert.

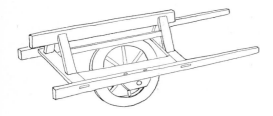

Chinese Wheelbarrow

Today we tend to think of pack animals in terms of horses and mules, but nonliterate peoples who had them packed loads on almost every available domestic animal. The Central Asiatics, whose nomadic life called for a maximum of transport, packed loads on horses, oxen, camels, sheep, goats, and yaks (on the Tibetan plateau). The only domestic animal they apparently did not pack was the dog, which was the sole pack animal of North American Indians until the horse was introduced in the sixteenth century. Camels and donkeys were the pack animals of the Near East and North Africa, in which areas the horse was reserved for riding. Cattle were packed in East and South Africa. The East and Southeast Asians did not, by

and large, pack their animals, though the Koreans regularly packed loads on cattle. Australia lacked suitable animals, the dingo being too wild, and the islanders of the Pacific had no real need for animal transport. In South America the llama was used as a pack animal by Andean natives. Lastly, the domestic reindeer of northern Eurasia were packed as well as used for sled traction and, less frequently, as riding animals.

Most of the larger domestic animals of the Old World were ridden in addition to packing and traction uses. This included the members of the cattle family. More often than one might imagine the animal was led instead of being directed by the rider; the human rider, in these instances, was just another form of cargo.

The diffusion of domesticated animals was part of a functional complex which included the ways in which they might be used and the appurtenances for such use. Therefore, with the animals there diffused saddles, bridles, stirrups, lassos, methods of marking, and personal equipment for the riders.

The travois was probably the simplest transport device used with animal traction. Basically it consisted of two poles, the upper ends of which were fastened together across the animal's back, while the lower ends trailed on the ground. The load was lashed between the poles about half-way of their length. Originally used in the Plains area of North America with the dog, the travois was later used, in a larger model, with the horse. It was also known in Central Asia for the horse.

The sled, previously mentioned with human traction, again comes to our attention. Among the Lapps of northern Europe the sled was canoe-shaped with a single, keel-like runner. Elsewhere in the Old World it had two runners supporting a substantially open framework. The two-runnered style was also found in northern North America. The Lapps used only the reindeer to draw their sleds, a single reindeer being harnessed to each sled. Trains of reindeer with sleds were led by one man, each animal's lead-rein being tied to the rear of the sled in front. Northwestern Siberians harnessed more than one reindeer to their sleds and also used teams of dogs. In addition to dogs harnessed in tandem to their sleds, the Eskimo used fan harnesses. In this mode each dog was fastened by its own trace directly to the sled, with the lead dog on a slightly longer trace. Fan harnessing enabled each dog to find its own way and to obtain better footing where the surface was irregular.

In Europe the land sled was used until quite recently. This sled (sometimes "stone boat") was generally heavily built, drawn by oxen, and used to move heavy loads (stone, logs) over rough, roadless terrain. A lighter version was sometimes used in the same context to haul hay or brush.

We have come to associate wheeled vehicles with more advanced cultures, though the correlation was by no means perfect. Despite the elaboration reached by some American cultures, the principle of the wheel and axle was completely unknown in the New World prior to the coming of Europeans. The wheel was also unknown or unimportant in all of Africa except along the Mediterranean shore. Elsewhere in the Old World it was absent from aboriginal Oceania and Australia. In the remaining areas the two-wheeled vehicle was logically, and historically, the forerunner of more elaborate forms. It remains quite widespread, possibly because of its simplicity (no problems with steerable wheels) and its ability to negotiate rough roads. Four-wheeled vehicles appeared in the early historic period in the Near East and Europe, but remained for a long time as an infrequent form. In western Asia an interesting development occurred as some yurts were mounted on carts and carried from place to place without being dismantled. Though pulled behind a team of

animals rather than another vehicle, they demonstrate that the house trailer is not a new idea at all.

The most ancient form of watercraft was doubtless a float used to sustain a swimmer or to carry his goods. Rafts represent an elaboration much better documented. The native Tasmanians, among the most primitive people known ethnographically, used bark rafts with which they evidently were able to cross Bass Strait (separating their island from continental Australia). Coastal dwellers of western South America used rafts of balsa and other wood for offshore fishing. In the Near East two distinctive raft types were used. One of these, principally made by sedentary peoples, had open-mouthed pots (ceramic) lashed upright in a pole framework. It floated well, though subject to disaster from hard blows or shipping water. The other raft, mostly made by nomadic pastoralists, used inflated animal skins as floats under a pole framework. Technically speaking, the "balsas" used on Lake Titicaca in the Andes and by California Indians in the San Joaquin Valley were rafts. These were made of bundles of reeds formed into a boat-like shape.

Dugout canoes have a substantial antiquity. They have been recovered, archaeologically, from contexts dating to the Mesolithic period in northern Europe, being perhaps 10,000 years old. Their widespread occurrence, in all continents, suggests that they are ancient elsewhere. The dugout canoe was especially elaborated in two areas. On the Northwest Coast of North America very large canoes (up to seventy feet long, with six- to eight-foot beam) were made. While their size is in part attributable to large, easily worked logs, it is equally due to having the sides of the canoe softened by boiling water and then forced apart to increase the original beam. The elaborated dugout canoe of Oceania was much smaller, but possessed some refinements not found elsewhere. It was equipped with outriggers, either single or on both sides. These parallel floats gave the canoe considerable additional stability, enabling the use of sails. When a single outrigger was used the drag it created tended to turn the canoe toward the side. On some islands of the western Pacific the body of the canoe was made asymmetrical to exert a compensatory force. This refinement seems to fall in the same class as the curved blowgun tube, and demonstrates mastery of complex hydrodynamic principles.

Plank boats, which we now take for granted, were evidently a rather late development when compared with other forms of watercraft. Several plank boats have been recovered from prehistoric Iron Age Europe. The keel and sides of these boats are formed of a few large planks, which were carefully fitted together and then lashed to each other with blind stitching. Internally, ribs and thwarts were fitted to hold the shape. A substantially identical mode of construction was used to make plank boats in Oceania. Here planks were used to make larger canoes as a solution, in the absence of very large trees. Analysts have held that the base of the boat was originally a dugout canoe of rather small size, to which two strakes were added on each side to increase the vessel's depth. Outriggers were added to the basic hull, as was the custom with smaller, completely dug out canoes.

The birch bark boat of the northeastern United States and eastern Canada is, doubtless, well known to the reader. It was made of birch bark sheets stitched together over a framework. One-piece bark boats were known in tropical areas, especially the Amazon Basin of South America. Most of the bark from the bole of a hardwood tree was removed as a unit. Preferably there were no branches along this section. The green bark was then molded to the desired shape and held in position with lashed thwarts. The bow and stern were closed by rolling the

bark upward to a smaller diameter than the body of the canoe. The shovel ends thus produced reached above the waterline.

Skin boats of various kinds were found among a number of separate cultures. One of these, the Eskimo kayak, certainly requires no extended description. A light, and cleverly made, frame of wood (and bone as necessary) was equipped with a sewn skin covering. The deck was fitted with holders for harpoons and other gear. Cargo, and an occasional passenger, was carried beneath the deck fore or aft. Of similar construction, but differing design, was the umiak (the so-called woman's boat). This was an open whaleboat used for groups of people, heavy cargo, and whale and walrus hunting.

American Indians living along the upper Missouri River used the bull boat, which derived its name from a buffalo bull skin (one whole skin) drawn over a pole frame. Being circular in outline, the bull boat lacked di-

Mesopotamian Basketry Boat (Gufa)

rectional stability, but it sufficed for river crossing and down-river trips. The coracle of the western British Isles was built of skin fastened over a pole frame. The frame might be elaborated with basketwork to strengthen it and give it better shape. This small boat, for two or three people, may have been more widespread prehistorically. Finally, the Mesopotamian gufa was a large, specialized basket with the interstices caulked with pitch. Round in form, like the bull boat and of about the same size, the gufa was used to haul passengers and cargo.

STUDIES IN TECHNOLOGY

The problems which may be undertaken in the study of technology are legion. Some are of long standing, while others arise with the special interest of the investigator. They may cover the entire range, from questions which are highly technical in nature, for instance, the tempering of African steel weapons, to those which are strongly social anthropological, for instance, the social organization of voluntary associations of workmen. That such a range of potential inquiry exists is, of course, indicative of the integrated nature of culture. In the following paragraphs we will outline some of the standing problems which exist with respect to technologies generally. Other sections will discuss some of the methods by which such problems may be investigated.

A substantial part of our present knowledge of technologies of nonliterate people stems from the work of archeologists. Two of their foremost questions regarding the artifacts they recover are: what was the function; how was it made? These two problems are inextricably related when one considers the whole inventory of tools and techniques of a culture. However, the entirety is very important, for if one were to be concerned only with these questions as they apply to nontool products of the use of tools, a whole echelon of the technology would be overlooked. This potentially lost range would be that of secondary tools, that is, tools to make tools. The third level of abstraction, tertiary tools, or tools to make tools to make tools, is rarely if ever found among nonliterates.

Hardly less basic is a concern with the histories, both historic and prehistoric, of techniques. There are many problems relating to the origination, introduction, diffusion, and development of existing or extinct techniques. Undertaking an inquiry into these may well deeply involve the investigator in general culture history.

Basic to any understanding, or investigation, of present technologies is an adequate description of these technologies. Adequacy of observation is closely linked to the background knowledge of the observer. He must already know something of the essential nature of the technology he is attempting to describe. To use Shakespeare's words, it goes without saying that a person who cannot tell a hawk from a handsaw will not make the best record of building construction.

There is a tendency to evaluate technologies and techniques as good, bad, or indifferent. Such evaluations may be highly subjective and naïve, but are not necessarily so. A major problem, when such appraisals are legitimately necessary, is to establish objective bases for the activity. It might be appropriate in this context to call attention to the important distinction between efficiency and effectiveness (Sonnenfeld 1960:172). Efficiency refers to the inherent capability of a device to perform the function for which it is used; this capability may be considered essentially invariant. Effectiveness refers to the results of the use of this device in a specific context. For example, a shotgun may be a very efficient means of killing birds; those birds it hits will be very dead. But if its loud report scares away all the surviving birds its effectiveness may be less than that of a quieter but less deadly weapon.

Another major problem area concerns the changes — technical, economic, and social — wrought by technological changes. Every cultural change may be expected to have repercussions in other parts of the culture and technical changes are not excepted. Investigations of the increasing use of cigarette lighters or of the introduction of computer-controlled automatic lathes will reveal effects beyond those in the match industry or in the educational qualifications of factory operatives, respectively.

Closely related are the problems of training and retraining of technicians. While this matter will be discussed at greater length below, it is well to note here that all people, technical operatives or not, are creatures of their cultures. As such they have certain trained capacities (and incapacities) and certain mental biases which affect their approach to the technical situation.

Finally, in outlining problems in technology we must not forget the social and economic side. The orientation toward our subject may not be wholly technical, for all manner of other aspects intrude and are vitally important. It is not in the least difficult to imagine a hypothetical situation in which native technical personnel, being workers, are socially segregated from that part of the society which has contact with Western culture. The higher class people, having little direct interest in technology, fail to transmit such new technical information as comes their way. The lower class workers, being illiterate, lack this avenue through which they may establish their own contacts with information sources.

The methods of technological investigations are many and varied. Those chosen in a particular case must, obviously, be appropriate to the problem in hand. The following section will explore the range of possibilities. It will be up to the investigator to decide for himself the methods to be employed in a given instance. Some of the following methods are almost universally applicable, while others have utility in a very restricted context. Not all of them are usable when studying the technologies of nonliterate peoples.

Direct observation of a technical pursuit is certainly the most obvious of techniques. The investigator watches the technician at work and makes note of the tools, materials, and methods he uses. A photographic record, ranging from a few still photographs taken at significant points in the process to a continuous motion picture, is quite appropriate and useful. The record may be examined repeatedly after the fact to fill gaps in the notes or to expand the notational record. However, a photographic record in any detail is not satisfactory as the sole information source. Sketches, while slower and more laborious, are sometimes superior to photographs in that they may be made to show particular details which escape the camera.

A full observational record should include the postures and movements of the technician. These are extremely difficult to record in any longhand fashion. Even the simplest takes some time and many words to describe. Though the writer knows of no instance in which use has been made of them in anthropology, it might be possible to adapt to our purposes the shorthand recording systems which have been developed for kinesics, choreography, or time-and-motion studies.

The personal interview is another potential method. Through this one might learn, from the technician, the history of his recruitment, training, and experience in the technique. His attitudes toward himself, his fellow technicians, or his craft may be revealed. Direct inquiry, even without formal interview, may answer many questions which arise. Verbal contacts, to be most fruitful, will necessitate a knowledge of the technical terminology.

Analysis of the products of technology, both the artifacts and the tools themselves, is another method of investigation. In this activity it will often be necessary to enlist the assistance of other specialists who can identify woods, minerals (in ceramics or paint), and metals. The investigator himself should be able to detect the ways in which fabrics or baskets are woven and pottery is formed.

Additionally, the sources of materials incorporated in artifacts may tell us something about the trading activities of prehistoric peoples.

Experimentation has its place in our group of methods. Lacking other information, it may be desirable to reproduce certain products of technologies. A series of experiments may reveal what techniques will yield a product matching the artifact in question. If more than one productive means is possible, then a choice must be made between them when suggesting the final solution to the problem. Experimentation may also be used to reproduce certain special effects observable on an artifact. For example, a tool may show wear, scratching, dulling, or some analogous condition. The question raised about the effect can frequently be answered, to any degree of satisfaction, in no other way.

When dealing with historical studies in technology some aid as to origins and diffusion can be gained from investigation of present or past techniques. In addition to the techniques themselves, either noted in the present or in the literature, the products of such techniques provide presumptive evidence for their presence. Such products remain long after the techniques which produced them are gone and may be found in the field, in museums, or in private collections.

The study of technologies of literate societies may use published and documentary sources. First, there are the papers of the crafts and industries themselves. These may include business records (such as invoices), catalogs and advertising, contracts, specifications, manuals for journeymen and apprentices, and guides for the operation of these businesses. There are various relevant public records: legislative acts, administrative codes, permits, customs invoices, and probate court proceedings. Personal documents might include letters, diaries, travel accounts, and the reports of migrants to those remaining at home.

Pictures can be very useful because they often include, inadvertently, items about which no one would bother to write. This extra information is frequently found around the edges 'of photographs whose subject may be a group of people. While the camera can be made to lie, in these cases it is likely to be truthful. Paintings and engravings may be of some help to research, but less so than photographs. Unless the artist characteristically produces very detailed pictures or has a special interest in the technical items, he is likely to gloss over them. One caution on the use of engravings is that the actual engraving was frequently done by an engraver following a field sketch made by the artist. The engraver might well use his imagination to supply missing details or to fill in an unoccupied corner of the scene. Also, with respect to pictures, those which portray historic events often have tools, weapons, costumes, and other details of the period of the artist, not of the event. For example, there are many paintings of the Holy Family, done in the Middle Ages, which show Joseph, the carpenter, with medieval tools.

Methods of research into technology are far from being fixed. Imagination, ingenuity, and improvisation are constantly required. Source materials may turn up in the most unlikely places and must be recognized for their worth. It goes without saying that the investigator of technologies, unless he is extraordinarily specialized in his interests, must have a tremendous range of information at his command.

The bulk of the literature of studies in technology dates from the last decades of the nineteenth century and the first decades of the twentieth century. While a number of landmark papers have come down to us from this period, papers without which we would be substantially poorer, most studies did not display the breadth and depth we currently feel desirable. They tend to be concerned with processes or products, rarely with both. We find concentration on a particular type of artifact in a number of cultures, for example, on bows and arrows (Pope 1923), or snowshoes (Davidson 1937). Concentration may, instead, be on a given craft either in one culture or in a variety of cultures, for example, on Navaho pottery (Tschopik 1941), or on American Indian basketry (Mason 1904). Finally, the emphasis may be on a given process in one or more contexts, for instance, on methods of fire-making (Hough 1926).

Exceptionally, when we learn of basketry from such a study we also learn about the basket-weavers (O'Neale 1932). More commonly we find details only on the particular product, craft, or process, and very little about the context in which it occurred. If, for example, one were to ask about the production rates of nonliterate technicians, he would look a long time before finding the answer. His quest for details on the economics of these technologies might be rewarded only a bit more often.

Motor habit patterns, which are discussed elsewhere in this chapter, have barely been mentioned in the past literature. This is especially true of those motor habits directly related to technical pursuits. Only one explicit study of this kind comes to mind (Bailey 1942). When motor habits have been the topic they are usually postural habits (Hewes 1955), and postural habits are the ones which find their way into the general ethnographic literature, if any are mentioned at all. Modern studies, which are strongly oriented toward social organization and social function, mention motor habits even less frequently than did more generalized studies of the past.

The literature in technological change is remarkably narrow in scope. Little attention is paid, in detail, to the existing or previous technological state of the people under dis-

cussion. There are few concerns expressed for technical practices, standards, or habits. Instead we find an emphasis on social circumstances or cultural attitudes as they affect the process of technological change. While these are certainly vital, they do not tell the whole story.

For all that the foregoing review may seem to be couched in a rather critical tone, this is no effort to decry the accomplishments of the past. Within the tasks these investigators set for themselves they did a fine job and we are greatly in their debt. However, in the interim anthropology has changed, as one might expect and hope, and we now see our purpose in a different light, with a broader scope. Paradoxically, today, when the task looms much larger, there are fewer anthropologists, both relatively and absolutely, interested in pursuing it. We may only hope they will prove equal to the task if no others can be recruited to an interest in technology.

By way of illustration of approaches to the study of technology, let us look briefly at two case studies. Each poses different kinds of problems and each shows different methods employed toward their solution.

The first is a study of Mexican mold-made pottery (Foster 1948b). Molding of pottery is the most widespread modern Mexican pottery-making technique and is found in two basic forms. In one of these the clay, already flattened into pancake form, is pressed into two halves of a vertically-split female mold. While still in the mold, the

Pottery Anvil-Mold

edges are trimmed and the two halves cemented together. After some drying the molds are removed and the seam is erased by scraping and smoothing. Patterns may be incised on the interior of the molds to produce a design on the exterior of the finished vessel. In the other technique, the flattened clay is pressed over the exterior of a male mold which is often mushroom-shaped. The mouth of the pot must be at least as large as the largest inside diameter so the mold may be removed. Designs, if any, on the mold are impressed on the interior of the bowl. Once molded, such a piece of clay may be used as a base for further additions to make larger and more elaborate forms. The additions may be made with the aid of the potter's wheel. Two male molds may be used, one to form the bottom of the vessel, the other to form the upper part. These two, after trimming, are then joined horizontally at the widest point. These basic techniques, and variations of them, are known from field observations made by the author.

Three problems are engaged. First, are these molding techniques pre- or post-Conquest? Second, what is the origin of these molds? Third, what is the relation between the primitive molding system and the use, or nonuse, of the potter's wheel?

In answering the first question, the investigator made use of the structural characteristics of vessels which reveal their mode of manufacture. Museum specimens which date from before the Spanish Conquest were examined and found to show the weld resulting from horizontal juncture. Vessels made in vertically-split molds are much more difficult to identify, but some few vessels and a greater number of effigies from Guatemala were found to have been so made. Cultural affinities between Guatemala and Mexico at this period were such as to make reasonable an assumption of co-existence of the vertically-molded vessels in Mexico. The presence of the molds themselves from archeo-logical sources at the proper date would similarly testify to their pre-Conquest presence. Only a few of these molds have been located. The author feels that the manner in which molds were treated after breakage and the lack of knowledge of molds on the part of archeologists may both have contributed to their sporadic recovery.

When seeking the origin of the molds, the author drew upon ethnographic literature to find that finished pots are occasionally used in Meso-America as male molds over which to form the bottom of a new pot. Forming a special thick-walled piece for this purpose is a simple, logical step. Field observation has shown such pieces to exist, often without a handle. The handle is added to facilitate manipulation of larger, heavier molds when trimming the lower edge of the clay. The author then showed that some archeological pieces from sites in California, the Southwest, and the Middle West, previously identified as pottery anvils, may well be molds. (The paddle-and-anvil technique involves holding an anvil inside a pot while paddling the soft clay from the outside. The anvil is often mushroom-shaped.) He believes that the mold was of Mexican origin and was adapted in these northern areas to use in the pre-existing paddle-and-anvil technique.

Some Mexican villages have made a total adoption of the potter's wheel, some have rejected it, and others make only limited use of it. Partial use of the wheel occurs when it is used to add to a pot bottom already made on a mold; this can be done only when the mushroom mold is used, for the seam is then horizontal. Prior to the advent of the wheel, the process of addition involved turning the pot by hand while pieces of clay were added and smoothed into place. The wheel is not used in conjunction with the vertically-split mold nor when the mushroom mold produces a finished vessel not further elaborated. Working from historic sources, ethnographic literature, and personal observation, the author accordingly concluded that the wheel was adopted in two circumstances, first, where its introduction was through industrial and trade schools or through the training provided workers by an entrepreneur establishing a pottery. In this instance the "workers learned to make pots on wheels, just as they might have been apprenticed to learn any other trade" (Foster 1948b:368). Second, the wheel was employed when its use was compatible with previous practices, as the work had already been turned by hand in the process of adding on.

The reader may thus see how archeological evidence, historical data, ethnographic accounts, and field observation may all be brought to bear on the problem.

The second of the case studies is an investigation of the work habits and tools of Chinese immigrants to the United States (Spier 1958). These people, almost exclusively men, came to the United States in the mid-nineteenth century, originally as contract laborers, but they later branched into other activities. They brought with them few tools and had no intent to remain as permanent settlers.

The problem concerned the reactions of the Chinese to an encounter with a tool inventory based on motor habits markedly different from their own. Where we push a saw to make it cut, the Chinese pull theirs. Where we have a stiff-handled sledgehammer, that of the Chinese is limber to deliver a whip-like blow. In light of the fact that any individual has become well habituated to certain motor patterns by adulthood, would the Chinese be able to adapt to the use of Western-style tools?

The principal context of investigation, as planned, was the building of the western end of the first transcontinental railroad (completed in 1868) for which the labor force was more than 80 per cent Chinese. Though the direct records of the Central Pacific Railroad and the construction contractor were not available, enough evidence was garnered from news accounts, contemporary photographs, and correspondence concerning material orders for the job to be certain that the Chinese were furnished no special tools but used those supplied by the contractor. Photographs assure us that these tools were in a Western style. The Chinese adapted.

However, it was felt that additional information would strengthen the case. Therefore, the investigation was expanded to include other activities of the Chinese. To the foregoing data sources were added agricultural reports, fisheries reports, invoices from the United States Customs House at San Francisco, general descriptive literature on California (then one of the wonders of the world), literature on the gold rush in California and adjacent areas, and a survey of Chinese artifacts in local historical museums.

It was found that the Chinese were not slow to import their own goods from China or to make such items in California. California was much closer, in terms of time and convenience of transport, to the Far East than it was to the eastern United States. The Chinese farming techniques used when working on their own account were very close in style to those practiced in China. Their fisheries were also in the Chinese style — boats, lines, nets, and all. As hired labor in agriculture and on heavy construction jobs they had no difficulty in using tools furnished by their Occidental employers. In gold mining the Chinese were restricted, by custom and law, to placer mining. Here they generally behaved as did Occidental miners, with the addition of some Chinese pumps for draining the workings.

The conclusion reached was that, despite what we may have believed regarding the fixity of motor habit patterns, the Chinese were able to adapt freely to the use of Western tools. Nonetheless, when working for themselves, or for Oriental employers, they continued to use Chinese-style tools and to use them in the Chinese fashion. The whole problem then resolved itself into a question of preference rather than capability.

Studies in technology may, accordingly, work from a wide variety of data toward a similar variety of goals. The studies may stem from questions regarding specific techniques or specific artifacts. They may be more broadly derived from concerns with whole technologies and with cultural change. The need for more studies of technology, especially those with broad theoretical implications, is evident in a world such as our own, possessing a strong technological bias.

TECHNOLOGICAL CHANGE

Although technological change may be seen as a separate entity and dealt with accordingly, it is basically little more than one aspect of the general subject of cultural change. Those principles and considerations which apply to the latter are also applicable to the former. The major sources of technological change lie, without doubt, in diffusion and innovation. A diffusionist viewpoint, with many fine analyses of specific cases, is to be found in Dixon's work (1928). Innovation has more recently come in for its share of attention (Barnett 1953). Because artifacts and technologies, which may form complexes by themselves, are often parts of larger complexes, technological change should not be studied totally divorced from the general topic.

The period since the close of World War II has seen a marked rise in activities which may be lumped under the general heading of directed technical change. In the following discussion we are primarily concerned with technical change resulting from the overt activities of a change agency. These agencies have proliferated in recent years as aid to war-torn areas and their ref-

ugees was begun, and then converted to aid to the so-called developing countries. The creation of many new countries from the remains of colonial empires, countries which wish to become independent economically as well as politically, has intensified both the need and the response. Agencies engaged in technical assistance programs have arisen under the aegis of supranational and national governments, of religious organizations, and of secular welfare groups.

If one may draw any conclusions appropriate to our immediate concerns from the actions of these technical assistance agencies they would include the following. The emphasis is strongly economic and social. No special reference is made to the previously existing technologies or technical habits in the cultures to be aided. There is an assumption that any person is capable of learning the proper handling and care of machinery. Even such a simple, yet basic, matter as the immutable relationship of nuts to bolts, which cannot be altered in any ordinary fashion, is assumed to be understood. Many other examples, real or hypothetical, may be cited. Perhaps no substantial difficulty arises on these scores, but it seems a matter of chance rather than of investigation and planning that it does not do so.

There have been two interesting criticisms leveled at the technical assistance programs. The first is that the more technically advanced cultures are supplying those less favored with cast-off goods and outmoded techniques. The critics say that these are deemed satisfactory for peoples who, by comparison, have nothing. If this criticism is correct, then these programs have something in common with some of our domestic practices of charity. But it must be stressed that the technical assistance programs are not charity. While some of the aid is rendered gratis, a great deal of the assistance is purchased outright or through the medium of long-term loans.

The second criticism is that technical assistance programs are designed to recapitulate, on a compressed time scale, the technological history of the Western world. In other words, the cultures receiving assistance are being led rapidly through certain developmental stages from their original technological position to that of the technologically advanced cultures.

These two criticisms are clearly different aspects of one basic problem. Quite aside from the question of basic philosophy which we cannot answer here, there remain a series of important questions which are relevant. In light of what has been said about cultural experience with technology and culturally-induced habituations, is it possible to take shortcuts in arriving at a given state of technological development? Is not our present technological state based upon a wealth of experience with less complex circumstances? Can a man be successfully catapulted from the use of a digging stick to the operation and care of a bulldozer? The answers are not to be found in philosophic inquiry nor in the literature, but only in the field. Meanwhile the problems of aid may be considered so pressing as to forbid allocation of the time necessary to arrive at answers to these questions by any scientific method.

Within the United States various agencies have been created to deal with technical changes, especially automation, and their consequences. Here, planning of change to cushion its impact is less evident than the task of picking up the pieces after it has struck. While virtually everyone favors ameliorative action, certain fundamental differences of opinion regarding large-scale planning as it affects private industry have restricted thoroughgoing control of technical change.

Forms taken by these ameliorative efforts have included vocational education and re-training. In the former, a strong effort is made to keep abreast of the changing needs of employers, even to keep ahead of them if possible. In its optimal form such vocational training might well be coordinated with planned technological developments so that the training may be appropriate and that planning not call for skills which cannot be readily communicated to trainees. In the latter, re-training is undertaken for those who have been displaced from their jobs by technological changes or who have failed, by reason of inappropriate education, to find a job in the first instance. Additional technical training, at a higher level of skill, may be in order. However, there are people whose basic education or native capacity lies at such a low level as to prohibit this. These people must be trained and directed in ways commensurate with their skills.

As a consequence of these training activities we may find that direction is given to technology by the schools. Certain technological potentialities may be realized or denied by the availability or scarcity of trained personnel. Again, as in international technical assistance (mostly rendered cross-culturally), there is a substantial neglect of the cultural experiences and habits of the trainees. Fortunately, an assumption of experiential homogeneity is possible with all save groups of the most marked ethnicity, for the work tasks and work conditions are usually set forth by members of the same culture as the trainees. It is highly unlikely that they would consciously or unconsciously violate the general cultural standards which apply. But the point is stressed here that success is achieved in spite of, not because of, the lack of complete understanding of the situation.

Technological change is, then, a most fertile field for study, offering a dynamic context from which we may extract the major effective factors in this species of cultural change. It may contribute substantially to general anthropological theory and it may offer an area in which social science can again demonstrate the predictive value of its conclusions. For the moment, with comparatively few decisive studies behind us, our role will be primarily cautionary. Unable to evaluate the weight, in general terms, which is to be placed on this factor or that, we must content ourselves with making sure that no major factor already recognized is overlooked when technological changes are planned.

SUMMARY

We have attempted to show that technology and material culture are integral parts of culture and that their study may illuminate for us certain aspects of culture which can be seen in no other way. The techniques man employs in environmental control and the products of these techniques form an important part of his life. One need not entertain a materialistic bias to see that this is so.

Every bit as important as an understanding of cultural integration, and the way in which technology contributes to culture, is a realization that technological activities are subject to the same considerations in terms of general cultural theory as are man's social, economic, religious, or other activities. Techniques are learned, diffused and innovated. Standards and habituations are developed and transmitted. In brief, the whole range of cultural dynamics is found in the technological realm.

The shield technology has increasingly interposed between man and his natural environment has freed him from a close, continuous dependence upon this environment. The technological and other aspects of his culture have jointly created a new, artificial (cultural) environment in which he lives. Within certain limits he may pursue his way without regard for weather, season, darkness, or other natural phenomena. The more complex the technology generally, the broader are these limits.

However, the creation of the technological shield has had its costs. Increasingly, technology plays a part in his everyday life. A total loss of this shield would leave man one of the most helpless of creatures. At a very early stage in human existence man's physical characteristics were altered because these features were no longer necessary; their possession conferred no particular selective advantage. Having lost his hairy covering, his prognathous face, and other simian traits, man is no longer as well equipped biologically as he was in the remote past to deal with the unmodified natural environment. The possession of culture, and especially the capacity to cushion nature's blows, has done this to him or made this possible — whichever way you wish to view it.

We have traced, in a limited way, the growth of technology from its early crudities to its present complex state. We have seen that each successive development was dependent upon that which had gone before, perhaps upon some specific prerequisite, perhaps upon a general accumulation of knowledge and experience. It is probably through an understanding of this long background that the student of man can best come to appreciate his present condition, its problems and its potentialities.

Suggested Readings

A classic consideration of primitive material culture and its underlying technologies is R. U. Sayce' *Primitive Arts and Crafts* which has fortunately again become available (Sayce 1933, reprint 1963). On a topical basis, period by period, is *A History of Technology,* edited by Charles Singer and others; the five volumes are primarily directed toward western European technologies and their antecedents, but the first two volumes are of considerable value to the anthropologist (Singer 1954–1958). A shorter summary of the same general topic is found in R. J. Forbes' *Man the Maker* (Forbes 1958). C. Daryll Forde's *Habitat, Economy and Society* offers a fine discussion of subsistence types and environmental adaptation with sketches of illustrative cultures (Forde 1948). A discussion of the craftsman, his habits, tools, and media in relation to his products is found in Franz Boas' *Primitive Art,* still the classic work on that subject (Boas 1927). Three works on technological change, each with a different perspective, are *Traditional Cultures and the Impact of Technological Change,* by George M. Foster, *Cultural Patterns and Technical Change,* edited by Margaret Mead, and *Human Problems in Technological Change,* edited by Edward H. Spicer (Foster 1962; Mead 1955; Spicer 1952).

CHAPTER 6 introduces a major branch of cultural anthropology, or, as some practitioners would have it, a quite separate and more productive alternative approach to the study of man, social anthropology. Professor Gearing examines the social structural basis of human life by stressing the critical importance of three fundamental technical ideas, the social anthropological distinctions between the "individual," the "social person," and "role." These three concepts, at once simple and subtle, are shown to be of great value both as analytic devices in their own right and as building blocks for the development of larger anthropological constructs, notions of social groupings, institutions, communities, and society itself. The writer shows how, using these few pivotal concepts, one may unravel the riddles and complexities (for an outsider) of the social life of an acculturated community of American Indians; and he demonstrates how the same ideas make comprehensible the seemingly bizarre features, classifications, and distinctions of non-European kinship systems. In the teaching of cultural anthropology two topics have with good reason been most frequently used as devices to generate in the student something more than just cursory insights into the inner workings of alien cultural and social systems. These topics are the structure of language and of kinship, two subjects about which anthropologists know and write a very great deal. As was the case for Professor Chafe's illustrations of the analysis of the morphology of the Dakota language, the careful application of a few basic ideas and of simple analytic techniques will here pay rich dividends in understanding.

THE AUTHOR has studied at the University of Chicago, where he received his Ph.D. in anthropology. He has taught at the University of Chicago, and is currently Associate Professor of Anthropology at the University of California in Riverside. For several years he was Assistant Director of the Tama Indian Project, whence comes his personal knowledge of the Fox of Iowa, and which expressed his interest and involvement in the use of anthropology as a means of assisting and guiding programs of social change. He has conducted community studies in modern Greece as well as ethnohistorical and ethnographic studies of American Indian peoples. He is author of *Priests and Warriors: Social Structures for Cherokee Politics in the 18th Century* and several journal articles dealing with territorial organization, social control, and action research.

6

Social Structure: Societies
as Arrangements of Personnel

FRED GEARING

University of California at Riverside

INTRODUCTION

If, through some fantastic mental black-out, some simultaneous and universal mass forgetfulness, one simple idea were to vanish from men's minds, a great deal of social science would at that instant disappear. Most of social science sets out to observe behaving humans and to describe and perhaps account for that behavior with some economy and precision. Very little of all that could transpire without this one simple idea: the recognition that the *individual* is one logical kind of thing and that the *person* is a second, logically very different kind of thing. Both are constructs — inventions of the mind. Insofar as social scientists hold firmly in mind the distinction between individual and person, observation and inference can and often do move steadily, and insofar as social scientists suffer the distinction to lapse from fully explicit awareness, observation tends to be-come murky and inference also becomes shaky.[1]

The notion of *individual* focuses the mind upon an organism, a being contained within skin, or an array of such organisms. An organism is born with a genetic inheritance; it lives some while in some series of environment and circumstance and through this time assumes some series of physical and mental shapes, each shape growing out of the earlier ones; and it dies. This seems the more "nat-

[1] Several realms of social study are clearly exempt from these bald assertions: one can study the syntax of a language without this distinction in mind; one can proceed some further distance in the same direction, as a description of a people's cognitive view of the world, or a description of the patterns of their art styles or their music; or one can describe the technology of a people, narrowly construed; outside anthropology, one can study certain dimensions of perception, or the various shiftings of a demographic profile. All these realms permit in common that the observer "bracket off" the human interactions which seem, for these analytic purposes, invariant.

ural" construct with which to think about the human scene; among more scientific modes of observation and thought, all those which involve, for example, learning, *must* so move in terms of the notion of individual. The notion of *person,* as we shall note, focuses the mind quite differently, upon a set of public ideas shared by a people, ideas as to *the social identities men can assume,* as, around a dinner table, "father" or "dinner host," ideas by which men publicly and appropriately identify themselves and are identified by their fellows. Thus any one individual is, in any day, many persons, varying according to the social contexts in which he finds himself that day: father vis-á-vis a son, host vis-á-vis a dinner guest, and so on. Conversely, any one person identifies numerous individuals, the many men who on appropriate occasion see themselves and are seen as fathers or hosts or what-have-you.[2] Studies of social structure move in terms of this latter notion, person.

It is quite doubtful whether a human being could survive twenty-four hours in a modern city unless he effectively (even if unconsciously) used this distinction in his normal goings and comings. One can interact effectively with strangers momentarily encountered who by dress or other signals are identified as professor, grocery clerk, and so on; and one can interact effectively with life-long friends insofar as one notes that this friend is at this moment professor or grocery clerk and that, irrespective of any predilection, certain constraints are established by those identities. To a man-on-the-street, "know-

ing" these things usually is like knowing the phonemic system of his native language: he knows, but he does not fully know he knows. It would follow, and frequently has, that men of letters sometimes draw this knowledge out from the welter of implicit human experience and make it explicit to some poetic or dramatic purpose, as Shakespeare's, "All the world's a stage. . . . And one man in his time plays many parts." The implicit knowledge, occasionally and fleetingly made explicit, has been always with us and all men, doubtlessly as an aspect of the human condition.

It similarly would follow, and frequently has, that minds of early scholarly observers of human behavior have tended to run more in terms of the one or the other of these pivotal terms. On the side of person (the sense, if not the term), mention must of course be made of Karl Marx (from 1867), Thorstein Veblen (1899), and others whose observation pivoted on class stratification; Sir Henry Maine (1861), J. J. Bachofen (1861), and other students of comparative law; early sociologists such as Émile Durkheim (1893). In early anthropology, it seems clear, those workers who chanced to hit upon kinship phenomena, as John Ferguson McLennan (1865) and pre-eminently Lewis H. Morgan (1870), found themselves, in effect, working almost exclusively in terms of the notion of person.[3]

However, the critical notion of person could not come to explicit, full, and (potentially) precise awareness until it was explicitly placed alongside the equally critical notion of individual. It is the logical contrast which makes each clearly evident. *This* full awareness was remarkably late arriving. Looking back, one can, as almost always in such cases, find any number of phrasings which recommend the authors as the original donors. But it is usually acknowledged: that

---

[2] This basic distinction is employed virtually throughout the social sciences; but the terms used to denote the second part of the distinction vary. I have used the word "person" (which is etymologically appropriate, at least, stemming as it does from the Latin *persona,* which meant an actor's mask). The word "status" is perhaps the most frequent usage (and can claim equally appropriate origins, being Latin for legal position or standing). "Role" is a related notion, used together with person and/or status.

[3] For an excellent overview of the history of kinship studies, see Tax (1955c).

phrasing which was made with sufficient clarity (and perhaps at just the right time) and which brought these twin notions fully into the public realm of social science came from the pen of the anthropologist, Ralph Linton, in 1936. Linton wrote (using the term "status"):

> A status, as distinct from the individual who may occupy it, [read, for our purposes: 'A person, as distinct from the sundry individuals who may assume that identity,] is simply a collection of rights and duties. Since these rights and duties can find expression only through the medium of individuals, it is extremely hard for us to maintain a distinction in our thinking between statuses and the people who hold them and exercise the rights and duties which constitute them. The relation between any individual and any status he holds is somewhat like that between the driver of an automobile and the driver's place in the machine. The driver's seat with its steering wheel, accelerator, and other controls is a constant with ever-present potentialities for action and control, while the driver may be any member of the family and may exercise these potentialities very well or very badly (Linton 1936:113).

From 1936 on, the notion of person (in its several phrasings) was integral to the work of great sections of social science disciplines. It is one of those ideas which quite transforms what an observer sees when he looks. As such, the notion of person is not unlike (though it is to date primitive) the physicist's notion of the atom. To a physicist, a table never quite looks like the thing you and I see; and to an observer of the human scene, once the notion of person is seriously entertained, that scene never looks quite the same again.

PERSONS AND ROLES

"Out there" in the phenomenal world are sounds and light (and smells, and the like), sensory reflections of sundry swirls of behaving humanity. These assault the senses, but what usually is recorded to the conscious mind of an observer are not mere sounds and light, nor even discrete items of the reflected behavior. Instead, the observer imagines he has seen some unfolding sequence of events, big and little packages of connected phenomena. He imagines he has seen, say, a family preparing dinner, and eating, and cleaning up afterwards (and lesser events making up these, and grander events subsuming them). This mental packaging of sense phenomena goes on unbidden by the observer, largely beyond his control, probably out of deeply ingrained habits of mind. This unreflective packaging, simply because it is unreflective, ought to be suspect. But all modes of observation of the human scene seem to start from this possibly risky base. The study of social structure conspicuously does.

The study of social structure is one way (of several) of selectively looking at any and all such human events. To observe the social structure of a people requires always that one focus his mind on a single, analytically separable facet of each event which regularly occurs among that people. To observe a social structure is to discern how that population, engaged variously as actors and audience in this or that event, imagines itself to be sorted, and how that population, so sorted, imagines the entailed work or play to be properly or expectably divided and ordered. Thus, more particularly, to observe social structure is to ask: what social "things" (among all the enduring social things of this kind imagined by that people to exist, as "uncle," "chief," "stranger," and the like) is this particular man deemed by his fellows publicly to be, in this context, at this moment? And what patterns of public conduct are expected or preferred of him by those fellows, his being by them so identified? (Thence, similarly, the next man and the next, thence to another event and another through some adequate array of the range of events which regularly occur among that people.) At that family dinner table, as we imagined, one man is deemed by all to be "father" (vis-á-vis his son or daughter), "husband" (in respect to his wife), "host" (to a guest), and so on, and each such identity implies for him a different pattern of expected or preferred public conduct; such notions he and all others involved carry with them to the table, and those notions may determine and will certainly affect what goes on there.

A student of social structure sets out, then, to discover certain ideas in the heads of a people. He may observe more (and most students, in a variety of ways, attempt to observe or otherwise note how far men do in fact conform in their actual conduct to these public expectations and preferences). But all studies of social structure must discover those ideas in the heads of the actors, must control that one separable facet of any human event, the primary data of any social structural study.

These primary data are usually derived, in some part, from the observation of actual events as they unfold (in contrast to sitting down with informants or to the administration of other, perhaps elegant, interview instruments). Insofar as the data are derived from actual observation of actual events, an observer, to prepare his mind to receive these primary data of social structural study, may hold in mind (more or less explicitly) a little model consisting of three human individuals, three fellow members of some community: A acts vis-á-vis B and with an eye to C who sees and visibly reacts with surprise or its opposite and with approval or disapproval in varying degrees. As among these three, the most immediately revealing and directly relevant data come from C. The utterances and other cues C publicly gives off, of anguish, praise, shock, awe, and the like, are the very stuff of social structure. A student of the social structure of some people, hav-

ing observed long and well, will find himself frequently surprised, in circumstances he thought he understood, by the actions of some A toward some B — for men do not always conform to the public expectations and public preferences of their fellows. But observation ought virtually to eliminate surprise as to the public reactions given off by those C's.

That is, the study of social structure — this very selective look at human events — requires, in the first instance, observation of sets of actions-and-reactions (both together, neither alone), and requires from that the inference and some listing of certain shared, public ideas in the heads of the actors — public notions about the several social things each man (at that moment, in the context of that event) is deemed to be, and public notions about the preferred or expected conduct of each man, being this and that social thing. We deal (exclusively so far) with a complex code in the heads of people, publicly understood guidelines for behavior; about any particular people, the student of social structure wants first to elicit the particular details of their particular code.

Thus the student of social structure seeks to learn, about any people, their full battery of *persons* (the full array of such assumable public identities) and their battery of corresponding *roles* (the patterns of expected or preferred public conduct). Every man in any society is deemed by his fellows to be many persons in a day or lifetime, and for each such person a man is, some role is deemed appropriate.[4]

---

[4] We might now more closely paraphrase the earlier passage from Linton (p. 163): A *person*, as distinct from the sundry individuals who may assume that identity, is a publicly recognized identification; each such public identification carries with it a *role*, a collection of recognized rights and duties and other such expectations as to public conduct. Since these *persons-with-roles* can find expression only through the medium of individuals, it is extremely hard for us to maintain a distinction in our thinking between persons-and-roles and

Mesquakie Fox Social Structure

In Iowa, near the town of Tama, there live today a community of some 600 Indians, the Fox (or Mesquakie). In many of the things these people do they hardly resemble the Indians they once were, they resemble more the white men who are their close neighbors; most earn their livings, for example, in the small factories or plants in the general area, or as members of construction crews. In some other activities the Fox remain quite unlike those neighbors. All this, the "old" and the "new," seems to an observer to unfold in some sequence of events, and in any such set of human events, by definition and by empirical fact, one can "see" that facet we call social structure. I choose to mention an "old" sequence of events the likes of which still unfold in general outline each year in this community.

One July Sunday morning (of 1953 as it happens), numerous Fox men, women, and children, began to gather near the house in which old Pete Bear (the name is fictional) lived. Some brought packages of meat or dried corn. A few men received the food as it arrived, cut up the meat when necessary, and added the contents of the packages to a stew boiling in a large cast-iron pot, and occasionally they stirred the pot. Pete Bear, at one point, squatted down by the fire for three minutes or so, on occasion sprinkling powdery tobacco into the fire and mumbling inaudibly. And so on, into the day. All these actions are quite rare in the Fox community; people do not habitually congregate in large numbers, at Pete's house or any other house, nor hand packages of food about; women, not men, usually cook; Pete rarely squats by a fire and mumbles. But no one gave indication of surprise at any of

these behaviors. More than that, these actions were evidently approved, as indicated in special instances as when the son of Pete's dead brother (the son being a young man, highly unpredictable, given to bouts with the bottle) — when this young man materialized and busied himself with the matters at hand, to the visible pleasure of the old man and several others who took note. And so, through the day, a series of events unfolded. Through all this Fox were doing things to other Fox in the presence of still other Fox who variously gave off indications of surprise or its opposite, and sometimes approval or its opposite.

The sequence of events that Sunday was one instance of a kind of occasion which regularly occurs in the Fox community. Each year, during the summer months, there occurs a round of ceremonial feasts. This is the traditional Fox religion. There has been a Christian mission in the community for two generations. Perhaps half the families go to one or another of the various mission activities, but only two or three families attend the mission exclusively, rejecting the traditional ceremonies.

For these ceremonial purposes the Fox population sees itself as sorted into a series of ceremonial groups. These are named: Wolf, Thunder, War Chief, *et al.* Each ceremonial group owns one or more sacred packs, bundles of sacred items. These sacred items represent salient events in Fox history, remote and not so remote, for example, the skin of an animal or bird, a Union Jack, a weapon. The packs are protected and handled with respect. Each pack or set of packs, in turn, "owns" a ceremony, a set of songs, prayers, dances which requires most of a day to complete. At least once each summer, each ceremonial group acts as host to the remainder of the community and performs the ritual of its packs for the assembled community.

Members of each ceremonial group, when

the people who hold them and exercise the rights and duties which constitute them.

For an extended recent treatment of person and role, see Nadal (1951).

their group's turn to serve as hosts comes around, begin in the morning to bring quantities of meat, obtained at Tama stores, and varicolored Indian corn, grown in Fox gardens; men of the group tend the cooking in large cast-iron pots over open fires. Most of the community gather — men, women, and children — and sit and stand about under the trees or sit in cars. Most seem relaxed, chatty but not boisterous; children are scolded if their play becomes too loud. By midmorning, men from the host group begin singing inside a ceremonial house, a rectangular plank house with an earth floor. One of the singers has a small tight drum and others have notched sticks upon which they make sounds in rhythm as with rasps; they sit in a group, cross-legged, at one corner of the house on a waist-high bench that runs full length along each side. Small groups of other Fox of all ages drift in, listen awhile, then leave, to return later. With some of the songs there is restrained dancing — a line of men and women who move in a circle or dance in place. Between songs, singers may joke a bit at the expense of one whose voice cracked, or threatened to give out; there is some stretching of cramped legs. The songs go on for an hour or two, then the community is fed. Members of the host group have not eaten since the day before and do not eat now. Then more songs and more dancing. Finally, in late afternoon, the ritual ends. The community moves off. The hosts then sit down together and break their fast. Then they disband to their homes.

Such a generalized description of recurrent Fox behavior is possible. That it is possible implies, if it does not directly examine, certain dimensions of Fox social structure. Pete Bear, that Sunday, was some array of persons and was playing some array of corresponding roles. During this round of ritual occasion each year analogous sets of identities with analogous recommendations as to conduct are held up to each Fox. Most Fox,

most of the time, more or less adequately, perform accordingly. Thus, the possibility of such a summary description of these recurrent events.

But what in detail is this array of persons? These Fox ceremonial groups are, it happens, basically kinship groups. Pete Bear is, on such Sundays, sundry kinds of relative to the members of his ceremonial group and sundry kinds of relative (or, in rare instances, no relative at all) to each remaining Fox. This, to an observer, is possible: to identify Pete Bear as this or that kind of relative to each other Fox (and similarly every Fox with every other); to discover the conduct expected or preferred between such pairs of relatives; and to note any particular forms, specific to the occasion, of those recommended patterns of conduct; thus to elicit a code for conduct, that much of the Fox code which is based on kinship. Since the ceremonial groups are kinship groups, it could be that this alone of the total Fox code provides Fox the guidelines for carrying out these recurrent feasts. It *could* be. To discover how far this is true, it is necessary to look at Fox reckonings of kinship. We shall see that the Fox reckoning of kin and the patterns of conduct recommended between pairs of various Fox kinsmen do facilitate the ordering of the round of ceremonial feasts, but do not by themselves provide the total blueprint and indeed occasionally (as it were) mislead.

To calculate how one man is related to another, the Fox make different discriminations from those customary to most other Americans. Figure 6-1 shows some of the relatives of American males.

A hypothetical American male is called EGO, and certain of his relatives are named as he names them. This familiar manner of reckoning kin seems natural enough. But by stepping back, as it were, and looking again, it may occur that no self-evident, compelling reason exists for naming as identical

Selected American Kinship Terms

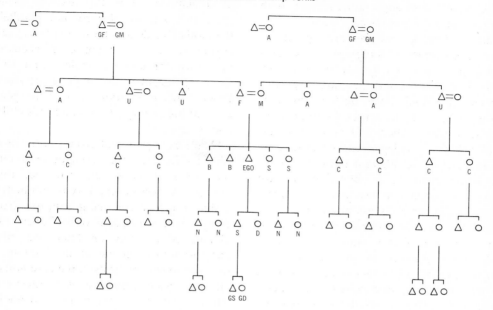

Selected Fox Kinship Terms, After Tax (1955b)

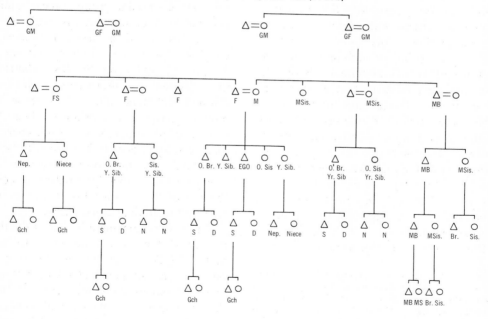

FIGURE 6-1

Selected American and Fox Kinship Terms

two distinct individuals: for example, one's mother's sister and one's father's sister, both of whom most Americans call "aunt."

Human kinship systems are systematic sets of such arbitrary lumpings and separations of persons variously connected to each other by genealogy and marriage. When a man calls two individuals by the same kinship term, he generally senses a similar set of obligations toward them and enjoys a similar set of rights or privileges, and when he calls two individuals by different terms he senses contrasting rights and obligations toward them. If a child can ask one aunt for a nickel, he can generally ask any aunt.

This American way of reckoning kin is bilateral, meaning that a man has the same kinds of kin connections with his mother's relatives as with his father's: aunts, uncles, cousins, and so on, identically on both sides.

Figure 6-1 also shows the same selected kin connections of any male Fox — EGO (read Pete Bear if you will) — but named according to Fox reckoning. Some relatives that most Americans lump together (father's sister and mother's sister — that is, "aunts") the Fox refer to by two different terms and thus think of as two different kinds of relatives; and some relatives that most Americans distinguish (father and his brother — "father" and "uncle") they consider as basically the same kind of relative and refer to them with a single term; similarly they use the same terms for those kin Americans separate as "brother" (or "sister") and "cousin"; and so on.[5] Of course, Americans do not confuse their father's sister and mother's sister when they call both aunt, nor do the Fox confuse a biological father and that

[5] Figure 6-1 employs a device which, without caution, misleads: we look to the Fox EGO's biological father, note a Fox term "X," translate that to the English term "father," and whenever the term "X" reappears we use again the English "father." Of course the semantic sense of the Fox word "X" and the English "father" cannot be the same. See below, p. 180.

man's brother; the terms denote common sets of obligations. Note also that the terms of these Fox kin are skewed, not parallel on the mother's side and father's side; especially curious is the line of common terms descending down through the males from EGO's mother's brother, to include persons in EGO's own generation, and in the generations of his children (and children's children and on down).

The Fox ceremonial groups carry responsibilities for the ceremonial observations of the Fox religion and are, we said, kinship groups. At birth every Fox is automatically assigned to a ceremonial group; for virtually every Fox it is the group of his father. (Individuals may, then or later, be ritually adopted into a second or third group, and thus participate as hosts in the ceremonies of all these groups, but that is another matter which I put aside; these men, so adopted, are considered to be only "borrowed," and their children are in turn members of the original ceremonial group, unless similarly adopted.) A group, then, is made up of a few old men, their respective sons and daughters, their sons' children (but not their daughters'), and so on: the descendants from those few old men down from each of them through the male line. Thus these ceremonial groups are patrilineal clans (plus those borrowed members). Since every Fox man or woman goes at birth into a clan, the total Fox population forms a series of clans.

Figure 6-2 is merely a rearrangement of the kin of the average Fox man, the same data that were diagramed earlier.

The new arrangement is that of the line of patrilineal kin, which descends from any male. EGO is put among his own (his father's) line of patrilineal kin; within this line of relatives there are several kinds of kin, distinguished by sex and generation. With these relatives, in terms of his various kin obligations to them and theirs to him, he cooperates in such things as the performance

EGO'S Patrilineal Kin:

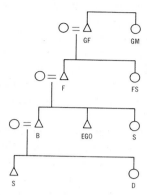

The Patrilineal Kin Group of EGO'S Mother:

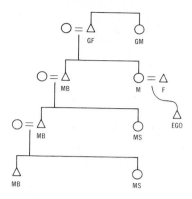

FIGURE 6-2

Two Patrilineal Lines of Fox Kin

of the clan's ceremonial duties. (Any clan, we saw, is made up of several such lines of kin — a few old men, their respective sons and daughters, their sons' sons and daughters, and so on.) But this Fox, EGO, looks out upon a second group, the patrilineal line of kin to which his mother belongs, also shown in Figure 6-2; she is a member (determined at her birth) of the clan of her father. These relatives are to EGO important but less centrally so; for example, during a clan ceremony being performed by EGO's clan, his mother and these her clansmen are jointly guests. For such reasons there is less necessity for EGO to distinguish among them; most of them are lumped according to sex as two kinds of kin.

In short, I have said that these kin terms, as selectively given here, seem to facilitate a sorting that goes on recurrently in Fox society. For certain purposes, the total population arranges itself into a set of clans. Each clan is in turn composed of a few lines of patrilineal kin. The terms with which any man — the hypothetical EGO in our charts — refers to his relatives reflects the way he sees them sorted into these patrilineal lines:

in the samples given, his own line (the line of his father and his children and his sons' children), and his mother's patrilineal line. We could look wider afield, to the patrilineal line of EGO's father's mother and that of his mother's mother; most of the relatives in both these lines are called grandfather and grandmother, irrespective of age.

In this manner, the Fox have elected, as it were, to arrange themselves as personnel to get certain tasks accomplished; one of those tasks is the performance of the round of clan ceremonial feasts. A clan feast is not an elaborate event in terms of the physical arrangements required. A day must be set; food must be collected; on the morning of the ceremony a fire must be made and the cooking begun; the guest clans must be fed; finally, the host clan must eat. All this requires some coordination of effort, but relatively simple *ad hoc* arrangements probably would, if necessary, get those tasks accomplished. *Ad hoc* arrangements there surely are, but the ceremonial groups need not depend solely on them.

Within EGO's lineal kin group each man is to EGO brother, or father, or grandfather,

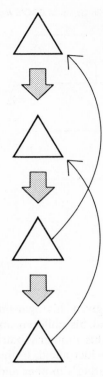

FIGURE 6-3

The Chain of Authority Within a Fox Patrilineal Line, Schematic

or son, or grandson. These represent together but three pairs of relationships: grandfather to grandson, father to son, brother to brother. Rights and duties are entailed in each paired relationship. Brothers are expected to be comradely, but to show some restraint (for instance, it is unseemly for brothers to talk about sex or to joke boisterously). A Fox son is expected to respect and obey his father; the father has the right to require his son, while the son remains young, to fast when he disobeys or otherwise behaves improperly, and this mildly disciplinary relationship seems to carry over into the son's adulthood. On the other hand, when a father exercises such mild duress against the son, the grandfather is expected to take the side of his grandson, to mitigate the duress and to give kindly advice; this is a more kindly supportive role.

These kinship relations appear to facilitate a nice balance within this body of men between discipline and unity, both of which are necessary if the group is to act effectively. In Figure 6-3 I simplify and imagine a line of men, father-to-son.

Between each father and son there is the firmer, mildly disciplinary relationship, represented by the heavy arrow. But each grandson can go to his grandfather for support, represented by the lighter arrows. As diagramed, EGO may feel it necessary to discipline his son; the son should yield, but may seek consolation from his grandfather; the grandfather does comfort, and may in turn, should it seem necessary, exercise his disciplinary authority as father to EGO. Clearly, influence and authority flow consistently in such a set of relations from old to young, but not through the exercise of constraint alone.

The suggestion is reasonably strong that if such a group of men are frequently joined in some common tasks and if they in some reasonable measure are guided in their behavior by the dictates of these kinship roles, the group will form an effective unit.

This is not the occasion for a complete examination of Fox kinship. But it must be briefly mentioned that Fox kinship falls conspicuously short of fully setting the stage for the round of ceremonial feasts. For example: a Fox clan consists of *several* lines of patrilineal kinsmen, but Fox kinship provides no systematic articulation among the several lines within a clan (as could be provided, for instance, if there were the device, frequently encountered in other groups, of considering those who are fellow clansmen but not of one's own line "clan-brothers"); and Fox kinship reckoning gives to certain relatives outside one's lineage the same kinship term as others inside the line (as mother's sister's husband is "father," mother's brother's wife is "father's sister," and mother's sister's children are "brothers" and "sisters," and there exist a host of "grandfathers" and "grandmothers"), yet during a clan feast, those "fathers," etc., inside one's line and clan are fellow hosts, while those others outside the line (and outside the clan) are guests.

We set out to identify Pete Bear (or any particular Fox) as this or that kind of relative to all other Fox; we set out to discover, that is, the many persons Pete Bear is and the many corresponding roles he might play, as established by the Fox mode of reckoning kin. During clan feasts *some* Fox code lays out the complex guidelines for Fox conduct. It is evident that that code is, in substantial part but only in part, a matter of kinship.

Fox social structure is, in fact, remarkably many sided. For the ceremonial purposes here briefly examined, the Fox see themselves sorted as to patrilineal line and clan; probably at an earlier time, the people saw themselves similarly sorted for political purposes, as during village councils; but beyond these, the patrilineal lines serve to order nothing. Beyond the clan feasts, the Fox have a series of other traditional religious practice. For some of these, men draw themselves into a few purely voluntary religious societies; for others, kinship again provides the ground plan, but without reference to the clans. For the array of economic tasks (wage-work, gardening, and so on), the Fox see themselves as sorted into relatively autonomous households, households variously put together according to whim and circumstance to include husband's relatives, or wife's relatives, or neither. For certain competitive sports (and earlier, apparently, in the competition for honors among warriors) the Fox sort themselves still another way which systematically crosscuts all the above: when a child is born he is assigned to one

of two categories, *token* or *gishgo,* the next child of that couple is assigned to the other category, the next to the first, and so on, hence the community and any grouping in it is divided approximately equally, and for any competition the sides are ready-made.

To elicit the primary data of Fox social structure is to describe all these — the full set of persons and roles deemed by Fox relevant in each recurrent event and, cumulatively, the full battery of persons and roles ascribable by Fox to themselves. As human societies go the Fox are a small community, and their social structure is therefore relatively simple. But the overwhelming complexity of even such a simple structure is evident. A Fox child knows that structure in large part; any Fox man knows virtually all of it. But an outside observer has his work cut out for him. It is clear that no observer has ever, for the Fox or for any human community, quite finished the task.[6]

DIMENSIONS OF SOCIAL STRUCTURE

In general, for the study of social structure descriptions of such primary data are required. The descriptive task has the following dimensions, irrespective of the human society involved:

Sex Categories

Every human society sorts its members into categories of sex. Two categories are usually employed, but frequently more (as in societies where men may with near or complete legitimacy assume female dress and occupations, or unusual women analogously adopt otherwise male tasks, either becoming in effect a third sex).

Age Categories

Every human society sorts its members as to age; as between societies, the categories

[6] For a brief description of Fox social structure, see Tax (1955b).

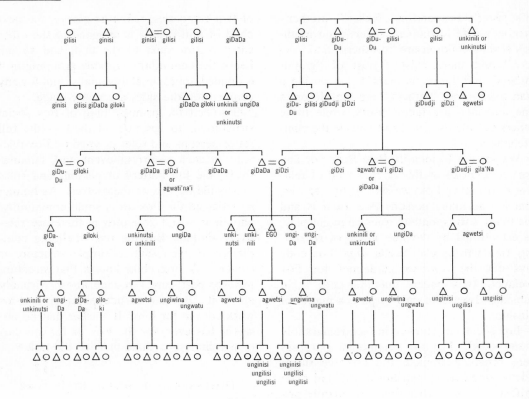

FIGURE 6-4 *

Cherokee Kinship System

Chart of Cherokee kinship terminology. Ego = male. For a female ego the same terms are used except for siblings, where *ungiDa* is used for "brother" and *ungilu'i* for "sister." Also, a woman classes her sister's children with her own. The father's brother's wife is called *agwati 'na' i* ("stepparent"), if she is of another clan than ego. The terms in the second descending generation follow the pattern.

* Reprinted from *Social Anthropology of the North American Tribes* by Fred Eggan by permission of The University of Chicago Press. Copyright © 1955 by the University of Chicago. Typographical errors in original corrected.

drawn are highly various and the boundaries more or less precise. Where the boundary is drawn precisely, the transition (as when a boy becames, in the public eye, a man) is usually marked by ritual, "rites of passage" in one form of that class of ritual. Usually age categories for males differ from those for females and the ritual marking of transitions usually differ for males as against females.

Kinship

All societies sort themselves as to kinship. Rarely are any two societies found to use altogether identical configurations of lumpings and separations. Conversely, a few basic patterns of configuration remarkably reoccur in all corners of the world. In gross outline these are: bilateral systems (as the

English and American system); generational systems, in which sibling terms are widely extended to cover all "cousins," parental terms almost as widely, grandparental terms very widely again, and so on (as among the Cheyenne); patrilineal systems (as, a case less confounded than the Fox, the Omaha Indians); matrilineal systems, which in configuration are rather like a mirror image of the patrilineal (as the Cherokee). To exemplify these, a diagram of the Cherokee matrilineal system follows; the sorting into matrilineal lines is evident, by the configuration of kin terms. All these types of kin configuration in turn break down into a host of subtypes.

The study of kinship has pre-empted the bulk of the energies of students of social structure, partly because kinship tends to be a major dimension of social structure in the small-scale societies usually studied by anthropologists.

Groupings

Every human society draws itself into certain groupings for certain recurrent purposes, other groupings for other purposes. Sex and age and kinship are used variously to determine membership in these. Membership may be ascribed to a man or be voluntary, but in either event his entry is almost always marked by and for the society at large in some evident fashion. Of all such groupings, the domestic family is everywhere important and almost everywhere overridingly so. To describe the constitution of the family is to discover at least these: rules as to courtship and marriage (including the boundaries of incest and exogamy as defined everywhere, but variously, in terms of kinship, and including patterns of marriage as monogamy, polygamy, polyandry, and including the mode of identifying, among all unions, some as marriages); rules as to the location of the residence of a new family (as with husband's parents or wife's brother, or

away from any other family, and so on); rules of assigning membership to offspring (generally, the matter of legitimacy as variously defined, and adoption); and, beyond the constitution of the family, the structural guidelines as to the general division of labor and other distribution of authority and responsibility, within the family and between families, as in the care and training of children. A battery of technical vocabulary has been devised to handle, with some precision, the major kinds of groupings which are found in small societies in all corners of the world: families are *elementary* if they mainly consist of parents and unmarried children, or *extended* if other relatives are included in the same household; *lineages* (patri- or matrilineal lines of kin) and *clans* we have briefly encountered; when clans are joined into pairs these are termed *phratries;* when all the lineal groups in a society are joined so as to form two major groups, these are *moieties;* when the society is otherwise divided into two halves (as the Fox), this is usually termed a *dual division;* and the like.[7]

In respect to all these sundry items of social structure, we are well advised to keep in mind the often dramatic and always telling degree in which men are "taken in hand" by their fellows, are made to be this or that social thing and in the process are handed a set of guidelines for subsequent public conduct. Engaged couples, it is clear, do not in most senses become man-and-wife at a moment: the process of mutual adjustment and mutual involvement began at first encounter, continues, and will continue indefinitely. Yet that special man says: "I now pronounce you . . ." and the pair become that, at that exact moment, effectively, in all public respects. It is a matter with which, as it were, the society wishes to take no chances and so removes the ambiguity (as much as that is possible with recalcitrant human materials).

[7] For a total array, still more or less standard, see Murdock (1949).

And so it tends to be, perhaps less dramatically in most instances, throughout the total battery of social "becomings" which every human experiences many times over in any day in every human society.

Thus the primary building blocks of any social structure: the battery of persons-and-roles, those public ideas carried in the heads of people which guide them in sorting and resorting themselves as personnel so as to get on with their work, play, and worship.

SOCIAL STRUCTURES AS SYSTEMS

All studies of social structure seek, not merely some listing of a society's battery of persons-and-roles, but some orderly arrangement of those items in their interconnections one with the other. A gross example is the division of labor within a household, as when men hunt and women tend the gardens. A social structure is a system of parts which mutually impinge. When societies are small in scale such systems tend strongly toward internal coherence. The main analytic task in studies of social structure has been to reveal those structures as systems.

Stepping thus beyond description to analysis, a new dimension of observable phenomena is usually — I think invariably — introduced: it becomes now crucial not only that one records that men hold in their heads certain ideas as to the public identities they may assume; now it becomes at junctures crucial whether men do in fact assume those appropriate identities and whether they do in fact act in conformity to the patterns of expected or preferred conduct. This would seem to call for new observation and would seem necessarily to lead to the reporting of frequencies of conforming and non-conforming behavior. Students of social structure have, however, generally taken a short-cut — through the assumption, roughly confirmed by impressionistic observation, that

most men most of the time do act more or less adequately according to the (relevant) expectations of their fellows.

In the earlier outline of Fox social structure we moved slightly beyond a mere listing of persons and roles; Fox kinship reflected, I suggested, a recurrent sorting of the Fox population into patrilineal groups (for ceremonial and, earlier, perhaps other purposes). That suggestion was already a half-step toward accounting for those separable "parts" — the kinship configuration and the ceremonial groupings — by showing their mutual fit. It is evident that unless the Fox did in fact aggregate as clans on concrete occasions (for one example), the suggestion would make little sense. We now move to certain studies which continue in the same vein.

This look at the variety of modes of interpretation must be most cursory. Excellent overviews exist, as Eggan (1955b), and Radcliffe-Brown (1950). In general, attempts at analysis have treated social structures as open systems, which is to say as *systems* within which "parts" affect other parts, but as *open* systems, affected by other things outside the system. In general, too, the sets of kinship terms, those configurations of lumpings and separations used as reflected in those verbal labels, play central parts in virtually all analyses.[8]

I shall here briefly treat one study of a particular people; suggest certain contrasting ways studies of this kind are intellectually exploited in comparative study in order to generate general propositions about social structures; name one recent development; and suggest one unresolved problem.

The study is Eggan's (1955a) analysis of Cheyenne (and Arapaho) kinship. The Cheyenne, as most other tribes who came to occupy the Great Plains, moved onto the Plains late, after the coming of Europeans

---

[8] This last is less consistently true in British than in American anthropology.

who had brought the horse to the New World. The horse permitted extensive exploitation of the buffalo herds and thus permitted the "filling up" of the Plains and the cultural florescence we know as Plains Indian culture. Tribes came into the Plains from east and west (the Cheyenne from the east) and, in spite of their diverse backgrounds, became culturally much alike, out of their common adaptation to life based on hunting the buffalo and war.

The terms of the Cheyenne kinship system are given by Eggan as in Figure 6-5. But to the Cheyenne, in the words of one Cheyenne informant, the kinship system is "just like three horizontal lines." To a man looking out, as it were, upon his array of relatives, the categories of relatives would appear as they are shown in Figure 6-6. Eggan further reports on the patterns of role conduct of such as father-to-son (and son-to-father), father-daughter, mother-son,

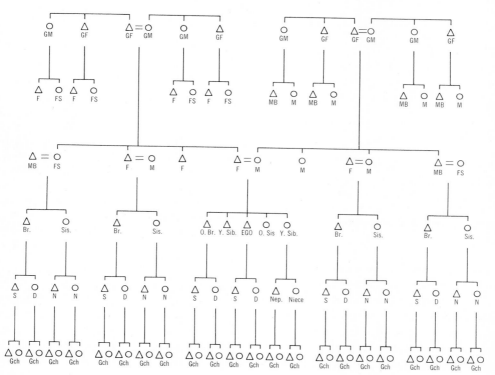

FIGURE 6-5 *

Cheyenne and Arapaho Kinship System

Basic terminological structure of the Cheyenne and Arapaho. In this chart, *F, M, FS, MB, GF,* etc., refer to father, mother, father's sister, mother's brother, grandfather, etc. . . . Ego = male. When Ego = female, the terms remain the same except that her sister's children are "son" and "daughter" and her brother's children are "nephew" and "niece," respectively.

* Reprinted from *Social Anthropology of the North American Tribes* by Fred Eggan by permission of The University of Chicago Press. Copyright © 1955 by the University of Chicago. Typographical errors in original corrected.

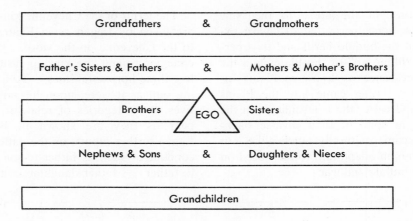

FIGURE 6-6

Cheyenne Kinship Categories, Schematic

mother-daughter, and so on, through the range of combinations, and, especially important, among brothers:

[It is preferred and expected that] two brothers work and play together, protect each other from danger, and revenge each other. An older brother [should look] after a younger brother; the latter should heed his brother's advice (Eggan 1955a:50–51).

Eggan then treats the organization of the household (in which the married couple typically live with the wife's family) and the analogous pattern of terms and role conduct among these in-laws. We here skip past that interesting discussion. Then Eggan returns to the above configuration of blood relatives, and briefly surveys the similarities and differences in these configurations throughout the whole plains area, and continues:

But from the standpoint of the Plains area it is perhaps . . . significant that tribes coming into the Plains with different backgrounds and social systems ended up with similar kinship systems. It seems probable that the conditions of Plains life favored a rather amorphous and mobile type of social organization which could vary to meet changing conditions.

Certain of these conditions have been indicated above — the uncertain character of subsistence and the need for protection. Leadership was also of uncertain and varying quality. Perhaps the outstanding adjustment to these conditions in the Plains is seen in the tremendous importance of the relationship of brothers. Everywhere in the Plains brothers formed the most dependable and solid group; among the Dakota "if a man has no brothers or cousins (and this was possible in the days of wholesale death from war parties) he says, 'I am related to nobody.' " Here is a basis for the wide recognition which brotherhood receives in the kinship system. The Cheyenne and Arapho extend the relationship to all cousins, and fictitiously extend it through the institution of "friends" and by means of common society affiliations. The Kiowa and Kiowa-Apache do likewise, a group of brothers assuming special importance among the Kiowa. We have seen that the Dakota consider cross-cousins as "brothers," even though they are segregated in the terminology, and there is some evidence that the Plains-Cree and Plains-Ojibway likewise attached more importance to the concept of "brothers" than did their relatives to the northeast. The Piegan have carried this principle even farther, so that all collateral relatives, not only in ego's generation but in the first ascending and descending generations as well, are considered "brothers" (or "sisters"). The Crow Indians furnish a crucial instance. Fundamentally, their system of kinship seems to have been in the process of changing from a pure Crow type, such as their close relatives the Hidatsa possess, to a "Generation" type, such as the Cheyenne and Arapaho have developed. Part of this process was the extension of the sibling relationship to cross-cousins. Both the Crow and the Hidatsa also extended the term for brother to the mother's brother and sister's son, though the Mandan preferred to use separate terms.

It is possible, therefore, that the relationship of brothers, because of its importance in Plains life, was one of the factors modifying kinship systems in the direction of a "Generation" type. If this is so, this factor and others may be the important agents in bringing about observed uniformities, and hence it seems worthwhile to look for and isolate them, rather than to attribute the uniformity to simple diffusion (Eggan 1955a:93–95).

What were the critical survival activities on the Plains? Hunting buffalo and war. Both require stamina and athletic prowess; both therefore fall to men in their prime — one generation. Both are risky and both require close timing and close coordination of effort, if there is to be optimum result; both thus require that the involved young men mutually regard and trust one another.[9] It seems evident that the relationships among brothers, as these were variously patterned among the Cheyenne and these other tribes prior to their moves onto the Plains, served as a kind of model; and that that relationship fit the new needs and was extended to embrace others heretofore called "cousins," and so on.

The Cheyenne in particular came originally from the area which is presently Minnesota.[10] There, life circumstance put a premium on the relationship between a man in one generation and another in the next. (There, the game, as deer, did not run in large herds and could be hunted by lone hunters or small groups, including men well along in years. Intimate, detailed knowledge of a relatively small tract and its flora and fauna was critical, the kind of knowledge which takes generations to accumulate and which, to be passed, say, from father to son, requires some years of tutelage.) Thus the configuration of kin, though its detail cannot be well known, was probably not vastly unlike what we have seen among the Fox. In Minnesota, there was a premium on accumulated knowledge of minute detail and no premium on unusual strength, and on the Plains there was less premium on such a fund of detailed knowledge and great premium on athletic stamina; in Minnesota, probably, there was a kinship system which sorted men into lineal groups, and on the Plains, a system which sorted men according to generation and which made brothers of all related men in each generation.

We thus see an array of structural facts tending toward internal cohesion, a system of mutually impinging parts; but we see those facts tending toward this particular system, rather than some other, in virtue of the effects of nonstructural facts as buffaloes, horses, and competing alien groups.

THE COMPARATIVE STUDY OF SOCIAL STRUCTURE

Over a century ago, it was becoming evident to students of non-Western men that certain basic configurations of kinship kept turning up in all quarters of the world.[11]

---

[9] Of course a tightly hierarchical organization with great powers of reward and punishment (as modern armies) would also serve; but no American Indian tribes, and perhaps no small-scale society in any quarter, happened upon that solution.

[10] I go now beyond Eggan's study.

[11] Of course, the statistical chance is nil of any such complex set of facts occurring twice by accident (that is, without being caused by some recurring condition); and these very configurations occur scores of times, on all continents.

Morgan (see above) launched a worldwide compilation of kinship terminological systems in the middle 1800's, as one dramatic example. This kind of experience was irresistible and the study of social structure has thus been comparative, from the outset. Beyond the analysis of any single society, the aim has been to compare several or all societies.

Eggan himself, and in the passages quoted above, exemplifies one mode of comparative analysis. Elsewhere he emphasized:

. . . the importance of controlling the comparative framework in as many directions as possible, so that variations in one set of factors or phenomena can be matched with other changes . . . (1955b:550),

and has termed this the method of "controlled comparison."

Earlier, Julian Steward (1955) similarly set out, on a wide-ranging scale, to inquire as to the structural effects of the exploitable ecological base. He makes note (as does Eggan in respect to the Plains) of the kinds of natural resources and the technological means available to a people for that exploitation; thence he moves (as Eggan) to note the various premiums on size of the group and relationships within the group entailed in those subsistence tasks; and (as Eggan) he sees the social structure as a kind of precipitate, an institutionalization of the-group-at-that-work. Around the world, Steward finds these basic forms of society: autonomous families; patrilineal bands; composite hunting bands; clan-organized societies; and complex urbanized societies. Steward calls his realm of work "cultural ecology." [12]

George Peter Murdock's *Social Structure* (1949) is still grander in scale. Murdock embraces data from 250 societies and sets out to put to statistical test many suggested connections between some one structural

[12] See Chapter 18 for an extensive discussion of Steward's ecological approach.

fact and another. We earlier discussed certain features of Fox kinship and briefly alluded to analogous features of Cherokee kinship. To illustrate Murdock's manner of comparative analysis, let us watch him handling features of these same phenomena; one is advised to refer back, as he reads, respectively, to the Cherokee and Fox systems as diagramed earlier.

Theorem 20: In the presence of exogamous matri-lineages, matri-sibs, or matri-moieties, unless exogamous patrilineal kin groups are also present, kinship terms for FaSi tend to be extended to FaSiDa, and those for BrDa to MoBrDa.

This theorem is conclusively validated in Table 41 by similar high positive coefficients of association with maximal reliability.

Parallel reasoning accounts for cross-cousin terminology of the Omaha type, in which the children of FaSi are classed with SiSo and SiDa, and the children of MoBr with the siblings of one's mother. Omaha nomenclature is normally found in societies with patrilineal descent. Under this rule, MoBr and MoBrSo are members of the same kin groups, as are MoSi and MoBrDa, and the similarity resulting from their social participation favors the extension of kinship terms across generation lines. The reciprocal terms for SiSo and SiDa tend to be extended to the opposite cross-cousins, the children of FaSi, partly by analogy and partly because paternal cross-cousins and sororal nieces and nephews are all children of the women of Ego's own patri-sib or patri-lineage.

Theorem 21: In the presence of exogamous patrilineages, patri-sibs, or patri-moieties, unless exogamous matrilineal kin groups are also present, kinship terms for MoSi tend to be extended to MoBrDa, and those for SiDa to FaSiDa.

This theorem is decisively substantiated by the data in Table 42.

Most of the cases in Tables 41 and 42 of the occurrence of Crow or Omaha terminology

FIGURE 6-7

Statistical Measures of the Effects of Lineal Descent on Selected Kin Terms *

TABLE 41

Pairs of Relatives	Exclusive Matrilineal Descent with Exogamy		Patrilineal, Double, or Bilateral Descent		Statistical Indices	
	Same Term	Different Terms	Same Term	Different Terms	Q	X^2
FaSiDa-FaSi	21	29	8	181	+ .88	1000
MoBrDa-BrDa	15	33	7	181	+ .84	1000

TABLE 42

Pairs of Relatives	Exclusive Patrilineal Descent with Exogamy		Matrilineal, Double, or Bilateral Descent		Statistical Indices	
	Same Term	Different Terms	Same Term	Different Terms	Q	X^2
MoBrDa-MoSi	21	68	3	144	+ .87	1000
FaSiDa-SiDa	24	66	6	143	+ .79	1000

* Reprinted with permission of The Macmillan Co. from *Social Structure* by George Peter Murdock. Copyright 1949, The Macmillan Company.

with other than the expected type of social organization are accountable on other grounds. Thus the Pawnee and Siriono have Crow terms with matrilocal residence; the Manus, Pentecost, and Yuchi have Crow terms with double descent; the Fox have Omaha terms with non-exogamous patri-sibs, and the Takelma with patrilocal residence. The only genuinely negative cases are the Bachama, Koranko, and Seniang, who have Crow terms with patrilineal descent and patrilocal residence.

Only about one third of the exclusively matrilineal societies in our sample are characterized by Crow terminology for cross-cousins, and only about one fourth of the patrilineal societies have Omaha terminology. This reflects the fact, already noted, that the inherent distinction of generation, which must be overridden to produce them, is the most resistant, or has the strongest relative efficacy, of all such differentials. To overcome it presumably requires both time and the full elaboration of unilinear institutions. This accords with the hypothesis advanced by White that Crow or

Omaha terms tend to appear only when a system of unilinear kin groups is fully developed "and comes to exert its influence more and more upon the social life of the tribe." †

Murdock finally undertakes to inquire from the same sample of 250 societies how and by what causes various forms of social structure develop, one out of the other.

Most recently, beginning in the mid-1950's, an older interest among students of social structure re-emerged in some force. Kroeber, and later Tax (1955a), had held that any kinship system is a set of categories of mind having an internal "logic" of some sort to men who lived that system, and that, beyond any other modes of explanation, it is necessary somehow to get at that implicit logic. Goodenough (1956a) and Lounsbury (1956), armed with the highly technical sys-

† Reprinted with permission of The Macmillan Co. from *Social Structure* by George Peter Murdock. Copyright 1949, The Macmillan Company.

tems of notation and inference appropriate for computers, opened the field of inquiry termed "componential analysis." They wished to get away from certain distortions wrought by using genealogical diagrams (and English terms) as the basic points of reference in describing a people's kinship system. They wanted instead to arrive at the few distinctions (as, say, generation, sex, and so on) which, in some hierarchical arrangement, actually define the range of application of each kin term as used by a people — that is, the "components" which define a given term, according to the usage of that people. Thus, in America the term "father" is defined by noting that it is applied to males, one generation above ego, directly ancestral to ego; father is applied only to individuals meeting all three components in the definition. Further, it seemed possible to define each American kin term by sundry combinations of the same three components.[13] The guiding notion has been that by such analysis one gets at the semantics of a term like "father" as established by the usage of that people.[14]

CONCLUSION

The unresolved matter to be mentioned here revolves around the connections between the way a people think and the way they actually act, in respect to these public identities and public expectations or preferences as to conduct.

But there is a prior difficulty. We have in these pages referred too casually to "shared public notions" as to the array of identities and the array of corresponding notions about conduct. *Shared?* What about heterogeneity of mind? It is probably true that, when societies are small in scale, the degree of likeness of mind (in these respects) is large. But even in these societies, change is always underway in *some* dimension of the social structure and at *some* rate, and during such change minds are necessarily not alike. Minds are even more unalike as one moves from tribal peoples to peasants, and dramatically so as one moves to urban societies. *Public?* We seem to have suggested that there is little risk in discerning the public cues given off by members of a society, as distinguished from the perhaps involuntary winces and grins which stem, for example, from private interests in the matter, interests not necessarily congruent with the public code. One should doubt that the matter is so safe, until one is told precisely how such public cues were and can be recognized. Thus, there remain substantial difficulties in eliciting a people's code.

Anthropology has been even more casual in its handling of the degrees of correspondence between such codes and the way in which peoples actually behave. It must here suffice to recall the phrase often used above, that roles are patterns of "preferred or expected" conduct, and to note that those two words create four boxes (at least four, since there are degrees of both): some patterns of role conduct are, by a people, both preferred and expected; other patterns are expected of many but not necessarily preferred; and still other patterns of role conduct are the obverse, preferred but not often expected. All three, distinguished or not, might find their ways, as role conduct, into a given study of social structure. (The fourth box, conduct neither preferred nor often expected would, most likely, be put down as some form of psychological "deviance," if noted at all.) Students of social structure have tended to translate directly from a people's ideas about behavior to the behavior itself, by assuming that most men most of the time conform (and by further noting that, when men fail to conform, the society has this or that cor-

[13] Two sexes, five generations, and three kinds of lineal relationship were employed.
[14] See Wallace and Atkins (1960) for an excellent overview of componential analysis, its successes and inherent problems.

rective or compensating measure). This assumption is clearly risky in all but the first box. Other students, perhaps of more cautious bent, have tried to count actual behavior (as the frequency of married couples actually living with the wife's parents, where that is the preferred arrangement in some society); such counting is clearly desirable in confirming that a preferred pattern *is* in fact expectable, and counting seems quite necessary in those two boxes wherein preferences and expectations fail to run together.

However, in the longer run, there is but one way to handle adequately these matters of conformity: by directly confronting the question of how public preferences or expectations enter, together with many other things, the *total* motivational systems of men, and how all that together determines conformity or its absence. And to do that requires leaving the notion of person behind and organizing one's analysis instead in terms of the notion of individual; see Spiro (1961) and Gearing (1962). Thus for this task, studies of social structure provide only some of the data and none of the method.

CHAPTER 7 discusses the convergence between cultural anthropology and economics. Although anthropological concern with the economic life of primitive and peasant communities is an old one, only recently have we seen a really studied effort aimed at testing the utility of the theories of Euro-American economists in non-Western cultural settings. While part of the convergence represents purely scholarly, scientific efforts to improve knowledge, it stems also in part from our Western commitment to the economic and cultural development of the many societies still isolated from the transformations of the Industrial Revolution. Thus the questions Professor Bradfield asks about Chimbote and the answers he obtains have a relevance beyond pure theory, for here is described one kind of anthropology applied to problems of practical concern. What is the nature and workings of non-Western economic systems? This question is nearly as old as anthropology. What do we do with Euro-American economic theory when we confront economic systems wherein the scheme of production is simple (all men being nearly equal in their economic skills), yet wherein the scheme of allocation is exceedingly complex, quite the converse of the situation in France or the United States? What different types of allocation systems can be discovered? Is man, or, for that matter, even Western man, indeed rational in his economic calculations? How do societies, to borrow Professor Gearing's phrasing in the preceeding chapter, sort themselves into separate structures for production or exchange and control of wealth? Why are some societies capable of swift and comprehensive adaptations to the impact of Western economic enterprises and development programs? Why are others exceedingly resistant to change? These are some of the issues brought forth in this chapter, in which the author shows that although we can pose relevant questions, firm answers are not always easy to come by.

THE AUTHOR received his education at Cornell University where he was trained, first in economics, then in anthropology. He has taught at Pennsylvania State University and is presently Associate Professor of Anthropology at Kalamazoo College. His research interests include economic and cultural development, and the cross-cultural study of the urbanization and industrialization process and of economic systems. He is the author of several articles dealing with these problems in Latin-American settings.

7

Economic Anthropology

STILLMAN BRADFIELD

Kalamazoo College

INTRODUCTION

As the title suggests, economic anthropology combines the methods, concepts, and interests of the anthropologist with those of the economist. The title also suggests that it is a branch of anthropology rather than of economics. Although it is sometimes difficult in practice to separate one from the other, at least at a conceptual level it is useful to distinguish between two viewpoints on the study of the economic life of primitive and peasant peoples. One approach uses the concepts and methods of cultural or social anthropology to study the economic life of a particular group of people. In this case, the field is clearly one of the many subfields of anthropology. The other approach employs the concepts and methods of the economist, to the extent that this is possible, in studying primitive peoples. I suppose we could term this second approach "anthropological economics."

The two approaches serve different purposes. In the first, the concern is mainly to record fully the economic life of a people and to integrate knowledge of their economic system with other aspects of their culture. The primary intent may well be a general ethnographic study of a people, and their economic life is studied as only one part of the whole culture. Or, the focus may be on the economy itself, with data from other aspects of culture brought in to permit a fuller understanding of the economic system. The second approach is used mainly to test the validity of economic concepts originally developed in the industrial societies of the Western world in a wide variety of cultures, and to integrate the principles of economics of primitive peoples with those of modern nations. Both approaches are alike insofar as each uses many of the standard categories of Western economic theory.

In the first section of this chapter, we will look at economic anthropology from the viewpoint of an anthropologist, and see how the subject reflects the interests of that science. In the next section, the second approach will be used to indicate the way in which the interests of the economist are integrated with the data of the anthropologist. In the final section we will examine in some detail procedures, problems, and possibilities of field work in economic anthropology in a particular place.[1]

ECONOMIC ANTHROPOLOGY AS ANTHROPOLOGY

Anthropologists have been interested in economic life since the beginning of the discipline. This is to be expected, since a major part of any people's time and effort is necessarily spent on economic pursuits. Given the crucial relationship between economic life and the survival and growth of a people, we would also expect that economic aspects of culture would be integrated in some fashion with many other aspects of their culture.

One of the earliest manifestations of interest in economic anthropology derived from the theory of evolution. It was thought that since man had evolved biologically he must have also evolved culturally. Obviously, there were marked differences between modern industrial economies and their associated cultures and the economies and cultures of peoples in the non-Western world. It was argued that there were definite sequences in development from simple hunting and gathering societies to herding, hand agriculture, plow agriculture, and industrialization. The key element in such schemes was technology. Given a certain technology, it was argued, only certain economic and social arrangements were possible. Theories of evolution and ecology are still being revised to

bring them into harmony with the facts as we now know them. For example, Steward has attempted to show the functional interrelationships that exist between a particular environment and the culture that has developed to exploit the environment. Moreover, he has shown that in some places and periods, there has been an evolutionary development through a series of parallel stages. Since there is no record of contact at this period of time between the old and the new worlds, these developments are presumed to be evolutionary (Steward 1955).

No one presumes today that cultures move through a neat series of stages, from lower to higher. It has been recognized for some time that one of the major differences between biological evolution and cultural evolution is that biological evolution is essentially substitutive, whereas cultural evolution is mainly additive. Peoples who depend mainly upon hand agriculture for their subsistence may also hunt and collect. While the United States is undoubtedly in the industrial stage, all the other stages can also be found, although they may only be sports, rather than important sources of livelihood. Commercial agriculture and fishing are highly mechanized in our society, but hunting, fishing, and collecting are still carried out by "primitive" hand techniques, mainly for sport. Similarly, hand agriculture is still practiced in home flower and vegetable gardens. Herding is still of considerable importance in some parts of the country, and plow agriculture using animal draft power is also still found in some sections.

Early anthropological field work revealed an enormous range of human behavior and also that the societies of interest to the anthropologist were being drastically and swiftly changed by contact with the West. Partly from the fear that their subject matter was disappearing, anthropologists became concerned with the rapid collection of ethnographic material on non-Western peoples

[1] The study reported on in the fourth part of this chapter was carried out under the auspices of the Cornell-Peru Project, with support from the National Institute of Mental Health, research grant No. M–5558, and fellowship No. 5 FI MH–17, 358–02.

before the aboriginal culture was lost. Their interests included all aspects of these cultures, and therefore a good deal of descriptive material on economic life was gathered. Unfortunately, a large part of this early data is of limited value, as much of what was assumed to be the description of economic life was in fact limited to, or confused with, a description of the technology and material aspect of life, rather than with the organization of men to produce and distribute these things, and the principles involved in their economic organization.

When the early evolutionary classifications of cultures were found to be unsatisfactory a new theoretical system was developed. Working with artifacts from American Indian tribes, Boas and Wissler found a marked similarity between artifacts and their associated culture traits and particular geographic areas. The culture-area classification was based on the argument that similar geographic environments present the same climate and resources to the peoples in that area. Since all people have to adapt themselves to their environments, people within the same physical environment are more likely to achieve similar adaptations than peoples in other habitats. The original migrants into an area such as the eastern woodlands of North America had to develop the ability to survive in this new environment. Other Indians, coming later, could pick up the necessary traits by means of diffusion, instead of having to develop them independently. Coming much later, Europeans learned some things from the Indians already in the area, such as the cultivation of particular crops. However, since much of the European technology was useful in the new environment, they did not have to abandon their own technology and learn that of the Indians. In some other areas, Europeans found it necessary to take over much more of the native culture. In the Amazon Basin, for instance, European agricultural technology could not be adapted to local conditions, and the Europeans had to learn how to survive there from the natives of the area. Steward (1955) and Forde (1963) continued to work with the culture-area classifications in an effort to clarify the interrelationships between geographic environment and culture. Both the evolutionary classifications and the culture-area classifications are of interest here since they indicate the importance anthropologists have always assigned to economic life in the portrayal of total culture.

Malinowski was among the first anthropologists to do serious, intensive, firsthand work on the economic life of a single primitive group. Upon analysis of his material on the Trobriand Islanders, he did indeed find a close functional interrelationship between their exchange systems and other aspects of culture — particularly their system of magic. But rather than argue that the nature of the interrelationship was from the economic to the noneconomic aspects of culture, he specifically pointed out the ways in which the magic system affected economic activity (Malinowski 1922, 1935). He found magical rites associated with the principal economic activities of gardening, fishing, and trade. Knowledge of magic itself could be regarded as property, since it could not only be inherited by a son from his father, but could also be purchased (Malinowski 1961:192). The important point Malinowski made was that the Trobrianders regarded magical rites as an essential part of economic undertakings when it was necessary to assure the outcome. He noticed an absence of magical activity in inner lagoon fishing where they regarded their technology as sufficient (1955:30–31).

Before the anthropologist can begin to integrate the economy of a people with the rest of its culture, he must undertake an analysis of the economy itself. A recommended procedure has been to describe the economy of a primitive or peasant group in terms of the traditional problems of the field of economics. These problems can be conviently grouped under four headings: production, distribution, exchange, and consumption (Committee of the Royal Anthropological Institute, Chapter 6). In describing the solutions of these four basic problems, anthropologists have normally used terminology already developed in the field of economics. The production problem can be broken down into a description of the resources available to the group, the resources utilized and their relative proportions, and the means used to produce certain amounts of particular goods. The anthropologist is also concerned with the way the people are organized for economic production, what technology and equipment they use, the amount and kind of labor used in the production of goods and services, and the amounts and kinds of capital available and used. The distribution problem is concerned with the nature and functioning of the reward system connected with economic activity. On what basis do a people determine who gets what share of the goods and services produced by the society? Can the system be described in terms of wages paid for work performed, interest paid for the use of capital, rent paid for the use of land or equipment and buildings, and profits for the owner of the means of production? These Western economic concepts are useful in some peasant societies, but are not generally useful in describing less monetized economic systems, in which there may be no local equivalents to such concepts as wages and profits.

The exchange problem has received a great deal of attention from anthropologists because of the great variety of principles and mechanisms involved in trade in primitive and peasant economics (for instance, Bohannan and Dalton 1962). Anthropologists want to know how the goods and services produced are exchanged. All societies must have some system of allocation, since some sort of division of labor, at least that based on differences of age and sex, is found universally. What types of goods are exchanged in the market, and what is the medium of exchange? Do they use money, barter, or some other system? How important is the exchange of gifts? In many societies there are different spheres of exchange in which different goods are handled by different principles and with different substances serving as money (Polanyi 1959). Finally, some attention must be devoted to the question of how the value of a particular good or service is determined. For instance, do prices of some goods respond to changes in supply and demand, while other prices remain constant?

The consumption problem is concerned with the final purposes or uses for the products of the society. How much is consumed relative to the amount saved? If there is "conspicuous consumption," what forms does it take in this society? Of the amount that is saved, the anthropologist would want to know whether and how it is invested, or hoarded. In what forms is wealth accumulated? What is the real income of the different groups in this society?

Although in some senses the anthropologist is interested in the same problems as the economist, he frequently wants this economic data, not as an end in itself, but to integrate with the rest of his data on the culture of the group in question to understand the functioning of the total culture. To this end, the frame of reference must be widened beyond the categories traditionally used in economics. In addition to economic organization, anthropologists usually assume that there are nine other universal categories of culture that apply to all human groups. These are language, technology and material culture, social organization, political organization, religion, recreation, fine arts, knowledge, and education (including socialization). If it is true that economic organization and its associated behavior makes up a core institution in a society, we would expect to find a connection between these various aspects of culture and economic behavior. The nature of the influence of one upon the other could flow in either or both directions. That is, economic behavior can in many cases be regarded as the independent variable influencing the other categories of cultures, or dependent variables. On the other hand, there are many cases in which we might find that the economic organization is best thought of as the dependent variable, responding to a stimulus from some other area of culture. In other cases, it is not possible to specify which is the independent variable. In these instances, there is an interaction between variables and dominance cannot clearly be assigned to one or the other.

The relationship between economics and some of the other categories of culture is either unclear or unimportant or both. Very few observations have been made on the interrelationship between language and economic behavior beyond the notion that vocabulary size varies with the complexity of culture. There may be a relationship between vocabulary and perception of economically important items in the culture. For instance, the Bedouin use many words for "camel." Perhaps, because it is crucial to their economy, small differences in color, size, and other physical characteristics appear to them to warrant separate names. Little work has been done to specify the relationship between customarily used grammatical forms and values and attitudes associated with economic activity. One might hypothesize a correlation between a relatively high incidence of the passive form of the verb and avoidance of responsibility for one's actions. Collaborative research of linguists and other behavioral scientists now under way should soon shed light on the interrelationships between language and economic behavior. In some other areas, such as recreation and fine arts, the economic anthropologist might be interested only in the extent to which these aspects of culture use the time, energy, and resources of the people.

The other categories of culture are of more direct relevance to the economic anthropologist. The technology and material culture of a people are so intertwined with their economic life that they can be treated as separate only conceptually. The problem here is to specify the techniques and the tools with which they deal with their environment. It is both unfashionable and scientifically indefensible to believe in any one-factor determinisms. Yet, we probably have rejected economic determinism with greater reluctance than other determinisms. The close interrelations between the knowledge of how to deal with the environment, the toolkit used in doing so, and the human organization required to do so are obvious. But these in turn are also related to other aspects of culture. The type of economy a people possesses places limitations on the type of social organization they have. For instance, the relationship between the technology and the environment of a hunting band precludes the possibility of large, settled villages, dense populations, and a series of other associated traits. In a more narrow sense, a good deal of work has been done on specific aspects of social organization, such as kinship and the economy. This is particularly true with respect to the four basic economic problems. In many societies the anthropologist cannot understand the way in which these four basic problems of production, distribution, exchange, and consumption are dealt with without first thoroughly understanding the kinship structure.

The system of political authority is normally little elaborated in hunting and gathering bands, but as the complexity of the economic organization increases, the complexity of the authority system normally does also. The interrelationship here with the rest of the social organization is also close. Differentiation into social classes with a definite hierarchy seems to require a more productive economy than is normally possible with a hunting and gathering base. Similarly, the support of specialist personnel who do not produce their own food requires an economic base which provides more than a bare subsistence for the food-producers. The causal relationship also runs in the opposite direction. Authorities can also use their power to affect directly the ways in which the society deals with its basic economic problems.

Social scientists have long been impressed with the ties between religion and economic behavior (for example, Weber 1930; Malinowski 1922, 1935; Tawney 1926). Economists who are trying to bring about economic development in many of the underdeveloped countries today are frustrated in their efforts by what they consider the adverse effects of religion on economic growth. In many areas, religion proscribes certain economic activities and prescribes others. Perhaps the most serious aspect for economists is that in some countries religious practices lead to a substantial diversion of energy, capital, and other resources into "nonproductive" investment and consumption. These nonproductive activities include such things as the construction of temples; and time, energy, and resources are spent in the celebration of religious holidays. To the extent that resources are thus used, they are not available for economic development.

In recent years, social scientists of various disciplines have become increasingly interested in the relationships between economic behavior and the state of knowledge of a people, particularly scientific knowledge. Similarly, they are concerned with education and socialization processes, particularly as they relate to the inculcation of values and attitudes which affect economic behavior.

People act at least partly on the basis of the assumptions they make about the physical universe and other people. These assumptions are for the most part learned from other people in their culture. A considerable amount of work has been done recently by anthropologists on the relationships between value-orientations and economic behavior (for example, Florence Kluckhorn 1956a). This is one of those areas mentioned earlier in which it is extremely difficult to trace a simple causal sequence. Do Americans tend to take the view that man is dominant over nature because they possess a technology that affords a good deal of effective control over the vagaries of nature, or do they have this technological control because they had a prior faith in their ability to gain control over nature through the development of modern technology? If the fatalistic position that man is subjugated to nature is more common to peasants all over the world, is it because they do not have an effective technology, or do they not have the technology because they have a fatalistic outlook? The causal relationship probably runs both ways — fatalism leads to a lack of effort to improve the technology, and a failure to improve control over nature reinforces the fatalistic attitude. Psychologists have also turned their attention to the relationship between value-orientations and economic development in the underdeveloped areas. McClelland (1961) urges that differences in the amount of need-achievement between different populations are directly related to both the emphasis given to economic activities and to success in economic development. Breer and Locke (1965), on the other hand, take the position that values and attitudes are in large part the *result* of task experience. That is, new situations may require new behavior, and if the new behavior is found to be rewarding, values and attitudes will change to support or rationalize the new behavior.

The methods used by the economic anthropologist vary considerably from those used by the economist. When working with nonliterate peoples, the anthropologist has little or no access to written history, documents, records, or statistics. His methods are essentially those of the ethnographer. He learns what he can from direct observation of people's behavior. Beyond that he must interview his respondents to find out what they think and the reasons they give for their behavior. In recent years projective tests and other research techniques have been used in working with nonliterate peoples, but reliance is still mainly on observation and interviewing. As anthropologists work more in peasant societies, and the urban centers in basically peasant societies, they are able to find more statistics and historical documents which aid in understanding the economic process through time.

In this section we have briefly examined one approach to the study of economic life of primitive and peasant societies. This approach involved using the problems and categories recognized in economics in conjunction with the concepts and methods of cultural and social anthropology. The emphasis has been on the description of economic life and its integration with the rest of culture. This functional integration can be seen by systematically relating economic behavior to the other universal categories of culture. The approach has largely reflected the interests and methods of anthropologists. We turn now to the approach that leans more toward the interests of the economists.

THE ECONOMICS IN ECONOMIC ANTHROPOLOGY

Relatively few anthropologists have shown much inclination to attempt systematically to apply Western economic theory to primitive peoples. The few who have tried to do so have in recent years been joined by a few

sociologists and economists (for example, Polanyi *et al.,* 1957; Firth 1939, 1946, 1959, 1964; Herskovits 1952; Tax 1953; Belshaw 1955; Nash 1958; Bohannan 1963; Dalton 1961, 1965; Smelser 1963; Salisbury 1962; McHale 1962). In attempting to use modern economic theory in primitive economies, the investigators have made several approaches with different results. Some have tried to apply the categories of Western economic theory to primitive institutions, and, in some cases, have forced the data to conform to the concepts. Others have tried to test the cross-cultural validity of economic theory. Is Western economic theory really useful in analyzing a primitive economy? In many ways, Herskovits used the first approach, employing the traditional concepts of economics to describe the workings of primitive economic institutions (Herskovits 1952). Others, such as Polanyi, Bohannan, and Dalton, have challenged the utility of Western economic theory when applied to primitive economic systems. Part of the reason for the different approaches and the different results derives from different conceptions of what the economic anthropologist is trying to do.

Burling has considered five different definitions of the field of economics as it applies to primitive societies. He argues that most anthropologists have in fact tried to study the same areas of life in primitive societies which economists study in Western society. Since only certain types of goods and services are priced in our market system, and economists are primarily concerned with prices, the equivalents of these sorts of goods and services are what anthropologists study in primitive societies. Burling feels this is an ethnocentric approach that cannot yield useful results since the phenomena studied are a result of the workings of the price system itself, and the categories cannot be fruitfully applied where there is either no price system or one of limited applicability. He also rejects the definition that economics is concerned with the production, distribution, and consumption of goods and services, because it does not specify which goods and services are truly of economic importance and which are not. The definition Burling favors is one involving a maximization postulate. Here it is presumed that time, energy, and other means for achieving ends are limited and ends are of differing order of importance. Therefore, man has to choose how to allocate his resources so as to maximize goal attainment. Burling recognizes that this considerably alters the subject, since it means that in all behavior there is an economic aspect. This being the case, there is no such thing as economic behavior per se, but an economizing, or choice-making element in all behavior (Burling 1962). If this definition were to be accepted by economic anthropologists there would be little possibility of comparing Western and non-Western economics, as there would be no common base.

The problems of delimiting the field and specifying its central issues are not the only ones facing the economic anthropologist. Increasing attention has been devoted to the problem of applying economic theory to the economic behavior of primitive peoples. Polanyi called attention to the problem by showing that there are really two definitions of "economic," and only one applies to primitive economies. The first, or substantive, meaning of the term "economic" refers to providing goods and services to supply social and biological wants. This definition applies at all times and places, since all peoples have to use resources to maintain themselves. But this definition does not specify how people do this, either in terms of their social organization or the specific technology used. The formal definition of "economic" implies economizing; that is, people strive to attain their ends with a minimum effort. Economic theory is based upon the latter definition. Anthropologists and other social scientists who have studied the economies of primitive peoples have had difficulty in applying this definition and its necessary correlates to these systems (Polanyi 1959). It is difficult at times to discover the economic "rationality" in a good deal of Western economic behavior. Among non-Western peoples who cannot convert all sorts of things into a commonly measured "cash price," it is much harder to decide whether or not a given behavior is economically rational.

Anthropologists usually classify the economies of the world according to the main subsistence base. Bohannan (1963) uses a five-fold classification of hunting and gathering, herding, horticulture or gardening, agriculture, and factory industrialism. Factory industrialism differs from the others in several important social senses. In the first four types, groups are normally organized for both production and consumption on the basis of kinship, and there is consequently little separation of the two functions in organization; that is, the family (nuclear or extended) is the basic unit of both production and consumption. In factory industrialism, on the other hand, there is a separation of the production and consumption units, as they are organized on different principles. The major consumption unit of final products is still the family, although other institutions such as the government also become important consumers. But production activities are organized on the principle of contract rather than that of kinship. Producing units and consuming units are linked through the mechanism of the market under factory industrialism, whereas markets are of less importance in the other four types of economies. In factory industrialism, all factors of production as well as finished products enter the market and their prices are determined by market forces. This means they must all be measurable in terms of money and subject to contract (Bohannan 1963:208–265).

The science of economics was developed to explain these market processes which arose after the Industrial Revolution. Economic theory addresses itself to the economic processes of factory industrialism and its associated market economy. One crucial fact in such an economy is that everyone derives his income from the sale of something in the market — his labor, his products, his natural resources, or his capital. The price mechanism serves to allocate resources to alternative uses. While, in principle, economics could be concerned with a wide range of problems, it has for the most part concentrated on the question of what forces determine prices in an industrial economy organized on the market principle. Earlier investigators believed that economic theory was so firmly founded on principles derived from nature and logic that it must be cross-culturally valid. A number of recent investigators are convinced that the opposite is true.

Dalton (1961) has summed up the case for the inapplicability of economic theory to primitive economies. He argues that not only are the institutions of Western society different from those in primitive society, but that the economic motivations of the people differ also. The proposition that wants are insatiable and that means to satisfy these wants are invariably in short supply is one of the assumptions upon which economic theory is built. Dalton argues that these are both socially determined and therefore vary considerably from people to people. One of the main reasons for economizing calculation in industrial societies is that machine technology is expensive and must be utilized efficiently to attain the owner's goals. In technologically simple societies each producer typically owns all the tools possessed by his fellow producers. Moreover, no price or economic value is associated with time; therefore, the cost-accounting rationality associated with economic behavior in the West

may not be present at all in simpler economic systems.

Polanyi and his associates have argued that industrial economies are integrated on at least three principles that are not normally found together in primitive economies. These are the economy-wide market, the materially self-gainful economizing that motivates the people, and the monetization of both internal and external trade (all-purpose money that serves as a common denominator for all kinds of transactions). Polanyi (1959) argued that one might find primitive groups having market exchange which appears at first glance to be similar in principle to the Western market system. But, upon closer examination, we find that many non-Western markets do not handle all sorts of transactions. Other principles such as reciprocity and redistribution are also important in the movement of goods and services among primitive peoples. Moreover, there may be special-purpose monies that are used only in certain kinds of transactions. Dalton notes that:

Some of the most respected comparisons between primitive and Western money fail to go deeply enough into comparative economic and social structure. Even Malinowski and Firth do not explain that it is nationally-integrated market organization which accounts for those Western monetary traits they use as a model of "real" money: . . . The question is not — as it is conventionally put — are shells, woodpecker scalps, cattle, goats, dog teeth, or kula valuable "really" "money"? It is, rather, how are the similarities and the differences between such items and dollars related to similarities and differences in socio-economic structure (1965:44–45)?

One way of noting the differences between a market-integrated economy using all-purpose money and a marketless economy or one with peripheral markets is to study what happens when Western money enters into one of these other systems. In these cases, Dalton argues that:

Western money does much more than merely displace primitive monies where the latter were not media of (commercial) exchange in indigenously. It allows non-commercial payments and obligations of traditional sorts (such as bridewealth) to be discharged with general purpose money earned in market transactions — instead of with traditional items of special-purpose money. In economies which formerly were marketless or had peripheral markets only, a structural link — Western cash — now exists between spheres of exchange which formerly were separate. Western money therefore has inevitable repercussions on traditional social organization and cultural practices. In brief, market earnings can now be used for reciprocal and redistributive payments (just as in Western economy goods purchased on the market enter gift-giving, and money earnings are used to pay taxes and tithes) (1965:61).

Bohannan sums up the differences in economic integration between industrial and primitive economies by noting that in industrial economies the technological processes are very complex but the distribution process is relatively simple, depending mainly upon the market principle. The reverse situation is found in primitive economies where the technological processes are very simple, but the distribution system may be very complex in both the organization and the principles involved (Bohannan 1963:229). In the simplest societies the division of labor is based on age and sex. This means that the members of each family together control the total technology of the whole society. Even in peasant societies it is common to find that most of the families in any given village are engaged in the same agricultural activities, using the same tools and technological skills. Thus, simplicity in technology is not normally associated with or a cause of simplicity in exchange.

Another major difference between industrial and primitive economies can be derived from the fact noted earlier that the production unit in primitive societies is almost invariably also a kinship unit. This production unit, usually the family, is limited in the personnel it can recruit for the work at hand, and also in the amount of capital at its command. There is normally no market for the factors of production in such societies. Labor is rarely, if ever, for hire, as is true for capital and land. The production unit in primitive societies is not organized just for production, as is usually the case in industrial societies, it is a multi-purposed social unit with economic production as only one of its many functions (Nash, in Tax 1964:173–174).

The argument in this section has been that economic theory was developed to explain the economic phenomena of an industrial society. However, the motives, institutions, and particular economic devices of industrial societies are not the same as those of primitive and peasant societies. Therefore, economic theory is of only limited utility in the study of primitive and peasant societies.

One of the major changes in the post-World War II world is that many of the underdeveloped countries, which have as their base either a primitive or a peasant economy, are trying to industrialize. In these countries, there is a considerable migration to the cities as people seek participation in urban life and the national economy. It is in the industrial cities that the rural peoples, the traditional subjects of anthropological research, meet the modern industrial system. Up to now we have considered the gulf between the industrial countries and their economic systems and those of the primitive and peasant societies. In the industrial cities of the underdeveloped countries the gap is closing. What kind of approach does the economic anthropologist find useful under these circumstances?

ECONOMIC ANTHROPOLOGY IN AN INDUSTRIAL BOOM-TOWN

In the newly industrialized cities of an underdeveloped country we would expect to find that in some ways economic theory applies as well as it does in the older industrialized countries. We would expect this to be the case since the system of production itself imposes certain restrictions on the forms of possible economic organization, and because such cities are bound to be integrated into the rest of the world economy in some manner. But since industry in such places is manned in part by people coming from a traditional peasant economy, there would probably be some evidence of only partial adjustment to the requirements of factory industrialism — that is, some of the traits traditionally associated with peasant peoples will be maintained in the city. Moreover, we should anticipate finding that some of the traits associated with factory industrialism are more slowly acquired than others. One of the most interesting and important questions for which we have as yet no answer is, what are the necessary social and cultural correlates of an industrial society? We do not yet know which of the cultural traits we find associated with industrial societies are really functionally necessary. Similarly, we do not know which traits of nonindustrial societies can aid, or at least not inhibit, industrial development. In this section we will examine briefly the approaches to his subject that might be made by an economic anthropologist working in Chimbote, an industrial boom-town on the north coast of Peru.

One of the first things to be done is to find out the reasons for the city's rapid growth. If there are books that mention the area, these should be consulted first. Similarly, the anthropologist would want to be as thoroughly grounded in the culture and language of the country as possible before going there

to carry out his study. Through interviewing some of the older residents of the town and consultation of official records some idea of the patterns and causes of growth could be gained. From such sources, we would find that Chimbote increased in a relatively normal fashion between 1920 and 1940, its population doubling from 2000 to 4000. In the '40's, the Santa Corporation was formed on the pattern of the TVA to develop the region. One of its major tasks was the construction of a hydroelectric plant in the mountains to supply electricity to the region in general, and to Chimbote in particular for a steel plant to be constructed there. Chimbote has the best natural harbor on the Peruvian coast, and the Santa Corporation set out to improve its equipment, for a larger volume of trade. The construction activity associated with improving harbor facilities, the hydroelectric plant, the railroad, and the steel plant attracted the first major wave of migration to Chimbote during the '40s. By 1950 the population had increased to 15,000. In the early '50s the fish canneries expanded and a new industry came into being — fish meal. By 1955, the population had expanded to 27,000, and by the time of the 1961 national census it had grown to 64,000. In 1964, some observers estimated that it had reached 85,000.

Who were these people, and where did they come from? Many came from other cities on the coast, but about three-quarters came from the mountain districts nearby. Information about the total population, their reasons for migrating, their attitudes and values, and their background characteristics can be gained from a questionnaire survey of a sample of the population. This medium also collects their opinions about life in Chimbote and their work. However, some independent information is needed to get at their problems of adjustment to industrial life. Interviews with labor leaders, foremen, employers, and government officials help round out the picture. The anthropologist also can learn a great deal from simple observation of the way in which work is organized and carried out, business practices that are observable to him as a customer, and the consumption habits of the people. For example, he could not help but notice from the way most businesses are conducted that the employer normally has very little trust and confidence in his employees and the public. He also learns a good deal about the facilities, goods, and services available to the population, and something of the behavior expected of people, since he is resident there and a member of the community for a period of time.

Besides gathering data about the people, the economic anthropologist would also be interested in gathering data about the main businesses in the area. If he has contacts with some of the companies, or with accountants, he might be able to get statistics on the cost of production in different types of business. At a minimum, he should get some idea of the scale of operations in terms of production. Since these commodities, particularly fish meal, are sold on the world market, he would need to know what world prices are in relation to the costs of production and the degree of fluctuation in prices, as these would have a pronounced effect on the volume of production, the stability of employment, and the rate of failures in business.

Once the field worker has a general overview of the area, he can begin to analyze the data already gathered, discover gaps in his information, and set out to collect the data needed to fill the gaps. The sorts of observations he might make about the four basic economic problems noted above will be discussed briefly, and some attention will be devoted to the question of integrating knowledge about economic behavior with some of the other areas of culture.

With respect to the production problem,

one of the first things to know is what resources are used to produce what goods and the origin and costs of these resources. In the case of Chimbote's fishing industry, the resource cost is relatively low as there are abundant supplies of fish in the offshore waters. However, not only is this industry subject to regular seasonal fluctuations in the supply of fish, there are also occasional years of scarcity, irregular in their appearance. Therefore, the fishing industry tends to fluctuate a good deal in the volume of activity. On the other hand, the steel industry is relatively stable all year. In terms of employment, these two industries are dominant in Chimbote, and the fishing industry is the larger. The Santa Corporation owns the railroad, the port facilities, a hotel, and most of the first-class housing in Chimbote, and thus counts as a third major economic organization. Given the instability of the largest industry of the city, the economic tempo and mood of the city seems to fluctuate with the fishing catch. The commercial and service establishments are the most obviously affected businesses, as the incomes of a great many families fluctuate widely during the year. Insecurity of life in the city for many of the migrants is one factor that favors keeping a foot in two camps; many migrants retain ownership of land and animals in their home villages, to which they can return in times of need. This insecurity also favors retaining close ties with relatives outside the nuclear family. Obligations to help cousins and nephews who come to the city are both recognized and honored. It is common to find households consisting of a nuclear family plus assorted relatives of either the husband or the wife. Strong kinship ties are apparently maintained in the urbanization process in Chimbote.

In the rural areas of Peru there is a good deal of association between economic activities and ritual activities such as fiestas. Are these practices continued in Chimbote?

Since the fiesta pattern is generally associated with the agricultural cycle we would expect that it could not be maintained in the city in precisely the same form known in the highlands. For a number of reasons it dies out, or assumes minimal importance. There are no clear breaks in economic activity for most of the people in the city at any one time; therefore, there is no particularly appropriate time to hold a fiesta. Another reason for its decline is that the people in a city come from many different places and have loyalties to different patron saints. The patron saint of Chimbote commands the loyalty of only a relatively small proportion of the total population and the celebration in his honor has been declining in importance as the city grows in size. Another factor favoring the decline of fiesta celebration is the size of the population. What individual or group could afford to sponsor a fiesta for the whole city? This does not say that the custom has died out altogether. It is maintained in two distinct ways. Those who can afford to do so arrange their vacations and return to their villages to celebrate the fiesta of their patron saint, and those who cannot go home frequently get together and have a relatively small celebration in the city. In 1962, the sponsorship of the fiesta of San Pedro, Chimbote's patron saint, was taken over by one of the national beer companies to promote its product, as no single committee was willing to undertake the responsibility.

Another important area to be investigated is the attitude toward work and production. What is the value of work? Do different groups feel differently about it? In Chimbote, for instance, it is commonly said that the people from the mountains are harder workers than those from the coast. Some types of work are much more highly esteemed than others and the bases for these distinctions must be noted. Certain types of work are not done by people with education, and some are afforded low prestige by virtually everyone. What values and attitude underlie the assignment of differential status to jobs? The organization of work must be studied in terms of who hires whom for what kinds of work. The large factories hire, for the most part, on a purely contractual basis. Smaller businesses, such as retail stores and craft workshops, exhibit a greater preference for kin.

The third factor of production, capital, requires some investigation in terms of the amounts and kinds available, and the cost. The cost of money capital is interest, and interest rates in underdeveloped areas are typically higher than in already industrialized countries. Banks in Chimbote have a series of charges, including interest, which add up to about 20 per cent per annum. Interest rates when borrowing from a friend are considerably higher than bank rates. One informant claimed that the regular rate was 20 per cent per month. Given the high cost of capital, the borrower must either be very sparing in its use, or earn a high profit from it to make borrowing worthwhile. The high cost of capital can be expected to influence the size of the productive units, and the relative proportions of capital and labor used in the productive process.

We have seen that the returns to the owner of capital are high. In general, this is also true for the owners of land and buildings. In a city growing as fast as Chimbote, housing is in constantly short supply. Profits vary a good deal, depending not only upon the effectiveness of the owner, but also upon the nature of the industry and the type of ownership. For instance, the Santa Corporation consistently loses money, and can do so as it is a public corporation. On the other hand, a fish company that loses much money will soon find itself in the hands of its creditors. An investigation of a few businesses revealed that profits of 50 per cent on investment were not unusual in good fishing years. Wages also vary with the industry. Where work is steady and unions are strong, wages and fringe benefits are considerably higher than for the independent worker making an individual bargain with an employer. Since fishermen are paid on shares, their incomes fluctuate widely during the year. Moreover, they, and the workers at the fish factories, suffer periodic unemployment due to the shortage of fish. A category of labor that is not normally counted by economists in developed countries, but which is of some importance in Peru, is unpaid family workers. These may function as household servants or work in family-owned businesses. Since they earn no wages, it is difficult to calculate the economic value of their services.

The exchange system in a city like Chimbote is more like one in any modern industrial economy than one in a primitive or peasant economy, in that there is all-purpose money, and virtually everyone is directly connected to the market. One of the interesting phenomena is the proliferation of petty traders, not only in small shops or stalls, but also in street vending. Since a large number of people are supported by such activities, one cannot but believe that a considerable amount of the cost of the final product is paid for these services.

The principles guiding the decisions of businessmen, their methods of competing, and the like, should also be investigated. Here we would find that most retailers do not compete on price or quality of goods, but rather on the basis of friendship with the customer and easy credit terms. As the city grows it is necessarily less possible to keep up this method of establishing personal ties between buyer and seller unless there is an increasing proliferation of traders and a small volume of business for each one.

The consumption problem is concerned with the final uses of the goods and services produced. Here we are not only interested in the money income and the ways in which it is spent, but also in any other nonmonetary income that contributes to the real total income of the family. For instance, one custom of rural peoples in Peru that continues for a long time in the cities is the habit of raising a few animals for both food and company. On the other hand, there may be an outflow of cash to aged parents back in the home village that takes part of a man's income. In Chimbote, we would be interested in the consumption patterns of individuals for several reasons. We would want to know how their level and style of living changed after coming to the city, as compared to what it was in a village. We would also want to know their consumption patterns, to compare it with the experience of other countries that have undergone industrialization, or with groups in other countries who have recently migrated to the city. In Chimbote, we find that the consumption patterns are very similar to those noted among North American migrants to the city who are earning a good wage for the first time in their lives. Just as is true of poor, rural migrants to North American cities, Chimbotanos spend a good deal of money on beer, watches, clothes, radios, and so on, and relatively little on improving the house they live in or its furnishings. Some people have argued that it is the tensions of urban life which causes migrants to drink a good deal more in the cities than they did in the country. However the migrants themselves say it is a function of their higher incomes. If they had had the money they would have drunk a good deal more in the highlands. The same logic holds for the greater amounts of promiscuity in the city — it is a more anonymous place that presents better possibilities, qualitatively and quantitatively, than a small village.

Economic behavior does not occur in isolation from the rest of social life, and the anthropologist cannot but notice the many interconnections between economic behavior and the rest of the culture. These interconnections are particularly close between the economic organization and the rest of social organization. Just as the pattern of economic organization changes with industrialization and urbanization from what it was in a rural society, so does the social organization. The greater complexity of the technological process requires greater occupational specialization and role multiplication. Occupational roles become separated from other social roles to a greater degree than is found in peasant societies. The relatively simple class structure normally associated with peasant society becomes more elaborate in the cities. Moreover, the bases for ascribing class status are more varied in the city. In a city changing as rapidly as is Chimbote, it is fairly easy to trace the alterations in the social structure that have taken place as it has altered from small village to major industrial city. New economic elites are being created, and are rapidly moving to the top of the social scale. The traditional behavior expected when persons of different classes meet is also changing rapidly, owing largely to the changes in the economic structure. With unions to represent them, common laborers no longer have to exhibit the obsequiousness once required of them. The personalistic ties between employer and employee are also weakening rapidly.

The class system is more flexible in an urban industrial setting than it is in the rural area. People in a city are a heterogeneous lot, coming from many places and many different backgrounds. The general tendency is to pay less attention to the family background of the migrant than was the case in his village. Correspondingly, achievement counts for a good deal more in the city than it did back in the village. The city presents more variation and more opportunities for upward social mobility than a village, and migrants are very much aware of this fact. These possibilities are, after all, the main reason given by migrants for coming to Chimbote.

Without making any special effort to do so, the anthropologist in Chimbote will discover a number of connections between economic life and political organization. One connection of great importance is an effect of the centralization of political power in Lima. Lima is not only the seat of political power for the country, but also the headquarters for all the major institutions of the society. Almost every business large enough to do so has its main office in Lima, where the owners and managers can live in comfort, and where they can have access to the centers of political power that are important to their economic success. This means that in a place like Chimbote, little real authority is held by the plant managers. Decisions of even minor importance are forwarded to Lima. For instance, the decision to lend a man enough money to buy a car is made in Lima, since the manager of a local branch of the bank has no authority to make a loan of that size. Labor disputes are settled with the company's labor lawyer in Lima, though the company may also have a labor lawyer in Chimbote.

The lack of political power at the local level has direct economic consequences. For example, the taxes reserved for the local government are almost invariably those which are most difficult and expensive to collect, and which produce very little revenue. Taxes such as those on scales in stores cost more to collect than they yield, and the city government is allowed to collect this sort of tax. Taxes on the fish companies go mainly to Lima. With the poor tax base, there is little the municipal government can do to meet the increasing needs for urban facilities. As in many countries, there are sometimes direct connections between the acquisition of political power and economic success. All these interconnections between the economic and the political structure must be well understood if the economic anthropologist is to gain a thorough understanding of this particular economy and the way in which it works.

The relationship between economics, the state of scientific knowledge, and the education and socialization processes, is extremely important to the anthropologist. One way to study this interrelationship is to examine economic behavior in terms of adaptation to the requirements of machine technology and its associated economic organization. Once the behavior patterns are known, the anthropologist can see in what ways the values, attitudes, and education procedures of the society support this behavior or are at variance with it. In many cases the outcome, in terms of economic rationality, is mixed. For instance, many cases can be found wherein the response of the individual workman indicated what the economists would call an economically rational response on his part. But the effect of this response may not be economically rational as far as his employer is concerned. An example would be the widespread habit of fishermen to work only when they are actually pulling in the fish, and not to use other free time for preventive maintenance on the boat while going to and returning from the fishing grounds. One result of this practice is that boats depreciate very rapidly and the capital cost to the owner is considerably higher than would be the case if proper care were given to the boat. Yet, as far as the individual fisherman is concerned, his response is the height of economic rationality, since he is paid on shares. The only factor that affects his income is the amount of fish caught. This is a common system of payment among fishing peoples everywhere, but is probably inappropriate where there are no traditions of seamanship and customary obligations on the part of fishermen to maintain the boat and its equipment.

In general, when a group of people move to the city and work in industry for the first time, we would expect that certain behavior patterns would change rapidly in response to the pressures and possibilities in the new situation. However, we would also know that some of the values and attitudes that normally underlie behavior are slow to change. Some of these values and attitudes are common to peasant societies everywhere and some are probably more pronounced in a Latin-American peasant society (Foster 1960). These values are also found in the cities of these societies, in part because much of their population comes from the rural areas. It was noted earlier that there was a shift to a contractual type of relationship in industrial areas. There is also considerable evidence that such a shift does not occur easily. Loyalties remain tied to people rather than to either corporations or particular roles in the hierarchical structure. Chimbotanos tend to distrust others, to feel that they are out to cheat you, that you really cannot count on their word. These feelings are part of the reasons why it is difficult to amass the capital necessary for a large-scale operation, and why by preference an individual may feel safer with a small family firm where he can control everything personally. Another general characteristic of peasant societies found in places like Chimbote is a rather well-developed fatalistic outlook. Peasants frequently feel that their environment is capricious and cannot be controlled. This outlook does not suddenly change upon migrating to the city and, this being the case, then how can one accept responsibility for what happens? If machines break themselves, how can the operator be blamed for this? The other side of the coin is that success depends a great deal upon luck, rather than upon rational action by the individual.

In this section we have briefly considered some of the problems that might interest an economic anthropologist working in a city in Peru. Many other problems could be dealt with, and some of those mentioned here could be subjected to studies in considerable depth. Once the anthropologist has completed the collection of his data, he is in a position to test the hypothesis developed prior to his field-work period. His data can also be used to test new hypotheses developed after being in the field. Although there is no statistical support for this notion, it is probably a fact that the anthropologist in the field discovers many interesting problems and possibilities he had not counted on when planning his field study, and that he commonly alters his research design while in the field to take advantage of these. It is probably the exception, rather than the rule, when an anthropologist accomplishes in the field all that he set out to do and finds no surprises.

Economic anthropology cannot yet be regarded as a highly developed subdiscipline of anthropology, as there are still very few anthropologists working in this field. Yet, the contribution to be made in this area is considerable. Professionals of many disciplines are devoting increasing attention to the problem of understanding the processes involved in economic development in the underdeveloped countries. It has become clear to economists, as well as others, that economic development does not occur apart from major changes in the rest of the culture. Anthropologists are peculiarly equipped to deal with the process of total culture change, as this has long been a specialty in anthropology. Economics can specify the basic economic requirements that must be met if there is to be development. Anthropologists may be able to supply much of the knowledge needed about the culture and the integration of the economy with other aspects of culture. With this knowledge they should be better equipped than others to make predictions as to what the effects of particular policies or changes will be on the different aspects of culture. This is probably the area in which economic anthropology will make its greatest practical contribution. It is also to be hoped that anthropologists will be able to make significant contributions to economic theory from their study of non-Western societies. Finally, we can expect that an increasing understanding of the economic life of non-Western peoples will contribute significantly to our understanding of the total way of life of these peoples.

Suggested Readings

The only attempt to date to bring together the findings of economic anthropology is Herskovits' book, *Economic Anthropology* (1952). Earlier, more limited attempts at synthesis include Thurnwald (1932) and Forde (1934, reprinted in 1963). Readers interested in a brief summary of the arguments against the applicability of economic theory to primitive economies are referred to Polanyi (1959) and Dalton (1961). Two collections of essays have appeared recently, each edited by an anthropologist-economist team. These are Bohannan and Dalton (1962), and Firth and Yamey (1964). The reader interested in ethnographic accounts of field work, with a heavy emphasis on economic behavior, are referred to any of the following: Malinowski (1922); Firth (1939, 1946, 1959); Foster (1942); Holmberg (1950); Tax (1953); Nash (1958); or Salisbury (1962).

CHAPTER **8** introduces anthropological approaches to the study of law and the sources of social control, and continues a discussion of issues raised in earlier chapters. How does the anthropologist set about creating a concept of law — or for that matter, economics, or the community, or art — which is validly applicable to many other cultures? If the arena of law cannot be dissolved into a "mass of omnipotent custom," and if narrowly defined Euro-American views on the nature of law are patently ethnocentric and have little cross-cultural validity, where does the anthropologist turn for a conceptual starting point and how does he build analytic definitions? Professor Pospisil argues convincingly that it is insufficient to accept only those particular concepts of law peculiar to given societies. We cannot substitute for Western ethnocentricity equally ethnocentric Cheyenne or Papuan ideas about law and techniques of social control. Here a weakness of the often touted position of "cultural relativism" is made clear. Purely ethnographic recordings of "folk" law-ways can only be one reference point against which to check the utility of broader theoretical formulations. The cultural anthropologist, aiming at analytic, theoretically meaningful definitions and working towards cross-culturally valid generalizations, has a larger responsibility. As Professor Pospisil makes clear, this responsibilty cannot be executed without fundamental rephrasings of our ideas about the nature of society itself, about leadership and decision-making processes, and about formal societal controls over norm-violating behaviors.

THE AUTHOR was born in Czechoslovakia and has studied law at Charles University in Prague, philosophy in Germany, anthropology at the University of Oregon and at Yale University, where he took his doctorate in Anthropology. He is currently Professor of Anthropology at Yale and Curator of Anthropology at the Peabody Museum. His long-standing interest in the comparative study of law, political organizations, and social control have required field research among the Alaskan Eskimo, the Kapauku Papuans of New Guinea, and the peasants of the Austrian Tirol. He is the author of *Kapauku Papuans and Their Law, The Kapauku Papuans of West New Guinea, Kapauku Papuan Economy,* other monographs, and numerous articles on his areas of professional interest.

8

Law and Order

LEOPOLD POSPISIL

Yale University

Aurea prima sata est aetas quae vindice nullo
Sponte sua, sine lege fidem rectumque colebat.
Poena metusque aberant nec verba minantia fixo
Aere legebantur nec supplex turba timebat
Iudicis ora sui, sed erant sine vindice tuti.[1]
　　　　Ovidius: *Metamorphoses* (1719:8)

These words of Ovid, written almost two thousand years ago, still characterize in some specific aspects the thinking of some social scholars who deal with the problem of law in primitive societies. According to these authors, conformity with basic values and general order in such societies is maintained not through an application of law in authoritative decisions, formally or informally rendered by the societies' judges, chiefs, headmen, or important men, but by the power of custom, which is well known to everyone and needs little restatement, determination, or elucidation by an individual or a body of individuals endowed by the society with judicial powers. This position was assumed by many early anthropologists and sociologists, leading them to conclude that an absence of law is a special characteristic of primitive societies.

Sidney Hartland expressed this position quite well by portraying primitive man as "hemmed in on every side by the customs of his people, . . bound in the chains of immemorial tradition, . . whose fetters are accepted by him as a matter of course; he never seeks to break forth" (1924:138). The law to him would be equal to "the totality of the customs of the tribe" (1924:85).

W. H. R. Rivers identified the force that accounts for conformity and order in primi-

---

[1] The golden age was first; when men, yet new,
No rule but uncorrupted reason knew:
And, with a native bond, did good pursue,
Unforc'd by punishment, unaw'd by fear,
His words were simple, and his soul sincere;
Needless was written law, where none opprest:
The law of man was written in his breast:
No suppliant crowds before the judge appear'd
No court erected yet, nor cause was heard:
But all was safe for conscience was their
　　　guard.
　　　　Ovidius, *Metamorphoses;* tr.
　　　　John Dryden (1815:4)

tive societies in Durkheimean terms, calling it a "group sentiment which makes unnecessary any definite social machinery for the exertion of authority"; people conform because of the presence of "the spontaneous, or, as it might be called, intuitive mode of inflicting punishment" (1924:169). Similarly, Hobhouse concluded that "in quite the lowest races there is, as we have seen, scarcely anything that is strictly to be called the administration of justice" (1906:80).

This tradition of regarding the primitive societies as being regulated by omnipotent custom known to everyone, as existing without a need for leaders of even the greatest informality who would restate, determine, and mold the custom in their advice or decisions pertaining to settlements of disputes, did not perish with the early generations of anthropologists who were affected by the Durkheimean jargon of generalities and the speculative stages of unilineal evolutionism. Indeed, it is being continued today by some contemporary authors who in their field work have failed to recognize the subtlety of informal authority and who insist upon a virtual absence of leadership in the groups they investigate. Accordingly, Meggitt describes a leaderless society when he writes of the Walbiri of Australia: "In short, the community had no recognized political leaders, no formal hierarchy of government. People's behavior in joint activities was initiated and guided largely by their own knowledge and acceptance of established norms" (1962: 250). As far as the mechanism of social control is concerned, Meggitt observes that "there are explicit social rules, which, by and large, everybody obeys; and the people freely characterize each other's behavior insofar as it conforms to the rules or deviates from them. The totality of the rules expresses the law . . ." (1962:251). Strangely enough, several pages later one reads that in this leaderless society with rules that by and large everybody obeys; the effective punishment of lawbreakers involves a person knowledgeable of custom who passes a decision as to the guilt of the offender and his proper punishment (1962:255). Of these two statements, which seem to contradict each other, I regard as more accurate the more specific latter one. Consequently, when one looks closer at the social reality, and abandons such generalities as "public opinion" (Meggitt 1962:254), and does not insist upon a legal authority as having "permanent and clearly defined legislative and judicial functions" (Meggitt 1962:251), one finds that justice is not expressed spontaneously by an expression of mystifying "public opinion," but that its administration is usually vested in the decision-making activity (irrespective of its informality or subtlety) of an individual or a group of individuals of influence.

As a reaction to this trend of dissolving law into the mass of omnipotent custom (or "norms of behavior") which is relatively static, known to every member of the primitive society, and to which most or even all the natives conform without the need of inducement through decisions of a leader, there emerged another set of anthropologists who tried to define law rigorously, to make it a useful ethnographical tool. These authors did not try to derive their concepts of law from comparative studies of various societies, but, influenced by Western legalistic tradition in general or by some legal scholars in particular, conceptualized law too narrowly, so the concept was inapplicable to many primitive societies. In other words, they concluded that some societies were simply lawless.

The early representative of this trend of anthropological thought was Radcliffe-Brown. He accepted Pound's definition of law and confined the term to "social control through the systematic application of the force of politically organized society" (Radcliffe-Brown 1952:212). This narrow definition led him inevitably to the conclusion that "some simple societies have no law, although all have customs which are supported by sanctions" (1952:212). Accordingly, the Yurok of California and Ifugao of Luzon, as examples, were judged to lack law (1952: 216–217). Along with the theories of the first group of anthropologists, the trend of thought of the second group continues to be manifest in the writings of many contemporary authors. We will consider here two recent examples of the second type of legalistic thinking.

In his recent book (1962), Van den Steenhoven, writing on the law of the Caribou and Netsilik Eskimo of Canada, states a certainly acceptable and praiseworthy premise: "Firstly, we should avoid the adoption of a law concept which, though perhaps it may be useful for application to one or more simple societies, will be unfit for utilization in the study of *all* societies" (1962:100). Bearing this claim in mind the reader would expect a definition of law based on a broad, cross-cultural research, and applicable at least to those societies well covered in the anthropological literature. This modest expectation is not fulfilled and, incredibly, the author defines law in such a way that it does not even apply to the society whose analysis constitutes the content of his book. His intuitive, arbitrary, and narrow definition of law leads him to the following conclusion in his work, entitled *Leadership and Law Among the Eskimos of the Keewatin District, Northwest Territories:* "The conclusions to be drawn from the evidence presented seems undeniably negative as regards the (threat of) physical force, the 'official' authority, the regularity of application and the non-spontaneity of community response which in this study are used as the elements to identify law" (1962:112). The claim of an absence of law among these Eskimos is a consequence of a definition of law based on several misconceptions about the nature and function of those phenomena of social control which usually are called by that term. First, in common with many authors of books on law, Van den Steenhoven seems not to be quite sure whether law is a concept (1962:103, 112) or a phenomenon (1962:100, 101, 112). One almost gains the impression that he uses the two terms interchangeably. Second, following the suggestion of Hoebel, he unduly stresses (unlike Hoebel) the importance of physical sanction as a criterion of law to such an extent that he not only neglects the most devastating sanctions in the Eskimo society, which are psychological (ostracism, ridicule, name-calling, and the like), but his emphasis upon physical violence causes him to select only those cases for consideration that in our law would be termed "criminal." Consequently, disputes that a Western lawyer would call "civil" are not touched upon at all. Third, in his emphasis on violence Van den Steenhoven identifies legal authority with agents who mete out physical punishment (1962: 103, 108, 111). He fails to recognize that the essence of the legal procedure is the decision-making process and that even in Western society the legal authorities (judges, juries) relegate the execution of their verdicts to the executive organs of the state (e.g., police, prison wardens, guards, executioners, and so on). Fourth, the author makes the existence of law dependent upon an ambiguous, vague, and exclusive criterion that he calls "non-spontaneity" (1962:103, 104), which postulates that law exists only where a "spontaneous" reaction of a group of people may be absent. Aside from the very vague and undefined nature of this criterion, I fail to understand how, after a research lasting only six weeks, without a knowledge of the native language, and using only cases of the past history interpreted to him by a missionary, Van den Steenhoven could determine whether the group in question "reacted spontaneously" or upon the decision, advice, or informal and subtle inducement of the native leaders.

In a joint account with three other scholars, called *Society and the Law,* F. James Davis, a sociologist, defines law as *"the formal means of social control that involves the use of rules that are interpreted, and enforceable, by the courts of a political community"* (1962:41). This definition, then, is assumed to have universal validity and to be applicable to all societies in the world. However, by designing a Western-biased definition, which makes interpretation of abstract rules as well as existence of formal courts of law prerequisites for the presence of law in a given culture, the author has excluded most primitive societies from his consideration of law. Furthermore, this narrow concept of law is not only impractical from the anthropological point of view but it unfortunately eliminates some non-European civilizations from the legal scene. For example, the Chinese civilization is clearly excluded by the author's insistence upon the Western conceptualization of legal process which is made explicit by the following statement: "Unless there are official agencies to decide disputes by interpreting and applying legal rules to given situations — that is, unless there are courts — there is no law as defined here" (Davis, *et al.,* 1962:45). Chinese magistrates were not concerned with "interpreting and applying legal rules" in their settlements, but used the rules only as advice, as helpful models, which they had no obligation to follow in their adjudication of cases. The deficiency of this definition can be made even more dramatic by applying it to those European societies to which we traditionally impute the existence of law. Since neither the Greek nor the Roman civilizations forced their judges to follow abstract rules and "interpret and apply [them] to a given situation," their law being basically casuistic, the social controls in these two ancient civilizations would not qualify by Davis' definition as "law." To claim that ancient Rome had no law would be difficult even for the most ethnocentric, narrow-minded, and traditionalist Western lawyer to accept.

As a reaction to this narrow, ethnocentric approach to the question of the concept of law, a third trend in legal thinking has arisen, which, while castigating ethnocentricity in anthropological and sociological jurisprudence, tries to comprehend legal phenomena through the frame of thought of the members of the particular society whose legal structure and content are being investigated. Bohannan characterizes the objectives of this endeavor as follows: "Obviously, the human beings who participate in social events interpret them: they create meaningful systems out of the social relationships in which they are involved. Such a system I am going to call a 'folk system' of interpretation, by analogy with 'folk etymology' " (1957:4). Although Bohannan very meaningfully distinguished this kind of system from the analytical system "which sociologists and social anthropologists create by more or less scientific methods" (1957:5), in his book, *Justice and Judgement Among the Tiv,* he almost exclusively concentrates upon the "folk systems." Thus his work presents a description of the Tiv conceptualization of this system, but does not deal with broader theoretical considerations ("analytical systems," in Bohannan's terms). While I certainly agree with Bohannan that a good *ethnographer* "should also give the folk system," I have to add very emphatically that a good ethnologist (as distinguished from a purely descriptive ethnographer) should also work with an analytical system. However, Bohannan's actual presentation of the Tiv folk system seems to contradict his more abstract statements. In the introduction to his book, for example, he makes the following statement concerning the Tiv folk system: "But I have tried *not* to 'explain' it *in terms* of our own system of 'law,' which would do violence to the Tiv ideas and folk system" (1957:5–6). Yet he uses Western legalistic terms which even some notoriously ethnocentric writers on non-European legal systems have not dared to use. Accordingly, Bohannan classifies Tiv cases as "criminal" and "civil." He tries to justify this obvious violence to his principles by the fact that a scribe of Mba Duku *jir* (a native court) used these terms himself (1957:113). It is my strong suspicion that this Western dichotomy, despite the native scribe's use, is a poor expression of the actual native conceptualization. In their discussion with the white man the Kapauku Papuans, whom I investigated, refer to their *tonowi* (informal headman) with the Malay term *kapala,* which in Indonesia stands for a strongly formalized type of leadership, an appointed head of a locality. In spite of the Kapauku "translation" of their folk concept of a rich informal headman (who is actually not a village leader but a leader of a lineage or confederacy of lineages) by the term *kapala,* I would reject such a misleading usage in my writings, and would rebuke the native informant for misinterpreting his society's "folk reality." In conclusion I would say that Bohannan's theoretical statements concerning the "folk and analytical systems" are certainly very sound, but he can be criticized for neglecting the analytical approach and for possibly violating the principles he set for the presenting of his folk system.

Bohannan's sound theoretical differentiation between folk systems and analytical systems was seriously misinterpreted by S. J. L. Zake, one of his students. Instead of understanding this conceptual dichotomy, Zake embraced the folk definition of law as the only proper approach to the problem of law, disregarding the analytical approach altogether. In his thesis he claims that definitions of law should change with time and provenience, where phenomena regarded as legal are to be found (1962:66–7). As a consequence, he himself refuses to define law (1962:67) and in his purely library work attacks most anthropologists who have written about law (except Bohannan), criticizes them for their theoretical attempts to arrive at a cross-culturally valid definition of law, labels them ethnocentric, and, in a rather arrogant way, lectures them on what the legal systems of the Cheyenne, Barotse, Kapauku, and others really are like. I shall not deal here with Zake's quotations out of context, his gross misinterpretations, and his omissions of relevant material, but will concentrate upon his theoretical misinterpretations that are of general importance and affect less dogmatic and more concrete writers on law, who have based their publications on field work. First, Zake's most serious mistake is that he does not realize clearly that "law" is a term applied to a concept, not a phenomenon (1962:esp. 67, 68, 157, 158). He does not seem to understand that law is a concept whose justification lies in its heuristic value, in its efficiency as an analytical tool in the hands of an ethnologist (and not necessarily a descriptive ethnographer). Second, Zake does not differentiate between social control in general and law as one of its specialized and institutionalized forms (1962:esp. 165). Had he understood this difference he would not have insisted that law accounts for practically all conformity within a culture. Third, Zake does not understand what Bohannan meant by the term "analytical system," a notion that reaches to the fundamental conception about science.

What Zake talked about in his dissertation were "folk systems" of law — descriptions of native laws with the natives' conceptualization pertaining to their own legal systems. As Bohannan correctly pointed out, inquiry into this subject is an important step in the research procedure every ethnographer must undertake. Indeed Gluckman, Hoebel, Bohannan, Schapera, and other anthropologists including myself have discussed the concepts of natives pertaining to their law. However, Zake does not seem to have realized that this is but the first and, even in Bohannan's implied terminology, only a descriptive step. The second, and much more important step for anthropology of law as a science, is a conceptualization of an analytical system (to use Bohannan's expression) or, better, the formation of an analytical and cross-culturally applicable concept and theory of law. Zake failed to discuss this in his work and, consequently, it is not surprising that he could not understand Hoebel's statement of fundamental importance: ". . . acceptance of everyone's folk system as an end in itself — an insufficient stultifying end . . . this would preclude the development of any useful theory of anthropological jurisprudence" (1961:432).

In his dissertation Zake labeled virtually all legal anthropologists as ethnocentrists. He criticized their "analytical conceptualizations in the field of law" for not conforming to the first concept of Bohannan's dichotomy — "the folk legal system." A cross-cultural theory of law cannot be composed of a mishmash of contradictory concepts derived from the various cultures whose only common denominator and virtue (in Zake's opinion) would be their "folk system origin." His insistence and fixation upon folk systems leads him to fantastic claims about anthropology in general which make it doubtful that he has grasped the very basic principles of the science he studies:

There is, therefore, no substitute for using the terminology of a nonliterate society. In studying other aspects of the culture in nonliterate societies, like religion or social organization or authority systems, this is what has in fact been done and there is no reason why the same principle should not be followed in the sphere of legal research (1962:165).

To this statement I have only to add my profound doubt that descent, genealogy, Crow or Omaha kinship systems, reduction rules, avunculocal residence, and so on, are concepts that belong in any of the world's folk systems (with the exception of the Western anthropological). To conclude my reaction to this "hypononethnocentric (or hypo-folk) trend of thought" I restate the position I have already expressed in "Kapauku Papuan Laws of Land Tenure" (1965). Scientific inquiry uses as its tools concepts, categories, apparatus, and procedures designed or selected by the scientist and not by the subjects he studies. Even if the purpose of the study is cognitive (or folk-oriented), one studies the native categories and cognitive processes as facts, as phenomena presented by the native informants. One does not necessarily adopt these categories for one's own cognition or for cross-culturally valid theories (unless they are of a cross-cultural validity). To analyze Kapauku, Cheyenne, Barotse, or any other people's thinking and their cognitive categories one does not have to think and speak as these people do.

THE MANIFESTATION OF LAW — A THREEFOLD POSSIBILITY

I have discussed above three traditions in legal-anthropological thinking concerned with the problem of the definition of law. The first tradition, which identified law with custom or norms that are somehow automatically observed without requiring leadership, legal authority, and adjudication, made the term "law" obsolete by identifying it with prescribed behavior and divorcing it from the decision-making process of authority (or group leaders). The second tradition represents a reaction to the first in attempting to define law by rigorous criteria, thus dissociating it from the body of prescriptive customs and making it an analytically meaningful concept. The failure of this tradition lies in the fact that law has been defined not on the basis of extensive cross-cultural research and experience, but in ethnocentric, narrow terms in the legal tradition of Western civilization. The third tradition, the most recent, tries to correct the extreme of ethnocentricity by moving to another extreme, that of cultural relativity. As a result, no analytical definition of law is given: only dogmatic statements concerning folk classifications, and criticisms (often unjustified) of anthropologists who have designed analytical legal definitions, are offered to the puzzled reader (see esp. Zake 1962). In the subsequent discussion we shall concentrate upon efforts that deal more realistically with the problem of an analytical definition of law. Folk classifications and folk semantics have their place in a chapter in particular ethnographies but not in a chapter on law as a theoretical-analytical device.

Since in their ethnographic accounts several recent authors regard the concept of law as a "phenomenon" (esp. Zake 1962:67–68, 157–158; Van den Steenhoven 1962: 100–101, 112) I am forced to state a premise which most anthropologists will regard as needless, superfluous, or obvious. I have to stress that law as a theoretical and analytical device is a concept which embraces a category of phenomena (ethnographic facts) selected according to the criteria the concept specifies. Although it is composed of a set of individual phenomena, the category itself is not a phenomenon — it does not exist in the outer world. The term "law," consequently, is applied to a construct of the human mind made for the sake of convenience. The justification for a concept of law does not reside in its existence outside the human mind, but in its value as an analytic, heuristic device. Since phenomena of social control often represent a continuum rather than qualitative clusters with clearly defined gaps between them,

there cannot be sharp divisions between the categories of the various types of social control. Instead, one must conceive of transitional zones between the categories, wherein the criteria of the neighboring categories overlap and, consequently, wherein it is difficult to determine which ones dominate the field. The blending of the phenomena of one category of social control into those of another does not invalidate the justification for those categories, for the same reason that we keep the concepts of, for example, the colors orange and red. Although there is a transition rather than a sharp dividing line between them in both instances, most of the pertinent phenomena can safely be placed within the boundaries of the categories. Furthermore, unlike color concepts, categorization of phenomena of social control into law, custom, political decisions, religious taboos, and so on is done for each of these categories on the basis of a different set of criteria (rather than just on the basis of a different quantity of the same criterion, as is the case with different colors). Consequently, I refuse to be a humble man in terms of those followers of Radin who adhere to his motto which states: "Those of us who have learned humility have given over the attempt to define law" (1938:1145).

In the following discussion I shall restate my definition of law originally arrived at through an intensive cross-cultural study of thirty-two cultures and a survey of an additional sixty-three, and subsequently tested in three societies: the Nunamiut Eskimo hunters of Alaska; the Kapauku Papuan horticulturists of West New Guinea; and the Tirolean peasants of Austria. Instead of concentrating upon the analytical attributes of law which I have discussed elsewhere (Pospisil 1958a), I shall deal here with the basic methodological problem of the form in which the legal phenomena are manifested, a problem that confronts every field worker interested in the subject of institutionalized social control.

In their book *The Cheyenne Way* Llewellyn and Hoebel identified three main "roads into exploration of the law-stuff of a culture" (1941:20). These roads constitute three possibilities of the way one may conceive of manifestations (or form) of law: first, abstract rules that either form the content of legal codifications in literate societies or that are to be found as a set of verbalized ideals in the repository of the minds of knowledgeable individuals in a nonliterate society; second, patterns of actual behavior of members of a society; and third, principles abstracted from decisions of legal authorities passed while solving disputes within their groups. To be sure, there are other possibilities of conceiving of the form of law. However, most of the theories of social scientists have tended to follow one of the three roads identified above.

It may be argued that all three categories of the phenomena are so important for the investigation of institutionalized social control that the term "law" should apply to them all. Although it is imperative that a student of law investigate all three bodies of data, the term "law," as we shall see, cannot be applied to all of them, because not all three instances would necessarily relate to social control, which constitutes the core of the law concept — the institutionalized social control. Furthermore, this use of the term would make "law" co-terminous with ideals, and, at the same time, with the concept of custom. Consequently, a concept of law so conceived would become so broad and all-comprising as to preclude any effective analytical application of it.

Abstract Rules

The legal thought that regards abstract rules, embodied within the coded law of civilized peoples or in the memory of preliterate peoples, as the proper and exclusive manifestation of law, represents the major legal tradition in Western Europe, especially on the Continent. Because of its paramount importance and general acceptance there, one may regard this as Europe's "folk category of law." The origin of the emphasis on abstract rules in the legal sphere has a long cultural history and dates back to the Babylonia of Hammurabi and to the origin of the notion of natural law (ca. 2,000 B.C.), a conception of law which was considered universally applicable and an abstract divine command to all mankind (Needham 1956: 533). Although Heraclitus (ca. 500 B.C.) had already made a claim that divine law nourishes all human laws, the idea that all of nature and, consequently, man's behavior also is subject to a universal law was firmly embodied in Greek philosophy with the Stoic School about two centuries later. According to Needham, this idea was a consequence of a direct diffusion of thought from Mesopotamia (1956:534). Through the Greek settlements in southern Italy and on Sicily, the Stoic ideas influenced Rome, as witness Cicero's work *De Legibus,* in which he claimed that "human life is subject to the decrees of the Supreme Law" (tr. Keyes, 1928:461). Old Roman Law, true enough, had its base in the *Lex Duodecim Tabularum* (Law of the Twelve Tables) which consisted of sets of abstract principles. However, these principles did not mechanically bind the Roman *jurisconsults* (lawyers) or magistrates; they were treated as a framework to be interpreted and adjusted to the problems arising from actual disputes. They were guides, not to be blindly followed by the jurist, but to help him write his *responsa prudentium,* advice to the parties of a dispute (Sommer 1933:15; Maine 1963:33). Because the Roman magistrate, the *praetor urbanus,* was often a political appointee, he relied heavily on the writing of these jurisconsults in his adjudication of cases. Thus these lawyers' opinions, written in response to particular cases, were the actual source of Roman law, which thus became a law of cases rather than a law based exclusively upon abstract rules. When the Stoic philosophy began to be studied in Rome, the casuistic nature of ancient Roman law was slowly influenced by the Eastern emphasis on abstract rules. Accordingly, as the Roman Republic approached its end, the responses of the jurisconsults were reduced to systematized compendia reflecting the praetor's edict. The edict, originally an annual proclamation of policy of that Roman republican magistrate, gradually incorporated more and more abstract legal precepts which became further sources of Roman law (Maine 1963:39). With the advent of the Roman Empire abstract statutes promulgated by the emperors (*constitutiones*) slowly accrued importance. Because the praetors incorporated the contents of previous edicts into their annual statements, the praetorian annual edict itself developed into an *edictum perpetuum,* a perpetual edict adopted mechanically by succeeding praetors from the time of Hadrian (Maine 1963:61). Thus the edict lost its function as a dynamic mechanism of Roman law. Finally, dating from Emperor Alexander Severus, Roman law became the exclusive domain of imperial constitutions (statutes). There were periodic attempts to codify the body of existing law. The evolution of Roman law ends with the reign of Justinian and his successful codification known nowadays as Corpus Iuris Civilis (ca. A.D. 533). Thus the originally casuistic law of Rome evolved into a legal system which relied on abstract rules and on their codification.

After being forgotten for several centuries this codified Roman law was resurrected and "received" in Northern Italy. Although this process started in the eleventh century, it was not until well over half a century later, with the renewal of the studies of Roman law at Bologna, that the Western world regained firm possession of its lost legal treasure. Because of its consistency, its admirable and precise juristic logic, and its systematic treatment of legal matter, Roman law rapidly gained tremendous prestige and became a subsidiary law to the legal systems in Italy and Central Europe. For political reasons the German emperors accepted Roman law as valid in their Holy Roman Empire: they thus tried to strengthen the fiction of the continuity of the German Empire with the Old Roman Empire (Sommer 1932:12–13). The prestige of the abstract tenets of the Roman law was so high that it became a subject of studies in a succession of several "juristic schools," such as Glossators (thirteenth century), Commentators (thirteenth-fourteenth centuries), Humanists (sixteenth century), and Romanists-Pandectists (nineteenth century) (Stone 1950:424–427). At the close of the eighteenth and the beginning of the nineteenth century, when there was an era of widespread codification of European legal systems, Roman law was invariably incorporated into them as a "spiritual backbone." Most of these codes are still in force on the Continent.

From the cultural point of view this historical sequence of events resulted in a type of legal philosophy and practice that is usually termed "legalism." In essence, legalism is an extreme emphasis upon abstract rules which are regarded as the objective revelation of the legislator's will, as the exclusive manifestation and source of law. The individual rules themselves are seen as the exclusive and concrete answers (solutions) for particular disputes. Parties to disputes are viewed by the legalists as playing a single role, namely, that specified in the rules. Consequently, unlike many non-European societies, the total status of the litigants is dismissed from the court proceedings as irrelevant. Furthermore, all evidence that may be actually related in various degrees to the case but that fails to illuminate the specific points stressed by the pertinent rule, is ruled inadmissible. The juristic method of legalism, ideally speaking, relieves the judge of all legal creativity. His function consists essentially in extrapolating from a given legal case the essential, "legally relevant" features, and equating the resultant legal situation with a similar situation in the codified rules which in its essential features comes closest to it. What follows is basically a fiction by which the two situations are literally held identical, with the consequence that the rule's provision (judgment· and sanction) is mechanically applied to the case. Because the "letter of the law" is held by "legalistic" lawyers to be sacrosanct, flagrant injustice may sometimes ensue as the result of "legal technicalities."

However, law is a category of social (rather than purely philosophical) phenomena and, consequently, it changes with time. Also, because of the complexity of social life the assumption of legalists that coded rules can encompass the totality of social relations and behavior remains a myth. In order legally to accommodate disputes involving relations and claims obviously absent from the inventory of rules, and at the same time keep the myth (and dogma) of the full adequacy of the code of rules, the legalists resorted to further methodological fictions which they called "analogies." Essentially two types of these fictions have been distinguished: *analogia legis* (analogy of a rule), which consists of solving a legal problem not mentioned in the codification by deciding the case on the basis of a principle contained in a rule dealing with a "similar" problem; and *analogia iuris* (analogy of law) which helped to solve legal problems not resembling any of those solved in specific rules, by applying to them principles which were thought to permeate the legal system as a whole (Sommer 1933:20).

This legalistic thinking was not limited to the legalistic schools that were preoccupied with the reception of Roman law. Through its domination of the legal philosophy of continental European law schools as well as courts of law, it affected to a greater or lesser degree most of the legal thinking of such authors as John Austin, Ernst Roguin, Hans Kelsen, Josef Kohler, and others. Further, the influence of legalism and its emphasis on abstract rules affected Durkheim and, through him, the Western social sciences, especially modern sociology (see, for example, Max Weber 1954:5). An outstanding and recent American example of this influence is presented by F. James Davis in his definition of law cited above, according to which not only do most nonliterate peoples have no law, but even the Chinese as well as Casuistic Ancient Rome have to be regarded as without "law." Thus the reception of Roman law and the attitude toward it expressed in the teaching and practice of legalistic scholars have provided Western civilization with a folk category of law whose component parts are abstract rules, preferably organized in a code.

Law conceived of as a system of abstract rules, codified or remembered, has been used by legalists, and contemporary scholars who have been influenced by legalists, as an analytical device intended to be applicable cross-culturally. The problem with studies that assign such an analytical value to abstract rules lies in the fact that this legal category has not been selected on the basis of its heuristic value in a comparative research involving several non-European cultures, but has been dogmatically adopted because it was the "folk category" of the writer. Unlike Zake (1962:66–67), I have no objection to the use of a writer's folk concept as an analytical device in his investigation of other cultures, as long as the cross-cultural analytical value of such a concept is positively established. Consequently, I shall argue against the use of the legalistic conception of law (as a set of abstract rules) purely on the basis of its value as an analytical tool, and will try to demonstrate, logically as well as empirically, its inapplicability in cross-cultural research.

Probably the best opening for my argument is to state the simple fact that, if abstractly worded rules are regarded as the manifestation of law, then, because of a virtual lack of rules in many tribal societies, there would be many "lawless peoples." Law would cease to be a universally usable concept, being limited in its applicability only to those societies which have either written legal codes or sets of rules deposited in the memories of their "wise men." As a consequence of this definition of law, people like the Cheyenne (Llewellyn and Hoebel 1941: 313), Comanche (Hoebel 1940:6), and the Barama River Carib (Gillin 1934:331), because they lacked systems of abstract rules, would have to be regarded as societies without law, and the three authors as having written their legal books and essays on chimeras.

The second argument centers around the incidence of legalistic ideas outside the sphere of Western civilization. To my knowledge there has been just one non-European parallel to Western legalism in the whole world. A legalistic philosophy developed independent of the West and became the dominant doctrine in the juristic thinking and legal practice in China during the rule of the Chhin dynasty (221–206 B.C.). Although this school of thought had already developed in the northeastern state of Chhin at the close of the fifth century B.C., its doctrine did not became the leading philosophy of China as a whole until the third century B.C., when policies based upon it enabled the Chhin dynasty to assume power over the whole country, and its last prince "to become the first emperor of a unified China" (Needham 1956:204). The tenets of Chinese le-

galism, so radically different from the traditional Chinese Confucian philosophy, were determined and elaborated by several Chinese scholars, of whom Han-Fei and Kung-sun Yang supplied the most significant contributions. These tenets of Chinese legalism, closely paralleling those of legalistic Europe, could be very briefly summarized as follows. The exclusive form of law was *fa*, a positive law consisting of abstract rules promulgated by the emperor. These rules were required to be definitive (no exceptions allowed), public, logically consistent, universal to all peoples in China, and binding not only the subjects but also the emperor himself. This type of law could not be questioned because its validity was considered to be derived from the authority's consent (promulgation) and not from morality. The judges were forbidden to change or adjust the law with regard to special circumstances of particular cases; they were expected to apply the pertinent rules mechanically. The abstract rules were believed capable of solving concrete problems arising from any type of relationship that might be present. Because of its radical and rather abrupt departure from Confucian thought, legalism died in China with the fall of the Chhin dynasty. In the twentieth century a European brand of legalism was introduced, after about two millennia of Confucianism. Rather than supporting the legalistic conception of law and the notion that abstract rule is the form or source of law, the Chinese exception confirms the inapplicability of this conception of law on a cross-cultural basis.

If we turn our attention from the societies having no rules to those that do have abstract rules, I will still argue that even in these societies the conception of law as a body of abstract rules is untenable. My argument here may well start with the observation that almost all authors of treaties dealing with law agreed upon one basic characteristic of the phenomena that should belong to this conceptual category, namely, that they should be a form of institutionalized social control. Consequently, those phenomena that do not exercise social control, that cannot be regarded as containing principles of behavior which are to some degree binding by being enforced, cannot be called law. It is often tacitly assumed that the sole existence of abstract legal rules in a society constitutes by itself an evidence that they exercise social control by being rigorously enforced by the authorities. Unfortunately, hardly anything can be farther from truth than such an assumption. In many societies in the world abstract rules play a different role from that which the Western legal scholar would expect. There were, and are, societies in which abstract rules are not expected to be enforced, where these are not regarded as inflexible orders to the judges.

An excellent example of a society with a radically "non-Western" conception of the role of abstract rules is Imperial China. Throughout its history, excepting the brief legalistic interlude discussed above, the Chinese legal sphere was dominated by Confucian ideals. These did not place *fa,* the positive law of abstract rules of the numerous dynastic legal codices, at the apex of legal importance. On the contrary, *fa* was much inferior in prestige (and consequently also in the judicial practice) to *I* and *Li.* While *I* may be briefly defined as the spiritual justification of *Li,* which in some instances may be compared with the Western idea of equity, *Li* consisted of ethical principles contained in social customs. However, unlike the West, the Chinese did not make sharp distinction between social laws and those of nature, with the consequence that they regarded man's social world as closely interrelated with the natural world. This interrelatedness was considered to be so close that human actions were believed to affect nature: good behavior had a positive effect; crimes, on the contrary, caused natural catastrophes, such as drought, floods, and famine. *Li,* then, were ethical principles permeating the whole universe — that of man as well as nature. The effect of this conceptualization upon Chinese law was well stated by Needham:

If, then, all crimes and disputes were looked upon in ancient China, not primarily as infractions of a purely human, though imperial, legal code, but rather as ominous disturbances in the complex network of causal filaments by which mankind was connected on all sides with surrounding Nature, it was perhaps the very subtlety of these which make positive law seem so unsatisfactory (Needham 1956:528).

The knowledge of *Li,* of the uniform ethical principles regulating nature as well as human society, meant title to power. Since the emperor had most of the power, he was expected to know *Li* well. His statutes (*fa*) were expected to reflect *Li* and were regarded as binding only as long as the magistrates could see a basic correspondence between the two. This philosophy allowed the possibility that a wise judge might know *Li* in a given case better than the emperor, which allowed him legally to disregard the statutes. Essentially, abstract rules of Chinese legal codifications were just models the judges might use for formulating their decisions in specific cases. However, the rules were never binding, a decision contrary to the rule was very often the case. In accordance with this conclusion Jean Escarra stated:

Enfin, la loi n'étant qu'un modèle, un modèle dont on demande à l'individu de s'approcher le plus possible sans toutefois exiger qu'il s'y conforme intégralement, la sanction, par sa sévérité voulue, garde un charactère idéal et théorique (1936:74).

Van der Valk arrived at a similar conclusion when he observed:

The law was always considered as a model according to which other cases might be solved.

Therefore the rule *nullum crimen sine praevia lege poenali* could not exist. This idea moreover involved that the written law was not necessarily always implied. It was only a model to be followed under certain circumstances and had no binding force as such (1939:11).

The role of abstract codified rules in Imperial China therefore was, from the point of view of actual social control, relatively unimportant, and the study of the Chinese codices alone would tell little about the judicial practice and law, if by the latter was meant behavioral principles which are actually enforced.

The legalistic doctrine which considers the exclusive source of law to be a set of abstract rules is inapplicable equally to Ancient Rome. True enough, the *Lex Duodecim Tabularum* was already in existence during the Republic as a form of codified law. However, some of the statements of this codex were expressed in a casuistic form (as decisions of concrete cases, functioning here as do our modern "precedents"), referring to specific legal decisions rather than to abstract principles (Sommer 1932:51). Furthermore, the codex, as in Imperial China, did not bind the Roman magistrates, who possessed the explicit power to formulate their own law. Sometimes their decisions clearly contradicted it (Sommer 1933: 15). One may go even further and argue that Ancient Roman law (until the onset of absolutistic empire) was by nature casuistic rather than legalistic. It relied primarily upon the *responsa prudentium,* which were in essence opinions written by Roman *iurisprudentia* (lawyers) for the parties to particular disputes. These opinions became, in effect, the main source of Roman law by which actual disputes were adjudicated. Although they were regarded as "interpretations of the principles and of the thoughts contained in the codex adjusted to concrete cases, in actuality they became the primary

source of the law, objectively rather independent from *Lex Duodecim Tabularum*" (Sommer 1933:15). As a consequence Rome was another civilization with a legal code whose abstract rules were not rigorously enforced (as we understand enforcement nowadays): in some cases they were even utterly disregarded. Here, too, one would not gain too much of an insight into actual Roman judicial practice or into the behavior that was actually enforced in Rome by studying the Twelve Tables alone.

The case for abstract rules as the source of law does not look much better if we turn to societies in which it has been assumed that the provisions of the codified law (written or memorized) are actually enforced. The first obstacles encountered are the so-called "dead rules." These are abstract norms, usually but not always outdated, whose provisions are tacitly disregarded in practice, the judiciary deciding legal cases as though these rules did not exist. As a consequence, all pertinent decisions contradict this kind of abstract rules. In European collections of statutes they are so notorious one need not bother with examples. However, it would be a mistake to believe that they are a specialty of European legal systems. For example, in the Quechua region of Peru, "The haciendas are required by law to maintain schools for their peones, but Government educational officers whom we met admitted that this law was largely a dead letter and that a majority of the estates did not even pretend to observe it" (Rycroft 1946:79). Similarly, in Republican China, the Civil Code of 1931, Article 1144, stated: "Each spouse has the right to inherit the property of the other and his or her successional portion is determined according to the following provisions . . ." (Ching Lin Hsia *et al.* 1931:50). This rule belonged to a group of several that may be regarded as dead, and of which Marion Levy said: "Again it must be observed that these laws are not enforced" (1949:332). Even in some of the nonliterate societies, we find, with amazement, that those having abstract "mental codifications" also have dead rules. Among the Kapauku of Western New Guinea, who have a rather sophisticated system of abstract remembered rules, we find several that are not enforced, although they are recited verbatim by the informants as the ideal. One of the rules regulating incest clearly states *keneka bukii daa* (it is prohibited to marry a sibmate). Yet in the Ijaaj-Pigome political confederacy of the southeastern corner of the Kamu Valley this rule is disregarded and incestuous relations, which should be punished by death, are not only condoned by the local headmen but even advocated as correct (for detail see Pospisil 1958a:165–166, 252; 1958b). Another rule in this confederacy specifies that an adulterous wife should be executed. However, in actual cases of adultery the Kapauku *tonowi* (headmen) request that the woman should only be beaten, and the husband is threatened with prosecution and punishment should he kill or even attempt to kill his spouse. Another such rule clearly calls for a full indemnity payable by a garden owner to the owner of a domesticated pig which is killed by a spiked trap set for a wild boar. This provision may be considered "dead," because in the headmen's decisions it became customary to request from the trapper a payment of only half the value of the killed animal, and to permit him to keep that quarter of the pig's carcass that was pierced by the spikes (Pospisil 1958a: 252).

But even if we ignore these cases we face a much broader problem pertaining to the enforcement of abstract rules: the rules are usually not enforced in the form in which they appear in the codes owing to various circumstances and factors. In other words, here too a study of the abstract rules alone would tell little about social control in the group. For example, of the 176 trouble cases reported for the Kapauku Papuans only eighty-seven, or less than 50 per cent, conformed to the provisions of the pertinent rules (for the various reasons for these discrepancies, see Pospisil 1958a:250–251).

There are many other arguments against the form of law conceived of as abstract rules. One may point out that rules cannot exercise proper social control because they are known to relatively few people in a society (judges in the West, headmen and old wise men among the Kapauku). Another objection claims that it is not the provision of the rule that is important, but what the judges actually decide. Even if they try to follow the "letter of the law," their decisions will differ, due to individual variations in interpretation and semantic understanding.

Some words in Western codes or rules are often deliberately vague in order to encourage the individual judge to "legislate" in a given case. Expressions like "due care," "due respect," "reasonable doubt," "reasonable person," "in due time," "criminal negligence," almost beg for variations among the judges and for discrepancies among the interpretations at different times of history: while the written word remains unaltered, its semantics changes in time. These changes can be detected and ascertained in the actual decisions, but never in the rules themselves. To pretend legalistically that one is, for example, detecting the "intent of the legislator" in a rule which is 200 years old amounts often to conscious self-deception.

Abstracts from Actual Behavior

The limitations and ethnocentric bias of the theoretical position that equated law with abstract rules were clearly realized by Eugen Ehrlich during his stay in Galicia. There he had an opportunity to discover that the "law" expressed in the Austrian legal codification of 1811 was an element completely foreign to the natives of the Austrian province upon which it was rather ruthlessly imposed by the government. Ehrlich, being a most perceptive man, noticed that the life of the peasants, that is, their behavior, followed very different canons from those contained in the official codex. He called these principles of actual behavior "living law," thus introducing a second path for legal thought that regards law as the principles abstracted from the actual behavior of members of the society (Ehrlich 1936:esp. 493–497, 502). This kind of "living law" he contrasted with "norms for decisions" — actually abstracts from actual court decisions (1936:175) — and "legal propositions" (statutes). The latter he regarded as the basic principles abstracted from the norms for decisions, "couched in words, proclaimed authoritatively with a claim to universal validity" (1936:174). Thus to Ehrlich the living law was "the law which dominates life itself even though it has not been posited in legal propositions" (1936:493). Over and over again he stressed the behavioral attribute of his living law: "The living law is not the part of the content of the document that the courts recognize as binding when they decide a legal controversy, but only that part which the parties actually observe in life" (1936:497). He suggested that to acquire the knowledge of this law one should study its provisions "quite independently on the question whether they have already found expression in a judicial decision or in a statute or whether they will ever find it" (1936:502).

It should be mentioned that Ehrlich's position has sometimes been misinterpreted. Preoccupied with the notion that actual behavior of people is controlled and guided by the various leading philosophies of the nations, Northrop implicitly equated Ehrlich's living law with these philosophies. He concluded that to understand, for example, the Chinese living law, one would have to study

Confucian philosophy, while to understand modern Russians one must turn to Marx-Leninism (1951:111). Besides the fact that an overwhelming majority of the Chinese were Taoists and Buddhists, and ignorant of the official Confucian philosophy, nothing can be farther from Ehrlich's living law than principles of well-formulated scholarly philosophies which usually are the property of very few in a given society; "living law" derives from the actual behavior of people, not from officially recognized theories posited in scholarly treaties.

In his conception of law, Bronislaw Malinowski came very close to Ehrlich's concept. Although in his writings he used the term "rules" when referring to the nature of law, to a careful reader it soon becomes obvious that Malinowski's rule has little in common with abstract rules (written or memorized) aimed at adjudication or informal settlements of disputes. What Malinowski had actually in mind were rules of conduct of members of the society as seen in (or abstracted from) the actual behavior and dictated by belief in their efficiency. Thus legal phenomena "do not consist in any independent institutions" (1959:59), such as codified abstract rules used by the courts, for example. Among the Melanesians "Law represents rather an aspect of their tribal life, one side of their structure, than any independent, self-contained social arrangements. Law dwells not in a special system of decrees, which foresee and define possible forms of non-fulfillment and provide appropriate barriers and remedies" (1959:59). Rather than a decree, "the positive law governing all the phases of tribal life, consists then of a body of binding obligations, regarded as a right by one party and acknowledged as a duty by the other, kept in force by a specific mechanism of reciprocity and publicity inherent in the structure of their society" (1959:58). According to Malinowski the nature of the mechanism of reciprocity that exercises control over the behavior lies in what I would term "superrational behavior" of the people: "The tribesman discharges his duty towards his neighbor, however painful or onerous it may be, with a long-range view of the situation. He anticipates and balances rewards quite as much as penalties, approval as well as condemnation" (1961:xxxv– xxxvi). In my own experience, in full honesty, I could hardly point out one Eskimo, Kapauku Papuan, Austrian peasant, or even a European city dweller with such a rational approach toward his behavior. I am far from denying that consideration of reciprocity motivates some behavior. However, the assumption that it motivates all behavior, and of every person, I must reject as highly unrealistic.

The basic premise for an adequate concept of law, advanced in this chapter and reflecting an almost general agreement among lawyers and social scientists, has been the requirement that the phenomena included in this concept constitute some form (usually institutionalized) of social control. In this respect rules and principles abstracted from the actual behavior of the people present several difficulties. First, the behavior of different people varies; its supposed identity is only a fiction used for ease of presentation by various authors. In every society, moreover, and in every subgroup, there are individuals whose behavior is considered more important than that of other members. To speak of law as an "average behavior" computed by the research worker would be equally futile because people are unaware of "averages." To "follow" averages as an ideal would often be impossible; imagine a "law" stating that "five and a half persons, on the average, form a household group among the Kapauku." Furthermore, the actual behavior of all the members of a social group lacks the ideal attribute, which is so important in

making people conform, and so essential for the concept of law. After all, if law were identified with behavioral patterns then the concept of law would become utterly meaningless and superfluous.

Finally, I must insist that law often differs from actual behavior (a statement that may come as a shock to Durkheimean-minded sociologists and anthropologists). For example, Timasheff presented a well-taken criticism of Malinowski's conception of law. He argued that if obligation were the essential criterion of law, then a challenge to a duel and its acceptance, which certainly was a generally recognized obligation in eighteenth-century France, should have been law. Actually, however, according to the state law, duelling was illegal and punishable by imprisonment (1938:871). There are many so-called "authoritarian laws," imposed ruthlessly upon whole populations against their will by a ruling minority (sometimes amounting only to a clique). They certainly not only fail to constitute abstractions from the "actual behavior" of the people, but often are diametrically opposed to it. During World War II most of the Nazi laws imposed upon the Czechs in Bohemia and Moravia were antithetical to actual behavior, and, in spite of Draconic penalties, were not obeyed by the Czechs. Most of the Czechs listened to broadcasts from London, although this transgression, if detected, was punishable by death.

For a last argument, I will turn to a situation in a primitive society. The Kapauku Papuans of West New Guinea steal whenever opportunity presents itself. Thus a "living law" would necessarily state that the law concerning theft indicates stealing whenever the chances are good that it will go undetected. Such a "legal norm," in addition to its absurdity and neglect of the Kapauku ideal rule, oma peu, oma daa (theft is bad, theft is prohibited), would completely ignore the numerous trials and wide range of institutionalized punishments for thieves for which this society is famous.

Principles Upheld by Legal Decisions

The third path to a definition of the form of law leads, according to Llewellyn and Hoebel, toward investigation of cases of conflict, toward the identification of law with principles of social control that are actually upheld in legal decisions. To be sure, although Llewellyn became one of the most effective and eloquent advocates of this path, the conviction that legal decisions offer the best way to investigate law (viewed as principles abstracted from judicial decisions) did not originate in his writings. It was Oliver Wendell Holmes who, in his work *Path of Law,* pointed out this approach toward investigation and conceptualization of law. He stated his concept of law quite bluntly in his now famous assertion: "The prophecies of what the courts will do in fact, and nothing more pretentious, are what I mean by the law" (1897:461). At this early date he advocated a more scientific and less dogmatic, philosophical, or speculative investigation of law by pointing out that "The life of the law has not been logic; it has been experience" (1881:1). According to him, law should not have been isolated from other social phenomena. It should have been studied as an integral part of the rest of the culture, not as an autonomous system of petrified abstract rules set in the old codices. To Justice Holmes, anthropology, especially, was the most appropriate discipline to deal effectively with this conceptual problem (1886:741). The Holmesian position opened up the third path toward investigation of law and became a foundation upon which a school of legal realism developed.

In his work Llewellyn went far beyond Holmes' work, becoming the most prominent representative of the realistic legal thought. His criticisms of legalism were devastating, and he not only accepted Holmes' philosoph-

ical and theoretical position, but actually implemented what Holmes only suggested. He joined forces with an anthropologist, E. Adamson Hoebel, and with him produced an outstanding contribution to the study of law, which nowadays is regarded as a classic: *The Cheyenne Way* (1941). In addition to an unusual richness of theoretical observations and constructs, the book demonstrates most effectively the value of the "case-study approach" to law. Among the Cheyenne Indians of the Great Plains, law was exceedingly rarely "clothed in rules" (1941:313). Yet the book contains a great wealth of theoretical as well as substantive legal principles of the Cheyenne, most derived from case material supplied by Hoebel. The two authors properly claim that this material can justifiably be compared with Roman law. If their investigation had used a concept of law based on abstract rules, this wealth of knowledge would have been missed and the authors would have been empty-handed. The value of the case-study approach could hardly be better demonstrated than by this work on Cheyenne law. It is with full justification that the authors conclude their theoretical discussion of the various approaches to the study of law by writing: "The trouble-cases, sought out and examined with care, are thus the safest main road into the discovery of law. Their data are most certain. Their yield is richest. They are the most revealing" (1941:29). The book itself includes fifty-three cases, of which five constitute the introductory chapter. The rest are distributed throughout the book wherever a theoretical point is to be documented. Thus the cases provide support and illustrations for the more abstract discussion and conclusions, and a vivid matrix from which the various principles are skillfully abstracted with what I would call anatomical legal precision. However, they are not used as a consistent matrix which, as a whole, would be subject to a rigorous formal analysis.

Cases of conflict have been utilized in the anthropological literature by several other authors for illustration and documentation. However, in their writings the cases do not appear for extrapolating principles of broad theoretical validity; they serve merely as documentation for statements concerning the substantive law of the society under discussion. This type of casuistic approach is rather old, dating back to anthropologists like Barton (law of the Ifugao of Luzon; 1919), and including such authors as Lips (Naskapi law; 1947), Holleman (Shona law; 1952), and Berndt (law of the Kamano, Usurufa, Jate, and Fore of New Guinea; 1962). Of the many authors working with the case-study approach to abstract and elucidate the substantive law, Howell and his work on Nuer law deserve special mention (1954). On the basis of an extensive study of several thousand decisions of the Nuer tribunals (founded by the British Administration, but deciding cases under the heavy influence of the old Nuer customary law) Howell presents the main principles of the native law by systematically abstracting them from the case material. Although the actual presentation limits itself only to summarized cases illustrating the various legal observations, there is no doubt that the generalizations are solidly based and "induced from" an impressive number of decisions. Thus the decisions are not used for illustrations and vivid presentation only but form the actual raw material from which most of the general statements were derived.

In his book, *Judicial Process Among the Barotse of Northern Rhodesia,* Max Gluckman employs a modified casuistic approach. Unlike the authors cited above, Gluckman defines law in terms of abstract rules: "First, it is a body of rules which theoretically are certain and have socially permeated 'intrinsic' meanings. Secondly, the law also exists in court decisions in which concepts are specified for extrinsic referents in a particular dispute" (1955:354). In his dualistic conception of law, Gluckman regards the form of the abstract rules that Lozi courts "ought to apply" as basic (1955:164), and the decisions are regarded as application of these general rules to concrete cases, thus forming "the law for the cases" (1955:227). Although one may suspect a European legalistic influence in this definition, Gluckman was obviously more influenced by the Barotse "folk concept" of law whose essence is abstract rules (1955:esp. 256–257). Unlike the European legalists, Gluckman does not limit himself to the emphasis on abstract rules. The second part of his legal definition, which emphasized legal decisions, induced the author to present a series of legal cases which nonsystematically but quite effectively document his generalizations. One may criticize this modified casuistic approach and dualistic definition of law on the basis of logical inconsistency. Since rules that ought to be enforced often deviate in a remarkable way from the principles that are actually enforced in legal decisions, one can hardly call both sets of principles, that sometimes differ to the point of contradiction, by the same term, "law."

Systematic analysis of matrices of legal cases did not remain limited to the investigation of substantive law only. Recent anthropological research employs systematic casuistic analysis for theoretical purposes, thus transcending the boundaries of the field of substantive law. In their work entitled *Zuni Law* (1954) Smith and Roberts subject to their casuistic analysis ninety-seven legal cases adjudicated by the Zuni Bow Priest Society and the Tribal and Great Councils. Unlike Howell's work, all the cases are fully described and organized under topical headings. Influenced by Kluckhohn's writings, the purpose of the analysis is to abstract from the case material cultural values that are upheld by the bodies mentioned. The abstracted, legally relevant values are then related to some aspects of the Zuni culture, especially to the dichotomy of the secular and religious. Since this study omits consideration of abstract rules, I would call it a purely casuistic approach.

Working systematically with extensive case material, Laura Nader used the casuistic approach for an effective inquiry into the relationship of law and some aspects of the socio-political structure of the Zapotecan society. Accordingly, her case analysis elucidated the relationship between the distribution of conflict resolutions and patterns of authority (1963), and types of conflict and their outcome (1964). The case analysis also shows the kinds of individuals who bring their grievances to the attention of courts, the range of grievances, and the age of delinquency. These comparative and relational efforts constitute an important contribution not only to the study of law itself but also to general ethnography, demonstrating to the anthropologists, who in general have shown remarkable disinterest in legal matters, how investigation of court decisions may contribute in a significant way to a fuller understanding of social organization.

Whereas Smith, Roberts, Nader, and Metzger used the case-study approach for investigating relationships between law and extralegal aspects of culture, my own casuistic efforts have so far been directed toward clarification of the concept of law itself, at empirically scrutinizing the effectiveness and importance of the various criteria of law, and at distinguishing between two types of law on the basis of the degree of their internalization (or support by the members of the particular group in which they are enforced). The work with the case material allowed me to investigate the nature of legal change, and, by relating the various legal cases to the locus of their adjudication within the "societal structure" (segmentation of the society), led me to the conception of "legal levels" and to the recognition of the multi-

plicity of legal systems within a given society (1956, 1958a, 1958c, 1965). Thus my use of case material was directed primarily toward the investigation of the legal field itself. In this endeavor I have abandoned the purely casuistic approach and, with my legal cases, I have also analyzed the pertinent abstract rules. The analysis of the comparisons between the abstract rules and the pertinent decisions clarified the relationships between the two sets of phenomena and their role in the field of social control in general, thus providing me with an empirical basis for construction of a general theory of law (1956, 1958a).

The fruitful and manifold use of the case-study method gives ample testimony to the heuristic value of viewing the form of law as principles abstracted from legal decisions. To this evidence, which supports the third, casuistic pathway to the study of law as the correct one, I can add other arguments that may further demonstrate its significance. First, by accepting the casuistic solution to the problem of the form of law, the concept of law becomes universal, leaving nowhere in the world a residuum of "lawless societies," which gives the concept a value for cross-cultural comparisons. Second, unlike the abstract rules concept, legal decisions are widely publicized, thus becoming a form of effective social control known to all — not the property of a few. Third, legal decisions incorporate no dead rules that obviously do not play a role in the field of social control. Fourth, legal decisions are positive statements in intelligible and definitive language; unlike abstract rules, they do not incorporate a vagueness that allows different interpretations. In other words, decisions clearly delimit and make specific the broad and ambiguous concepts stated in the rules, such as "due care," "reasonable doubt," and the like. Fifth, unlike abstract rules, legal decisions are not "outdated," or "obsolete"; reflecting minute changes in law, the adjudication process itself may be seen as a continuum of change in the institutionalized social control of a society. Sixth, legal decisions reflect the contemporary culture and "life" of the society, and are actually part of it. Llewellyn and Hoebel expressed this argument very well: "Not only the making of new law and the effect of old, but the hold and the thrust of all other vital aspects of the culture shine clear in the crucible of conflict" (1941:29). Seventh, through the idea of legal precedent, principles contained in the legal decisions become ideals not only for the public, but also for the authorities themselves, thus providing for public awareness and for continuity and certainty of the law.

Some folk-minded Western lawyers may object that this conception of form of law, which differs so much from the traditional legalistic one of abstract rule, is misleading by being labeled "law." But according to Webster, the casuistic conception of law does no violence to the semantics of modern English, and the definition in Webster does not actually exclude it (Neilson *et al.* 1940: 1401). Critics holding to a traditional orientation may further argue that even if the dictionary's meaning of the term "law" is not violated, then certainly the common legal jargon is. To be specific, they may argue that one refers to an abstract rule passed by the Congress as "a law." This is of course true. However, in this case we face a problem peculiar to the English language. In European Continental languages one distinguishes between an abstract rule (for example, *lex* in Latin, *Gesetz* in German, *zákon* in Czech, *loi* in French) and "law proper" (*ius* in Latin, *Recht* in German, *právo* in Czech, *droi* in French). The English language makes no such distinction, applying to the abstract rules of the law books (*leges*) as well as to the other kind of law (*ius*) the same term. What anthropologists are obviously arguing about is the more basic concept of *ius,* not the obvious and clear concept of an abstract rule designated in Latin by *lex.*

There is one more problem to be clarified. The Western folk tradition views as proper legal decision a formalistic act by a formally instituted authority pronouncing a formal verdict, which is then physically enforced. In most of the nonliterate, and in some literate but non-European societies, legal decisions may assume forms undreamt by Western jurists, of such informality that an anthropologist with even a slight Western folk-bias would disregard them as of no legal consequence. As an illustration I shall describe a decision-making process among two Papuan tribes of New Guinea — the Kapauku of the Kamu Valley and the Manga of the Jimi River Area.

The Kapauku "process of law" starts usually as a quarrel. The "plaintiff" accuses the "defendant" of having performed an act which causes harm to the plaintiff's interests. The defendant denies this or brings forward justification for his action. The arguments are usually accompanied by loud shouting which attracts other people, who gather around. The close relatives and friends of the parties to the dispute take sides and present their opinions and testimony by emotional speeches or by shouting. If this sort of arguing, called by natives *mana koto,* goes on unchecked, it usually results in a stick fight (Cases 40, 55, 57, 59, 118: Pospisil 1958a) or in war (Case 16). However, in most instances, the important men from the village, and from allied communities, appear on the scene. First, they squat among the onlookers and listen to the arguments. As soon as the exchange of opinions reaches a point too close to an outbreak of violence, the rich headman steps in and starts his argumentation. He admonishes both parties to have patience and begins questioning the defendant and the witnesses. He looks for evidence that would incriminate the defendant, at the scene of the crime or in the defendant's house (Cases 62, 74). This activity of the authority is called *boko petai,* which can be loosely translated as "finding the evidence." Having secured the evidence and made up his mind about the factual background of the dispute, the authority starts the activity called by the natives *boko duwai,* the process of making a decision and inducing the parties to the dispute to follow it. The native authority makes a long speech in which he sums up the evidence, appeals to a rule, and then tells the parties what should be done to terminate the dispute. If the principals are not willing to comply, the authority becomes emotional and starts to shout reproaches; he makes long speeches in which evidence, rules, decisions, and threats form inducements. Indeed, the authority may go as far as to start *wainai* (the mad dance), or change his tactics suddenly and weep bitterly about the misconduct of the defendant and the fact that he refuses to obey. Some native authorities are so skilled in the art of persuasion that they can produce genuine tears which almost always break the resistance of the unwilling party. A superficial Western observer confronted with such a situation may very likely regard the weeping headman as a culprit on trial. Thus, from the formalistic point of view, there is little resemblance between the Western court's sentence and the *boko duwai* activity of the headman. However, the effect of the headman's persuasion is the same as that of a verdict passed in our courts. There were only five cases in my material wherein the parties openly resisted and disobeyed the authority's decision (Cases 54, 94, 105, 119, 168; 1958a:254–255).

The Manga of the Jimi River area afford an instance of an authoritarian "decision" in which, fantastically enough, not a single word was spoken. Only a research worker with a discernment and knowledge of the native language and the subtleties of informal social control equal to that of Cook would notice it, recognize its significance, and report it in the proper perspective. Briefly, a subclan leader named Wando of the village Kwiop, trying to stop a quarrel over a girl's marriage and punish the "guilty party" for being a public nuisance, shot and killed a man with an arrow in 1956. Six years later, during Cook's research among the Manga, a similar quarrel resulted over an elopement. As he had done six years before, Wando decided there had been enough quarreling by the girl's agnatic relatives. Not uttering a word, he went to his house, picked up a bow and arrow, came back to the scene of the dispute, and silently began to sharpen the arrow. In this wordless way his decision that the girl's agnates should stop arguing was made public. By linking it to the "precedent," the parties to the dispute were made aware of the decision as well as of their potential danger. As a result the quarreling stopped, and the threat of an open conflict subsided (Cook: 1965).

CONCLUSION

On the basis of the arguments presented in this chapter I conclude that law (*ius*) manifests itself in the form of a decision passed by a legal authority (council, chief, headman, judge, and the like), by which a dispute is solved, or a party is advised before any legally relevant behavior takes place, or by which approval is given to a previous solution of a dispute made by the participants before it was brought to the attention of the authority. This form of law has two important aspects: a decision serves not only to resolve a dispute, which represents the behavioral part played by the authority while passing the sentence, but it also represents a precedent and an ideal for those who were not party to that controversy. They regard the content of the decision as a revelation of the ideally correct behavior. Consequently, a legal decision may be considered a culturally important behavior insofar as the authority's act of passing his verdict (opinion) is concerned, and as an ideal insofar as the effect upon the "followers of the authority" is concerned. Whereas the abstract rules lack the behavioral aspect, the actual behavior, or "living law," lacks the ideal. This is another reason why legal decisions should be preferred over the two other possibilities as manifestations of law. Thus the field of law consists of principles abstracted from the decisions of authorities. These may be identical in content with corresponding abstract rules (*leges*), in which case we may regard the rules as being actually enforced. Those rules that are not enforced — the dead rules — are, by their lack of exercise, omitted from the legal field; they have no corresponding principles abstracted from decisions. Thus the legal nature and importance of enforced abstract rules is here neither denied nor diminished. I object solely to the inclusion of dead rules in the legal field, to the exclusion of legal decisions from it, and to the denial of the latter's paramount importance for the study of law, if by law is meant a form of institutionalized social control.

CHAPTER **9** places the scientific comparative study of religion into its existential setting. Out of the skeptical philosophic traditions of Europe and America came a variety of efforts to comprehend the causes for as well as the essential nature of religion. With the development of a cross-cultural, anthropological approach to the study of "religions," an effort worldwide in scope and not limited to a scholarly absorption in the grand cosmologies and theologies of the great traditional religions, comes an intellectual difficulty similar to that posed for the comparative study of law, language, and other aspects of human social life. In one sense, Professor Wax points out, "religion" is no more than a Western folk category, but it is a notion anthropologists and other social scientists are attempting to refine into an analytic concept of general applicability. In this context Professor Wax discusses the theoretical contributions of J. G. Frazer, Émile Durkheim, Bronislaw Malinowski, and Radcliffe-Brown, and offers a discussion of the "primitive world view," which is contrasted with the polytheistic religious systems of the world's high civilizations, a comparison which affords insight into the functions of cult, ritual, and magical practice.

THE AUTHOR was born in St. Louis, Missouri, and has studied at the Universities of Pennsylvania and Chicago. He has taught at those universities, and also at Emory, Temple, and the University of Miami; he is currently on the faculty of the University of Kansas. He has long experience in applied social research, while at the same time pursuing his scholarly interest in intercultural relations, world view, and anthropological theory. In recent years he has focused his research energies on problems of American Indian education, which has resulted in the monograph *Formal Education in an American Indian Community*, written jointly with his wife, Rosalie Wax.

9

Religion and Magic

MURRAY WAX

University of Kansas

THEORISTS AND RIVAL THEORIES

Western civilization has been intimately associated with the Judaeo-Christian religious complex. Wherever the civilization has spread it has been paced by its Christian missionaries, who have felt the call to take their religious message to people they regarded as heathen and superstitious. Conjointly, Western civilization has borne a strong rationalist tradition which has insisted on subjecting Judaeo-Christianity to the acid test of reason (Weber 1958b:13–27). In medieval times this rationalism found its expression in the theological endeavor to demonstrate that reason and faith were complementary in reaching the truths of the Catholic religion. With the passage of time, the application of reason became ever more critical, and from the eighteenth century onward, increasing numbers of scholars endeavored to disenchant (or debunk) Judaeo-Christianity and its Holy Scriptures by showing that these institutions and artifacts were the consequence,

not of divine revelation, but of conventional and irrational processes occurring everywhere in human society. So, for example, Friederich Engels analyzed the development of early Christianity and of Protestantism in Germany as instances of radical and revolutionary movements among proletarians and peasants (Marx and Engels 1964; Engels 1926). Or, as another example, James George Frazer argued that Christianity was an integration of a series of cultural traits such as the ceremonial slaying of the divine king and the communal cannibalism of his flesh and blood, traits that were widespread among human societies. Or, as a final example, Sigmund Freud argued that the fundamental traits of Judaeo-Christianity reflected the same kind of mental processes as were operative among his neurotic patients, and, in particular, that the severe and repressive moral (and sexual) codes associated with the teachings of Moses and Jesus were sustained among Western man by the *guilt* deriving from the communal slaying of these great leaders — a guilt which he believed was transmitted unconsciously from generation to generation (1939, 1949a, 1949b, 1950).

In each of the foregoing examples it is clear that the rationalistic analysis of Christianity was an aspect of and was dependent upon the empirical study and understanding of conventional social processes. Whether or not we choose today to accept the interpretations of Marx and Engels, or Frazer, or Freud, their efforts at disenchanting have plausibility only to the extent that they relate to a more general theory of man and society. Thus, Engels' essays reflected his and Marx' studies of revolutionary movements and the dynamics of social change. Frazer could not have written *The Golden Bough* unless he had been able to compile and organize a vast body of information about the beliefs and practices of the peoples of the world. And Sigmund Freud's studies of Judaeo-Christian religions were integrated with his development of the psychoanalytic theory of personality and society. In retrospect, it is clear that one significant byproduct of this scholarly effort at criticism and disenchantment was a great impetus to the creation of the various social sciences, especially anthropology. Of course, several other movements such as the concern over urban poverty and the task of administering colonial possessions contributed to the development of the social sciences; yet it is significant that many of the most important figures — both those cited and others to be mentioned later — were participants in this critical activity. Marx and Engels could well assert that "the criticism of religion is the premise of all criticism" (1964:41).

In some measure at least, this critical assault on Judaeo-Christianity was predicated on the comparative study of the beliefs and practices of other peoples. This fact brings us, as it brought earlier students, to the issue of the nature of the entities suitable for comparison with Christianity or Judaism. To use the phrase "other religions" simply begs the question, as it leaves us with the basic query, *what is religion?* For pious Christians and Jews the answer was contained in their Scriptures and their traditions: Judaism and Christianity were intolerant and exclusive and what their prophets and priests had denounced as the worship of "other gods" (than Yahweh) could be taken to be "other religions." But, for social scientists, this procedure was to make considerable difficulty, since the entities so defined as "other religions" were radically different from Judaeo-Christianity, and the task of discerning something common to all of them was to prove very difficult. Yet without being able to specify this essential commonality, the notion of "religion" would have to remain as a vague undefined entity. The confusion is apparent in the accounts of the travelers, administrators, and missionaries of the nineteenth century, for some spoke of the peoples they observed as having "no religion," others spoke of them as being the "victims of superstition" and "heathen beliefs," while still others spoke of such peoples as having beliefs and rites that were noble and pure, even if unchristian and, therefore, fallacious. True, some of these differences in description reflect differences among the customs of the peoples observed as well as the differing viewpoints of their observers, but underneath is the lack of consensus as to what was "religion" (that is, other than Judaeo-Christianity).

Edward Burnett Tylor, regarded as the founder of cultural anthropology, handled this confusion about "religion" by remaining very close to the empirical data (1958). As a result, his writings and those of other Britons such as R. R. Marett still have an interest for the student today, even though no one would accept their definitions of "religion" or their theories as to how it arose (1914). However, other scholars were much bolder and more speculative in their theoretical efforts, and several tried to define or characterize "religion" as a universal social phenomenon and to demonstrate how it must have arisen and what its role was in individual and social life.

A contemporary sociologist, Talcott Parsons, has been much interested in this historical development and has singled out as of especial importance the theories of Max Weber, Émile Durkheim, Vilfredo Pareto, and Bronislaw Malinowski. Surveying their work a few years ago, Parsons concluded that the theoretical development of the sociology of religion "represents a notable advance in the adequacy of our theoretical equipment to deal with a critically important range of scientific problems" (1949:52).

Eminent though he is, Parsons' appraisal is not shared by all scholars interested in the comparative study of religions. A few years after his statement appeared, another eminent scholar, E. E. Evans-Pritchard, declared (1954:7) that the study of religion "has hardly begun to be a scientific study"! The radical difference between these appraisals can hardly be resolved by identifying Parsons as a sociologist and Evans-Pritchard as a social anthropologist, because at least half of the figures singled out by Parsons would be claimed by anthropologists as ancestral to their own discipline. Nor can the difference be resolved by such a device as identifying Parsons as American and Evans-Pritchard as British, since Parsons did much of his graduate work abroad, and the influence of his studies with Malinowski at the London School is clearly visible in his subsequent essays on religion and primitive thought. A more significant ground for the difference in their appraisals may derive from personal research experiences, for Evans-Pritchard has done field work among several folk and devoted much of his research among the Nuer and Zande to their religion and magic, while Parsons has had no such direct and personal encounter with peoples of simple technology and primitive world view. Lest

this consideration lapse into the fallacy of the *ad hominem* argument, let us turn more directly to the theoretical issues.

As the reader might have expected from the foregoing discussion, part of the difference between the appraisals of Parsons and Evans-Pritchard rests in their disagreement about "religion": Parsons thinks progress has been made toward an adequate definition of an entity universally present in human societies; Evans-Pritchard disagrees. Another part of their difference rests in disagreement as to the nature of social science and thus as to the nature of a "scientific study" or an adequate "sociological study"; the nature of this disagreement will become more apparent when we review the theories of Émile Durkheim. Meanwhile, let us discuss further some of the circumstances complicating the definition of "religion."

RELIGION AS A FOLK CATEGORY

The student may be surprised that there is so much disagreement as to the scientific definition of "religion," and he may be inclined to think that this reflects the intractability of the subject matter, that "religion" cannot be subjected to scientific analysis. For comparison, we may note that quite a similar problem has long plagued the anthropological study of kinship. There the difficulty was that scholars were attempting to apply Western kinship terminologies to the practices and relationships of non-Western peoples. In so doing, they were acting as if such Western terms as "father," "sister," and "uncle" were *universal* categories of social relationships, rather than being *folk* categories peculiar to Western societies (and not all of those!). Until this terminological ethnocentrism was perceived and corrected the attempt to organize data about non-Western kinship systems led to repeated paradoxes and incongruities. Today, we recognize that of the Western categories of kinship, only a few, for example, marriage and incest, seem to be universal or nearly so.

With this as a cautionary example, we may say that "religion" is a folk category of the Western Judaeo-Christian tradition. Social scientists in general and anthropologists especially have been trying to transform it into a scientific and universal category, but have not yet achieved a consensus about how this should be done. Other Western folk categories often used in religious discourse include magic, sacred, witchcraft, miracle, superstition, supernatural, heathen, spirits, divinities, and sorcery. Since their universal applicability remains to be demonstrated, the student should be wary of all these terms, lest he (or an author) apply them without suitable caution.

The foregoing may help to explain why I phrased the initial paragraph of this essay on "religion" as carefully as I have. I did not wish to begin by implying that there was some definite, universal social entity which all could agree was "religion," and that this entity was to be the focus of our inquiry. Rather, I wished to communicate that much of the social-scientific and anthropological discussion of religion is limited and biased by the peculiarities of Western traditions and, especially, the central place of Judaeo-Christianity in Western history.

Islam, Buddhism, Confucianism, Hinduism (and to a lesser extent, Zoroastrianism) have occupied a place in the history of other civilized societies that is comparable to Judaeo-Christianity in the West. Some scholars (for instance, Max Weber) have referred to them as "world religions" or "universal religions" in order to counterpose them to "folk religions," but for us this nomenclature still prejudges the question of what is "religion." We must note, for example, that in its pure or ideal form Buddhism has nothing whatsoever to do with the worship of a deity or deities, and should note, also, that while Hinduism has its sacred scriptures, it

can scarcely be said to have a creed which its participants must endorse. A better system of nomenclature by which to denote this collection is the term, "Great Tradition," and correspondingly for folk peoples, the term "Little Traditions" (Redfield 1956:chap. 3; Singer 1960). At the moment, we cannot take time for the further elaboration of these concepts; however, let us conclude this section by commenting that it may well be more significant to compare Christianity, not (as did Frazer) with the beliefs and practices of primitive peoples, but with such other Great Traditions as Islam, Buddhism, and the like.

DURKHEIM'S TWO-SIDED DEFINITION OF RELIGION

We are now prepared to consider the way in which some of the most influential social scientists have proposed to define "religion." Émile Durkheim, it will be recalled, was one of the quartet of theorists singled out by Parsons for their contributions to the theoretical development of the sociology of religion, and so he represents an appropriate initial point of departure. His most important work here was *The Elementary Forms of the Religious Life,* and he began it with a cogent and critical review of the attempts by earlier scholars to differentiate "religion" and the "religious" from other aspects of social life (1947b: chaps. 1–3). In particular, Durkheim objected to the equating of the *religious* with the *supernatural,* because, as he pointed out, the notion of the supernatural hinges on the contrary notion of a *natural* order of things. Lacking the notion of a *natural order,* people cannot have the notion of the *supernatural* as that which violates the logic of that order. Since the notion of a *natural order* is of recent origin, being a product of Western scholarship and science, it follows that primitive peoples cannot have the contrary notion of a *supernatural.* Accordingly, Durkheim argued that the dichotomy of natural/supernatural cannot be used to differentiate and define the dichotomy of the secular/religious. The student should note that by the very structure of his criticism Durkheim is insisting on the importance of the scientist's grasping the categorizations of the peoples themselves; this is a methodological principle we will shortly discuss more fully.

In like manner, Durkheim criticized several other qualities or characteristics which his contemporaries and predecessors had proposed as universally true of "religion" and had used as the basis of a definition, for example, the sense of mystery, or the notion of spirits or divinities. Concerning these qualities he was able to show that each is not present everywhere among the phenomena scholars have agreed are religious: for example, the sense of mystery, or the notion of religion, even though it worships no divinities.

Having thus eliminated the rival proposals, Durkheim presented his own. He argued that the universally present quality of the *religious* is the differentiation between the *sacred* and the *profane* as two distinct classes of things, two worlds which share nothing in common. Religious *beliefs* are then systems which express the nature of sacred things, and religious *rites* are the rules prescribing the way men must conduct themselves in relationship to sacred objects. "Religion," then, is "a unified system of beliefs and practices relative to sacred things, that is to say, things set apart and forbidden — beliefs and practices which unite into one single moral community called a Church, all those who adhere to them" (Durkheim 1947b:47). This definition is quite a mouthful, and he himself devoted a sizable book to explaining and defending it, while numerous later scholars have, in turn, devoted many pages to analyzing it and criticizing its implications. Our limited task here is twofold: first, to comprehend the definition by understanding what is included and what is excluded from *religion*

in this sense; and second, to clearly distinguish the two sides of the definition, that is, the two perspectives integrated within it. From the perspective of the people participating in the religion, there is (according to Durkheim) the division of objects into the *sacred* and *profane;* from the perspective of the detached, scientific observer, there is the *uniting* of individuals into a single *moral* community. In Durkheim's definition and in his argument, the two perspectives are so neatly fused that the reader is not particularly conscious that their separation is possible, but as we shall note later, one of the major problems as to whether "religion" is universal hinges on whether or not the data do lend themselves to this fusion.

Standing within the Durkheimian tradition, the scientific observer regards and analyzes the society under his scrutiny much as if it were a biological organism. Mentally, he is as detached as if it were such an organism, and, like the biological scientist, he analyzes the constituents of the society and the processes within it in terms of the contribution they are making to the maintenance (or disruption) of the equilibrium (or homeostasis) of the system. In the lexicon of modern social science, this observer is said to be operating with a *structural-functional* or *systems-theoretic* model, and in that model "religion" is the social institution which unifies the society (or social system) about its moral values. So in *The Elementary Forms of the Religious Life* Durkheim himself wrote of the great annual ceremonials of the Australian aborigines as uniting them about the sacred totem; and in the same way, he would have seen the Catholic Church in the French peasant village as serving through its rites to unify the inhabitants about the sacred symbols of Christianity. These unitings, which are based on allegiance to a set of *sacred* symbols, may be contrasted with the earlier philosophical notion of a social compact, which would be agreed to on *rational* and utilitarian grounds by an aggregate of previously disunited men (as in the governmental theories of John Locke).

Distinguishing the systems-theoretic perspective of the outside observer from the perspective of those participating in the rites is important because, otherwise, we are apt to overlook that fact that as applied, say, to the United States, Durkheim's definition would include as "religious" many rites and institutions which we participants would not usually classify as such. Put in other words, we can say that Durkheim's definition does not exactly match the United States folk category of "religion"; and while the scientific and folk categories need not match, the disparity poses a certain risk, insofar as it may lead us to errors in reasoning if we are careless in handling the terms. To be more specific, we should point out that patriotism or nationalism — with its rites and beliefs — would classify as a "religion" in Durkheim's sense. Those students who are familiar with the Mediterranean societies of classical antiquity will not find this usage novel, since the Roman Emperor and the Egyptian Pharaoh were explicitly identified as deities, and in city-states such as Athens the body politic was symbolized by a deity (Athena) who was worshipped by all citizens as a patriotic duty. Similarly, in some traditional African societies, the monarch was more of a priest or spiritual symbol than a political ruler backed by the armed force of the state (Fortes and Evans-Pritchard 1940). However, in the contemporary United States, where we think of church and state as separated by the First Amendment of the Constitution, it may be more surprising to realize that Durkheim's usage would require us to classify a Memorial Day celebration as a religious rite (Warner 1959), and we would have to pause, reflect, and recall that in many towns this celebration is a cultic rite involving sacred things (flags, anthems, cemeteries, military parades) and serving to unify the participating townspeople into a "nationalistic church."

Not only does Durkheim's definition include as "religious" social phenomena that do not fit the particular folk categories, it also excludes from the "religious" other phenomena that do fit within the folk category. Whatever an individual does wholly by himself — prayer, solitary religious exercises, meditation, personal retreats or withdrawals (including hermitage) — can only be considered as "religious" in Durkheim's sense by stretching his original definition or fudging its boundaries. Without such an alteration there would be the danger that these individualistic actions would be classified in Durkheim's terms as *magic,* for "magic is opposed to religion as the individual to the social" (p. 45n). As he contrasted the two, *magic* is individualistic and does not unite its believers or practitioners into a moral community: "there is no Church of magic" (p. 44). Responding to these statements, many American anthropologists, familiar with the Plains Indians and their Vision Quest, have been uncomfortable with Durkheim's argument (Lowie 1948:chap. 7; Goldenweiser 1922).

In the typical form of the Vision Quest the individual isolated himself for days, mortified his body, and prayed for an encounter with some divinity who would convey to him a grant of Power (*manitou, wakan,* and so on). While the quest was a solitary individual activity and the Power, if obtained, was personally held, among many tribes the quest was regarded as a moral duty of all adolescent males. Again, if we look to the history of Judaeo-Christianity, we can find similar cases wherein individuals retired, sometimes briefly, sometimes lengthily, to pray and worship "in the desert" or elsewhere, isolated from their fellows. Durkheim and his disciples were aware of these cases and argued that they fitted into their definition of the "religious" rather than the "magical," but in order to perform this classification, they had to blur the phrase within the definition, "the single moral community called a Church," and replace it by the vaguer, more flexible notion of the common cultural-moral background of the community.

In categorizing these individual activities as "religious," Durkheim was clearly responding to the view of the participants in the Church or community. Palpably, the individuals engaging in solitary exercises were not uniting with their fellows in joint activities based on allegiance to a set of sacred symbols; in fact, the Christian hermit may have intended to disaffiliate permanently from the fellowship of any actual community or Church. Nevertheless, the members of the community or Church they had quitted saw them as engaging in moral or holy conduct. Consideration of this paradox brings us to a discussion of the other "side" of Durkheim's definition, that which is concerned with the perspective of the participants. Within European social science, research from this perspective has come to be spoken of as *Verstehen* (the German word for "understanding"), and within the fields of history and sociology there has been considerable debate over the scientific utility and validity of the *Verstehen* approach. However, cultural anthropology is based upon a research technique which is unavailable to historians — the extensive field trip involving intense participant observation and requiring a high degree of socialization into the life of an exotic people. Ever since the pioneer investigations of Malinowski and Radcliffe-Brown, the intimate understanding (*Verstehen*) of how another people view and experience their world has come to be one of the major goals of cultural anthropology. Durkheim, like Tylor, was of an earlier generation whose ethnological analyses were based on intensive study of whatever fragmentary accounts (from missionaries or travelers) were available to them. That men like Durkheim and Tylor were able to accomplish as much as

they did using such uneven data is a tribute to their insight and sagacity. Radcliffe-Brown, who himself worked among the Australians, judged that Durkheim's major thesis as to the social function of the totemic rites was valid but that his understanding of Australian totemism was defective (1952: chap. 8). More significantly, Radcliffe-Brown simply avoided in his own writings the usage of the dichotomy of the *sacred* and the *profane*, and it is quite plain that he regarded it as not corresponding to any dichotomy universally present in human societies. Since Radcliffe-Brown was much influenced by Durkheim, his negative judgment on these issues must carry considerable weight; however, further consideration of this topic must be postponed until we deal directly with Radcliffe-Brown's own theories of religion.

We may conclude our review of Durkheim by referring to the contrast initially posed between the appraisals of Parsons and Evans-Pritchard. Parsons would see Durkheim's accomplishments as both positive and negative (that is, critical): positively, there is the view of "religion" in terms of its social origin and social function; negatively, there is the refutation of the popular views which see "religion" as a species of intellectual ignorance and error. On the other hand, Evans-Pritchard would see Durkheim's accomplishment as only negative: he helped to dispel an inaccurate conception of "religion," but his own proposal is itself unacceptable because it is not derived from a detailed ethnographic understanding of the institutions and social processes of the peoples of the world.

MALINOWSKI AND SAVAGE SCIENCE

While Malinowski's theorizing about religion was not of the profundity of a Durkheim, a Radcliffe-Brown, a Parsons, or an Evans-Pritchard, he wrote with a vivid and impassioned rhetoric that students generally have found attractive. Having lived intimately for several years among the peoples of the Trobriand Islands, he was able to describe their lives in such fashion that the reader is carried along as though he too were gliding in an outrigger canoe across the South Pacific seas. His celebrated essay on "Magic, Science and Religion" (1955) is of this character and is likely to persuade the unwary reader with its current of eloquence. Properly to appreciate this essay, we must bear in mind its polemical intent. Malinowski was more interested in refuting what he believed to be derogatory conceptions about "savage society" than he was in building a positive theory. The principal target of his argument was Lucien Lévy-Bruhl, who had amassed considerable evidence and exercised fine insight to demonstrate that primitive peoples reasoned differently than did Europeans. Malinowski interpreted this piece of scholarship as an example of European ethnocentrism, and took as his task the rebuttal that would show that, even though primitive peoples (such as the Trobrianders) practice rites which Europeans disdain or derogate as "magic" or "superstition" or instances of "pre-logical mentality," nonetheless the reasoning underlying these rites is as creditable and sound as that which underlies European practices.

In this essay and generally throughout his writings, Malinowski was more interested in that which he observed and labeled as "magic" than that which he labeled as "religion." As we shall note, he thought of these entities differently than did Durkheim, although he did not present formal definitions as had the French scholar; hence direct comparison between the two is not simple. However, in terms of perspectives, contrast is possible. On the one hand, Malinowski attempted to explain "magic" by communicating an understanding of the view of the native participant (the "magician"); on the other hand, he explained religion from the viewpoint of the detached observer studying the dynamics of native society. So, where Durkheim tried to fuse the results of the two perspectives, Malinowski alternates between the two, depending upon his subject matter. Let us see how this is so.

As Malinowski presents them, the Trobrianders have acquired a great stock of empirically grounded knowledge concerning their environment. They grow a variety of crops and skillfully adjust their agricultural activities to the varying local situations. They build fine outrigger canoes in which they undertake long voyages for trade and for fishing. But, says Malinowski, they know that their "science" is limited and that there are factors beyond their control. Yam gardens made with the best of care may be blasted by one or another natural phenomenon; sudden storms may drive a canoe far off course or even capsize it. In such situations the Trobrianders have recourse to magic; and, insists Malinowski, they distinguish it sharply from their "science" and, for that matter, from their religion. Magical rites, then, are performed by the Trobriander with a specific and definite goal in mind and with a clear consciousness of their reinforcing or complementing mundane procedures. The best comparison would be with the gambler, who, having assessed the situation carefully and laid his wager, then rubs his rabbit foot or prays to some divinity; the ritual is not intended to substitute for the previous exercise of intelligence in choosing the most likely among alternatives, but rather is a response to the unavoidable risks. As Nadel says, Malinowski's is a pragmatic and explicitly utilitarian view of magic (Firth 1964: 195). We may also add that the division he makes between "magic" and "science" is like that which Durkheim makes between the *sacred* and the *profane;* both scholars claim to be formalizing and making explicit a distinction made universally by all peoples.

Malinowski's perspective on native religion does not involve this kind of understanding, for there is nothing to "understand." The savages, he says, have no end in view as they perform the rite, except the performance itself. As a typical example, he describes a postnatal ceremony (the public presentation of the newborn) as having no purpose but being an end in itself. A detached observer (for instance, Malinowski himself) can however discern the "sociological function" of these rites, namely, preserving the cohesion of society. Here Malinowski appeals, not to the formation of a moral community through allegiance to sacred symbols, but more generally and more vaguely to the necessity of tradition. Ceremonies of initiation serve to sanctify tradition as they transmit it formally from generation to generation; hence, they insure that traditional knowledge will not be lost and that traditional social relations will be maintained. Thus, Malinowski as observer is able to conclude that these kinds of religious rites have a survival value for a society of this level (1955:40).

By way of summary criticism, we may remark that the difficulties with the understanding side of Malinowski's argument are much like those mentioned in the case of Durkheim. The question is whether or not peoples generally (primitive or civilized) do themselves distinguish between magical and scientific activities (or between the *sacred* and the *profane*). Whether or not an outside observer can impose such a distinction analytically upon their conduct is something else again. While we will later discuss this question more fully, it is appropriate to remark here that Malinowski's opinions here have been challenged, even in the case of the Trobrianders he seemed to know so well (cf. E. R. Leach in Firth 1964). To be fair, we must note that there are prominent scientists (e.g., Parsons) who adhere to Malinowski's position in the matter. As for Malinowski's functionalist views on *religion,* these enjoy less repute; Nadel has remarked that they are "loose and disjointed" and that their author had grossly oversimplified the variety and multidimensionality of religion in order to emerge with a simplistic definition and unity of function (Firth 1964:205–206).

RADCLIFFE-BROWN: A NEO-DURKHEIMIAN SYNTHESIS

Where Malinowski's theorizing was limited by his devotion to the shallow arguments of J. G. Frazer and his ire at the interpretations offered by L. Lévy-Bruhl, Radcliffe-Brown's theoretical efforts arose from a richer, more scholarly matrix, as is exemplified by his attempt to revise Durkheim's proposals. Again, where Malinowski confined the empirical basis of his arguments to his single, major field experience in the Trobriand Islands, Radcliffe-Brown had engaged in a greater diversity of field researches and, moreover, had maintained a scholarly interest in the history of civilized societies, especially traditional China. The student will not find in Radcliffe-Brown's pages the poetic and polemical rhetoric of Malinowski, but he will enjoy a clear, incisive style.

In his famous essay on "Religion and Society" (1952:chap. 8), Radcliffe-Brown begins by adopting a systems-theoretic perspective. Citing the discussions of Confucian philosophers, such as Hsün Tzǔ, as well as European scholars and historians such as W. Robertson Smith and Fustel de Coulanges, he emphasizes the importance of *rites* (or practices) as compared to religious *beliefs,* and argues that rites are essential to the maintenance of the society (1952:164): the rites renew and strengthen the sentiments which solidify the society; they do so by giving solemn and collective expression to these sentiments.

Having thus rendered homage to the sociological functionalism of which he was such an exponent, Radcliffe-Brown then directed his essay toward the Australian peoples who had formed the empirical referent for Durkheim's *The Elementary Forms of the Religious Life*. Radcliffe-Brown had himself worked among these peoples, and as he depicts their beliefs and rites, his approach shifts from the systems-theoretic position toward that of *Verstehen*. Vividly he communicates to us the principles by which the Australians perceive and organize their universe, that the social-and-natural order of the universe was brought into existence by the great mythical or "totemic" ancestors, the "Dawn Beings," and that "Australian totemism is a cosmological system by which the phenomena of nature are incorporated into the kinship organisation" (1952:169). Since a particular clan group perceives the kangaroo species as their clan elder-brothers, it is understandable why they would engage in certain ritual activities directed toward the species, and at the same time it is also clear that the holding of these rites would be a reaffirmation of the strength and solidarity of the clan organization. Thus, Radcliffe-Brown integrates in his brief description a structural-functionalist approach with the approach of one who understands the world view of the people themselves.

His very familiarity with the life and perspectives of simple peoples made it impossible for Radcliffe-Brown to accept Durkheim's conceptions of "religion." For one thing, most peoples have a variety of rites, each involving differing congeries of participants. For example, the Australian aboriginals have two major types of ritual, one performed by local groups at particular "totem centers," and another performed at meetings where a number of local groups come together. Were the student to apply Durkheim's definition in its strict sense, he would have difficulty because instead of *one* moral community, he would apparently have several. For another thing, Radcliffe-Brown perceived that the dichotomy Durkheim had proposed between "religion" and "magic"

was simply false to the facts. Accordingly, Radcliffe-Brown tended to avoid not only counterposing these two terms but even the use of them. Apparently, he believed that these crucial terms were too freighted with Western traditions, and he instead used "ritual" (or rite) and "ritual attitude" as the basic terms of his analysis.

Substituting ritual for religion (or magic) has clear advantages insofar as discussion is concerned, since it means that the ethnographer and the reader are less likely to assume an identity in meaning and attitudes between, for example, the Australian aboriginal and Martin Buber. Identities or similarities in ritual performances or symbolisms may exist between the aboriginals and the Judaeo-Christians, but they have to be demonstrated, not unwittingly assumed via a process of labeling (or mislabeling). Yet, the elimination of misleading culture-bound terms does not resolve the problem of conceptualization. If the Western dichotomies of religion/magic and sacred/profane do not accord universally with the views of primitive peoples themselves, are we likely to find that they apply a distinction that we could translate into English as ritual/nonritual? According to Jack Goody, the answer is negative: the distinction between the ritual and the nonritual is in the eyes of the Western observer; it is not part of the grammar of native conduct (1961).

CONCLUSION:
THEORISTS AND RIVAL THEORIES

Influenced by the role of Judaeo-Christianity in Western civilization, scholars have attempted to find in primitive or uncivilized societies a corresponding entity, "primitive religion." Since economists have been unable to find a "market" in such societies and political scientists have been unable to find a "state," we should not be surprised by the difficulty in locating and defining some entity that would correspond to the Judaeo-Christian institutional complex. A resolution can be achieved via a systems-theoretic approach in which religion is regarded simply as a device for integrating a social system; however, this procedure tends to empty religion of its meaning for the participants. The greatest figures in the history of the scientific study of religion have tried to integrate the systems-theoretic approach with the "understanding" approach of the person who has been socialized into the perspective of the participants themselves. Our brief review of the major theoretical efforts and of the criticisms that have been levied at them indicates that there are intrinsic difficulties in performing this integration. However, we will not fully understand why this difficulty exists until we compare the primitive and Western civilized views of the world, as we will proceed to do in the next major part of the chapter.

UNDERSTANDING OF RELIGIONS:
THE MAGICAL WORLD VIEW

This review of theories about "religion" has shown how that term reflects Western preoccupations and biases. If we are to avoid such ethnocentrism, we would do better to begin by studying how primitive (or other non-Western) peoples view their world and organize their experience; thence we could proceed to single out those patterns of their existence which seem most closely related to the Western phenomena that are labeled as religious. By this procedure, we would avoid imposing narrowly Western categories on non-Western institutions, and we would hope to understand whether or to what extent there is something shared by all peoples that could be classified as "religion."

In this section we will delineate the principal features of a world view that has been associated with people labeled "primitive" (Redfield 1953; Wax and Wax 1962;

Diamond 1963). We shall present this view as a scientific construct in the sense of an "ideal type" (Weber 1958a) or a "natural whole" (Redfield 1960:chap. 1), and we shall not here inquire as to which peoples at which times have shared how much of this view. Similarly, we shall not here enter into the discussion of whether or not all the peoples who are "primitive" by technological or other standards are alike in sharing this view. Rather, we have proposed this ideal type as the basis for an independent scheme of classification of peoples, and, by this scheme peoples may be classified as more or less "magical" or "primitive," depending upon the extent to which their view of the world rests on premises similar to those we will now delineate.

To those who inhabit it, the magical world is a "society," not a "mechanism," that is, it is composed of "beings" rather than "objects." Whether human or nonhuman, these beings are associated with and related to one another socially and sociably, that is, in the same ways as human beings to one another. These patterns of association and relationship may be structured in terms of kinship, empathy, sympathy, reciprocity, sexuality, dependency, or any other of the ways that human beings interact with and affect or afflict one another. Plants, animals, rocks, and stars are thus seen not as "objects" governed by laws of nature, but as "fellows" with whom the individual or band may have a more or less advantageous relationship. Specifically, if a hunter is successful in his quest, then this means that his relationship to the game animals and to the other beings associated with hunting has been a good one. If the cultivator harvests a good crop, then his relationship to the plant species, to the earth, and to the other beings associated with its fertility has been a good one. Conversely, if a man's family is ailing, or if his group is beaten in battle or humiliated in competition, the beings who are presumed to be supporting them are either enfeebled or otherwise indisposed to assist them, or other beings are exercising malevolent powers against them.

This view of the world is so utterly different from the view of the sophisticated men of the contemporary West that it is not easy to understand it or even to perceive its presence as shaping the actions of an exotic people. Ethnographers as able as Malinowski have misinterpreted it. Furthermore, scholars have emphasized distinctions that have no significance within the magical world. So, for example, J. G. Frazer defined the distinction between "religion" and "magic" on the grounds that in the first man supplicates and beseeches, while in the second he attempts to manipulate and command the deities. However, in the magical world, the relationships among human and nonhuman beings may be as varied as the relationships among humans alone, and the patterns a society will stress will most likely be those that are dominant among the human members. So, if kinship obligations are emphasized within the human society, it is likely that the same patterns will be utilized by humans dealing with nonhumans; or if feudal-type authority relations are the norm within the human society, it is likely that humans will approach powerful nonhumans submissively and humbly, offering gifts that may be bribes; or, again, if trickery and slyness are the norm among humans, this pattern may be manifested toward the nonhumans; and so on. Consequently, we may anticipate finding instances of both supplication and manipulation in the relationships between humans and deities within the magical world, and it is unlikely that this distinction will be of such significance that it could be the basis for differentiating magic from religion (cf. Wax and Wax 1963).

A kindred error is the Frazer-Malinowski notion that the performance of magical rites is intended to control the future, as if the "magician" thought of himself as an engineer or scientist able by the exercise of his craft to determine the course of events. In a world that is a "society" and not a "mechanism" and that is composed of beings who interact in human fashion, control in a mechanical sense is inconceivable. Moreover, if the world is a great society, there is no point in seeking the general "laws of nature" (the knowledge of which has been so important in Western history). In dealing with a particular fellow human being even the most scientifically oriented psychologists will grant that the laws of human nature (whatever they may be) are less helpful than prolonged, detailed, and intimate study of that person. So, in the magical world, the emphasis is upon the individual, the particular, and the concrete, and the actor in this world does not seek a "mechanical control" of his destiny but rather to establish and maintain a beneficial relationship with the beings he views as influential in his life.

Needless to say, the principle of success in the magical world is not mechanical or scientific. It could be called spiritual (although this might sound too ethereal to contemporary students), and it could be called interpersonal (although this might sound too social-scientific). There does seem to be a set of comparable terms by which various societies have referred to it, namely, *mana, wakan, orenda, baraka, manitou.* We will hereafter term it (magical) "Power." Fundamentally, its presence is manifest, not in the electrical discharges of ancient, Grade C, Hollywood horror movies, nor in dazzlements of eye and ear, but in prosperity, good fortune, and success. The hunter who returns with game, the cultivator whose harvest is bountiful, the woman whose children are numerous and strong, the gambler who pockets the stakes, the girl who ravishes the hearts of the young men — these are people of Power. Nowadays, when we read the Old Testament, we are more likely to see Power in the parting of the Red Sea or other supersessions of the "laws of nature"; but to those who transmitted Old Testament tales and to many other folk today, an equally if not more significant Power was manifest in the prosperity of Abraham and the others blessed by God.

THE MAGICAL WORLD AS DEPICTED BY JAIME DE ANGULO

A perceptive and insightful ethnographer, Jaime de Angulo did his principal field work among the Pit River Indians of California and presented his discoveries outside the formal framework of the anthropology of his time. His *Indian Tales* may be enjoyed by those who are innocent of anthropological researches, yet will furnish the serious student with much material for reflection (1953). In the following passages de Angulo describes his early contacts with the magical world of his friends among the Pit River Indians (1950:23, 32–33). The student should note that the Indians conceived of human beings as living amid a greater society of animals who observed human actions thoughtfully and who were capable of human speech. From time to time, an animal being chose to enter into relationship with a young man whose plight had moved him, and when he did so the man was thereafter lucky in some particular range of activity. Through his relationship with his animal protector, the human acquired Power.

It was Robert Spring who first made me understand about the *dinihowi*. "That's what we Indians call *luck*. A man has got to have luck, no matter for what, whether it's for gambling, or for hunting, for making love, for anything, unless he wants to be just a common Indian . . . like me."

We were lying flat on our backs under a juniper. After a silence he started again: "When a fellow is young, everybody is after him to go to the mountains and get himself a *dinihowi*. The old men say: 'You'll never amount to anything if you don't go and catch a *dinihowi*.' And then you hear other fellows brag about their luck at gambling, or how they got a good *dinihowi* for hunting. Well, there come a time when a young fellow starts to feel uneasy, kind of sad, kind of worried, that's just about the time he's getting to be a man grown up. Then he start to 'wander,' that's what we call it, wandering. They say: Leave him alone, he is wandering. That's the time you go to the hills, you don't come home, you stay out all night, you get scared, you cry; two, three days you go hungry. Sometime your people get worried, come after you, but you throw rocks at them: Go away, I don't want you, leave me alone. You get pretty hungry, you get dizzy, you are afraid of grizzly bears. Maybe you fall asleep and someone come wake you up, maybe a wolf push your head with his foot, maybe bluejay peck at your face, maybe little fly get in your ear, he say: Hey! Wake up! What you doing here? Your people worrying about you! You better go home! I seen you wandering here, crying, hungry, I pity you, I like you. I help you. Listen, this is my song. Remember that song. When you want me, you come here and sing my song. I'll hear you, I'll come. . . ."

We were still sitting in the same spot. Jack says, out of the blue: "Yes, I got a *dinihowi*. Must be a damn poor Indian without a *dinihowi*. When I was a young fellow, old people always get after us. You go get luck for yourself. You can't live without luck. Go and run up the mountain in the afternoon. Try to beat the sun, the red light, to the top, get there first. Keep your breath. Run steady. . . . You know, Doc, I used to be a good runner. We used to have foot-races in the old-time days. All the young Indians we used to try beat each other going from one place to another, maybe five mile, maybe ten mile. Run through the sagebrush, keep your breath in, don't slow down, don't sit down and sleep, don't get scared, keep running through the brush, sometimes awful high brush, higher than your head. . . . I was pretty good runner in them days. Now I make my race-horses run. . . . Well, the old people kept after me. You beat the sun to the top of the mountains, then you'll be a man. I tried, and I tried. Then one day a big frog was standing in the road, right in the dust of the trail. He says: You'll never get to the top without me helping you. I been watching you. It's awful how hard you try. I'll help you. . . ."

"Did you get to the top that day?"

"Yes, I got to the top. There ain't nothing there."

"Then what?"

"Then I came down."

"Oh. . . ."

"What do you mean, oh? I got my *dinihowi*, didn't I? I am always trying to tell you things, Doc, but you are worse than a young Indian." [1]

So skillfully has de Angulo relayed the story and the difference between the two viewpoints, his own — as the naïve listener — and the Indian narrator's, that Jack's final response is startling and witty. But this, of course, was de Angulo's intent: he wanted to dramatize the difference in views of the world. The reader, being of the Western tradition, tends to convert the tale into his own folk idiom and — like de Angulo — sees the Indian narrator as striving to achieve a materialistic goal, climbing the mountain. Moreover, the reader tends to feel that if there is a reward, it should follow the achievement. But the Indian narrator disregards the notions of achievement or of materialistic goal; for him the important issue was that he had reduced himself to such a desperate and pitiable condition that an animal being could not resist his plea and offered to befriend him, then and thereafter. So Jack Folsom (the second narrator) acquired the assistance of a Powerful protector, while Robert Spring remained "just a common Indian."

POLYTHEISMS, PROPHETS, AND PHILOSOPHERS

The polytheistic configurations of the societies of classical antiquity and the tradi-

[1] The sections from "Indians in Overalls" are reprinted from *The Hudson Review*, Volume III, No. 3 (Autumn, 1950). Copyright 1950 by The Hudson Review, Inc.

tional Orient seem to have been social and cultural formalizations of the magical world. The more elaborate division of labor that developed with the rise of civilized society was mirrored in the formal organization and specialization of the nonhuman society; and the diverse beings of the latter were arrayed, like humans, into social systems and hierarchies, crowned by beings of great Power, the gods. Gods and lesser beings became specialized for the various masculine activities and for the feminine, for particular occupations (cultivator, goldsmith, sailor, warrior), for particular ranks of people (artisan, noble, and serf), and for the various life crises (birth, puberty, marriage, illness). Associated with each deity was a temple or series of temples and its corps of priests, while lesser spirits lived a less sheltered existence, attached to "holy places," serving as protagonists in occasional modest ceremonials. Elaborate ceremonials were conducted at the temples in relation to occupational specialties and crises, as for warriors departing for battle or for cultivators at key periods in the agricultural cycle. In addition to the usage by a particular mass audience, there was also the use of the temple and its priests by individuals with special needs, for example, by an infertile woman seeking to bear children, by a cultivator whose crops were blasted, by a person who had lost a valuable object. Because of the rationalistic, disenchanting heritage of Western history, we are now inclined to think of the priestly corps as spiritual (and so impractical, if not actually fraudulent and deceitful) in their functioning, yet it is certain that at least some of these persons were wise or learned men. The priests who were associated with the deities of healing were students of illness and the Egyptian priests associated with agriculture were able to regulate the agricultural cycle by virtue of their knowledge of the connection between the astronomical year and the flood stages of the Nile. There is reason to believe that the role of the medieval monastery as the repository and distributor of the practical and scholarly wisdom of earlier ages may well have had its roots in the role of the temple priesthoods of polytheistic ages. From the perspective of modern science, it is clear that a good part of the temple lore was based on fallacious premises. So, within the logic of the magical world, it was plausible to interpret a quarrel among human lineages or societies as the response to an antagonistic relationship among ancestral beings who were symbolized in planetary figures; however, the polytheistic attempt to rationalize this linkage via precise description of planetary movements conjoined with the chronicling of crucial political events was foredoomed to failure. Nonetheless, we should not forget that the modern sciences of astronomy, mathematics, and chemistry have roots in the lore and studies of the priests of polytheistic antiquity.

Polytheistic configurations have endured for millenia within civilized societies and are still present in Asia. Nonetheless, they do seem to engender their own radical critique, the rational prophet and the ascetic philosopher (Weber 1958b). The most familiar and striking example is the great tradition of Hebraic prophecy — Amos, Isaiah, Job — including the founders of Christianity, Jesus and Paul. Parallel phenomena seem to be represented by the Hellenic Sophist tradition — Socrates, Plato, Diogenes, Epictetus — and by the Indian tradition climaxing in Gautama, the Buddha. While it is customary to regard these men as radically individualistic, we should note that from an anthropological perspective each appeared within a cultural background of literacy, which served to transmit to him a set of ancient sacred texts, and served as well to record his own words. We should also note the frequent record of schools of disciples, and that the presence of such schools may be inferred even when the formal record of them is lacking, since without such disciples it is dubious whether the words and deeds of the prophet or teacher would have been so carefully preserved. Let us turn to a consideration of a central theme of the prophetic message — ascetic rationality.

To peoples who view the world magically, the man who is prosperous — whose wife bears many children, whose family is healthy, and whose larder is full — must be having correct relationships with the human and nonhuman beings of Power. Conversely, if a man and his family are poor, or ill, or enslaved, then his relationships with the beings of Power are not the most desirable kind. These attitudes toward prosperity and toward correct conduct are singled out for criticism by the rational prophets of the great traditions.

Within the great tradition of Western civilization, one of the most forceful and clearly stated of such criticisms is contained in Plato's *The Republic*. In the course of this dialogue, one of the characters mentions the (mythical) ring of Gyges, which was supposed to render its wearer invisible, and he argues that every man in his heart would like to have this ring and would consider himself the happiest of men if he did possess it, as by means of it he could enjoy any woman, taste any meal or liquor, own any object, and govern any state. In riposte, Socrates argues that true happiness comes from a balanced and harmonious state of the personality. The power a man should strive for is not a mythical power allowing him to deceive and humiliate his fellows, but an inner power designated by achievement of the four great virtues: courage, temperance, wisdom, and justice.

The Hebraic Book of Job constitutes a similar critique of the notion that external prosperity is a reliable index of the correctness of a man's behavior (Wax and Wax 1964). For, as the biblical story starts, Job is a man in the pattern of Abraham: his conduct is righteous, and as a consequence he enjoys prosperity and health. Then, at one fell swoop, he is deprived of his children, his possessions, and his health, so that he can but curse the day of his birth. To people who view the world magically, Job's miseries are signs of his having displeased some beings of great Power, and his proper course is to review his past conduct, discover his errors, and placate the offended beings. Job's Hebraic friends offer similar counsel, arguing in effect that the magnitude of his calamities testifies to the extent of the sins he must have committed against God. Yet Job's response is utterly unmagical: he insists that there are norms of pious and correct conduct and that he has abided by those norms. Job will not agree to the proposition that prosperity is a measure of morality and piety, and he thinks it would be a mocking of God to pretend to sins of which he feels innocent and thus to surrender his faith in a moral religiosity.

These illustrations from the Hellenic and Hebraic books could be augmented with others from the great traditions of other civilizations. In essence, the prophet or philosopher is preaching a critique of conventional morality and its creed of material success. In opposition, he urges a moral code and a control of the self (including a subjugation of the passions) that will prove to be its own reward. Needless to say, the logic of this self-restraint has never been convincing to more than a small minority in any generation, but the moral codes have been socially very potent when they have been reinforced by millenarian or intense otherworldly expectations. Both Judaism and Christianity have succeeded in imposing extraordinarily stern moral codes on their mass participants for long periods of time, so long as these were sustained by hopes of participation in a transfigured world.

For the anthropological student of religion, it is important to bear in mind the ob-

verse of these facts. If ascetic rationality is one of the special messages of great traditional prophets and philosophers, then it will not be found — or, at least, certainly not to the same extent — among peoples of the little tradition, whether they be peasant peoples attached to urbanized civilizations or folk peoples comparatively isolated from urban centers. While every society is a moral system, and while peoples who view the world magically will share sets of norms and values, the moral logic by which they apprehend and organize their experience is quite different from that associated with Judaeo-Christianity or other great traditions, which is an additional reason for being wary about classifying under the rubric of "religion" the beliefs and practices of peoples of radically different world views.

These great traditions of radical prophecy became the nuclei for new organizational structures. At their inception and often at later dates in their careers, Judaism, Christianity, Islam, and Buddhism each developed organizational forms separate from and even antagonistic toward the existing political and social structures. Thus, we have the emergence of the notion of a "religion" and a "church" — as distinct from the conventional organizations of the civilized society about them — and incorporating together as brethren congeries of deracinated urbanites. The participants were lured by the promise of a glorious reward in a transfigured world and united together under the bonds of a strenuous morality and a novel and rational creed.

Yet if there is one word that characterizes these great traditional religions, it is tension. They are not at peace with conventional existence, and the message they preach is critical of conventional morality and goals. Accordingly, these religions can never really succeed, except in a millenarian sense. When they appear to be most successful by claiming large numbers of adherents, it is at the price of a watering down and adaptation of the original great traditional message. The New Jerusalem is not a viable community in the present earth.

Thus we find mutual processes of influence between the great and little traditions. The emissaries of the great tradition are constantly trying to bring the conduct of the folk into line with the true message, while the folk are equally occupied trying to convert the pure message into counsel that is meaningful and helpful in their daily lives. With reference to India and its great traditions of Hinduism and Buddhism, McKim Marriott speaks (1955:171–222) of the twin processes of parochialization and universalization. In Western societies, we can illustrate parochialization with the folk employment of images of the saints or the Virgin Mary as if these had a magical Power that could be utilized for the secular benefit of the possessor, as when a Catholic motorist ties a rosary to his dashboard. A similar instance (illustrating the circumvention of the prohibition against worship of graven images) is the Judaic custom of fastening a small prayer scroll to the doorpost of a house. With universalization, we find local customs and beliefs incorporated into the great tradition, as for example when the ceremonial of Yule, celebrated by the pagan folk of northern Europe, is integrated into a holiday, called Christmas, supposedly marking the birth of Jesus.

RELIGION: FUNCTIONAL, DYSFUNCTIONAL, OR NEITHER?

Durkheim, Malinowski, and Radcliffe-Brown all agreed in characterizing religion as a social entity that was functional in the sense that it contributed to the maintenance of social stability or equilibrium. In this view they were not alone but in accord with the general conservative philosophy that thinks of religion as good for the stability of the

political community. In this regard note the statements of Dwight Eisenhower:

Our government makes no sense unless it is founded in a deeply felt religious faith — and I don't care what it is. . . . I am the most intensely religious man I know. That doesn't mean I adhere to any sect. A democracy cannot exist without a religious base. I believe in democracy (Berger 1961:63).

We are now in a position to appreciate the various objections that may be offered against this functionalist image of religion. Because of its familiarity to the reader, the case of early Christianity offers as good an example as any of the difficulties of employing the functionalist analysis — at least in any simple and clear-cut fashion. Within the polytheistic societies of classical antiquity, there were cults which signified the unity of the political state. The Athenian demonstrated his patriotic allegiance by performing a ritual directed to Athena, the Roman, by corresponding rituals directed to the Emperor, and the Egyptian, Syrian, and others proceeded similarly. However, the early Christians were regarded as seditious atheists because they refused — on religious principle — to perform these patriotic rituals. In this and other ways the early Christians made such troubles for the Empire that the historian, Gibbon, regarded them as a principal cause of its decline and fall. While we need not go as far as Gibbon, we certainly must recognize that the criticism of convention and the ascetic indifference to wordly achievement that was characteristic of early Christianity (and kindred great traditional religions) must have had a thoroughly disorganizing effect on existing socio-political structures. Of course, it may be replied that while Christianity was being dysfunctional to the equilibrium of the western Roman empire, it was also serving to create new and potent congeries of organizations, the various Christian churches, and that these were to integrate millions of people into new types of communities. Moreover, with the passage of time, increasing numbers of Christian churches did emerge that functioned as the nationalistic and patriotic cults of the state organizations of the Near East, Russia, and Europe (such as the Orthodox Church of Tzarist Russia or the Anglican Episcopalian Church of England).

The fallacy that besets the religious concepts of Durkheim, Malinowski, and even Radcliffe-Brown derives from their focusing upon the isolated little society as if it were the natural unit for the analysis of human existence, rather than a convenient unit for ethnographic field work. As a result, these theorists have tended to overlook the tumultuous, all-encompassing growth of human culture and to read into the little society social processes that are distinctive of civilizations. In its great traditional sense religion can no more be interpreted with regard to a single small group than can art, or mathematics, or economics. Great traditional religions are like violent reactions that defy the capacity of the social vessels that presume to contain them and, instead, transform the very ingredients of the vessels into something new.

Suggested Readings

Rather than singling out works focusing narrowly on "primitive religion," the student will derive most value from excellent ethnographic monographs which convey the perspective and spirit of the human actors. Some of the classical ethnographies, such as those by Knud Rasmussen of the Eskimo or by Vladimir Bogoraz of the Chukchee are still unsurpassed. Among more recent works, Colin Turnbull on the Pygmies (1962) and Kenelm Burridge on the Melanesian Cargo Cults (1960) are vivid human documents of great value.

Of works which are more analytic or systematic, a useful starting point is Placide Tempels, who clearly delineates many of the basic presuppositions of Bantu thought and action (1959). With this background, the student will be prepared for the more formal discussions of great and little traditions, and of world and folk religions, via the writings of Robert Redfield (1953, 1956), Milton Singer (1960), and Max Weber (1958a). The collection of essays edited by Frankfort (1946) may prove of great value as illustrative of the great traditional background to our contemporary society, since it contains outstanding essays on the religious and philosophical developments of the civilized societies of classical antiquity. As a way of perceiving the contemporary contrast between Judaeo-Christianity and folk attitudes, the student might well browse in the journal, *Practical Anthropology,* which is edited by anthropologically sophisticated missionaries and which reports their difficulties in relating to and communicating with non-Western peoples.

The richest ethnological literature on the subject of religion and magic continues to be the essay. Of the many which could be cited, I single out Winans and Edgerton (1964), Gluckman (1944), Bharati (1963), Wax and Wax (1963), Goody (1961), and Diamond (1963). The collections edited by Charles Leslie (1960), by Lessa and Vogt (1962), by Middleton and Winter (1963), and by Schneider (1964) are generally weak and unsatisfactory in their theoretical structures and excerpts, but nonetheless contain some outstanding essays; reading with discrimination, the student will find in them materials of marked value.

CHAPTER **IO** introduces some of the major ideas and problems associated with the cross-cultural study of values. Professor Ayoub makes it clear that there is now little room for valid doubt as to the possibility of subjecting values — those of other societies as well as our own — to meaningful scholarly and indeed scientific inquiry. As a universal aspect of human choice-making behavior, when objectified as the standards of conduct or idealized preferences of a community, values are a legitimate part of the domain of interests of cultural anthropology as well as the other social and behavioral sciences. Beyond the issue of values as an object of study, however, are other critical matters which have a particularly intimate association with this subject. Although a useful and favored principle of analysis, the interpretation of value systems only in the context of or "relative" to the sociocultural systems in which they occur is not, as the author points out, an entirely satisfactory guideline. In one sense, accepting the relativism of values means assuming a position of noninvolvement, a kind of detachment which provides the student of man with a perhaps spurious sense of objectivity. Professor Ayoub, arguing that the impact of science on society cannot be ignored by scientists, suggests that the cultural anthropologist cannot be less than involved. Thus the topic of values has a meaning larger than just the empirical quest for "knowledge *about*" an aspect of human behavior, for here the issue of "knowledge *for what purpose*" is unavoidable.

THE AUTHOR received his undergraduate education at Antioch College and his graduate training at Columbia and Harvard Universities. He has done field work in Lebanon and in Iran, and is currently Associate Professor of Anthropology at Antioch College.

IO

The Study of Values

VICTOR F. AYOUB

Antioch College

INTRODUCTION

"Values" is a concept of importance in anthropology, as well as in any discipline having to do with man's behavior. It points to a significant element in the complex of activities and states of mind, including the symbolic transmutation of physical objects and environment into cultural artifacts, which is human behavior. These activities, these states of mind, these objects are not values. They are as they are. Making bakery goods. Preparing toast. Performing the Eucharist. Feeling confidence, affection, devoutness. A piece of bread. A toaster. A chalice. They are as they are. All these things may be valued. They may not be.

The concept of "values" also points to the matrix in which human behavior is embedded. This is the network of social relationships which shape our activities into the mold of institutions and our mental states into the mold of public experience. These molds are not values. They are as they are. Being an employee (to an employer). Being a wife/mother (to a husband/child). Being a priest (to a parishioner). The expectation of particular rights. The acceptance of specific obligations. The recognition of a state of grace. The particular content of these molds may or may not be valued. They may determine direction in the act of valuing. They are not, in and of themselves, values.

The concept points, finally, to the end products of conceptual acts, the reflective enquiry upon our experience which results in the beliefs we hold, the goals we pursue, the ideas we project, and the standards of judgment we define. Work as the avenue to grace. The achievement of material well-being. A universal moral order to assure the brotherhood of man. Moral edification as the basis for judging art. These are phrases reflecting the product of mental states at a conceptual level more abstract than those kinds hitherto mentioned. It is sometimes difficult to separate them, even with analytically sharp tools of linguistic discrimination. But they too

245

may or may not be valued. And they too, as ideology, the conceptual composite of beliefs, goals, ideals, and standards, may determine direction in the act of valuing. They are not, in and of themselves, values.

It is through acts of selection that the transmutation to values eventually takes place. Much of the discussion which follows will have to do with the development of this statement.

Values. The word has been used several times in the short span of the preceding paragraphs. And without definition. That has probably not been bothersome thus far. It is doubtful that anyone preparing to read this chapter looked up its meaning in a dictionary, as he might "rebarbative," or scores of other words I had to search out before I decided to use that one. The notion of worth as of a person, place, or thing consisting thereof is surely understood by all of us. Even used as though there were a reference to an object, a Value, rather than imputation of worth to an object, the context of use does not raise problems of communication for us in ordinary discourse.

The situation is different in the study of values. There is need for greater precision in the use of the word. The work it must do to advance our understanding is subtler. Several times I have illustrated remarks with content from experience, concluding each time that the substance of the illustrations, and their like, were not values, though they might be valued. Obviously, I was using the generic and lexical definition suggested above. I should not have been so emphatic. I was intent upon suggesting a problem in definition, not in obscuring one with an immodest display of certainty where the certainty would only be my own, not shared. My purpose in this essay is, on the contrary, a modest one. It shall be stated as a conclusion to this introductory section.

A mapping of the ground the study of values presumes to cover will constitute the substance of this essay. And it is an "essay" in the generic sense of the word. The analogy will be pushed a little further to make my purpose clear. The discussion is intended to identify the distinguishing features of the territory which can attest to the credibility of studying "values" as such, to designate general perimeters within which sovereign rights (fortunately without closed frontiers) are claimed by philosophy and social science, with an applied area representing an international zone, and to mark the rough terrain and dense foliage of definition and conception which obscures the paths of understanding we might best take. The metaphor is done. The remaining remarks will elaborate the point of the analogy. The end result will be a series of discriminations of various kinds. They should make clear the issues and the problems involved in studying values.

FOUNDATIONS

The world of events does not provide its own explanation or its own assessment of itself, revealing them to us in a fashion immediately apprehended. If this statement cannot be taken as an axiom, it is still important working premise. Events transmuted by our reasoning, doubting, wishing, or wanting into beliefs, desires, and preferences become intelligible to us. They come to have meaning for us.

The process might be likened to a process of refraction. The events are deflected into beliefs and attitudes through the medium of language. Within that same medium the beliefs and the attitudes are themselves objectified as events, that is, they become part of the world as we experience it. As Santayana once defined beauty as pleasure objectified, it might be said that knowledge is belief objectified and values are desires and preferences objectified.

That world of events comprised of knowledge and values is a cultural world. It is part of nature, as much a part as are the organic and inorganic aspects of nature. But as the spider's web is to the spider, this cultural mesh of knowledge and values is woven by men and independent of them as well. Its objective aspect, the transformation of belief into knowledge, of desires into values, is formed by the social nexuses which bind men together as society.

Whether described as the result of the mental operations of individuals or as the objective residuum of those operations, which is the cultural world of knowledge and values, the conceptual order of experience is a necessary condition of man's adaptation to his environment.

The wherewithal that enables men to cope with the world into which they are born, that is, their adaptive capacity, is learned. In effect, man's adaptive processes have become largely cultural, not only genetic. The idea is a fundamental one in anthropology. It is not necessary for us to have an elaboration of it here.

The products of our activity — the things we do, the manner in which we relate ourselves to one another, the objects we construct and the significance we give them as well as natural objects — are artifacts of learning as well as artifacts learned. They are means by which man adapts himself to the ultimate problem of survival.

But the notion of survival means more than the avoidance of physical extinction. It means also maintaining the identity of the species regardless of what adaptive changes take place over time. For man, the interdependence of individuals in some kind of social matrix is a necessary condition of survival and a necessary element in the definition of "survival." The fact of such interdependence is a biological one. Man shares it with other animal species. The modes of such interdependence are not a biological fact. If it were otherwise, learning would not

be such a fundamental part of the adaptive process.

Cultural adaptation depends significantly, if not entirely, upon the way we conceive the world, upon the way we order it. If we treated every event as a novelty, learning would be pointless. Our conceptual responses to the world of events is a process of fitting our experiences into a general and ordered set of ideas which make these experiences credible and relevant in our effort to survive. Such phrases as "design for living," "a way of life," and "world view" have been used to identify a conceptual order of this kind when it is represented as the objectified, cultural world of knowledge and values. In this respect, this order of ideas represents unstated premises which guide our conduct in a manner we accept as credible and relevant. Under critical circumstances, when a decision between alternatives must be made, we can be forced into a consideration of the basis and justification for making a choice. At such times, unstated premises may come to the surface of consciousness and be stated. Otherwise, such premises are inferred from our conduct.

Even as I try to explain these notions, I am subject to the condition I am trying to explain. My present behavior, the exposition of certain ideas, reflects premises which have not been made explicit about the way I conceive of things. These are conceptions held by others also, as they represent a segment at least of the cultural world of knowledge and values in which I learn.

The classifying of experience into general categories and the statable relations between them which in some degree form a system of ideas may be referred to as cognitive behavior. It is the fount of belief and belief as knowledge. The source of values must be fitted into the account.

I remarked earlier that the world of events does not give its own explanation of itself; it is not revealed to us as something directly apprehended. There is always an arbitrary element in the way we order the world. Experience — as we discover new events, uncover different facets of the same events, suggest different relations between events — overflows our categories and the conceptual order we have provided as a basis for understanding it. That order, to use an old but useful metaphor, is as a procrustean bed into which we fit experience. Not so diabolical as the original, of course. There is never a perfect fit, but we adjust the bed, not the occupant.

It is this indeterminate relation between the world of events — our experience — and the world of knowledge — our cognitive organization — which opens the way to values. It does so from two points of view.

The hiatus between events and the particular way in which we understand them must be bridged by criteria which legitimize the specific conclusions we draw at any time. Since the events themselves do not give us the indisputable grounds for choosing once and for all between modes of understanding or even specific judgments based upon such modes, choice is always possible. The imputation of relative worth and a preference must be elicited. Such acts presuppose criteria for deciding. Evaluative behavior is joined to cognitive behavior in the process of organizing our experience. Objectified criteria are standards of judgment and part of the cultural world of knowledge and values.

There is another aspect from which the source of values may be gleaned. It was noted that man's adaptation to his surroundings is principally through learning, which depends upon the generalizing and ordering of experience born of cognitive behavior, and objectified as knowledge. Adaptation through learning consists of acting in the light of our understanding of the nature of things so as to maintain a relationship between ourselves and the environment, such that survival may be assured. Knowledge is

converted into the means which will serve this ultimate end.

Here again there is an hiatus. When converted into action, our understanding does not provide one unequivocal path insuring survival. The gap between our knowledge and the consequences of action taken upon that knowledge to serve an end must be bridged by a decision. There is always a choice possible between available means. A choice made betokens a preference by some standard of judgment. A preferred means becomes itself an end. It may be sought in its own right even as it is made to serve another purpose. It is a cultural end since it is a product of the adaptive function of learning. In turn, it calls for means to serve it. As long as choice is possible, such means may also be ends. Thus, the artifacts of learning represent a means-ends continuum of activities, objects, and relationships. As they are elements in the process of cultural adaptation, they are a means to an end, survival. But as they are themselves preferred means, finite sets drawn from the continuum, they are ends, themselves requiring means. As such, they are objectified in institutions as goals and prescribed ways of achieving those goals. They form the social matrices which are a necessary condition of survival.

Seen as the objective counterpart of preferred means and ends, the artifacts of learning are values and are independent of the choice that produced them. They reflect different modes of cultural adaptation. Thus "values" sometimes refers to the standards of judgment, themselves ultimately a product of choice, according to which choices are made. But the term can also refer to the objectification of decisions, that is, the objectification of the actual choices made. The most inclusive use of the term is "things valued."

Just as the conceptual bridge between the world of events and our understanding of them is cognitive behavior, the conceptual bridge between our understanding and our actions is evaluative behavior. They come together as they are the condition of adaptation. We constantly strive to bring our understanding in line with our experience and with our actions. This has been described as a striving towards consistency or a strain towards consistency. That striving is the cultural adaptive process. It may be referred to as conative behavior. It is not independent of cognition and evaluation, but underlies both as the means by which man maintains some kind of stable relationship between himself and his environment in his ultimate effort to survive, in his effort to maintain species identity.

It was noted earlier that learning as the medium through which the adaptive process operates would be pointless if we treated every event as a novelty. In the context of action, the same may be said of choice. Things preferred by some standard of judgment and therefore things desired are the end-products of evaluative behavior. Like beliefs, they are objectified into the world of knowledge and value, the conceptual coalescence of the artifacts produced through the adaptive process. They become part of the world of events independent of the adaptive process even as they are an integral part of that process. Artifacts to be learned as well as artifacts of learning, they become subject to our understanding as well as guides to our actions through our understanding.

Such adaptations are culturally prescribed, institutionally limited ways of behaving. They are fixed in experience through a process of conceptualization that gives them credibility and justification. They must fit beliefs we hold about the nature of our experience and the criteria of appropriateness we hold in the light of those beliefs. At the same time, objectified as knowledge and value, such beliefs and criteria are themselves artifacts of learning, but at a level of discourse in which they are used to reflect

upon experience even as they are transmuted into experience. At the same time that they are instruments we use to interpret our experiences, they become part of that experience, subject themselves to interpretation.

As the process of conceptualizing is made concrete in knowledge and value, the affirmation of end results of adaptation, it contributes to experience as a finite order of cultural events, which in turn prompts adaptive responses because an indeterminate relationship between experience and understanding may always be posited. Adaptation is a process of mediation between the need for conceptual permanence and the fact of existential change.

Those artifacts of learning which at any time have adaptive viability are fixed in our experience as culturally appropriate means and ends embodied in institutions. Knowledge and values, a cultural world of events, affirm the means and ends by which a stable relationship is maintained between ourselves and our environment, a condition of survival as that notion has been defined. The stability is never fully achieved. There is always a striving towards it. Adaptation is a constant process.

However, if conative behavior did not include some sense of fruition, the notion of maintaining identify would have no significance. Thus the ultimate problem of survival is transformed to mean more than biological survival, more than the persistence of species identity. It means cultural survival as well, the persistence of cultural identity. As the world of knowledge and values is an independent world of cultural events which affirms modes of adaptation men have realized in the ultimate effort to maintain identity as a species, becoming thus an integral part of those modes, the adaptive process is directed not only towards maintaining that identity, but also towards maintaining cultural identity. Man's conceptualizing is part of the natural world and must be understood as part of his total behavior.

The study of values is a study of cultural identities, finite cultural orders of knowledge and values in an adaptive continuum of means and ends. It is also a study of their action consequences.

CONTEXT

This section will consist essentially of a series of illustrations, providing substance to some of the argument in the preceding exposition. Any further elaboration of the argument will therefore be realized through examples rather than dialectics.

The concept of "values," however defined, reflects a concern with two related problems. It is meant to play a part in the understanding of these problems. The relationship between the way in which we conceive the nature of the world around us and the behavior we exhibit in that world is one problem. The other concerns itself with the variations found in the conceptual ordering of experience which are different enough to mark distinctive cultural identities. Persian culture is not the same as American culture is not the same as Navaho culture, because in each instance the world in some manner is conceived differently, thus behavior of people within each culture is different from others to some extent. Each culture, taken as a whole, constitutes different modes of adaptation. They are different worlds of knowledge and values.

Neither the basis and extent of the relationship between conception and behavior nor the basis and extent of variations which distinguish cultural identities is altogether clear. An understatement. However, there is little doubt that the significance we attach to objects, to actions, and to our associations with others through a conceptual act of interpretation sets down paths which guide our conduct in what we accept as a meaningful and appropriate fashion. And this tie between understanding and action varies in important ways between groups of people, especially sets of groups which constitute different societies.

The wine a devout Catholic sips decorously and sparingly at an altar railing, fulfilling in action and state of mind the duty of Communion, is not conceptually the same as the wine he may drink expansively at the dining table in his home, realizing in action and mental state the pleasures of aesthetic nourishment. Nor is the priest, the man, who "serves" him at the altar railing, conceptually the same as the man, the priest, whom he may serve at his dining table. An interpretive act changes the significance of object and relationship, even if ever so slightly, and conduct shifts accordingly.

For the Turkish gentlemen, earlier in the century, who were made to doff the fez in favor of the European fedora, that strange headgear held added import for them other than that it held for the Europeans from whom it was borrowed. It was a mark of modernization insisted upon by a ruling and intellectual elite intent upon transforming Turkey into a European-like nation. Some approved, some disapproved. Among those who disapproved, some resisted, some did not. Much ado about a hat. But headgear in Middle-Eastern culture has had longstanding significance, other than aesthetic or protective, since it has in many cases been a mark of religious, ethnic, or class identity. Little wonder that the governing elite chose it as an item upon which to focus in the effort to transform Turkish habits of mind and behavior. It was a highly visible object and also had meaningful continuity with the past. In effect, its significance was part of the cultural world of knowledge and values, a world of conceptual generalization. As with any generalization, there is some measure of independence of time and space or, to say it another way, there is continuity through time and space. This continuity furnishes more or less fixed conceptions of experience which prompt particular responses to particular experiences. Whether opposed to such conceptions surrounding headgear or fundamentally guided by them, Turkish gentlemen for a while gave the fedora a significance no contemporaneous European would likely have given it.

The process of organizing our experience through the imputation of meaning is not, in effect, activated by us as individuals at all times. In most instances, the end-products of such conceptual acts are provided for us through the continuity of our associations in time and space, in tradition and community. It may be said that tradition is the community of human associations seen temporally; whereas community is the tradition seen spatially.

These end-products of knowledge and values borne in the continuity we share with others in tradition and community may be cited as cultural premises which steer us through a labyrinth of variegated experience, not conceptual acts entirely our own.

"Dear Abby," a woman wrote. She felt "proud" that her two sons were born with cleft palates because it was a "manifestation of God's work." Whether applied as a rationalization or as an honestly held belief, a not always easily discriminated matter, the premise that " 'what is' is God's doing and man can find contentment in that understanding," identifies a cultural prescription inferable from the woman's remarks. She applies the prescription to the unique circumstances of her experience, but it is the end-product of a conceptual act objectified and supported through tradition and a community of believers. She has assimilated it as her own through one or another process of learning, though she might never state it as a premise.

But there is no fixed, determinate relationship between a particular cultural premise

and an act, as I have already suggested. Believe this, apply it thus, do that. "Dear Abby," another woman wrote. She was moved to comment on the mother's sentiment regarding her son's cleft palates. It was not credible, she argued. Did not the mother know that such deformities could be corrected through surgery? As though to say that no one knowledgeable about the advance of medicine in this respect could subscribe to such a sentiment. In the query there could be hidden another cultural prescription, a belief interpretable as a guide to conduct because if brought to consciousness, if made explicit, it could be recognized as grounds justifying the particular behavior: " 'what is' is and it is man's work to shape it, transform it, to his own designs and for his own well-being."

However, the illustration so far only suggests that different premises may arise in the same social environment, perhaps to conflict with one another within the same individual, or to be applied unwittingly or otherwise by some but not by others without direct conflict. The second woman, obviously, would not be expected to behave in the same manner as the first, without special cost to either. These remarks do not clarify the issue raised above. The indeterminate relationship between premise and act does not emerge as a reasonable conclusion. There is more to be added. In her comment, the second woman goes on to say that God does not manifest His work "by deforming infants at birth. If He did, He wouldn't give the surgeon the knowledge and skill to correct such deformities" (*Ann Arbor News* 1965). We can still be confident that this woman would not act, would not express the same sentiment, as the mother under the same circumstances. At the same time, her comment does not deny the premise inferred from the mother's remarks, but it does represent a different conclusion drawn from it.

The qualification must be registered that

the first woman may be ignorant of or unable to take advantage of medical advances and is therefore rationalizing in order to endure her plight, while the hypothetical nature of the second woman's position does not tell us about her actual behavior should she ever be faced with the same problem without the resources to resolve it, but these qualifications only enhance the indeterminate relationship posited. Of course, this indeterminacy creates strategical and tactical problems of research for the student of behavior.

This lack of fitness between our conceptions of the world and our behavior leads to another point. The premises provided for us through tradition and community of association with others can be viewed as an incrustation of the mind. They do not form a pervasive hardening, but a firm boundary, almost unbreakable for some, brittle or elastic for others, within which there is always considerable interplay between perceiving and conceiving such that the act of appraising our particular experiences in the light of given premises may be accompanied by the reappraising of the premises in the light of experience. As a result of such interplay, they may be gradually modified or even discarded as their credibility and appropriateness to experience comes into question.

An incident related to me illustrates. A few years ago, an American college girl married a Persian student, who was studying in the United States. Not an uncommon occurrence. Soon after she found herself in a strange culture and in the midst of a conservative Moslem family, her affines. She faced usual problems of adjustment — the abrasive strangeness of sights and sounds, the uncertainty about expected behavior, the food, the water, the loneliness of the outsider deeply dependent upon others who have long-standing association with one another — in an understanding and forebearing manner. On one occasion, however, she

refused to defer. She compromised, but she refused to defer.

Within her first few months in Persia, the girl became pregnant. The physiological responses to unaccustomed food and water, in addition to the pregnancy, made a doctor's attention more imperative for her than it might for other women under normal circumstances. One day, shortly before her doctor's appointment, she sneezed. In the presence of her mother-in-law!

There is a Persian folk belief — who knows how far back it goes? — which warns that should someone sneeze just prior to setting off on a journey some misfortune will result unless the departure is postponed (Donaldson 1938).

The trip to the doctor must be cancelled, said the mother-in-law. Absolutely not, said the girl. Implicit in those responses was the acceptance and rejection of a notion of causation, which assimilates the event into a meaningful order of experience for one person but not the other. It continues to be a belief held by some Persians, perhaps in no more than a furtive, almost subliminal, uneasy manner (as so many folk beliefs are held by even the most "rational" among us) that a sudden sneeze opens the way for an evil spirit to enter the body. Unless another sneeze casts it out immediately or it is exorcized properly, its host must take care to avoid becoming a victim of its evil power.

The conversation between the girl and her mother-in-law might be reasonably well reconstructed with a little imagination. It is safe to say that neither of them is likely to have gone into an exegesis of the epistemological and ontological implications of the event to support their responses to it. But such implications are always there to be drawn out of our actions and found to be in tradition and community as a superstructural mesh which might be likened to an exo-skeleton supporting the mental constructs of individuals within it.

Whatever the substance of the dialogue, the girl remained firm. She must go to the doctor and that same afternoon. Her husband, not altogether comfortably, sided with his mother. His justification? Twenty-five hundred years of Persian culture gave more credible grounds for accepting the belief than the briefer span of Western culture could give for rejecting it. Little avail. But out of the give and take came a compromise resolution. An immediate appointment was made with a different doctor.

From the compromise came a restriction in the scope of the belief. Obviously a single incident does not mark a modification or the rejection of a cultural premise. It does point toward a process of attrition whereby cultural premises, which give the fixed aspect to our mental constructs as aids to the understanding and the manipulation of our experiences, must always weather the richness and variability of a reality never completely encompassed by them.

These illustrations have been restricted in scope. They have, in each instance, had a singular emphasis, giving little sense of the elaborate order into which the results of our conceptual behavior fall as elements of knowledge and values. It is a logical order to some extent, the elements always partially articulated into a system, but never completely so.

It was argued earlier that the adaptive process is characterized by a striving towards consistency. It mediates between conceptual permanence and existential flux as an effort to maintain a stable relationship between ourselves and the environment. There is a corollary to this proposition applicable to the conceptual order itself. In this realm as well, a striving towards consistency can be assumed. The adaptive process serves to maintain a stable relationship between the elements which make up any particular cultural world of knowledge and values.

A final illustration will emphasize this point. Not long ago it was reported in a newspaper that the 177th General Assembly of the United Presbyterian Church in the United States had passed resolutions for significant creedal changes, including the resolution that there are no religious barriers to interracial marriages (*Ann Arbor News* 1965). The resolution was carried in the assembly with only a scattering of "nos." This resolution also urged the denomination to work for repeal or nullification of anti-miscegenation laws in nineteen states. The church, it was concluded, found no scriptural or theological grounds either to condemn or prohibit such unions.

The news article went on to say that much of the assembly debate concerned itself with a section of the Bible which declares that "the Scriptures are the words of men." The new confession emerging from this General Assembly describes the Bible as the "normative witness" to Divine revelation.

Here is an act of men. No one can be unaware of the civil rights movement during the past decade. As members of the same religious community, these men are responding to issues of concern to themselves as members of a far larger community. Their response is meant to be legislation not simply for themselves but for all members of the faith, present and absent from the assembly, now and into the future. Nor is it unreasonable to presume that it is meant to be exemplary for other religious communities within the society, in the hope they will follow suit. Much as we may tolerantly express otherwise at times, if we conclude a judgment to be a right one for ourselves, under specified nonexclusive conditions, then we believe it to be right for anyone who falls within those conditions.

There is not likely to be any serious disagreement with the assertion that one basic premise in American society hinges on the notion of "equality," whether or not all or any Americans do in fact behave fully in accordance with it at all times. The notion may be understood as an existential proposition, a statement about the nature of things: "men are equal" or "men are created equal." It may be understood as a normative proposition, a legal statement as part of a theory of justice: "men are equal under the law." It may be understood as a normative proposition of another kind, a moral statement implying an imperative condition without the firmly founded sanctions to insure it: "men ought to have equal opportunities" (whatever the context). These interpretations as well as others have been elaborated in volumes of exegeses on the subject of "equality" in American society.

History, law, and myth have supported this premise. And the strains in this nation's development have recurrently been due in some measure to social movements intended to implement the premise behaviorally in the interests of one or another segment of the society. The current struggle on behalf of Negroes is an example.

Through its resolution disclaiming any religious barriers to interracial marriages, the 177th General Assembly of the United Presbyterian Church has striven to keep the cultural premises of its own special community of co-religionists behaviorally consistent with a significant cultural premise associated with the more inclusive society of which it is a part. Marriage choice is one context in which the manifestation of that premise takes on considerable import for many Americans. The resolution does not imply the moral imperative that marriage ought to be interracial. It does imply that "race" ought not to be a criterion by which to limit marriage choices. It extends equality of opportunity. What justification? Not that "race" as a social concept is a fuzzy one at best from the point of view of interested and knowledgeable natural scientists and social scientists, although such views may well be influential in some fashion; but that the be-

liefs and judgments which make up the scriptural and theological premises of the community — its own cultural world — do not provide grounds for condemning or prohibiting such marriages. Thus elements from the cultural world of a particular society, while drawn from different sources, are worked into a consistent pattern, although never completely achieving the state of a system, a self-contained logical order of relationships independent of actions outside it.

The illustration suggests more. If scriptural and theological grounds cannot be found today as a support against interracial marriage, we might presume that, had the matter been given concerted thought fifty or a hundred years ago or even much earlier, those grounds would have been wanting then also. After all, the Corpus from which justification is ultimately sought has not changed. Of course, the presumption would be ill-founded. But it does bear upon the point.

The article hints, without providing much evidence for confident elaboration, that the assembly's striving toward consistency was operating also on an issue obviously related to the resolution but more fundamental for the community. Even as scriptural sources are appealed to as the standard of judgment, that standard itself falls under scrutiny (to make it more relevant to contemporary events, more consistent with contemporary ideas?), an inference not unreasonably drawn from the report of the assembly's debate about the source of the Scriptures and its judgment about their relationship to divine revelation.

It was argued that species survival meant maintaining species identity, and, in turn, that such identity was closely bound to cultural identity. The adaptive process, operating at the conceptual level, works towards retaining that identity in the face of the constant change which the significance of our specific beliefs and judgments undergoes. Again, it mediates between conceptual permanence and existential flux, as a striving towards consistency which keeps the elements of the cultural world in some logically ordered interrelationship.

Conceptual permanence is realized in the objectification of beliefs and judgments into a cultural world of knowledge and values. It is part of the natural world, and may be so studied, since man as we know the species could not survive except through being interdependent and developing culture.

The student of values formulates problems and methods as an effort to identify the elements of specific cultural orders, their variation within and between such orders, and their consequences to the behavior of members of the societies with which each order may be identified. Let us turn to them, briefly.

PRACTITIONERS

The following discussion represents an effort to provide perspective from which to look at work done in the area of "values." It does so through general remarks and a few brief illustrations of work that has been done.

As I described the incidents and subject matter that made up the several illustrations of the last section, I took care not to use the word "values." When it did appear, it was used in the context of those comments which link the illustrations to the general exposition of the first section, wherein the term denotes the inclusive class of relationships, beliefs, conditions of being, and objects which are the objectified end-products of the evaluative behavior fundamental to the adaptive process. In this respect, it has modest, if any, interpretive significance.

In effect, the illustrations were not seen from the viewpoint of an investigator, engaged in reflective enquiry at a level of discourse wherein the concept of "values" might be meant to have analytic and ex-

planatory purpose. They were seen by an expositor, someone mapping out, through the use of examples, the domain of such enquiry.

Undoubtedly, "value" was recognized as implicit in the content of the illustrations. For example, the idea of "equality" is treated as presumed knowledge about the natural status of men; it may be treated as a standard against which to judge the actions of men in their relations with one another; or it may be treated as a goal towards which behavioral choices are made as means to an end. Possibly all simultaneously. Whatever the case may be, the imputation of worth to it such that it might be conceptually transmuted from a condition valued to a "value" lies hidden in the fact that it is recognizable as a cultural attribute of a particular tradition and community. To be made explicit, it must be elicited somehow from participants in the culture. This is, of course, a problem of enquiry, the conceptual behavior of an observer interested in understanding an aspect of the conceptual behavior and related actions of members of a society always at work through the adaptive process developing and maintaining the cultural superstructure of knowledge and values.

As participants in a culture, we are seldom aware of the "presence" of values. We do without thinking about the significance of what we are doing. "Poetry," W. H. Auden has written, "makes nothing happen; it survives in the valley of its saying." Something similar may be said of values which presumably guide our conduct. They do not so much make anything happen, but exist in the valley of our doing. Each of our acts is not viewed as related to a set of beliefs we share with others about the world of man and nature and thus made credible; nor is each act viewed as related to a set of standards we share with others about what is good or what is right and thus justified. But our actions, including that level of discourse which is handmaiden to them and not a comment upon them, reflect in the fact of their performance beliefs and standards and goals we do hold and do share with others. And it is the investigator's use of the concept of "values" in his work as he elicits and infers these beliefs, standards, and goals and interprets their relation to one another and to the acts of men with which the next few paragraphs are concerned.

The distinction made between participant and investigator is an obvious one. But it is especially important to note it here. It has been stated that evaluative behavior, whether seen as a process or the objectified end-products of that process, is a fundamental characteristic of man. To study man as distinct from any other object of nature is inevitably to study his valuing and his values. His actions, his beliefs, his normative judgments, his goals, all reflect choices made and choices objectified. However, the concept of "values" has not been long in the service of the social scientist, aside perhaps from the economist. Often enough, it is used in discursive discussion much as a special member of that class of useful, almost all-purpose words, such as "thing," "matter," "gear" (archaic), "stuff," that is, as an unspecified array of "things valued."

Some qualification is necessary. Two aspects of the "problem of values" in which the concept is extensively used has had longstanding currency in the social sciences. The first aspect is related to the issue of objectivity in the study of human behavior. The question often asked from this point of view is whether there can be a value-free social science. The second aspect concerns itself with the relationship between knowledge drawn from the rational-empirical study of human behavior and judgments made in the process of evaluation. Here, the question is often asked whether such knowledge can validate values. Both these matters will be touched upon in the final section.

Among anthropologists, the tendency to project culture as an ordering of the objectified end-products of conceptual or symbolic behavior has produced several concepts intended to have some interpretive significance, and to provide some understanding as to the relationship between the conceptual order and action. They incorporate ideas bound up with the effort to give singular identity to particular cultures, that is, to particular modes of ordering experience, characteristic of different peoples, which constitute their distinctive "ways of life."

Such concepts as "configurations," "patterns," "culture themes," "unconscious canons of choice," "world view," "ethos," "unconscious system of meanings," point to work done by American anthropologists [1] which anticipated the use of "values" in this area of study. The identification of "values" as basic elements of a culture and their distribution in some organized fashion as the distinctive character of a particular cultural order, as well as the effort to determine what those values are and how to characterize their ordered distribution within specific cultures, is an approach which got underway after World War II. Illustrations will be drawn from this later work.

It will be useful to name three categories into which studies of values may be put. They will suggest some perspective from which to identify the work to be cited. Borrowing from a set of terms used to classify legal study (Stone 1950), I shall discriminate among the analytical study of values, the sociological (anthropological, psychological) study of values, and the philosophical study of values.

The first category refers to any work which concentrates on the nature and distribution of values within any society, as well as the relations among them as they are

---

[1] Among them must be mentioned Ruth Benedict, Clyde Kluckhohn, Morris Opler, Edward Sapir, and Robert Redfield.

made to exhibit a logical order. The second refers to any work in which the problem is the relation between values and human action. The third refers to any work which concerns itself with the rationale that lies behind the basis of justifying judgments of values.

I shall begin with this third category because it need not be illustrated here by any specific work. The problem it covers is one that generations of philosophers have taken hold of and elaborated in great detail. It is of particular interest to all of us insofar as decisions made are choices made. We cannot escape them, and they always involve values and evaluating. Never is this fact clearer than on hearing that favored ploy, fashionable at one time at least during heated student discussions, which ensures stalemate when checkmate is out of reach: "That's just a value judgment." Behind such an assertion there is a view as to whether a basis for justifying judgments of value can or cannot be agreed upon.

The issue is simple; its resolution has not been. There are two possible ways to account for values acknowledged. Particular experiences of the individual or the community may be described and interpreted as an explanation suggesting how these values came to be held. Causes are inferred. At the same time, it might be shown how the values have been justified. The grounds which have prompted belief in them may be cited. Reasons are given.

Much of the philosophical discussion of values has to do with "grounds." The range of dispute has been wide. It has been argued that there are no grounds by which any values may be justified independent of the fact that they are held and the causes which account for their being held. This position is opposed, of course, to one which insists that grounds can be determined. But even among those who hold the latter view, there is considerable disagreement as to

what those grounds are, that is, what sort of justification can discriminate genuine values from spurious ones.[2]

The problem is not directly of concern to the social scientist, who takes the presence of values as a "given," working to identify them, classify them, analyze the significance of their being held, generalize about them in one or more or (ideally) all societies. For this reason, the issues have not been elaborated here. Actually, they will be implicit in the discussion of applied problems in the final section.

The work of Florence Kluckhohn and her collaborators illustrates the "analytical study of values" as I have defined that category (Kluckhohn and Strodbeck 1961). The concept of "value orientation" is a central one in an enquiry intended to elicit dominant and variant profiles of basic values distinctive of five small communities (Mormons, ex-Texans, Spanish-Americans, Zuni, and Navaho) living in the same area in the American Southwest. Defined in the most comprehensive sense, it refers to principles held regarding fundamental problems which deeply influence behavior.

The concept rests upon a central assumption: there are basic human problems, limited in number, common to all people, for which solutions must be found. Several corollaries to this assumption may be stated: the solutions to these problems vary between and within societies; the range of possible variation is limited, therefore ordered;

---

[2] The philosophic literature on this subject is voluminous. The following list of publications are recent studies which cover different points of view: Aiken, H. D. *Reason and Conduct* (1962); Baier, K. M., *The Moral Point of View* (1958); Edel, A., *Method in Ethical Theory* (1963); Hare, R. M., *Freedom and Reason* (1963); Taylor, P., *Normative Discourse* (1961); Singer, M. G., *Generalization in Ethics* (1961); Toulmin, S., *Reason in Ethics* (1960); Waddington, C. H., *The Ethical Animal* (1960); Zink, S., *The Concepts of Ethics* (1962); Kerner, G. C., *The Revolution in Ethical Theory* (1966).

the total range of variation is found in all societies but may be discriminated along two dimensions — in any society, an order of preference will be reflected in the presence of a dominant set of solutions accompanied by one or more variant sets, and within any set, the range of solutions will also be present, probably ranked in an order of preference. Value orientations are the "content" of these solutions, that is, they are the type of answer which is given to these problems.

Dr. Kluckhohn has enumerated five problems as crucial to all peoples, problems to which answers must be given so as to provide orientation or direction as the activities of living are pursued. Men must concern themselves with a conception of human nature — for example, whether it is intrinsically good or evil, neutral or mixed, and whether for each postulated condition it can be changed or must remain inexorably fixed. They must concern themselves with a conception of man's relation to man, whether he is subjugated by nature, is master over it, or is in harmony with it. There must be concern with a conception of man's relation to man, to time, and to activity as a reflection of self-expression. And in each instance, as I noted with two of the problems, she has postulated a limited range of variation.

The organization Dr. Kluckhohn provides for ordering the value orientations of any society consists, then, of five basic problems of orientation, four of which have three categories of variation. The fifth orientation, "human nature," is slightly more elaborate. Compare it above with the "man-nature" orientation cited. The large number of permutations possible within this order of categories and the potentially complex elaboration for characterizing societies when the notion of dominant and variant sets is superimposed upon the scheme can readily be imagined.

Questions based upon this classifying scheme, which has been partially described, were asked of individuals from each community. The purpose was to elicit the kind of responses for each problem from which dominant and variant sets of value orientations in the five communities could be inferred through statistical and discursive analysis. The responses to the questions involved the selection and ranking of alternative solutions to basic human situations. For example, "livestock dying" is one item under the "man-nature" orientation. A man has lost most of his livestock, the respondent is told. Three ways by which others might account for such an event are listed. One is intended, by the investigator, to reflect subjugation of man to nature, another, mastery over nature, and the third, harmony with it. The respondent is asked to indicate which reason he thinks "true," which of the remaining two he thinks "more true," and which one most other persons in his community would think is "true." [3] There are twenty-two items in the schedule, classified under one or another problem orientation, each describing situations for which there are alternative solutions covering the postulated categories of variation for each orientation.

The results need not detain us long. Each group did show a distinctive order of preference on any orientation dimension. For example, on the "man-nature" dimension, the Texans showed greater preference for the view that man was master over nature rather than subjugated by it, whereas the "value orientation" of the Spanish-Americans reflected the latter view. The Mormons, however, contrasted with the Texans along this dimension with a "value orientation" which

[3] The example is not representative in one respect. For two other items, "right" and "more right" are the appropriate responses. In all others the alternative solutions to the situations presented require "best" and/or "better" as answers.

gave more stress to "harmony with nature." On the "time" dimension, the Texans were more future-oriented than the Mormons or the Spanish-Americans; the Mormons more past-oriented than the Spanish-Americans or the Texans; and, the Spanish-Americans more present-oriented than either of the other two. In spite of differences, the English-speaking communities were most alike; the Indian communities showed most similarity to each other along the "man's relation to man" (relational) orientation, but in other respects were quite different from each other as well as different from the non-Indian communities. The Spanish-Americans stood apart from all the rest in their distinctiveness.

Describing societies by sets of value orientations characterizes them along one dimension of "values." A "value orientation" is a basic value. The specific content of any "value orientation" characteristic of a society, for example, is held in preference to the specific content of others. In this respect, it is a "value," as any content of a society may be a "value." But a "value orientation" is also a criterial principle which generates other values in that it guides and is generally consistent with objectified preferences for the specific content of a vast array of relationships, objects, beliefs, states of feeling, prescribed and prohibited modes of behavior which invest any society with order and any individual with a "map" of the well-trodden paths in that society. In this respect, it is a "basic value." The "value orientation" concept may be viewed, then, as at the apex of a hierarchical order of values, that is, of specified conceptual and physical entities which have been objectified as valuable, and exhibit some logical relationship to one another. Dr. Kluckhohn has been concerned with the ordering of values at this "apex," that is, the classification of basic values which are the fundamental criterial principles of the logical or-

der of values characteristic of particular societies.

An article by Dr. Ethel M. Albert offers a paradigm for the classification of values illustrative of an approach which aims at classifying the entire order of values characteristic of a particular society (1956). Briefly, she postulates a "value system" of which cultural values are the basic elements. This system is embedded in a philosophical order of metaphysical, logical, epistomological, and psychological assumptions. This philosophical order represents a cultural world view. Metaphysical assumptions, for example, include ideas about space and time, principles of causation, and reality, while logical assumptions have to do with rules of reasoning characteristic of a particular culture, and psychological assumptions with conceptions of human nature. These assumptions apparently generate "value premises" which stand at the head of the "value system."

The "premises" seem to have a "Janus" aspect. Dr. Albert defines them as existential statements which provide the rationale behind the system of values, while being part of the system. In this respect, they appear much like the content of the world view in which the system is embedded but of which it is presumably in some sense independent. In fact, the Navaho "value premises" are defined by Dr. Albert, quite intentionally, in virtually the same way as she defined the philosophical order of assumptions on which they rest. Nevertheless, "value premises" are also defined in a normative sense, as the most general views about what are desirable and undesirable modes, means, and ends of action. And in this respect, she includes Dr. Kluckhohn's "value orientations" as "value premises," but seems to contrast them with other "premises." In effect, "value orientations" are members of the class of "value premises," but do not exhaust that class. Therefore, some "value premises" are existential propositions but not normative ones, and some are both existential and normative. These subclasses are clearly defined, but as they are members of the same class, the definition of that class becomes uncertain to me. I think there is some lack of clarity here, either in my understanding or in Dr. Albert's argument.

However, for my purpose, there is no need to trip over this point. My main concern is not a critique but a description of approaches to the study of values. Quickly, then. At the next level of the paradigm, "focal values" appear. In any culture, values of central import cluster about a limited number of areas. Among the Mormons, for example, work, health, education, and recreation are focal points for value clusters. Such a set of "focal values" would be different for the cultures of different societies.

Since the "value premises" serve as rationale for the entire system of values, their relation to "focal values" is of that nature. They differ from the latter in at least one important respect. Whereas the "value premises" must be inferred by the investigator from verbal and other behavior, "focal values," although they can be inferred, may well be explicitly embodied in the discourse of the cultural participants. In fact, specific "focal values" are used to justify and account for other values in the cultural order, including those at their own level, that is, other "focal values."

At the next descending level of the paradigm, the concepts of "directives" and "character" are introduced. The former refers to the various modes by which conduct is regulated, the prescriptions and prohibitions embodied in such concepts as laws, obligations, taboos, rights, and privileges; the latter, to those qualities of personality deemed "virtues" and "vices" within the culture and regulated accordingly. The justification behind the specific content of this

level in the "value system" is found in the existential and normative content of the "focal values" and, more generally, of course, the "value premises": "you must work; work is good; man fulfills nature's (God's) purpose when he works."

Finally, there are "valued and disvalued entities," the most elemental features of the "value system." They are the activities, objects, situations, and mental states valued by virtue of their relation to the higher order of values in the culture. They serve as means to satisfy them. Moreover, contrasts between cultures are most easily observed at this level — as one might guess. After all, the more general the principle, the greater the diversity encompassed and neutralized by it.

Dr. Albert has programmed a paradigm which, if superimposed, as it were, upon the actual values in a society — disregarding the problem of eliciting those values — would form them into an interdependent hierarchical list of belief, norms, qualities, behaviors, objects, and situations which characterizes that society's cultural world of knowledge and values.

The two works described should be contrasted. In the first, the most general principles in a cultural order of values are taken as the subject matter of investigation and classified according to a paradigm which permits comparison between and within societies as they exhibit dominance and variance in the specific content of those principles. In the second, a society's entire order of values is taken as the subject matter of investigation and classified according to a paradigm which shows that order to consist of a series of increasingly more inclusive valued entitites. All such values are related to one another. Those at the more inclusive levels of generalization are sources of justification and explanation of those at the less inclusive levels. The latter, in turn, serve as a means of satisfying the former. The entire order ultimately rests upon a rationale about the existential nature of things. It could be argued that the first paradigm attempts to formulate a system out of its subject matter, while the second attempts to exhibit a system in its subject matter. These are not mutually exclusive efforts, but rather complementary.

Both approaches concentrate attention on the conceptual order in itself. The interaction of that order with actual behavior is not explicitly a matter of concern. Not to say that Drs. Kluckhohn and Albert are not interested in and fully aware of this aspect of study; they have simply not made it a foreground issue.

I want to turn, then, to illustrations in which the relation of values to behavior are the explicit concern of the investigators. These examples fall into the category identified above as the sociological (anthropological, psychological) study of values. The tradition of social enquiry in this area has been long and rich. It is usually marked by a concern with ideology and its impact upon social action, that is, the concept of "values" has not always been central and explicit in the interpretive discussion. In this category, the work of Max Weber is of classic significance, no work being more renowned than his "The Protestant Ethic and the Spirit of Capitalism." The idea is the thing wherein to catch the content of the act. Marxian ideology would seem to have it the other way, thereby hinting at a genuine paradox.

These prefatory remarks are meant to provide a general context for two articles to be hardly more than resumed. "Values" enters as a central idea in both of them.

It is appropriate to begin with a study done by Evon Z. Vogt and Thomas F. O'Dea (1953) because it is part of the same extensive program of research which gave impetus to the work of Kluckhohn and Albert. Between 1949 and 1955, the Laboratory of Social Relations, Harvard University, undertook "A Comparative Study of Values in Five Cultures." In this article Vogt and O'Dea describe a comparative study of two New Mexico farming communities: a Mormon village and a settlement of migrant Texans. They were intent upon demonstrating the importance of "value orientations" in shaping a contrasting aspect of the social organization of these communities and concomitant behavior of the respective community members.

The environmental situation was the same for both communities. In this respect, both faced the same problems of maintaining a community. The authors sought the source of the different solutions developed by each group in the ways they conceived of their situation; in effect, in their "value orientations."

Among the Mormons, the church was the center of the village organization. Family and family partnerships provided the organizational base for farming. Although private initiative was valued, the Mormon Law of Consecration emphasizes a socialistic attitude manifest in cooperation and cooperative enterprise. For example, irrigation of the land was achieved by the village only through a cooperative undertaking.

In contrast, the Texans stressed individual independence. Family rivalries and religious denominationalism were indications of the looseness of the community integration.

Cooperation was a dominant orientation among the Mormons; individualism, among the Texans. Both communities had faced the same three issues: a tight land problem; the opportunity to gravel their streets; and the advisability of constructing a high school gymnasium.

The Mormons created a cooperative to purchase land, contributed equally to gravel the streets, and invested both labor and money in the building project. The decision process was of the town meeting sort under the aegis of the church. The Texan community, oriented towards individualism, failed to purchase land, witnessed some gravelling of their streets through individual initiative only, and sold their labor to the school in the uncompleted (1953) gym building project.

Although the authors do not discount the possible relevance of other factors in the situation and in the personalities of those involved to account for this difference of behavior between the communities, the difference in value orientations is presumed the dominant one. These contrasting orientations set the tone of the two communities. Reinforced in action, they repeatedly determine the choices of the group. Thus, the authors argue that the scattered residence pattern of the Texans is a matter of deliberate choice. And, in keeping with their orientation, the Mormon community's choice of a site which allows irrigated farming as opposed to the dry-land farming of their neighbors was, to the authors, motivated by the desire to establish a particular cooperative form of society.

Comment on this study will be brief. Explication is hardly required. The notion of "value orientation" has been covered by our earlier discussion. The elements of comparison which occasion the inferences linking a mental construct — such as a "value orientation" — with actual behavior are easily recognized in the resumé: postulating a common environment and several common problems, the authors must suggest what accounts for the responses of individuals within two communities which significantly distinguishes those communities from each other.

The second illustration of the category I have labelled the "sociological study of values" provides a problem of somewhat different emphasis. In an article describing a study in which the locus of investigation was the class structure of American society in general, Dr. Herbert H. Hyman argued that values represent a significant factor in perpetuating the existing class organization (Hyman 1953).

The study's focus is upon the limitation of upward mobility among members of the lower economic and social strata of society. Dr. Hyman recognizes that inadequate resources such as lack of education and special training due to financial restrictions, which by definition is a characteristic of lower classes, regulate movement upward on the social scale. However, these "objective" factors do not exhaust the limiting conditions. He contends that a system of values intervenes between low status and lack of upward mobility, creating a barrier to improvement which is self-imposed, because it restricts voluntary action (initiative?) even within the degree of freedom which in fact does keep the way at least partially open to improvement of class position. In effect, even if he has the means to improve his social position, his values impose upon the lower-class individual in such a way that he is apt to be immobilized in his place. Thus the existing social order tends to be perpetuated.

This lower-class value system, according to Hyman, consists of three elements: there is less emphasis on the traditional American goal of success; the limits of opportunity to achieve success are more acutely perceived; and there is less emphasis upon those goals which are means to the success goal.

The evidence of the differential presence of these "values" in the American class structure provides the inferential base for the author's conclusions. For example, willingness to strive, as well as ability, is a prerequisite to achievement, including the willingness to obtain the formal training necessary to achieve many high positions in the society. Identified along several dimensions, including occupation, economic and education level achieved, the lower strata of the population put less value upon college education in contrast to higher classes.[4] To the extent that a college education enhances the opportunities for upward mobility, the inference is reasonable that as something evaluated it operates upon members of the lower classes so as to help maintain the present order.

Dr. Hyman's discussion is considerably more elaborate than this account suggests, recognizing, among other things, the possibility that "values" may not be a relevant issue because the unwillingness to aim higher and behave accordingly may result simply from the reduction of aspiration which is prompted by a realistic accommodation to fewer opportunities, as a guard against frustration and failure. However, there is no need to extend his argument here since I am using the work as an illustration of an approach, not as a substantive statement about American social patterns.

Drs. Vogt and O'Dea were concerned with values as criterial principles which guided behavior in the choice of alternative solutions to specific problems consistent with different modes of social organization. In contrast, Dr. Hyman concerned himself with values as specific states of mind valued, representing an addition to "objective" factors by which the limitations on upward mobility are increased so as to help maintain a particular social order.

Both tend to highlight the conservative force of value elements, which regulate conduct so as to perpetuate the conditions giving rise to them. Reasonable enough. Insofar as a cultural order of values in society points to what is believed and what is recognized as appropriate conduct, it affirms the social order the beliefs and the conduct generate. It conserves. As I argued earlier, the ultimate goal of survival must be defined to include the maintenance of identity, species

and cultural identity. Conceptual behavior, of which evaluative behavior is a part, imposes permanence upon our experience through identification, generalization, and abstraction. And maintaining species and cultural identity is a product of this sense of permanence.

Even in the context of social change, the conserving process is fundamental. Permanence is a vital factor in such change, which, as we distinguish it from existential flux, is inevitably bound up with conceptual processes. An advertisement for the Volkswagen makes the point neatly. After noting that some 5000 changes had been made since 1948 on a car known and acclaimed for the longevity of its basic model, this was added: "A few purists feel we kill the bug each time we improve it. But we have no choice. We've got to keep killing the bug every chance we get. That's the only sure way to keep it from dying" (*Newsweek* 1965). The adaptive process, as I wrote in the first section, mediates between conceptual permanence and existential flux. Social change would have no meaning unaccompanied by the sense of permanence.

The two articles discussed draw our attention to another issue, a central problem in the sociological study of values: making the inferential link between mental construct and behavior reasonable. There is not a necessary fit between the two. The idea is hardly novel that what we think and what we do may not conform to one another. Even if language should intervene in the sense of explicit statements about what we are thinking and what we would do, the problem obviously remains for the investigator. The modes of comparison and the substance of the arguments in these articles can be viewed, as I tried earlier to suggest, as strategy and tactics meant to resolve the problem. It would be foolhardy to pursue the issue any further here, since it carries important methodological implications, not to speak of

---

[4] The author's evidence was drawn from a nationwide survey done in 1947 by the National Opinion Research Center, using a total sample of about 2500 adults and 500 youths.

metaphysical ones which extend well beyond the study of values.

PROBLEMS OF DEFINITION

The notion of values is made to do a great deal of work. Evidence of this has certainly been suggested in the preceding discussion. This fact contributes to lack of confidence in the concept among many social scientists. The word — whatever the range of its uses — points to a fundamental aspect of human experience. It seems unfortunate that it often provokes more confusion than clarity.

In this section, some attention will be given to the sources of confusion. In the introduction, I insisted that it would not be my purpose to try and resolve the problem of definition. Except insofar as an individual strives to be consistent in usage, the resolution of such a problem is a community affair, a matter of agreement among interested parties. Of course, explication as to why one particular usage is to be preferred above others falls prior to such agreement, but such a discussion takes us far off the track of the mapping operation I set as my purpose.

Actually, the lexical meaning of "values" does not cause much difficulty. As a verb, it refers to the act of imputing worth to anything. As a noun, it is a common class term which subsumes any entity — object, relationships, and so on — to which an imputation of worth has been given such that the attribute of its being valued takes precedence over any other attribute in the appropriate universe of discourse. Both these senses would be recognized and agreed upon, it is safe to say.

However, the question of semantic domain provokes concern. The overlapping boundaries of its use in various contexts do not always appear consistent. The confusion lies not in any notion of the central meaning of the word, but in the range of its application, which might easily lead a venturesome spirit

to argue that the problem is a matter of homonymous terms being mistaken for *a* single term. It is this contextual source of confusion which I want to make explicit through two or three illustrations.

Mention has been made of the contrast between Kluckhohn's use of "value orientation" and Albert's use of both this concept and that of "value premise." The weight of the difference may seem to rest upon the two end terms rather than the common modifier. However, that is not altogether so. Besides being a phrase which refers to a "basic value," the former concept also refers to that "basic value" as an orienting principle in the act of valuing, as it directs our actions by influencing the choices we make. The phrase "value premise," in turn, refers to a principle about the nature of things which serves as a rationale to make credible a "value system" taken as a whole, whose elements are also identified by the term "value." Thus, "value" is not used in the same way in these two concepts. The point might be strengthened by arguing that grammatically the weight of meaning in "value orientation" falls on the concept as a whole as a noun phrase; whereas with "value premise," the end term takes the brunt of meaning as a noun modified by an adjective.

In his book on American culture, Dr. Jules Henry (1963) puts a stamp of his own on the notion of "values." He would appear to exclude from the category of "value" those sentiments and behaviors to which we were compulsively addicted. For example, the ideas of "achievement" and "success" and the behavior associated with them are generally acknowledged as significant attributes of American culture and society. It is not uncommon to find them noted as "values" (see especially Williams 1963). But Dr. Henry explicitly and emphatically denies them such status. For him, they are "drives" or "urges." As the chemistry of the body generates the drives of hunger, thirst, and such, our culture generates the "drives" of competitiveness and achievement. We are compelled by the latter much the same way we are compelled by the former. "Values," however, refer to such sentiments as gentleness, kindliness, and generosity, which act as opposing "urges" to offset the destructive expansiveness of the achievement and competitive drives. The analogy to the "chemistry of the body" would suggest that it is the compulsive force of a sentiment which determines whether or not it will be identified as a value. At the same time, those sentiments he does acknowledge as "values," he also refers to as "urges," implying therefore a compelling quality about them as well. In effect, the conclusion which seems most reasonable is that "values" are good "urges" and "drives" (of the cultural sort at least) are bad "urges," provoking the uneasy feeling that Dr. Henry is not talking about American values but about his own likes and dislikes.

My own use of the concept in this discussion can contribute to the illustration of the contextual variability which gives it such instability. It has been my intention to use the word to refer only to the objectified end-products of evaluative behavior, that is, to those preferences, desires, and interests which, no matter how they may have arisen, are held in common by members of a group. From this point of view, any reference to "personal values" or "individual values" would seem out of place. Nevertheless, both uses are common. Even "idiosyncratic" is given modifying weight equivalent to "personal" and "individual" in this context (von Mering 1961). I have tried to avoid this usage. Perhaps it can be made to serve some distinctive purpose, but at present it lends itself too easily to ambiguity. It may serve too many purposes. It can be interpreted as "not held by anyone else," or as "not recognized by the individual to be held by anyone else," or as "recognized to be held by others but stated from a personal point of view in order

to serve as a shorthand expression." More needs to be said on the matter. However, as another example of contextual variability nothing would be added by doing so here.

Another context of use which burdens the concept is found in the notion of "negative values," or "disvalue." [5] In one sense, the idea of a "negative value" does not seem justified; in another sense, it does. If the notion of "value" has in it the idea of approval, then it seems odd to speak of "negative value," because it must be interpreted as "all of those things which are not approved" or "disapproval of the approved." In the first instance, if "A" is the set of all things approved in a given culture, which we must presume to be a finite set, then "not-A" is the set of all things not approved within that culture, which is potentially an infinite set. I do not believe this is what is meant by "negative value," but if it were, I can see no use in identifying a limitless class for this subject. In the second instance, a "negative value" has the sense of being the negation of a "value." "A" is a "value," by some measure, which is disapproved of in the culture. In the context of intercultural comparison of values such an interpretation might have some relevance. However, this is not, so far as I can understand, the context intended for the idea of "negative value." Rather, it points to a category accompanying that of "value" within the same culture, and its content is made up of those sentiments and behaviors which contradict the prevailing "values." In this context, it seems a pointless notion, because the negation is always implicit in and understood by the statement of the value itself. The contradiction of "A" is "not-A." If "honesty" is a value, then "not-honesty" or "dishonesty" is not valued, but there seems to be little gained by

[5] Dr. Albert, *op. cit.*, makes use of "disvalue" primarily, but so far as I know it is interchangeable with "negative value."

identifying a special category of "negative values" by which to make this fact understood.

I think the reason the notion appears to be relevant in this context stems from comparison of two different levels of generalization. If "honesty" falls into the category of "value," then the "negative value" associated with it is construed as the specific content which identifies "dishonesty," that is, cheating, lying, defrauding, and such. But this specific content should be set beside the specific content which identifies the notion of "honesty" as a "value," for example, "telling the truth," in order to make the level of generalization comparable and relevant. The statement of the "value" should be " 'A' $(A_1, A_2, A_3 \ldots A_n)$." The "negative value" would then be " '−A' $(−A_1, −A_2, −A_3 \ldots −A_n)$." And, therefore, again, the notion of "negative value" is implicit and understood in the statement of the "value." There is no need for the additional category.

However, there is a context in which the idea of "negative value" may indeed be relevant. If our universe of discourse about "values" concerns itself with the problem of relative worth, then we might try to string those entities which are valued in the culture along a spectrum of sharply discriminated rank orderings of most and least, more and less. In any case, I believe I have given some reason as to why "negative value" adds to the uneasiness felt about the concept of "value" due to its contextual variability.

Perhaps the greatest source of difficulty rests in the most inclusive contrast that can be made. The problems it raises have been among the most difficult ones from which social scientists in particular and all scientists at one time or another have had to extricate themselves as a community. As stated earlier, we are observers of our culture even as we are participants in it. We are also participants in our culture even as we are observers. Each within his culture uses the same language for reflective enquiry as he does for performance, and, most significantly and ambiguously for the matter at hand, much of the same lexicon in particular. The level of discourse is different, however. In effect, the natural language — English, French, Russian — is both the language of performance and the language of reflective enquiry. Moreover, as the language of performance it is an important part of the subject matter for which the language of enquiry is developed as an instrument for understanding. There is a constant borrowing from one dimension of discourse to the other, which has consequences for both.

Our reflection upon what we do and what we say as participants in a culture obviously has influence upon our performance. This is most strikingly seen through language. Even when the lexicon of reflective enquiry has been initially different from the lexicon of performance, as the productive consequences of such enquiry pass into our acts they are often carried over with the lexicon of reflective enquiry. When Moliere's Monsieur Jourdain, to fall back upon a perennially sturdy source of analogy, realized that he had been speaking "prose" all his life, just such a transposition took place. So it has been with "values" and many other terms, which have either been taken over from the language of performance and given special attributes of meaning in the dimension of reflective enquiry or have been coined new in enquiry and incorporated ultimately into the dimension of performance. Thus, dimensional variability is added to contextual variability, and vagueness of use can be increased, particularly since the boundaries of discourse in the language of performance are never as sharply delineated as those in the language of enquiry.

The notion of "values" is, it must be acknowledged, an important one. For that reason it needs careful examination as a concept. Dr. Harold Fallding, a sociologist, has contributed to such an examination most recently (1965). He argues that the concept should be restricted to those ends which may be deemed self-sufficient, that is, those satisfactions towards which all other satisfactions are directed. These are penultimate goals, "organizing ends" secondary only to the ultimate end, that of survival.

If a limited set of such ends can be identified such that all other interests, desires, satisfactions, acts can be shown to be organized by them and therefore subordinate to them as means, then, he argues, it is reasonable to say that only those few ends are values. All other things are included because they are necessary to gain those penultimate and self-sufficient satisfactions. There is no point in referring to them as values.

In effect, if the means-ends continuum, in which any entity may be viewed both as an end and as a means, could be eliminated, the notion of value could be successfully restricted in scope. It cannot be so long as it refers indiscriminately to "things valued."

Dr. Fallding's argument deserves attention. His point might be better taken, however, if he had adequately demonstrated, as he recognized it was necessary to do, the means by which such ends might be empirically isolated so as to be recognizable as self-sufficient, except only as they are means to the ultimate goal of survival, and, therefore, distinguishable from all other preferences, desires, and interests which are sufficient only as they serve penultimate ends. Nevertheless, such efforts are necessary.

It might be thought from my remarks in this section that I am counseling despair. Not at all. I am counseling care. Until such time as the concept of "values" is given a thoroughgoing examination, and dialectical discussion has justified the restriction of its use to the satisfaction of the community of social scientists, that is all one can counsel. Naturally, the enterprise is an ongoing affair. The problem will not be resolved by fiat, but by the productiveness of the ideas generated by it.

CONCLUSION

Much ground has been covered, however briefly. The mapping analogy has played itself out. The discussion has been intended to mark off several aspects from which the study of values should be viewed so as to discriminate boundaries and issues which identify the study as an enterprise.

All our actions are embedded in assumptions and premises which serve as a rationale for them, at times explicit, more often than not, implicit. The study of values is itself a mode of action, an enterprise, as the study of any subject is. Therefore, I began by outlining a rationale which was meant to provide credibility for the study of values.

In man, conceptual behavior is a major mode of adaptation. Evaluation is an integral facet of conceptual behavior because there is never a perfect fit between experience and our rendering of it into belief and knowledge. There is, therefore, choice; and choice presumes preferences that reflect desires, interests, wishes, or other such inclinations, whatever the mode of expression used. Objectified, the end-products of evaluative behavior form a cultural order of values, a super-structure which in turn affects evaluative behavior since it serves to guide conduct.

Since it has a conceptual base, which includes evaluative behavior, the adaptive process may be seen as a constant mediation between conceptual permanence and existential flux directed ultimately towards survival, which is defined to include the maintaining of both species identity and cultural identity.

The rationale stated, the remainder of the essay merely illustrated the following matters: (1) the kinds of observations out of which particular cultural orders of values may be constructed and interpreted; (2) different approaches which have guided social scientists' interpretations and analyses of values in a society; and (3) some of the conceptual difficulties which surround the concept of "values" as it has been used in social enquiry.

This brief summary might be enough. But it would not constitute, in my mind, the appropriate conclusion. Any enterprise, including that of scholarship, scientific or otherwise, forms a social order of its own with a conceptual apparatus of ideas and values which make it, in some respect, a thing in itself. It can provide its own relevance for being. Easy enough then for its practitioners to lose themselves in the labyrinth of their own thoughts. Important enough, too.

However, there are always those of us outside the domain who must have issues and problems presented in such a way as to reflect a more inclusive range of relevance. There are such issues bound up with the study of values, as well as with social enquiry in general. I shall mention three of far-reaching significance. The first is the matter of "cultural relativism"; the second that of a value-free social science; and, the third, the relation of social science enquiry to the formulation of social policy. These are the "applied problems" mentioned earlier. Each has been shrouded in substantial dialectics. Introducing them in the conclusion of an essay, for whatever reason, can lead to hardly more than a bare beginning at unveiling. It is therefore my purpose only to identify them as practical problems related to the study of values. I shall cite what I believe to be the major points in each issue and hint at the direction a satisfying resolution of them might take, giving most attention to "cultural relativism" since it has been a subject most particularly associated with anthropology.

The primary object, then, of this concluding section is to illustrate the kind of problems which bridge the self-contained world of social enquiry and the more inclusive so-cial order, the society, for which enquiry ultimately performs a service.

The French baccaulaureate examinations for 1965 posed a question which has the first issue at its core: "Has one the right to talk of inferior societies?" Different societies are characterized by different cultural orders of values, although observation of specific things valued might quickly disclose overlapping at many points. The issue is whether discriminations between values of different societies can be made such that valid arguments may be adduced supporting judgments of comparative worth: the relative value of different orders of values.

The phrase "cultural relativism" labels a particular response to this issue. The position can be stated briefly. The content of a people's culture must be evaluated on its own terms. Any evaluation presumes a standard of evaluation. But there is no legitimate standard outside the culture by which to judge it or any of its elements. In this guise, "cultural relativism" is an ethical doctrine. It is a statement having to do with the kind of justification to be adduced for specific judgments of good and bad in the context of comparing different cultures.

The doctrine rests upon a premise. It is a premise of methodology which has dominated much of social anthropology for thirty years or more and to which I have alluded. Any element of a culture is related to and interdependent with other elements in such a way as to maintain a distinctive configuration, even a necessary one, from the point of view of the participants in the culture. There is, in effect, a cultural order for each society which partakes of the qualities of a system. It is in some measure a self-contained entity.

To judge any particular cultural order, that is, the complex of elements which make it up, by a standard not intrinsic to it is to judge it out of context. It may be done obviously, but the judgment can have no legitimacy outside the simple act of making it, because the standard of judgment would be the product of a different cultural order. Such is the case, then, that in judging the values of others we are implicitly, at least, judging our own as well. "It is not permitted to the most equitable of men to be a judge in his own cause," Pascal wrote. So too might we say of cultures.

Implicit, of course, is the conviction that a meta-standard independent of any particular cultural order of values by which all cultures might be judged is not possible. Some effort has been made towards positing cultural universals which might serve as such a meta-standard. I believe it is safe to say, however, that they either do not escape the dilemma of being a product of a particular culture, or they serve mainly to classify and not judge, or the statement of them is so general as to have little relation to actual things valued in different cultural orders.

Unfortunately, the position of "cultural relativism" does not free us from the dilemma. Right enough, the elements of a cultural order may be judged valid by reference to other elements within it. Dr. Albert's work, cited earlier, suggested just such a relationship in a "value system." However, nothing within the order can validate the order as a whole. Since there is a tendency to treat cultural orders as something of a logical system, it might be pedagogically useful to make my point by reference to the general idea in mathematics associated with Godel's theorem. Although simple elements of a logical system may be proven to be consistent within the system itself, the system as a whole can never be. It seems to me that Dr. Albert tried to resolve this particular aspect of the problem by finding the validation of a "value system," which is normative, in a system of "value premises," statements about the nature of things, which is existential. But, as I suggested, the line between the existential and the normative as

she deals with them is not sharply discriminated. I am not confident that it can be. As a matter of fact, the projection of any meta-standard would always leave us the problem of validating it by a standard outside of itself. The "cultural relativist" and the "cultural universalist" are faced with the same dilemma.

"Cultural relativism" does not, then, resolve the problem of making comparative judgments of value between cultures. It promotes the inclination to ignore it. Only a few years ago the phrase "cultural relativism" was popular in the literature. It was a topic much discussed. One hears much less of it now. Not because the issue to which the phrase pointed was satisfactorily resolved. More than likely because it ceased to stimulate interest. The arguments marshalled around the problem began to sound the same each time they were presented. Not an uncommon event in any field of enquiry.

Such a state is an unhappy one in which to leave matters. The practical aspects of the issue reflect a situation wherein such comparative judgments are always being made. The world grows smaller and the interaction as peers between people of different cultural orders of values increases. (It often disconcerts me how embarrassing it can be to express the uncontroversial). Comparative judgments are inevitable. It is in the emergence of different cultural orders out of such interaction — out of conflict, compromise, agreement, much like the tussle between the young American girl and her Persian mother-in-law — that a resolution to the problem of "cultural relativism" may be found. The problem resolves itself, then, in the formation of new social orders. But this is to say that it is to be found ultimately in the adaptive process which produces new modes of conceptual permanence in the effort to mitigate existential flux. Of course, the adaptive process destroys even as it maintains and produces anew. Sadly, perhaps, one cannot make a tragedy out of the necessary.

The second issue concerns itself with another type of query. The scientific enterprise is presumably a detached, impersonal one. Objectivity is its keynote. However, social scientists labor under the yoke of being participants in the making of what is eventually their own subject matter. Under such circumstances, the question of detachment would seem to be quixotic. The tilt light is always on, exposing "not objective"!

Conforming to the mode of expression already used, the issue may be stated in the following manner. The social order of enquiry is part of the more inclusive social order which is the subject of enquiry. Its practitioners are thus faced with the problem of detaching themselves from the cultural conditions which identify them as participants in order to attain the cultural conditions which can best identify them as investigators.

Again, the issue has a methodological and a moral aspect. The possibility of attaining detachment from the values of the society in which we participate is a methodological issue. The difficulty inherent in this situation has been suggested. The shadow cast by the cultural order of which we are inevitably a part may not mean a total eclipse of disinterested enquiry into the nature of it and its social counterpart, but a penumbra between it and its probing satellite there seems to be. In this sense, a value-free social science is a fiction, regardless of what procedures are developed to promote "objectivity."

The moral issue I have in mind is related to this striving for objectivity. It is frequently argued, increasingly so, that the contemporary social scientist has relinquished his responsibility to make judgments about the society in which he lives. He has so thoroughly subscribed to his job of description and analysis that he abjures moral comment. He neither condemns nor condones. Thus, he resists choice. He becomes, in a sense, value-free as a participant in his culture, if hardly as an investigator of it. In this respect, it has also been argued that many social scientists, unwittingly or not, support the status quo, the existing order of society, whatever it may be. The failure to make judgments is a tacit acceptance of what prevails. A far cry, especially among sociologists, from an earlier reforming zeal and liberal political tradition.

The criticism is levelled, often enough, against social scientists by social scientists. Whether or not the indictment is a fair rendering of the dominant state of affairs, it still points to a prevailing state of mind in the ranks. There is some irony in the situation. To keep things critically discriminate is the aim of all disciplined work, whether infused ultimately with the spirit of reform or not. What makes the social scientist such a good prospect for the role of reformer is the fact that he knows his subject — human behavior. But he knows his subject because he has concentrated his attention upon discriminate understanding of it. If methodological detachment and moral detachment do indeed have a positive relation to each other — the former increases as the latter does — then the problem is unresolvable.

There is a way out, I believe. Define "objectivity" as a function of attachment, not detachment. It is not a state of mind but a state of community which produces it. The interaction of scientists, in their various guises, out of which the several social orders of enquiry emerge, maintains and perpetuates the cultural order of values associated with them, including that of "objectivity," and in turn is maintained and perpetuated by that cultural order. "Objectivity" as a state of mind is developed and sustained to the extent that "objectivity" as a state of community — the judgments of one's peers according to the standard of shared understanding in language, methods, techniques, problems, aims, and knowledge — prevails. This view does not mean that objectivity will be seen as more in evidence within the social sciences than it has been once it is accepted, or that it will come to them any faster. It means only that by defining "objectivity" in this fashion, the commitment to its attainment in the world of reflective enquiry cannot be used as a justification for moral detachment in the world of performance.

The justification for knowledge revealed through the rational-empirical study of experience is ultimately grounded in the credibility such knowledge can maintain in society as it is made to serve as a basis for decision-making.

Decisions made are choices made. What is at issue, then, in the third problem is the basis for evaluative behavior as a purposeful and organized reformulation of the elements which constitute a cultural order in the light of experience. The revelations of science as the foundation of values — that is our concern. The issue may also be stated from another perspective: the problem is to what extent and in what way the adaptive process can be made subject to that part of our understanding which is a product of rational-empirical enquiry.

The question is not asked so much anymore. Science, even as it has become identified with the study of human behavior, has won its battle. Not so much by conviction as by pervasiveness. Of course, conviction as it is an experience attributed to a society may be but the offspring of pervasiveness. A mark of its ideology.

Therefore, I want to do nothing more than suggest the basis of my own conviction on this matter. It may serve as a fitting conclusion to an essay on "values."

I have said that there is never a perfect fit between experience and our organization of that experience into an order of under-

standing. In the realm of enquiry that hiatus is filled by inference and the procedures of investigation and argument that make specific inferences reasonable. In the process of decision-making — the process that transmutes the knowledge of experience gleaned from the world of enquiry into related social policies in behalf of the more inclusive society — there is also a hiatus. It derives from one source, but has two aspects.

Policy must be made within the fullness of experience. Even if one cannot juggle all the variables of experience which would be appropriate to consider in the making of any particular decision, he must face the consequences of not having done so. The scientific enterprise, in contrast, rests significantly on the practice of drawing limited sets of variables from experience and isolating them to examine their relationship to one another. Any particular "examination" leaves out much of the reality of experience. Science is no more a mirror to nature than art is a mirror to nature. It provides conceptions of nature.

In the process of decision-making, conceptions limited in scope must be applied to situations potentially unlimited in scope. Moreover, the rational decision based upon the revelations of scientific enquiry, which, in a manner of speaking, is always "ideal" knowledge, must face the potential restrictions of implementation. The implementation of any decision involves the allocation of resources — those of mind as well as matter — to it. The limitation of resources means the limitation of the "ideal" decision based upon "ideal" knowledge. It is in these situations that we find the gap between the knowledge drawn from rational-empirical enquiry and the values produced through purposeful adaptation. It must be filled by a conception of science and experience far beyond the scope of this essay.

However, I can state one conviction which the ideas touched upon here have impressed

upon me. There are sciences of human behavior as well as sciences of nature's behavior. But there is no science of living.
There is an art of living. Science is intended, like any worthy craft, to help us
understand that art well enough to attain the
most inspiring results.

The conviction does not, by itself, solve
any problems. But it is the beginning.

Suggested Readings

As will be obvious by now the topic of
values is shared throughout the social and
behavioral sciences and concern with this
subject extends beyond the limits of science
proper. For the thoughts of two anthropologists on values, see Clyde Kluckhohn's
"Values and value orientations in the theory
of action" (1951) and Melville J. Herskovits' "Tender- and tough-minded anthropology and the study of values in culture"
(1951). Other useful supplementary readings are T. Parsons and E. A. Shils (1951),
Gunnar Myrdal (1953), M. Stein and
A. Vidich, eds. (1963), Stephen Toulmin
(1960), Abraham Edel (1963), and C. H.
Waddington (1960).

CHAPTER **II** offers an overview of anthropological efforts to understand the nature of culture and social systems when set into the dimension of
time, or — to phrase this differently — to think clearly about the processes of cultural stability and culture change. Unlike other social scientists, few anthropologists have ever been entirely satisfied with viewing cultural and social systems in terms of static, immobile models. The very large issue of the causes and
nature of cultural change has been raised repeatedly. This continuing interest in
cultural change may result from the fact that the discipline grew up partly in response to the recognition of the reality of wide variations in local cultural adaptations and of vast modifications in the nature of human existence since early
Pleistocene times. In general, anthropologists have felt it insufficient simply to
document the facts of cultural diversity across time and in space: temporal and
regional cultural differences must be accounted for and explained. More specific
questions such as the origins of cultural practice and belief, the diffusion — or
intercultural transmission — of material inventory and ritual act, the social and
psychological consequences of culture contact or acculturation, and the old concern
with cultural evolution are raised recurrently, but they are not simply anthropological chestnuts. Interest in these issues does not dissipate since they are very
important, and because they are as yet not satisfactorily resolved. Further, as
Professor Lurie suggests in her discussion of the Omaha case, sound scientific
knowledge of the nature of cultural change is a very necessary prelude to the use
of anthropology as a means of rationally guiding change, so that practical value
may be added to our purely scientific need to know and understand. From the
mass of research in this field, whether "developmental" or "operational" in approach and orientation, the writer has abstracted a set of principles of change, key
statements or firmly grounded hypotheses about the nature, causes, and consequences of change in cultural systems.

THE AUTHOR was born in Milwaukee, Wisconsin, and today is Professor of Anthropology at the University of Wisconsin in that city. She obtained her professional
training in anthropology at Northwestern University and studied earlier at the
Universities of Chicago and Wisconsin. She has also taught at the Universities of
Michigan and Colorado. Her interest in and extensive knowledge of the ethnohistory of and cultural change among North American Indian peoples has been
put to work repeatedly in her role as expert witness before the United States Indian
Claims Commission and as consultant for several Indian tribes. Her special interest
is the Winnebago, who have witnessed much cultural change, and her scholarly
publications include *Mountain Wolf Woman, The Autobiography of a Winnebago
Indian,* and numerous articles and other publications.

II

Culture Change

NANCY O. LURIE

University of Wisconsin at Milwaukee

INTRODUCTION

Studies of culture in its time-dimension aspects are as old as cultural anthropology itself. Yet, paradoxically, this field of theory and method is currently weak and not well-integrated (1953:1).

This was Felix Keesing's opinion in regard to his extensive bibliographic review and analysis of culture change studies up to 1952. Although a bewildering variety and amount of research has been devoted to the subject in the decade and more since Keesing's publication appeared, we have yet to see a coordinated, generally satisfactory theoretical assessment. Methods of study have certainly improved, but have tended to bring to our attention ever more variables, complexities, and large and small scale theorizing and provocative speculation which must be accounted for in any general conceptualizations. Part of the difficulty has rested on the simple question of what different scholars mean by culture. Culture in the sense of language, social organization, material objects, and other broad universal categories may be viewed as an adaptive evolutionary attribute of the whole human species, comparable to bipedal locomotion and freeing of the upper limbs for transport and manipulation whatever the environment. Or, cultures may be viewed as contributing to survival in the sense of local adaptations in types of bipedal gait, such as the mariner's roll or the steel worker's toe-to-heel track, and the things that are transported or manipulated for given purposes to survive in a given environment. In somewhat simplified terms, the first view has underlain what for convenience here will be called developmental theories, while the second has underlain what will be called operational theories. It remains to adduce convincing and rigorous scientific testing of both approaches and to explore fully the possibility of reconciling them in a single, unified body of theory.

DEVELOPMENTAL AND OPERATIONAL APPROACHES

For some scholars, the major objective has been to discern whether there are logical, consistent, and predictable features in the nature of culture change taken as a whole, apart from the actual societies which may manifest them. The question is whether it can be said with confidence that for B to occur, it must have been preceded at some time and in some place by A, and that C relates equally consistently, congruously, and necessarily to a forerunner in B. Whether all cultures at different periods are made up of integrated clustering of all A or B or C features is unimportant, the assumption is that either a single grand path or a limited number of different but parallel paths lay out the direction cultural change has followed and must inexorably continue to follow, whatever the dallyings and detours along the way in specific cases. That given cultures may even go from B features back to A features is equally unimportant, since A still had to exist for B to have ever occurred.

For others, the major objective has been to find regular processes to explain why and how change occurs at all. In some cases, concern with process accepts the possibility or even probability of a grand A-B-C or a limited number of such logical unfoldings. In other instances, the possible or probable existence of the major chronological sequence transcending local occurrences is either denied or left unconsidered. In any event, the underlying assumption is that certain definable and recurrent conditions and dynamic procedures are implicit in the nature of culture, or of man, who is the vehicle of culture, as some prefer to visualize it, to account for change, whatever its direction or content in any given case.

Disagreements, differences of opinion in interpreting data, and refinements of original formulations have naturally marked the course of scholarly exchanges on the topic of culture change. Where arguments have occurred within the two major schemes, developmental and operational, they seem to have been productive of more concrete evidence of careful theory building. Differences between proponents of the two approaches have often devolved upon the philosophical or intellectual propriety of pursuing one objective or the other, or even the failure to recognize fully the different assumptions and objectives involved. Data have been used to assail the other point of view, but have often only supported the assailant's arguments without touching the opponent because two different objectives were under discussion.

However, it appears that the two approaches are not mutually exclusive or that one must succeed while the other fails. Both raise valid theoretical questions about the nature of culture and both require carefully designed testing from existing data and further fact-gathering directed toward obtaining ethnographic information relevant to the questions. One or both views may test out positively, but certainly no major formulations are possible until these questions are settled satisfactorily, without rancor based on partisan preferences or out-of-hand rejection of ethnographic and ethnological information, whose significance is not yet fully explored, by labeling it "nonanthropological," "abstractions," "speculative," "humanist," "psychological," "irrelevant," "mere neologism," or "eclectic."

At present, both approaches seem to have merit, and eventually they may be coordinated as integral parts of our overall understanding of the nature of culture change. This optimistic view is based on more than the hope of a harmonious synthesis to unify divided anthropological opinion. Through time a body of knowledge has passed from the condition of working, or mere implicit, assumptions to the status of tested and validated principles. The process of arriving at these principles has been so gradual and the principles themselves so obvious that it is sometimes surprising to realize that they had to be formulated and that they are with us still because of their demonstrated utility and reliability. Furthermore, while we can separate the growth of theory within the developmental and operational frameworks, each has been productive of insights and generalizations of use to the other. A few writers have begun to make explicit efforts to reconcile the approaches.

Developmental Approaches

The first theoretical constructs in ethnology took culture change for granted. This is reflected in the very terms with which we commonly characterize these nineteenth-century approaches, cultural evolution and the diffusionist school. Both sought the origins of cultural phenomena and assumed the existence of stages or logical progressions of culture. Contemporary people with varying cultures were looked upon as exhibiting phases through which Culture as a whole passes. The scientist's task was defined as the reconstruction of the logical sequence of stages. Several important principles began to take form at this early period in the discipline of anthropology:

1. *Change and persistence are both implicit in the nature of culture. Although major sequences of growth were perceived, their reconstruction depended upon the existence of what were deemed "survivals" of older elements in otherwise more evolved settings and the existence of whole groups exhibiting total life-ways exemplifying early evolutionary stages.*

2. *Culture change is crescive, building upon itself. Whatever shortcomings existed in the bald evolutionary scheme of barbarism to savagery to civilization, and criteria of progress such as the bow, agriculture, and*

writing, they established a habit of anthropological thought to expect change to follow from preceding conditions. Whether change is thought of in highly localized terms of a given culture or in regard to overall sequences, it is a logical and continuing process depending upon a pre-existing cultural inventory.

3. *Culture is learned. This principle, growing in part out of the early evolutionary concept of the "psychic unity of mankind," has proven of inestimable value. It permits the social scientist to eliminate confidently any theories of cultural differences, and by implication, cultural-change, resting on assumptions of innate biological superiority or inferiority of intellect. It means that from an operational or developmental point of view, we must look only to universal human thought processes, such as the ability to solve problems, and the nature of culture itself to explain change. Paradoxically, the principle has also been a source of controversy in theory building. Developmental theories have often used it to mean that the individual, man, as the agent of culture, is irrelevant as a simple constant, with culture itself providing the significant variables to be dealt with. In at least some operational formulations, however, the study of individuals in culture cannot be dispensed with but is deemed highly relevant in terms of, for example, motivational psychology, conditioning, frustration-aggression levels, to attain as full an understanding as possible of the dynamics of culture change.*

4. *Change can be initiated from within a given culture or borrowed from another culture. This important and, to us, obvious principle is owed to scholarly differences of opinion in the formative years of the discipline. It laid the foundation for explicit and ultimately refined concern with process as well as sequence, and generalizations con-*

cerning conditions underlying acquisition or rejection of innovations.

For the cultural evolutionists, the advantage of one condition of life over another was sufficient reason to account for change. Food production must follow upon food gathering as a logical generalization and, given the opportunity, one will follow upon the other in actuality. Opportunities of environment vary, but generally it was simply accepted that, all else being equal, food gatherers would eventually get the idea of food production. Although clearly cognizant of the fact of diffusion in specific instances, the British and American evolutionists were most concerned with demonstrating how each stage carried the seeds of invention for the next, whatever the location and spread of a particular stage. Given time and the right conditions, culture evolves (e.g., Tylor 1958; Morgan 1963).

In Europe, especially among German scientists, the view became popular that, while one condition may logically underlie another, people as a rule are not all that inventive and good ideas are hard to come by. These German ethnologists accepted the possibility of independent invention but saw major ideas and concomitant traits spreading from one or a few limited wellsprings of cultural inspiration. Further, they set some rather rigorous tests of diffusion. If multiple cultural variables bearing no logical relationship to one another, such as curvilinear designs and patriliny, occurred as clusters in different places, the probability was high that they came from a common source, no matter how geographically remote they might be from each other. The diffusionists sought not only to designate the logical stages of culture, but also the course by which a more actual culture history in all its richness of curious detail might be reconstructed in terms of who got what, when, and from whom (e.g. Graebner 1931:421-445).

However, both evolutionists and diffusionists were profoundly aware that many of their ideas required better data than were then available for proper tests. Cultural information occurring in accounts by missionaries, colonial administrators, casual travelers, traders, and others engaged in activities unrelated to the science of anthropology were likely to be incomplete, biased, equivocal, or inaccurate.

In time, the search for reliable data and the development of rigorous observational methods were to become almost ends in themselves. However, as more accurate information became available, many shortcomings were revealed in the initially ambitious, overarching theoretical constructs. Franz Boas, whose influence in American anthropology began to be felt at the close of the nineteenth century, is usually held responsible for the opinion that the data should be gathered first, hypothesizing confined to clearly testable cases, and broad formulations developed only when far more extensive data were secured. However, many anthropologists were already in the field during the last quarter of the nineteenth century and were concerned with intensive investigation of local conditions. They had already begun to show that lack of environmental opportunities or diffused inspiration to change were inadequate explanations for disparities in cultural evolutionary stages from place to place. Cultural evolutionary theory was hardly threatened by the fact that, in an Arctic environment, agriculture would not develop or could not even be accepted if diffused there. However, the bolstering theory that conditions must be right for particular groups to exhibit particular phenomena had to be stretched to transparent thinness to cover all cases. At the very least, the nature of conditions would have to be redefined until eventually the point would be reached at which each case was so special that recurrent regularities were lost to sight. Instances were noted wherein former incipient gardeners, such as the Cheyenne, became full-time hunters in response to moving onto the plains. It could be argued from later theories such as those of Leslie White, to be discussed, that in short-range terms at least the Cheyenne's acquisition of the horse for hunting was a more efficient energy utilization than the kind of gardening they had practiced, and was thus also a "progressive" change. However, such refinements were stimulated by scholarly criticism of the early cultural evolutionary formulations which reflected the biases of the nineteenth century in terms of agrarian values.

In addition to reversals, there were reported instances of outright rejection of opportunities to change to the next predicted stage. In time, evolutionary theory was redefined to disregard the question of local exceptions, which were considered ephemeral and of no account in overall reconstruction of major sequences. But this clarification was not made until some tests, both unsuccessful and sometimes tragic in their consequences, had been made on the assumption that cultural evolutionary stages were reliably predictive in local cases. For example, during the 1880's, while Alice Fletcher was engaged in ethnographic research among the Omaha, she saw an opportunity to render humanitarian assistance reinforced by the most modern anthropological conclusions of her day. Confined to a reservation, fearful of losing even that bit of homeland, and unable to continue an existence based on the buffalo hunt, change was clearly indicated for the tribe. That the Omaha were seeking to change and harbored no illusions of a possible return to a golden age of plains culture is reflected in the fact that the keeper of the sacred buffalo bundle entrusted that object and information on accompanying ritual to Fletcher for preservation in a museum as a record of the Omaha past.

Fletcher set about hurrying the Omaha from a stage of tribally organized hunters and gatherers into a civilized stage of full-time agriculturalists dependent upon market economy. Since increased and elaborated concepts of private property were adduced as a hallmark of civilization, she saw the means of breaking "the tribal relations by giving each individual ownership of lands and homes, and extending over these lands and homes our laws of property and legal descent . . . and the way opened" for total accession of a civilized state for the Omaha (Fletcher 1855).

Fletcher's energetic efforts led to a special act for the allotment of the Omaha Reservation in 1882, which was followed in 1887 by the Dawes Act and the allotment of many other reservations. Fletcher herself served as a special allotting agent to the Omaha and other tribes so that she had control over both implementation and administrative phases of the plan. The succeeding course of events was similar on all allotted reservations. First, there was a period of unprecedented prosperity in the form of new goods and homes paid for with the proceeds of sales of tribal lands left over after individual allotments were made. Once the period of protection from alienation by sale or taxation ran out, twenty to twenty-five years on most reservations, material hardships, social chaos, and incredible administrative complications followed. Not only was the remaining tribally-held property gone but individual homesteads were sold to avoid the actual threat of starvation, in some cases, or to obtain manufactured goods upon which the Indians had become dependent. Those homesteads remaining in Indian hands were soon put in protective status again but became ever more divided by the combination of population increase and our laws of property and legal descent. Today, it is common for an individual on an allotted reservation to own forty or more acres, but as six acres inherited from one relative at one end of the reservation, half an acre from someone else at the other end, two acres in the middle, and so on. There is little administrative recourse but to rent land out in large parcels and divide the proceeds among the many heirs.

Ostensibly, with the granting of private property the conditions had been provided for both internal invention to follow predictable evolutionary lines or for diffusion of the next stage to have occurred by borrowing of agricultural practices from neighboring whites. The latter possibility was reinforced by the fact that farmer-teachers were provided on many reservations to assist Indians in learning techniques of productive use of their property. Neither invention nor diffusion occurred in expected forms. Existing conditions were thrown into chaos and the Omaha and other tribes continue to survive by piecemeal government relief, a conscious limiting of desires if meeting them means economic and social activities threatening to their identity as Indians, and adaptations to wage work, often using their farming skills in the employ of local whites (Mead 1932). Today they continue to look upon prosperous periods as windfalls of game or other natural resources are considered by the hunter, to be spent and enjoyed rather than husbanded to build capital for making greater profit. The spending and enjoyment come as often as not from acts of generosity within the tribal community aimed at winning esteem and the assurance that, in the inevitable lean times to come, a man's standing will be sufficiently secure that he can depend without shame upon those more fortunate at the moment.[1]

Reactions against unreconstructed evolutionism may be traced in part to such early attempts to direct cultural change "scientifically," as well as to the aid and comfort ideas of primitive versus civilized gave to apologists for colonial exploitation; that civilization would prevail anyway as a matter of scientific "law." Whether these reactions were "unscientific" because they were humanitarian is not so important as the fact that evolutionism was tested empirically and found wanting as a predictive tool (cf. Reining 1962). Scholars had become uneasy at many of the assumptions and a good deal of the methodology of evolutionism. Basically, there was the nagging question of ethnocentric bias. In cases in which actual data from contemporary observations of different peoples or historical sources were used, questions arose about the ponderously documented and unassailably "logical" schemes. Did the evolution of graphic and plastic art from realism to abstraction, religion from polytheism to monotheism, kinship from matriliny to patriliny, exist in the data, or in the mind of the investigator who could select cases from around the world and fit them into his pre-existing framework as illustrations rather than tests of his chronological sequences (Herskovitz 1950:388–392)? The highest forms were drawn from the culture peculiar to the investigator unless some inconsistent detail was designated a "survival" of the past for illustration. Similarly, there was concern for methodology in the practice of wresting phenomena out of their historical and cultural contexts and arranging them in sequences as if they had developed in that fashion rather than out of their own developmental unfoldings. The preceding stages, if known in each case and taken as a whole, might not line up as neatly as the original scheme (Lowie 1937:81–84).

That evolutionary ideas were most convincing in regard to technology and that technology remains the keystone in modern evolutionism is understandable on several counts.[2] First, there is the record of archeology showing chronological sequences from

---

[1] Discussions of Omaha and Winnebago not otherwise cited are based on the writer's field work.

[2] See Chapter Five for a fuller exposition of these points.

tools for hunting to tools for agriculture. Historical records bear out that succeeding technological improvements brought population increases, which in turn required concomitant complexities of social organization relating to environmental exploitation and the general ordering of human affairs. Second, technological improvement, in the elaboration of transportation and communication, carries within its very self the capacity for greater diffusion of many elements of the total culture it represents. Civilization, as characterized in technological development, prevails because it is prevailing. However, to call these traits higher in the evolutionary scale, with the absolutistic implication of superior, continues to raise doubts. Our thing-laden culture has potentials for destroying the human species as well as contributing to survival of greater numbers expending less individual energy to survive (cf. Commoner and Daly 1964:18–24; Snow and Wolfe 1964:26–33).

As our review unfolds, it will at least suggest that a certain ethnocentric bias blinded investigators for a long time to questions of degree and function of technological diffusion from place to place. Evolutionary theories are now refined, and many if not all criticisms of earlier formulations have been met or shown to be at times carping rather than constructive. Yet, in all seriousness, we cannot be entirely sure that in accepting the cumulative growth of culture as highly significant — some would say most significant — to anthropological theory we do not still labor unduly under the overpowering appeal of the value system of the anthropologist's culture. The idea of history as progress is implicit in Western tradition and antedates the discipline of anthropology, while in the formative era of anthropology as we know it today, the industrial revolution was beginning to have profound social consequences which are of continuing and increasing general concern.

Certainly from about the turn of the century Boas and his students contributed to the partial eclipse of cultural evolutionary theorizing. If they offered no new theoretical constructs, they contributed enough embarrassing tests of existing constructs to force later theoretical refinements. However, by implication even Boas saw eventual theory building along evolutionary lines. Boas was not so much opposed to theory as to speculating on matters such as the origin of religion for which there were no data, or using speculation when data might be obtained if scholars would just get out of their armchairs and into the field before vital information was irrevocably destroyed by — it must be noted — encroaching "civilization." Thoroughness, self-conscious objectivity, and accuracy of field observations and interviews became the rule. If customs were no longer practiced, the next best thing was to pan the memories of the oldest informants for nuggets carried down from antiquity. The great-grandfather was asked what he learned from his great-grandfather. Terminology and categories became established, sometimes by design, sometimes by the consensus of literary usage, and monographs became standardized in terms of sections on religion, social organization, and technology and economics. Games, warfare, music, education of children (when mentioned at all), the dance, and other obviously cross-category phenomena were either given separate treatment or fitted for convenience under one of the major chapter headings to which they seemed to have the greatest relevance.

A sort of historical cut-off point was usually implied, if not mentioned explicitly. Historical reconstructions were restricted to the period or condition that the scholar discerned a cultural destruction setting in, beyond selective borrowing, and replacement by his culture. It was noted that some things "survived" or "lagged" from the past, but these disparities were prized not as sources of understanding of the nature of change, but for their own sake in helping to reconstruct the past in terms of cultures or even Culture, since interest in broad evolutionary theorizing was never entirely abandoned by all scholars. However, the question of retentions as relating to process, along with the question of what a proper cut-off point is in one's observations, eventually took on tremendous importance.

Concern for process and conditions of change which would in time become basic to operational theorizing were already becoming evident in work done both prior to and during Boas' time. The still plaguing term "acculturation" which everyone uses and yet is hard put to define was employed as early as 1880 by Major J. W. Powell, the first director of the Bureau of American Ethnology. He used it initially in the sense of profound destruction of an existing culture and replacement by another, in discussing the problems attendant on gathering data on American Indians: "The force of acculturation under the overwhelming presence of millions has wrought great changes." He and others were shortly using the term as a synonym for diffusion, cultural borrowing in general, or as an antonym to invention, the producing of innovations within a group (Herskovits 1938:3).

Although commitment to the objective of gathering data while they were still extant in memory or practice led to a consideration of the effects of the scholar's culture as an annoyance and hindrance to scientific inquiry, a few people began to recognize at least the more dramatic effects of such contact as productive of scientific insights. For example, between 1908 and 1913 while Paul Radin was studying the Winnebago in Nebraska, he chose to ignore the devastating effects of allotment which were then just beginning to set in and simply let photographs of individuals, groups, and landscapes illustrate fortuitously the amount of

borrowing and local adaptation of white material culture.

However, Radin was among the first to take purposeful account of the dynamics involved in the adoption of the peyote religion then newly introduced among the Winnebago. He was fascinated with myth-making and traced the conscious attempts of peyotists to bridge old Winnebago concepts and Christianity in equating the benevolent culture hero Hare with Jesus Christ, peyote hallucinations with the vision quest, and the creation of an ethical framework out of two heritages to bring some order and meaning into a world which had become confusing and distressing to the Winnebago. He further observed that peyote was not equally attractive to all Winnebago but appealed primarily to those with some education in Christianity and estrangement from their own culture due to absence from the group in boarding schools during their formative years. They fitted comfortably in neither the white world of which they knew only the boarding school intimately nor the society of conservative Winnebago "intellectuals" whose exclusive commitment and sense of worth and identity were in the native religion (Radin 1915–1916:388–426).

Even earlier, James Mooney had seen the Ghost Dance of the Plains tribes, embodying new supernatural and white material elements, as a distinctive last-ditch response to the threat of conquest. Studies such as those by Mooney and Radin were to form the foundation for many later works having a largely operational orientation in which certain regularities from chaos to reorganization came to be discerned in what are now termed revitalization movements (Wallace 1956).

Other students of Boas expanded upon their teacher's interest in diffusion, such as Boas' charting of myth motifs throughout the Pacific Northwest, which noted distribution of similar traits within a given geographical area (1896:1–11). Clark Wissler (1926) developed the age area-culture area hypothesis in an effort to create meaningful museum displays from myriad disparate material objects. This was no simple geographic determinism. Wissler observed that conventionalized design motifs and other items unconnected with environmental necessity lent themselves to spatial groupings along with associated tools and utensils adapted to exploiting a given environment. This in turn led to an analysis of diffusion from centers, like waves radiating out from a pebble dropped in a pond. It was suggested that traits with the widest distribution would be the oldest and the peripheries of distribution would coincide with natural boundaries. Environment was seen as a limiting rather than a determining force. Wissler was most concerned with the source of traits and felt the center would be where one found the most traits of wide-to-narrow distribution occurring throughout the entire area. A. L. Kroeber built upon Wissler's schemes, profiting from critical refinements of the original formulation evoked from the anthropological profession. Kroeber concentrated on the peripheries of areas and the limiting and moderating effects of subareas of vegetation, climate, and the like within major areas (1939). This concern for diffusion and chronology harkens back to older evolutionary-diffusionist approaches, albeit much refined and limited to cases for which adequate data were considered to exist for proper testing. Kroeber also applied himself to the concept of diffusion in operational terms in his concept of stimulus-diffusion, distinguishing the diffusion of actual elements from culture to culture from diffusion of an idea which stimulated local innovation quite different from the original form. The Cherokee syllabary, for example, was developed by Sequoyah, an illiterate Indian who grasped the principle of writing in symbol-sound from watching English speakers read and write. He went on to develop symbols, not for individual sounds, but for a finite number of sound clusters or syllables characteristic of Cherokee (1948:368–370).

Despite such operational interests which became even more evident in Kroeber's later years, he expressed the view that theory should concern itself with culture as a "superorganic" obeying internal laws of its own without regard to causality in terms of human agencies or instrumentalities (1917). He was later to modify this concept, but this famous pronouncement and his concern for criteria of "progress" in culture as a whole are indicative of the fact that, Boas' teaching notwithstanding, the view continued to prevail that the proper approach to the study of culture change should be the discerning of A-B-C sequences as abstractions in the sense of distillates from specific data in specific settings. Kroeber's three criteria of progress are interesting on two counts. While accepting the primary importance of technological complexity, he relegates it to third place in his enumeration. If this is an implied disclaimer of ethnocentric bias, Kroeber nevertheless reveals an astounding blindness to the commonplaces of his own culture. His first criterion is magic and "superstition." As a culture is less reliant on these, it is more progressive. Wolf, as we shall see, relegates this feature to the category of "recurrent" component, unrelated to cumulative evolution and as likely to occur in highly technological as in other cultures. The second criterion is "the obtrusion of physiological and anatomical considerations into social situations, or with the related matter of taking human life." Kroeber had in mind both the magical and nasty — "unpleasant and useless" — features of segregation of women at parturition and menstruation, preoccupation with the dead body in mummification and skull ornamentation, and public interest in physiological functions (1948:296–304). Even the most casual television viewing or scanning of advertisements in popular magazines reveals that our own society, which Kroeber considered highly progressive, is able to make many more "unpleasant" features highly public because of its technology. Not only are murders reenacted nightly on television screens but the actual shooting of Lee Oswald was captured by the camera and shown over and over so everyone could see it. Dripping noses, constipation, diarrhea, tooth decay, bad breath, and perspiration are big unabashed business and there is no question as to our preoccupation with the dead body (Mitford 1963).

During the last twenty years, however, the most active and influential modern proponent of evolutionary theory has been Leslie White of the University of Michigan. In 1953 Felix Keesing could write with fair justification that, while White's views since 1943 had become "considerably publicized by vigorous presentation, no professional following has fallen in behind him" (40). Such is certainly no longer the case and the student is now faced with both a Whitean evolutionary approach and the multilinear approach of Julian Steward, as well as various interpretations and modifications on these themes. White, like Kroeber in his concept of the superorganic, sees the individual as irrelevant to questions of culture change. Although claiming to be no more than a latter-day disciple of Lewis Henry Morgan, White has dealt in most original terms with the old problem of criteria of progress so as to delineate the major stages of cultural change. The old clustering of traits in stages designated savagery, barbarism, and civilization which remained basic in the formulation of another modern evolutionist, V. Gordon Childe, is replaced in White's formulation by the concept of the quantitatively increased harnessing of energy, either as per capita per year, or as technological methods and their efficiency in putting energy to work (1949:362–396). White also insists that both culture and the evolution of culture are "real," not "abstractions," a word he professes not to understand as it is used by other scholars in describing evolutionary generalizations. He has also introduced certain neologisms into the anthropological literature, "symbolates," the cultural realities to which his theories refer, which come about through the process of "symboling" (1959a).

In the search for universal laws of culture change and growth, Julian Steward has endeavored to combine both evolutionary and operational approaches in a purposeful fashion with the concept of multilinear evolution. He contrasts this with White's theories, which he designates as unilinear or universal evolutionism. Steward notes that in the operational camp there is a highly particularistic or so-called relativistic insistence that each culture has undergone its own evolution and must be evaluated in its own terms, reserving generalizations for recurrent processes of change, generalizations which would not involve any attempt to equate one culture or type against another in a cumulative rating scale. On the other hand, there are generalizations such as White's which are supposed to state universal laws of cumulative change, exclusive of local variations and even exceptions. Steward suggests that the first approach suffers from a kind of can't-see-the-forest-for-the-trees blindness, and says of the latter that "the postulated cultural sequences are so general that they are neither very arguable nor very useful" (1955:17, 24). Steward sees cultures as classifiable into a number of evolutionary types which depend upon different ecological conditions and run parallel but different courses, sometimes diverging and sometimes converging with each other in the forms they take. He notes them as recurrent but not necessarily universal phenomena leading to certain sequences of complexity. He introduces the concept of levels of integration within cultures, the family, the community, and the nation, as a means of establishing parallel sequences of development. The greatest integrative influence in a total culture, and consequent complexity, occurs in turn at these different levels, with some societies manifesting only the first level, others, the first two, yet others, all three. However, the evolutionary stages may take varying forms and relate logically only to each other within their own developmental channels.

Steward makes a convincing case for the use of operational constructs in evolutionary theory. He relates any cumulative innovation to its own foregoing cultural inventory and cuts the number of special cases into types understandable in terms of recurrent ecological adaptive considerations. However, he denies the probability of ever achieving a universalistic scheme that would be both inarguable and useful as a predictive tool. That one channel might combine with another and work out a common destiny is accepted, but whether this is the inevitable course of cumulative evolution remains an open question.

The criticisms leveled at classical and even Whitean evolutionary theory as having no utility in understanding specific cases have been dealt with in recent years by a number of White's followers who acknowledge the influence and utility of Steward's formulations, although at times protesting a rather belligerent loyalty to White as the one voice of reason through the period of Boasian and relativistic chaos. A growing distinction is now made more explicit between specific and general evolution. Following this distinction, the evolution of local cultures is nothing more than culture history, illustrating the myriad modifying effects of environment, diffusion, persistent local style, particular conditions of culture contact, and the like. On the other hand, general evolution en-

compasses and transcends the local instances. Importance is attached to precise ethnographies at the local level. As for adaptation for survival, it is not only warranted but probably necessary to understand specific cultures from a relativistic-functionalist point of view in assessing how they accomplish this end. But the methods and formulations for gathering data and analyzing cultures at the local level are different from those applied to the analysis of general evolution in terms of energy utilization and technological efficiency (Sahlins and Service 1960). This would appear to argue as though the laws of mathematics applied up to the number 1,000,000, at which point other laws take effect, but such criticism is perhaps unfair when the distinction is admittedly in a formative stage. However, that a sense of rating by absolutistic criteria is implicit even in comparisons on the level of local cultures is seen in the "law of cultural dominance," in which specific and general evolutionary forces, in the sense of environmental adaptations, may be in conflict. Thus, "a higher, more progressive type in the general evolutionary sense of efficiency of energy utilization has adaptability which *extends* the ecological horizon" at the expense of less well adapted systems. It is defined as higher because it has extended its horizon. Lower cultures on the other hand, are so defined because they occur in marginal environments, and the areas are so defined because low level cultures occur in them (Sahlins and Service 1950:69–92).

Accepting this evolutionary framework, it could be suggested that relativistic criteria may be as useful to general evolution as absolutistic criteria are implied to be even in specific evolution. For example, the tribally organized and by evolutionary criteria lower level Gypsies are denizens of the cities and populated rural countryside. Their main economic activity was once itinerant horse trading, but is now itinerant dealing in used cars, which probably involves some increase in efficiency of energy utilization but does not seem to have changed them significantly in other features of their culture except to permit their maintenance in a changed socio-ecological environment. To dismiss such examples as quaint but inevitably doomed holdouts begs the implications of the frequency and astonishing persistence of such exceptions and the practical questions of processes of persistence and change with which operational approaches deal in detail.

Similarly, an interesting case is presented by American Indian communities, notoriously conservative and driven into marginal regions either on reservations or by their own choice as civilization spread into the more ecologically desirable regions. The very technological efficiency of the American culture as a whole has created far more leisure time for the average American. The once undesirable hinterlands, simply because they are "unproductive" hinterlands are now the locus of the industry which has risen to great importance in many states, touristry.[3] In Michigan, for example, only the automobile industry takes precedence. Indian people on reservations which escaped the chaos of allotment who still control large tribally-held areas are looking to the successful models already developed among the Eastern Cherokee, Umatilla, and White Mountain Apache in providing tourist facilities. Explicitly excluding some of the efficiency or convenience of urban life, they maintain as much as possible of the wilderness aspect of the environment and the asset of their own ethnicity.

[3] Except for Nunez (1963), anthropologists have generally disregarded the growing tourist industry as an area of research. However, it is beginning to attract serious study, as is illustrated by the fact that a special symposium, organized and chaired by James M. Silverberg, was held at the 1964 annual meetings of the Central States Anthropological Society, Milwaukee, Wisconsin, May 15: "Tourism: A Neglected Area of Culture Change Research and Applied Anthropology."

Now, it is noted by evolutionists that the path of cumulative evolution is neither straight nor smooth, but is marked by zig-zags and potholes, with different specific societies picking up the burden of culture and carrying it along another lap until it exhausts its evolutionary potential for further progress. The case of the American Indian groups cited may perhaps fit into the "law of evolutionary potential." This law is set forth to answer the question of critics as to what evolutionary theory can *do* as a scientific tool. It is stated as, "The more specialized and adapted a form is in a given evolutionary stage, the smaller is its potential for passing to the next stage," or "specific evolutionary progress is inversely related to general evolutionary potential" (Sahlins and Service 1960:97). Thus,

For the advanced societies, in displacing backward peoples or harnessing them to their own progress, become agents of a disruption that frees the backward region from the dead hand of its own past. . . . While advanced and dominant cultures create the circumstances for their own eclipse . . . they themselves become specialized. Their development on a particular line commits them to it: they are mortgaged to structures accumulated along the way . . . (143).

Two questions remain if the law is to fill its role as a predictive tool. While this could happen, will it? And, how and when are we to judge if a culture is either too backward or too specialized to have much internal potential? The work of Homer Barnett, who provides the most intensive analysis of innovation available today, while suffering from its own defects of vagueness as an operational formulation for predictive purposes, nevertheless makes clear throughout that the process set forth as "law" does not always take effect (1953). Other variables, and presumably variables that can be tied down to a few wieldy yet reliable types, must be at least included as clarifiers if not qualifiers of the "law." Perhaps the basic defect in the law of evolutionary potential as it is stated is the implication that progressive spurts form at the level of specific evolution and require a violent destruction of specific systems, the forcible raising of the "dead hand" of the past. This assumption is a legacy of conflict ideologies underlying certain nineteenth-century theories and philosophies of social change, theories which have undergone considerable critical modification (cf. Martindale 1962:4–30). The point is that a thoroughly deculturated group sometimes has only the alternative of replacing its culture with that of the dominant or progressive group, thus losing distinctive cultural identity. Innovative potential is lost by assimilation. It is noteworthy that the American Indian tribes now cashing in on touristry did not suffer the destructive disorganization of allotment, and consciously resisted forcible change and assimilation. They sat out proffered opportunities to improve and progress until they discovered means of obtaining on their own terms what they deemed desirable from the dominant group, and only then began to make massive and rapid changes.

As shall be shown, operational analyses of cultural change have revealed, if nothing else, that the one thing we can be sure of is that change is made on the specific level by analogy to the features of the existing system. If violence must be done to a system to free it for innovative progress, there appear to be quantitative and qualitative limits to the amount of violence a system can sustain and still keep its potential.

It is certainly an acceptable concept that because things occur together, such as people and culture, they are not necessarily relevant to each other, but it is important to distinguish irrelevance from methodological inconvenience. It is more than unscientific humanitarianism to be concerned about how people feel if better theory can spare them anguish, at least in directed change. The burgeoning field of applied anthropology becomes an important means of actually testing our theoretical constructs and, if we do not care to be humane, we should at least hope to be right. There is need to review the concept of human irrelevance, even in general evolutionary theory, and to keep an open mind to the chance to use insights developed in anthropological studies of personality. We cannot dispense with the possibility that need for social identity, whatever its local content, is a biological evolutionary attribute of the human species. There may be outside numerical limits of groups including subgroups within larger societies for effective social interaction to make a culture work — including the process of adaptive changes. Or, the long physical maturation of the human individual and types of enculturation of the individual may produce predictable rates of change in "unlearning," "innovating," "reformulating," and "relearning."

These and other questions must be considered if developmental theory in a prospectively dynamic rather than a retrospective sense is to rest on a more solid foundation than the nineteenth-century assumption of an inventive drive now restated as "evolutionary potential."

There have been many reactions against the terminology of both evolutionary and operational approaches in that, if not intended to be pejorative terms, they come through that way to the people who are called "backward," "underdeveloped," "lower," and "primitive." A major criticism is set forth by Francis Hsu (1964), who, among other scholars, feels that terms come to dictate habits of thought, and that by categorizing neat boxes or stages as higher and lower, civilized and primitive, we may be forcing data into compartments that obscure regularities of culture that admit of no such sharp delineations. Violent change is exceptional at the level of specific cultural evolution; as presently set forth in evolutionary writings, it appears to be a necessity in general evolutionary stages. If cultures usually change by slow, crescive processes, can Culture change only by upheavals? Perhaps, but the case is not proven. Even Childe's term, "the Neolithic Revolution," relating to the invention of food production, and Hockett and Ascher's term, "the Human Revolution," relating to the development of language, are used in a qualified sense. The revolutions came on gradually but carry potential and stimulus for a greater number and variety of changes than many other gradual innovations. Perhaps the reactions of both anthropologists opposed to such terms as primitive and those of the people so designated rest not just on resentment of an implied insult and factual distortion. They also tend to imply mayhem and impending doom not only for given ways of life but for the very people who carry them. The incorrigible relativist may take some comfort in the current state of general theory by contemplating a New Guinea village of the future, which, having gone through the violent throes of a revitalization movement, has reached the stage of stable reorganization, and is making plans to send a Peace Corps to the overdeveloped areas of the world.

However, that a reasoned and nonpolemical synthesis of developmental and operational theories is not only possible but likely in the foreseeable future is illustrated in a brief but perceptive and provocative article by Eric Wolf. Wolf reviews the many criteria used or possibly useful to establish evolutionary stages and progress, criteria such as energy utilization, control over environment, population increase, the ratio of prestige positions available to the number of people capable of filling them, and so on. He points out both their potential value and need for further testing. A major question is whether all these various measures occur simultaneously and to the same degree at a given stage. Wolf further distinguishes two major orders of cultural phenomena, recurrent and cumulative. Recurrent phenomena, a particular concern of operational orientations, are merely adverted to in comparison to the more extensive consideration of cumulative phenomena which make up the stages of evolutionary growth. He finally suggests that the old bugbear of parts of different stages occurring simultaneously in the same local culture can be resolved by first distinguishing whether certain components ought to be excluded from a consideration of stages as culturally necessary, or whether differences in cultural content merely express recurrent interchangeable phenomena. The analysis also suggests that the conceptual position of the individual might be rehabilitated and seen as relevant to cultural theory, insofar as recurrent variations in culture content seem to be most often the least specialized and related, for example, to the individual and family. Thus, in an industrial order,

. . . magic — or religion akin to magic — persists on this level, even where science has made the behavior of statistical aggregates of people quite predictable and comprehensible. We may know . . . how many children are killed in automobile accidents . . . but the individual can take little comfort from this knowledge. For he must still come to terms with his unique personal fate if . . . his child is run over by a car (Wolf 1964:117).

Even seemingly incompatible cultural components may occur together. Wolf does not specify whether two incompatible cumulative components may be involved, or whether he refers exclusively to logical incompatibilities between two or more recurrent phenomena or recurrent and cumulative components as illustrated in his examples. However, what is important and basic to his analysis is his designation of the "third component" which acts in a mediating fashion and "neutralizes the effects of their incompatibility," and contributes to functional integration (Wolf 1964:116). This seems to open the door to consideration of purposiveness in the study of culture change. A choice is posed between accepting cultural chaos and destruction or at least loss of one perhaps "lower" or "specific" component at the expense of another "higher" or "general" one, and adaptive reconciliation of otherwise dysfunctional components. In tending to modify the chaos or violence implicit in the present formulation of the law of evolutionary potential, the notion of the third component raises the questions of whether, how, and why chaos may really account for change in some instances but not in others.

Wolf's concept of the third component has been of singular use in understanding an apparent cultural paradox observed among the Wisconsin Winnebago over the last twenty years. As progress in the technological sense has increased and shown its greatest acceleration to date over the last three or four years, older components of clan organization, chieftainship, traditional practices of naming, social dances, gift exchange at the time of marriage, wakes, and the like have undergone an equally dramatic increase and acceleration in the activities of the group. The third component is the Business Committee formed in 1962, when the tribe voted to organize under the Indian Reorganization Act of 1934. It has begun to handle problems of an economic and educational nature in relating the group effectively to the dominant society. Traditional institutions were not designed to handle such problems. The problems themselves led to dispersal of the group and to piecemeal and even somewhat dysfunctional retentions of old components while individuals or local communities struggled to make even a bare living. Pooling the limited capital in the group for long-range planning as well as successful action of a more immediate nature

have demonstrated the utility of organized unity. People have reason and, further, are now economically enabled to meet together more often in local community and all-tribe gatherings. Old components designed to order internal affairs by defining roles and responsibilities for group action in meeting crises or carrying out projects have a renewed utility. The Business Committee was the finally successful form arising out of many smaller successful and unsuccessful experiments to better material conditions and to organize for action of various kinds. The Business Committee is now established as the accepted form to achieve generally agreed upon economic objectives, but will have to experiment continually with various means of accomplishing its purposes. This case is of particular value in the context of innovative potential because the Wisconsin Winnebago are descendants of a faction of the total tribe that once occupied southern Wisconsin and northwestern Illinois and remain in the state because they consciously resisted atempts to remove them. The other "treaty abiding" faction lives on a reservation in Nebraska where there has been considerably more direct pressure to give up old organizational features. The Nebraska enclave, long organized under the Act of 1934, has never approached the Wisconsin group in successful use of opportunities inherent in the provisions of their constitution. The difference seems to lie in the fact that there was less choice and experimentation involved in their formal organization, which was encouraged by the Bureau of Indian Affairs. The Wisconsin group actually had to argue strongly to be allowed to organize in 1961. The Business Committee in Nebraska was looked upon as a total replacement of older internal organizational components. It is no more designed to achieve this end effectively than the older institutions were able to handle problems imposed from outside. Taken as a whole, the Winnebago were upset and reorganized in the course of expansion of the fur trade and were changed from settled agriculturalists in a developing phase of chiefdom to seasonally nomadic fur trading bands with a simple tribal organization, to, on the one hand, a reorganized tribe increasingly availing itself of and contributing to the larger technological economy and, on the other hand, a still rather dispirited community lacking purpose and direction. Hence it would appear that the innovative potential of the Wisconsin group could be stimulated only because destruction of the existing culture was limited and they were freer to develop a third component in their own terms.

Self-proclaimed evolutionists are free to disagree with the final tentative conclusions concerning comparison of the Wisconsin and Nebraska enclaves of the tribe. However, generally we see in more recent evolutionary approaches an increasing utilization of operational or specific analyses, attempts to relate generalizations back to local cases, and greater concern for precise conditions accounting for resistance and reversals rather than excluding these embarrassing exceptions from developmental theories.

Operational Approaches

Basically, operational interests concentrate on predictable processes of why and how change occurs, compared to developmental emphasis on delineating stages and sequences of what changes. Although operational considerations were implicit in even the earliest studies, they began to be made explicit and became a source of interest for their own sake with the advent of functionalism in anthropological theory. By and large, they have found most frequent expression in acculturational studies, and, most recently, in applied anthropology.

Bronislaw Malinowski and A. R. Radcliffe-Brown are generally associated with the concept of functionalism. Malinowski related his ideas of the integration of culture to concepts of primary and derived human needs met by culture. Radcliffe-Brown's efforts, often called structuralism, were concentrated on discerning what he perceived as virtually mathematical patterning in the congruity of relationships integrating social systems (cf. Malinowski 1944; Radcliffe-Brown 1935, 1940). Both Malinowski and Radcliffe-Brown drew their inspiration from sociology, particularly the French school of Emil Durkheim, rather than from history or political geography which had influenced developmental approaches. Stressing synchronic studies, that is, observations at one point in time, the early functionalists struck out vigorously at developmental or diachronic approaches, whether traditionally evolutionary, diffusionist, or historical reconstructions in the Boasian sense. Where Boas and his students had chided the overly ambitious evolutionists who wrested data out of their temporal and spatial contexts to fit pre-existing frameworks, the functionalists raised further questions. Did not the standardized categories in which monographs were generally written also imply preconceived constructs? Was the account of a Plains Indian culture, for example, drawn from observed "survivals" and received recollections going back over four generations, really much more valid as a description of an actual culture serving a group at any time than the abstractions developed by evolutionists for Culture as a whole?

We need not go into the acrimony that marked debate between proponents of functionalist and traditionalist orientations in the 1920's and early 1930's, but merely note that it did occur and may account for some resistance to theoretical synthesis even today. But, for all that, functionalism soon took its place in the general anthropological toolkit. To continue our enumeration of principles, those derived from functionalist theory were brought to a more clarified expression rather than newly discovered by it. For example:

5. *Culture is more than the sum of its parts. Culture is integrated and the interrelationship of parts as well as the parts themselves explain how culture operates as an adaptive complex for human survival. In this context, function is used in a mathematical sense. As one angle of a triangle is changed, at least one other must change to retain the triangular structure. This does not mean that all cultures everywhere are similarly or even perfectly integrated, but change tends to work in the direction of maintaining integration. As we have seen, change is implicit in the nature of culture. If one part is changed in terms of additions, alterations, or deletions, reverberations are felt throughout the system. Such effects must in turn be dealt with to maintain effective integration so that culture, in the persisting phase of its nature, can carry out its adaptive responsibilities. Innovations, inequities of power or goods, or loss of a resource may all create dysfunctional situations, hence more changes are set in motion to bring about a more satisfactory state of affairs for the group concerned. Recognition of this fact underlies another principle.*

6. *Cultural components exist for a purpose. In this connection Malinowski's early formulations of basic and derived needs were met with scorn. Kroeber, for example, could see little distinction between some of Malinowski's rather fine-spun "psychological needs" to account for every detail of a given culture and the evolutionists' futile and speculative search for the ultimate origins of traits (Kroeber 1948:309). But the point did eventually emerge that a trait is not simply a trait. It forms part of a social and cultural network. No matter how bizarre or seemingly inconsequential, it persists for a reason. If lost, its functional tasks will be met in some other way.*

Early functionalist writings stressed intensive study of local cultures as they operate here and now. Concern for the dynamics of cultural integration led to a disparagement of the concept of "survivals" so dear to the hearts of developmental theorists. Whatever their original purposes or historical depth in a culture, all cultural components in evidence at any point in time can be treated as comparably contemporary because of their current integration to serve current needs. This approach is sometimes known as a relativistic view insofar as a culture is studied and described solely in terms of its own time, place, and values, rather than those of the observer's culture or some general, absolutistic criteria. Overall comparisons between cultures so described then seek to distinguish universal processes, such as those regarding change and persistence, rather than the establishment of stages of change based largely on content (Herskovits 1950:63–70).

However, as scholars began to take the injunctions of functionalism seriously, they found they seldom happened upon such stable, isolated, and well-integrated societies as Malinowski's Trobriand Islanders or Radcliffe-Brown's Andamanese or Australians were alleged to be. Even small, seemingly remote groups in the post-World War I period began to show evidence of the technological expansion of Euro-American and some Asiatic cultures. Furthermore, many still culturally distinctive groups had long been under colonial authority of one kind or another, a circumstance that had wrought changes but had brought about adaptations rather than the outright cultural destruction anticipated in the dire prophesies of Boas and others that soon there would be no more data to gather. More important, many changes were in the process of occurring, sometimes at a startling rate, and dysfunctions and functional reintegrations were available for the perceptive student to observe and analyze. Both Radcliffe-Brown and Malinowski were to become reconciled to the need for work on diachronic problems and both were involved in the revived interest in applied anthropology (Malinowski 1945, 1930; Radcliffe-Brown 1930).

As an outgrowth of the functionalist approach, studies of culture contact became increasingly prominent. Although the distinction between internal invention and borrowing eventually was modified insofar as certain common processes seemed to underlie acceptance of innovation whatever its source, the opportunity to study change was more frequently and clearly presented in culture-contact situations. Particularly after World War I, improved technology in a number of societies contributed to enormously increased communication and transport of goods throughout the world. However profound and sometimes devastating the effects of so-called Western civilization on groups heretofore considered isolated and unchanged, scholars had long been aware through diffusion studies that culture contact was an old and ubiquitous phenomenon accounting for culture change. However, studies of change in process sharpened awareness of contacts unrelated to the expansion of Western technology. Note was taken of long stabilized relations, sometimes called cultural symbiosis, in which groups require one another to survive while each maintains its own identity, such as the relations between Pygmies and Congo tribes in Africa (Putnam 1948) and the settled and nomadic peoples of Manchuria (Lindgren 1938). Similarly, such preindustrial contacts as the spread of Islam and the other great religions with their associated secular elements are matters of common knowledge. Studies designated acculturational appeared with increasing frequency, but the

term began to lose precision as it was applied to a multitude of results of contact, from long established exchanges of goods over great distances by established trade routes, to American Indian schooling deliberately aimed at the obliteration of the Indians' original identity and their assimilation into the larger society. Consequently, formal steps were taken among anthropologists to arrive at a generally satisfactory definition of the term "acculturation." In 1936, Melville J. Herskovits, Ralph Linton, and Robert Redfield, as a committee of the Social Science Research Council, studied the question carefully and prepared "A Memorandum on Acculturation," discussing the need for a definition and offered the following:

Acculturation comprehends those phenomena which result when groups of individuals having different cultures come into continuous first-hand contact, with subsequent changes in the original cultural patterns of either or both groups. Under this definition, acculturation is to be distinguished from *culture-change*, of which it is but one aspect, and *assimilation*, which is at times a phase of acculturation. It is also differentiated from *diffusion*, which while occurring in all instances of acculturation, is not only a phenomenon which frequently takes place without the occurrence of the types of contact between peoples specified in the definition given above, but also constitutes only one aspect of the process of acculturation (Redfield, Linton, and Herskovits 1936:152).

Generally, this definition continues to be used in establishing what kind of a situation is under consideration when a study is labeled acculturational. But scholars still wrestle with the questions of what kinds of subsequent changes are likely to occur and in which group. In 1938 Herskovitz published a small volume entitled *Acculturation* in which he reviewed a number of anthropological reports and even novels pertinent to the question of acculturation, pointing out problems for further study. He noted that things are never just accepted from one group by another, but are reinterpreted to suit the accepting group; acculturation is a two-way street and changes worthy of study occur in both groups which have continuing cross-effects; and frequency and similarity may be seen in systematized religious reactions, such as the Ghost Dance, which seek to create new integrations when contact produces disorganization and inability to continue accustomed ways. The book also includes a rather extended outline developed by the committee enumerating points that appear to require special attention in acculturational analysis. Among these are the type of contact — friendly, hostile, and so on; the contact situation, whether involving political and social equality or inequality of the parties; processes such as selection and integration; psychological mechanisms, for example, the personality of individuals leading the way in acceptance of innovations; and results of acculturation — acceptance, adaptation, and reaction. The outline is, in effect, a checklist whereby sufficient comparable data on given topics might eventually be gathered to permit generalizations.

Review of Keesing's annotated bibliography on culture change up to 1953 shows a high preponderance of specifically acculturational works in the two decades preceding its publication. As data accumulated, more effort was required to find order and predictability in a mass of details. In 1953, the Social Science Research Council sponsored a summer seminar on acculturation which attempted to review and classify existing ideas and information (Barnett *et al.* 1954:973–1002). The participants admitted that the discipline was still far from a coordinated analysis of the subject, but concentrated their attention on types and situations of contact as suggesting definable variables which could be utilized with some degree of precision in predicting acculturative developments. Their definition was, in effect, an extension and elaboration of the 1936 statement as suggested by the backlog of both descriptive and theoretical information available to them. Acculturation was defined as:

. . . culture change that is initiated by the conjunction of two or more autonomous cultural systems. Acculturative change may be the consequence of direct cultural transmission; it may be derived from noncultural causes, such as ecological or demographic modifications induced by an impinging culture; it may be delayed, as with internal adjustments following upon acceptance of alien traits or patterns; or it may be a reactive adaptation of traditional modes of life. Its dynamics can be seen as the selective adaptation of value systems, the processes of integration and differentiation, the generation of developmental sequences, and the operation of role determinants and personality factors.

The term "autonomous systems" is somewhat misleading as one follows the subsequent discussion, but it does denote an important distinction between changes flowing among role groupings of a single system and changes occurring between different systems with their distinctive clusterings of roles. Thus, contacts and resulting changes between factions or classes or occupational groupings of a single society are not considered acculturational. The term is reserved for relationships between ethnic groups and their encompassing societies as well as cultural contact between more autonomous systems. These systems in contact may share some roles or have parallel roles, but the total clusterings of roles are distinctive and derive their distinctiveness from the fact of different and meaningful traditions underlying them. Distinguishing such changes has proven of value in understanding the differences in selective adaptations to industrialization made by peasants as compared to those made by ethnic and tribal minorities within larger national enclaves. Despite certain vested interests underlying peasant conservatism, the peasant looks to the city and the urban conational elite for inspiration and prestige (Friedl 1964; Nunez 1963). On the other hand, groups such as American Indian tribal communities look to other Indian groups, ranking them as models to emulate in adaptive adjustments to the larger society which allow continued Indian identity.

Out of the great variety of items listed in the 1936 outline and suggested by subsequent studies, many drawn from work in applied anthropology, the 1953 seminar arrived at four key points in the study of acculturation:

(1) characterization of the properties of the two or more autonomous *cultural systems* which come into contact; (2) the study of the nature of the *contact situation;* (3) the analysis of *conjunctive relations* established between the cultural systems under contact; and (4) the study of the *cultural processes* which flow from the conjunction of the systems.

The discussion suggests typological categories, admittedly as examples rather than as an exhaustive list, that might be used with some degree of precision in predicting acculturative developments.

In characterizing autonomous systems, older dichotomies such as simple-complex, folk-urban, Appollonian-Dionysian, and the like were rejected by the S.S.R.C. seminar in favor of looking to the kinds of boundary-maintaining mechanisms which distinguish systems as "closed" (e.g., Hopi) versus "open" (e.g., the United States); "rigidity" or "flexibility" of internal structure; and self-correcting mechanisms. In regard to the contact situation, special importance is seen in the ecological context and demographic characteristics of the respective peoples where types of interdependent or competitive environmental exploitation and populational differentials may set changes in motion. Among conjunctive relations, note is

taken of intercultural roles and quality and quantity of communication. The discussion of cultural process includes consideration of the need for close attention to intercultural transmission, cultural creativity, cultural disintegration, reactive adaptation, progressive adjustment, cultural fusion, assimilation, stabilized pluralism, and differential rates of changes.

Although the results of the 1953 seminar are more provocative and stimulating than concretely informative, it is understandable that the state of actual generalizations should trail the clarification of questions to be asked to gain broad understanding. Of special interest, however, is the fact that the study ends on a note clearly indicative of a purposeful drawing together of operational and developmental interests:

In the search for uniformities in acculturation processes, the possibility of regularities in sequential developments over long time-spans should not be neglected. Are there, in fact, processural regularities in acculturation comparable to those suggested for the development of early civilizations . . . and for the transformations of the primitive world . . . ?

A curious feature of the publication is that the list of processes of change is really a list of results or extensions rather than basic processes. By 1953, some understanding had already been gained in this matter and perhaps it was taken for granted by the seminar participants. Among the noteworthy concepts developed in operational studies regarding cultural change, it is probably justifiable to list at least one as a principle in common use.

7. *Change occurs by analogy of potential innovations to the existing cultural inventory and social system. Cultural inventory is used here to mean the aggregate of definable things, material and nonmaterial, characteristic of a given culture, while social system*

refers to the patterned integration of the parts of a culture.

Linton and Barnett set forth remarkably similar analyses, and comparable conclusions were drawn by Herskovitz, Ruth Benedict, and others. Linton felt that any trait, complex, or other distinguishable component of culture has at least four significant facets: form, function, meaning and use — or principle, in Barnett's terminology. Any item, whether kettle, song, kinship system, or ax, has a definable and describable form. An item is functionally integrated into a total culture in terms of the purpose it serves, such as promoting law and order, disciplining children, assuring an adequate food supply, or placating spirits. Similarly, it evokes meanings — pleasure, hard work, fear, amusement. Finally, the item is used, applied, handled, and activated in culturally prescribed ways (Linton 1936; Barnett 1940, 1942).

Consider, for example, the case of long red flannel underwear, which became a popular trade item with the Hupa Indians of California. In the donor culture it is a limp, woven red garment, tailored to cover most of the human body. Its function is utilitarian, to keep one warm in cold weather, thereby promoting greater efficiency and comfort in outdoor work or recreation, and sometimes also providing cozy apparel for sleeping. Its meanings are mildly humorous as an intimate and rural or old-fashioned item of clothing and, therefore, both suggestive and amusing, given the value system of the donor culture. Its use or principle rests in the fact that it is worn next to the skin and that it is covered by other garments.

To the Hupa Indians, "the functional analogue was to the deerskin blanket, but because of its color, rarity, and naive elegance of pattern it was converted into an article of display with prestige associations.

It became an article to be paraded at dances . . ." (Barnett 1940:37).

By way of comparison, negative analogies can lead to rejection of an innovation. As Herskovits noted:

Manchester-made copies of Ashanti cloths, for instance, lay on the shelves of Gold Coast shops for want of buyers, despite the fact that these exact replicas were far less expensive than the native weaves. The reason for their rejection was a puzzle to those who charted their course in terms of economic theory based on concepts of price and value. Prestige and position, however, mean more to the Ashanti than an advantageous price. These cloths are marks of rank, and a man who appeared wearing one to which he was not entitled was subjected to unmerciful ridicule. Those upper-class persons who were entitled to wear them, on the other hand, had no need to take price differentials into account, even if considerations of their rank did not dictate their obligation to have cloths made by native weavers (1950:559–560).

Ruth Benedict used the principle of analogy formation in a broader context than the simple tracing of acceptance or rejection of a single trait or complex. In "Two Patterns of Indian Acculturation," she observed that in Middle America, Spanish conquest merely replaced a nascent native feudalism with Spanish feudalism in Indian peasant communities. Little cultural disorganization and disruption occurred as elements were exchanged between highly analogous systems. By contrast, in North America, culture contact between Indians and Europeans was fraught with resistance, opposition, and cultural confusion for tribal peoples who could only select randomly analogous items from European cultures, while the cultures in contact remained alien and irreconcilable as total systems (1943).

Retrospectively, the reasons why changes were or were not made are often easily discerned (cf. Paul 1955). However, applying the principle of analogy formation in a prospectively predictive fashion to specific cases is exceedingly difficult. It requires that the outside observer have an unusually complete familiarity with the cultural inventory and social system of a society, including the implicit values underlying meanings evoked by various kinds of stimuli. Edward Spicer's textbook, *Human Problems in Technological Change* (1952) offers fascinating exercises for the student to test his predictive skills on a number of different cases. The innovation and significant features of the culture are provided and the student is asked to trace the reasons why changes occurred.

Innovations generated from within a group are even more difficult to anticipate. However, the old question of the relative importance of borrowing versus independent invention in accounting for change generally has undergone some modification. Culture change in an operational sense appears to require three phases of development. First, there is the stimulus to innovate which may come from exposure to another culture, accidental discovery, felt need to solve some problem, a positive cultural value on innovation for its own sake, and other definable circumstances (Barnett 1953). As early as 1936, the difference between stimulus and innovation was pointed out by Linton in a classic example, using the terms "discovery" and "invention." A child discovers that if he pulls a cat's tail, the cat is likely to scratch him; but with this stimulus he is on the way to invention if he pulls the tail so that someone else holding the cat gets scratched (Linton 1936:306). Similarly, the Hupa Indian people discovered long red underwear on the trader's shelves and were stimulated to create a decorative innovation.

Thus, whether introduced from within or outside a culture, an item is merely a stimulus before it enters a second phase and becomes an innovation in terms of relating it to the culture in some significant fashion.

Finally, there is the phase of actual integration into the culture, so that an innovation is more than an ephemeral curiosity. The shared cultural inventory and social system promote a consensus making an innovation acceptable to a representative number of the entirety or definable subgroupings of a society. Sometimes it is possible to accept an item with little reinterpretation, but even straightforward attempts at outright imitation always involve some process of adaptation.

Language provides many examples of the process of adoption of innovations through analogy in both loan words and neologisms. When the Soviet Union launched its first satellite, Sputnik, American newscasters automatically changed the initial *shp-* of the Russian pronunciation to *sp-,* and the soft Russian *kh* final sound to an English *k.* For a time there was disagreement about the *u* sound as to whether it was analogous to *oo* as in the exclamation "pooh!" *u* as in "put," or *u* as in "spud." The "spud" analogy is now generally favored, probably because it also includes analogy to the *sp* sound.

The creation of brand names clearly reflects the influence of the existing linguistic inventory of sounds and meanings: Pream, Duz, Fab, and the like. A neologism or loan word such as *smrz* would be inacceptable to English speakers, who would automatically introduce a vowel between the *m* and the *r,* to achieve consistency with consonant-vowel relationships in English. Even fictitious languages reveal no more creativity than an exploration of mathematical possibilities of combinations of sounds and structures drawn from a variety of extant languages (Fraenkel 1961).

There is little doubt that no innovation is entirely independent or original, despite the dramatic speed, ingenuity, and magnitude of changes noted in some cases. New ways are found to do old things, or old ways are recombined to do new things, as in the case of the mother of ten who mass-produces toasted cheese sandwiches for her large brood by laying the sandwiches between strips of aluminum foil the length of her ironing board and running a hot iron over the foil. An innovation depends upon analogies to the existing culture, but once accepted, it carries the potential stimulus for further innovations insofar as it expands or alters the existing culture from which different analogies may then be drawn.

However, the study of cultural change is also by definition the study of cultural continuity because, despite changes, a group of people sharing a culture persists and has a vested and indeed inevitable stake in social and cultural continuity. Our biological evolutionary heritage means that we must learn our cultural adaptations for survival, and for this vital technique to work, a culture must be firmly implanted in the members of the society which shares it. The term "enculturation" is sometimes used to describe this process. Cultural behavior must be virtually habitual in order to bring organization, predictability, and direction into what would be an otherwise impossibly chaotic and uncontrolled universe for a species almost totally devoid of any genetically programmed behavior patterns. Our biological make-up with its long infant dependency and slow maturation suggests that we must exist in groups and agree upon ways to live and work together. Perhaps of greater importance, the evolutionary test of survival has also shown that beyond at least maternal responsibility in the care and teaching of children, culture is contributory to survival as it also promotes cooperation and allocation of mutually interdependent tasks among adults.

Flexibility and the purposefulness of problem-solving distinguish cultural evolution from biological evolution. In the latter, chance mutations must be present to assure survival of some of the members of the

group should the environment become so altered that other members lacking adaptability do not survive. Here the difference between the evolution of the social behavior of wasps and man is obvious.

Sociocultural systems must be stable enough to assure survival insofar as the learning of one generation can be used to prepare the next to survive and adults can operate within a reasonably predictable universe. They must also be flexible enough to adapt to changes in the social and natural environment or take advantage of opportunities to improve chances of survival.

The concept of social identity has proven useful to operational studies (cf. Goodenough 1963:176–251) since it takes into account both the conservatism (sometimes called ethnocentrism) of specific cultures as well as the means by which changes occur. We may define social identity as the total and distinctive clustering of roles, cultural inventory, and social system *experienced* by a group and derived from the group's own viable historical tradition of changes through time. It gives both a sense of continuity and the background for common analogies to occur to produce innovations permitting change. At this point another principle may be introduced.

8. *Cultural change is selective. We cannot always predict what analogies will be made in specific cases, but a few qualified generalizations can be drawn. All evidence to date seems to indicate that cultural changes on an operational level of analysis occur as they are perceived or interpreted to improve, enhance, enrich, or preserve social identity. Potential innovations are rejected as they evoke distasteful analogies or are threatening to social identity.*

Turning to qualifications, we must note the phenomenon of assimilation, adverted to in both the 1936 and 1953 studies of acculturation but not defined. Individuals can be absorbed into another culture, but this involves only the exchange of one identity for another and the acquisition and utilization of accompanying cultural components in the new identity. The reasons are varied, but usually assimilation occurs among some but not all individuals in a group where an alternative is posed between adaptive changes in the individual's culture or rejection of it in favor of another. In some instances, such as many North American Indian groups, the opportunity for assimilation into another society of the dissatisfied or somewhat aberrantly encultured selects and removes elements threatening to the group and contributes to strengthening of its identity since the more like-minded remain to perpetuate the culture. If the original group can keep up its numbers despite losses through assimilation, it is likely to persist indefinitely in a state of cultural pluralism, making its own adaptive cultural changes within its own framework of identity.

Many factors may be operative in assimilation. Where racial or other barriers exist and dissatisfaction with one's identity occurs, a few individuals may manage to "pass" while the rest are obliged to seek ways in which existing identity can be enhanced. In recent years, various news stories indicate that increased education among the "untouchables" of India has led to growing dissatisfaction with the social disabilities inherent in their identity as presently defined. However, there are differences of opinion as to the best way to overcome these disabilities. Some individuals reject their identity as untouchable and manage to "pass" as members of castes which are not untouchable. Others accept Gandhi's ideal of working to reform the Hindu religion and abolish the concept of untouchability. Such people wish to retain their ties of religion, communities, and families but strive for more satisfactory definitions of their own

historical identity. Others have chosen the course of rejecting caste and Hinduism entirely and seek a new identity as Christians or Buddhists.

Among immigrants, as in the United States, the reason for immigration may include a desire for a change in identity, and assimilation occurs rapidly. However, some immigrant groups seek sanctuary in order to maintain their identity more effectively than was possible in their original homeland, and cultural pluralism may be achieved if the receiving environment permits it. Glazer and Moynihan's recent book (1963) contains rich examples and analyses of the persistence of ethnic identity in urban settings, contrary to older sociological "melting pot" notions concerning the extent of assimilation of immigrants into American culture.

Sometimes fusion occurs rather than assimilation or pluralism, so that a culture is eventually made up of two or more cultures with an awareness of identity from two or more traditions. Redfield (1936) and Elsie Clews Parsons (1936), working in different areas of Mexico where there had been long contact between Spanish and Indian cultures, observed that the effects of initial contact led to further innovations. It often became impossible to determine whether a given trait was of Spanish or Indian origin. Similarly, the Métis communities of central Canada illustrate a fusion of French and Indian cultures.

Another qualification to the concept that change moves in the direction of persisting social identity is that changes are sometimes stimulated by the need to adapt to conquest or natural catastrophe. Groups will strive to maintain identity, but the amount of selectivity that can be exercised is limited. Thus, while a few remnants of tribes of the Powhatan Confederacy remain in Virginia and adjoining states, they retain no more of their cultural identity than recollection of their history in terms of continuous occupation of the same area since contact times. The loss of population through warfare and disease meant that an elaborate political structure designed for some thirty tribes and over 9000 people simply could not be maintained or changed selectively in adaptation to conquest. Individuals survived by assimilation into the surrounding societies, white and Negro. A few larger tribal communities remained in social isolation, with wholesale acquisition of the traits of rural neighbors. Indian identity, albeit only a historical claim, is prized since white identity is denied them by surrounding white people, and Negro identity is undesirable to them (Lurie 1959).

Even where changes are made voluntarily a group cannot always anticipate destructive effects that may eventually result from an innovation which appears innocuous at the outset. Lauriston Sharp reported how a seemingly minor change, the substitution of steel axes for stone axes among the Yir Yoront of Australia, happened to strike at a critically important integrative feature of the culture. The relatively few stone axes had been used by all, but were considered the property of certain old men who derived a wide variety of powers from control of the axes. This fact defined the key roles in the network of social relationships. When a few steel axes first reached the Yir Yoront through trade, they could be easily integrated into the culture by simple analogies to stone axes. However, steel axes were then introduced by missionaries in great quantity and were given to people of both sexes and all ages. This completely undercut the traditional allocation of rights of ownership and use and the mutual interdependencies among the people so that the entire culture was disrupted (Spicer 1952:69–90).

The myriad and qualifying circumstances underlying cultural change as seen from an operational point of view have tended to create more confusion than any solid understanding of process. Various typologies have been suggested to try to distinguish orderly categories, such as material and non-material changes, voluntary and involuntary, primarily and derived. Or, circumstances regarding the role, prestige, or powers of persuasion of the innovator or initial acceptor have been explored. All have merit in given situations but tend to be only slightly less particularistic than taking each case as if it were unique. It is tentatively advanced that changes in general may be seen in regard to a typology which appears under such headings as cultural and social or minor and major changes. For clarity and to avoid specialized connotations implied in such terms, we will simply designate them as Type I and Type II changes.

Type I changes are those which are made to fit the innovation to the existing inventory and system. For example, thimbles were a popular item in the fur trade among Great Lakes Indian people. However, their form did not immediately suggest analogies to sewing and protection of the finger tip since at the time they were introduced Indian women used awls and a stiff sinew element rather than eyed needles with soft thread. To the Indian people, a thimble looked like a jangler and a hole was accordingly punched in the top, with a knotted cord drawn through the hole. Bunches of such thimbles were attached to cradleboards and clothing to make a visually attractive and sound-producing decoration comparable to use of false hooves of deer or animal claws. As we have seen, language affords many instances of Type I changes. New words, whether borrowed or invented, are made to conform to the accepting language in patterns of sound and structure. Type I changes build cumulatively since once an innovation is accepted, the culture is changed and holds the potential for stimulating yet other heretofore impossible combinations. A compounding of Type I changes also holds the potential for Type II changes.

Type II changes are those which require changing of the inventory and system to accommodate the innovation. For example, automobiles were accepted initially as analogous to other sources of locomotive power, particularly horses. Analogies were readily made to meanings and functions associated with horses and wagons, and even analogies in form can be seen in the continuing use of such terms as "dashboard." However, as the automobile was adapted to a variety of purposes previously served by horses it accomplished familiar tasks more effectively — that is, it promoted continuity with a sense of improvement and enrichment of the existing state of things. Horse-associated features were soon discontinued or greatly reduced in manufacture and the stimulus to innovate automobile-associated features resulted in tremendous changes both in the cultural inventory and the social system. Today, we see such things as cross-country, multilane highways, service stations, even religious fetishes made for the express purpose of protection from automobile accidents. The entire social system has also been accommodated to the automobile; types of insurance and credit buying, courtship patterns, consolidation of school districts, crimes dependent upon the automobile and laws and means of enforcement designed to deal with them, and the involvement of a large percentage of the national labor force in the production, sale, and servicing of automobiles. Although the typology of changes is useful, as the case of automobile illustrates, Type I changes sometimes build up by such imperceptible degrees that it is difficult to pinpoint the actual transition to Type II changes.

On the other hand, the distinction combined with the concept of analogy formation is useful in understanding the nature of changes within a given group. For example, massive changes which may impress the observer as overwhelming evidence of incipient loss of identity are sometimes only huge aggregates of Type I changes with minimal Type II accommodations. Ojibwa Indian people of the Great Lakes region have undergone tremendous change since fur trade contact was first established with them in the seventeenth century, yet they remain identified as distinctive Ojibwa communities. Personality and culture studies show that they have remained remarkably consistent in modal personality over a long period of time. From a functionalist point of view, this poses a seeming paradox in that congruity is expected between the parts of a culture, in this case, components of modal personality and the rest of modern Ojibwa culture. The Ojibwa in virtually all phases of material culture — food, housing, clothing, transportation — closely resemble their white neighbors. The resemblance even extends to matters of skills, such as literacy, farming, lumbering, automobile repair, construction work. Finally, these items and habits relate to a money-wage economy of white origin. A paradox exists for the outside observer who sees these forms of his culture in terms of his culture's meanings, functions, and uses. He holds technology and its material forms as an important value. For the Ojibwa person, there is no puzzling paradox, because from his point of view his culture simply has not changed as radically as all the borrowed forms would seem to indicate. He invests the forms with his own functions and meanings, and regards forms, particularly material objects, rather lightly. He does not cherish objects as a hedge against a rainy day or indicative of his personal worth in the manner of his white neighbor. Furthermore, there is a distinctive clustering of philosophical values or themes among the Ojibwa that has permitted many Type I changes: events are considered finite; the socially adequate and admirable individual is one who is resourceful and able to turn a wide range of alternatives to his advantage; change is implicit in the nature of the universe; and the fortunate should share with the less fortunate because neither good nor bad fortune lasts.

These attitudes, fostered by the exigencies of a hunting and gathering existence, have allowed for Type I changes in adaptation to an industrialized and even rural wage-work setting. The Ojibwa learned farming skills in the course of Indian Bureau policies designed to teach them to be self-sufficient, but never took to farm life in the sense of white agricultural entrepreneurship. They used the new skills as opportunities arose, and as the need and inclination at given times dictated working for farmers so as to buy the necessaries of life no longer available through hunting and gathering. Butcher's beef substituted easily for venison, textiles for tanned skin clothing. Skills in speaking English and literacy promoted other skills so that other opportunities could be exploited, such as lumbering, carpentry, performing Indian dances for paying audiences, or appeals to the welfare office. Each instance tends to be considered finite as abundant game or a bumper crop of blueberries were considered and exploited in an earlier day (Friedl 1956). Conscious selection of material items has occurred in order to benefit by conveniences and comforts of white material culture — automobiles, stoves, wooden houses, and the like. But the Ojibwa lack meanings involving the acquisition of goods for their own sake and arranging them tastefully for display. There is an appearance of poverty in the eyes of white observers even in those Indian households in which the family considers itself and is considered by other Ojibwa to be financially comfortable and secure. Whether one wishes to see this as an illustration of evolutionary potential discussed earlier is a matter of opinion. The fact remains that in moving from a life based on hunting and gathering into a wage economy, groups such as the Ojibwa have been able to put interpretations on borrowed items that members of the so-called donor group find difficult to comprehend, bound as they are to the meanings and functions they associate with given forms.

An important source of stimulus for the intensive analysis of the processes of cultural change in operational terms has been afforded by the increased emphasis on applied anthropology since World War II. The Society for Applied Anthropology was organized in 1940, reflecting the development of a corps of workers in this field interested in exchanges of information. Significantly, the basic definition of applied anthropology as directed change draws together data and theory related to both internal and acculturational changes. Among the early and continuing applied anthropological studies have been analyses of differential productivity among groups within one industrial setting, labor-management relations, intergroup relations within hospitals, and differential success of health programs in sections of the same urban environment. Acculturational changes are noted in the introduction of Western health practices and technology to areas heretofore entirely lacking such opportunities to change. Actually, it is sometimes difficult to say in the latter cases whether acculturational or nonacculturational considerations are more importantly involved, insofar as the requests for assistance frequently come from the national elite although actual work is often carried on in the remote hinterlands which may stand in an ethnic tribal or nationally identified peasant relationship to urban centers. Whatever scruples "pure" scientists may have about applied anthropology, the field has contributed importantly to the beginning of integrated syntheses of theories of cultural change. Various approaches in the social sciences as a whole as well as the developmental and operational differences within anthropology are being drawn upon without regard for academic parochialism. The horrible nineteenth-century examples of well-intended but premature and ill-advised meddling in other cultures' developments should, however, remain sobering and cautionary reminders that in avoiding past errors we are still capable of promulgating equally unfortunate albeit different errors today. Nevertheless, our understanding and knowledge have increased, at least on the level of changes in specific cultures. For instance, there is a clear appreciation that the people involved in planned change together with social scientists and technicians can better evaluate differential consequences of alternative courses of action than outside experts alone. For such work to be effective, the people involved must be thoroughly informed of opportunities and prospects and assured that agreed-upon programs can be carried through as promised. An appreciation for the crescive nature of change means that we now know that programs may require continuing adaptations as specific and untoward effects may occur, admittedly unpredictable in our present state of knowledge (cf. Holmberg and Dobyns 1962).

Originally, the new applied anthropology was directed almost entirely toward specific and relatively limited changes on the local level. Within the last few years applied anthropological work and operational studies have been moving in the direction of questions of cumulative change on a worldwide scale. Illustrative of the closing of the gap between operational and developmental interests is exploration of the concept of the "third culture," defined in a recent study as "the behavior patterns created, shared and learned by men of different societies who are in the process of relating their societies, or sections thereof, to each other" (Useem, Donoghue, and Useem 1963:169). By way of examples we may cite the United Nations, the European Common Market, the ecumenical movement of the Christian church,

the diplomatic community, international cartels, and even world-wide crime syndicates.

Discovery of third cultures in our time has promoted probing into historical data which show that the phenomenon is not new, merely made strikingly obvious at present. Intelligent planning of change through third cultures may hold the key to more effective survival of the human species, through sharing of innovations by more effective means than were possible in an age of simpler and slower methods of transportation and communication.

Whether a particular third culture is pervasive or restricted, functional or dysfunctional, from a world view, it exists. It always has. An anthropologist would say that throughout history, the diffusion of man-made artifacts, information, ideas, beliefs and aspirations has taken place between societies via cultural contacts and human interaction. In retrospect, we classify these men and their activities as incipient third culture phenomena. Now man has become one and thousands are engaged in the common human process of sharing mankind's social heritage. In our times, coordinate cross-cultural programs have become man's newest instrument to quicken the pace and organize the means. In fact, the administrations of cross-cultural programs in bi-national third cultures is but an expression and a product of an expanding, world-encompassing third culture (Useem, Donoghue, and Useem 1963:179).

Formulation of the concept of the third culture is new and even its most enthusiastic proponents agree that it requires testing and critical evaluation. The questions remain whether localized distinctiveness and social identity are to be blurred and flattened in a monolithic world culture based on shared technological achievements, or whether third cultures act or can be directed to permit localized creativity for the development of uniquely rewarding community life. It should be noted that, while anthropologists have tended to form two camps, developmental and operational, in the study of cultural change, the problem of relating these views has long attracted some scholars. In 1924, Edward Sapir published a prophetic essay, "Culture, Genuine and Spurious." In it he distinguished specific cultures, with their distinct traditions, from technological developments of a cumulative nature, along with social forms for making such general advances widely available to humankind. In philosophical terms, he anticipated such recent and more rigorously scientific formulations as Wolf's recurrent components as a modification of developmental theories and the enlargement of scope of operational approaches seen in the concept of the third culture. In defining genuine culture as encompassing both material and nonmaterial features shared by distinctive groups which are comprehensible to and wielded by the individual, Sapir observed:

Does this mean that we must turn our back on all internationalistic tendencies and vegetate forever in our nationalisms? Here we are confronted by the prevalent fallacy that internationalism is in spirit opposed to the intensive development of autonomous cultures. The fallacy proceeds from the failure to realize that internationalism, nationalism and localism are forms that can be given various contents (Mandelbaum 1957:115).

Linton, in 1936, expressed a similar view in regard to the impact of the machine:

. . . unless all past experience is at fault, the society will once more reduce itself to order. What the new order will be no one can forecast, but the potentialities of the local group both for the control of individuals and for the satisfaction of their psychological needs are so great that it seems unlikely that this unit will be dispensed with (230).

The local culture is still not well enough understood in terms of its persistence, its possible necessity to survival in serving as a wellspring of variation like the mutations of biological evolution, and its flexibility, to be disregarded as a continuing object of study. It is tempting but premature to set forth in the exclusive pursuit of new, broad generalizations now hinted at in narrower problems as yet only partially understood. At the same time, such formulations as cumulative developments and the third culture underscore the need to look not only at but beyond the local culture to major interrelationships, just as we have learned to look beyond the isolated trait to the integrated patterning of traits in cultures to understand more fully both the trait and the patterning.

Suggested Readings

For a more complete exposition of the several developmental positions, see White (1949) and (1959a) for a statement of the position of unilineal evolutionism, Steward (1955) for the alternative multilineal position, and Sahlins (1964) for an attempt to reconcile these two points of view. Wolf's 1964 essay seems to be an effort to bridge what we have termed the developmental and operational approaches to culture change. Clifton's 1965 article attempts to link features of social structure with high rates of culture change.

A more complete presentation of the operational approaches to a comprehension of cultural change will be found in Barnett (1944, 1942), while his 1953 volume is fascinating but difficult. Linton's chapter on "Function" in his 1936 book should also be read in this connection. The Barnett, *et al.* seminar report on that aspect of culture change called acculturation is highly theoretical, and attempts to set new directions for future study. Finally, Useem, Donoghue, and Useem's concept of the "third culture" attempts a reconciliation of the operational and developmental positions from the operational side.

CHAPTERS 12-13 discuss the ways in which anthropology and psychology approach the comparative cross-cultural study of human psychological functioning. Jointly and singly, psychologists and anthropologists have for years used one or another laboratory, experimental, or clinical procedure to measure various dimensions of the human psyche. These efforts are not always articulated. To the extent that psychology, like anthropology, is concerned with generating valid general knowledge about *human* nature, rather than narrowly validated knowledge about middle-class American nature, there is a broad-scale area of mutual relevance cutting across traditional disciplinary lines. Recognition of this fact has insured recurrent development of cross-disciplinary fields, culture *and* personality, psycholinguistics, and so on, and has stimulated considerable collaborative effort between the two sciences. Yet to date, the amount of cross-cultural psychological research by no means approaches the great volume of research accomplished with or on Euro-American subjects. Too, in recent years most work in ethnopsychology has consisted of comparative studies of personality, generally with a strongly Freudian psycho-dynamic orientation. On the one hand, this convergence of interest represents efforts to join two grand ideas of the early twentieth century, to test Freudian and Neo-Freudian propositions about human nature against the fact of diverse sociocultural settings; on the other hand, it represents (in anthropology) the tremendous growth and dominance of concern with social organizational phenomena. As social anthropology has expanded, comparative studies of personality — of motivation, of emotional adjustment and disorder, and of individual adjustment to diverse sociocultural settings — have understandably occupied ethnopsychologists. The psychological conception of personality, with all its constituent subdimensions, remains a key term when set beside social person, role, and cultural change, especially for those concerned with such processual phenomena as the sociocultural origins of mental disorders, the diffusion of cultural innovations, or the varieties of child-training practices. For most anthropologists largely interested in social phenomena, their associates have been clinical or social psychologists or psychiatrists. Very few experimental psychologists have joined anthropologists to work on questions like those Professor Spier raised in Chapter 5 about learning and re-learning of the motor skills associated with different technologies. Frequently, as Professor Price-Williams says, this is due to lack of coordination, and to a seeming absence of mutual relevance between their activities. Yet cross-disciplinary problem-centered fields constantly crop up, and the issues and research discussed in these chapters may well contain seeds ready for intellectual fertilization.

THE AUTHOR was educated at Uppingham, a public school in England, and later at Birkbeck College, University of London. He took his bachelor's and doctor's degrees at the University of London. For ten years he held a lecturing position in psychology at the London School of Economics. In 1962–63 he was Visiting Lecturer in Psychology at the University of Kansas, and is now Professor and Chairman of the Department of Psychology at Rice University, Houston. His interest in psychological anthropology stems from field work with the Tiv of Central Nigeria in 1959, and he has also done work in Guatemala. He has written a book and several articles in psychological, anthropological, philosophical, and social work journals, and is currently engaged in ethnopsychological research in different parts of the world.

12

Ethnopsychology I:
Comparative Psychological Processes

DOUGLASS R. PRICE-WILLIAMS

Rice University

INTRODUCTION

The term "ethnopsychology" appears to have been used in the same sense as the German word *Volkerpsychologie,* or folk psychology, which was introduced into psychology by Wilhelm Wundt in a series of volumes under that general heading (Wundt 1900–1920). Wundt took the term from a philosopher and a philologist — Lazarus and Steinthal (1860) — who had given it a Hegelian overtone of the Volksgeist. The notion of ethnopsychology was brought more into line with modern psychology by Werner (1961) who gave it a developmental interpretation. In anthropology Murdock (1950) has employed the term in a strict sense as indicating particular societies' notions of drives, concepts of sensations, standards of pleasantness and unpleasantness, ideas about mental states, and so forth. We will use the concept both in the latter sense and in the rather wider meaning the older psychologists gave it.

Wundt made a sharp distinction between the study of elementary psychological processes, which was to be carried out by laboratory procedures, and the comparative study of the languages, myths, and customs of different peoples, which was to be contrasted with presumably universal psychological processes in which all mankind shared. Since Wundt's scheme was outlined, and indeed even before and during the time it was written, the combined efforts of psychologists, anthropologists, and linguists have tended to confuse this simple division of labor. It is relatively correct to state that psychology has concerned itself with asserting general propositions about human nature, drawn mainly and perhaps parochially from investigations of people living in Europe and America, but even in the very first years of the twentieth century a group of scholars was applying laboratory procedures to what used to be called primitive peoples (Haddon 1901). In the last two decades, at least, a vast amount of experi-

305

mental data on elementary mental processes has accumulated from people all over the globe.

To some extent the notion of a psychology of particular societies has also been developed by scholars in the field of culture and personality (discussed in the next chapter). Recently Hsu (1961:1–15) has suggested the term "Psychological Anthropology" to replace "Culture and Personality." This new rubric appears to include material other than that exclusively related to the concept of personality; in Hsu's volume, for example, there is material devoted to dreams and to mental illness. What has come to be considered under either title has largely, though certainly not exclusively, been determined by anthropologists. The contributions of psychologists, when interested in psychological processes for their own sake, not in particular societies or cultures, are simply labelled cross-cultural studies. Cross-cultural investigations pertain to general psychology, as in studies of the perceptions of people from Alaska to Oceania; to developmental psychology, as in work on different methods of child training; to abnormal psychology, which considers the incidence, formation, and variations of mental health; and further to social psychology, where textbooks are giving more and more attention to cross-cultural work, as Hsu points out (1961:12).

A discussion of ethnopsychology in the different perspectives of anthropology and psychology entails some consideration of the mutual relevance of the two disciplines. This has been extensively treated by scholars who have bridged the two disciplines, such as Brewster Smith (1954:32–66), Hallowell (1954:160–226), and French (1963:388–438). At the outset it must be emphasized that what may be considered important by the psychologist frequently has minimal interest for the anthropologist. To take a recent example: Allport and Pettigrew (1957) enlisted Zulus as subjects to test whether a particular visual illusion, generally observed by Western people, was attributable to learning mechanisms or to innate factors in the nervous system. The apparatus which produces this illusion is a figure cut in the form of a trapezoid affixed with horizontal and vertical bars to give the resemblance of a conventional window. If this figure is attached to a motor so it can revolve on its axis, an illusion is produced in that the trapezodial figure oscillates backwards and forwards and appears to behave not as it in fact does, namely, to go round in a circle. This phenomenon has been explained in terms of the observer bringing certain expectations to the figure, expectations based on familiarity with rectangular shapes and particularly with conventional European-style windows. The conflict between these expectations and the particular shape of the figure in motion induces in the observer an impression of sway or oscillation.

Now traditional Zulu culture is marked by familiarity with circular rather than rectangular shapes and one group of Zulus tested had never seen windows. The illusion is most salient when the figure is viewed monocularly, and under this condition the unacculturated Zulu group, those with little or no experience of urban South African life, failed to report the usual illusion. While this finding is very relevant to the study of perception, it is of no very great import to anthropology. The only reason why such a study might be included in any survey of psychological anthropology would be that the subjects were Zulus. The interests of psychologists lay in the nature of the problem, not in the particular people or culture in itself.

In contrast, the psychological studies of Hallowell, as for example his investigations of Salteaux perception of space and their methods of measurement (1955:184–202, 203–215), tell us a great deal about this particular society as well as psychological processes in general. It is clear that there is a difference in orientation between the two examples given. This difference may sometimes be noted on the same subject matter. The study of dreams, for instance, may be undertaken cross-culturally, to find out what the dreams of a particular society can provide for our knowledge of the general nature of the dream mechanism, or as another source of data for our knowledge of the particular society. While it would not be altogether correct to generalize and state that psychology uses the cross-cultural method to check, compare, and amplify our knowledge of psychological processes, and that anthropology focuses on particular societies and peoples and the comparison between them, it is safe to say that the theoretical interests of the two disciplines are not always aligned with each other.

Another point of difference lies in the descriptive units the two disciplines use. Very often units used by anthropologists, and, for that matter, sociologists, are not necessarily relevant to the problems of the psychologist. What may be of significance in the study of perception, for instance, is not so much the social form of one people as against another, as the differing habitat. Very much depends upon the level of the problem. The subject matter of values is one both anthropologists and psychologists find equally meaningful. When descriptive units merge in this way the tendency is for an intermediate discipline to transcend to a major discipline in its own right and with its own categories. This is noticeable in the fields of ethnolinguistics and trans-cultural psychiatry which have now become full-fledged disciplines, for which reason we will not discuss them here.

The idea of a proper "Comparative Psychology of Peoples" is lacking in academic psychology as it exists today. The interests of scholars and investigators have led to a diversification of problems which cannot al-ways be easily compared, owing mainly to the lack of any fundamental and agreed basis of comparison. What exists is a compendium of research areas, very loosely connected under the umbrella title of cross-cultural studies. This chapter is intended as an illustrative outline of the kinds of problems which exercise psychologists working in this field and some of their methodological difficulties.

PROBLEMS OF METHOD IN CROSS-CULTURAL PSYCHOLOGICAL RESEARCH

Campbell has contrasted what he calls the descriptive, humanistic task of recording all aspects of a specific cultural instance with the abstracting and generalizing intention of asserting propositions across cultures (1961:333–352). This is a methodological and ontological dichotomy which tends to recur in the social sciences. It is seen in the opposing viewpoints of those who interpret social anthropology as history, on the one hand, or as the comparative study of societies, on the other. It is seen in the field of personality theory, where Allport (1937:22–23) borrows the terms "nomothetic" and "idiographic" to contrast two distinct approaches. In this context the nomothetic approach seeks general laws across individuals; the idiographic approach fastens on the unique person in the matrix of his time and place. French (1963:398–401), following the linguist Pike, has emphasized what the latter called the "emic" and "etic" standpoints (terms taken from the suffixes of phonemic and phonetic). This last distinction is based on the same principles as the former but differs in the method of categorizing the data. An emic classification represents the way in which members of a society chop up their universe into its various domains. An etic approach employs an external method of analysis wherein all observations are categorized by a scheme of classification which is logically prior to the observations. Different types of psychological investigations can be classified with these approaches.

The emic approach has been used mainly by anthropologists interested in the field of cognition. The technique of componential analysis has encouraged investigation of "ethnoscience," which portrays any one society's ideas about a particular domain: thus we find an ethnozoology, an ethnobotany, and an ethnohistory (Romney and D'Andrade 1946). It is in this specific sense of how people structure their universe that the term "ethnopsychology" can be used, and there is an interesting article by Valentine (1963) showing how the Lakalai of New Britain categorize personality.

There are two subtypes of the etic approach. The first is exemplified by the method used by those of the Whiting school (for a summary of this approach, see Whiting 1961:355–380). The essence of this method is to make correlations between two sets of data across a large number of societies. For instance, the two sets of data may be the degree of harshness with which children are treated by their parents or elders, on the one hand, and the degree of benevolence or malevolence of the gods or supernaturals in these same societies, as regarded by the inhabitants. The intention is to discover whether there is a significant correlation between these two sets of data, whether societies who bring their children up harshly also have harsh gods. By using a large number of societies and statistical measures to determine significant comparisons, this method can yield general statements about cultural instances. It is predominantly etic in that the observational indices are selected on the basis of what is considered to be a meaningful variable in socialization. The indices are not selected according to the way in which the various societies studied might interpret them. This subtype is marked by reliance on the Human Relations Area Files as the source of observations. These files have been compiled over time from the various reports of ethnographers and social anthropologists, and categorized under various headings. In using them the exponent of the Whiting school thus relies on second-hand observations, as he himself has not actually made the observations he requires.

It is obviously better to make first-hand observations over which one has complete control, which is in fact the criterion of the second subtype of etic approach. In this subtype research workers are trained in advance to restrict their observations to an agreed codification. The severe practical limitations of training a sufficient number of research workers is the main reason why this subtype is relatively rare in psychological investigations. It has been carried out recently (B. Whiting 1963) by co-ordinating husband and wife teams in six different societies. The teams planned their observations in the area of personality characteristics and child training on a proper comparative basis.

As a subject, psychology tends to be biased in the etic direction. Even in the largely idiographic accounts of Margaret Mead in the South Seas, the reports on child upbringing, attitudes towards sexual behavior, and adolescent behavior are shot through with comparisons to the Euro-American way of life (Mead 1928, 1930).

In personality studies the idiographic approach often uses personal documents. In psychological anthropology, Hallowell's study of the self-image of the Ojibwa Indian (1955:172–182) is a prime example. The notion of self is related to other factors in the environment and full use is made of a personal account by an Ojibwa Indian on the nature of what he himself regarded as his "Self." This approach avoids enforced categorizations on the data one is interested in collecting, particularly with respect to such difficult and subtle concepts as self, soul, body, and spiritual beings. The events are made to speak for themselves and the observer or reader can perceive a representation of life which may be alien to his own way of thinking. This is, of course, the anthropological way *par excellence,* but when psychological aspects are considered, it must be contrasted with the nomothetic strategy, which tends to ride roughshod over nuances of difference and must needs conform to the investigator's own logical scheme. No comment on the merits or demerits of either method is intended here, only an indication of the differences where they exist (for objections and counter-objections to the nomothetic strategy see Campbell 1961:346–348).

A major problem in cross-cultural work, especially in the nomothetic, is the equivalence of the particular variable being investigated across the different societies in which it is presumably embedded. When something like a visual illusion is studied, a subject has merely to point or make a simple verbal answer, and there is little confusion. However, when a particular variable is studied which calls for some kind of judgment by the ethnographer, the difficulty emerges full blown. This is clear in a cross-cultural enquiry into the incidence of schizophrenia (Wittkower *et al.* 1960). The authors listed a number of symptoms which were thought to be sufficiently characteristic of this mental illness, and which were to be checked by psychiatrists in twenty-five countries. The symptoms were grouped under various headings: delusions, hallucinations, hypochondriacal ideas, catatonic states, social and emotional withdrawal, loss of control both of behavior and body, disturbances of emotion, and depersonalization. There appeared to be fairly common agreement, from the returns, that social and emotional with-

drawal, hallucinations and delusions, and flatness of emotion were regarded as being characteristic of the patients investigated, but contrary to the expectations of the authors and to psychiatry in general, the reported data revealed an infrequency of inappropriateness of affect, hypochondria, and depersonalization. The important methodological problem here is whether the reported infrequency of these well-established symptoms was due to actual lack of incidence, or to the variance in the concept of what constituted schizophrenia among the psychiatrists themselves.

Sears has examined this problem in detail (1961:445–455). He points out that variables used in cross-cultural work must be *trans*cultural; that is to say, they must be measurable on an equivalent basis in whatever society is chosen. He makes an important distinction between instrumental acts and goal responses, which he exemplifies in the case of aggression. There are many possible indices of aggressive actions, such as murder, hitting people, noncooperation. These are instrumental acts and may vary in form from one society to another. The goal response is the recognition by some person of any action as constituting aggression. Sticking a tongue out at another person is recognized in English and American society as a rude and possibly aggressive action; in China it is said to register embarassment. Thus if we were prepared to take sticking the tongue out as a transcultural index for aggression we could go wrong in China.

The equivalence of indices problem is intimately connected with the type of research instrument used. It is now generally recognized that intelligence tests constructed and standardized for Western populations cannot readily be thrust on non-Western peoples. The criticisms have been well summarized by Anastasi and Foley (1949:725–726). Quite apart from the inappropriate comparison with the results to Western and literate populations, there are many other technical difficulties. There is the unfamiliarity with test procedures; motivation for doing a test differs widely in ethnic groups, and for that matter, in socio-economic groups within the same culture (Eells *et al.* 1950:20–21). And many of the conceptual problems included as tests items are thoroughly unsuited to the ecology of the group being tested (for example, maze tests would be meaningless to a group living in desert regions). There seems little doubt that when Western-type intelligence tests are applied to, say, African people, the results are markedly inferior to those for European and American subjects, but there is a strong hesitation to draw conclusions from this owing to the difficulty in allowing for environmental factors on test performance (Cryns 1962). The difficulty is not restricted to intelligence tests. Jahoda (1956) has shown that the Goldstein-Scheerer Cube test, intended to measure the degree of abstraction, was similarly influenced by environmental influences when applied to adolescent boys in Ghana.

We shall examine personality projective tests in detail in the next chaper. Here we need merely mention their role in the equivalence problem. The cross-cultural validity of these tests is somewhat undecided. Henry and Spiro (1953:417–429) considered that the Rorschach ink-blot projective test was culture-free. On the other hand, Dennis (1951:154–158), who culled the evidence of various cultural influences upon the responses to the figures in this test, quite plainly showed the influence of experience. Thus Samoans displayed numerous open-space responses, which seem associated with the fact that white is a favorite and symbolic color among the Samoans. Pilaga Indian children produced an abundance of sex responses which Dennis interpreted as reflecting the sexual freedom permitted them. The

stimulus meaning of the Rorschach cards not being culturally equivalent has spurred Adcock and Ritchie (1958) to suggest that the Rorschach should be adapted variously in different cultures, and different norms established for the different societies in which it is used, though Clifton (1959) has argued cogently against this step. Many personality tests have of course been adapted in this way. Chowdhury modified the Thematic Apperception Test for Indian subjects (1960). As the author insisted, Indian social situations do not have the counterparts in European and American society portrayed in the original Murray cards. Contrariwise, in these cards there is no religious theme which would be very necessary for Indian people.

The equivalence problem which appears to cut across all psychological tests would seem to require some special procedure. One may concentrate on the single society, as Biesheuvel has done for South African populations (1949:87–117; 1952a, 1952b), indicating the various environmental deficiencies or merits which could account for bad or good test performances, and construct specially prepared tests for the particular group. Or one can adopt the experimental procedure Doob (1957–1958) advocated. He compared representative samples of male Africans from three different tribes, the Ganda, Luo, and Zulu, on a battery of tests which included projective techniques. By comparing results on items aimed at the same question he could see that different tests might produce different responses in the same tribe. Among the Ganda, for instance, there were more "human" responses on the Rorschach test than in the projective drawing the subjects made. As Doob states "a single item, therefore, *may* give a misleading impression of a society or it may yield a score different from one secured via another item." On the other hand, this procedure can yield a positive finding. One item which was intended to probe favorable attitudes towards the Europeans was very low among the Zulu on four different tests, indicating unanimity of an item across tests. In this way ambiguous items in any test can be weeded out, and what remains is unequivocal.

THE FINDINGS OF GENERAL PSYCHOLOGY IN CROSS-CULTURAL PERSPECTIVE

The discovery of regularities in the field of general psychology has on the whole been gained from using Western subjects. A simple form of inquiry is merely to find out whether these regularities are substantiated or negated by the study of non-Western peoples, particularly so-called primitive peoples. This intention was doubtless in the minds of the distinguished group of anthropologists and psychologists who composed the Cambridge expedition to the Torres Straits at the turn of the century (Haddon 1901). The expedition entailed the study of the senses, visual illusions, and other perceptual phenomena. River's contribution (1905; Haddon 1901:Vol. 2 Part 1) showed that two of the societies approached were less susceptible to one classic visual illusion and more susceptible to another. This seemed to argue for the influence of environmental factors in perception, and subsequent research has been aimed at studying what modifications of general psychological regularities are imposed by specific cultural conditions. For example, a well-established finding is that of the perception of size constancy. As we see them, objects do not appear to fluctuate in magnitude under differing conditions of perspective and distance to the extent which would be expected if only physiological factors in the retina were to be considered. A man in the near distance still appears to us to be of much the same height as when he

is close. This constancy of perception was labelled by Thouless (1931) as a phenomenal regression to the real object. As the regression is a relative matter, bounded by the real object as one limit and the retinal image as the other limit, it can be asked whether there is not some variation in different cultural populations. Thouless himself found with Indian students, as compared with British students, that the former displayed a high degree of shape constancy (1933), while Beveridge, working with West African college students, showed both a high degree of shape constancy and size constancy (1939). Both related their findings to the prevailing artistic styles of their cultures, which may or may not be the case: the interest for us is that there is undoubted variation in phenomenal regression throughout the world.

A search for differences or similarities is not made merely to form a comprehensive catalogue. What is at the heart of the inquiry is the controversy of nativism versus empiricism. How much of what we see and think can be attributed to the workings *in vitro* of our generically human nervous system and how much is to be attributed to learning and experience in different cultural context, the relative weighting of which will vary from one society to another? Consider a well-established perceptual principle of organization, a Gestalt law known as closure. This is the tendency to complete perceptually a drawing or figure that is actually incomplete. In the experimental situation, if a circle which has a small part of its circumference missing is briefly presented to an observer, the perceiver tends to complete the gap and report the circle as perfect. The Gestalt psychologists presented this demonstration as evidence of existing laws of perception which are governed by factors in the nervous system. As this is a nativistic explanation, it is important to look for exceptions to the general rule, in which case the postulation of innateness would have to be modified. Suitable subjects for testing this principle are the Navaho, since their values reportedly maximize incompleteness. Michael compared white Americans living in New Mexico with adult Navahos, choosing as the task the perception of incomplete circles of varying magnitude, briefly projected (1953). As far as this study is concerned, the results (which showed no difference between the two groups) support the Gestalt position and thus the nativistic viewpoint.

Visual illusions have given cross-cultural psychologists a considerable body of data with which to assess the factors of nativism and empiricism in perception. Over fifty years after Rivers' early study, Segall and his associates carried out a large-scale testing of three types of European cultures (Segall, Campbell, and Herskovits 1963, 1965). Behind this ambitious study was the notion that the varying ecology of peoples' visual world and the varying familiarity or lack of familiarity with straight lines would heavily influence the direction in which each illusion would be perceived. There is little doubt that the results showed that previous habits of perceptual inference tend to influence the perception of space thus portrayed. But there is less agreement as to what exactly these habits may be. Campbell (1964) had outlined the view that people living in such contrasted environments as a desert and a forest, for example, would have visual expectations which would be portrayed when faced with a visual illusion. This ecological hypothesis is partially confirmed in the Segall, Campbell, and Herskovits data, but other studies fail to confirm it, and yet others partially confirm it and partially do not (Jahoda 1965–1966; Gregor and McPherson 1965; Mundy-Castle and Nelson 1962).

A further factor interlinked with ecology is the degree of familiarity with two-dimen-sional representations, which in cultures with little educational background is a rarity. Take, for example, the perception of depth represented in drawings and photographs. People who are accustomed to representation of depth, realize that when a person is shown as small he is not a pigmy but a person of normal height in the background. But what are the facts for people without this familiarity with drawings or photographs?

Some of the ensuing difficulties have been met by investigators who showed movies to people who had never experienced this manner of depiction. Sellers (1941), operating with movies in Nigeria, revealed some interesting points. A vertical "pan" shot of a building conveyed the impression that the building was sinking into the ground. Sellers considered that his audiences focused their eyes flat onto the screen and did not see stereoscopically. While this point was made from good observational inquiry the same feature has been found by a formal experiment. Hudson (1960) contrasted literate and illiterate groups in South Africa in the perception of certain three-dimentional cues such as object size, superimposition, and perspective, using pictorial matter. He demonstrated convincingly that the literate sample more frequently perceived depth in the pictures than did the illiterate sample, and that white subjects in the former sample were more prone to this than black, native subjects. Apparently not a single illiterate saw a photograph as three dimensional. These findings argue for the preponderance of experience and instruction in depth perception.

The diversity of ecological and occupational forms throughout the world entails a source of environmental factors which become manifest in the perceptual area. The Eskimo is said to have about thirty words for snow, indicating a variety of categories where we have only a few; some reindeer-herding peoples have more than two dozen names for the pattern of reindeer hides. The present writer noted that the Tiv of Nigeria gave special examination and different names to the grooves on the lamina of a leaf. The Ga people of West Africa are said to tell by the way a woman places her feet in walking whether she has ever borne a child (Field 1937:147). Classical illusions can be influenced by familiarity with certain kinds of objects. The Muller-Lyer visual illusion consists of two straight lines identical in length, the one affixed by inward-turning arrows, the other by outward-turning arrows. Generally the line with the outward-turning arrows is perceived as longer. It was thought that the reason some native groups in the Torres Straits failed to observe the illusion was the similarity of their spearheads to part of the Muller-Lyer figure. The list of ecological, social, and occupational influences can be multiplied.[1] They serve to show the range of environmental factors which direct, mold, and modify psychological processes. Selectivity of perception due to interest, familiarity, and value is no new finding in experimental psychology; the examples drawn from cross-cultural work provide a variety of — and sometimes novel — instances of this central fact.

Selectivity is not restricted to perception. The process of remembering also contains this feature. The method of serial reproduction, which is used in memory studies, consists in a narrative or passage being passed on from one person to another. Stemming from the classic work by Bartlett, the method allows for the analysis of modification of the verbal matter as it proceeds sequentially (1932). Bartlett found that the background and interests of people involved in telling the subject matter tended to rationalize the material and shape it to their conventional forms of thought. He originally submitted a North American Indian folk story to his Cambridge, England, undergraduates. The different cultural background of these students produced distortions in the narrative sequence which conformed to their interests and expectations. Nadel followed the same procedure with two Nigerian tribes, the Yoruba and the Nupe (1937a). In this case the prevailing art styles of the two tribes were the cultural differentiating factor. The Yoruba have a highly developed imagery in their art and drama, whereas Nupe art concentrates more on spatial and symmetrical arrangements than on the qualities of meaning Yoruba art encourages. Nadel used both story and picture material from the two tribes with school boys up to the age of fifteen to eighteen. In the story experiment one tribe stressed logical and rational elements, while the other made more of situational facts and connections of time and place. In the picture experiment, the two tribes diverged according to their relevant artistic differences — the responses of the one were orientated towards meaning, while the other's responses were in terms of spatial arrangements.

Nadel saw more in this experiment than a simulation of a Bartlett-type experiment (1937b). He argued that the content of a culture changes more rapidly than the psychological organization of the group. He regarded a psychological inquiry such as this with the two Nigerian tribes as an indicator of the way they would react to culture change. He hoped that an analysis of the detailed changes in the account of a story or a picture might tap more complex psychological dispositions such as sentiments, ways of reasoning, and psychological values.

Cultural studies on the process of thinking have been fewer than those on perception and it is only relatively recently that the task has been attacked in any systematic manner. The writings of Levy-Bruhl (1923,

---

[1] These examples (and others) are mentioned in Bruner (1951:135–137), Dennis (1951:150–151), and C. Kluckhohn (1954:931–933).

1926) on the notion of primitive mentality were advanced purely on philosophical suppositions and the observations of older type ethnographers. The study of primitive classification by Durkheim and Mauss was concerned with the linkage of thought with varying social forms (1963). When psychologists first approached this field conventional tests, formulated and standardized with Western subjects, were used. At this point the concepts of abstraction and concreteness of thought became salient frameworks in which to understand the thinking of non-Western peoples. In psychological usage these terms are polar opposites. A concrete attitude means dependency upon an individual object or its context in the environment, an attitude which cannot single out particular properties of an object and manipulate them independently. An abstract attitude is the facility to select any attribute from an object or event and the ability to class it with similar attributes of other objects. Certain tests which involve blocks of varying colors, shapes, and sizes are used to distinguish principles of classifications. These have been used throughout the world. For instance, McConnell used the Kohs Block test with the Tepehuen Indians, and found that they had a marked ability to abstract (1954). Wintringer, working in French North Africa, noticed that there was a heavy reliance on a concrete attitude in the thinking (1955).

The difficulties of achieving a wider framework than that of the abstract-concrete dimension, and of providing experimental material which is less culture-bound than conventional psychological tests, have been partly overcome by applying the type of task established by Piaget (see Flavell 1963 for best summary). Piaget has studied the specific thought processes through which children progress as they reach certain concepts. For instance, he has established the approximate age at which children can es-

tablish the concept of conservation. He found that there was a chronological sequence in which they first relied heavily on perceptual qualities, then advanced to true conceptual ability to realize what was involved in the idea of conservation. The sequence was observed by examining their reactions to liquid being poured from one container into others. With children below the age of seven, approximately, judgment of how much water is in the different containers is heavily influenced by the number of containers used and by their size. Children below this critical age report that there is more liquid in the initial vessel if the level is higher than in the vessels into which the liquid is poured, or that there is more liquid in the receiver containers if they exceed the number of original containers. Only after the age of seven or thereabouts does it occur to the child that the amount of liquid in the containers is a constant quality that does not alter in its various transfers from one set of vessels to another.

This procedure is relatively simple and can be applied from one culture to another. Price-Williams (1961) carried it out with children of the Tiv tribe in Central Nigeria and found a similar sequence of thinking, although the difficulty of establishing exact chronological ages with these children made it difficult to say at what age level the transition from one kind of thinking to another took place. Jacqueline Goodnow (1962) investigated conservation ideas relating to weight, space, and volume in Hong Kong with Chinese children who had only had one or two years of schooling. She found that they did as well on these tasks as educated English children of the same age. However, other investigators using Piaget's tasks in various cultures have observed differences in age levels from those observed in Western society.

Peluffo (1962), working with three different socio-economic classes in Italy, in an age range of eight through eleven, found age differences, from Western children, in conservation ideas relating to physical quantities — substance, weight, and volume — and also to ideas of causality. Similarly, a recent comparative study across Alaska, Senegal, and Mexico using Piaget's tasks (Bruner *et al.,* 1966) has also found such differences.

As with perception, the search for cultural factors that influence cognitive structuring is the important element in all cross-cultural analysis of thinking. Linguistics is one such factor and a whole field of inquiry — ethnolinguistics — has arisen which takes the relationship of thought to language as its target; it is outside the scope of this chapter to give an account of the vast amount of work in this field. Other factors are the degree of education in any culture, the differences between children living in urban milieux with those living in rural settings, and the kind of occupations available. In some cultures there also appear to be sex differences. Using an object-sorting task originally designed by Gardner, Mercado and others found differences in abstraction between Mexican girls and American girls, but little between boys in the two cultures (Mercado *et al.* 1963). As Triandis said in reporting this study in his chapter on cultural influences upon cognitive processes

(Triandis 1964), if it is established that there are cultural influences on cognitive styles then an important new field of inquiry will have been created. The task is to establish what is common to the process of cognition for all cultures, and what specific cultural factors contribute to the differences.

Suggested Readings

The most detailed historical account of the relationship between anthropology and psychology is that of Hallowell (1954), whose book *Culture and Experience* (1955) is further recommended as showing the contribution of psychological analysis to ethnographic reports. The place of perception and cognition generally in anthropological perspective is best reviewed by French (1963), and Triandis (1964). Systematic cross-cultural researches in these fields are best illustrated in the Segall, Campbell, and Herskovits monograph (1965), and in the book published by Professor Jerome Bruner and his associates (1966). The contribution of linguistic methods to cognition is well covered in the special number of the American Anthropologist edited by Romney and D'Andrade (1964).

13

Ethnopsychology II:
Comparative Personality Processes

DOUGLASS R. PRICE-WILLIAMS

Rice University

HISTORICAL

When considering the concept of personality in its social setting, the tendency has been to focus not on the individual person so much as on the typical person in a given milieu. When the typical personality of an American or an Englishman is examined, a generalization is made which allows for a certain statistical distribution. The traditional field of "personality-and-culture" has a perspective which permits this typical instance. If we change our perspective to allow for general statements about human nature, the molding of personality by the various social structures can be ironed out. Similarly, if we focus our attention down to a very refined margin, then everybody is in some ways different from everybody else. The term "personality," both as we use it in everyday life, and as it is used in the technical vocabularies of the professional psychologist, has this range of meaning. When the concept of personality is linked with society, it is thought that institutional forces in some way place a premium on certain personality characteristics so as to form a type, which is special to that institution. To be sure, there may be various kinds of personalities arrayed around a social institution, but amidst the multifarious traits there is one trait or a clump of traits which stands out, either because it is dominant or because it is the most frequent characteristic. The institution may be large or small; it may be a nation or a social class or an occupation or stratum; it may be a small tribe or a small group or a handful of individuals. Whatever the extent of the institution, many people have believed that it is possible to attribute to it the characteristic of a typical personality.

While the contemporary emphasis on personality-and-culture can be traced to anthropological theories in the 1920's and 1930's, theoretical concern with the linkage of character and society can be extrapolated back many centuries. Indeed, a case might be made that it is a special class of the general phenomenon of characterology which dates back to Theophrastus (372–287 B.C.). Literary characterology has in the main been concerned with ethical or moral types and temperamental types. But attention was also paid to the personality or character of social classes, of occupations, and, especially, of nations. The seventeenth-century characterologists showed marked attention to the social scene.[1] John Stephens [1615], for instance, besides illustrating moral types such as "a good husband" or "a contented man," also had pieces on the character of "a jailor," and another on "a farmer." John Earle wrote a small classic called *Microcosmographie* [1628] with the subtitle *A Piece of the World Discovered: In Essays and Characters. Newly Composed for the Northerne Parte of This Kingdome,* and his collection included such social characters as the "Tobacco Seller," "Attorney," "A plodding Student," and a "Plain Country Fellow." Francis Lenton [1631] was more specific in his social reference. He covered such individuals or "typical instances" as "The Low Country Common Soldier," "The Sempster Shopkeeper," and "The Gentleman Usher." What is significant in these contributions is the wandering away from the pure ethical type to the mixed social and moral type. As Boyce comments in his book on these writers:

Hall in his "Good Magistrate," Breton in his "Estates Characters" as well as Overbury, Stephens and Earle, contributed to the shift from moral to social bases of classification, and Lenton was by no means original. What makes his "Sempster Shopkeeper" so effective is not the pretty woman's greed nor her slack morals but her amusing way of appearing in the window among cobweb lawn and delicate needlework to surprise the passer-by into coming inside to do business. It is a delightful little picture of London life . . . (Boyce 1947:262).

A similar trend can be seen in the ascription of character to actual nations.[2] In the sixth edition of the Overbury Collection, I. Cocke [1615] alluded to "A Braggadocio Welshman" as "the oyster that the pearl is in, for a man may be picked out of him. . . . He hath the abilities of the mind *in potentia* and *actu* nothing but boldness. His clothes are in fashion before his body, and he accounts boldness the chiefest virtue." The Character of an Irishman by Edward Ward (1698–1700) indicates a similar trend in satire and generalization: "He is commonly a huge Fellow, with a little Soul; as strong as a Horse, and as silly as an Ass; very poor, and yet proud; lusty, and yet lazy, foolish, but yet knavish; impudent, but yet cowardly; superstitiously devout, yet infamously wicked. . . ."

At this level analysis of national character is a complex amalgam of national sentiments, satire, and what modern psychology would call stereotypes, that is, preconceived beliefs about classes of individuals or groups. As such the imputations are likely to change from time to time. As Ginsberg (1956: 250–251) in his essay on national character and sentiments says, it is difficult to estimate the degree of permanence or stability to alleged national characteristics. Energy is a characteristic now attributed to the English by Continental writers, but in the sixteenth century many other nationalities considered the English as lazy as Spaniards. Personal cleanliness is another facet that has changed over the years: commentators on English life in the fifteenth and sixteenth centuries consistently remarked on the un-

---

[1] An account of the characterologists quoted here is taken mainly from Boyce's book (1947) on the Theophrastian Character.

[2] These examples are taken from Greenough's article (1940) on the "Characters of Nations."

cleanliness of the habits and persons of English people. No doubt it is difficult to ascribe personality aspects to social groups with any degree of consistency over the centuries, since people and groups change. And it is also difficult to subtract subjective biases from an objective state of affairs. It does not follow, though, that social characteristics are a myth. Thoughtful social scientists have concluded that there is something here to be delineated. As Donald Macrae (1961:101) has put it, "in the thirties it was usual to attack such concepts as 'national character' as meaningless, but common experience renders this merely silly. There *are* uniformities of group behavior and outlook between societies and also within them."

The shift from literary characterology and the judgments of historians to the professional social scientist reflected a change in analysis in two directions. One change lay in the language in which social characteristics were framed. Due to the interest of psychologists and psychiatrists in individual types in the nineteenth century a whole new range of terms was available, terms that were technically expressed, such as "extroverted" and "introverted." For example, the anthropologist Seligman (1932) attempted to use these very terms (which Jung [1923] had first made prominent) with the personality characteristics of certain tribes in which he was interested. The second direction of change was that of the level of analysis. The technical nomenclature turned on certain theories to which they were related. These theories, in turn, necessitated certain methods by which to assess them. Hence any ethical or sterotypical overtones were of necessity withdrawn from the analysis; the theory of social and personality characteristics was represented as any other scientific theory might be, with postulates, hypotheses, and evidence. In other words, a scientific attempt was made to see whether there was any truth in the suppositions that

thoughtful impressionistic writers had made over the centuries.

In this scientific attempt two psychological schools made their impact in anthropological spheres. These two schools were responsible for entire programs of research and gave issue to what might be called programmatic theories. Chronologically, the first was psychoanalysis, the second, behaviorism. The contribution of Freud and his followers (and also deviates) has been extensive in ethnopsychology. Classical psychoanalysis and the analytic psychology of Jung have illumined much of folklore, myths, totemism, dreams, and expressive culture generally. A great deal of what could be called the psychoanalytical contribution to psychological anthropology belongs to headings other than personality, for the majority of psychological anthropology studies are in fact underpinned by Freudian theories. We will use two aspects of Freudian notions to show how cross-cultural work is related to them and to explain their application.

In the Huxley Memorial Lecture for 1932 the noted British anthropologist Seligman listed five questions he considered could be answered by aligning anthropological field work with psychoanalytic theories. Two were concerned with the developmental stages postulated by psychoanalysis as crucial determinants of later personality. Subsequently the three primary stages known as the oral, anal, and sexual or phallic stages have been the focus of a considerable body of research. The researches have been either on the developmental side *eo ipse* or planned with the socialization aspect in mind. Certain areas of the world have unusual and often exotic forms of child training which allow a crucial testing ground for Freudian theories of child development. For example, the process of weaning is held to be of marked significance in the life of the infant. Sudden weaning is thought to introduce persistent personality effects. The characteristic of Zulu society to wean suddenly on a day set in advance is the kind of situation that provides a valid setting for inquiry on this point. Albino and Thompson carried out what might be called a short-range project to test the extent of subsequent disturbance (1956). We call it a short-range project to distinguish this study from the more numerous studies which correlate child-training procedures with adult and sometimes institutional traits. Albino and Thompson compared six Zulu infants from a rural neighborhood with ten other Zulu children from an urban environment who had been weaned considerably earlier. The rural group was investigated intensively before, during, and after weaning, and the authors point out that expected traumatic effects on the traditional Zulu child is all the more likely for he is given unlimited access to the mother's breast before the weaning date. It was certainly noticed that there were immediate disturbances in the child's emotional and social life following abrupt weaning, but these tended to clear up over time and the authors felt the experience served a useful social purpose. Specifically, they noticed that the Zulu child became more mature and independent, and that the undoubted aggressiveness that was persistent as a result of the experience was channelled to socially approved ends. A typical cross-cultural child development study such as this investigation has more than one advantage. It enables a check to be made on a specific point of theory; it tells us something about the particular people tested; and it ramifies into quite other subject matters than child development. Many Freudian hypotheses and concepts have an intrinsic generalizing quality which is attractive to varying social customs and odd ways of life that are distributed throughout the planet.

The second aspect of Freudian theory to be discussed, also related to the developmental thesis, is the child's relationship to his parents. Freud maintained, with some dramatic impact to the social thought of the time, that in the early years of life — approximately at the age of five — a boy formed a significant relationship with his mother, which was thought to have effects on the relationship of the boy to his father, and more residually, on his later personality structure. To be more precise, it was held that the young son was erotically attracted to his mother, that the father was regarded as a rival to his affections, and that abnormal fears, inhibitions, and fantasies persisted in the personality structure if the relationship remained fixated. This is the classic Oedipus complex; the complementary relationship of the daughter to the father was labelled the Electra complex. Freud's clinical observations were made in the framework of European people and thus in families which were patriarchal in type. The first cross-cultural dissent came from the fieldwork of Malinowski (1927:80–82) who was able to show in the matrilineal Trobriand Islanders that whereas friction certainly developed in the family, it was with the mother's brother (the *pater* in sociological usage) that the boy became hostile. The social distinction of *genitor* and *pater* does not become clear in European society, for with the exception of stepfathers, they are one and the same person. The Trobriand example steers the Freudian conception of the Oedipal situation away from the biological instinct viewpoint in which it was couched towards a more social structural orientation. What has come to be known as neo-Freudianism, with its exponents such as Kardiner, Horney, and Fromm, has long since followed up the implications of this finding. Cross-cultural checks of the Trobriand Islanders kind are necessary to counter the error of overgeneralizations.

The Oedipus relationship is associated with a number of specific customs. These include, for example, the degree of incestuous prohibitions, menstrual taboos, type of kin avoidance, and presence or absence of initiation ceremonies for boys at puberty. Recently Stephens has compiled the evidence on the comparative distribution of these customs by adopting a nomothetic approach with the use of the data in the Human Relations Area Files (1962). He was able to demonstrate correlations as follows: the duration of postpartum sex taboo was correlated with the presence or absence of initiations for adolescent boys, with severity of mother-in-law avoidance, and with the extensiveness of menstrual taboos. The extensiveness of the latter in its turn was connected with a number of other variables such as whether or not the father was a severe disciplinarian. From first principles Stephens put forward sixteen predicted correlations; nine turned out to be significant and only one was in the negative direction. From such correlational evidence Stephens felt that there was left only a small margin of doubt concerning the world-wide distribution of the Oedipal complex, though he was careful to state that none of the correlations directly showed the direction of causality.

The second theoretical school is behaviorism. The concepts of behavioristic psychology have their root in animal behavior with the emphasis on learning mechanisms. The fruits of behaviorism, however, have flowered in most branches of psychology, personality and social included. Insofar as psychological anthropology is concerned, the effect of behaviorism is not so much in forming precise theories which can be tested by ethnographic data as in the application of new conceptual frameworks which help to clarify data already obtained or to suggest fresh ways of looking at new data. Many behavioristic concepts are focused on the learning mechanisms of habits and their production and extinction. Very early in the game, Malinowski recognized the value of this line of inquiry when he argued that the extinction

of learned habits through lack of reinforcement was a fundamental law at the root of the growth and change of human institutions, which he felt had to satisfy basic needs or disappear (1944:142). In this passage there are two concepts which are deeply rooted in learning theory language. These are needs and reinforcement. Many learning theorists have taken as their fundamental framework a cyclical sequence of stimulus and response units; the initial step is a basic human need, either innate (like hunger or thirst) or acquired (like prestige or economic gain). Steps further taken to act on the impetus of a need result in a drive which propels a person towards a goal which is considered to satisfy the initial need and reduce the tension which has been aroused. Goal satisfaction or dissatisfaction serve to act as a reinforcement or nonreinforcement to the drive and the habits associated with it.

Although behavioristic notions have not been applied in cross-cultural research as extensively as psychoanalytic ideas, there is evidence in the literature that they have been considered. Anxiety is counted as an acquired drive by learning theorists, and some social scientists have not been slow in recognizing that this particular drive is very relevant to anthropological data. In 1942 Gillin showed how conditions of change in a culture would result in anxiety which in turn would lead to new forms of acquired drives. He had in mind such disturbances as the increase or decrease of population, reductions in the numbers of one sex, and the failure of methods of exploitation of the natural environment. Re-adaptation to the disturbed state of affairs, it was argued, leads to new drives with perhaps new goals. That there are varying cultural preferences for reinforcement was noted by Mischel in a Trinadadian study, in which the tendency for delayed reinforcement there was linked with personality characteristics (1958). That some people insist on immediate gains or reinforcement for their labors while others are ready to wait for larger rewards is perhaps a casual observation; what must be searched for is institutional pressures encouraging one or the other. This feature of habit formation may not so much be best analyzed on a cultural level as on some other dimension which cuts across it. The caution comes from a project on Arab refugee children by Melikian, who certainly found a tendency for delayed reinforcement, but it went with the more intelligent children who were the subjects of the experiment (1959). They preferred to wait for a larger monetary reward for a simple drawing, rather than a lower immediate reward, in contrast to the less intelligent children.

One of the most conscious applications of learning theory principles to ethnographic data comes from LeVine's extension of stimulus generalization (1960). The principle states that the more a new stimulus is perceived as being similar to an older stimulus which was linked with a response, the greater is the similarity of the response elicited by the new stimulus. One sees this in fear reactions caused by artificial means on the old Watsonian conditioning model. By presenting a white rabbit together with a loud noise a child can be frightened when the white rabbit is displayed without the associated noise. The stimulus however generates a gradient of response. Similar fear reactions can be elicited by anything which resembles something furry and white, to tail off gradually as the new stimulus becomes less identical with the initial white rabbit. Now in non-Western cultures ethnographic reports have commonly reported that the family idiom is extended to political relationships, a feature not observed in more complex societies. LeVine shows that the intervening link consists of an extension of attitudes which are initially associated with family relationships and which are then paired with political units. In other words, the family idiom expressed basic orientations of value which in turn influence political processes. Evidence from a number of societies is given in LeVine's article, but the intention is largely programmatic, provided to demonstrate the utility of a behavioristic concept to anthropological data.

CONCEPTS OF PERSONALITY

The field of personality-and-culture has dealt with a particular segment of personality. For proper perspective on this segment it is necessary to delve into the concept of personality as it has been regarded both by psychologists and by personality-and-culture theorists. There is a bewildering plurality of definitions of personality. Allport (1937) in his classic volume on personality listed at least fifty different definitions and we might now consider this an underestimate. It is probably fruitless to try and pin down a definition in the same manner as we might pin down a botanical definition. Hall and Lindzey are probably correct when they state that "no substantive definition of personality can be applied with any generality" (1957:9). They propose that "personality is defined by the particular empirical concepts which are a part of the theory of personality employed by the observer" (1957:9). In this chapter we should notice, first, that psychologists on the whole tend to frame their concepts of personality abstracted from the context of society (which does not necessarily mean that they lean on the biological side); second, that they tend to posit their definitions in terms of abstractions and generalizations; and, third, that they educe their generalizations from the first-hand evidence of individuals. Gardner Murphy provides (1947:3–9) a useful method of considering ways to represent personality by postulating three levels of complexity. At the first level, we can regard personality without respect to internal structure. We may think of it just as individual differences: merely contrasting this person with that person, men with women, Chinese with Japanese. The second level now takes into account the internal organization of people. Parts or attributes of a person are defined which are specifically interrelated. The third level takes into account the environment; organization within the organism is considered in relationship with organization outside the organism. At this third level the majority of personality-and-culture theories start.

How to define the organization within the organism or individual is the crucial question. It must be recognized initially that all personality definitions and constructs are inferred from an individual's actual behavior. When we talk of personality structure we have made an inferential step from observing how a person performs in a variety of situations. We construct a scheme or model which spells out in detail how we think personality is organized, then apply the scheme to the actual performance of the individual or groups of individuals. In this inferential process two terms have become important: "trait" and "type." A trait has been defined by Cattell (1946) as "a collection of reactions or responses bound by some kind of unity which permits the responses to be gathered under one term and treated in the same fashion for most purposes." Guildford (1959) has defined a trait as "any distinguishable relatively enduring way in which one individual differs from others." Whereas the theory of traits has been applied to behaviors, the theory of types has applied to the classification of individuals. For example, Freud (1925) and later Abraham (1927) classified individuals by reference to characteristics linked with early infantile experience. The "oral type," for instance, is an individual whose character has been generated by a demand for the reinstatement of the full mothering experience. The contrasting terms "introvert" and "extrovert" differ in the basic orientation of individuals to the world about them. Traits can

be related to types through some theoretical model: Eysenck (1953), for example, regards types as higher order contructs than traits, several different traits being assimilated under a type.

Whatever theoretical frame of reference is used, the techniques of assessing its validity is the same: the study of individuals through questionnaires, interviews, experimental procedures, and tests. The validity of the theory turns on the degree of assessment the particular battery of tests gives.

As noted above, concepts of personality-and-culture begin at the level of interaction with the environment. They are postulated to explain differences of individuals who exist in different cultures. One of the big differences between personality-and-culture concepts and those of psychology proper is the source of inference. Whereas the latter has come from the study of individuals, the source of the former has mainly been institutions, or institutional behaviors. There are several varieties of personality-and-culture concepts. All share the assumption that every culture has a typical personality which is characteristic of that culture, although the meaning of the word "typical" varies from one theoretical approach to another. Singer (1961) distinguishes four varieties: Basic Personality Structure, Modal Personality, Configurational Personality, and National Character. We will take each of these in turn.

Basic Personality Structure

This was a theory originally propounded by Abram Kardiner (1939, 1945) and supported by Ralph Linton (1945). It maintains the following points. First, a distinction is made between primary and secondary institutions. Primary institutions include such matters as family organization, subsistence techniques, and, particularly, child-rearing practices. Secondary institutions include such areas as mythology, art, folklore, and religion. A causal sequence is implied in that the constellations of the primary institutions find their expression in the secondary institutions. Such constellations are postulated to be unconscious in the individuals of the culture studied. A hypothetical construct called the Basic Personality Structure is defined, and is said to mediate between the two institutions. It is presented as an explanatory construct to explain these unconscious constellations. Thus we have the sequence: Primary Institutions (mainly child-rearing practices), Basic Personality Structure, Secondary Institutions. It is thought, under this scheme, that once a set of nuclear trends could be identified as exemplifying the Basic Personality Structure, then a connection was established to bridge the earlier personality influenced by the primary institutions and the later personality manifested in the secondary institutions. We have here a personality explanation of behavior involved in social institutions early in an individual's life. Continuity between the two behaviors is explained by this inferential step of a kind of personality structure.

Modal Personality

This concept was first introduced by Cora Du Bois in her book on the people of Alor (Du Bois 1944). Here the statistical term "mode" was amplified to mean that an examination of various individuals who share a common culture would reveal a common set of personality characteristics. Although in any given culture there is obviously a wide range of personality structures, there is enough of a central tendency to justify talking of a "typical" personality. Singer (1961) has pointed out that modal personality is implicit in the other concept of Basic Personality Structure, but the former emerges as an explicit concept when there are psychological data on *individuals* to be considered. In other words, whereas the idea of a Basic Personality Structure infers personality through

social institutions, modal personality is inferred through specific observations or tests on actual individuals.

Configurational Personality

Ruth Benedict's book *Patterns of Culture* (1934) established the notion of a configurational personality which occurs in different cultures. By this term she meant that, although in any given culture there would be a variety of individual temperaments, nevertheless there would be a dominant set of characteristics which would be encouraged by the pressures of the society. This dominant set would be regarded as normal by the members of the society and any departure from it would be considered as abnormal or deviant. Such a dominant personality type, or configurational personality, was not necessarily related to individuals as such but rather to the ethos or value system of the culture. Benedict spoke of large collections of individuals — that is, cultures — as exemplifying types. In her earlier writing Nietzsche's classical distinction of Apollonian and Dionysian types are attributed to the Zuni and Plains Indians groups respectively. In her later writings psychiatric typologies are used: the Dobu are "paranoid" and the Kwakiutl are "megalomaniac paranoid" types. It must be noted that these terms apply to the cultural productions of people — ceremonies, songs, war practice, and social and economic organizations — there is no reference to documentation of, or observational studies and psychological tests on, individuals. The notion of a configurational personality is an impressionistic one, originating in a psychological analysis of social institutions expressed in terms of personality characteristics.

National Character

The idea that a specific culture gives rise to a distinct personality reaches a logical conclusion in the thesis that a specific character can be affixed to a nation. As a matter of fact, as many different characters can be referred to as many different social units as one may think relevant. Singer (1961) classifies cultural character, social character, tribal character, and even the personality of small groups. The notion of national character singles out specific nations as the social index. As already observed, the idea that different characteristics of temperament can be attributed to national groups antedates professional psychology by several centuries (see Pearson 1896; Barker 1927). The innovations that psychologists and anthropologists made in the subject, apart from techniques, stemmed from theoretical notions. A segment of these theories came from psychoanalysis with its thesis of personality determinancy in the first few years of life. Thus Gorer, one of the main modern advocates of the national character approach, discusses modern Japanese character in the perspective of early child-rearing practices in that country (Gorer 1943).

Whereas the preceding concepts of personality are linked to relatively large-scale units such as cultures, nations, or entire societies, other personality concepts are allied to particular parts of a society. In their definitive chapter on the study of modal personality and sociocultural systems, Inkeles and Levinson (1954:1006–1007) have enumerated occupational roles and political structure. The ordering of institutions for this purpose depends largely upon how one wishes to cut up the institutional cake. In their book, *Character and Social Structure,* Gerth and Mills (1953) outlined five orders of institution: the kinship order; the religious order; the political order; the military order; and the economic order, with all of which character can be associated. This classification harks back to Spranger's six types of men (1928), the theoretical, the economic, the esthetic, the social, the political, and the religious. Subdivisions of large units become more salient as the social structure becomes increasingly heterogeneous, with marked boundaries of political and social life. As subcultures arise, it becomes possible to identify certain personality traits which are increased by the values pertaining to the subculture. Indeed, it becomes possible to identify different value systems, even to streets which geographically may be very close to one another (see University of Nottingham 1954). A novel by Arthur Morrison, first printed in 1896 (1946 ed.), gives a good descriptive picture of street-values in Shoreditch, London. There are also social divisions which cut across country and state by virtue of an attitude or equivalent position in society. For example, Elkins can write persuasively (1961:243–267) of slavery and personality, bringing together such different kinds of people as the Negroes imported from Africa to the New World, and the victims of concentration camps under the Nazis. Again, it is possible to view characteristics right across societal systems and attempt to link personality with industrial life as against rural life (see Inkeles and Levinson 1954: 1007), or with political modes of thought, as in the case of the authoritarian personality (Adorno *et al.* 1950). Such definitions, various as they are, work into the concept of personality such factors as attitudes, role behavior, values, and temperament. What then becomes crucial in assessing the part that society plays in the individual person is the method of assessment itself. These methods operate at different levels, from the analysis of cultural productions such as folk tales, to detailed analysis of actual persons. Talking about comparative personality processes therefore requires a close watch on the methodology involved.

METHODS OF CROSS-CULTURAL PERSONALITY ASSESSMENT

Practically all cross-cultural personality studies can be referred to by invoking three dimensions of method: first, the question of the target of inquiry — simply, what or who should be studied; second, the question of design: given the choice of a subject of study, how should the study be done; third, the choice of instruments.

It might be supposed that if the area of study is personality then there would be no question of target choice; one would obviously analyze the personality structure of individuals. However, many studies have focused not on the specific individual but rather on the cultural productions of individuals, such as folklore, myths, ritual, and values. This was the approach of the early pioneering works in the personality and culture field. For example, Ruth Benedict's analysis of three societies, Pueblo, Dobu, and Kwakiutl (Benedict 1934) is at the level of the set of values these peoples entertain, which might further be described as a world-view. However, the world-view is not inferred from specific members of this society; it is inferred from their ceremonial habits, such as religious dances and initiation rites at puberty. What Benedict was concerned about with these particular groups was an abstracted idealized image, represented in terms of a typology borrowed from Nietzsche, as noted before. Contrasting types were taken from Nietzsche's distinction of the Dionysian and the Apollonian values of existence. The Dionysian mode seeks to escape from the bounds of existence limited by the five senses into a world of ecstatic experience. The Apollonian way of life is the exact opposite; it adheres to the common round of mundane existence, distrusting mystical experiences. Extending from a general world-view certain temperamental differences were put forward. Apollonian features are seen as gentleness and submission, Dionysian features are characterized as harshness and cruelty. In Benedict's analysis the Pueblo Indians are seen as idealized Apollonian types and the Kwakiutl as Dionysian types. The evidence from

which this typology is drawn turns on an impressionistic analysis of religious ceremonies, inferences from homicide and suicide rates, the role of punishment in child training, and attitude to drinking of liquor. For example, among the Kwakiutl there is a series of religious rites, called the Winter Ceremonial, in which frenzy and fasting are marked characteristics in the principal actors. In the same society there is another dramatic ritual, called the initiation of the Cannibal Dancer, in which biting of onlookers, carrying of corpses, and apparent uncontrolled behavior by the main dancers are characteristic events. Whether or not these events are realistic or merely mock simulations (see Barnouw 1963:50–51 for a discussion of this point), the thematic characterizations which are salient in the ceremonies are taken by Benedict as indicating a certain kind of value system, which she called Dionysian. Similarly, examples of self-torture, fasting, and the use of various drugs like peyote and alcohol are seen as further exemplifying this mode of existence. In contrast, the Apollonian nature of the Zuni Indians is inferred from the strong disapproval of drinking, from the comparative lack of harsh punishment by Zuni parents and elders, and from the relative lack of suicides. It is important to note again from the point of view of method that in *Patterns of Culture* there are no life histories of individuals, indeed, no investigations of individuals as such. The value system is drawn from such behavioral events as illustrated above. The concern is with the concept of ethos, which is interpreted variously by different authorities (see Gould and Kolb 1964: 246–247 for definitions), but which definitely includes the values of a culture.

The question of ethos crops up in the psychological and cultural analysis of recurring themes which can be observed in some societies. For example, Bateson and Mead (1942) drew attention to a recurring theme or "plot" in Balinese life which plays on the notion of a seductive female arousing a responsive male, only to dash his hopes at the last moment. This notion is dramatized in ceremonial dances, can be seen in adult heterosexual situations, and plays an important part in mother-child relationships. Obviously, then, the theme would seem to be integral to the Balinese outlook on life. From this one is tempted to invoke certain personality characteristics among the Balinese generally, in keeping with the recurrent plot. Such an approach assumes that the involvement of individuals in certain kinds of interpersonal situations and ceremonial events indicates that personality traits inferred from the latter are identical with personality traits in the individual. If, for example, anxiety is a theme which runs through many cultural productions of a society, it is expected that anxiety is also present in the individuals of that society. However, as Inkeles and Levinson have properly pointed out in their discussion of collective behavior (1954:996), a theme or plot, while an undoubted psychocultural characteristic, is not itself a personality characteristic. It can only be regarded as reflecting personality trends. If, then, the analysis of cultural productions and values can only result in an inference about personality, it would seem that direct attention should be paid to individuals as such.

A determined effort to relate observational material by way of standard ethnographic field work with actual studies of individuals has been the hallmark of those researches which come under the heading of modal personality. Cora Du Bois' pioneer work among the Alorese in Indonesia (Du Bois 1944) included the application of psychological tests to individuals, observations on child-rearing systems, and analysis of the social and economic system. Specifically, thirty-seven Rorschach tests were given, fifty-five subjects were given the Porteus maze test, thirty-six individual Alorese were given word association tests, and fifty-five boys and girls were asked to make drawings. The total number of individuals thus tested may represent only a very small fraction of the total population; nevertheless, the conclusions drawn about the population at large could at least justifiably be defended in that they did not rely on ethos or analysis of the social structure alone. In addition to these tests, eight long autobiographies were collected and submitted to independent analysis. It was clearly recognized that there would be individual variation in the results of the tests; but it was also recognized that there would be a central tendency effect, which indeed gives the name to this theory. From the interrelations of these various methods, both from the macroscopic view of the culture at large and the microscopic analysis of the people making up that culture, a synoptic viewpoint is reached which represents a typical Alorese personality.

In a true modal personality study the issue of sampling is extremely important. Gladwin (Gladwin and Sarason 1953) attempted to lay a foundation for sampling by devising a previous rating of the islanders of Truk through a random selection of five males and five females. These ten people were asked to rate all other people on the island on a four-point scale of like to dislike. Then, from this, entire population extremes of liked and disliked were selected together with a middle range, culminating in a total sampling of twenty-three subjects who were assumed to represent the typical Truk personality. Each of these Truk men and women were then given two projective techniques. The "blind" analysis of these tests was matched against an anthropological description based upon standard ethnographic data.

Adequate sampling of course depends upon many factors; the extent of the total population is not the only one. In the Truk study over 13 per cent of adult males and over 14 per cent of adult females were taken. From the point of view of actual labor and time involved, from sheer practical considerations, it is clearly easier to gather sufficient psychological data when the total population is relatively small. This was the case with the Tuscarora Indians which Anthony Wallace took as his modal personality target (Wallace 1952). Yet even when the total population is small, difficulties of sampling for a modal personality remain. Wallace applied the Rorschach test to seventy people, and by using a special statistical technique, abstracted from the various categories involved in the Rorschach test, a modal range or class. He found out that 37 per cent of his sample fell into this class, representing the largest single type of a group of personality characteristics. Naturally the majority of the population still remained to be considered. Apparently a further 23 per cent of his sample could be considered as clustering about the modal type, although not be fully included in the modal range. There still remained 40 per cent which could fit neither of these categories. The question of a genuine modal type, then, seems more difficult to establish than it would at first appear. However, there did seem to be a good congruence in the Tuscarora study, between the cultural observations and the psychological data.

Whether attention is directed to the cultural products of individuals, to the nature of individuals themselves, or to the way in which the two are related, there remains the problem of the framework or design in which this is done. There are three types of design: longitudinal studies, cross-sectional studies, and correlational studies. Tracing the history of an individual from infancy to puberty, say, would have enormous value in an area of study in which the central thesis is that the early years of the child are linked with the later cultural life of the individual. Perhaps due merely to pragmatic difficulties, longitudinal studies of this kind have been scarce in the personality-and-culture field; the majority of investigations have used the other

two types of design. Cross-sectional merely means that an individual is inspected at some specific point in place and time and inferences about him are extrapolated, either to the past or to the future. In the history of personality-and-culture researches, cross-sectional studies of individuals have been linked with the correlational design. In this combination the emphasis fell heavily on the observation of child-rearing techniques. This was especially salient in the approach of the supporters of the idea of a basic personality structure. This is because child-rearing methods are thought to produce those kinds of personality characteristics which make up what Kardiner called secondary institutions (Kardiner 1939). We will later discuss more fully the Freudian hypotheses about child-rearing which have had important implications in anthropology; here it will be noted that the kinds of observations Kardiner and others of the basic personality structure orientation used were those relating to the postulated stages of early life: weaning, toilet training, and sexual experiences. The emphasis in this theoretical framework is, as in configurational theory, towards collective representations of people and away from specific individuals. However, basic personality theory centers on the interpersonal aspect; mainly the particular relationship between the child and its parents. What is being searched for in these child-parent relationships, and later in attitudes expressed in folklore and religious beliefs, is precisely a syndrome of attitudes or what older psychologists would have called sentiments. The method is basically observational; only the observations are narrowed to a common strand of correlations.

Quite similar methods have been employed by some writers on national character. The best example is that of Geoffrey Gorer (Gorer 1943) in his analysis of the Japanese national character. The apparent Japanese concern with ritual and tidiness is linked with the severity of Japanese toilet training. Again the observational practices follow the same line as that of the basic personality school. Certain forms of compulsiveness and attention to meticulous detail were observed in ceremonial activity and in everyday activity. However, it is very important to notice that the word "observed" in this sentence refers to studies made from Japanese books, movies, and journals. Japanese living in the United States were interviewed, but as it was war-time when this first report was issued, there was no first-hand observation of people living in Japan. What emerges is a kind of content analysis of Japanese material from which is drawn a portrait of the average Japanese character. Nevertheless, the linkage between early childhood training and institutional activity is the same as that of the Kardiner approach. Gorer also made inquiries into the Russian national character (or at least into those people who occupied a geographical region called Great Russia) where actual interviews were made (Gorer and Rickman 1950). Again there is postulated a linkage between early childhood disciplines and later adult characteristics. In this case the Great Russian habit of tightly swaddling infants, thereby inhibiting their motor activity, is said to be a determinant of the swings of extreme mood, from depression to elation, which is thought to be characteristic of these people. Despite the interviews cited, the method seems to fall back upon observations (either at first-hand in the field or second-hand from analysis of novels and the like) of collective actions.

The third dimension of method to be considered concerns the nature of the instrument used. In many cases it has simply been that of controlled observation. However, certain actual techniques have been commonly employed by workers in this field. The most used tool is the projective test. The general form of this test is such that the material presented is relatively ambiguous or un-structured, so that the perceiver introduces traits of his own personality into his judgment of material. While there are a number of projective techniques which clinical psychologists have used for many years, two have been most used in the personality-and-culture field, the Rorschach ink-blot test and the Thematic Apperception test. In 1961 Kaplan calculated that there had been as many as 150 studies using projective techniques in more than seventy-five societies. From an ethnographical point of view, projective techniques have a real pragmatic advantage. They are simple to administer and need only the simplest instructions. The Rorschach instructions tell the subject to report what he sees in the ink-blots; in the Thematic Apperception test (T.A.T.) subjects are asked to tell a story about the figures or scenes they see. The difficulty about these tests does not lie in their administration, it is in evaluating the results.

To review this evaluation would require considerable more space than allowed for in this chapter. Lindzey has devoted an entire book to this task. In the final chapter of his book concerning the contribution of projective techniques to anthropological research, he draws certain conclusions; he mentions the following (Lindzey 1961: 311–312):

First of all, there appears to be enormous variation in personality even within apparently homogeneous, nonliterate societies. This finding points to the difficulty of formulating a clear one-to-one relationship between the individual and his culture, which is implicitly assumed in so many personality-and-culture theories. Second, varying levels of acculturation are accompanied by varying personality attributes. Third, individuals representative of different socialization practices and different cultural backgrounds respond differently to most projective techniques. As Lindzey goes on to state, these differences can also be found in subcultural or within-culture groupings. This group of findings narrows down the sociological unit with which personality is considered to be allied, and perhaps re-directs the relationship to social structure as distinct from the broad category of culture. Fourth, a more tentative conclusion is that personality inferences based upon projective techniques appear to be consistent with parallel inferences derived from ordinary field-work methods. This is a reassuring finding, if the tentative evidence strengthens into more solid evidence, as otherwise the projective techniques, when used in the field, would always be suspect. Indeed there has always been some degree of doubt about projective techniques in this respect. In his review of the cross-cultural use of these techniques, published at the same time as Lindzey's book, Bert Kaplan concluded that only a modicum of validity and value can be obtained from their use (Kaplan 1961:252). What seems unmistakable is that considerable more attention needs to be paid to the methodological implications involved in the application of these techniques, a point both Lindzey and Kaplan pay close attention to in their reviews.

In his account of the differences between European and American theories of personality Gordon Allport (Allport 1957:3–24) has commented on the different philosophical traditions which have appeared to influence the theorist from these different cultures. He pointed out that continental theories have tended to focus on the whole man, while Anglo-American theories have been more often concerned with parts of the whole, that is, with traits, syndromes, factors, or performances. This is reflected in methods used, so that continental theories of personality are more apt to use such techniques as biographies or life histories. Although it may not have been due to continental influence, anthropological incursions into personality certainly appear to have been influenced by the whole man approach, and we find that life history material is another important instrument in the battery of measures used. Sometimes such material is presented at the purely descriptive and informative level, and one is presented with autobiographies written or dictated by informants; *Sun Chief, the Autobiography of a Hopi Indian,* edited by Leo Simmons (1942) represents a classic example. There are also attempts to go beyond the purely descriptive level to an analytic interpretation. The Leightons' interpretation of the life history of Gregorio, the Hand Trembler, which is an account of a personality study of a Navaho Indian (Leighton and Leighton 1949), shows how this can be done. The uses of personal documents such as life histories are extremely interesting and provide the reader with an intimate "inside" picture of the people depicted. However, there are vast methodological difficulties involved in using such methods, which have been well discussed in Allport's "The Use of Personal Documents in Psychological Science," and again in Gottschalk, Kluckhohn, and Angell's "The Use of Personal Documents in History, Anthropology, and Sociology" (Allport 1942; Gottschalk, Kluckhohn, and Angell 1945). As far as the study of personality-and-culture is concerned, the prime consideration is to what extent the narrator is representative of the culture he belongs to. It might be supposed that the kind of person who is prepared to give an account of his life to an ethnographer in the first place is already somebody special, as it were, and may not prove to be in any sense typical of his community. As with projective techniques, the validity of life histories turns on the use to which they are put; the issue lies again in the inferences that one draws from them. As descriptive commentaries, as is the case of the edited tape-recordings of a Mexican family in Oscar Lewis' "The Children of Sanchez," life-histories are an important research tool (1959).

SOCIAL PSYCHOLOGY AND PERSONALITY PROCESSES

Socialization

The dividing-line between general and social psychology is not sharply demarcated and systematic positions like those already briefly outlined, namely, psychoanalysis and behaviorism, could just as well have been included under the heading of social psychology. Indeed, psychoanalysis in particular has often been considered as an inverted social psychology, and many of the behavioristic concepts have been just as applicable in the sphere of interpersonal relations as in individual reactions.

As traditionally treated, the process of socialization has been analyzed with help from both psychoanalytic categories and those from behavior theory. There is no rule concerning what particular category should be taken for tracing developments from early childhood to adult life, and the literature reveals a plurality of behavior: oral behavior, excretory behavior, sexual behavior, aggression, dependence, and achievement (Child 1954:655–692). Many socialization analyses have been content to rely on correlational designs. These have been of two kinds: childhood behavior has been correlated with certain kinds of institutional features, folk stories for instance; and childhood behavior has been correlated with traits in adults of the same society discovered by projective techniques or questionnaires. The simple connection between antecedent and consequent insinuated by correlational designs is made more complex by considerations of the duration, age limits, and severity of the system in mind. Conclusions are then based on the qualification of the system investigated.

Whiting and Child (1953) established a highly significant correlation between severity of weaning and the presence of explanations of illness which were attributed to oral

activities by the peoples concerned. Many other correlations have been established. Nevertheless, evaluations of the validity of the persistence of childhood systems have not been encouraging (Orlansky 1949; Child 1954:661–677). There appears to be more success when so-called projective systems such as folktales, beliefs about supernaturals, and beliefs about causation in illness, are taken as the consequent, than when traits in actual adult individuals are chosen. In a correlational design, of course, there is no necessary indication as to causation; a *tertium quid* may be involved.

A proper disentanglement of any socialization system should call for longitudinal researches, but this is rarely found in cross-cultural work. More detailed concentration on one socializing system in a single society sometimes avoids the gross level of abstraction which has to be made by a nomothetic correlational approach, and may pick up interior differences the latter overlooks. Tracing the dependency system in Java, Danziger (1960:65–74; 75–86) found that within the same society there was more than one attitude towards bringing up children and more than one attitude as to how they should be trained for independence. He noted that there were in fact two typical patterns of parent-child relationship. One derived from Western middle-class culture which looks upon the child as a separate individual with its own rights, and the other resembled the traditional Javanese attitude which treats the child as part of a social collectivity. The two patterns also differed vis-à-vis their expectations on the age at which the child should fend for himself, that is, independence training. As might be expected, the professional group of Javanese society chose a lower age than did the working-class group for requiring independence of their children, while the Javanese middle-class group adopted an intermediate age.

Danziger's studies are relevant to the

point that many psychological variables are better related to socio-economic levels within the same society, a point made earlier by Malinowski (1927). To have talked about Javanese child-training attitudes in general would have been insufficient, for this dependency system at least. This kind of variation is what we find in our own culture and what will, no doubt, invariably be found in any society with pronounced socio-economic strata or classes. Perhaps one of the most valuable lessons cross-cultural socialization studies brings is the fantastic contrast throughout the world, so that we are able to regard our own socializing agents through fresh categories and with proper perspective.

Values

What the child has to be trained for and the severity or laxity with which it is done depends in the final analysis upon the values which are held to be important in the community. Thus, as Ruth Benedict cites in her example from the Papago of Arizona, the responsibility of a definite status role is laid down very early in this society and, as she again points out, sex roles in societies as wide apart as the Dakota and the Marquesas are early indoctrinated according to the varied values the two communities hold on sexual matters (1955:21–30).

Values from the psychological point of view are regarded on a continuum from specific goal-states to a somewhat nebulous ethos. In the explanatory machinery of social psychology, values are theoretically linked with attitudes, on the one hand, and norms, on the other. When attention is turned to the mechanism of attitudes, we are led back to habit formation and the socialization process. When a particular attitude is inspected in terms of its associated goal-state, the study of values for their own sake is emphasized. At its most superficial level the study of values merely acknowledges the

cultural diversity of goal-states and their motivational determinants. Varying evaluations placed on the role of competition, on co-operation, on the place of sexual behavior in society, and on approved expressions of aggression are simply noted throughout different societies. These values are very often no more than descriptive categories taken from the communities' overt behavior. When descriptive categories of value are taken as the starting-point their diversity is truly overwhelming, and cultural relativism the rule. A step towards placing some order in this diversity is taken when the numerous values are themselves classified under some principle of division, in other words, when we turn from descriptive to explanatory categories. The contribution of Florence Kluckhohn is on this scale (1956b). Her basic assumptions are that there is a limited number of fundamental human problems that all peoples at all times and in all places have had to solve; and that while the solutions have undoubtedly varied, they have done so only within a range of possible variations. The dimensions which she selects as basic to human nature are fivefold: peoples' view of human nature; their view of man's relationship to nature; the valuation they place on time; their preferred activity orientation; and the dominant modality of man's relationship with other men.

An empirical application of these five dimensions was worked out as part of the huge Values Project sponsored by the Department of Social Relations at Harvard University. The area undertaken for detailed working-out of values was a small ecological zone in New Mexico in which there exist five very different communities: a settlement of Navaho Indians; the Pueblo Indian village of Zuni; a Spanish-American village; a Mormon community; and a recently established farming village composed of Texas and Oklahoma homesteaders (F. Kluckhohn and Strodbeck 1961). To give some idea of the variations anticipated within the dimensions, let us take the third — the valuation placed on time. It is really time orientation that is the important point, whether a man looks to the past, the present, or future for his anchoring point. As the authors state by way of example, preferences for varied temporal focus have always existed. Historical China had the past as a first-order value preference; Spanish-Americans heed little of either the past or the future but pay attention to what is occurring at the moment; Americans look to the future. The research instrument in the New Mexico project consisted of items directed to economic-occupational, religious, recreational, and intellectual-aesthetic fields. Within their fields the importance of time orientation could be given a hierarchy of preferences, and then generalized for the whole community so that between-cultures differences were made.

Results of this study showed that the Spanish-American people orient themselves, as expected, in the present, but regard the future with higher preference than the past (on religious items the order is a little different — the past was relegated to second position). The Texas and Mormon communities display a slightly different pattern: they equate the future and the present in that no significant difference was found between these time orientations and the past is evaluated last (Kluckhohn and Strodtbeck 1961: 351). The present also comes first in precedence in the two remaining communities, Zuni and Navaho, and the future last, but in the case of the Zuni there was no significant difference between the present and the past, and with the Navaho none between the past and the future. In this way constellations of human values can be identified within a fine pattern of possible arrangements. In the past, psychological studies of values in cross-cultural work have centered on the dominant ethos which is thought to identify and characterize a society. This new approach enables the student to inspect variations both within a society and between societies and to group common patterns of value where they exist.

Acculturation

Advancement of communication in our present civilization inevitably means that isolated cultures are forced to reconcile themselves with new social and economic systems, fresh methods of technology, and shifting systems of value. In traditional psychology there has been no little attention paid to the problems of resistance to change and the difficulties involved in the formation of new habits. With respect to acculturation both problems are in the forefront, except for the fact that the scale of magnitude of the problems has changed from the individual to a whole mass of people and institutional factors have entered the picture. The function of the psychologist in attempting to grapple with elements of acculturation is to select particular modes of behavior within the setting of a social context, then to hypothesize and test assumptions taken from general or social psychology concerning the effects of interaction. An illustration is taken from three African societies, the Ganda, Luo, and Zulu (Doob 1957). The realms of behavior were those of education and leadership, within which psychological mechanisms of frustration and aggression are treated. The hypothesis is adopted that people with relatively greater contact of new ideas feel generally frustrated, which in turn leads to general aggression. The cause is thought to be that such people are motivated to learn new modes of behavior either because they are dissatisfied with the old or because they are dissatisfied as a whole, but this impulse places them in a condition in which they find difficulties. Such peoples may encounter difficulties in learning their preferred new modes of behavior; or they may be actually prevented from learning them; or new and unexpected complexities may emerge. The increased frustration the acculturating experience generates makes them aggressive. The hypothesis is tested through a variety of techniques.

The results of this African study indicate that care must be taken in generalizing assumptions such as the above. In all three tribes, frustration and aggression were certainly prominent but only in the case of the Luo was there evidence for both realms of behavior, education and leadership. For the other two tribes, Ganda and Zulu, there was no evidence that frustration or aggression emerged in contact with European officials. On the other hand, the situation at schools did appear to precipitate these mechanisms. The psychological complexities underlying acculturation may be appreciated by inspecting Doob's (1960:324–326) twenty-seven hypotheses, which range from assumptions about motives, through cognitive factors, through changes in personality. It is not only the broad assumption that people who change from old to new ways are likely to be more discontented than those who remain unchanged that is considered, but also less obvious processes such as that increased facility in abstract thinking is likely to develop in people who have changed from old to new ways, or that they become proficient in judging time intervals.

The degree of subtlety with which a psychological research in this area may become involved is shown by examination of the acculturating process among the Banyankole tribe of Uganda (Segall 1963). Here, as in many other areas and other situations, the acculturating group adopts the values and attitudes of the external authoritarian group, in this case, the British colonials in the Uganda Civil Service. If, as was the case here, the latter held fairly disparaging opin-

ions about the people, the acculturating group seems to be placed in the odd position of self-disparagement. On the surface this appears to be a paradoxical state of affairs which has been termed "identification with the aggressor." Following the reported opinions of Banyankole one would conclude that this kind of identification was taking place with them. But careful analysis of the items in the attitude questionnaire reveals that the adoption of the out-group's values amounts only to acquiescence at a superficial level. There was acceptance of the anti-African statements formulated by Europeans, but there was no real evidence that the negative attitudes behind the values were assimilated. This finding cautions the investigator in such a tender field of inquiry to question responses to items which are not supported by cross-checking.

CONCLUSIONS

The subject of personality across the cultures of the world has long attracted the attention of diverse scholars, as we have seen. This chapter has attempted to trace the history of this concern, to describe the varying concepts employed, and to relate the topic of comparative personality to allied problems of social psychology. Owing to varying theoretical positions and the difficulty of achieving a common definition of the key term "personality," a certain degree of conceptual complexity is present in the field of personality and culture. Some thinkers, like Spiro (1951) have attempted to disentangle the conceptual issues involved, and it may be that such attempts will be more rewarding than the addition of further empirical data. Be that as it may, the student's attention should be drawn to the historical antecedents of this field and to the theoretical positions of scholars within it.

Suggested Readings

The field of culture and personality has been so well covered in the past that it is very difficult to find anything very new to say about it. Two edited books are recommended: Kaplan (1961) and Francis Hsu's volume on psychological anthropology, both quoted in the text of the present chapter. A previous book edited by Professor Hsu, not mentioned in the chapter, *Aspects of Culture and Personality* (New York: Abelard-Schuman 1954) can be recommended. Victor Barnouw's recent book on the subject (1963) is very comprehensive and can be thoroughly recommended as beginning reading for the student.

The subject of projective techniques is best reviewed in Gardner Lindzey's book (1961), while the various field researches of Du Bois (1944) Gladwin and Sarason (1953), and Anthony Wallace (1952) show how these are actually used. Anthony Wallace, incidentally, has also written a small but excellent introduction to this subject, indicating the evolution of culture and the evolution of the brain (matters often neglected in the usual personality-and-culture reviews) (1961).

CHAPTER **14** opens a section of the book given over to a discussion of the classic research procedures used by anthropologists in pursuit of knowledge about man, culture, and society. We have elected a progression from ethnographic through microethnology, or small-scale comparative studies, to macroethnological research methods, because in one important sense ethnographic research is the foundation for and the pathway to the tasks of classification and correlation, which in turn lead to statements about regular, recurrent, predictable cultural processes, or, if you will, scientific laws. Yet although the major task the ethnographer sets himself is to discover, to describe, and to understand the customs and traditions of other peoples, no ethnographer can willingly see himself as simply collecting data to be indexed and lodged in the archives of the Human Relations Area Files. For all ethnographic research is, intrinsically, comparative, and all modern ethnographic work is problem-centered, focused by some hypothesis or circumscribed by some overriding theoretical concern. Professor Berreman makes it abundantly clear that the ethnographic research task is not a passive social survey type research activity, with so many preselected alternatives to be ticked off. Rather, the ethnographer spends a good deal of time attempting to discover what questions he must ask, and waiting for the opportune moment to ask them. Ethnographic research is a dialogue between what is known, or what we can reasonably assume we know, and what is discoverable in the ways of an alien society. In this sense, regardless of his concentration on the unique patterns of a particular culture, the ethnographer is also engaged in a variety of ethnology. Hence the distinction we have made between ethnographic and ethnological research is partly artificial; each presumes the other, and together they contribute spirally to building knowledge. Professor Berreman scrutinizes and provides rich insights into the way cultural anthropologists go about one aspect of their work, whether their special interest is in the field of technology, or social structure, or the processes of enculturation.

THE AUTHOR was born in Portland, Oregon, and has studied at the University of Oregon, and at Cornell University, where he took his doctorate in anthropology. In addition to the work in North India reported in this chapter he has done ethnographic research among the peoples of the Aleutian Islands. He has been at the University of California, Berkeley, since 1959, where he is now Professor of Anthropology. His major interests are cultural change, social organization, social stratification, and — as will be evident from this chapter — research methods. In addition to a number of scientific articles on culture, society, and change in the Aleutians and in India, he has written *Hindus of the Himalayas* and *Behind Many Masks: Ethnography and Impression Management in a Himalayan Village*.

14

Ethnography: Method and Product

GERALD D. BERREMAN

University of California, Berkeley

ETHNOGRAPHY

Every science depends upon observed phenomena for its analytical and interpretive statements. In some cases the observation is aided by instruments such as microscopes, cloud-chambers, or seismographs, just as analysis may be facilitated by symbolic systems such as mathematics, and by data-handling devices such as computers. These are simply aids to human observation and analysis — extensions of the person who uses them. No nonhuman device can make observations or analyses except by human design, manipulation, and interpretation.

Anthropology, in common with other social sciences, depends for its data upon observations of human behavior, including verbal behavior. The process of making such observations has been called "ethnography." "An ethnography" is a written report summarizing the behaviors and the beliefs, understandings, attitudes, and values they imply, of a group of interacting people. Thus, an ethnography is a description of the way of life, or culture, of a society.

Everyone who does empirical research in cultural or social anthropology engages in ethnography as a process, though by no means everyone reports his research in the form of an ethnography. An ethnography is generally expected to give an overall view of the culture of the people about whom it is written, within the limits inherent in ethnographic research and in prose exposition. As such, it attempts to cover all aspects of the culture of a given society. In practice, it covers those aspects which the ethnographer considers relevant to an understanding of the main features of the culture he studied.

The manner and sequence of written presentation differ, of course, according to the outlook and style of the author and according to the nature of the culture being described. As we shall see, in recent years there has been increasing emphasis on organizing ethnographic descriptions along lines which represent the organization of the world as seen by the people who live the culture, rather than simply according to the preconceived notions and categories of the ethnographer. So far, however, there have not been whole ethnographies written in this fashion, chiefly because in the year or two available to most ethnographic researchers, it is not possible to accumulate the data necessary for acquiring a complete subjective view of a culture; and even if such data were collected, recording them would be a formidably massive undertaking. Therefore, to the present, most ethnographies comprise the scientist's description of a way of life he has observed in detail, described as it seems to him to be organized and to function. He combines indigenous concepts with his own analytical concepts in organizing his data.

Typically, the ethnographic account includes an introductory section on the geographical and historical setting of the people to be studied, their racial, linguistic, and cultural affinities. Following that are relatively detailed chapters on their means of making a living (often called economics), their political and legal organization, their religion, their social organization (frequently the most detailed section of all, covering family and other kin-based groups, rules and terminology regarding kinship, social stratification, and various kinds of groups based on criteria other than kinship). There may perhaps be sections on such topics as how they rear their children, their values, "expressive behavior," such as folklore, art, and music, or special topics relevant to the society in question, followed by a closing section on the changes the people are undergoing as contacts with other groups or with urban centers and modern technology increase. Most often the account is written in the "ethnographic present," which means that the present tense is used after the author has identified the time period for which the account is accurate. This is especially important to bear in mind for ethnographies describing former eras or "memory cultures." Often the accounts are written as though the culture being described were static — un-

changing. Actually, of course, all cultures are dynamic and ever changing. The ethnographic account is like one frame of a motion picture, arbitrarily selected for display as a "still," for continual change is impossible to convey in the stillness of the printed page.

Other sequences of presentation and of organization besides that described above have also been effectively used. For example, M. E. Opler approached Apache ethnography by focusing on the sequence of life events through which an individual typically passes, revealing the culture by unfolding a generalized Apache lifeway (Opler 1941), while Homer Barnett depicted the culture of the Palauans of Micronesia through the eyes of the people — by telling what it is to be a Palauan (Barnett 1960).

Whatever the method of presentation and analysis, the aim of ethnography is to report the culture studied in sufficient depth and breadth to enable one who has not experienced it to understand it. Understanding may be assumed to have been achieved if the reader learns how participants in the culture see themselves, others, and their environment, and how they deal with each. Ideally, this requires that the ethnographer convey information sufficient in quantity, variety, and quality, and so organized and analyzed, that it would enable the reader to understand events of the culture if he were to experience them, to anticipate the reactions of members of the society to the events they experience and, ultimately, to behave appropriately in that society in a manner similar to that of a person who has lived the culture. In this respect, the ethnography is analogous to a linguist's description of a language. It may not enable the reader to speak the language easily, but it enables him to understand how it works. An ethnography comprises, essentially, a statement of a set of rules which describe how people act in their culture. Given time, the reader of an adequate ethnographic (or linguistic) description can understand what is done (or said), can act (or speak) correctly and meaningfully in the culture (or language), can anticipate the responses he will evoke in others, and can respond to them in ways they deem appropriate.

Ethnographic research often goes unreported in the form of an overall ethnography simply because the author preferred not to collect data on such a wide range of topics or was unable to do so, or because although he had such data, he preferred to present them in less inclusive form focused on a particular and restricted problem or series of problems.

It is sometimes assumed that the broadly descriptive ethnographic report is not theoretical — that it represents the results of theoryless fact-collecting — and that while it may interest the reader who has a taste for esoterica, it is unlikely to lead to advances in the science of man. A reply to this position is that there can be no pure observation and no straight description without underlying assumptions — without a theory or theories — which determine what will be observed and what will be recorded. There is no day in the life of any people, family, or individual which could be observed or recorded in all its detail. The events and circumstances are simply too manifold. In fact, a single five-minute interview has been the subject of a 260-page book (Pittenger, Hockett, and Danely 1960). Even there the written account was not exhaustive; much was left undescribed.

The point here is that all observation is selective, all recording of observation is selective again, and the published account is selective of the recorded observations, since researchers rarely if ever publish all the records of their field research. Thus, between the event and the report there are at least three stages of selectivity on the part of the researcher. The underlying assump-tions by which he selects what he will observe from the mass of stimuli with which he is confronted in his research, what he will record from the innumerable observations he has made, and what he will report from the multitudinous records he has kept, comprise his theory or theories. If he regards it as more important to record a ceremony than a bull session, a song than an epithet, how and where people eat than how and where they defecate, the rules by which they marry rather than the infractions of these rules, the circumstances in which they take grievances to court than the circumstances in which they become embarrassed, what they do when someone dies than when someone belches (or vice versa), it is because he has a set of understandings or assumptions about the nature of human society, how it works and what is important in it. A theory is nothing more than a coherent set of assumptions.

There are wide differences, of course, in how aware individuals are of the theories upon which they base their research and in how explicit they are in conveying them to the readers of their reports. It is because they often do not realize or make explicit their assumptions that many authors of ethnographies are accused of being theoryless fact-collectors. Often the result of being theoretically unaware or inexplicit is that the account is incomplete, inconsistent, internally contradictory, or illogical. This does not mean that the researcher had no theories; merely that he was theoretically unsophisticated. If so, he is certainly as culpable as the oft-maligned theorists who do not relate their elaborately stated assumptions to empirically derived facts.

It is clear, therefore, that theory is inherent in ethnography and that good theory is essential to good ethnography. As theory becomes more explicit, observation becomes more perceptive, and as observation becomes more perceptive, theoretical formulation becomes more explicit. To evaluate a theory, one must know the observed facts which support it; to evaluate reported facts, one must know the assumptions of the observer. If these elements are made explicit in any particular study, it is even possible for either facts or theory to remain useful if one or the other is discredited. Facts may outlive the theory which led to their being recorded; a theory may prove to be valid even though the presumed facts on which it is based are discovered to be in error. But this can occur only if the theory and facts are known so that their limitations or defects can be assessed.

ETHNOGRAPHERS AND THEIR CRAFT

Ethnographic research differs from research in the nonsocial sciences in that it is above all a human undertaking. The ethnographer studies human beings from the point of view of a fellow human being. He is of the same order as the phenomenon he studies. Every scientist faces the problems of minimizing irrelevant external influences on the subject matter he studies and on his perception of that subject matter. Many also face the problem that the devices by which they study a phenomenon in some degree affect that phenomenon. But the social analyst faces the unique and acute problem that he is part of his own subject matter — of any social situation he attempts to study. His very presence alters the situation he studies, and alters it in ways and to an extent which cannot be fully anticipated, compensated for, or even known.

The method of study adopted by most ethnographers is loosely termed "participant observation." This refers to the practice of living among the people one studies, coming to know them, their language, and their lifeways through intense and nearly continuous interaction with them in their daily lives. This means that the ethnographer converses with the people he studies, works with them,

attends their social and ritual functions, visits their homes, invites them to his home — that he is present with them in as many situations as possible, learning to know them in as many settings and moods as he can. Sometimes he interviews for specific kinds of data; always he is alert to whatever information may come his way, ready to follow up and understand any event or fact which is unanticipated or seemingly inexplicable. The methods by which he derives his data are often subtle and difficult to define. He may have learned some of them by reading accounts of how research is or should be done (for instance, Becker 1958; Bennett 1948; Paul 1953), or by reading accounts of how particular studies were done (for instance, Berreman 1962; Malinowski 1932:5–25; Thomas and Znaniecki 1918:1–86; Whyte 1955), or by talking with and being taught by experienced ethnographers. Often he has little advance preparation for the methodological and technical problems which will confront him in his field research. This is partly because of the subtlety of the ethnographic research process as it is usually carried out, and partly because, until very recently, it was widely assumed that the process need not, and perhaps could not, be taught, that it was an ability or knack which came naturally or not at all. Recently, as we shall see, this view has been undergoing revision. Concerted efforts are now being made to explicate methods of research with the aim of communicating them so they can be taught, and so that any particular study can be put to the test of replication.

A famous and experienced American ethnographer thirty years ago came to a view that still strikes a responsive chord among many of his profession, when he noted that "any individual who has received the requisite training [in the facts and theories of anthropology] and who possesses, in a moderate degree, the attributes of honesty, intelligence and humility has all that is necessary" to do successful ethnographic research (Radin 1933:ix). While we might well question the assumption that training in research methods is unnecessary or useless, it seems obvious that he is correct in his implication that a successful ethnographer is, above all else, a person who is successful in everyday interaction with others. The reason for this is clear, for ethnographic research — participant observation — is a process of social interaction similar in many ways to the interactions of everyday life. Aaron Cicourel has referred to this in his book on methods in sociology:

The difficulties in obtaining data through participant observation and interviewing are no different than those which persons living their daily lives would encounter if they were placed in a comparable situation though devoid of its research implications. Moving into a new neighborhood, starting work at a new job, applying for a new job, starting school, meeting groups whose customs and language are different from one's own, attempting to befriend someone so as to obtain certain information, trying to sell a customer some merchandise, trying to pick up a girl, and obviously any number of similar and divergent social processes include the same features which are found in field research (Cicourel 1964:68).

To describe the attributes of good ethnographers, one might refer to those factors which Gordon Allport (1937:213 ff.) has identified as characteristic of the mature personality, for maturity is essential to effective adult social interaction in any context. Of crucial importance is a sense of perspective: the ability to distinguish the important from the unimportant, the inevitable from the results of choice, the part from the whole, the self from society. This entails an ability to see oneself and one's society with insight and a sense of objectivity or detachment. An aspect of this, I think, is a kind of generic skepticism. The ethnographer, like any social analyst, has to be a doubting Thomas if he is not continually to be led astray by his informants or his preconceptions. A sense of perspective, objectivity, and skepticism are associated closely with a genuine sense of humor, which I would see as necessarily combined with humility — what the poet John Ciardi has called "the ability to chuckle wryly and ruefully at one's self." To take oneself too seriously is unlikely to allow one to go through the trying physical, psychological, and social circumstances which field research in an alien culture entails. To take one's subjects too seriously is likely to distort one's perspective on what they are doing and is apt to lead one to become too caught up in the events of their lives to view them as subjects of inquiry. Peter Berger has argued that

. . . the social scientist who does not perceive [the] comic dimension of social reality is going to miss essential features of it. One cannot fully grasp the political world unless one understands it as a confidence game, or the stratification system unless he sees its character as a costume party. One cannot achieve a sociological perception of religious institutions unless one recalls how as a child one put on masks and frightened the wits out of one's contemporaries by the simple expedient of saying "boo." No one can understand any aspect of the erotic who does not grasp its fundamental quality as being that of an *opéra bouffe*. And a sociologist cannot understand the law who does not recollect the jurisprudence of a certain Queen in *Alice in Wonderland*.

These remarks, needless to say, are not meant to denigrate the serious study of society, but simply to suggest that such study itself will profit greatly from those insights that one can obtain only while laughing (1963:165).[1]

A crucial consequence of perspective and a crucial concomitant of humor is empathy — the ability to put one's self in the place of others, to experience the world as they experience it. Empathy is insurance against

[1] *From Invitation to Sociology,* by Peter L. Berger. Copyright © 1963 by Peter L. Berger. Reprinted by permission of Doubleday & Company, Inc.

narrow complacency, ethnocentrism, and sterile scientism. Only through empathetic ability can the scientist hope to understand the phenomenal world of the people he studies, to comprehend their motives, their hopes, joys, and fears, and their reactions to himself.

In addition, an ethnographer must be flexible, adaptable, and open-minded. In his work he will have to adjust to a variety of physical conditions and to a variety of people making diverse demands upon him. He will have to adjust his research to the exigencies of the situation, which will often be largely unanticipated. In the vast majority of cases he will have to alter more or less drastically his research plan to accommodate to field conditions and opportunities. He will also have to accommodate to the social conditions, personalities, and even the idiosyncrasies of his informants.

In personal relations the ethnographer will succeed best if he is straightforward, modest, tolerant, and adaptable. He must be liked and trusted as an individual to win the trust and confidence of those with whom he works. There are no shortcuts on this score. People seem to be basically alike in their ability to identify a phony, a con man, an operator, a dissembler, an egotist, or a selfish person, and in their inclination to reject or mislead him. Everyone, of course, tailors much of his behavior to impress others favorably or to accord with the view of himself he wishes to project to others (cf. Goffman 1959; Berreman 1962). This is inherent in social interaction. But there is a difference between this and crass dissimulation which spells the difference between normal social interaction and deviousness, between research and exploitation. Successful ethnography is based on the former, as are most successful human relationships.

All social interaction is reciprocal. The ethnographer must be prepared to give as well as take in his relationships with those among whom he works. He cannot expect them to give him their time and trust unless he is willing to give of himself. Often material benefits are important. He may find it necessary, appropriate, or advantageous to reimburse his informants for their time in money or goods. Frequently, gifts will be acceptable and appreciated where formal payment will not. Services of various sorts, such as simple medical aid, instruction in English or in technical fields, and advice and help in dealing with official agencies, are often highly valued ways in which the ethnographer can reciprocate. Willingness to participate in an exchange of information — to tell about his own experiences and way of life — may greatly enhance his informants' willingness to provide information on themselves, for the situation is then defined as exchange rather than as prying. People are likely to be most appreciative of the simple fact that the ethnographer provides entertaining diversion by talking with them, demonstrating his possessions, sharing his radio, showing his magazines, distributing photographs. All these and many more are means by which the ethnographer can establish with his hosts the mutuality of which successful interaction, hence successful ethnography, is made.

Closely related to this is a requisite ability to listen. The ethnographer must be an interested, sympathetic, and patient listener if he is to learn. If he is not willing to listen to his informants' opinions and information on subjects which he deems irrelevant to his research he will find it difficult to get them to talk on subjects in which he *is* interested. He will, of course, guide conversations in the direction of his research interests, but to win rapport he must not limit himself to such topics. To do so is indicative of lack of genuine involvement with the informants, or is likely to be so interpreted.

Energy, determination, and persistence are equally necessary to successful ethnography. One cannot learn about a culture unless he interacts with those who live it. Therefore, the ethnographer has to expose himself continually to social situations and project himself into them. He must keep talking to people, participating with them in their daily lives, and observing them. Even when he has no specific information in mind which he wishes to collect he must be on hand, talking, participating, and observing, for only by so doing can he hope to get new, unanticipated, and sometimes crucial information. He never knows when or how such information will become available, but it will not unless he is there to obtain it. This may be exhausting psychically and physically, but it is the only way to learn what the ethnographer wants to know. In addition to awaiting the unpredictable information or insight, the field worker may spend months passively awaiting or engineering an opportunity to ask a crucial question or observe an important event. Earning the necessary confidence or acquiring the invitation may take great effort and cause considerable anxiety lest the effort be to no avail. Yet this is an important part of the ethnographic process. To ask too soon or in an inappropriate context may jeopardize further research.

An ethnographer must be inordinately curious about the human condition in its various manifestations and at the same time be sympathetic and empathic. Without these qualities, he would be unlikely to sustain himself over the long, often trying and lonely period of research. Like the sociologist described by Berger he

. . . is a person intensively, endlessly, shamelessly interested in the doings of men. His natural habitat is all the human gathering places of the world. . . . Since he is interested in men, nothing that men do can be altogether tedious for him. He will naturally be interested in the events that engage men's ultimate beliefs, their moments of tragedy and grandeur and ecstacy.

But he will also be fascinated by the commonplace, the everyday. He will know reverence, but this reverence will not prevent him from wanting to see and to understand. He may sometimes feel revulsion or contempt. But this also will not deter him from wanting to have his questions answered. The sociologist [or ethnographer], in his quest for understanding, moves through the world of men without respect for the usual lines of demarcation. Nobility and degradation, power and obscurity, intelligence and folly — they are all equally *interesting* to him, however unequal they may be in his personal values and tastes (Berger 1963:18).[2]

Curiosity is not enough, obviously. To make anything of what one's curiosity leads him to learn, there must be a sense of the problematic — a fundamental creativity which leads the observer to seek and find relationships among his observed data, to see relationships between his observed data and other facts and ideas with which he is familiar, to see their relevance and to weigh their importance. This is roughly what C. Wright Mills meant by the "sociological imagination," which "enables its possessor to understand the larger historical scene in terms of its meaning for the inner life and the external career of a variety of individuals" (Mills 1959:5). He who possesses this imagination will see in specific behaviors and events indicators of structures, processes, and functions in the society at large, operative in significant historical context. It is "the capacity to range from the most impersonal and remote transformations to the most intimate features of the human self — and to see the relations between the two" (Mills 1959:7). If one lacks this creative and synthesizing ability, he will be immobilized by the field experience simply because of the overwhelming number, immediacy, and variety of potential observations

[2] From *Invitation to Sociology*, by Peter L. Berger. Copyright © 1963 by Peter L. Berger. Reprinted by permission of Doubleday & Company, Inc.

which confront him. He will either be unable to rise above the welter of facts to see their significance and relationships, or he will be unable to descend from his theories and assumptions to relate them to events in the empirical world.

Finally, I think successful ethnography depends upon a thorough understanding of the nature of social structure and social interaction on the theoretical and practical planes, both in the culture being studied and in the most general human sense. The ethnographer needs an adequate theory of society. This is both the goal and the prerequisite for good ethnography. Successful ethnographic research depends upon it and enhances it.

These, then, are some of the characteristics of successful ethnographers. If they sound like the Boy Scout Law, it is because ethnography is a human undertaking. Boy Scouts presumably want to be effective human beings and this is precisely what it takes to be a good ethnographer. No Boy Scouts or ethnographers attain the ideal perfectly. There is a wide range of degrees to which the ideal is approximated. Success may be achieved despite conspicuous shortcomings, but the basic list of attributes can still be regarded as sound.

ETHNOGRAPHIC RESEARCH

We turn now from our discussion of what the ethnographer is (ought to be or would like to be), and what ethnography is, to what the ethnographer does. How does he go about his task of participating and observing? How does he use the virtues cited above in pursuit of his goal? What are the difficulties, hazards, and frustrations he faces?

Choice of a region and locality in which to work, like the ethnographer's theoretical orientation and his choice of research problem, is the product of a complex of factors

which need not concern us here.[3] Suffice it to say that availability of the prerequisite training in language and area studies and of financial assistance for field research are important limiting factors. Political considerations are also important. Some nations do not admit American scholars to study their people and the American government does not allow its scholars to study the people in some nations. Whole regions of the world are therefore closed to the ethnographer, and the number and extent of such areas seem to be increasing. Once in a country, the choice of locale may be limited by considerations of internal politics, by the availability of transportation, by health facilities, by housing, and many other conditions, as well as by the requirements of the research itself. The specific site for intensive study is often selected on the basis of such a variety of explicit and implicit factors that the researcher himself cannot fully explain his choice.

Time for research is never unlimited. Typically, the hopeful ethnographer spends a year — sometimes two — living with the people whose way of life he intends to learn. The duration of his or her stay is determined by many factors. The generosity of the foundation which supports the research must be considered. The academic calendar makes a year a convenient, often a maximum, period for research. Health and morale seem often to be capable of being sustained for a year under circumstances which would have telling effect over a longer period, and it is generally assumed to be possible to witness most things that happen in a society in the period of a year. There is also the assumption that it takes about a year to attain sufficient facility in the language, sufficient rapport with the people, sufficient familiarity with the culture, and sufficient notebooks full of information, to

---

[3] For an account of one such set of factors, see Fischer's description of his experience in Micronesia, detailed in Chapter 15.

write a creditable account of the way of life of the people one has studied.

Because of limitations of time, the ethnographer must begin his research soon after his arrival in the field. To search for the ideal location might lead to endless delay. Therefore, after visiting a number of potential sites, the researcher usually settles on one which seems promising, and hopes for the best. If, of several comparable sites, one strikes him as intrinsically more interesting or attractive than the others, it is without doubt the one most often chosen and certainly is the one which should be chosen. Field research is sufficiently difficult, frustrating, and at times discouraging, that such subtle characteristics as interest or attractiveness can become important in sustaining the ethnographer's morale, attention, and energies. If, in addition to fulfilling his research requirements, the people he studies fascinate him, the ethnographer will find his work much easier and more rewarding.

At best the choice is an uncertain one. McKim Marriott (1957:423) mentions that he was politely thrown out of three villages in which he attempted to work in India before he was allowed to settle in the one upon which he subsequently published his research results. Official permission, both from such national and regional agencies as the police and district offices and from the local authorities such as village headmen and elders, is important, but it may not be enough. Two anthropologists who had obtained permission from the chief of a village of Mexican Kickapoo Indians were formally ejected after only two weeks of work (Ritzenthaler and Peterson 1956:9). This did not prevent them from publishing an account of their findings, but it certainly attenuated those findings.

Having chosen a place to work, the ethnographer is faced with two crucial and simultaneous problems: to account for himself to those among whom he plans to live; and to set himself up in housekeeping. The latter often seems to be the more pressing and the difficulties therein are not infrequently great, but the former is just as important and may ultimately prove to be the more difficult. Local conditions and attitudes are vital to the success of both.

In some areas the ethnographer will have to live in a tent, build his own dwelling, or hire someone to build it for him. In others he will be able to stay in a guest house, borrow or rent an unused dwelling or portion thereof, or board in the home of a local resident. No general rule as to which is preferable can be adduced, except that the ethnographer should be prepared to do that which seems most likely to meet with the approval of the residents, consistent with his research aims.

Housekeeping can be a serious and time-consuming problem. It may take so much time as to preclude intensive research, in which case a housekeeper has to be sought. On the other hand, at least during the initial period when the ethnographer is seeking to establish understanding, trust, and friendship, housekeeping and associated endeavors may give him an invaluable opportunity to engage in understandable activity and to meet people in a natural way. It may be an excellent way to become a participant in local society.

Food itself can be an acute problem. In some areas there may be so little food available locally that the ethnographer will have to take his own. In others the local food may be insufficiently nutritious to maintain his health, or may be sufficiently unpalatable to him that, again, food must be imported. In many parts of the world considerable caution must be exercised in the preparation of food and drink to avoid acquiring the internal parasites and other ailments which, at best, may delay the research. These are largely mechanical details which every field worker must resolve as best he can in the circumstances which face him. They are, however, real and immediate, and they can be extremely important in their effect on the research.

Little has been written on the social and psychological conditions of ethnographic field research, the role the ethnographer's morale plays in his research, the incidence, causes, and effects of fear, anxiety, loneliness, frustration, and despair. These are not data the ethnographer conventionally records, and he may even hesitate to admit them. Anecdotal but informative glimpses are to be found in introductions to several classic ethnographies (for example, Evans-Pritchard 1940:8–15; Firth 1936:1–12; Holmberg 1950:1–4; Malinowski 1932:5–25); in *Behind Many Masks* (Berreman 1962), in *The Savage and the Innocent* (Maybury-Lewis 1965), in *The High Valley* (Read 1965), in *Stranger and Friend* (Powdermaker 1966), and in the fictionalized account entitled *Return to Laughter* (Bowen 1954). The researcher's morale is a palpable factor in all ethnographic research, and is vital to the success of the endeavor. Often the causes are obvious. Debilitating or dangerous illness or the threat thereof to oneself or one's dependents, hostile individuals or groups including officials as well as members of the society being studied, lack of easy-going, friendly, and understanding companionship, lack of respite from continual and stressful interaction in an unfamiliar context, inability to escape from the scrutiny of curious observers — these are factors which are not uncommon and cannot fail to have effect on the ethnographer. He is, after all, only human. The effect may be to cause the ethnographer to fail in his work; more commonly, it is to restrict the scope or depth of his findings. Not infrequently such facts cause the ethnographer to have recourse to research methods other than participant observation. Stories of ethnographers who did their work by summoning informants to the resort hotel of the region, or by hiring assistants to report data back to the hotel, are rife, if perhaps most often apocryphal.

More frequently discussed in the literature, and no less difficult and important, is the problem of establishing one's role before the people with whom one wishes to work, and to establish good relations with them, once one has established his physical presence among them. In some regions the role of anthropologist is only too well known. The Zuni household of the American Southwest has been described as typically comprising a mother, a father, three children, and an anthropologist. The Nayar of the southwest coast of India, famous for their matrilineal kin groups, have been studied sufficiently that a Nayar youth is reported to have told an ethnographer recently, "Please go away and do not bother us; we have no customs." Occasionally an ethnographer in a well-studied society has been referred by his informants to the standard published ethnography on their way of life. The people of some nations or regions identify the anthropologist with the study of "primitives" and therefore resent his presence. But more frequently, the role of the anthropologist is unknown — and therefore it is often suspect.

Few individuals are capable of such complete participation in an alien culture as to be able to act as if they were members of it. Participant observation does not imply or require that the anthropologist become one of those he studies. In the literal sense, this would be impossible in most cases, especially in the relatively short time available to most ethnographers. But circumstances vary widely; the relative proportions of participation and observation vary widely from one study to another. Some people urge the inquisitive outsider to emulate and interact with them in every possible way; others prohibit him from doing so. In the brief but insightful introduction to his account of research in the Sudan, the British ethnographer E. E. Evans-Pritchard compared two groups with whom he had worked: "Azande would not allow me to live as one of themselves; Nuer would not allow me to live otherwise. Among Azande I was compelled to live outside the community; among Nuer I was compelled to be a member of it" (Evans-Pritchard 1940:15). Most peoples fall somewhere between these extremes. To become a member of the group one studied would doubtless inhibit the opportunity and perhaps the inclination to do research. There are cases on record of anthropologists who have become so closely identified with the people they studied that they have refused to divulge what they have learned, or even to come home.

Therefore, while some ethnographers pride themselves on having adopted the way of life of those they studied and having been accepted into their society, successful research is most often the result of being viewed and accepted as a trustworthy, interested, and sympathetic outsider. This has advantages in that an outsider can be naïve. He can ask blunt, embarrassing, trivial, or simple-minded questions, he can do or say the wrong thing, he can repeat his queries and pursue his interests ad nauseum, he can consort with people of every status and reputation. Such behavior would not be tolerated in an insider, yet it may be crucial to the research. The outsider derives the benefit of an immunity borne of difference and ignorance.

It is a widespread if not universal human trait to be interested in and communicative about one's way of life when confronted with someone who is unknowing and interested. Being, in effect, a neophyte, the ethnographer is in a position to receive indulgent instruction such as no other adult could expect. Any progress he makes in language, custom, and information is likely to be hailed, seemingly out of all proportion to the magnitude of the accomplishment. In the process he learns the lifeways of his instructors.

A role which is known or at least understandable in many societies, and one which the ethnographer can legitimately claim, is that of the student. This role, broadly defined, is probably the most widely successful one for ethnographic research. It is simply a special instance of the role of the interested person who wants to learn. It is not always easy to come by. People will suspect that other motives underlie those the ethnographer claims. Missionaries and governmental officials have often preceded the ethnographer with apparently similar interests or activities but with intentions which prove threatening to those who receive them. To avoid being identified as such, the ethnographer can only identify himself straightforwardly and behave in ways consistent with that claim and inconsistent with the suspected roles.

Thus, the more comprehensible the role of the ethnographer, and the less threatening he is to the community in which he works, the more successful he is likely to be in insinuating himself into the social life and conversation of the people he studies. Consequently the likelihood of ultimately successful research is greater.

Having established his role, the ethnographer has to find people with whom to talk. They may be suspicious or hostile. They may consider even the most discreet inquiries to be not worthwhile, impertinent, or even threatening. Whole segments of potential informants may be unavailable to the ethnographer because of age, sex, social status, factional alignments, and so on. People may be too busy or too tired to talk at length after a hard day's work. In an absolute sense, these constitute obstacles to obtaining data. They also influence the kind of research that is possible, and the reliability and validity of the research results, by influencing or limiting the choice of informants.

There is a wide range in the representativeness of the sample of informants upon whose word published ethnographies have been based. Raymond Firth derived information from all of the 1,300 living Tikopia (Firth 1956a:49). Cornelius Osgood, by contrast, worked some 500 hours with a single Inglalik Indian informant (Osgood 1940:50–55). Circumstances may make a choice impossible, as when one is working with a culture which exists only in the memory of one or a few informants — a situation which is not uncommon in the study of American Indian groups (see T. Kroeber 1961). Even in societies with large populations whose ongoing culture is the ethnographer's interest, it is likely that a few individuals will become the ethnographer's best friends and confidants because of their interests, capabilities, free time, alienation from their own society, hope for rewards from the outsider, or their position in the social structure (for instance, the "old man" who is expected to talk, reminisce, and speculate at length). These people may become sources of extensive information, and often of information that could not be obtained from more casual and diffuse contacts.

The methodological question arising here is one of representativeness, reliability, and bias. Can one individual give reliable information on all phases of his culture? Can a man adequately observe and report women's culture, especially in a society such as that of India where the sexes are systematically segregated in many of their activities? One of the serious problems in ethnography is its heavy androcentric (male-centered) bias, since most ethnographers and most informants are men. This may be unavoidable, but it should be recognized as a fact and as a problem. Can one occupational group, social stratum, or ethnic category suffice to give information on a multi-group society? Can a blacksmith know enough about the farmer's or priest's life to report it adequately? Even if he knows, will a white man in Mississippi report accurately the nature of race relations there, and are his observations and his definition of accurate reporting the same as would be those of a Negro in the same vicinity? Is the man who seeks out and cultivates an inquisitive stranger as a friend likely to report his culture in a way consistent with that of a man who shuns outsiders? These and similar questions have led most ethnographers to conclude that a fairly representative selection of informants from different groups and strata within a society should be used wherever possible so as to minimize bias and error, and to bring out divergent viewpoints extant in the society so they can be further investigated. The question is not whether the male or female informant is more correct, the blacksmith or Brahmin, the white or Negro, the committed or the alienated individual. All are equally correct and equally revealing in their ways, but no one alone provides a complete picture. A complete picture of the culture can be derived only by considering and collating the full range of views and experiences which comprise it.

Getting people to talk, once their confidence is won, is not as difficult as one might anticipate. It seems to be a universal human trait to like to talk about oneself to interested people one trusts — to tell one's accomplishments, misfortunes, and suspicions, to display one's knowledge, and to propound one's theories. It is almost as universal not to like to listen to the same kind of conversation by others, at least not by others whom one unavoidably hears often on the same topics. These traits are a boon to the ethnographer, especially if he is unafflicted with the second, or can suppress it in the research situation. If he has the trust of those with whom he works — largely as a result of not repeating what he is told in confidence and not appearing overly interested in sensitive subjects — he is likely to be deluged with information, opinions, anecdotes, complaints, and gossip from people who have been unable to find an audience or whose audience has long since left them. It is as a sympathetic neutral confidant that the ethnographer receives much of his data.

There are always some things which individuals or groups consider private or secret and which are therefore not communicated to the ethnographer — at least not intentionally. Many such things are considered secret only by those individuals for whom their revelation would be embarrassing or damaging, while others in the society are only too willing to reveal them if the fact or source of the revelation will not be communicated to others. By utilizing a variety of informants, and by being discreet, it is possible to learn much about even those aspects of a people's life about which they are sensitive (see Berreman 1962).

THE ETHNOGRAPHIC EXPERIENCE

In order to illustrate the nature of the ethnographic experience and factors relevant to that experience as it affects research results, I will briefly describe my own research in a tightly knit, socially closed, and highly stratified community. Special emphasis will be placed on the way in which I accounted for myself to the people with whom I worked and among whom I lived, and on the differential effects on the research of the fact that I worked first in the company of a high-status assistant and later in the company of a low-status assistant. The research experience to be reported here is described and analyzed in detail in my monograph, *Behind Many Masks: Ethnography and Impression Management in a Himalayan Village* (Berreman 1962), in which much of this account originally appeared. The results of the research are presented in full in

Hindus of the Himalayas (Berreman 1963).

This ethnographic research took place in and around *Sirkanda,* a peasant village of the lower Himalayas of North India. Its residents, like those of the entire lower Himalayan area from Kashmir through Nepal, are known as *Paharis* ("of the mountains"). The village is small, containing some 384 individuals during the year of my residence there in 1957–1958, and is relatively isolated, situated as it is in rugged hills accessible only on foot, nine miles from the nearest road and bus service.

Strangers in the area are few and readily identifiable by dress and speech. People so identified are avoided or discouraged from remaining long in the vicinity. To escape such a reception, a person must be able to identify himself as a member of a familiar group through kinship ties, caste ties, and/or community affiliation. Since the first two are ascribed characteristics, the only hope an outsider has of achieving acceptance is by establishing residence and, through social interaction, acquiring the status of a community-dweller, a slow process at best.

The reluctance of Sirkanda villagers and their neighbors to accept strangers is attested to by the experience of those outsiders who have dealt with them. In 1957 a new teacher was assigned to the Sirkanda school. He was a Pahari from an area about fifty miles distant. Despite his Pahari background and consequent familiarity with the language and customs of the local people, he complained after four months in the village that his reception had been less than cordial:

I have taught in several schools in the valley and people have always been friendly to me. They have invited me to their homes for meals, have sent gifts of grain and vegetables with their children, and have tried to make me feel at home. I have been here four months now with almost no social contact aside from my students. No one has asked me to eat with him; no one has sent me so much as a grain of mil-

Interaction between ethnographer and subjects may be formal and polite (left), or informal and exuberant (below), depending upon circumstances.

Gerald Berreman, Hindus of the Himalayas. University of California Press, 1963.

The village blacksmith who became the author's closest friend and informant.

Sharing aspects of his own way of life (top), and learning local skills (right) are ways the ethnographer can join his informants in mutually rewarding activity.

Good rapport can be facilitated by the use of a camera, which resulted in these self-conscious portraits
at a local fair (right), or even by small family members, in this case the ethnographer's daughter and his
assistant's son (below).

Ethnography is not entirely work with informants. The ethnographer's
life must go on, and the way in which it goes on affects his research.

The ethnographer's family
must accommodate to village
conditions.

Home is where the hearth is: ethnographer and assistant beside the
house they shared with the two buffalo in the background.

The ethnographer's life is not easy: ethnographer and impedimenta enroute to
Sirkanda, a five-hour walk, to carry on
the research.

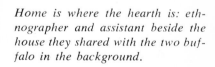

let; no one has asked me to sit and talk with him; no one has even asked me who I am or whether I have a family. They ignore me.

He fared better than the teacher in another village of the area who had to give up after three months, during which he and his proposed school were totally boycotted.

Among the forestry officers whose duty it is to make periodic rounds in these hills, the villagers' lack of hospitality is proverbial. The officers claim that here a man has to carry his own food, water, and bedroll because he cannot count on villagers to offer these necessities to him on his travels. Community development and establishment of credit cooperatives, two governmental programs in the area, have been unsuccessful due largely to their advocates' inability to establish rapport with the people. My assistant, who had worked for more than a year in an anthropological research project in a village of the plains, was constantly baffled at the reticence and lack of hospitality of villagers. As he said:

In Kalapur when you walked through the village men would hail you and invite you to sit and talk with them. Whether or not they really wanted you to do so, they at least invited you out of common courtesy. Here they just go inside or turn their backs when they see you coming.

The reasons for such reticence are not far to seek. Contacts with outsiders have been limited largely to contacts with policemen and tax collectors — two of the lowest forms of life in the Pahari taxonomy. Such officials are despised and feared not only because they make trouble for villagers in the line of duty, but because they also extort bribes on the threat of causing further trouble and often seem to take advantage of their official positions to vent their aggressions on these vulnerable people. Since India's independence, spheres of governmental responsibility have extended to include stringent supervision of greatly extended national forest lands, rationing of certain goods, establishment of a variety of development programs, and the like. The grounds for interfering in village affairs have multiplied as the variety of officials has proliferated. Any stranger, therefore, may be a government agent. As such he is potentially troublesome, even dangerous.

Villagers' fears on this score are not groundless. Aside from the unjust exploitation such agents are reputed to employ in their activities there are many illegal or semilegal activities carried on by villagers which could be grounds for punishment and are easily used as grounds for extortion. In Sirkanda, national forest lands and products have been illegally appropriated by villagers, taxable land has been under-reported, liquor is brewed and sold illicitly, women have been illegally sold, guns have gone unlicensed, adulterated milk is sold to outside merchants, children are often married below the legal age, men have fled the army or escaped from jail, property has been illegally acquired from fleeing Muslims at the time of India's partition. Any of these and similar real and imagined infractions may be objects of a stranger's curiosity and therefore are reasons for discouraging his presence in the village.

Paharis are thought by people of the plains to be ritually, spiritually, and morally inferior. They are suspected of witchcraft and evil magic. In addition, they are considered naïve bumpkins — the hillbilly stereotype of other cultures is shared by Indians. Paharis try to avoid interaction with those who hold these stereotypes. Alien Brahmins may seek to discredit their Pahari counterparts by finding evidence of their unorthodoxy; alien traders may seek to relieve them of their hard-earned cash or produce by sharp business practices; scoundrels may seek to waylay or abduct village women; thieves may come to steal their worldly possessions; lawyers or their cohorts may seek evidence for trumped-up legal proceedings which a poor Pahari could not hope to counteract in court; and Christians may hope to infringe on their religious beliefs and practices. Thus strangers are suspected of having ulterior motives even if they are not associated with the government.

The only way to feel sure that such dangers do not inhere in a person is to know who he is, and to know this he must fit somewhere into the known social system. Only then is he subject to effective local controls so that if he transgresses, or betrays a trust, he can be brought to account. The person who is beyond control is beyond trust and is best hurried on his way. This is therefore a relatively closed society. Interaction with strangers is kept to a minimum; the information furnished them is scanty and stereotyped. Access to such a society is difficult for an outsider.

Within this closed society there is rigid stratification into a number of hereditary, ranked, endogamous groups — castes — comprising two large divisions: the high or twice-born castes, and the low or untouchable castes. The high castes, Rajputs and Brahmins, are landowning agriculturists who are dominant in numbers, comprising 90 per cent of the population. They are dominant in economic wherewithal in that they own most of the land and animals while the other castes depend upon them for their livelihood. They are dominant in political power, for both traditional and new official means of control are in their hands. They dominate in ritual status as twice-born, ritually clean castes, while all other castes are "untouchable." In most villages, as in Sirkanda, Rajputs outnumber Brahmins and so are locally dominant, but the ritual and social distance between them is not great and the economic difference is usually nil.

The low castes, whose members are artisans, are disadvantaged in each respect that the high castes are advantaged. They are dependent upon the high castes for their livelihood and are subject to their will in almost every way. Ideally, their relationship to the high castes is one of respect, deference, and obedience. In return high-caste members are supposed to be paternalistic. In practice there is a good deal of tension in the relationship, and it is held stable largely by considerations of relative power.

In addition there are nonhierarchical cleavages within both the high and the low castes, cleavages based upon kinship ties (lineage and clan lines being paramount), and informal cliques and factions. As a result, the community is divided within itself. While there is consensus on some things there is disagreement on others. Acceptance by one element of the community does not imply acceptance by the whole community and frequently, in fact, precludes it.

It was into this community that my interpreter-assistant and I walked, unannounced, one rainy day in September, 1957, hoping to engage in ethnographic research. On our initial visit we asked only to camp there while we visited a number of surrounding villages. We were introduced by a note from a non-Pahari wholesaler of the nearest market town who had long bought the surplus agricultural produce of villagers and had, as it turned out, through sharp practices of an obscure nature, acquired land in the village. He asked that the villagers treat the strangers as "our people" and extend all hospitality to them. As might have been expected, our benefactor was not beloved in the village and it was more in spite of his intercession than on account of it that we ultimately managed to do a year's research in the village.

The note was addressed to a high-caste man who proved to be one of the most suspicious people of the village. He was the head of a household recently victorious in a nine-year court battle over land brought against it by virtually the entire village, the leader of a much-resented but powerful minority faction. That he gave us an unenthusiastic reception was a blow to our morale but probably a boon to our chances of being tolerated in the village.

The interpreter-assistant who accompanied me was a young Brahmin of plains origin who had previously worked in a similar capacity for a large research project carried out in the plains village of Kalapur. I shall hereafter refer to him as Sharma.

For the first three months of our stay in the village, most of our time was spent keeping house and attempting to establish rapport, both of which were carried out under trying circumstances.

According to their later reports to us, villagers at first assumed that we were missionaries, a species which had not previously invaded this locality but which was well known. Several villagers had sold milk in Mussoorie, a hill station sixteen miles distant that is frequented by missionaries. When we failed to meddle in religious matters or to show surprise at local rituals, this suspicion gradually faded. We had anticipated this interpretation of our motives and so were careful not to show undue interest in religion as a topic of conversation. We purposely used Hindu rather than areligious forms of greeting in our initial contacts to avoid being identified as missionaries. As a topic for polite and, we hoped, neutral conversation, we chose agriculture. It seemed timely too, as the fall harvest season began not long after our arrival in the village. Partly as a result of this choice of conversational fare, suspicion arose that we were government agents sent to reassess the land for taxation, based on the greater-than-previously-reported productivity of the land. Alternatively, we were suspected of being investigators seeking to find the extent of land use in unauthorized areas following the nationalization of the surrounding uncultivated lands. My physical appearance was little

comfort to villagers harboring these suspicions. One man commented: "Anyone can look like a foreigner if he wears the right clothes." Gradually these fears too disappeared, but others arose.

One person suggested that our genealogical inquiries might be preliminary to a military draft of the young men. The most steadfast opponent of our presence hinted darkly at the machinations of foreign spies — a vaguely understood but actively feared type of villain. Nearly four months passed before overt suspicion of this sort was substantially dissipated, although, of course, some people had been convinced of the innocence of our motives relatively early and others remained suspicious throughout our stay.

One incident nearly four months after our first visit to the village proved to be a turning point in quelling overt opposition to our activities in the village. We were talking one afternoon to the local Brahmin priest. He had proved to be a reluctant informant, apparently because of his fear of alienating powerful and suspicious Rajput farmers whose caste-fellows outnumbered his own by more than thirty to one in the village (his was the only Brahmin household, as compared to thirty-seven Rajput households in Sirkanda) and in whose good graces it was necessary for him to remain for many reasons. However, he was basically friendly. Encouraged by our increasing rapport in the village at large, by his own feelings of affinity with the Brahmin interpreter, Sharma, and by the privacy of his secluded threshing platform as a talking place, he had volunteered to discuss his family tree with us. Midway in our discussion, one of the most influential and hostile of the Rajputs came upon us — probably intentionally — and sat down with us. The Brahmin immediately became self-conscious and uncommunicative, but it was too late to conceal the topic of our conversation. The Rajput soon interrupted, asking why the Brahmin was telling us these things and inquiring in a challenging way what possible use the information could be to an American scholar. He implied, with heavy irony, that we had ulterior motives. The interview was obviously ended and by this time a small crowd of onlookers had gathered. Since a satisfactory answer was evidently demanded and since most members of the audience were not among the people I knew best, I took the opportunity to answer fully.

I explained that prior to 1947, India had been a subject nation of little interest to the rest of the world. In the unlikely event that the United States or any other country wanted to negotiate regarding matters Indian its representatives had merely to deal with the British who spoke for India. Indians were of no importance to us, for they were a subject people. They, in turn, had no need to know that America existed as, indeed, few did. Then in 1947, after a long struggle, India had become independent; a nation of proud people who handled their own affairs and participated in the United Nations and in all spheres of international relations on a par with Britain and the United States. Indians for the first time spoke for themselves. At once it became essential for Indians and Americans to know one another. Consequently India sent hundreds of students to America, among other places, and we sent students such as myself to India. We had worked at learning their language and we also wanted to learn their means of livelihood, social customs, religion, and so on, so that we could deal with them intelligently and justly, just as their students were similarly studying in and about America. Fortunately I had an Indian acquaintance then studying a rural community in Utah, whom I could cite as a case comparable to my own. I pointed out that Indian and American scholars had studied Indian cities, towns, and villages of the plains so

that their ways were well known, but that heretofore the five million Paharis — residents of some of the richest, most beautiful, historically and religiously most significant parts of India — had been overlooked. I emphasized that Paharis would play an increasing role in the development of India and that if they were to assume the responsibilities and derive the advantages available to them it was essential that they be better known to their countrymen and to the world. My research was billed as an effort in this direction.

I would like to be able to report that on the basis of this stirring speech I was borne aloft triumphantly through the village, thereafter being treated as a fellow villager by one and all. Needless to say, this did not happen. However, my questioner was evidently favorably impressed, or at least felt compelled to act as though he were before the audience of his village-mates. He responded by saying that he would welcome me in his house any time and would discuss fully any matters of interest to me. He also offered to supply me with a number of artifacts as exhibits of Pahari ingenuity to be taken to America. I might add, anticlimactically, that in fact he never gave me information beyond his reactions to the weather, and that the Brahmin, evidently shaken by the experience, was never again as informative as he had been immediately prior to this incident. This is partly attributable to the substitution, soon afterwards, of a low-status interpreter in place of Sharma, a circumstance to be described below.

The Rajput challenger, however, ceased to be hostile whereas formerly he had been a focus of opposition to my presence. General rapport in the village improved markedly and the stigma attached to talking with me and my interpreter almost disappeared. One notable aftereffect was that my photographic opportunities, theretofore restricted to scenery, small children, and adolescent boys in self-conscious poses, suddenly expanded to include a wide range of economic, ritual, and social occasions as well as people of all castes, ages, and both sexes. Photography itself soon became a valuable means of obtaining rapport as photographs came into demand.

The degree to which I was allowed or requested to take photographs, in fact, proved to be a fairly accurate indicator of rapport. One of the more gratifying incidents of my research in Sirkanda occurred at an annual regional fair about eight months after the research had begun. Soon after I arrived at the fair a group of gayly dressed young women of various villages had agreed to be photographed when a Brahmin man, a stranger to me, stormed up and ordered them to refuse. An elderly and highly respected Rajput woman of Sirkanda had been watching the proceedings and was obviously irritated by the fact and manner of the intervention. She stepped to the center of the group of girls, eying the Brahmin evenly, and said, "Please take my photograph." I did so, the Brahmin left, and my photography was in demand exceeding the film supply throughout the fair.

The incident described above, in which the Rajput challenged my interviewing of the Brahmin priest, came out favorably partly because of the context in which it occurred. For one thing, it occurred late enough so that many people knew me and my interpreter. Having no specific cause for doubting our motives, they were ready to believe us if we made a convincing case. Also, there was a sizeable audience to the event. My explanation was a response to a challenge by a high-status villager and the challenger accepted it gracefully. It was the first time many of these people had been present when I talked at any length and my statement was put with a good deal of feeling, which fact they recognized. It was essentially an appeal for their confidence and cooperation in a task they knew was difficult and which I obviously considered important. They were not incapable of empathy. In fact, an effective appeal for accurate responses from villagers was to picture my academic examining committee in America as made up of relentless and omniscient taskmasters who would unerringly detect any inadequacies or inaccuracies in my report and perhaps fail me on that basis so that I could not pursue my chosen profession. This evoked empathy and cooperation from several informants, one of whom said he would assume personal responsibility for the accuracy of all information obtained from or checked through him.

One man had said, early in the research, "You may be a foreigner and we only poor villagers, but when we get to know you we will judge you as a man among other men, not as a foreigner." With time, most of the villagers demonstrated the validity of his comment by treating me as an individual on the basis of their experience with me, rather than as the stereotyped outsider or white man.

Most important, my statement placed the listeners in a position of accepting what I said or denying their own importance as people and as citizens — it appealed to their pride. They have inferiority feelings relative to non-Paharis which account in large measure for their hostility, and my presence as defined in this statement counteracted these feelings. It was especially effective in response to the Rajput who put the challenge; a man with an acute, and to many aggravating, need for public recognition of his importance. He had gained some eminence by opposing my work; he now evidently gained some by eliciting a full explanation from me and magnanimously accepting it.

Although I remained an alien and was never made to feel that my presence in the village was actively desired by most of its members, I was thereafter tolerated with considerable indulgence. I became established as a resident of Sirkanda, albeit a peculiar one, and no one tried to get me to leave. I have heard strangers en route to or from further mountain areas inquire of Sirkanda villagers as to my identity, presuming that I was out of earshot or could not understand, and be left to ponder the succinct reply, "He lives here."

Other, less spectacular rapport-inducing devices were employed. Unattached men in the village were considered, not unjustly in light of past experience and Pahari morality, a threat to village womanhood. This fear with regard to my interpreter and myself was appreciably diminished when our wives and children visited the village and when a few villagers had been guests at our house in town where our families normally resided. We won some good will by providing a few simple remedies for common village ailments. One of the most effective means of attracting villagers to our abode in the village during this period was a battery radio which we brought, the first to operate in this area. It was an endless source of diversion to villagers and attracted a regular audience, as well as being a focal attraction for visiting relatives and friends from other villages.

At first there had reportedly been considerable speculation as to why two people of such conspicuously different backgrounds as Sharma and myself had appeared on the scene as a team if, as we claimed, we were not sent by the government or a missionary organization. The plausibility of our story was enhanced when Sharma made it clear to villagers that he was my bona fide employee who received payment in cash for his services.

Villagers never ceased to wonder, as I sometimes did myself, why I had chosen this particular area and village for my research. I explained this in terms of its relative accessibility for a hill area, the hospitality and perspicacity of Sirkanda people, the reputation Sirkanda had acquired in the area for being a "good village," and my own favorable impression of it based on familiarity with a number of similar villages. The most satisfactory explanation was that my presence there was largely chance, that is, fate. Everyone agreed that this was the real reason. Villagers pointed out that when the potter makes a thousand identical cups, each has a unique destiny. Similarly, each man has a predetermined course of life and it was my fate to come to Sirkanda. When I gave an American coin to a villager, similar comment was precipitated. Of all the American coins, only one was destined to rest in Sirkanda and this was it. What greater proof of the power of fate could there be then that the coin had, like myself, found its way to this small and remote village?

All our claims of motive and status were put to the test by villagers once they realized we planned to remain in Sirkanda and to associate with them. Sharma's claim to Brahmin status was carefully checked. Extensive inquiry was made about his family and their origins. His behavior was closely watched. His family home was inspected by villagers on trips to town. Only then were villagers satisfied that he was what he claimed to be. When all the claims upon which they could check proved to be accurate villagers were evidently encouraged to believe also those claims which could not be verified.

That suspicions as to our motives were eventually allayed did not mean we therefore could learn what we wanted to learn in the village. It meant only that villagers knew in a general way what they were willing to let us learn, what impressions they would like us to receive. The range of allowable knowledge was far greater than that granted a stranger, far less than that shared by villagers. Although at the time I did not realize it, we were told those things which would give a favorable impression to a trustworthy plains Brahmin. Other facts would be suppressed and if discovered would be discovered in spite of the villagers' best efforts at concealment, often as a result of conversation with some disaffected individual of low esteem in the village. Our informants were primarily high-caste villagers intent on impressing us with their near conformity to the standards of behavior and belief of high-caste plainsmen. Low-caste people were respectful and reticent before us, primarily, as it turned out, because one of us was a Brahmin and we were closely identified with the powerful high-caste villagers.

Three months were spent almost exclusively in building rapport, in establishing ourselves as trustworthy, harmless, sympathetic, and interested observers of village life. In this time we held countless conversations, most of them dealing with the weather and other timely and innocuous topics. A good deal of useful ethnographic information was acquired in the process, but in many areas its accuracy proved to be wanting. Better information was acquired by observation than by inquiry in this period. We found cause for satisfaction during this frustrating and, from the point of view of research results, relatively fruitless time in the fact that we were winning the confidence of a good many people which we hoped would pay off more tangibly later. When the last open opponent of our endeavor had evidently been convinced of our purity of motive in the incident described above, we felt we could begin our data-collecting in earnest.

Until this time we had done all our own housekeeping, cooking, dishwashing, carrying of water and firewood. These activities gave us an opportunity to meet people in a natural setting and to be busy in a period when rapport was not good enough to allow us to devote full time to research. As rap-

port improved we found our household chores too time-consuming for optimal research. We attempted to find assistance in the village but, unable to do so, we added as a third member of our team a seventeen-year-old boy who was of low-caste plains origin but had lived most of his life in the hill station of Mussoorie and was conversant with Pahari ways and the Pahari language. His role was that of servant and he assumed full responsibility for our housekeeping in the village. His informal contacts with some of the younger villagers were a research asset and his low-caste origin was not overlooked, but otherwise he had little direct effect on our relations with villagers. His contribution to the research was primarily in the extreme reliability of his work and his circumspection in relations with villagers.

At this point of apparent promise for productive research, Sharma, my interpreter-assistant, became ill and it was evident that he would be unable to return to our work in the village for some time. Under the circumstances this was a disheartening blow. It plunged my morale to its lowest ebb in the fifteen months of my stay in India, none of which could be described as exhilarating. I cannot here go into the details of the causes for this condition of morale: the pervasive health anxiety with which anyone is likely to be afflicted when he takes an eighteen-month-old child to the field in India, especially if, as in this case, he is away from and inaccessible to his family a good share of the time; the difficulties of maintaining a family household in town and carrying on research in an isolated village; the constant and frustrating parrying with petty officials who are in positions to cause all kinds of difficulty and delay; the virtual lack of social contact outside of one's family, employees, and the villagers among whom one works; the feeling of being merely tolerated by those among whom one works and upon whom one is dependent for most of his social interaction. In such circumstances research is likely to become the primary motivating principle and its progress looms large in one's world view. Therefore, to lose an assistant whose presence I deemed essential to the research when I was on the threshold of tangible progress after a long period of preparation was a discouraging blow. I shall not soon forget the anxiety I felt during the five-hour trek to the village alone after learning of Sharma's illness and incapacity. To await his recovery would have been to waste the best months for research because his illness came at the beginning of the winter slack season when people would, for the first time since my arrival, have ample time to sit and talk. In two months the spring harvest and planting season would begin and many potential informants would be too busy and tired to talk.

After a period alone in the village, I realized that I could not work effectively without assistance due to my inadequate knowledge of the language. Although I dreaded the task of selecting and then introducing a new and inexperienced assistant into the village, this seemed to be a necessary step to preserve the continuity of the research. My hope and intention was to utilize a substitute only until Sharma would be able to work again. Not wishing to spend too much time looking for a substitute, and with qualified people extremely scarce, I employed with many misgivings and on a trial basis the first reasonably promising prospect who appeared. Happily, he proved to be an exceptionally able, willing, and interested worker. He differed from Sharma in at least three important respects: age, religion, and experience. Mohammed, as he will hereafter be called, was a middle-aged Muslim and a retired school teacher who had no familiarity with anthropological research.

These facts proved to have advantageous as well as disadvantageous aspects. I was able to guide him more easily in his work and to interact more directly with villagers than

had been the case with Sharma simply because he realized his inexperience, accepted suggestions readily, and was interested in helping me to know and communicate directly with villagers rather than in demonstrating his efficiency as a reseacher and his indispensability as an interpreter. As a result of his age he received a certain amount of respect. As a Muslim he was able to establish excellent rapport with the low castes but not with the high or twice-born castes. Perhaps most importantly, he had no ego-involvement in the data. He was interested and objective in viewing the culture in which we were working, whereas Sharma had been self-conscious and anxious to avoid giving an unflattering view of Hinduism and of village life to an American in this unorthodox (to him often shockingly so) example of a Hindu village. Moreover, the Brahmin, almost inevitably, had his own status to maintain before the high castes who lived in the village, while the Muslim was under no such obligation.

Since it seemed probable that Sharma would return to work after a few weeks, I decided to make the best of the situation and utilize Mohammed in ways that would make most use of his advantages and minimize his disadvantages, for he was strong where Sharma had been weak, and vice versa. While high-caste people were suspicious of Mohammed on the basis of his religion, low-caste people were more at ease in his presence than they had been with Sharma. Further, low-caste people proved to be more informative than high-caste people on most subjects. I therefore planned to use this interpreter to get data about low castes and from them to get as much general ethnographic data as possible. I was counting on Sharma's return to enable me to return to the high castes and my original endeavor to secure information from and about them. However, after several weeks it became evident that Sharma could not return to work in the village. By then we were beginning to get a good deal of ethnographic material with the promise of much more. In addition to remarkably good rapport with the low castes (greater than that Sharma and I had had with anyone in the village), we were also winning the confidence of some high-caste people. In view of these circumstances I felt encouraged to continue with Mohammed and to broaden our contacts in the village in the remaining months of research.

I had not anticipated the full implications for research of the differences in status of my associates, Sharma and Mohammed. For example, villagers had early determined that Sharma neither ate meat nor drank liquor. As a result we were barely aware that these things were done by villagers. Not long after Mohammed's arrival villagers found that he indulged in both and that I could be induced to do so. Thereafter we became aware of frequent meat and liquor parties, often of an intercaste nature. We found that these were important social occasions, occasions from which outsiders were usually rigidly excluded. Rapport increased notably when it became known that locally distilled liquor was occasionally served at our house. As rapport improved, we were more frequently included in such informal occasions. Our access to information of many kinds increased proportionately.

Mohammed's age put him virtually above the suspicion Sharma had had to overcome regarding possible interest in local women. Mohammed's association with me in my by then generally trusted status precluded undue suspicion of missionary intent or governmental affiliation. Probably his most important characteristic with regard to rapport was his religion. As a Muslim he was, like me, a ritually polluted individual, especially since he was suspected of having eaten beef. For most purposes he and I were untouchables, albeit respected for our presumed wealth and knowledge.

LESSONS FROM THE ETHNOGRAPHIC EXPERIENCE

Had I been alone in the village I would have had a relatively free hand in attempting to determine with whom I associated, so long as I did not infringe too freely on the private life of villagers or on matters of ritual purity. However, since I was in almost constant association with an assistant whose behavior was closely tied to my own, my status and his were interdependent. The definition of ourselves which we cooperated in projecting had to correspond to known and observable facts and clues about ourselves and our purposes. Since to villagers my assistant was more conventional, hence more comprehensible as a person than I, it was largely from him that impressions were derived which determined our status. For this reason the characteristics of the interpreter-assistant were of crucial significance to the research effort.

In such a society as this the ethnographer is inevitably an outsider and never changes. He is judged by those among whom he works on the basis of his own characteristics and those of his associates. He becomes identified with those social groups among his subjects to which he gains access. The nature of his data is largely determined by his identity as seen by his subjects. Polite acceptance and even friendship do not always mean that access will be granted to the confidential regions of the life of those who extend it. The stranger will be excluded from a large and vital area if he is seen as one who will not safeguard secrets, and especially if he is identified as a member of one of those groups from which the secrets are being kept.

Sharma was a high-caste plainsman and was consequently identified with very important groups outside the village — groups rigorously excluded from large areas of the life of both high-caste and low-caste villagers. As such he could likely never have achieved the kind of relationship to villagers which would have resulted in access to much of the life of Sirkanda. Access to that information was essential to the ethnographer because it constituted a large proportion of all village attitudes and behaviors in this closed group. Mohammed was able to gain substantial rapport with the low castes. In view of the attitudes of villagers and the social composition and power structure of the village, the low castes were the only feasible source of information which high-caste villagers considered to be embarrassing, damaging, or secret. They were a reasonably satisfactory source of such information on the entire village because all castes were in such close contact that they had few secrets from one another and did not differ greatly in culture. This is not to say that the information obtained was complete or totally accurate, only to assert that it was much more so than would have been the case had Sharma been the assistant throughout the research.

In a highly stratified society the opinions and behaviors of one stratum are insufficient for an understanding of the whole society. An ethnographer coming into such a group inevitably becomes more closely identified with one or more strata than with others, a fact which largely determines the information he acquires, therefore his analysis of the system. In choosing his employees and other associates he has to bear this in mind. In making his analysis he must be aware of the distortions in his data which result from the fact that he is identified by his subjects with certain groups or individuals and that the impressions and facts he perceives are largely determined by that fact.

Once one has been identified with a particular social group, it may be difficult or impossible to change this identification or to get information that is not colored or determined by it. Early choices have fateful results. The choice of the house in which one will live, of one's first acquaintances, one's associates and employees, are all crucial because they define one's role in the community. The first people one meets — the friendliest locals — are often the very ones who are marginal to their own culture and who therefore seek outside friends and allies. They may be excellent informants, but their probable biases and the effects of their friendship on further contacts in the community must be appreciated if the research is not to be seriously distorted by them. If, as is often the case, the community is riven with factions, rivalries, intrigue, and gossip, one can early and permanently become identified with a group of whose existence he is unaware but which has major effects on his research. Generally, he will come to know of his predicament eventually (often too late to do much good), but the extent of its effects is likely to remain indeterminate.

In the ethnographer's relations with those he studies, as in all human relations, there is some conscious effort on both sides to maintain a definition of the situation and of the individuals and groups within it which is socially acceptable and which is in fact advantageous to those involved. This is a crucial factor in research.

Erving Goffman, in *The Presentation of Self in Everyday Life,* has presented a description and analysis of social interaction in terms of the means by which people seek to control the impressions others receive of them. He has suggested that this "dramaturgical" approach is a widely applicable perspective for the analysis of social systems. In this scheme social interaction is analyzed "from the point of view of impression management."

We find a team of performers who cooperate to present to an audience a given definition of the situation. This will include the conception of own team and of audience and assumptions concerning the ethos that is to be maintained by rules of politeness and decorum. We often find a division into back region, where the performance of a routine is prepared, and front region, where the performance is presented. Access to these regions is controlled in order to prevent the audience from seeing backstage and to prevent outsiders from coming into a performance that is not addressed to them. Among members of the team we find that familiarity prevails, solidarity is likely to develop, and that secrets that could give the show away are shared and kept (Goffman 1959:238).[4]

The ethnographic research endeavor may be viewed as a system involving the social interaction of ethnographer and subjects. Considered as a basic feature of social interaction, therefore, impression management is of methodological as well as substantive significance to ethnographers.

The ethnographer comes to his subjects as an unknown, generally unexpected, and often unwanted intruder. Their impressions of him will determine the kinds and validity of data to which he will be able to gain access, hence the degree of success of his work. The ethnographer and his subjects are both performers and audience to each other. They have to judge each other's motives and other attributes on the basis of short but intensive contact and then decide what definition of themselves and the surrounding situation they want to project — what they will reveal and what they will conceal and how best to do it. Each will attempt to convey to the other the impression that will best serve his interests as he sees them.

The bases for evaluation by an audience are not entirely those which the performer intends or can control.

Knowing that the individual is likely to present himself in a light that is favorable to him, the [audience] may divide what they witness into two parts; a part that is relatively easy for the individual to manipulate at will, being chiefly his verbal assertions, and a part in regard to

which he seems to have little concern or control, being chiefly derived from the expressions he gives off. The [audience] may then use what are considered to be the ungovernable aspects of his expressive behavior as a check upon the validity of what is conveyed by the governable aspects (Goffman, 1959:7).[5]

In their awareness of this, performers attempt to keep the back region out of the range of the audience's perception and to control the performance insofar as possible, preferably to an extent unrealized by the audience. The audience will attempt to glimpse the back region in order to gain new insights into the nature of the performance and the performers.

An ethnographer is usually evaluated by himself and his colleagues on the basis of his insights into the back region of the performance of his subjects. His subjects are evaluated by their fellows on the basis of the degree to which they protect the secrets of their team and successfully project the image of the team that is acceptable to the group for front region presentation. It is probably often thought that this presentation will also satisfy the ethnographer. The ethnographer is likely to evaluate his subjects on the amount of back region information they reveal to him, while he is evaluated by them on his tact in not intruding unnecessarily into the back region and, as rapport improves, on his trustworthiness as one who will not reveal back region secrets. These tend to be mutually contradictory bases of evaluation. Rapport establishment is largely a matter of threading among them so as to win admittance to the back region of the subjects' performance without alienating them.

The impressions that ethnographer and subjects seek to project to each other are, therefore, those felt to be favorable to the

---

[4] From *The Presentation of Self in Everyday Life,* by Erving Goffman. Copyright © 1959 by Erving Goffman. Reprinted by permission of Doubleday & Company, Inc.

[5] From *The Presentation of Self in Everyday Life,* by Erving Goffman. Copyright © 1959 by Erving Goffman. Reprinted by permission of Doubleday & Company, Inc.

accomplishment of their respective goals: the ethnographer seeks access to back region information; the subjects seek to protect their secrets since these represent a threat to the public image they wish to maintain. Neither can succeed perfectly.

If the ethnographer does not gain access to back region information he will have to content himself with an "official" or public view of the culture he studies, derived from publicly accessible and approved sources. This, in any culture, is a limited view at best, which cannot result in accurate and thorough understanding of the culture.

LANGUAGE AND INTERPRETERS

Language poses a problem in most ethnographic field work for the obvious reason that the researcher works with people who speak a language which is foreign to him. Usually, now that training in many languages is available in universities and other institutions, the ethnographer tries to become at least minimally competent in a language known to the people he studies. His imperfect knowledge of the language introduces limitations to the research. The language he learns is sometimes a second language to his informants, known perhaps about as well by them as by him. In this case the limitations are even more severe. In any case, there are bound to be problems in translating ideas from one language to another. People of different cultures and different languages categorize their experiences and the world around them differently, and they verbalize them in different ways. Literal translation of words for objects, ideas, attitudes, and beliefs is often impossible. Even close approximations fail to communicate culturally specific connotations, and the consequent mistakes in communicating with informants, and in recording, interpreting, and analyzing material can distort research greatly. "The field worker should be frank to admit that no matter how much care he devotes to the translation process, it is in absolute terms an unsolvable problem, and the best that he can hope for are good *approximations* between the meanings of the two languages" (Phillips 1960:291). Problems of communication across linguistic barriers are also suggested in Atkinson's facetious and fictional account of an ethnographic expedition (Atkinson 1960:770). He comments that the Mugus (pronounced, he says, to rhyme with "fingers") "speak a kind of bastard D'hoi. . . . They were also adept at making themselves understood by signs. At any rate I *hope* they were, because otherwise much of the information we brought back is not going to be worth a row of beans."

Some anthropologists have made it a point to learn the language of their informants as well as they could, and then to rely entirely upon their knowledge for research purposes. Others have employed bilingual interpreters. The anthropologist, Clyde Kluckhohn, has discussed the problems of doing research through an interpreter:

At worst, an interview carried on through an interpreter resembles, as someone has said, "an exchange of telegrams." At best, an awkward third set of variables have been introduced into an already complex problem. What the subject says and fails to say will be influenced by his fear of, admiration for, social relation to, the interpreter as well as by the manner in which the interpreter puts questions, his general bearing, his aside comments, etc. What the investigator hears will be entirely filtered through a selective screening which is hard to allow for with any precision. The interpreter will suppress and distort both consciously and unconsciously. He will omit what seems to him unimportant or irrelevant or whatever is embarrassing to him. These omissions can largely be checked if the field worker has a measure of control over the native language. But the subtle distortions of translation cannot be prevented unless the anthropologist knows the language so well as hardly to need an interpreter or unless the whole interview is first recorded in native text and then worked out with, preferably, a battery of interpreters (Kluckhohn 1945:123).

In a few instances, research has even been done via two interpreters where, for example, the people studied speak only Language A and the ethnographer speaks only English, and where no one can be found who speaks both. Then one interpreter will be employed who knows English and Language B, and another will be employed who knows Language B and Language A. All information must then be filtered through two intermediaries. Use of any interpreter inevitably results in cumbersome inquiry procedures, but does not preclude useful research.

Most field workers agree that for effective use of an interpreter, the ethnographer himself must be able to follow much of what the interpreter and informant say. This enables him to check the accuracy of interpretation, to clarify points, to catch instances when, as inevitably happens, the interpreter simplifies, summarizes, or injects his own information, opinions, or impressions in his interpretation. If the ethnographer cannot understand any of the conversations between interpreter and informant, he is completely at the mercy of the interpreter; what he learns is filtered and inevitably interpreted, and to an extent, distorted before he hears it. Ambrose Bierce, in fact, has defined an interpreter as "One who enables two persons of different languages to understand each other by repeating to each what it would have been to the interpreter's advantage for the other to have said" (Bierce 1958:69).

Some ethnographers use an interpreter even when they are quite fluent in the language themselves, simply to enable them to probe deeply into meanings that otherwise might remain obscure, and also to guard against the natural tendency for an informant to simplify answers for a foreigner. An in-terpreter can also keep a conversation going while the ethnographer makes notes, or he can follow up on side issues with some informants while the ethnographer continues the main conversation. While fluency is a goal for nearly every ethnographer, its lack has not prevented successful research. John Gumperz, a linguist, has mentioned that some kinds of inquiry and information became closed to him in his research in a village in north India when he achieved fluency in the colloquial language. Prior to that time, many naïve and trivial questions asked in his imperfect, foreigner's Hindi were indulgently answered. When he knew the language well and spoke it like a villager, he was no longer considered the naïve stranger, and his questions were dismissed as stupid or impertinent, as they would have been if asked by a local resident.

Communication between people occurs in many ways other than by verbal means, as Edward T. Hall has made abundantly clear in *The Silent Language* (1959). Human behavior is largely symbolic, that is, arbitrary meanings are attached to it. Thus, many of the problems of nonunderstanding and misunderstanding which apply to problems of language apply to a wider range of behavior and interaction as the ethnographer confronts those whose way of life he studies. As a stranger to that culture, he is likely initially to be unable to behave correctly — to convey, for example, politeness, to detect impatience, to identify sensitive subject matter, or to appreciate the significance of many social situations. He is likely to make blunders and he risks alienating those whose friendship and trust he most wants and needs. In this context, caution, circumspection, and sincerity are invaluable traits, and the role of stranger or neophyte is most useful, for it generally excuses mistakes, or at least gives their perpetrator another chance.

SPECIAL TECHNIQUES

The techniques used by anthropologists for obtaining data, as distinguished from the overall participant-observation method, vary according to the training and interests of the ethnographer, the problems he wishes to investigate, and the people he studies.

The bulk of field research is done by the simple but difficult method of living among the people one wants to learn to know, talking with them, observing them, and writing down that which seems significant. Various kinds of aids have been devised to facilitate this task (cf. Rowe 1953). Most notable among mechanical aids are the camera and the tape recorder. Neither substitutes for observation, but both are aids to it.

In another sphere altogether are particular techniques of inquiry. These range from the census (Richards 1938) and the genealogical method (Rivers 1910) to a vast array of psychological tests including, prominently, projective tests (Henry and Spiro 1953; Henry 1961). Census-taking is simply a way of getting considerable information on a variety of topics in a systematic way in a short time. It involves finding out who lives in the society or group to be studied, where they live and with whom, their occupations, possessions, and many other kinds of information. It is a detailed listing of facts about the people who live in a locality. The genealogical method gathers similar information about people who are related to one another. It is acquired by asking people to remember their relatives as far into the past as possible and as remotely related as possible. This method focuses on the kin group rather than on the locality, and emphasizes antecedents as well as contemporaries. It affords information on a wide variety of topics, including kin groups, kinship terminology, marriage rules, residence rules, adoption, inheritance, history of the people, trends in culture change, and many others. Both the census

and the genealogy are excellent means of initiating inquiries and of uncovering information which might otherwise go undetected. Thus, their value is as much in what is discovered incidentally in the process of their collection as in what is discovered intentionally as part of the formal collection of the data.

Psychological tests provide a wide variety of insights. Those which are projective in nature — which ask the informant to respond to an ambiguous stimulus (usually a visual image) — give the anthropologist an additional insight into the way his subjects see themselves and the world around them. Other ways to this end are the collection, on the individual level, of life histories (Dollard 1936), of dreams (Eggan 1961) and fantasies, and of folklore (Fischer 1963), art and other expressive forms on the group level. The aim in all these is to find out how people view their world.

ANALYSIS OF DATA

The mode of analysis of ethnographic data, like the method of its collection, is dependent in large part upon the training and interests of the ethnographer and upon his research problem. It is also dependent upon the ways in which he collected his data (which in turn was determined partly by how he intended to analyze it).

Traditionally, ethnographic data have been presented so as to provide a picture of the way of life of the people studied which is as complete as possible. Obviously no account can be entirely complete. In presenting their reports, ethnographers have found it necessary to organize the data under subject headings. Even though culture does not occur in compartments, much less in handily labeled compartments, it is inherent in the nature of language and exposition that to describe a culture, it must be described sequentially according to some principle of organization.

This means that, implicitly or explicitly, cultural facts must be categorized. G. P. Murdock has published an indexed list of such headings thought to be useful to ethnographers and, if used consistently, believed to be capable of producing categorizations which are valid cross-culturally, that is, comparatively. His list totals eighty-eight major headings of cultural facts such as "clothing," "settlements," "marketing," "marriage," and "social problems" and well over 500 subheadings, such as, under the heading "clothing," "normal garb," "special garments," "paraphernalia," and "clothing manufacture" (Murdock 1950).

The Royal Anthropological Institute of Great Britain and Ireland has published frequently revised editions of *Notes and Queries on Anthropology* since 1874. This contains lists of topics to be investigated in any culture, and suggestions on how to derive the necessary information on each topic.

Categorizations such as these have been used with success by many ethnographers, more often as reminders of what to look for or what data to collect than as bases for organizing their ethnographic research or report. The question is often raised whether by using predefined categories, the ethnographer does not in fact force his data into inappropriate molds, thereby distorting it. Is it possible, for example, to describe Hinduism, Christianity, and Eskimo religion under the same headings — according to the same categories? [6] This is an argument we cannot go into here except to say that those who have used such headings defend themselves on two grounds. (1) They use the headings with insight and caution, so that distortion is absent or minimal. Wherever necessary they adopt novel categories derived from the data, and (2) the headings are sufficiently abstract that cultural context and detail can be included under them, thereby preserving the

[6] See Chapter 9 for an argument as to why this is not possible.

nature of the phenomena as they occur in any particular culture, while maximizing the chances for comparison across cultural boundaries through the use of general criteria for categorization. Thus widespread and comparable phenomena are not obscured by their particular, unique manifestations. They point out that to refuse to use general categories is to focus upon the culturally specific, thereby eliminating comparison and generalization. There can be no science of the unique.

The desire to describe cultures in terms of their own structures and categories rather than in terms of imposed schemes has long been present in anthropology. Recently, an explicit technique of analysis has been devised for the purpose, adapted from linguistic analysis. Just as modern linguistics attempts to describe and analyze each language in terms of its own grammar, so culture can be analyzed in this fashion. For this approach the terms "componential analysis" and "ethnoscience" have been coined (Frake 1962b: Sturtevant 1964).

It is well known that people of different cultures construe their worlds in different ways. As the linguist Benjamin Lee Whorf has put it, "We cut nature up, organize it into concepts, and ascribe significance as we do, largely because we are parties to an agreement to organize it in this way . . ." (Whorf 1956a:213). More recently Ward Goodenough has made much the same point: "Culture is not a material phenomenon; it does not consist of things, people, behavior, or emotions. It is rather an organization of these things. It is the forms of things that people have in mind . . ." (Goodenough 1957:167). Thus we know that people of different cultures categorize colors in different ways despite the fact that the visual stimuli they categorize are in all cases the same. Some name more colors than we do, some less. Other cultures do not place the boundaries between named colors exactly where we do. The componential analyst would seek to discover the color terminologies and their referents in any culture he studied. He would attempt further to determine the rules or criteria by which the terminology is constructed and applied to the phenomena of the observed world. He would feel successful if he could devise a statement about rules or criteria for categorization of colors in terms of components such as hue, brightness, and so on, which would enable him or anyone else who knew them to categorize (that is, name) colors appearing in nature precisely as would a native of the culture he is analyzing. Such rules or criteria are derived by collecting detailed data indicating how people group and distinguish the phenomena in their world. The analyst notes carefully not only the content of the categories, but the context in which distinctions are made. His aim is to find significant usage as distinguished from insignificant variation, just as does a linguist looking for phonemes and the structures of which they are constituent parts among all the phonetic variation which occurs in a language. The method is based directly upon linguistic methods.

Whether the rules the analyst devises are or should be the principles upon which the native actually bases his categorization, or whether the rules merely "work" (and therefore may be only one of several alternative sets of adequate rules) is a point that has been much debated. Those who believe that a single, correct set of rules is immanent in any culture (and in any language), and that it merely awaits discovery, have been called the "God's truth" analysts, while those who believe that the ethnographer's (or linguist's) task is to manufacture a workable set of rules (and that there may be any number of different rules which will work) have been called the "hocus-pocus" analysts (Burling 1964a).

What utility such analyses will have for ethnography in the long run remains to be seen. So far they have been applied only to extremely limited kinds of data — those data which are highly structured, and generally those which can be studied as terminological systems or taxonomies, for instance, color categories, kinship terminologies, categories of disease, categories of plants, and so on. To study any one of these systems is painstaking, time-consuming work, which results in a detailed but very narrow description and analysis. Whether the procedure can be effectively applied to less obviously and formally structured data and to more subtle data (for instance, social interaction, attitudes, values) remains to be seen. Whether it can result in an overall ethnography is a question to be answered in the even more distant future. Its advocates would maintain that whatever it accomplishes analytically, it does so with a degree of validity which less formal analysis can never achieve. Therefore, it may not do much, as yet, but what it does, it does rigorously. Its aim, as stated by Frake is "eventually to provide the ethnographer with public, nonintuitive procedures for ordering his presentation of observed and elicited events according to the principles of the people he is studying" (1962b:85). Some would say that componential analysis is the only method adequate to the ethnographic aim of accurate description of a culture.

Its detractors and skeptics point out that they and their teachers and their teachers' teachers have been doing componential analysis inadvertently all their professional lives, simply as part of the ethnographic method, albeit in less rigorous fashion. They doubt that the added rigor pays off sufficiently well in insight or understanding or descriptive accuracy to make the restriction in scope worth the while. They express doubt that an ethnography will ever be written that is based on the method of componential analysis, simply because of the time required to gather the data and the space required to report it for even one small segment of culture. It offers to many, at best, an unrealizable ideal. They suspect that in the process of componential analysis, the human understanding of the culture analyzed is likely to be factored out, so that the product is sterile and in that sense untrue to life (Berreman 1966).

SCIENTISM, HUMANISM, AND ETHNOGRAPHY

In the quotation cited above, Frake stated that componential analysis aims ". . . to provide the ethnographer with public, nonintuitive procedures for ordering his presentation of observed and elicited events. . . ."

This leads to a crucial problem in anthropology: the extent to which it is or ought to be a science. Without broaching directly the subject of what science is, we can point out immediately that many social scientists — anthropologists and others — see ethnography as methodologically unsophisticated, intuitive, journalistic, and unfocused, and they therefore call for increased rigor. They call for increasing problem orientation, adoption of highly structured research methods, use of quantification, models, and formal analysis, and they place great emphasis on scientific rigor, objectivity, and verification. These might be called the scientific or scientistic anthropologists. At the other extreme are those who are suspicious of quantification and highly structured methods on the grounds that these lead the ethnographer away from people and their way of life, toward a sterile, dehumanized scientism. They urge an eclectic approach to research, letting the problems emerge from the data. They emphasize insight at the expense of rigor, discovery at the expense of verification. These might be called the humanistic anthropologists.

This polarization in the philosophy of ethnographic research is part of the general problem of social science: how and whether to treat scientifically human situations. Some see scientific rigor and human insight as being alternatives in ethnographic research. But I do not think the choice need be made. The question I see is not whether to be scientific or humanistic, but how to be both. That is, the ethnographer must strive to make his observations and analyses more rigorous than those of a casual observer and he must do so without losing the fundamental insights that are obtained by perceptive nonscientists (for instance, novelists). The humanistic view tends to overlook the advantages of rigor — especially of verifiability of findings; the scientistic view tends to overlook the advantages of insight. The humanist ignores the fact that findings are only as good as the theories and methods by which they are derived and are only convincing if they can be verified; the scientist ignores the fact that studying human social events is in itself a social event — that the observer is in and of his data, however hard he may strive to remain apart, however highly structured his tools, techniques, and analytical models. Attitudes, emotions, values, meanings, connotations are as important in the collection of materials by questionnaire as by interview, in materials recorded in numbers as in those recorded in anecdotes. To ignore them is to miss the crucial core of humanity. The appearance of scientific respectability in such a case is achieved at the price of insignificance (at best) or error (at worst).

Thus ethnographers, like all social scientists, are faced with the dilemma of how to be objective about a subjective research situation: how to be scientific *and* (not *or*) humanistic.

No definitive solution can be given, but one may be sought through making explicit and public the procedures by which research is accomplished and interpretations are derived. This requires essentially what we might call an ethnography of ethnography: a description of exactly how ethnography is done, how insights are derived, how judgments about data are made. One does not abjure insight and intuition, he simply treats his insights and intuitions as problematic. He attempts to define them. He makes as explicit as possible the cues which led him to them. He reports the bases for his inferences. Thus, the ethnographer can attempt to determine *why* he sought out Informant X and not Informant Y, *why* he found one report plausible and another implausible, *why* he considered Behavior A significant and Behavior B trivial, and so on. The scientific virtues of verifiability and replicability can be increased without sacrificing the humanistic virtues of insight, empathy, and understanding by defining the procedures by which the latter are accomplished. Frake has commented, in this vein, that "to produce ethnographic statements that can be demonstrated to be *wrong,* and not simply judged to be unpersuasively written, is, I think, some advance over the production of most current statements" (Frake 1964b:142–143).

Unless methodology is made explicit in ethnography, its practitioners are likely to diverge, on the one hand, into those (probably a large majority) who take refuge in scientism, who seek rigor at the expense of drastic reduction in content, insight, and understanding, and who get farther and farther away from the realities of human social life — from culture as it is lived. They are remote from research which has anything at all to say to the human condition and especially to the human problems in the world today. On the other hand will be those (probably a minority) who have no pretense of being scientific, whose statements, while at best insightful, bear no demonstrable validity, who are essentially creative writers on anthropological topics. Berger (1963:13) has rightly pointed out

that "in science as in love a concentration on technique is quite likely to lead to impotence." [7] But one need not conclude, therefore, that technique cannot be defined, improved, taught, and effectively applied to practice. The aim must be to do so without destroying the meaning and feeling which makes it worthwhile. If ethnographers can continue in the honored tradition of insight, empathy, and understanding, and make the achievement of these subject to verification through making the processes explicit, it can achieve this.

ETHNOLOGIST'S BIAS

No one can be completely objective in any undertaking. Human beings are by definition subjective. The problem of a science of human behavior is largely defined by this fact. The question then arises: is ethnographic research simply a huge ink-blot test for the ethnographer? To what extent is the ethnographic report a projection of the ethnographer's personality and to what extent is it a reflection of external "reality?" Several societies have been studied by more than one ethnographer. Sometimes the results have been quite divergent. Robert Redfield (1930) and Oscar Lewis (1951) both studied the Mexican village of Tepoztlan, about twenty years apart. The former described it as well integrated, peaceful, homogeneous, and populated with contented people; the latter described it as faction-ridden, tense, and populated largely by frustrated, fearful, envious, distrustful people (cf. Redfield 1955:132–148). John Bennett (1946), in an insightful article, described two major views of Pueblo culture in the American Southwest, as held by the many anthropologists who have studied that

[7] From *Invitation to Sociology,* by Peter L. Berger. Copyright © 1962 by Peter L. Berger. Reprinted by permission of Doubleday & Company, Inc.

culture. One view depicts that culture as integrated, harmonious, tranquil, and homogeneous. The other depicts it as marked by tension, suspicion, hostility, anxiety, and ambition. He noted that the first group focuses on the *end result* of the cultural process — on the apparently smooth-running cultural machinery; the second group focuses on the *means* to that end, and the costs at which the efficient functioning, and the apparent tranquility, are achieved. He analyzed these divergent views as reflections of the values and viewpoints of the respective ethnographers. Ralph Piddington (1957:546) notes, with reference to two classic ethnographic studies, *We, The Tikopia*, by Raymond Firth, and the various works on the Trobriand Islanders by Bronislaw Malinowski, that "a critic once remarked that the Trobriand Islanders are very like Malinowski, and the Tikopia very like Professor Raymond Firth."

Other sources of bias have been noted by various commentators on ethnographic reporting. It is often noted, for example, that anthropologists seek out and note the exotic and tend to overlook the commonplace and familiar (Naroll 1963). This is both an advantage and a disadvantage in studying an alien culture — more things in it are unusual, hence problematic than in one's own culture. Thus, less is likely to be taken for granted than in a familiar milieu, but because of the welter of unfamiliar material, crucial facts may be ignored simply because they are inconspicuous and therefore do not strike the observer as noteworthy.

Anthropologists, like all people, are to a large extent products of their culture. They see the people they study through their own cultural lens, with their own preconceptions and categories, and this introduces bias. A Chinese anthropologist has indicated how views of Zuni culture (one of the Pueblo cultures mentioned above) have been conditioned by the fact that those who have done the research have been Americans, and he gives his own interpretations derived from the same anthropological background but from a different national culture (Li 1937).

Some commentators have claimed that anthropologists tend to select their discipline partly because they are alienated from their own culture and therefore find the study and appreciation of foreign cultures peculiarly satisfying. Frequently anthropologists are said to favor the downtrodden and disadvantaged, to have a strong equalitarian bias; sometimes they are alleged to value stability and equilibrium over change, and otherwise to embody value positions which may conflict with objective reporting and analysis of social events.

Since man is a cultural animal, and since ethnographers are men, such problems are inevitable: objectivity in any absolute sense is impossible in the study of men. To deny bias is to mask the problem rather than to eliminate it. Perhaps the best advice is for the ethnographer to attempt to recognize his biases, compensate for them insofar as possible, and in any event to make them as explicit as possible so that readers will be able to take account of them in evaluating the ethnography. Obviously, even the most conscientious effort will fall short since no one is fully self-aware, but this, like explicating the research methods and the bases for inference, is a direction in which ethnography must go in the pursuit of increasing scientific validity, and it constitutes no threat to humanistic insight.

ETHICS AND RESPONSIBILITY

No discussion of research on human beings is adequate without some reference to the morality of the undertaking. I will not discuss the ethics of research into the functioning of human society as such. Obviously I believe it to be worthwhile. To the few remaining critics who see it as dangerous tampering likely to lead to too much knowledge, hence to destruction of the social order, I would quote Edward Shils' comment, "I do not think that all social order rests on cognitive illusions which the results of scientific social research must dissolve" (1959:138). To those who fear social research because knowledge leads to potential control and therefore is inimical to freedom, I would maintain that ignorance is not to be confused with freedom. One cannot be said to act freely if he is in ignorance of the consequences of his action. Knowledge is a condition of freedom.

More immediate and acute problems of morality in research are those which arise from the direct effects of research on those who are studied. Does the ethnographer give medical aid, legal counsel, and financial assistance? Does he settle disputes or enable an informant to come to America to get a Ph.D.? Or does he merely observe, record, analyze, and then depart? What if he is asked to do these things — or is asked not to? If he has become an important factor in the local social or economic system, or is essential to the status of one or more persons, what happens when he leaves? Allan Holmberg made one man into an important, respected, and successful figure among the Siriono simply by giving him a shotgun and shells and teaching him to use them. When he left, the man was faced with sinking back into his former position of low esteem, so he emigrated to a missionary outpost, there to live a different life altogether, isolated from his former fellows. Stories of this type could be multiplied many times over.

Occasionally the results of research are more drastic and even more unforeseeable. Cora Du Bois has described how five of her friends in Alor were executed during World War II as an indirect result of her presence there years before. They were accused by Japanese army officers of being pro-Ameri-

can. She concludes with the poignant statement, "there is no end to the intricate chain of responsibility and guilt that the pursuit of even the most arcane social research involves. 'No man is an island' " (Du Bois 1960:xv). Social research cannot fail to have effect on those who experience it.

There is indeed no escape from responsibility, but the ethnographer has scope for the exercise of discretion in the manner of his research and in the content of his report. Here he is faced with numerous difficult and fateful decisions. What is his responsibility to his informants with reference to the information they divulge and entrust to him? How much should he let them know of his intentions? How much should he reveal of his methods? When does research efficiency defer to moral responsibility, and what is moral responsibility in research? How much should the ethnographer reveal of his subjects' secrets in his published report? If they engage in illegal activities, should he report the fact, or not? If so, how can he protect them, or should he? Social researchers have long been faced with these problems, and it is clear that there are no simple answers to them. In this context, too, it must be remembered that ethnography, like all social research, is a human undertaking. It carries with it the responsibilities of all human undertakings — neither less nor more. These responsibilities must be borne by the individual researcher and must be made in human terms, just as are all social responsibilities. Sometimes he will find that the use of pseudonyms will suffice to protect his informants; sometimes information will have to be suppressed. Sometimes he will intervene as a result of moral commitment; sometimes he will remain aloof. He will always balance the human values of his subjects and himself. He can do no more; he should do no less. He may sometimes make a wrong choice and hurt someone, including himself. These are risks everyone takes. A good ethnographer is a successful human being, and as such he will make relatively fewer mistakes. But it is pointless to expect of an ethnographer superhuman insights or behavior.

I prefer to think of ethnography as a truly human and cultural undertaking. The ethnographer is as much a phenomenon of the contemporary world as has been the trader, the missionary, the soldier, the administrator, the revolutionary, the conservative. He, like any other person, is a creature of the world. The responsibilities he bears are human responsibilities. The justifiability of his intrusion into a society is of the same order as that of any other intruder. Happily, ethnographers have maintained a level of responsibility which has made it possible, in most areas of the world, for subsequent ethnographers to be welcomed back. In this dramatic proof of the pudding, ethnographers have surpassed other categories of intruders into alien cultures. In large part this is attributable to their combination of scientific commitment, insight, and human integrity. It is to be hoped that, through their published works, they will enable others to benefit by, and share in, their hard-won understanding of the peoples they have studied, and their welcome among those people.

Suggested Readings

Scattered through anthropological and sociological literature are books, chapters, articles, and more frequently pages or paragraphs which bear directly upon the topics raised in this chapter. A few of the most pertinent and insightful will be cited here for further reference.

Excellent and readable general introductions to social science as a research discipline are to be found in Berger (1963) and Mills (1959). General introductions to the research process itself are to be found in Selltiz et al. (1960), and Cicourel (1964). The interrelationship of theory and research is discussed by Merton (1957a). All these are written by sociologists, but what they have to say is equally relevant to anthropologists.

The development of ethnography as a science is surveyed briefly by Lowie (1959). Research design in anthropology is discussed by Lewis (1953) and by Spindler and Goldschmidt (1952). The comparative method in anthropology is the subject of articles by Eggan (1954) and Lewis (1956). McEwen (1963) investigates the problem of validation in ethnographic research, while Passin (1942) and Dean and Whyte (1958) present examples of that problem. Ethnographic methods are surveyed in excellent articles by Bennett (1948) and by Piddington (1957: 525–596). Perhaps the classic discussion of methodological problems in social research is that by Thomas and Znaniecki (1918:1–86). General guides to field work are provided by the Royal Anthropological Institute (1951) and by Junker (1960).

The ethnographic field experience is entertainingly and insightfully described in fictionalized form by an anthropologist using the pseudonym Elenore Bowen (1954), and is recounted in nonfiction by Berreman (1962), Evans-Pritchard (1940:8–15), Firth (1936:1–12), Haring (1956:52–65), Holmberg (1950:1–4), Malinowski (1932: 5–25), Maybury-Lewis (1965), Powdermaker (1966), Read (1965), and Whyte (1955:279–358).

Participant observation and interviewing as research methods are introduced in overview by Paul (1953) and by Dean (1954). Special aspects of these methods are discussed by Becker (1958), Dean and Whyte (1958), Kluckhohn (1940), Schwartz (1955), Vidich (1955), and Vidich and Bensman (1960). Goffman (1959) gives the classic discussion of how people present themselves before one another in attempting to control the impressions they convey. These ideas are extended to apply to the ethnographer's role in relation to his informants by Berreman (1962), and by Nash (1963). Problems of bias in ethnographic research are perceptively addressed by Bennett (1946), and are exemplified in discussions by Li (1937) and Redfield (1955:132–168).

Language and the use of interpreters has been the subject of several articles. Among the most stimulating is that by Phillips (1960). Mead (1938) and Lowie (1940) address the subject from a different perspective, as do Bohannon (1956, 1958), and those who replied to his statements in lively debate (e.g., Beals 1957).

A wide variety of works deal with special types of data, data collection, and analysis. Only a few of these, on a few representative topics, can be indicated here: psychological anthropology, Barnouw (1963), DeVos (1961), Henry and Spiro (1953), Henry (1961); folklore, Fischer (1963); community studies and censuses, Arensberg (1954, 1961), Colson (1954), Mandelbaum (1956), Richards (1938); genealogical method, Rivers (1910); componential analysis, Conklin (1964), Frake (1962b, 1964b), Sturtevant (1964), and critiques thereof by Burling (1964) and Berreman (1966).

The use of photography in ethnographic research is discussed by the Hitchcocks (1960) and by Mead (1956), while an overview of technical aids is given by Rowe (1953).

Ethics, responsibility, and freedom in social research are addressed by Barnes (1963), Berger (1963:151–163), Mills (1959, 1963a, 1963b), Shils (1959), and in an exchange of comments regarding a specific research project by Whyte and others (1958–1959).

CHAPTER 15 makes explicit the kinds of research processes involved in the qualitative analysis and comparison of a few societies to discover or suggest relationships between sociocultural variables. As a means of discussing the logic and promise of microethnology, Professor Fischer here systematically analyzes his own research tactics on two Pacific islands, Truk and Ponape. As he makes evident, small-scale ethnological comparisons are, in terms of basic research activities, not far from ethnography, although the aims and design do differ. The importance of this chapter rests in the fact that in anthropology and social science generally very little attention has been given to the logic and principles of research using qualitative, mechanical models, quite unlike the situation of the very sophisticated outpouring of treatises on quantitative, statistical, probabilistic research strategies. Yet a very great deal of comparative work in anthropology involves confronting and dealing with masses of detailed, particularistic, concrete, unquantified descriptions of sociocultural events, or people doing things in special places on particular occasions, descriptions obtained from informal if highly systematic ethnographic observations, informant interviews, life-histories, case studies, and similar techniques. As Professor Fischer points out, some of these comparisons and the ensuing conclusions are scientifically useful because they raise problems, because they conflict with what we think we know and what we anticipate seeing, while others are entirely novel and perhaps at first inexplicable. In part, then, microethnology involves deliberate comparison of qualitative cultural data, preliminary classification and sortings, attempts to build a typology and to proceed to a demonstrated statement of patterned relationships between variables, and an effort to derive a plausible explanation for such relationships. Microethnology thus is one more step in the direction of general knowledge about man. A word of advice to the reader: the paper on Trukese and Ponapean totemism appended to the chapter should be read first.

THE AUTHOR was educated at Harvard, where he obtained both his undergraduate and graduate degrees in anthropology, and at the New School for Social Research. Additionally, he studied Japanese in the Navy Language Training Program during World War II, a skill which he has since put to use both in the islands of Micronesia and in Japan. He has taught at Harvard and since 1958 has been at Tulane University. Between 1949 and 1954 he served first as Native Affairs Officer and then as District Anthropologist in Truk and Ponape Districts of the United States Trust Territory of the Pacific. His writings deal with the peoples of Micronesia, Japan, and the United States. They include *The Eastern Carolines,* a survey of the cultural anthropology of part of Micronesia, and *Orchard Town,* a study of culture and socialization practices in a New England community, which is co-authored by his wife, Dr. Ann Fischer.

15

Microethnology:
Small-Scale Comparative Studies

J. L. FISCHER

Tulane University

Ethnology has been defined as "the comparative study of peoples past and present" (Kluckhohn 1949a:300). "Microethnology" is a term which may be aptly used to refer to the sort of small-scale comparative study represented by Robert Redfield's *The Folk Culture of Yucatan* (1941) and Fred Eggan's *Social Organization of the Western Pueblos* (1950). These studies compare a small number of communities or societies which are historically related through substantial contact or common origin, but show contrasts on certain points. Since differences on most points are fewer and less sharp than would be found between unrelated societies, it may possibly be easier for the investigator to isolate functional or causal relationships explaining the relatively few differences which are great enough to attract attention.

The objective of this chapter is to discuss and evaluate a number of methodological issues in the practice of microethnology,

with reference mainly to a single brief study of mine, a paper entitled "Totemism on Truk and Ponape" (Fischer 1957), which is appended to the chapter. Before proceeding, the reader might profitably examine this research report, for because of its very briefness it may conveniently serve as a concrete example to make the discussion of methodological issues more meaningful. To begin, I will discuss something of the genesis of the Truk and Ponape research. This will be followed by a summary of the data and argument presented, with an evaluation of the degree to which the conclusions can be considered to be supported by the data, the possibility of drawing other conclusions from the same data, and further data which would be desirable and the way it might be gathered. Attention will be given to principles which can help guide future research of this type.

When I went to do field work in the Caroline Islands, I was a graduate student in

Anthropology in the Social Relations Department at Harvard in need of material for a thesis. The opportunity to go to the Carolines came up rather suddenly, before I had thought much about thesis plans. My teachers advised me to prepare a thesis prospectus and have it approved before leaving. I quickly read what literature I could find on Palau, where I was supposed to be sent, and concocted a prospectus which said I would study temporal orientations among the Palauans in many phases of their life: cooking, kinship, sex, and so on. This was promptly rejected by my teachers as vague and over-ambitious, for one thing, and I left without an approved thesis prospectus to guide my field work but with an understanding that once in the field I would no doubt find some suitable topic.

One point was clear: we anthropology students in Social Relations were not to write a simple ethnography of the cultures we studied, for our teachers strongly felt there was no point in piling up more ethnographies if we did not have some idea of what we would do with the data. We must have some guiding hypothesis and collect data to test it. One member of the committee (not an anthropologist, incidentally) explained further to me, "It would really be much easier if you studied two related cultures, not just Palau. Then you could make a comparison and observe differences between the two cultures, testing to see if these are related to differences on another set of variables, which might be supposed to cause the first set." It seemed outrageous to me that anthropologists in the modern age could not get along with a study of a single culture for their doctoral thesis, that the amount of field work required should be doubled in this fashion, but I agreed that I would be on the lookout for a possible second culture to compare with Palau. I would also try to think up some kind of hypothesis which might be tested by such a comparison. Of

course, I realized that those members of my thesis committee who were not anthropologists must have been secretly rather shocked at the idea that even two cultures were enough to test a hypothesis in which a whole culture was statistically only a single case. Of course two cultures would provide two points on a graph — enough to draw a line through — and even if they could not be regarded as proving a hypothesis, they could at least hint at the direction of the relationship of my variables, whatever they might be.

But when I went to the Pacific as a District Anthropologist for the American Administration of the Trust Territory of the Pacific Islands (Carolines, Marshalls, and Marianas, except for Guam), I went to Truk, a thousand miles east of Palau. And after a little over a year in the Truk District, an opportunity arose for a transfer to Ponape District, so the possibility of making some kind of "controlled" comparisons of two related societies could be realized. My doctoral thesis (Fischer 1955) and some publications derived from it (1956, 1960; Fischer and Swartz 1960) was such a comparison, as was the paper on totemism discussed below.

According to a popular view, it is desirable for an anthropologist to keep his theory-making and his data-gathering separate. In one phase, he ponders over ethnographies and constructs theories to explain already recorded ethnographic facts. In a second phase he goes out to some societies for which certain relevant facts are not yet known, collects them, and sees whether or not they fit his theory, whether or not the new societies behave like the previously recorded ones or extrapolations from them. Obviously I did not follow this program. Frankly, in my opinion, it is undesirable in most anthropological field work to do so, although I would agree that in some library work the separation of formulation and testing of hypotheses from data collection is a useful practice in testing hypotheses through evidence from recorded literature, in the fashion of the large-scale comparative studies of Murdock and Whiting (e.g., Murdock 1949; Whiting and Child 1953). In the latter case, what one does essentially is to read a fraction of the literature rather carefully and formulate hypotheses as to the relation between sociocultural variables, then predict what one ought to find in the bulk of the literature on other societies which one has not yet looked at, and pick a random sample of these and see if the prediction is borne out.

But in preparing for extended field work, one cannot as easily decide in advance to look just at certain phenomena in a culture and completely ignore the rest. Just to live and sustain himself in a foreign society the ethnographer must undergo a certain amount of general acculturation. What he learns during this process (which is sometimes called participant observation) includes the personal skills necessary for making his way in largely unfamiliar cultural surroundings; but he simultaneously acquires information of definite anthropological interest, and this cannot be ignored or thrown away. Moreover, to understand a people one must pay some attention to their main interests, which cannot always be known in advance. For instance, it would be possible to understand quite a bit about Trukese society without even knowing of the existence of Trukese yam cultivation, which is traditional but very minor, but to get very far in Ponape one cannot avoid yams (cf. Bascom 1948). On the whole, agriculture is a more central interest in Ponape because of the greater dependence there on yams, which require time and effort, than in Truk, where the people depend more upon the breadfruit tree, which produces fruit year after year with little care or effort other than to pick the fruit in season and perhaps preserve

some in a pit, dug in the ground and lined with leaves.

Anthropologists have boasted that one virtue of their discipline is that it sees sociocultural systems as wholes, it looks for interrelations among all parts of the system. This is said to be achieved especially through the experience of field work. But if field work is guided too narrowly by predetermined hypotheses this holistic view will be lost. Further, even the possibility of seeking evidence for alternate hypotheses to one's original hypothesis can be reduced if one determines in advance what data to collect.

How then did I decide in the case of the paper on totemism that it might be desirable to compare totemic practices in the two societies? The decision was a gradual one. To begin with, I needed to learn the local languages. One of the principal techniques I used for this was to spend all the time I could having informants dictate and explain texts which I transcribed. It was easy for many informants to dictate myths and folktales. Among the myths in both cultures were what could be called totemic myths: myths of the origin of particular medicines involving totem animals in Truk, and myths of the origin of clans from totem animals in Ponape. A general pre-existing interest in the problems of mythology and totemism no doubt sensitized me to texts of this sort, hence I encouraged informants to give them to me, overcoming to some extent their ordinary reluctance to impart esoteric details of myths to strangers. However, my primary aim in the field in choosing texts to transcribe was to get a wide variety of types of traditional literature, not just to collect totemic myths.

One night on Truk a centipede bit me on the cheek while I slept, causing considerable pain and sleeplessness for the rest of the night. This inspired some Trukese friends to tell me about a certain man of my acquaintance whose clan or lineage (the Trukese word is ambiguous) possessed the centipede medicine; centipedes would not bite him; he did not like to see centipedes killed in his presence, but he could if he wished give people a remedy which would relieve the pain of centipede bites. (The pain had stopped before I saw this man again, so I cannot vouch for his powers.) This seemed to me at the time to be fairly clear evidence of a kind of clan totemism on Truk, and inspired me to be somewhat more on the lookout for relevant material. The pattern of what is called in the paper "individual totemism connected with curing" emerged from this after a time, while the evidence for permanent clan totemism grew, if anything, weaker after talking with many informants. What most Trukese meant by a certain "clan" possessing a certain medicine animal was that a particular man in a particular *lineage* of the clan currently possessed the medicine. He probably would pass this on to one or two of his lineage mates and he might have received the knowledge from a lineage mate, but the medicine could also be given to his children or other relatives, or the man could refuse to transmit it to his younger relatives if he was dissatisfied with their care of him.

When I went to Ponape, I found much less interest in medicine animals associated with particular disorders and medicines, but much greater interest in what could be called clan totems in the classical sense. Most of the characteristics of totem animals regarded as typical by the nineteenth-century anthropologists can be illustrated in the Ponapean clan animals. But the Ponapeans told me little about medical animals, even when asked. Here then was a cultural contrast which began to loom out of the transcribed texts and other information. Since I was supposed to be on the lookout for cultural contrasts, I intensified my efforts, when time was available, to obtain information about any sort of supernatural attitudes

toward the animal kingdom in either culture. (I continued to work with Trukese immigrants on Ponape as well as with the native Ponapeans.)

Note that I cannot claim to have formulated a hypothesis about totemism in the two cultures on the basis of other information about some antecedent variable and to have then proceeded innocently to collect data to test my hypothesis. While I was in the field, it seemed to me that there should be something about the social structure and especially about relations with close kin which might help explain the difference between the two cultures in totemic practices, but what this might be I was not sure. In fact for some time I was rather hard pressed to find clear differences between the two societies in many respects. Before leaving for the field I had been instructed that the most important thing to look for in comparing cultures was clear-cut pattern differences: if one society happened to be matrilineal and another patrilineal this made a nice pattern difference, for instance, but if both societies were matrilineal but one allowed for more circumventions of matrilineal ties by adoption and so on, this made a rather sloppy difference which had to be quantified and might change from year to year. If only I could find a clear-cut pattern difference, I thought, it would probably explain a great deal, but apparent pattern differences kept disappearing and turning into differences of emphasis when I examined them closely. Perhaps due to this search for incontrovertible pattern difference between the two cultures, I never formulated, while in the field, a very clear opinion on the reasons for the cultural difference with respect to supernatural animals, which was itself rather close to a clear-cut pattern difference.

In working over my field data for my thesis the opinion grew on me that in comparing these two cultures at least, as Redfield found in comparing communities in

Yucatan (1941:xiii–xiv), the majority of the differences are not of the "yes" and "no" type, but are matters of emphasis. How much this is really a characteristic of the cultural materials involved and how much a characteristic of the investigator may be questioned, but at least it seems more plausible to me to formulate many of the major differences between Truk and Ponape in this fashion. When this is done, differences in social structure or almost any aspect of culture do appear. It is often rather easy to compare two cultures and say that one scores higher or lower than the other on some variable, although if one were asked to characterize crudely the cultures with respect to one of two polar opposites they might come out alike often enough. It would be hard to say, for instance, that Ponapean matrilineages are conflict-ridden while Trukese matrilineages are free from internal conflict. However, it seems to me fairly well established that there is more of a sort of pervasive conflict in Ponapean matrilineages, while in Trukese lineages there is a greater tendency toward union of close agemates against seniors and juniors, and that this age-grading tends to extend beyond any single lineage and across lineage boundaries, minimizing the psychological involvement of the lineage as a unified group in interpersonal conflicts. It was thus in the process of analysis of data after leaving the field that I developed the "hypothesis" of a specific connection between the forms of totemism and the social structures of Truk and Ponape.

Of course, there would have been nothing scientifically wrong with my having developed a hypothesis about the social determinants of totemism before going to the field, choosing two societies which were known to differ in totemic practices, and making predictions about the social conditions producing these; or vice versa, choosing two societies known to have different social condi-

tions and predicting the forms of totemism if these were unknown. However, had I done this, I probably would not have chosen Truk and Ponape to study, since the German reports from the Thilenius South Seas Expedition indicate some clan totemism for both cultures (cf. Krämer 1932:255–261). Moreover, it seems unlikely that I would have made the same hypothesis to test. Conceivably, such a test might have been more rigorous and elegant (if, indeed, I have really "tested" anything at all now), but the hypothesis or explanation might have been worse to begin with and would then not have been supported.

The explanation in the totemism paper almost certainly does not give a complete list of the necessary prerequisite conditions or determinants of classical totemism. The paper is mainly concerned with one condition: a coincidence or similarity in Ponape of an early conflict involving the mother and parents with a later conflict involving lineage loyalty versus personal ambition and the contrasting lack of such a coincidence in Truk. If I had formulated an explanation on the basis of published data on other societies, I might well have gotten at some other determinant which was operative in Ponapean totemism but which also operated in Trukese individual medical totemism. One might specify certain conditions of infant care as causal perhaps. This would do no harm, but if the determinant happened to operate in the same fashion in both Truk and Ponape, as it might in view of the historical relationship and similarity between the two, this would be of little help in explaining the difference between *these* two cultures, although it might explain the difference between two *other* cultures well enough. In brief, the suggestion here is that in comparing two cultures with regard to a variable of interest, such as totemism, which may be presumed to have a complex set of causes, one cannot tell very well in advance on which part of the set of causes the comparison is likely to shed some light. Insofar as anthropologists concern themselves with a wide range of phenomena and a wide range of possible causes for them, they should not expect too much from that part of their field work which is guided by specific hypotheses derived from examination of data from other societies.

To put it in more abstract and general form, let us suppose that some culture complex of interest, such as totemism, is "determined" by a set of several preconditions, A, B, C, D, and E, such that if any one of these are missing the complex does not occur. A comparison of one pair of societies may indicate that Condition A is necessary since it alone is absent in one society, in which the supposed resultant culture complex is also absent. But perhaps in the next pair of cultures one examines it is Condition B which is variable, while Condition A is present in both cultures. This does not "prove" that Condition A is irrelevant, only that in itself it is insufficient. But the comparison of the second pair of cultures will not then shed much more light on the operation of Condition A. At the same time, the mere association in the first pair of presence and absence of Condition A and its proposed result is in itself no very strong evidence that Condition A is necessary for the culture complex in question, although it may be suggestive. From a statistical point of view the value of the association as evidence is further weakened if it is hypothesized as significant only after observing that it exists. This is admittedly what happened with my totemism hypothesis.

At this point let us review the argument and findings of the paper in question. Briefly, the argument is that in many respects the two cultures are rather similar due to common historical origin, but that, in respect to classical totemism, one culture, Ponape, shows this in rather clear form, while the other, Truk, does not. It is further argued that social conflicts in adult life are differently organized in the two societies; that in Truk the most difficult conflicts in Trukese society are between age grades or generations, regardless of matrilineal relationship, and the most difficult conflicts in Ponapean society are those within the matrilineage. In both societies these particular conflicts are regarded as "difficult" or giving rise to social and psychological problems because, although they are fairly strong, there is at the same time positive support for the relationships involved, which necessitates the suppression of full and direct expression of these conflicts.

Note that while the cultural judgments about the presence or absence of clan totemism have been phrased as "yes" and "no" statements, the judgments about social conflicts are phrased as matters of degree. No attempt is made to deny that there are important conflicts in Truk between lineage members about such matters as the use of lineage property or the misbehavior of lineage members from time to time; nor is it denied that there are sometimes conflicts in Ponape between members of different generations which override matrilineage boundaries. I would go farther than this and state that I have not really even shown very well that in Truk generation conflict is more important than intralineage conflict, or that the reverse is true of Ponape. What I do feel fairly confident about, and this may be all that is necessary for the argument of the paper, is that the *balance* of the two types of conflict is different in the two societies; that however weak the generation conflict may be in Truk, it is still clearly stronger than in Ponape; and that however weak the intralineage conflict may be in Ponape, it is still stronger than in Truk.

The argument of the paper depends in part upon the premise that the two cultures are rather similar in many basic ways apart from those differences which are specifically brought out. Let us note some basic similarities and evaluate very roughly how close they are. To begin, the location and geographical environment are quite similar. Both are at about the same degree of north latitude and experience similar winds, currents, seasons, and rainfall. Ponape, since it is higher, gets somewhat more rainfall, but in both rainfall is abundant enough so that there is usually no problem of water supply. Both are high island groups in a lagoon. The land area of both is rather small, Truk having about forty square miles and Ponape about 130. However, in addition to the difference in size, there is a difference in distribution of the land area: Truk consists of a group of rather small islands in a rather large lagoon, while Ponape consists mostly of a single large island in a rather small lagoon. Both have the same basic kinds of crops: breadfruit, coconut, true taro and the giant swamp taro (Cyrtosperma), bananas, plantains, and yams. There are differences in subspecific varieties of these plants, but the most important difference is probably the much greater use of yams in Ponape and somewhat greater use of breadfruit in Truk.

Linguistically the two languages are clearly related and the pattern of sound shifts is not complex. They share about 40 per cent of the Swadesh basic vocabulary list, which may suggest a separation of a couple of millennia and prevents mutual intelligibility, but certainly the two languages are still closely enough related so that knowing one helps in learning the other.

In social organization, both peoples are organized into named, exogamous matrilineal clans, which are subdivided into matrilineages which formerly held rights to land in common, and still do in Truk. (Traditional land tenure in Ponape has been more altered by foreign administrations in this century.) Aboriginally there was some difference here in that the chiefs in Ponape

held more power over the matrilineage lands than in Truk. Theoretically they could reassign lands at will and received more tribute or taxes from landholders than did the Trukese chiefs.

Both peoples were divided into a number of petty states headed by chiefs whose offices were inherited matrilineally. Here again we may note that the political organization of Ponape was more complex, with various lines of promotion and many more specific political titles, than that of Truk. Personal achievement played a large part in assignment to most Ponapean titles, but to only a few Trukese titles (the so-called *itang,* who were orator-magician-strategist-ambassadors). Moreover, the petty states in Ponape were fewer and larger than those in Truk, which perhaps could better be called simply "independent communities" or "chieftainships," rather than "petty states" with the implications of territorial extension and political complexity.

Communication existed between the two societies before foreign contact, although it was not very regular or reliable. Ponape is nearly 400 miles east of Truk, with nothing much directly in between, and the people of the high islands had little occasion to leave their homes in seagoing canoes. But it appears that occasionally persons from one group who were lost at sea would be carried by storms to the other, and after repairing their vessels, refreshing themselves, and waiting for favorable winds, would manage to return to their homes. In view of the direction of the prevailing winds, it is likely that the Ponapeans were carried accidentally to Truk more often than the reverse. Also, the people of the low islands to the south, north, and west of Truk have traditions of occasionally sailing to Ponape. These people had to be better sailors than the high islanders in order to survive when their homes were devastated by typhoons or other calamities; they also had the urge to visit the great culture centers such as Truk and Ponape, whose inhabitants regarded the low islanders as rather rustic. The low islanders therefore provided some communication between the two high island cultures. We can perhaps assume that over a period of millennia there was enough communication (beginning with an original presumed near-identity of culture) so that information about any long-established basic feature of one culture became transmitted repeatedly to the other, though not necessarily very forcefully.

The list of similarities between the two cultures could be multiplied considerably or made more detailed. However, it would not on the whole be a list of cultural identities or exact equivalences. From the point of view of an approach to rigorous experimental design we must admit that most of the irrelevant variables we wanted to control are in fact controlled only rather roughly. The only variables which appear to be exactly equivalent for the two cultures are those which have negative values. Thus we can say that the two cultures are identical in that they did *not* have writing, metal working, popular secret elections, pottery, cultivated cereals, most domestic animals including all draft animals, the arch, market economy, and so on. We should not underestimate the importance of these negative features held in common by the two societies, but at the same time these are features which characterize many other traditional cultures in vast areas of the Pacific and other parts of the world. The similarities with respect to many positive features shared by the two societies, even if not perfect, are more important for justifying the comparison of this pair with each other rather than with one of the many other cultures on which some information is available. Thus, even if we cannot say that the geographical environment of the two is identical — even if Ponape has more land, higher mountains, less lagoon, and the like — the natural environments of Ponape and

Truk are much more alike than those of either as compared to any of the low coral atolls found in the Carolines and many other parts of the Pacific.

The fairly clear common historical origin of the bulk of both cultures is also important in establishing their comparability. For one thing, this implies strongly that even if there are some important differences between the cultures at present, these have developed as parts of ongoing systems in the present sites, and are not differences which each culture imported into the area from some unknown different area at the time of original settlement. There is also the hope that even if we do not succeed in recording and comparing the two cultures in their entirety, there may still be some important similarities due to common historical origin which we have failed to note, but which make the comparison more appropriate.

The existence of some degree of continuing intercommunication between the cultures throughout their development in Micronesia is an additional argument for comparability, although perhaps not of such great weight, since communication was rather tenuous in recent times. Certainly over a period of millennia there must have been castaways and lost vessels from many parts of the Pacific which landed in both Truk and Ponape, and the list of ports of origin of some of these would be different for the two cultures. Many of these visitors apparently had little effect in introducing changes into their host culture, for they would on arrival be outnumbered, impoverished, and unable to converse well at first, regardless of their status in their native land. But probably visitors from other high island Carolinian cultures would be the most likely to introduce innovations successfully: their home island would be known and mythological connections would exist between the clans, the cultures would be similar enough so that an element from one would be more likely to seem sensible and be functional in the other. Moreover, such visitors would be more frequent than those from remote islands.

Some cultural exchange between islands may be observed going on today in the Carolines and is perhaps increased by the greater frequency of contact provided by modern transportation. Some Trukese, for instance, have taken back Ponapean varieties of yams to plant in Truk. Some Ponapeans express the belief that Trukese practitioners of traditional medicine are superior to Ponapean practitioners. People in each culture know a fair amount about the other. On the other hand, there are or have been natives of other, more remote Pacific islands, especially on Ponape, who have made much less cultural dent on the local culture. They have been accepted as individuals much more by virtue of their adjusting to Ponapean culture, than by virtue of any contribution to the culture. These include people from Guam, the Moluccas, New Britain, Tahiti, Samoa, the Philippines, and so on.

One problem which often arises in any sort of comparative work is that of the effect of the observer on the comparability of the data. In the present stage of anthropological theory different observers who may think they are using similar concepts and terms can come to seemingly quite different conclusions. A nice example of this is the discussion between Ward Goodenough and myself as to the frequency of "matrilocal residence" on Romonum Island in Truk Lagoon (Goodenough 1956b; Fischer 1958a, 1959). Goodenough showed that seemingly great differences in the frequency of matrilocal residence in two censuses taken by different investigators were almost entirely the result of different definitions of the types of residence with kin. Presumably there are many "ethnographic" differences of this sort in descriptions of different societies which are never discovered because they have not been checked by a second observer. In short, some seemingly important cultural contrasts might turn out to be contrasts in ethnographers rather than in cultures. In addition to the confusion which is no doubt caused by conceptual and theoretical differences there is also the problem caused by differences in interest and coverage between ethnographers. While nonliterate cultures are much simpler than modern civilizations, human beings anywhere have enough culture so that they spend a large part of their life learning it. It is hard for an ethnographer to compress all this learning into a year or two of field work. It is especially hard since people normally learn particular items of culture in the appropriate context and do not even think about them much outside these contexts. The ethnographer who spends all his time talking to an informant in private may never even realize that certain things exist to ask about if he has not encountered the proper contexts. In any case, the ethnographer must usually make some selection of what he will investigate, and the selection of one ethnographer will differ from that of another.

If a single ethnographer can do field studies in two or more societies which he wishes to compare, the problem of ethnographer bias in selection of data to record is largely overcome, since one man's interests are not likely to change radically from one culture to the next. Of course, there is still the danger that what people like to tell ethnographers can differ from one culture to another. If the ethnographer is too passive and does not push his informants at times for answers to certain questions, he may still end up with quite different coverage of two cultures he hopes are comparable. But this is not too hard to remedy by a conscious attempt to seek the necessary data. The comparison of totemism on Truk and Ponape is at least not invalidated by a great difference from one society to the next in the observer's theoretical attitude toward the question of totemism or social structure or psychoanalysis or other relevant problems. However, if a romantic anthropologist fond of totemism had investigated Truk and an excessively hard-headed anthropologist who believed that totemism was meaningless had investigated Ponape, it is not inconceivable to me that a third anthropologist reading their data would conclude that Truk was the culture with well-developed clan totemism and Ponape lacked it.

In comparing large numbers of cultures, it is of course impossible for a single investigator personally to visit and do field work in all. This is often possible in comparing a small number of societies, however, and is very helpful where it can be done. Failing that, it would be best to choose cultures each of which has been investigated by several ethnographers to help reduce or cancel out the effect of their personal biases and special interests. Of course, it is always a help to be preceded in one's own field work by other competent ethnographers whose reports are available, even if they have a different theoretical and conceptual background — perhaps especially then. Certainly my own comparison of Trukese and Ponapean totemism was greatedly aided by my being able to consult the work of other earlier ethnographers, as acknowledged in the paper.

There is one flaw in ordinary anthropological field technique which probably affects the validity of the totemism paper to an unknown extent and which is not remedied by having a single investigator make the comparison on the basis of personal acquaintance with the cultures. This is the problem of the validity of anthropological generalizations which are gathered on the basis of informal observation and interviews with a limited and biased sample of informants. To be sure, this is not quite as serious as it may sound to a sociologist or social psychologist who spends much of his time perfecting his sampling techniques. The sort of question the anthropologist is likely to be most interested in is not so much of the sort "Who will you vote for for the president?" as "How is the president of this country chosen?" That is, the anthropologist is especially concerned to describe what everyone in the society or everyone in certain clearly specified positions in the society is expected to know, and probably does. For this sort of question elaborate sampling techniques are an unnecessary luxury, and are wasteful in that they require time which could be more profitably devoted to asking other questions. Therefore, the anthropologist in the field tends to ask one or two informants about a point and assumes their answers are correct until he sees something contradictory. Often it is only then that he checks with several informants and attempts to get something approaching a sampling of opinion.

With this approach a reasonably full coverage of a culture can be achieved in a year or two, but it would be wrong to regard all the statements of the anthropologist as firmly established. To give one example from the Truk-Ponape totemism paper, a casual reading of this paper will give the impression that the totemic food taboos on Ponape apply only to clan members and that the totem animal represents the mother and the matrilineal line of female ancestors. Strictly speaking, the matter is more complex than this, as was shown by Frank Mahony in later field work on the problem (Fischer, Fischer, and Mahony 1959). With more systematic questioning of a larger sample of informants Mahony found that there was a tendency for Ponapean *men,* not women, to respect the food taboos of their father's matrilineal totem more than those on their own matrilineal totem, which was of course also their mother's totem. Mahony even found two men who observed the food taboos on both their father's and father's father's matrilineal totem and not on their own totem. In brief, although clan membership is inherited matrilineally on Ponape and the totems automatically go with membership in a particular clan, for many Ponapeans the father's totem is quite important and evidently functions primarily as a male symbol rather than a female symbol. To account for this fully would certainly have rendered the argument in the earlier paper comparing Truk and Ponape more complex, although I still consider it valid as far as it goes. It would appear that the greater respect of men for the father's totem is one of spontaneous sentiment rather than of enforced custom, and is something of which an informant might be expected to be unaware as a general proposition. As far as tradition goes, it is generally agreed that one should respect the taboos on both totems and that violation of either will result in the appropriate supernatural punishment. Nevertheless, the distinction in actual behavior between the men and women would seem to be important in interpreting the practice and is the sort of information which all but the most thorough and focused anthropological investigation is likely to miss.

In most ethnographic work there are likely to be inadequacies of this sort. Such variability is often especially strong in features of expressive culture (religion, mythology, art, magic, and so on), where deviations from the cultural norm pose no immediate practical problems and may serve to adjust items of culture to the personality needs of particular individuals or small subgroups. When one compares two ethnographies, each with its undetected gaps and random distortions, one runs the risk of compounding error. If only two or three cultures are involved in the comparison, the effect of any particular error can be great. The lesson here is not to avoid small-scale comparative studies, but to retain a certain healthy skepticism about the data and conclusions until supported by a number of independent replications. Another lesson, always with us, is thoroughness of field work, insofar as time and circumstances permit.

In evaluating the conclusions of the Truk-Ponape totemism paper one must ask whether other explanations of the difference between the two societies are possible. It is impossible to foresee all the other interpretations of the data which might be offered, but one interpretation which is raised perennially is that of diffusion. One might argue that perhaps the two cultures were already somewhat differentiated elsewhere before they settled in the Carolines and that the proto-Ponapeans had clan totemism then and the proto-Trukese did not. Alternately, one might argue that the idea of totemism was a later introduction brought to Ponape by immigrant conquerors who never imposed their rule on Truk. I do not regard either of these explanations as very likely but even if one of them turned out to be true, there would still be the question as to why the totemic complex has been maintained to the present day on Ponape and what its psychological and sociological functions are. If these seem to be sufficient to justify the independent development of the complex over time, then from one point of view the historical origin from fairly remote diffusion is not too relevant. Actually, if I were to make a guess from the distribution of clan totemism in Micronesia, Melanesia, and Polynesia, and from possible survivals in Trukese culture, I would say that probably Truk had clan totemism a millennium or less ago and has since lost it because it became functionally trivial. In the absence of written records this would be difficult to establish very firmly and would require much sifting of myths and ethnographic data for perhaps a rather slight gain of information. Still, one must grant that it would be nice to have a reasonably conclusive answer on this point as an additional scientific datum, not just to satisfy antiquarian curiosity.

Truk and Ponape may be somewhat more historically differentiated than would be ideal for the comparison of totemic practices. Ideally, in a microethnological comparison one wants to find two societies which are as similar as possible in all respects except in the traits one is trying to relate to each other. The amount of historical distance needed to permit the development of a clear contrast in the variables of interest cannot be predicted and will certainly vary from trait to trait. If one is determined to compare a particular trait in two or more cultures so as to obtain understanding of functional or causal relations, a preliminary survey of the cultures will be necessary to determine the minimal historical distance required in that particular culture area to produce differences of interest.

An alternative procedure, followed in the totemism study under discussion, is to pick two related cultures and study traits of interest on which the two cultures seem to differ. In this case some difference will probably be found on any trait, but for some traits the differences may be trivial, while for others one may find that one could have picked even more closely related cultures, or perhaps two different communities in one of the cultures, and found the desired contrast. The line between microethnology and ethnography is not always too clear. When one studies two communities with "the same" general culture, one is approaching ethnography. Perhaps it is in part a matter of aim: when one is studying the two communities to compare differences involving local cultural tradition, it is microethnology, while if one is simply interested in certain ecological differences, assuming that there is "free" communication and movement between the communities, it is ethnography. Of course, ecological differences rapidly translate themselves into subcultural differences, since an

important part of culture is knowledge of the environment and how to adapt to it. And movement in and out of a community is rarely completely free. So microethnology of some sort can always be practiced within a culture possessing local differentiation.

The possibility of microethnological comparison involving cultures which have no close historical relations is also worth considering. Anthropologists sometimes like to make such comparisons to illuminate particular points in which they are interested. One might cite Francis Hsu's recent work comparing India, China, and the United States (Hsu 1963). Some may argue that the cultures considered are too different from one another to be worth comparing, that Hsu should have compared subcultures in India alone perhaps, instead of bringing in two other so disparate cultures. However, if he had done so, he would probably not have found the basic contrasts in family pattern and social organization for which he was searching; or if he had found them all locally in India somewhere, the Chinese-like and American-like local types would not have had the historical opportunities to develop as fully as the more typically Indian type. In other words, by taking cultures with great historical genetic distance between them, one introduces many uncontrolled variables but one simultaneously increases the range of variation of the variables in which one may be interested. One often finds that in studying very closely related cultures, the differences are so minor that they are not of very much interest. If one is concerned with major variations in basic sociocultural variables it may be useful to apply the microethnological method to more or less unrelated societies.

In conclusion, microethnology is a flexible technique which can be adapted to the study of many problems, although in particular studies one may have to change either the choice of problem or the choice of society if one is to make a fruitful comparison. It has become something of a cliche to say that anthropological methods are better at formulating hypotheses than at proving them. This is true of microethnology. However, it can at times give fairly convincing suggestions as to how some sociocultural phenomena may be explained, although using microethnology alone, it is impossible to make a conclusive demonstration of one's point or to quantify the probability of any statement. In any case, small-scale comparative studies help the investigator notice things and relationships he had not noticed before. Given the present development of anthropological theory and social scientific theory in general, and the extreme complexity of many sociocultural phenomena, microethnological studies can make a very useful contribution to the advancement of scientific knowledge about culture and society.

Suggested Readings

A classic statement of the uses of small-scale comparisons of historically related societies will be found in Eggan (1954). An application of this line of thought to the Western Pueblos is contained in Eggan (1950), while Calender employs essentially the same approach in his 1962 publication. One further example is Nadel's study of "concomitant variation" of types of witchcraft in four African societies, found in his 1952 article.

APPENDIX*

TOTEMISM ON TRUK AND PONAPE [1]

J. L. Fischer

In field work in the Eastern Caroline Islands from 1949 to 1953, while employed by the American administration of the Trust Territory of Micronesia, I was struck by several differences between Truk and Ponape, two genetically related high island cultures which are separated by nearly 400 miles of open sea. Some of these differences involved customs and beliefs about animals, often referred to as totemic. In brief, something like classical sib (or clan) totemism is present on Ponape, while on Truk there is what might be called individual totemism connected with curing. However, although both cultures have exogamous matrilineal sibs, the connection of animals with sibs is weak or lacking in Truk,[2] and the connection of animals with medicine and disease is generally weak on Ponape, except as the sib totems are thought to punish offenses against themselves or their human kin.[3]

The question arises, why is classical sib totemism rather well developed in one of two related cultures and not in the other? An answer is here sought by relating totemistic beliefs and practices to individual sociopsychological problems or conflicts, and to the social structures of the two cultures as they generate these problems for typical individuals.

More specifically, the nature of the lineage on Ponape — and in both cultures the lineage tends to be equated lexically and conceptually with the sib of which it is a part — is such that it becomes an object of marked sociopsychological conflict or ambivalence for its members. In this situation totemic beliefs, myths, and practices serve as psychological supports of the sibs and lineages, thus helping the individual to accept his role as a sib and lineage member.

In Truk, on the other hand, the lineage as such is less an object of sociopsychological conflict, but there are important conflicts between generations. Although much of the conflict between elders and youths occurs within the lineage, the opposition of generations divides the lineage into segments according to age, and splits the psychological unity of the lineage as an emotional object. Thus a conflict about persons of different generation, especially elders but also those markedly younger than oneself, acquires priority for the typical Trukese over the general conflict of each lineage member with every other member. In these circumstances we find that totemistic beliefs and practices are practically nonexistent in connection with Trukese

---

* Reprinted from the *American Anthropologist,* 59:250–265 (1957), by permission of the American Anthropological Association.

[1] This is a revised version of a paper originally presented at the 1955 annual meeting of the American Anthropological Association in Boston. The paper has been read in various stages and helpful advice offered by Thomas Gladwin, Ward Goodenough, Frank Mahony, Saul Riesenberg, and John Whiting. Goodenough and Mahony have also provided further field data as noted. Responsibility for the final form of the paper is of course my own.

[2] See also Goodenough 1951:84–85 for a further discussion. Goodenough's conclusions as to the present status of sib totemism in Truk are essentially in agreement with my own.

[3] See Riesenberg 1948 for a general discussion of Ponapean medicine.

sibs and lineages, while similar beliefs about personalized animal associates are elaborated instead in connection with traditional medicine, the practice of which is especially a prerogative of old people.

It will be noted that the attribution of significance to differences in the lineage as an object of sociopsychological conflict does not in itself imply anything directly as to differences in the amount of interaction with lineage mates in the two cultures. To be sure, there could hardly be a strong conflict about lineage members in Ponape unless there were considerable interaction of some sort with them, but it would be wrong to assume that psychological conflict is purely a function of the amount of interaction of the individuals in a group. It is just as much a function of conflict of individual interests. If the interests of the members were nearly always mutually reinforcing in group interaction, there might well be much interaction and little conflict.[4]

Before developing more fully the points made above, I wish to state that I consider unsatisfactory a diffusionist explanation that perhaps totemism never reached Truk. There are in fact some suggestions that classical totemism did once exist in Truk. One old Trukese informant told me that the *Pwe* or *Nipwe* sib, of which he was a member, was descended from the bat, *ni-pwe:pwe*, and that it was formerly taboo for members to kill or eat bats. This statement is disputed by some other informants. Another informant told me of the origin of a certain clan on Pulusuk Island, an atoll to the west of Truk, from a porpoise which a man caught and married there. These and other similar ideas appear to indicate that the bare idea of sib totemism may well be old in Trukese culture, but it simply has not been elaborated by the Trukese or integrated very extensively into the culture in recent times.

PERSONAL CONFLICTS OCCASIONED BY SOCIAL STRUCTURE IN TRUK AND PONAPE [5]

In order to understand the differences in the sociopsychological problems with which members of the two societies are preoccupied, and thus approach the question of differences in totemism, we must investigate certain differences between the two societies in interpersonal relationships as occasioned by social structure. Defined broadly, the most striking difference between Truk and Ponape is with respect to the political systems. For one thing, the sheer size of political units on Ponape

[4] While it is not directly relevant to the central thesis of this paper, I would note that although it appears to me that the lineage is an object of more intense conflict in Ponape, in terms of sheer duration of interaction with lineage members, the Trukese probably rank higher than the Ponapeans, since the Trukese prefer group activity more in daily routine. The point made here about the importance of considering sociopsychological conflict rather than amount of interaction alone in understanding the development of totemism and allied phenomena is analogous to Malinowski's well-known point about Trobriand fishing magic. Malinowski noted that the Trobrianders had no magic in connection with routine fishing in the lagoon, important though this was as a source of food and in terms of time spent, but that there was magic connected with deep sea fishing, where the catch was uncertain and personal danger was involved (1948:51). Malinowski's discussion emphasized conflict due to material difficulties, while I am here dealing with social difficulties arising out of conflicts of interest.

[5] For a discussion of Ponapean political and social organization, see Bascom 1946 and 1948, Riesenberg 1949. For a discussion of the same for Truk, see Goodenough 1951. For Trukese character, see Gladwin and Sarason 1953. Most of the material in this section has previously been presented by one or another of the above authors, although they should not be held responsible for my reinterpretations.

has traditionally been larger than in Truk. Truk is a group of many small, high islands of volcanic origin within a large, reef-encircled lagoon. More than a dozen of these islands were large enough to support permanent populations, and the larger ones each contained several traditionally independent communities with populations ranging perhaps from one hundred to five hundred. Ponape is a single, larger high island, which was traditionally divided into only five independent districts, each larger in area and population than the Trukese districts. The population of the Ponapean districts at present ranges from 1,000 to 2,500, and aboriginally was probably about three or four times this size.

Along with the greater size of Ponapean political units goes a much greater number of political statuses or titles, ordered in a number of hierarchical lines. Each title is unique and may be held by only one person at a time. Individuals start as youths at the bottom of one of these title lines and ideally advance progressively to higher positions. The lines themselves as well as the positions within them are of varying prestige, and individuals may be shifted from one line to another under certain circumstances. The rules for assigning titles are complex and the subject of perennial disagreement among the Ponapeans themselves, but they involve a combination of hereditary (primarily matrilineal) rank and achieved merit, with the highest chiefs of the two most important lines acting as final arbiters.

The Ponapean districts or states are divided into subdistricts, each of which has its own system of titles. Most men have at least two titles, a district title and a subdistrict title. Outstanding individuals may also be given honorary titles in districts or subdistricts other than their own, much in the manner in which European nations bestow decorations upon foreigners as well as on their own citizens.

The title system on Ponape is intimately connected with the system of feasts. Public feasts were formerly held frequently, on both regular and special occasions, and many are still held, though fewer than in the old days. Receipt and possession of a title both obligate the holder to make certain contributions at public feasts and give him certain rights to share in the distribution of food there. As one advances in the system of titles, one's obligations and privileges both increase, but the obligations tend to increase less rapidly than the privileges, so that high title holders receive somewhat more food than they give and young title holders contribute somewhat more than they receive. One of the principal ways of winning the favor of the senior chiefs and thus gaining promotion in the title system is to make outstanding contributions of food at the feasts. Each man vies with his rivals to contribute more and choicer food. Other service to the chiefs or the district, such as (formerly) bravery in battle, also gives merit toward promotion, but feast contributions are the most important single source of merit today and perhaps always have been. Following receipt of each new title, it is confirmed by a feast which the recipient and his relatives prepare for the bestower, epitomizing the relationship between title holder and bestower.

In Truk, on the contrary, political titles are few and their acquisition is not related to feast contributions. The principal political title is simply that of "chief." The traditional chief (leaving aside the "office chiefs" introduced by foreign regimes) is the oldest competent man in the chiefly lineage, and the measure of competence is simply the absence of obvious senility. The Trukese had what might be called competitive feasting, but the competition was between whole lineages or sometimes whole districts, and public attention was not brought to bear on the contributions of any single individual.

In Truk, a faint suggestion of the Ponapean feast and title system is seen in connection with the individuals known as *itang*. An *itang* was a combination of orator, diplomat, war-strategist, magician, and historian. An *itang* was supposed to be either of chiefly lineage himself or the son of a male member of chiefly lineage, but the title was not granted except upon thorough training in the subjects with which an *itang* should be familiar. There were two lesser titles or degrees through which men passed while studying to become *itang*. The candidates made gifts of food and valuables to their teachers, which are a little reminiscent of the Ponapean title feasts in function, but there was little element of competition about these gifts. The presentations were made in private, and if there were two or more candidates there seems to have been no special attempt to compare the contribution of each candidate with those of all the others and choose the best, as long as each made a reasonably acceptable contribution. Such personal competition as did exist was limited chiefly to feats of memorization. The title of *itang* and the two related lesser titles were not unique. Two or more men in a single community might hold the same title simultaneously, so the success of one did not automatically preclude the success of another.

The formal structure of sibs and lineages in the two societies contrasts less than do the political systems, but there are significant differences here too. In both societies a community contains a number of exogamous matrilineages, each of which is a part of a more widespread exogamous matrisib. A typical matrilineage in either society holds or formerly held property in common, acted as a unit in exacting vengeance for injuries done to its members and in compensating injuries done by its members, and in general formed a sort of mutual aid group.

The larger sib groups, consisting of groups of historically or traditionally related lineages, have fewer and weaker functions than the lineages, although in addition to control of marriage they formerly had some influence on war alliances and on hospitality extended to strangers. The sibs, and in Ponape the sub-sibs, are named, and a few of the sibs in Truk and Ponape have cognate names.

Sib and lineage structure contrasts in the two societies with respect to the methods of assigning seniority to members. In Truk an individual's seniority within his lineage is directly a function of age, while in Ponape it is first of all a function of birth order of his mother. Thus in Ponape the eldest son of the eldest sister is senior to the eldest son of any younger sister of his mother, even when chronologically younger. The Ponapean method of assigning seniority emphasizes the distinctness of the descent lines or sublineages within a lineage and their hierarchical order, while the Trukese method slights these. Accordingly, it is not surprising to find that the lineages within a sub-sib, and sub-sibs within single sibs on Ponape are more rigorously defined and hierarchically ordered than in Truk.

At the same time, while hereditary seniority of individuals and descent groups is sharply defined on Ponape, achievement can considerably modify the actual standing of groups as well as of individuals. One hears such statements as "Sub-sib A is really the senior sub-sib, but they were wicked so sub-sib C has replaced them as chiefs." Sibs, sub-sibs, and lineages on Ponape may all have their social standing modified by the achievements of individual members. If one member manages to achieve a high title, members of his descent group feel that another one of them should receive this same title when the first holder dies, although strictly speaking the conferring of titles is a matter for the discretion of the highest chiefs. Probably one reason for this sentiment of a moral right of the lineage to the higher titles of its members is the mutual assistance between lineage members. If a member has attained a high title by his feast contributions it is in large part because he has had the help of his brothers and other male lineage mates and of the lineage women, through the labor of their husbands, which the latter customarily owe their brothers-in-law. Moreover, the lineage in a sense shares in the possession of the high title of one of its members during his lifetime. All share in reflected glory and also benefit from the political influence of the holder of a high title.

But Ponapean individuals are not only in competition with members of other lineages; they are also in competition, suppressed though it be, with members of their own lineage. To be sure, not every member of a given lineage can hope to attain one of the higher titles. To retain the loyalty of their subjects and to maximize feast contributions, the chiefs feel it proper to distribute the choicer titles rather widely among the various lineages and sibs. But everyone, regardless of age, hereditary seniority, or wealth, may reasonably have some hope of achieving a better title than he now has, and the usual way of doing this is to prepare superior feast contributions, with important assistance from one's lineage mates. The result may be described as an each-against-all conflict in which the ambitious men in a lineage are covertly competing with each other for the labor and food supply of the lineage. This pressure tends to result in an abundance of food and hard work for all.

In Truk, with its lack of honorary titles, there is no such pressure for intralineage competition. The lineage makes feasts as a corporate unit, not for individual members in turn. Since there are few occasions for competitive feasting of any sort, even including competitive interlineage and intercommunity feasting, Trukese food production is more casual and is devoted mostly to satisfying daily needs. The labor required by the lineage of its members is thus more regular and predictable in Truk than on Ponape.

Since the Trukese have little reason to grow more or fancier food than they require for their daily diet, the food demands of the society can be met with considerably less labor in Truk. Moreover, since sublineage boundaries are less emphasized in Truk, lineage co-operation in food production and other aspects of life is facilitated, in contrast to Ponape, where lineage co-operation is often for prestige purposes and has a certain air of jealousy and reluctance about it. Since food production in Truk is oriented toward subsistence, the products are as a matter of course shared rather freely with lineage mates and members of extended families associated with a lineage.

This is not to say that there are no conflicts within Trukese lineages. There are, but the sort of each-against-all conflict described for Ponape is relatively unimportant. The most important conflict seems rather to be the generation conflict, which segments the lineage horizontally and extends beyond it as well. This emphasis on generation is of course connected with the previously noted Trukese patterns of automatically assigning seniority by chronological age and minimizing individual achievement. The psychological distinction emphasized here is not Ego versus all lineage mates individually but rather Ego and contemporaries as a group versus chronological seniors as a group, on the one hand, and juniors on the other.

The Trukese minimization of individual achievement within the lineage is correlated with a greater psychological dependence on the lineage and residence groups, and a greater physical dependence on them for subsistence needs. But with young adults in Truk there is not simply an absence of competitive pressures to produce: they are hardly expected even to pull their own weight. Trukese have traditionally taken the attitude that youth, including to a large extent the early years of marriage, is a time of relative irresponsibility when individuals are naturally preoccupied with romantic affairs. They seem to feel that it is both unrealistic and unkind to demand too much work from persons at this stage of life. Moreover, the older people express the sentiment that they must take care of the younger as long as they can, so that the younger people will feel kindly toward them when age renders them too feeble to continue working. Gladwin also suggests that since the old people are anxious about old age and feebleness, they are motivated to work by a desire to prove that they are still physically competent (Gladwin 1955). Consequently the burden of providing food falls, by our standards, to a disproportionate extent on the older people of the lineage and residence group.

As the older people grow feeble, they use their control of certain property to ensure that their juniors will care for them. By virtue of chronological seniority, the old people control the distribution of real estate among members of the lineage, and they are also the masters of valued esoteric lore. If their juniors fail to care for them adequately, the elders may transfer some of the lineage land to outsiders who have proved more thoughtful. Similarly, the esoteric lore may be taught to non-relatives who are willing to pay for it with food, valuables, and services.

Relations between old and young in Truk imply special sociopsychological conflicts. The elders are hesitant to demand much of their juniors until absolutely necessary and consider that it is difficult to get the juniors to work, but still the elders know that they must some day transfer the major subsistence responsibilities to their juniors. It is not surprising that even the elders often do not approach the job of food production whole-heartedly. The daily food supply in many Truk households thus tends to be erratic, although the climate is favorable and the soil fertile enough for a stable food supply. The juniors, on their part, are liable to resent the elders for not providing food regularly enough, and for the threat of giving to outsiders valuable real estate and esoteric lore belonging wholly or in part to the lineage.

One difference between Trukese and Ponapean age conflict appears in relations between siblings. In Truk, an older sibling is an object of considerable respect and formal behavior, which may be taken as indicative of a concealed resentment. The greater the age difference between two siblings, the greater seems to be the stiffness between the two. However, siblings or lineage mates of about the same age are treated as friends and confidants. In contrast, on Ponape the relations between siblings and lineage mates close in age seem to be as stiff or stiffer than relations between those with a greater age difference. Also, I have heard a number of complaints in Ponape that a certain sibling was a "favorite child," while I do not recall ever having heard a term for this concept in Truk. This again suggests the lesser importance of the age difference as a focus of resentment in Ponape, and also ties in with the Ponapean emphasis on individually achieved status.

TOTEMISM AND RELATED PHENOMENA

Having discussed the aspects of Trukese and Ponapean social structure which appear to me to be the foci of sociopsychological conflict for members of the two societies, I now wish to present for comparison some examples of totemistic beliefs and practices from the two societies. In this section I am defining "totemistic" quite broadly to refer to any serious belief or practice involving personalization of animals and an association of such personalized creatures with a human individual or limited human group. Totemistic phenomena in this broad sense occur in two general aspects of the cultures under discussion. These are, in the order of treatment below: (1) classical sib totemism, found principally on Ponape; and (2) individual medical totemism, found principally in Truk.

1. *Ponape*. As a sample of some Ponapean totemic material, I shall describe briefly the myths and practices associated with the Lasialap sib. I have chosen this sib because it is one of the largest and most important on the island and because I am most familiar with it. Incidentally, some sibs on Ponape have no known totem at present and probably have had none in recent precontact times. As a problem for further study I suggest that the sibs without totems may in general have had less political status over a long period of time. This would be consistent with points made below in the interpretive section.

Members of the Lasialap sib are the hereditary chiefs of U, one of the five petty states of Ponape. The name *Lasialap* means "Great Eels," *lasi* being an obsolete term for the freshwater eel, the sib's totem. The common name for eels today is *ke-misik*, literally, the "Frightful One." An outline of the origin myth of the clan is as follows: [6]

> The clan is descended from three generations of eel ancestors which married gods or humans. The first of these eels was female; its child, which was later eaten by its human parents-in-law, was male; and the third and last eel, and chief character of the myth, was female.
>
> Her human foster parents also attempted to eat the third eel, but she ate them instead. She then married an important chief, but left him when his people expressed their disgust with a gift of fish which she generously vomited up for them.
>
> After this she settled elsewhere, devouring the people of another part of the island. Lured out to sea by a magician, some smaller fish attacked her but desisted on her plea for the children in her womb. She then traveled around giving birth to human ancestresses of the various branches of the Lasialap sib.

Lasialap people express their identification and relationship with eels in a number of beliefs and practices, of which the following are illustrative but not exhaustive:

1. They formerly fed eels and caressed them.
2. It is believed that eels would bite members of other sibs but not of Lasialap.
3. Lasialap people are forbidden to kill or eat eels. Other people do not harm eels in their presence. One Lasialap man told me that he tried eating an eel when the island was blockaded in World War II, and that consequently his jaws swelled up like an eel's gills.
4. It is believed that eels are likely to crawl out of the water and visit the homes of dying Lasialap people, like good relatives, and also, less frequently, visit the home of a Lasialap woman giving birth. Reciprocally, the people used to mourn dead eels.

2. *Truk*. Ponapean totemism is well exemplified by the Lasialap case, but it is not as simple to pick out an equally suitable illustration of the totemistic medicine animals for Truk, because of the great variability of practices and beliefs. This greater variability may be attributed at least in part to the more private and esoteric nature of Trukese medicine as compared with Ponapean sib myths and sib totemic practices. On Ponape the sib myths are known by all sib members, in outline at least, and the outlines of the myths of the most important sibs are familiar to the whole community.

But in Truk, knowledge of a medicine is restricted to the owner and a few selected

---

[6] This is based on my own unpublished manuscripts in the native language. The German ethnographer Hambruch gives versions of parts of this myth which coincide rather well, as far as they go, with versions which I collected in 1950–1953 (Hambruch 1932, subvolume 2:48, 124–125; Hambruch and Eilers 1936, subvolume 3:146–147).

pupils. Variations can easily arise. New medicines, it is believed, are occasionally revealed by spirits or animals appearing in dreams. Old medicines whose owner has died without transmitting them are sometimes "rediscovered" by learning them "anew" in this same manner in dreams.

Mr. Frank Mahony, District Anthropologist at Truk, writes of Trukese medicines: "Many of them are named after various kinds of sea animals. . . . The name of the medicine frequently indicates the main source of the medicine as well as the principal taboo, though this is by no means always true" (Mahony 1955). The application of the food taboo is variable, but to generalize from Mahony's and my own data, the rules in several instances allow the practitioner more freedom to consume the medicine animal than is granted to his own lineage mates, his acquaintances, or his patients and their households.

For example, on the west side of Fefan Island, in one kind of medicine, *sewi,* which is associated with the magician-war leaders (*itang*), the male lineage head knowing the medicine may eat the *sewi* fish but others in his lineage may not. Patients are sometimes debarred for the remainder of their lives from consuming the animals connected with certain medicines, while practitioners usually may consume their own medicine animals, although Mahony notes that practitioners may refrain from eating their medicine animal if their lineage has possessed the medicine for a long time.

As for acquaintances, strictly speaking they may usually eat the medicine animal in the presence of the practitioner if they dare, but the act would have connotations of disrespect or presumptuous intimacy, and an acquaintance would often be afraid of sorcery. As both Mahony and I have noted, Trukese believe that every medicine has its "bad side" in addition to its "good side." Supposedly, if one partakes of a medicine animal in a routine meal accompanied by the practitioner, the practitioner may later sorcerize the other person by consuming a medicine or saying a spell. The magical practice presumably activates the identification of the practitioner with his medicine animal, which is physically divided between his own and his victim's stomachs, this being the link which magically transmits the practitioner's injurious wish.

Goodenough reports a case where such sorcery is obligatory on the possessor of the medicine. This case involves a resident of Romonum Island, the son of a famous *itang* who knew the medicine for needle fish: "Any needle fish . . . which he ate he had therefore to eat by himself. If someone else ate of the same fish with him he would have to mutter the spell afterwards to make that person sick (swelling of the throat) or become sick himself. After receiving a gift from his victim he would then perform the curative rite" (Goodenough 1955).

Most Trukese medicines are considered valuable esoteric lore because of the payments which treatment commands. Medicine is usually the property of old people. Formerly the payments sometimes included not only money, food, and valuables, but food trees and plots of land as well. The fruit of food trees given in payment for medicine became taboo to the original donors and relatives under pain of recurrence of the original malady.

Trukese often speak of a certain medicine as being the property of a certain matrilineal sib (*einang*). However, when I have pressed informants as to just what they mean by this, they have invariably said that the medicine is the property of one or more specific localized lineages in that sib and not of the sib as a whole. Moreover, they say that the medicine is not known to everyone in these lineages but to a select few; that usually an older person is the one who practices it and that he could, if he wished, teach it to his children or even, on receipt of payment or services, to nonrelatives outside the lineage. A younger person knowing medical lore would, I believe, be very hesitant about transmitting his knowledge to members of other lineages (except to his children) without the approval of both his elder lineage mates and his children, but an older person would feel less compulsion to keep the knowledge in the family, especially if he believed that he was being neglected by his children and younger lineage mates. Informants repeatedly mentioned this conditional bestowal by old people of medicine and other lore, and also of real property.

INTERPRETATION

It was postulated initially that differences in typical sociopsychological conflicts between Trukese and Ponapeans are functionally related to differences in totemistic beliefs and practices in the two cultures. This section tests the hypothesis by interpreting and comparing the symbolism of the totemistic phenomena in the two cultures presented in the preceding section with respect to the personal conflicts discussed at the beginning of the paper.

Before considering the data in detail, however, I wish to note some aspects of my approach to totemism and related phenomena. I assume, first, that totemistic phenomena are symbolic representations of typical human relationships in the society; further, that the native can not usually state fully the socio-symbolic nature of totemism — he assumes in the main that totemistic myths are literally true; and further, that the social meaning of totemism is nevertheless present in repressed form in the unconscious mind of the natives and is the greatest single source of the individual motivation for totemistic beliefs and practices. In accord with psychoanalytic theory, the reason that thoughts about the social relationships represented in totemism are repressed is that they are ambivalent and full of conflict, and their overt expression would be disruptive to social relationships and psychologically painful to the individual.[7] The concrete imagery of totemism may be a secondary and lesser reason for its development: a fable makes a more vivid impression than an abstract platitude.

Proceeding on the assumption that totemistic beliefs and practices in the main symbolically or metaphorically represent actual social conflicts, we can turn to the question of what conflicts are specifically suggested in the divergent totemistic practices in Truk and Ponape. I shall begin by considering the Ponapean material, which is more truly totemic, and then proceed to the Trukese material.

From a variety of evidence, examples of which are cited below, two distinct but not mutually exclusive interpretations suggest themselves for Ponapean totemism: (1) a narrower interpretation, treating the totemic animals as representing the mother within the nuclear family; and (2) a broader interpretation, treating them as representing the lineage and sib as a whole.

Considering first the interpretation of the ancestral eel in our example as a mother symbol, I would begin by noting the fact that the chief mythical eel is female, although initially there is a wavering between female and male eels.[8] Further indications of the eel as mother symbol include its large size (suggesting the

---

[7] This is essentially Freud's view of symbolism. For a recent presentation of this and other theories of symbolism, see Fromm 1951.

[8] Several other Ponapean totem animals are also clearly female in the myths, including even the stingray, which would seem to be especially suitable for a male symbol. I know of no totem animal conceived of as primarily male.

size of adults as they appear to children), the eel's attempt to feed her husband's subjects with food from within her and their ensuing disgust (suggesting the attitude of weaned children toward the breast), and the attack on the eel by lesser fish, who desist at her appeal for her unborn children (suggesting both the children's hostility toward the mother at the prospective birth of younger siblings and the eventual acceptance by the older siblings of the mother's reprimand for their jealousy).

Irrational totemic food taboos on edible animals such as the eel may be plausibly interpreted as signifying a general taboo on aggression or disrespect toward a parental figure — or in terms of conflict, as signifying an opposition of strong aggressive and disrespectful wishes against still stronger loving and respectful wishes. But a food taboo with specific reference to a mother figure, i.e., a taboo on eating the mother, further suggests a taboo on nursing and on the general dependence of small children on their mothers. Of course this is a taboo which must be inculcated in children everywhere as they grow older and younger siblings are born, but we also know that cultures vary in the manner of inculcation and in the resultant individual psychological traumata.

The portrayal of the eel in the myth as dangerous and cannibalistic, now being called the "Frightful One," is also consistent with the interpretation of the eel as a mother figure, in view of clinical studies in a variety of cultures showing the tendency of children to depict mothers in their frustrating and demanding aspects as hostile witches, monsters, etc.[9]

The above interpretation, that Ponapean totemism represents in part a conflict around initial dependence on the mother due to her subsequent efforts to weaken or break this tie, suggests that we should investigate differences in child training to account for the presence of sib totemism on Ponape and its absence in Truk. I believe that the childhood conflict over dependence on the mother is in fact stronger in Ponape than Truk and that this is relevant to the elaboration of totemism in Ponape. However, I shall not give detailed evidence for this point here, since I also believe that a strong childhood conflict over dependence could be expressed symbolically in other ways than totemism, e.g., in fear of ghosts or animals not associated with lineal descent groups. In other words, an intense childhood conflict over dependence on the mother appears to be a predisposing but not sufficient cause for the development of totemism in a society.

I believe that to explain why the eel and other animals on Ponape are totemic in the classical sense, i.e., associated with sibs and lineages, we must further consider the relationship of the individual Ponapean to his sib as a whole, and especially to his lineage, in addition to his relationship to his mother. There are a number of indications that the totem animal represents the lineage and sib in general, as well as the mother in particular. The totem animal is said to be a sibmate, and is thought to behave in some ways like a sibmate: allegedly, it is not aggressive toward its human relatives and, as a good lineage mate should, it visits them on birth and mourns

[9] Some of the totems are superficially benign, and include birds, edible fish, and even plants and fruit. However, regardless of superficial appearance to the outsider, the natives appear to conceive of all totems as ambivalent: potentially both hostile and benign on different occasions. Thus the apparently hostile eel defended her human children and generously offered people food, while the seemingly benign totems are thought to cause sickness if their taboos are violated. The culture has supplied, so to speak, the missing aspect necessary to represent the ambivalent mother and lineage. Thus if native beliefs as well as the objective characteristics of the totems are considered, the differences in the totems can be reduced to the question of which aspect has been supplied by the native imagination: positive or negative. With the eel and other dangerous totems the positive aspect has been invented, while with edible fish and the like the negative aspect has been supplied.

for them at death. Reciprocally, the sib members protect and formerly fed and mourned the animal as if it were a sib or lineage mate. We should also bear in mind that since Ponapean lineages are matrilineal, a female totem animal is an appropriate symbol for not only the mother but the whole lineage and sib as well.

When we review the typical sociopsychological conflicts for the two cultures as discussed earlier, we may note a considerable formal similarity between the Ponapean conflicts of mother versus child and lineage versus individual member. This coincidence is lacking with respect to the same conflicts in Truk. More specifically, as an adult, a Ponapean is dependent on his lineage for food and for protection from enemies; in childhood he was dependent on his mother for the same thing. As a child, the help his mother could give him was limited by his siblings' demands for help; in adulthood, the help the lineage may give is limited by the demands of other lineage mates (many of whom are terminologically "siblings"). The child's demands on his mother tend to be high because of his lack of experience and also, in Ponape, probably because of certain ways in which the mother handles her children, which will not be discussed here. The adult Ponapean's demands on his lineage tend to be high because of the competitive nature of the feast and title system. Once the child is weaned and becomes a responsible member of the nuclear family, he may not return to the breast or to his general infant dependence on his mother. Likewise, once the adult has learned to bear lineage responsibilities — which on Ponape he learns at a fairly early age — he must continue to bear them for the rest of his life as long as he is physically competent.

While mother-child conflict over the child's dependence on his mother is also found in Truk (although probably weaker than on Ponape), this childhood conflict does not coincide with a very strong adult conflict of lineage versus individual member over the individual's dependence on his lineage. Since Truk lacks the competitive feast and title system, lineage members make fewer difficult demands on each other and there is relatively little competition among adult lineage mates of the same generation for lineage labor and property. The limited competition that exists is more between the younger adults as a group versus the older adults. In view of the relative industriousness of the older Trukese adults, the mother and parental surrogates continue to be objects of dependence for young adults for many years. The parents are thus not neatly replaced in this respect by the lineage as a whole, and the psychological equation of lineage and mother is more difficult than on Ponape, and less adequately represents the social situation.

In view of this relative weakness of the intralineage conflict as such in Truk, the near absence of sib totemism there is not surprising and is in accord with the positive relation postulated between sib totemism and intralineage conflict on Ponape.[10]

[10] The point here is concerned solely with the strength of sociopsychological conflict about the lineage as a group for its members. The question as to whether Trukese or Ponapean lineages have greater solidarity is not under discussion here, and is irrelevant to the explanation of totemism advanced in this paper. Under this explanation, societies with highly solidary lineages but with little intralineage conflict as such would lack totemism, while a society with low lineage solidarity but highly ambivalent relations of lineage members to their lineage would have totemism. But since solidarity is irrelevant as an antecedent, a society with high lineage solidarity and highly ambivalent member-lineage relationships should likewise have totemism, and a society with low lineage solidarity and weak member-lineage conflict should lack totemism.

I would presume that the function or effect of totemism is to strengthen lineage solidarity in societies with strong intralineage conflict, but if the disruptive tendencies are strong the total resulting lineage solidarity may still be quite weak, even if totemic beliefs are very well developed.

While the each-against-all conflict typical of the Ponapean lineages is minimized in Truk, it will be recalled that the Trukese intergeneration conflict was described as relatively intense and as possessing obstacles to its free expression. And while we find little sib totemism in Truk, we do find the individual medical totemism, with traditional medicine being largely in the hands of the older adults. This suggests that we should examine the possibility that the medicine animal complex may be an expression of the generation conflict there.

What specifically is the evidence for such an interpretation? A number of facts suggest that there is a symbolic identification of the medicine animals with the medical practitioners in Truk. One obvious fact is that the practitioner relies on the animal as a sort of extension of himself in curing and sorcerizing people. Moreover, it is believed in some cases that the animal originally taught the medicine to some human. Normally, of course, the actual medicine teacher is an older adult. In two cases where I have been able to ascertain the sex of the original medicine animal, it was male in one case and a brother and sister in the other. This is consistent with the fact that in Truk males are considered better medical practitioners for most purposes, except for specifically female complaints such as difficulties in childbirth.

Food taboos on the medicine animal are not absolute in Truk; often the animal is used in the medicine which may be consumed by the patient. The occasional medicinal consumption of the animal by the (usually younger) patient appears to symbolize the sacrifice of self which the older people feel they make for the younger. I have heard Trukese express the attitude that work is debilitating, but have received amused skepticism from those to whom I have suggested that work, through physical exercise, would develop strength. Parallel to this reluctance about actual physical labor is a reluctance to use one's medical powers. For any one cause of illness, as classified by the Trukese, there is often a series of medicines graded in order of potency. The practitioners are generally suspected of using the weakest first (since it is generally the simplest and requires collecting the fewest ingredients) and only using the stronger if the weaker fails to work. This stinginess with medicine is regarded as a somewhat reprehensible but human failing. If the patient's medicinal consumption of the animal does symbolize the sacrifice of the elder practitioner (letting part of himself be consumed), then the existence of the practice itself and the reluctance associated with it are both symbolically consistent with the Trukese intergeneration conflict as described above.

In addition to these features of medicinal consumption, the food taboos themselves, though variable, also lend support to the symbolic identity of the medicine animal with the aged practitioners. It will be recalled that the practitioner himself is often permitted to eat the animal, although his patients, his younger relatives, and acquaintances, are often either forbidden to eat it or discouraged from doing so. If the medicinal consumption of the animal may be regarded as a symbolic imposition and dependence on the practitioner, the food taboos may be regarded as a symbolic deference to him. A practitioner is apt to regard violation of these taboos as a personal insult and an expression of contempt for his powers. On the other hand, if the practitioner eats the animal himself, this is purely his business and he is offending no one.

Mahony's statement that the practitioner himself may sometimes observe a food taboo on the medicine animal if the medicine has been in his lineage for several generations is of special interest. The fact that the medicine has not been transmitted out of the lineage for several generations is presumably an indication that in this particular lineage there has been less intergeneration conflict than average, since transmission of esoteric lore to nonlineage members is a common way for lineage elders to express their dissatisfaction with their juniors. In this special situation in Truk, the medicine animal tends to become in effect more of a lineage totem than a symbolic representation of the individual practitioner, and it becomes psychologically inappropriate for the practitioner to eat it. We may speculate that the sociopsychological situation in these "strong" Trukese lineages approaches that on Ponape, where food taboos on the sib and sub-sib totems are common. It seems likely, in fact, that if enough lineages in Truk managed to minimize the generation conflict for a long period, genuine sib totemism could be born (or perhaps reborn) in Truk within a few generations out of the possession of medicine animals by lineages.

CONCLUSIONS

Before summarizing the positive conclusions with respect to totemism in the two cultures, I wish to point out certain limitations in the aim of this paper. First, the ethnographic material reported is illustrative, and no full coverage of either Ponapean sib totemism or Trukese medical totemism has been attempted. Either subject treated in detail could easily fill a monograph.

Again, this paper is not primarily concerned with the relationship of child-care practices to totemism, although cross-cultural research being conducted by Dr. John Whiting and myself at the Laboratory of Human Development, Graduate School of Education, Harvard, indicates that highly significant relationships are demonstrable here. Of course a child-care and an adult social structure hypothesis need not be mutually exclusive. In fact, many of us would expect consistencies between child care and social structure, so that eventually knowing one should help predict much about the other.

I do not claim to have exhausted the symbolic meaning of totemistic practices in the two cultures discussed, not to mention other cultures. Since expressive institutions such as totemism often have multiple meanings, there are no doubt other complementary hypotheses about the meaning of totemism which might be investigated in an exhaustive study. One might inquire, for instance, why a mother figure on Ponape is represented by an eel, which is a phallic symbol in many cultures and in certain other contexts in Ponapean culture. An answer might be found in terms of child care, but it would require more field data and space to demonstrate.

The main conclusions of this paper are that a relatively intense conflict of individual and lineage interests on Ponape is consonant with the classic sib totemism found there, and a relatively intense conflict of interests between older and younger generations is consonant with the medicine animal complex on Truk. While both conflicts certainly exist in both cultures, the difference in intensity or priority seems to be the most significant factor in explaining the difference in totemistic practices. Probably also relevant to sib totemism on Ponape is a stronger conflict about dependence on the mother in childhood. At any rate, this childhood conflict is present and works in the same direction as the conflict about lineage duties and privileges.

These conclusions imply that we should look for classical sib totemism not merely in cultures with exogamous sibs, nor again merely where there is an intense childhood conflict over dependence on the parents, but where some factor intensifies the conflict for members of the society between their interests as individuals and their interests as sib or lineage members. I would further suggest that comparisons between pairs or groups of related cultures, at least one of each group possessing totemism and one lacking it, would be a form of cross-cultural testing on a larger scale which would help discount irrelevant variation due to separate historical traditions.

CHAPTER **16** continues our discussion of research strategies in cultural anthropology by introducing the methods employed in large-scale cross-cultural comparisons. Originally suggested by Tylor in 1889 as one method in the study of cultural evolution, this approach to the comparative study of cultures very early became an instrument devoted almost exclusively to the investigation of synchronic and functionalist problems in cultural dynamics. In recent years, however, along with other shifts in the interests and theoretical focus of cultural anthropology, increasing attention has been paid to the exploration of problems of cultural evolution as well as to research into the internal dynamics of single cultures or types of cultures, and data on many cultures are assembled and analyzed for both purposes. In addition to exploring both uses of large-scale comparisons, Professor Cohen here discusses some of the issues of an evolutionary approach to the study of culture, an approach which contrasts with the strongly functionalist position taken in other chapters, and one which must be appreciated if the reader is to understand the nature of contemporary cultural anthropology. The author opens his discussion by presenting an original cross-cultural study of eschatological beliefs, an illustration of the synchronic or functionalist use of cross-cultural comparisons. In later sections of the chapter, he reinterprets a large-scale cross-cultural study of patterns of food distribution he originally completed several years ago. This study of food distribution illustrates the use of macroethnology as a technique for studying issues in the evolution of culture. After this volume had gone to press, Professor Cohen completed two new cross-cultural studies which led him to rethink some of the basic tenets of the method of large-scale comparisons. At the end of this chapter, he presents an alternative approach to current methods in large-scale comparisons in an attempt to bring cross-cultural methodology into line with the study of cultural evolution.

THE AUTHOR was born in New York City in 1928; he took his B.A. at Brooklyn College and Ph.D. at Yale University. He has taught at Connecticut College, Columbia University, the University of Chicago, Northwestern University, and the University of California at Davis. He is Professor of Anthropology at Livingston College of Rutgers, The State University of New Jersey, which he recently joined. Professor Cohen will begin teaching at Livingston College in 1969 after spending two years conducing field research in Israel. He has done field work in Jamaica and Okinawa. His major research interests are in culture and personality, comparative institutions, and contemporary civilization. His publications include *Social Structure and Personality: A Casebook* and *The Transition from Childhood to Adolescence: A Cross-Cultural Study of Initiation Ceremonies, Legal Systems, and Incest Taboos.* Professor Cohen is currently collecting materials for several large-scale comparative studies in social and political organization and culture and personality.

16

Macroethnology:

Large-Scale Comparative Studies[1]

YEHUDI A. COHEN

Rutgers — The State University

WHERE DOES THE SOUL GO? AN EXAMPLE OF MACROETHNOLOGY

One of the principal themes of this chapter is that anthropology generally and the method of large-scale comparisons particularly must view with skepticism their nearly exclusive reliance on the methodologies of other sciences and explore the possible necessity of developing methodological procedures which meet the needs of the study of culture and social organization.

While I will elaborate on these points in greater detail later on, it is an essential starting point of this chapter that, like any other method in the social sciences, the technique of large-scale comparisons — what can be thought of as the comparative anatomy of culture — has many facets. Also like any

other method, the scientific utility of macroethnology depends upon the competence of the individual who is using it as well as upon the validity of the theoretical position to which it is anchored. Furthermore, large-scale cross-cultural research is not designed to investigate all problems of an anthropological nature, only some; the range of problems for which large-scale comparisons are best suited is still undetermined by anthropologists.

Cross-cultural research is facilitated by the degree to which the investigator has a clearly defined point of view about the ways in which sociocultural systems operate. A corollary of this is that he must have a clear notion of the role of large-scale comparisons in anthropology; that is, he must have some point of view about the ultimate goals of the study of sociocultural systems and about the place of cross-cultural studies within those disciplinary aims. Finally, the investigator who makes use of large-scale comparisons

[1] In the preparation of this chapter, the author received many helpful suggestions from Drs. Martin A. Baumhoff, Richard D. Schwartz, William C. Smith, and Stephen A. Tyler, which he gratefully acknowledges.

should always bear in mind that macro-ethnology is a procedure of *social* science, and that its stance and operational modes must be suited to the study of sociocultural phenomena vis-à-vis those which are investigated by the nonsocial sciences. Since human beings do not behave like pairs of dice, electricity, plants, or mice, the concepts and methods which have been evolved in the studies of the latter facets of nature might have only limited applicability in the social sciences generally and in large-scale cross-cultural studies in particular. In other words, whether the models of the nonsocial sciences are applicable to the data of anthropology, and to what extent they might be applicable, is a matter which still must be determined empirically.

These considerations are crucial, because the relationship between theory and method is indivisible. For example, in an extremely erudite discussion of the use of the Guttman scale in comparative research — and bearing directly on the point of view taken in this chapter, that cross-cultural research should be geared, at least in part, to the study of cultural evolution — Goodenough has observed:

If Guttman scaling . . . is applicable to cultural evolution, as I heartily agree with Carneiro [1962] that it is, it confronts us with some issues that must be resolved. It requires us to make more explicit just what it is the theory of uni-linear evolution is about. It requires us to pay close attention to the appropriate criteria for classifying the traits whose distributions we are to plot. Without this no application of scaling techniques can be reliable . . . [Thus, for example], should the data force us to conclude that evolution is a function of not one but several major variables, the minimum number of scales or quasi scales into which the universe of all culture traits can be sorted will indicate the minimum number of variables that we must take into account, if we are to develop a workable general theory of cultural growth and development (Goodenough 1963b:248).

I do not claim in this chapter to represent all points of view in the use of large-scale comparisons, only those to which I subscribe. This is not to suggest that I believe that the latter are the only valid or worthwhile points of view in this regard, but they constitute the position I know best and with which I am most comfortable; the presentation of this bias is the most that can be accomplished within the limited confines of one chapter. For those who wish to familiarize themselves with other points of view in cross-cultural research — as well as the history of this procedure, which I will also neglect to a large extent in this chapter — there are several basic references which, together with their fine bibliographies, can be consulted with considerable profit. The review by Lewis (1956) of the different approaches in cross-cultural research and the methodological article by Whiting (1954) are both reprinted, with other important articles, in *Readings in Cross-Cultural Methodology* (Moore 1961). The latter collection presents a point of view of cross-cultural research which is at some variance from the one proffered here (see Cohen 1962b for an explication of one aspect of this divergence). The interested reader should also be certain to consult Mead (1961:516–525) and Ackerknecht (1954), and the suggested readings at the end of this chapter.

As the basis of this chapter, I am going to use an example of a large-scale comparison of cultures with respect to a particular problem: "Where does the soul go?"

To the extent that it is possible, I will try to explicate the steps through which I generally go — logical, intuitive, mechanical, and procedural — in the course of a cross-cultural study. Of course, as I have already suggested, this is not the only correct or valid procedure in conducting cross-cultural research, but it is the way with which I am most familiar. Every cross-cultural investigator — as is true for the use of all other empirical methodologies — must find his own ways of operating; that is, he must find those ways with which he is most comfortable. He can best find these by first becoming aware of the procedures used by others, then modifying them to suit his own inclinations. The hypothesis about eschatological beliefs which I will attempt to verify empirically is the simplest kind of cross-cultural hypothesis, which makes it ideally suitable as an introductory teaching device before going on to more complex hypotheses.

FINDING A HYPOTHESIS

My thinking about beliefs concerning the soul's destiny begins somewhat as follows. One of the abiding interests of anthropology, since the days of Tylor, has been with the religious, philosophical, metaphysical, and eschatological beliefs held by different peoples. We have come a long way from the primeval notions of "primitive thought," "the primitive mind," "primitive logic," and the like in searching for different cultures' notions about the nature of the universe, about the ordering of life, and about the nature of the nonphysical world. But this process of discarding hypotheses sometimes leaves a theoretical vaccum. In lieu of better explanations, we are often left in the position of shoulder-shrugging, implicitly conveying the attitude of "that's culture for you."

When confronted with great variety among cultures with respect to any one institution, belief, or custom, the anthropologist who seeks to learn whether there is order or consistency in such differences has several tools at his disposal. First — and I am aware that not all anthropologists will agree with me — he begins with "the principle of limited possibilities." Originally suggested by Alexander Goldenweiser (1933:45–49), this principle asserts that there are a finite or limited number of forms which any institu-

tion, belief, or custom can take. In other words, there are a limited number of ways in which men can do or think something, and there are a limited number of solutions to any one problem. Thus, with respect to culture and social organization, variety is never endless or limitless.

This is an important starting point in large-scale comparisons; it has been demonstrated for almost every aspect of culture and social organization, and it is reasonable to expect that, within time, we will know the precise limits of variability for all aspects of culture and social organization. Thus, for example, as a result of the comparative studies of Kroeber, Lowie, and Murdock, among others, anthropologists have been able to uncover the limited number of principles and systems by which kinsmen are organized sociologically and terminologically in different societies. In brief, they have been able to illuminate the order and consistency in an aspect of cultural life which, at first impression, seems endlessly variegated, random, and fortuitous. Most outstanding in the comparative study of kinship organization, and in large-scale comparisons in general, Murdock's *Social Structure* (1949) is a landmark in what can be called the comparative anatomy of culture and social organization. The unmatched breadth of this study, incidentally, can be appreciated by the fact that it was conducted manually, before the era of computers.

The second important tool available to the anthropologist concerned with large-scale cross-cultural comparisons is the principle of "the psychic unity of mankind." Briefly stated, this principle asserts that all men, regardless of race, possess the same basic mechanisms of mind, that is, of thought and feeling. Specifically, "there are certain experiences and certain physiologically determined tensions, felt subjectively as desires, which no human being escapes, however differently he may seek to satisfy them and however different the level of satisfaction may be" (Du Bois 1944:2). This principle is especially important in the investigation of the ideational aspects of culture, such as notions of where the soul goes, though it is no less important for the study of others. All people must cope with the phenomenon of death; they must try to understand it, explain it, deal with their anticipations of it and their emotional reactions to it, and somehow fit it into their rational schemes concerning events in nature. One of the clearest demonstrations of this principle can be found in *Child Training and Personality,* in which Whiting and Child (1953), in a comparative study of seventy-five societies, established strong correlations between child training practices and adult explanations of illness.

With these tools in hand, among others to be discussed later, the investigator must determine the kind of cross-cultural study he wants to conduct. As Lewis has observed,

It does not follow that those studies which use quantification and express co-variation statistically are the only valid, useful, or scientific studies. Nor must all comparisons necessarily be directed toward testing hypotheses or arriving at general principles of societal development, worthwhile as these objectives are. Comparisons may have other values, depending upon the nature of the data and the objectives of the study. And so long as cultural anthropology feels a sense of kinship with the humanities as well as with the natural sciences, comparisons which increase our general understanding shall have their rightful place (1956:259–260).

Large-scale comparisons can be (a) descriptive or (b) designed to test hypotheses. The actual difference between these two types of research is much smaller than would be imagined from the designations, because while description does not necessarily involve the testing of hypotheses, hypothesis-testing must always rest squarely on description and taxonomy of cultural data.

A descriptive cross-cultural study seeks to determine the range of variability — that is, what people do in different societies — with respect to any aspect of culture or social organization. Thus, for example, a descriptive cross-cultural study would seek to learn the different ideas held in different cultures about the fate of the soul after physical death. It would not — at least initially — seek to correlate these views with any other factors, though such correlations might suggest themselves to the investigator in the course of examining his data. One of the most comprehensive large-scale cross-cultural descriptive comparisons ever carried out is *Patterns of Sexual Behavior,* by Ford and Beach (1952), in which 190 societies were compared. This study, which did not seek to evaluate any cross-cultural hypotheses, is also noteworthy for having combined cultural data with those of nonhuman mammals.

A large-scale comparative study which is designed to evaluate a hypothesis empirically — what is often referred to as "testing" a hypothesis — involves description but takes the additional step of linking one variable or set of variables with some other factor or factors. The study of eschatological beliefs in this chapter is designed to evaluate a hypothesis empirically.

Having begun with the principles that there are a limited number of ways in which people can conceive of life after mortal death and that such death is a "problem" with which all people must cope, I went on to the first element in my hypothesis, namely, that part of every culture has a set of beliefs concerning the nature of life after death. I then wondered why this should be so, assuming of course that it is so. I went through the obvious, but indispensable, step of noting that such beliefs cannot be based on experience of personal knowledge. Having noted this, I then considered alternative possibilities which might account for this postulated universality in culture. I was aware that other scholars, such as those in the tradition of Kardiner and Whiting and Child, might look to the nature of infantile and childhood experiences, assuming that these early life-events would lead to color the formation of such fantasies. For reasons which cannot be gone into here, I tend to be suspicious of such hypotheses; actually, I did look for correlations between early experiences and these adult beliefs while conducting the research, but was unsuccessful. Having rejected the "infantile experience" hypothesis, I asked myself, "What is being 'projected' — if anything — in these fantasies about life after death?" My hunch was that nothing is "projected" in them, in the strict sense of the term. Then how can people "know" the nature of afterlife? The thought that went through my mind at this point was, "People can only know what they know. What people really know better than anything else is their social organization."

EMPIRICAL EVALUATION OF THE HYPOTHESIS

The hypothesis to be evaluated here is that in societies in which there is a belief in a life of the soul after mortal death, the world of the dead is held to be ordered socially or physically, or both, in much the same way as the world of the living.

Every known society possesses the belief that the individual has a nonphysical — what Westerners sometimes call spiritual — life, in addition to a physical one; that is, it is believed in every society that the individual possesses a soul in addition to a body. It is held in almost all societies, with some significant exceptions, that the nonphysical part of the person continues to live or to have some existence after the individual's corporeal death. In some societies, it is also believed that an individual's soul leaves his

body during sleep (thus they explain the phenomenon of dreams), and that severely deleterious consequences can result from the soul's failure to return by the time its host awakens; death can be one of these consequences. Finally, in some societies it is believed that an individual has more than one soul.

In postulating a noncorporeal life after physical death, almost all societies also have definite notions of where the soul resides after physical death, though in some societies these ideas are more elaborated than in others.

I began the collection of the data on where the soul goes with a serious misconception. I was under the impression, from my general readings in ethnology, that every ethnographer made mention of life after death. And without realizing it at the time, I further assumed that every such mention would include a statement, however brief, about the nature or organization of the world of the dead. The first assumption was largely correct; the second was erroneous. There are data on the nature of the world of the souls for only slightly more than half of the societies in my original sample. (This sample is to be found in Cohen 1961a and b.) But the data that are available bear out the hypothesis that, in those societies in which there is a belief in a life after death, the world of the dead is held to be ordered in much the same way as the world of the quick.

In what follows, I am going to present the data for this study. Specifically, I am going to paraphrase and quote directly from ethnographic reports and monographs about the beliefs which are held in different societies about the destiny of the soul. My principal purpose in doing this, rather than merely presenting a tabular checklist, is to show the beginning student what kinds of data are used in a cross-cultural study, the ways in which they are used, and the nature of some of the conclusions which can be drawn from them. In the final sections of the chapter, I will discuss some of the alternatives to this mode of presenting data and the difficulties posed by this procedure and others.

The *Alorese* of the island of Alor in the Netherlands East Indies believe that every individual has two souls. One of these lingers about the village of the living for a short while after its host has died and then is forgotten. There do not seem to be any beliefs about the fate of this first soul, "whether it rejoins the other soul in the village of the dead, below or above, no one seemed to know. . . . Even the village of the dead seems to be no more than a reflection of earthly life" (Du Bois 1944:163).

The *Chiricahua Apache* of southeastern Arizona picture the world of the dead in the following fashion:

The same ways we have here are carried on down there too. Those people dance, eat, and sleep. A person down there can actually feel another in the flesh. The people remain the same age as they were when they died. . . . The same places, the same sacred mountains. The same ceremonies exist there as here. It is just as though everything is transferred to a different country. . . . There is no death there, but lots of good things to eat. Affairs go on in the same way, but better. Those who are there just go on living happily. Life means more. It is always the same life, the hunting, the raids, and all, as in the old days. There are the same puberty rites, masked dances, and sacred mountains. In the underworld they are just like a big community, but they are split up into the same groups as on earth. Each person is with his own group. And each does the same things he used to do when he was on earth. As the story goes, if you were an arrow-maker, you are there making arrows. If you were a good hunter, you are over there hunting. If you were a good warrior on earth, you are out at war (Opler 1941:78).

The *Arunta* of Australia believe that all people have souls, but they appear to have no belief in an afterlife, holding to the tenet that physical death leads to the complete destruction of the soul;

the Northern Aranda man has no illusions about death as far as the human individual is concerned: death is, to him, the last great catastrophe which leads to the eventual complete destruction of his own body and his own spirit. His life's work done, the ancestor merely went to sleep; but man must die, and his death ends all (Strehlow 1947:43).

The *Balinese* have developed rather elaborate theories of the reincarnation of the soul, one's birth into a superior or inferior caste depending on his previous behavior on earth.

A man who is guilty of serious crimes is punished by being reborn, often for periods of thousands of years, into a tiger, a dog, a snake, a worm, or a poisonous mushroom. Between incarnations, until the time comes for its return to this earth, the soul goes to Indra's heaven, the *swarga*, a reservoir where "life is just as in Bali, but devoid of all trouble and illness" (Covarrubias 1947:361).

The *Logoli and Vugusu,* Bantu peoples of North Kavirondo, in western Kenya, believe that the world of the dead exists underneath the earth.

The mode of existence which the spirits lead in this land of the dead is thought to be similar to the life of the living. They have wives and children (i.e., their wives and children join them after they have died), they own cattle and make the same social distinctions as the living people (Wagner 1949:163–164).

The *Basuto* of the Union of South Africa are uncertain as to whether the world of the dead is in the depths of the earth or in the heavens:

But wherever it is, existence there is much the same as here. People live in villages, on the familiar pattern of home life, though it is doubtful whether they marry or beget children; they have the same sort of social organization under the leadership of their former chiefs. They also continue the same pursuits, and so they must take with them the wherewithal to establish their new crops, herds and homes; accordingly seeds and *mohloa* grass [which symbolizes family and community life as it always grows where settlements are established] must be placed in the grave so that their essence may be taken by the spirit (Ashton 1952:113).

The *Bena* of Tanganyika believe that

the *kihoka,* the spirit or soul . . . is immortal and after death "goes to a place appointed for it by Mulungu" [Supreme Being]. It is usually assumed that the status of a man's *kihoka* in the next world corresponds more or less with his status while alive. One informant states, "No one really knows whether a man has the same status after death as he had on earth, but Mulungu would never think of making a slave a chief, or vice versa" (Culwick 1935:101).

Beliefs about a life after death have been strongly affected by Catholicism among the Indians of *Santiago Chimaltenango,* in Guatemala. But there is still a conception of a world of the dead in folk and traditional terms; this conception seems to reflect social divisions along lines of economic stratification:

There is no one clearly conceived heaven to which all people go after death. There are several kinds of after life and Chimaltecos are not clear as to why people are designated to go to one place or another. . . . Some people are called by the Guardian of the Mountains, or of the Volcanos, to work as *mozos* [hired laborers] inside the various mountains. Both good and evil people are called, it seems, and only chance determines who is chosen. In . . . various incidents quoted, we have a description of the scene inside the mountain where the dead live and work, but there is a difference in the treatment which they receive in the various moun-

tains. Inside of Santa Maria, with Juan Noq [its owner] the dead work constantly and forever. This is the worst kind of after life. In the volcano Takana, one remains young; one lives and works as we do on this earth. It is not bad (Wagley 1949:67).

The *Dahomeans* of West Africa maintain lineage boundaries in the world of the dead in much the same fashion as they do on this earth. "Therefore, the souls of those who cannot be called by name are not admittedly 'forgotten' but are remembered as groups" (Herskovits 1938b:208).

The *Dusun* of North Borneo place the world of departed souls on the slopes of the sacred high mountains which surround the areas in which they live:

Mount Antulai, more commonly known as Mount Aru (The Mount of Ghosts), is more equivalent to our idea of Paradise than of Heaven, for it is considered to be but a place of sojourn, a stepping-stone as it were, to the next world, which is the sky. According to Bur, a headman of the Tagul, it is a land much resembling Borneo, but not so difficult to live in: there is food in plenty and conditions of life are easier in every way (Rutter 1929:220).

The *Hopi* of northeast Arizona believe that life after death is a replica of human life on earth. As a matter of fact, "the myths tend to minimize the distinction between the living and the dead, and in a similar vein, other 'legends indicate that the deceased Hopi plant and harvest, that the dead have ceremonies and altars . . . [and] that the customs of those who occupy the abode of the dead resemble those living on earth'" (Titiev 1944:107).

Among the *Kurtatchi* of Bougainville in Melanesia, it is believed that the souls of men (*urar*) can make themselves manifest to the living in a variety of ways and that humans can communicate with the souls of deceased Kurtatchi. They differ from people in a variety of ways, especially in the things they eat. "Otherwise, they are thought to live much the same kind of lives in the place of the *urar* as they did when they were alive" (Blackwood 1935:508).

Paralleling the tripartite division of *Lakher* socio-political organization (in eastern India) into royal, noble, and commoner castes is the belief that "there are three separate abodes to which the spirits of the dead may be sent" (Parry 1932:396).

The *Lambas* of Northern Rhodesia appear to project their social structure only partially in their ideas of the nature of the world of the dead. This "is the great place of levelling. . . . In *ichiyawafu* there is no distinction of social status; no distinction is made between the persons of chiefs, commoners, or slaves" (Doke 1931:231).

Among the *Lepcha* of Sikkim in the Himalayan Mountains there are two separate sets of beliefs about the destiny of the soul after physical death. The first set consists of the formalized doctrines of the lamas, who maintain a hypothesis of reincarnation in human or animal form. In traditional belief, however, "the soul is conducted to the *rumlyang*, the child grows up to maturity and leads a happy and immortal life among all the other dead, a life similar to that here on earth except that there is no death or disease or want" (Gorer 1938:346).

There are no published data on the destiny of the soul of the contemporary Mandan-Hidatsa people of Lone Hill, but there is information of the beliefs of the *Mandan* Indians in their aboriginal state. Traditionally, it is believed that the souls of the dead "live in earth-lodge villages, plant gardens, hunt, and perform ceremonies much the same as

during their lifetime. One's status in the hereafter is essentially the same as when one died" (Bowers 1950:98).

In *Malekula* of the New Hebrides it is believed that the Land of the Dead resembles the land of the living, but with a few differences. "The women do not wear the mat-skirt of Seniang, but instead the petticoat of banana fibre which is worn in Mewum. Another distinction is that all the vegetation, in particular the yams, are red and not green" (Deacon 1934:556).

The afterworld of the *Marquesans* of Eastern Polynesia is a highly stratefied place, as is the land of the living, and one's place in the afterworld depends on the amount of wealth one can amass:

Those whose rank did not entitle them to a place in the sky world went to one of the three lower worlds. The lowest of these was the most desirable, while the highest one, the one immediately adjoining the world of the living and therefore the easiest to reach, was highly unpleasant, dark and muddy and short of food. The world to which a man went depended on the number of pigs sacrificed at his memorial feast. Those for whom there was only one pig, or none at all, went to the poorest world (Linton 1939:184).

The *Navaho* of Arizona and New Mexico, in line with their distaste for thinking or speaking of death, have very unelaborated ideas about the nature of the hereafter. "The afterworld is a place like this earth, located to the north and below the earth surface" (Kluckhohn and Leighton 1946:126).

The hereafter of the *Okinawans* in the Ryukyu Archipelago in the Western Pacific is by and large a replica of life on this earth. Cemeteries, for example, are often laid out as "grave villages," each tomb being in the shape of a traditional house, all of these tombs arranged in the same style and pattern as the villages of the living (personal field notes).

Among the Omaha of Iowa and Nebraska "the environment in the spirit world is similar to that on the earth, the avocations seem to be the same and it would appear as though interest in the affairs of this world never wholly ceases . . ." (Fletcher and La Flesche 1911:590).

The *Papago* of Arizona and adjacent Mexico believe that "the soul on its journey must pass through a gap, which was very dangerous. . . . Beyond the gap is the town where the dead live, just as people on earth do. . . . The life is like the life on earth, except that there is plenty of rain, for this is in the east, whence the rain comes" (Underhill 1939:191–192).

The afterworld of the people of *Pukapuka* of East Central Polynesia was largely a reproduction of life among humans, save that

there were no class distinctions in the Po; hence there was no special reception for a chief. Spirits did not grow old or mature in the Po. People who died old were looked after by relatives who had died young. Babies never grew up. The old cared for the children, and the young men and women provided food for the rest of the community (Beaglehole 1938:330).

The *Sirionó* of Eastern Bolivia appear to constitute a second exception to the generalization that all peoples believe in a life after death. Although one investigator seemed to think that they do possess a belief in a hereafter, their ethnographer "found no evidence to corroborate such a belief in a hereafter. While notions of an afterlife have crept in when the Indians have had contacts with the whites, these are clearly assignable to Christian influence. . . . One thing seems clear as regards eschatological beliefs: there is no

afterworld to which the soul departs" (Holmberg 1950:91–92).

Following living *Siuai* relationships, "in the realm of the dead there is no overall hierarchic arrangement of beings, although there are specific instances of some spirits being subordinate to others" (Oliver 1955:80). Also reflecting the looseness of form in Siuai social-structural arrangements, "accounts of [the spirits'] actions leave one with the impression that the Siuai believe them to behave according to individual caprice, within the bounds of certain patterns, of course, but not according to a comprehensive and ordered scheme" (Oliver 1955:80). The Siuai live in the Solomon Islands.

The people of *Suye Mura,* Japan, order the world of the dead along the lines of socioreligious affiliation in this world.

Most of the ideas of heaven and hell come from the priests' talks and are not very much thought about by the people except when they get old. . . . One characteristic attitude is that, according to one's belief in life, so will one's soul be disposed at death — if Shin sect, one goes to Amida's heaven; if Zen sect, to some other type of heaven; if Shinto, to the village shrine (Embree 1946:195).

Continuing one of the basic problems of their social structure into the social structure of the hereafter, the *Tallensi* of the northern Gold Coast take full account of "the rivalry of successive siblings in a number of . . . ways. Thus, successive siblings (this applies chiefly to brothers) may not be buried in the same grave. If they are, their spirits will be continually quarreling and persecuting their descendants until they are exhumed and separated" (Fortes 1949:254).

Among the *Tanala* of Madagascar, "souls who have been accepted by the ancestors live in villages and carry on an existence exactly like that while alive. They have chiefs, marry, have children, build houses, plant rice and raise cattle, go on journeys, etc." (Linton 1933:167).

The *Thonga* of southern Mozambique designate the soul of a departed man as a *shikwembu,* a god. It is generally believed that upon death "the departed go to a great village under the earth, a village where everything is white (or pure, 'ku basa'); there they till the fields, reap great harvests, and live in abundance, and they take of this abundance to give to their descendants on earth. Thus the life of the *Shikwembu* seems to be the exact continuation of his earthly existence" (Junod 1927:350).

Among the *Witoto,* an Amazonian tribe in Brazil and Colombia, the "land of the After-Life is a diminutive replica of the ordinary world, but with evil things eliminated and joyful things emphasized. All is on a lower scale, stunted forests and pigmy game" (Whiffen 1915:225).

The *Yurok* world of the dead was as clearly stratified and constructed of differentiations as was the world of the living. "People killed with weapons went to a separate place in the willows; here they forever shouted and danced the war dance. Contentious and thievish men also remained apart: their place was inferior. A rich, peaceable man, on the other hand, who had constantly planned entertainment for dances, came to the sky" (Kroeber 1925:47). The Yurok live near the Pacific Ocean in extreme northern California.

Thus, the foregoing data reveal several things. First, a society's conception of the world of the souls is a replication of the social structure of the living. The repeated statement by ethnographers that the world of the dead is a replica, often in miniature, of the world of the living does away with the need to organize these materials by types of social organization; hence, they have been listed alphabetically. Second, and stemming from this, these imageries of the afterlife cut across different types of social structure and there does not seem to be any relationship between the conceptualization of the afterlife and social-structural typologies. In other words, the generalization which can be drawn is that it is a characteristic of life in most societies for people to see the world of the dead as a replica of the world of the living. The nomadic Arunta and Sirionó appear not to have beliefs about an afterworld.

While collecting these data, it was inevitable that others would be gathered; these round out the picture of the destiny of the soul after physical death, and bear on two questions. First, in view of the Western notion that the desirable destination of the soul after death is "above," or in some general upward direction, these data shed interesting light on the cultural relativity of direction (see in this connection Bevan 1957:28–81). Second, and also from the vantage of Western thought, the question naturally arises about the types of societies which visualize the world of the dead in terms of "heaven" and "hell," and those which see the abode of life after death as a relatively undifferentiated system.

There are very few societies for which we are told whether the land of the dead is up or down; specifically, this information is available for only thirteen societies in the sample. Of these, five (Balinese, South African Bushmen, Ifaluk, Sanpoil, and Witoto) believe that the world of the dead is in the sky, that is, in an upward direction; eight societies (Chiricahua Apache, Bantu of North Kavirondo, Basuto, Lamba, Navaho, Pukapuka, Thonga, and Yurok) see the afterworld within the earth, that is, in a downward direction.

Each of these beliefs about the location

of the world of the dead is associated with a variety of social structures; social organization and belief about the site of the dead thus seem to be independent of each other. Although the number of cases for which there are data are small, it can nevertheless be concluded that this aspect of eschatological beliefs is unrelated to living social-structural arrangements. (For a discussion of one facet of this general problem from the point of view of linguistic theory, see Greenberg 1954, and Newman 1954:90–91.)

The second question raised by the data concerning the social structure of the dead is the dichotomization of the hereafter into what is called "heaven" and "hell" in Western culture. The data bearing on this problem are meager.

Thirteen societies in the sample appear to organize their world of the souls into two or more separate domains. Not all of these can be interpreted in Western terms, however. For example, some societies which dichotomize the world of the dead have separate abodes for those who have died natural deaths and those who have died violent deaths. It is difficult to interpret such theories, since there are very few data, if any, which might lend meaning to this organization in the land of the souls.

"The Alorese think that each individual has two souls. One of these goes to the 'village below' if the death was natural, and to the 'village above' if death was violent" (Du Bois 1944:119). Among the Chamorros of Guam, "according to Sanvitores, the souls of those who died a violent death were believed to go to a sort of hell called Sasalaguan, the dwelling of a demon who cooked them in a cauldron, which he stirred continually. Those who died a natural death were believed to inhabit an underworld paradise" (Thompson 1941:137).

The Chenchu do not divide the world of the dead, having a very nebulous conception of a hereafter, but they do consign different souls to different fates. Those who lived evil lives are refused admission to the land of the souls and are condemned to roam about in the vicinity of their former homes as evil ghosts (Fürer-Haimendorf 1943:196). As noted earlier, the Indians of Santiago Chimaltenango divide the land of the dead into separate entities, the destiny of individual souls apparently being determined solely by chance (Wagley 1949:67).

The Lakher have one abode for "all ordinary spirits" and a second for "people who have died unnatural deaths and . . . those who have died of certain loathsome diseases . . ." (Parry 1932:396). The people of Malekula do not divide people in the land of the dead according to the ways in which they have died, but have separate abodes in the afterworld for those who have lived good lives and those who have lived bad lives (Deacon 1934:557). The Spirit World of the Marquesans was divided neither according to the ways in which people died nor according to the moral quality of their lives on earth; instead, there were three levels, graded according to social rank and wealth (Handy 1923:251).

In the Underworld of the people of Pukapuka "was kept burning a hot fire, into which adulterers, for example, are supposed to have been thrown . . ." (Beaglehole 1938:329). The Siuai have three abodes for the souls of their dead. One is for "fortunate ghosts, whose deaths have been widely mourned and whose mourners have been suitably rewarded" (Oliver 1955:76). A second abode is for those who have not been properly mourned, and a third is for those killed in fighting. The people of Suye Mura apparently do believe in the existence of a heaven and a hell, but "some younger people (twenty to forty years of age) believe that there is no heaven and hell except in one's self" (Embree 1946:195). Like the Chenchu, the Tanala do not divide the world of the souls into separate abodes, but "a person who has been formally disowned, a notorious sorcerer, or a man of extremely evil life, may be rejected by the spirits of his ancestors and refused a place in their village. Such souls become vagabonds working evil upon the living and hanging about at sacrifices to intercept the good souls and seduce them into injuring their descendants" (Linton 1933: 167).

The Tarascans appear to have fully incorporated Roman Catholic beliefs about the divisions of the afterworld into their folk beliefs (Beals 1946:207; Foster 1948a:269). The Yurok not only divided the land of the souls according to rank, morality, and wealth, but "people killed with weapons went to a separate place in the willows; here they forever shouted and danced the war dance" (Kroeber 1925:47).

In conclusion, it appears from these data that the social structure of a group enters into the perceptual and motivational apparatus of its members, and that it functions as a cognitive basis for the construction and evaluation of reality. After completing the research for this chapter, new data which are being gathered for a different cross-cultural study suggest that there are important social-structural factors which influence the dichotomization of the afterworld into what we call "heaven" and "hell." While these data and their analyses are still incomplete, they indicate that such a bifurcation of the afterworld tends to occur in highly stratified vertically entrenched civil-state structures. One tentative conclusion which can be drawn is that the promise of an eternal reward of "heaven" — and the corollary threat of eternal punishment in a "hell" — is one of the ways in which the ruling classes exact obedience and conformity from the lower classes. However, why some people place their hereafters in an upward direction and why some place them in a downward direction appears to be unrelated to levels of institutional integration.

SEPARATING THE MYTHS FROM THE TRUTHS ABOUT CULTURE

I mentioned earlier that I had begun this research with a serious misconception about the availability of the data which would be required for this study; fortunately, however, enough data were available to make the study feasible. I had also begun with another anticipation — much more fundamental than the first — and this, too, was not borne out.

I had anticipated that different ideas of the destiny of the soul would covary with different types — or, more specifically, certain dimensions — of social organization, in much the same way that I had found that behavior with respect to food distribution, patterns of friendship, socialization practices, and legal systems covaried with particular types of social organization (Cohen 1961a, 1961b, 1964a, 1964b). For example, I was certain that different types of hunting and gathering societies would have their own ideas of the nature of life after death, that horticultural societies would have theirs, agricultural societies theirs, and so forth. I did not have any specific hypotheses about what kinds of ideas would be found in each type of socio-economic organization, but I was fairly certain that, with good fishing, I would find them. Clearly, there is no relationship between ideas of the world of the dead and those elements of social organization in my hypothesis. However, as noted earlier, research currently in progress suggests that political integrations play an important role in this respect.

Although I was wrong in one way, I found empirical verification for something most anthropologists know and of which I apparently needed reminding: there are areas of culture which do not parallel or coincide with social organization in strict fashion and which appear to be quite independent of social organization.

This is one of the great values of large-scale cross-cultural studies, namely, that this type of research — thought of as the comparative anatomy of culture — is one of the most valuable procedures by which we can determine the regularities in culture and social organization. Putting this in colloquial terms, this is the procedure by which we can find out what is really true about culture — as a system — and what is not true. Cross-cultural research helps separate the myths from the truths about culture.

One of the most fruitful sources of hypotheses for the cross-cultural determination of regularities in culture are the postulates and axioms which anthropologists hold about the principles which govern cultural development and functioning. When anthropologists assert that they are concerned with, among other things, uncovering these principles, they mean they are seeking the regularities which are present in cultural patterning and evolution. Anthropologists are not content with such statements as "culture changes," or "all cultures are constantly undergoing change," or "every culture is put together in a unique way." These are descriptive truisms, and although often necessary as starting points, they are insufficient to explain anything. Thus, in addition to knowing that culture changes, we must have some notion of priorities in change, that is, which phenomena or events are most likely to set changes into motion, and what their consequences are. We must also have a clear picture, or at least a set of verifiable hypotheses, about which aspects of culture (for example, language) are outside the mainstream of these chain-reactions of change. In addition to knowing that every culture is patterned in a unique way, we must know what the articulators and fulcrums of this patterning are: is it the system of exploitative activities which triggers the patterning and then holds it together; is it the system by which resources are allocated and by which people have access to the means of production; is it the

organization and filiation of kinsmen into different kinds of groupings and associations; is it the system of ideas which dominates and integrates the patterns of thought in a society, and the like?

These are questions about regularities in culture, although they far from exhaust the list; large-scale comparative studies of culture are one of the techniques of anthropology most admirably suited to the explication of such regularities. There are many different kinds of statements of regularity about culture and social organization which can emerge from such comparative studies. The finding in the present study that cultural beliefs about the location of the afterworld are independent of the social-structural arrangements of the living is as much a statement of regularity in culture as the finding that the nature of the world of the dead tends to be a replica of the social-structural arrangements of the living. (In a way, this hints at one of the most serious problems in contemporary science, namely, that only positive findings, and rarely negative ones, are ever published.) Without even attempting to exhaust all possibilities, the following statements are examples of cultural regularity which can be uncovered by large-scale comparisons:

There is a definite tendency for North American Indian cultures to develop in a direction of greater and greater integration of economy and social organization (Driver 1956:27).

Under matrilocal pressures, patrilineal societies can become bilateral, and thence perhaps eventually matrilineal. They cannot, however, undergo direct transition to a matrilineal form of organization (Murdock 1949:218).

In most of the societies that practice segregation and chaperonage to control the sexual behavior of adolescents, boys are less carefully watched than girls; and, in some cases at least, it appears that youths are able to circumvent the barriers with the result that sexual intercourse before marriage not infrequently occurs (Ford and Beach 1951:183).

Relative importance of love-oriented techniques of punishment by parents will be positively correlated with the importance of patient responsibility in the explanation of illness (Whiting and Child 1953:244).

In those societies in which children are brought up by their parents as well as by members of the children's descent group, and in which children are subjected to extrusion or brother-sister avoidance at the first stage of puberty, the concept of joint liability will be found. In those societies in which children are brought up by their parents plus non-members of the children's descent group, and in which there is neither extrusion nor brother-sister avoidance, only the concepts of several liability will be found (Cohen 1964b:141).

Regardless of the kinds of regularities a cross-cultural investigator seeks to uncover and regardless of which areas of culture he is probing, there is one stricture he must always keep in mind; this was mentioned at the outset of this chapter, but bears reiteration. Statements of regularity in culture — diachronic or synchronic — need not be formulated in terms comparable to those of biology, physics, chemistry, entomology, astronomy, and the like. Statements of cultural regularity need not model themselves after statements of regularity in the nonsocial sciences because the two branches of science deal with entirely different kinds of phenomena in nature, and it is possible that the methods of one are not strictly applicable to the other. While the logico-deductive method is common to both branches, it is also possible that cultural phenomena are neither comparable nor analogous to those studied in the nonsocial sciences. Man, among other attributes, is a feeling and decision-making being who is capable of reflecting about himself in third-person terms; this makes him unique in the known universe. Hence, laws and principles about human culture might have to be formulated according to entirely different standards from those pertaining to

other phenomena. In view of the importance of the nonsocial sciences to modern technology, and their consequent prestige, there is understandable temptation to use them as models; hence, it is essential to keep this stricture in mind.

One of the clearest statements of this skepticism with respect to nonsocial scientific models has been made by Driver who, in a remarkable cross-cultural study of patterns of economic and social organization in North America, has

shown how functional theory can suggest correlations which can be verified empirically by geographical distributions and correlation coefficients. The truth or falsity of a functional correlation cannot be satisfactorily expressed with words alone because correlations among ethnographic data are almost never perfect or zero. The all, some, and none categories of Aristotelian logic are of little value in ethnology, or any other social science, because practically all relationships fall in the same category. Since the same category includes correlations from .99 to .01 and from −.99 to −.01, it becomes imperative to express the degree of correlation in quantitative terms. Once the numerical correlations are known, they may be grouped in matrices and used to prove or disprove temporal sequences (Driver 1956:32).

In the study on which this important insight is based, Driver attempted to determine cross-culturally the degree of economic and social-structural integration in North American Indian societies. He found that statistical procedures were insufficient for the analysis of his data

because functional correlations are low and only a minority of tribes achieved complete or near complete integration. The others seem to have been disturbed in some manner. At this point functional and evolutionary theory are of no help because they cannot account for the negative instances. To stop at this juncture would leave at least half of the distributional facts unexplained. Therefore we must turn to history (Driver 1956:27).

Evidence, Probability, Exceptions, and Hypotheses

I am going to begin this section with a brief review of some problems in hypothesis construction in comparative research from an example in kinship organization and political leadership. The hypothesis I am going to construct will not be tested here, and is intended to serve only as a heuristic device in this context.

I will use this hypothesis to introduce this section for several reasons. First, it will serve as a bridge between the methodological caveats raised at the beginning of this chapter and the problems to be reviewed in this section. Second, it will help round out the picture I want to present of the range and kinds of hypotheses that can be analyzed cross-culturally; the beginning student should not come away with the impression, especially in delving into the methodological issues of this section, that the hypothesis about where the soul goes is the only valid type of cross-cultural hypothesis. Third, the hypothesis has several elements which can be put together in different ways; it also has the advantage that it can be tied to other hypotheses and to problems in other areas of social organization.

In the exploration of a hypothesis, the investigator must always be clear as to which factor is his dependent variable and which is his independent variable. (As we shall see, there can be more than one of each of these variables; however, I am confining myself for the moment to the simplest statements for illustration.) Thus, for example, in constructing a hypothesis about the possible factors responsible for different forms of kinship affiliation, such a hypothesis would read (after Murdock 1949:204–219): matrilineal or uterine reckoning of descent [the dependent variable] arises out of any system of food production in which the roles of the women are more important than those of the men

in the division of labor by sex, as in horticulture [the independent variable].

A dependent variable can also become an independent variable, as in the following hypothesis: societies which possess the principles of matrilocal residence and matrilineal descent [independent variable, composed of two elements instead of only one] will have political leadership which is weak and relatively ineffectual [dependent variable] (Cohen 1962a). (This, incidentally, is an inversion of the generally accepted notion that matrilineal descent is one of the consequences of weak political authority.)

Sometimes it is possible to construct a broad-spectrum hypothesis in which a dependent variable can become an independent variable within the same hypothesis. Taking the latter two hypotheses and combining them into one, we can see how this is accomplished: those systems of food production in which the roles of women are more important than those of the men in the division of labor by sex, as in horticulture [independent variable], will give rise to matrilocal residence and matrilineal descent [dependent variable, composed of two elements]; in such societies [rules of residence and descent are now the independent variable], political leadership is weak and relatively ineffectual [dependent variable].

As it stands, this hypothesis contains several pitfalls which I have deliberately included in order to be able to point to them. Every investigator must be aware of these before embarking on a study based on controlled comparisons. In order to appreciate the significance of these pitfalls, it must be recognized that large-scale cross-cultural studies are the closest anthropologists can come to a true laboratory situation. For a variety of reasons, anthropologists cannot conduct experiments with cultures. But even while realizing that all cultures will continue to evolve, history and nature have provided us with most of the imaginable cultural situations in which people can find themselves. The panorama of cultural diversity is our laboratory. By comparing cultures in all their dimensions, we can unravel the myriad combinations and permutations which have been established for us in this vast laboratory.

One aspect of the analogousness of cross-cultural studies to laboratory experimentation is that it should be possible to replicate every cross-cultural study, just as it is assumed that every laboratory study is replicable. But no two anthropologists will arrive at similar results in the study of the relationship between matrilocal-matrilineal systems and political leadership because, as the hypothesis now stands, the terms "leadership" and "weak leadership" are undefined, and there are many notions among anthropologists as to what such leadership is. Unless there is an unequivocal definition of each variable in a hypothesis, misunderstandings and confusions will inevitably result because, while different investigators will think they are studying the same phenomenon, they will actually be studying quite different phenomena. Thus, in the trial formulation of the latter hypothesis, the statement reads as follows: societies in which the rule of residence is matrilocal and the rule of descent is matrilineal, political leadership in the form of hereditary chieftainship will be weak and relatively ineffectual; weak and ineffectual authority is denoted by the absence of institutionalized means for the enforcement of decisions in predictable and consistent fashion (Cohen 1962a).

The difficulty with terms like "leadership," "political," "weak political leadership," and the like, is that they are abstractions. Anthropologists do not study abstractions, unless they are examined as cultural objects (for example, ideas of "good" and "beauty" in different cultures); they study the behavior and institutions of people in different societies in order to arrive at generalizations and

principles about the ways in which human culture evolves and operates. While these generalizations and principles are abstract — that is, they are derived from individual concrete instances and are intended to refer to many instances — they constitute the goals of comparative research rather than the raw data. In other words, in cross-cultural studies designed to evaluate hypotheses empirically, the hypotheses must be couched in the most particular and concrete terms possible, and they should always be designed to answer the question: do the people in these societies perform the behaviors posited in the hypothesis or don't they?

The difficulties which can arise from failure to follow this basic stricture of scientific procedure can be illustrated by a critical review by Leach of a large-scale cross-cultural study by Udy, in which Leach focuses on the proposition (which is one of fifty-eight) that "familial organizations tend to be basic-auxiliary, diffuse and permanent." Leach comments that

. . . the elaborate coded jargon which Dr. Udy has devised for the presentation of his argument is in itself an effective screen between author and reader. . . . For example, when proposition 27, cited above, first appears at p. 60, it is supported by the coefficients: $Q = +.99$, $x^2 = 97.23$, $P < .001$. This implies, I take it, that probably it is so! But what is so? What does proposition 27 mean in plain English? There is no index or glossary of special terms but the reader may perhaps remember that *basic-auxiliary*, *permanent*, and *diffuse* have been defined at pp. 42–44. These definitions seem to reduce proposition 27 to the profound statement that: "In many societies kinsmen can be observed to help one another on some jobs part of the time with no obvious objective." What an amazing discovery (Leach 1960b:136)!

For better or worse, and for a variety of reasons, it is the nonsocial sciences which, in the minds of many people, set the standards of "scientific" methods and thought; as a result, some social scientists often feel defensive about their procedures and concepts. Some, perhaps in the belief that only the non-social sciences can ascertain cause and consequence, have maintained that cross-cultural research is impossible because every culture is a unique and self-contained system, in which all parts are of equal valency, and that the only way to understand cultural phenomena is to know the history and structure of every society. Professor Leach, who also seems to feel that anthropology's only hope is to become a generalizing mathematical science, has seriously written as follows:

Comparison is a matter of butterfly collecting — of classification, of the arrangement of things according to their types and subtypes. The followers of Radcliffe-Brown are anthropological butterfly collectors and their approach to their data has certain consequences. . . . Now I agree that analysis of this kind has its uses, but it has very serious limitations. One major defect is that it has no logical limits. Ultimately every known society can be discriminated . . . as a sub-type distinct from any other, and since anthropologists are notably vague about just what they mean by "a society," this will lead them to distinguish more and more societies, almost ad infinitum (Leach 1961:2–3).

Such questions have a tendency to become ideological rather than empirical, and their discussion *as though* they are empirical is often pointless. Simply put, though I will return to some of these questions in detail in the final section of this chapter, I accept Steward's assertion that, underlying comparative studies is a

conception of culture [which] is in conflict with an extreme organic view, which regards culture as a closed system in which all parts are of equal importance and are equally fixed. It holds that some features of culture are more basic and more fixed than others and that the problem is to ascertain those which are pri-

mary and basic and to explain their origin and development. It assumes that, although the secondary features must be consistent and functionally integrated with the primary ones, it is these that are more susceptible to fortuitous influences from inside or outside the culture, that change most readily, and that acquire such a variety of aspects that they give the impression that history never repeats itself (Steward 1949:6–7).

Still others, especially outside anthropology, maintain that comparative research is not possible because the data of anthropology are "subjective," that is, information about people gathered by people in uncontrolled situations. Such objections are based on the confusion of science with the hardware of a windowless laboratory. As a noted biochemist has observed, "Science is not any particular method of techniques. It is a way of reasoning. The standards are intellectual rather than procedural. The method of observation, formalization, and testing must vary with the nature of the problem" (Miller 1949:291).

A key issue in the derivation of laws and principles about culture through large-scale comparative studies is the question of evidence and, by extension, the nature, definition, and meaning of an exception to a hypothesis. This problem was alluded to earlier in the quotation from Driver's cross-cultural study of economic and social-structural integration in North American Indian cultures, but it requires further elaboration.

One of the characteristics of any science is its ability to state conclusions together with their coefficients of probable error. We do not know yet whether this can be done in anthropology with any degree of certainty. Although there are a variety of mathematical and statistical procedures for indicating degrees of probable error, these procedures have been developed in connection with non-cultural phenomena. It has yet to be determined empirically whether these mathematical and statistical procedures can meet the needs of the study of culture.

The nature of statistical probability is central to this problem. The issue of probability in large-scale comparisons of cultures involves such phenomena as randomization in the data introduced by any one ethnographer, randomization introduced (and multiplied) by the presence of many ethnographers in each cross-cultural study, by errors in the collection of data by any one ethnographer and the multiplication of these possible errors by the presence of many ethnographers in the sample, and the like. When we are someday able to determine with some degree of precision the nature of probability in culture and the degree of probable error in our conclusions and statements of principle or regularity, we shall have reached a measure of scientific maturity far greater than what we possess today, and we will then be able to determine the degree of applicability of the mathematical procedures of the nonsocial sciences to anthropological problems and materials.

Putting this in slightly different terms, the degree of finality in the conclusions and propositions of a science is an indication of that discipline's empirical maturity. The evidence anthropology possesses for its propositions and conclusions is incomplete, although the reduction of this data gap in the last decade has been great. To the extent that the evidence is incomplete, our propositions and conclusions are, at best, only tentative statements of probability. Of course, this is true of all empirical sciences, nonsocial as well as social. But it has special relevance to anthropology generally and to large-scale comparative studies in particular, for several reasons. First, as I have just indicated, the methods of determining the degree of probable error, and the modes of expressing them, have been developed for the investigation of nonsocial phenomena and events in nature. Clearly, anthropology and the other social

sciences which deal with human behavior must determine the extent of the need to develop their own methods or to make radical modifications in the methods of the nonsocial sciences and adapt them to social-scientific needs.

Second, large-scale comparative studies depend upon the quality of the data collected by other investigators in the course of ethnographic investigations *in situs*. (This is a problem with many ramifications, and I will return to it in another context later on.) Thus, the cross-cultural investigator has to rely on the competence of other investigators. He must assume that there is some standardization in the observation of events and the recording of data by ethnologists whose published writings he is using; similarly, he must assume a standardization of terminology in these published works. There are few alternatives to these assumptions, and all are fraught with a variety of dangers.

Third, more so than in most other scientific procedures, the "data" of large-scale cross-cultural studies are not really data at all. What the cross-cultural investigator is really working with are abstractions and generalizations based on the data the ethnographer has collected and which, usually, no one else sees. This, of course, lends even greater urgency to the problem of probable error in our conclusions and statements of regularity, which I mentioned a moment ago. Since the methods of determining and expressing degrees of probable error were originally devised for disciplines in which inquiry is normatively based on true data, we must have methods of determining and expressing degrees of probable error in connection with the information used in large-scale comparative studies.

It is understandable from some points of view that social scientists are sometimes envious of the biochemist's advantage in being able to publish samples of his data, such as photographs of a virus or pictures of damaged cells, or of the physicist's ability to duplicate the impressions on a photographic plate of his experiments with a cyclotron. In view of the nature of the materials that these and other nonsocial scientists work with and the benefits afforded them by the society's technology (for example, electronic microscopes), they can now often enjoy the luxury of maintaining extraordinarily high standards in reporting data as well as conclusions. However, just as science is a way of exploring reality, every science must adapt to the reality with which it deals by, among other things, gearing its methods and concepts to the exigencies of that reality. There is no sense in an anthropologist using a cyclotronic experiment, an astronomical observation, or a biochemist's stained slide as a model for anthropological research. If he does, he is "doing" neither anthropology nor any of the other sciences. The modes of reasoning — for instance, the logico-deductive method — might be similar for both types of science, but it cannot be assumed automatically and unquestioningly that the same axioms and postulates can be used in all; it cannot be assumed unquestioningly that probability, evidence, and exception are the same, or even similar, in all the sciences currently known to us. The reason for this skeptical position, as I have already suggested, is that the data of the social scientist, especially when he is conducting large-scale comparative studies, are not always comparable to the data of other sciences.

For example, the information available to me for the study of the nature of the life of the dead are not necessarily the kinds of data for which most scientific methods have been devised. How many Arunta individuals made statements on the basis of which Strehlow said, "The Northern Aranda man has no illusions about death as far as the human individual is concerned: death is, to him, the last great catastrophe which leads to the eventual complete destruction of his own body and his own spirit. His life's work done, the ancestor merely went to sleep; but man must die, and his death ends all" (Strehlow 1947:43)? According to the information Strehlow provided, the Arunta of Australia appear to have no belief in an afterlife. Thus, they constitute an exception to my hypothesis. I note them as such, but are they truly an exception? What kinds of statements were actually made about the fate of the soul after mortal death; what would a formal linguistic analysis of their statements reveal vis-à-vis a translation of their concepts into Western ones?

There are no ready answers or solutions to these problems. Some anthropologists have at various times proposed that ethnographers publish their field notes, that is, their data. On the surface, this appears to be an ideal solution — especially for those wishing to meet the standards of the nonsocial sciences — but the cure in this instance might be worse than the original malady. For example, would this require that every cross-cultural investigator become proficient in the language of every culture in his sample? This is clearly a physical impossibility. The amount of time required to analyze raw ethnographic data in one's own language is formidable enough; to become proficient in dozens of non-Western languages is a task reserved for the polyglot linguist.

The growing use of sampling procedures and of standardization in data-collection among ethnographers considerably reduces the dimensions of this problem. These procedures make the available published information more readily comparable, and they also have the advantage of reducing errors in data-collection. However, at the same time that anthropologists turn increasingly to standardized procedures of data-collection, care must also be exercised not to neglect the types of problems which anthropology is best suited to investigate but which are not readily susceptible to standardized quantitative procedures; these are often the best grist for the cross-cultural investigator's mill.

One of the war cries of the Thomases who doubt modern anthropology is the relative lack of numbers, of tables showing ranges of variation, of statistical manipulations. In part, this dissatisfaction is justified. Cultural anthropologists have often been cavalier on the problems of representativeness and of validation. In part, however, these objections arise from a misunderstanding of the nature of "proof" in the cultural realm. What is significant in cultural phenomena is often not distance or intensity or other measurable quantities, but rather position in a pattern under a given set of conditions. The pertinent variation is alternation from one configuration to another, rather than movement in terms of measurable positions (Kluckhohn 1955:356–357).

Another important problem in the use of available information for large-scale comparative studies, and another facet of the principle that our cross-cultural generalizations are only as good as the materials presented in ethnographic monographs and articles, is that anthropologists' views of the nature of man and of culture periodically undergo revision (comparable to shifts in these areas in Western culture generally). This, of course, is a sign of intellectual maturity in the discipline and it indicates a reluctance to stand still and to accept conceptual blinders. But this liveliness of the discipline also creates some difficulties for the cross-cultural investigator. One is that his views of culture and social relationships sometimes outrun the available information, which was gathered within the framework of older conceptualizations of culture. When it is realized that a minimum of two or three years elapses between the initiation of an ethnological field investigation and the publication of its report (the average number of years is actually much greater), and that fewer such investigations are currently un-

dertaken compared to the number conducted prior to 1960, we can better appreciate that most of the ethnographic information available to us was gathered through filtering conceptual lenses, some of which are largely outdated.

For example, a few years ago a colleague and I conducted a seminar for two years in which the attempt was made to examine cross-culturally the nature of husband-wife relationships and to relate these to different aspects of social organization. One of the first things which became clear in that seminar was that the *kinds* of information we needed were difficult to find. In the course of comparing ethnographic reports from different periods, it was notable that anthropologists during the last decade have begun to examine and write about the nature of marital relationships in preliterate societies from a substantially different perspective than previously. Increasingly, anthropologists have been reporting explicitly and directly on the emotional, physical, social, and economic relationships between spouses in a manner and in terms that tended to be rare, though not entirely absent, in earlier ethnographic reports. As a result, we are beginning to get a much clearer view of what really goes on in the daily and nightly relationships between spouses in different cultures; the impressions conveyed in many of the earlier reports now appear to need drastic revision. Formerly, we were given the impression from ethnographic reports of great stability and orderliness in marital lives in different cultures (Margaret Mead's accounts of Manus marriage were among the several exceptions to this); this impression came largely from the heavy emphasis anthropologists placed on the formal rules and customs governing reciprocities between spouses, on the division of labor, on spouses' relationships with their own and each other's kin groups, on their expected behavior toward children, and the like. Currently, by contrast, and in addition to the formality of rules and reciprocities, we are being provided with stark descriptions of the nature of marriage in different societies. But the latter reports are recent, and therefore relatively few; hence, any contemporary cross-cultural study of marital relationships is correspondingly limited.

To cite another example from my own work — and I am certain that other anthropologists have encountered similar difficulties, but it is my own that I know best — I recently attempted to formulate an anthropological view or conceptualization of secular morality, basing my attempt on a postulate that every culture has a highly particular area of rules and interdictions which can be called "moral" and which are different from all other provinces of custom, law, and regulation. One of the serious problems which faced me in this attempt was that almost no ethnological reports say what the members of different societies regard as moral and what they do not regard as falling within the sphere of moral consideration. The dearth of such information forced me into the position of making these determinations and definitions myself, using little more than inference and arbitrary criteria. My alternative would have been to disregard the question entirely.

These two examples underscore and point directly to the close relationship between ethnographic investigation and large-scale comparative studies. Ethnographic reports provide the basic raw materials and information for cross-cultural studies; cross-cultural investigations can — among their other important uses — spotlight the gaps in our knowledge and encourage anthropologists to begin to collect the necessary data to remedy these lacunae. The mutual interdependence between the two methods is a continuing one, because as more and better data are collected ethnologically it will be possible to carry out better cross-cultural studies which will then point to the need for

still other bodies of data. This is one way in which a science grows.

To return to some of the formal and methodological issues in cross-cultural research, I mentioned a little while ago that the Arunta of Australia appear to constitute an exception to my hypothesis about beliefs about life after death. One of the issues with which anthropologists have yet to come to grips — especially those who conduct large-scale comparative studies — is the problem of what constitutes an "exception" to a rule or generalization about cultural processes. Intimately related to this, of course, is the nature of "probability" in culture. Driver, as we have seen, has demonstrated that problems which are investigated cross-culturally have to be carried out at several levels simultaneously, as in the juxtaposition of functional and historical analyses in the exploration of a problem.

Especially in regard to the problem of exceptions, we do not know, for example, whether exceptions to a cross-cultural generalization are alternatives which are equally possible or whether they are merely "chance" events. That is, can we assume that cultures or societal units which do not conform to an apparently true hypothesis are fortuitous events, or must each be examined separately in order to try to comprehend its deviance from statistical probability? As pointed out by Driver, the ultimate answers to such problems will be provided by a sophisticated methodology tailored to anthropological imperatives which combines functional and historical approaches into one.

I suggest that every cross-cultural hypothesis is, in effect, at least partially a hypothesis about the processes of cultural evolution or of the structures of levels of sociocultural integration. Exceptions to empirically verified hypotheses, from this point of view, can therefore be considered as divergent paths or routes along evolutionary continua. We now know with hardly a doubt that different cultures can reach the same stage of development (for instance, urbanism, civil-state organization, structural independence of the nuclear family) from different starting points, along diverse paths, and by different means. As a result, one of the goals of large-scale cross-cultural comparisons should be the development of hypotheses which, instead of containing one-to-one covariations, should provide for historical and evolutionary alternatives (see, for example, Adams 1966; Goode 1963).

In other words, we should begin to explore the feasibility of freeing our hypothesis-construction as well as our methods of verification from the models provided in the non-social sciences and devise a separate set of standards for hypotheses which attempt to formulate regularity in cultural phenomena. What I am thus suggesting is that even our most psychologically oriented hypotheses be cast in historical and evolutionary terms and within the frame of levels of sociocultural integration.

There are not many extant cross-cultural hypotheses which can serve as examples of this. But the point of view underlying it is clearly expressed, albeit implicitly, by Driver in his comparative study of degrees of integration of economy and social organization in North America:

The theoretical expectations for economic determinism would be positive correlations between forms of economy, residence, and descent. Perfect correlations would not be anticipated because the process takes time. For example, a sib would not necessarily arise the same year that residence first became 100 per cent unilocal. Conversely, if a unisexually dominated economy changed so that the opposite sex became dominant, unilocal residence and unilateral descent might lag behind for a time (Driver 1956:3).

Closely related to this, and complementing the interpretation that exceptions to a cross-cultural hypothesis represent divergent evo-

lutionary paths, are some of the suggestions which have been emerging out of the application of Guttman scaling to large-scale cross-cultural hypotheses (see, for example, Freeman and Winch 1957; Schwartz and Miller 1964). In a detailed and important exploration of the use of Guttman scaling in comparative research, Carneiro suggests that deviations from observed regularities can be due to "environmental limitations which operate to prevent the invention of certain kinds of traits" (Carneiro 1962:165) or to "supersedence," that is, that two traits "are inversely related functionally" (Carneiro 1962:165). As an example of the first, which he calls "skipping," Carneiro cites "the general absence of pottery and loom weaving among the moderately advanced societies of Polynesia [which] may well have been due to the lack of suitable clay and of textile fibers on those islands" (1962:165). As an example of "supersedence," he discusses the hypothetical absence of clans in a group of societies which, by all anticipations, should possess this element of social organization. Using the terminology of the Guttman scale, he notes:

A gap may also appear in a society's column of plusses, not because the society never developed the missing trait but because, having once developed it, the society later lost it. If a trait were to be superseded from among any considerable number of societies in our sample, we would ordinarily eliminate it summarily from our list of scalable items. But if the absences of such a trait manifested some kind of pattern on the scalogram we would do well to attempt to discover what regularity might lie behind its disappearance. . . . [In this hypothetical instance], the dropping out of clans coincides with the advent of . . . *territorialism*, that is to say, the basing of socio-political organization on territorial units rather than on the principle of kinship. The fact that these two traits appear on the scalogram as mutually exclusive *distributionally*, strongly suggests that they are inversely related *functionally*. In other words, something about the onset of territorialism seems to lead to the elimination of clans. Thus, what at first appeared to be a puzzling aberration turns out to be an instance of a regular and orderly process of change . . . (Carneiro 1962:166).

Even without using scaling techniques, I think I can best illustrate the way in which a hypothesis can be constructed in historical terms as well as in functional terms — and the possible advantages accruing from the former — by what I now regard as a serious lacuna in my first large-scale cross-cultural study. There I hypothesized:

(1) In those societies in which infants and young children are fed whenever they cry for food or ask for food, individuals will, as adults, share their food or money, or both, with other people. Conversely, in those societies in which infants and young children are not fed whenever they communicate the desire for food, individuals will, as adults, amass or hoard their wealth, and there will be few enforceable prescriptions to share that wealth with other persons.

(2) Those factors which make for social proximity between households will maximize the emotional predisposition to share food or money, or both, with other persons which was created by feeding on demand during infancy and childhood. Similarly, those factors which make for social distance between households will minimize this predisposition to share which was created by feeding on demand during infancy and childhood (Cohen 1961a:318).

I feel that there is a serious weakness in this hypothesis, as well as in its empirical analysis, for the following reason: one of the corollaries of the tendency of cultures to become increasingly complex within the limits of their environments (all other things being equal) is that one dimension of the evolutionary curve, from its beginnings, shows a movement from social fragmentation or atomism toward greater cohesiveness and then once more toward fissility or weakness in daily social relationships. However, this atomism or weakness in social relationships takes different forms at different points on the evolutionary continuum. At the lowest levels of economic adaptation, this atomism is generally based on a family level of sociocultural integration or, at most, on very small multifamily aggregates. At the highest levels of economic adaptation, this atomism takes place within the context of states and huge urban centers, and for very different reasons.

The principal omission in this hypothesis (or commission, depending on the point of view) is that it tends to view social systems as static and removed from any dimension of time or level of integration. Furthermore, because of this static view of social organization, the correlations set forth in the hypothesis stopped too far short of the true limits of the reality which they purported to reflect; that is, since it left no room for the dimension of time, the hypothesis was unable to account for the adaptive aspects of social relationships to the wider environment. If it is true, as the first cross-cultural study indicated, that degrees of fissility and cohesiveness in social relationships will minimize and maximize the psychological predisposition to share with others, and if it is also true that the quality and structure of social relationships is one part of a society's adaptation to its environment, then patterns of sharing and nonsharing of food and money must also be viewed as part of this system of adaptation. Hence, not only would a more complete analysis of this hypothesis require many categories of data which were not included in the first analysis, but it would also demand a more elaborate and complex theory to account for these fuller data. Specifically, this theoretical stance would have to rest more squarely on the ego-psychological concept of reality-testing (Brenner 1955:63–64; Freud 1946:87), on the awareness that the individual is in constant dynamic relationship not only with his social environment but also with his physical environment.

I do not want to imply in this formulation that all relationships in culture can be understood only in terms of the sequential relationship of two variables in which one necessarily precedes the other. Currently available evidence suggests otherwise. But the notions of sequence and the dependence of variables upon each other, diachronically as well as synchronically, are indispensable and indisputable nevertheless. However the extent to which our claims for evolution in social relations are established — as limited or narrowly specific — they will have to emerge out of empirical investigations in the years to come.

In terms of what I am proposing here, I would now recast my hypothesis about patterns of food distribution somewhat as follows: given the relationship between early experiences and psychological predispositions to share and be generous with others (which, I think, can be taken as having been demonstrated), such predispositions will find different expressions at different stages of sociocultural development. Specifically, at those levels of sociocultural integration at which there are strong pressures which create social distance between households and other indices of fissility in social relationships, the psychological predisposition to share will be minimized; at those levels of sociocultural integration at which there are forces which create great social proximity between households and in social relationships, the psychological predisposition to share and to be generous with others will be maximized.

This is a redundancy of my original hypothesis within only the narrowest limits;

I think the newer version is much better, for several reasons. As already mentioned, it places the hypothesis within a context of levels of sociocultural integration, which is one aspect of cultural reality. Because this dimension was omitted in the original version, I had to construct a quasi-artificial model of social organization ("the functionally significant unit of association") to help explain the correlations (Cohen 1961a:314–318). There is a very good possibility that this model would prove unnecessary in an analysis which included the dimension of levels of development, or it would at least prove to be less necessary.

Another reason for feeling that this version is much better than the first, and closely related to the foregoing, is that had I cast the original hypothesis in terms of levels of development, I might have been able to explain certain regularities of which I was aware but which I did not mention because the strict synchronic or functionalist frame of the hypothesis did not have room for them. For example, with the exception of the Kwakiutl (who, in view of their huge surpluses of fish, are not really an exception to this hypothesis at all), all the societies manifesting what I call "recurrent exchange and sharing" are horticultural. However, horticultural societies are also represented in the other types of food distribution ("mutual assistance and sharing in times of need," "narrowed and reluctant sharing," and "nonsharing"), as are other types of socio-economic systems. I think that a re-analysis of the problem of patterns of food distribution would show quite conclusively that "recurrent exchange and sharing" is a pattern which emerges as a characteristic of certain kinds of horticultural societies and then tends to become modified and lost in later stages of cultural development; "recurrent exchange and sharing" is largely unknown in historically earlier stages, although — and this is the important point — there are hints of it in some types of nomadic and collecting groups. When this hypothesis is cast in strictly functional terms, it would appear that this system of sharing grows directly out of the social organization of societies which are horticultural. When cast in terms of levels of cultural development, it becomes evident that the structures of certain horticultural societies not only maximize a psychological predisposition but also elaborate a pattern which had been present in earlier stages — specifically, in the modes of meat-distribution in multifamily hunting and collecting bands — as part of the total transition to horticulture.

In concrete terms, recurrent exchange and sharing is the regular, repeated, almost ritualized exchange of food, often of equivalent amounts, between households. In many hunting and collecting groups, mutual assistance in times of need often takes the form of the immediate distribution of meat to almost all the households of the community as soon as an animal is slain, even if the recipients of the meat have also killed an animal; these, therefore, also become donors themselves. I maintained in the original study of patterns of food distribution that although this resembles recurrent exchange and sharing, and brings the two patterns very close to each other, what distinguishes them is the following: where the pattern of food distribution is characterized by recurrent exchange and sharing, some food or other must be exchanged or shared at specified time intervals, depending upon the cultural rules; where the pattern of distribution is characterized by mutual assistance in times of need, and where there is immediate distribution of meat to almost all the families in the community, no other food is spontaneously shared in this manner if no meat has been captured — unless, of course, a related or neighboring family is in great need of other food (Cohen 1961a:321–322).

While the differences between the two patterns of sharing are not to be gainsaid, the similarities between the rules governing the distribution of slain animals and recurrent exchange are notable when viewed historically. The similarities suggest that recurrent exchange grew out of the rule requiring equal sharing in the meat, and that this emergence was part of the transition to horticulture from the hunting of animals in multifamily aggregates. In sedentary societies characterized by mutual assistance in times of need, this mode of distribution takes the form of aid which is rendered to kinsmen — real or fictive — when economic help is objectively needed.

In the original study, I lumped into a single category the "mutual assistance in times of need" of hunting and sedentary societies. But when looked at historically, it is possible to see that not only does this mutual assistance have different meanings in the two (or more) types of social systems, but there are also good and sufficient reasons for the fact that certain sedentary societies have not developed functional equivalents to the custom of immediately distributing hunted meat throughout the community. If we conceive of the evolution of culture as constituting, in part, a grand sweep and movement from simpler to more complex forms of social organization, we can think of the rule which requires equal and immediate distribution of slain animals as a significant step toward recurrent exchange and sharing, the latter being symbolic of and contributing to the cohesiveness of kinsmen in solidary communities. As the complexity of social organization increases — by a variety of criteria — the solidarity of kinsmen begins to wane; this is reflected in the loss of the pattern of recurrent exchange and sharing, without the substitution of an equivalent custom for immediate and equal distribution of meat throughout the community. Furthermore, as some of the historical analyses in the original study indicated (Cohen 1961a:335–

346), the category of "narrowed and reluctant sharing" tended to fit atomistic hunting and gathering peoples as well as horticultural societies which were in transition to more advanced economic adaptations; with a few possible exceptions, it does not appear to characterize stable horticultural and other sedentary societies.

Thus, the point I want to make on the basis of this reinterpretation of my study of patterns of food distribution is that the kinds of answers we derive from cross-cultural research depend to an important degree upon the theoretical perspectives with which we formulate our questions. The functionalist hypotheses I analyzed in the first study of patterns of food distribution yielded four types of distribution; the historically cast hypotheses this reinterpretation suggests appear to yield five, or possibly six, types of food distribution. To paraphrase Goodenough's stricture, cited at the outset of this chapter, no matter what methods we decide are applicable to our theoretical goals, they confront us with issues that must be resolved: we must make explicit just what it is our theoretical orientation (for example, historical or functional) is about. (For another approach to the study of economic exchange, see Sahlins 1965.)

In these terms, then, how would I evaluate the cross-cultural study of where the soul goes? In addition to its heuristic value for this chapter, I think the comparative study of beliefs about the destiny of the soul tells us several things. First, and very importantly, it points empirically to a basic tendency in almost all societies to believe in a systematically constructed world of the dead. This tendency is found at all levels of cultural development. Second, this proclivity takes the specific form of being a replication, even in miniature, of the social organization of the living. Thus, we would anticipate that as changes occur in the social organization of the quick, there will be comparable shifts in the social organization of the dead. Third, I think the data show that, with the possible exception of ancestor-worshipping societies and a few others which are not ancestor-worshipping, eschatological beliefs are largely independent of religious ideas and institutions. The latter can be regarded as a derivative hypothesis growing out of those discussed in this chapter, and it requires further investigation.

To summarize what I have said thus far in this chapter, one major lesson of the history of science in general — and one all too frequently overlooked by social scientists — is that statistical methods are greatly limited. However, the ethos of statistical methods and their corollaries (for example, in hypothesis-construction) have achieved an ascendancy in the social sciences and have, in turn, seriously affected anthropological preoccupations with methodology. This is not to say that statistical concepts and methods are without utility; the contrary is true. But such methods and concepts are effective in anthropological research only to the extent that their limitations are recognized and to the extent that they meet uniquely anthropological needs. Thus, anthropologists will only be able to deal with such phenomena as probability and exception in culture if they are able to free themselves from the restrictive concepts of nonsocial-scientific statistics and investigate the ways in which the laws of probability are applicable within the realm of culture and the framework of anthropology. Stating the matter succinctly, the laws of probability in throwing a pair of dice are not necessarily the laws of probability in cultural events.

GETTING AT THE FACTS

I would now like to turn my attention to some of the problems in the actual conduct of cross-cultural research and large-scale comparisons (much of the following is taken from and elaborates on Cohen 1964b:199–212). As already mentioned, there are different approaches to cross-cultural research, and there are probably as many cross-cultural approaches or methods as there are kinds of cross-cultural problems (see Lewis 1956; Mead 1961:516–525).

A considerable number of published cross-cultural investigations have, to varying extents, used the facilities of the Cross-Cultural Files of Yale University. In recent years, these facilities have been made available elsewhere, and have since become known as the Human Relations Area Files. The procedures and some of the rationale of these cross-cultural files are presented in the introductory sections of the *Outline of Cultural Materials* (Murdock *et al.* 1950) and in Murdock's publications (1940, 1954, 1957) on some of the research methods that can be employed in using the Files.

The mechanics of the Files, as well as the rationale behind them, make them very easy to use and they facilitate the speed with which research can be conducted. Ideally, one could gather all the information necessary for any large-scale comparative study within a matter of hours by using them, discounting the time it takes to record the material.

The bases of the Files are verbatim excerpts from ethnographic accounts, filed according to the coding system in *Outline of Cultural Materials*. This code outline is geared to snare every item in an ethnographic account, so that each statement by an ethnographer will appear somewhere in the filing cabinet of that culture. All these materials are filed by code numbers, each culture being filed separately. Thus, for example, if one wished to evaluate a hypothesis about the conditions under which moieties develop, he could go to each culture's filing drawer or cabinet, and select the section numbered 61 ("Kin Groups"). Within each two-numbered category (like 61), there are

up to nine three-numbered subcategories, each of which is a subdivision of the two-numbered category. Category 611 is devoted to "rule of descent"; 612, to "kindreds"; 613, to "lineages"; 614, to "sibs"; and so on. The materials for moiety organization are to be found in Category 616.

In conducting an inquiry into moiety organization, the investigator would select the material filed under Category 616 for all the cultures in the Files which are in his sample. If, for example, he wanted to evaluate the hypothesis that moiety organization is correlated with "ideas about probability" in different cultures — I am pulling this hypothesis out of a hat; it is not meant to be taken seriously — the investigator would then take Category 777 ("luck and chance") for all the cultural units in his sample and attempt to verify his posited correlation. (Each excerpted item has a coded bibliographical citation.) The speed with which one can find materials for specific items in hundreds of cultures explains the appeal of the Files to many anthropologists (and, increasingly, to other social scientists who use ethnological materials).

(In 1962, with the first issue of the journal, the editors of *Ethnology: An International Journal of Cultural and Social Anthropology* began the publication, at the end of each quarterly issue, of an "Ethnographic Atlas." This atlas presents coded ethnographic materials for a random sample of the world's societies, based on Murdock's "World Ethnographic Sample" [1957]. The ethnographic information in this atlas is set forth in such a way that it is easily transferred to punched cards for electronic processing [popularly known as IBM cards for computer analysis]. Thus, for example, one could, at a glance, scan 100 societies in order to learn [and then tabulate and intercorrelate] such information as that concerning community organization, religious behavior, economic and subsistence activities, legal concepts and practices, family organization, and so forth. The "Ethnographic Atlas," which is a rather ingenious innovation in anthropology, is thus intended as a quantified cumulative synthesis of ethnographic knowledge.)

For reasons discussed below, I no longer use the Files for cross-cultural research; since my purpose in this chapter is to present the point of view of comparative research to which I subscribe, I shall dwell on the method of large-scale comparisons I use. The advantages and techniques of using the Files are well represented in the published literature, and are easily available (see especially Moore 1961).

Instead of the Human Relations Area Files, I use only complete ethnographic and field reports for my large-scale comparative studies. From a previously selected sample of societies and communities throughout the world, I read, in their entirety, the reports on each culture. (Methodological issues in sampling and recording data will be discussed below.) Materials relevant to the problem I am investigating are marked off in the margin of the book or journal (lightly, with a hard pencil, so the markings can be erased when I am through with that source) and are typed verbatim onto 5 x 8 cards, usually by a secretary who does not know the hypothesis for the study. These cards are filed alphabetically by cultural groups or units. In each of the cross-cultural studies I have carried out thus far, this procedure had to be repeated several times because of the omission of relevant variables in my original working hypotheses. In other words, I continue to read and reread until I have collected all the necessary data for the problem on which I am working. I will return to this later on.

I began my cross-cultural research about a dozen years ago with the hope of achieving a truly random and representative sample of the world's societies. The criteria for this sampling are those accepted by most anthropologists, and they are essentially twofold. First, each culture has to be an independent unit, that is, unrelated to any other culture or society. Second, there should be a proportionate sampling of societies in each culture area. These criteria had to be abandoned very early in my research on the problem of patterns of sharing and nonsharing.

The choices I made, which I will mention in a moment, were elections in the general problem of whether to follow the methodological standards of the nonsocial sciences or the standards which appear to be dictated by the unique requirements and demands of anthropological research.

In testing the original hypotheses for the study of behavior with respect to food distribution, I required three sets of information: those reporting the experiences of infants and children in connection with feeding; those dealing with the behavior of adults with respect to food and money; and those covering patterns of settlement and kinship. (In the evaluation of the revised hypothesis, as outlined in this chapter, I will require several additional categories of information.) I had to abandon the second criterion — the random sampling of each culture area — because very few ethnographic reports contain all this information. I had also hoped that the reports for the societies in my sample would include data on toilet training. If I had insisted on this, I would have ended with an even smaller number of societies.

After completing the study of food-sharing and turning to the problem of patterns of friendship, I had to consider the question of sampling procedures more directly than in the first inquiry, and decide whether to retain the sample used in the first investigation or select a new sample that would be more representative of the distribution of societies. I elected the first alternative — that is, to continue with the original sample

— because of my long-range goals in these investigations. In other words, and to reiterate what has been said above, I chose between the standards and procedures which appeared to be dictated by strictly anthropological interests.

It could be maintained from one point of view that more rigorous sampling methods for each of my studies might have given more and sharper insights into the problems with which I was dealing. But if I had accepted the requirements of random sampling more strictly — that is, those of the nonsocial sciences — and if I had worked with entirely different selections of societies in each study, I would have done so at the expense of broader interests and theoretical considerations. Sampling methods, like any other procedures of research, can be made ends in themselves, or they can be used as expedient instruments for achieving other goals. The vehicles we press into service and by which we arrive at a destination are always dictated by the conditions under which we use them. I maintain emphatically that slavish adherence in anthropology to the standards of the nonsocial sciences is nonscientific because it defeats, or at least fails to serve, the aims of anthropology.

In brief, my selection of societies for these cross-cultural studies was originally determined by the requirements of certain minimal information for the study of food distribution. An attempt was made to locate representative cultures for each culture area within the limits imposed by the required ethnographic materials. What is important in connection with the studies conducted subsequently to the one concerning food distribution, and especially the inquiry into legal and value systems and initiation ceremonies (Cohen 1964a, 1964b), is the fact that regularities and consistencies in the information about different cultures have appeared so strikingly in a sample that was originally selected for an entirely different problem.

One of the principal difficulties in the resolution of the various issues involved in problems of sampling in large-scale comparative studies is the significant role played by diffusion in the evolution and development of cultures. It has been estimated, for example, that at least 80 per cent of the social and material elements in any culture have diffused from other cultures. Thus, it could be argued — and this is maintained by some anthropologists — that large-scale comparisons of cultures are inherently invalid because they do no more than trace the geographical distributions of diffused elements of culture and thus can shed no light on the structures of social systems or on the relationships among the various parts of a culture. While diffusion does pose some serious methodological problems in sampling for cross-cultural research, this phenomenon should not be permitted to cloud a much more fundamental set of processes, namely, that diffusion is not a mechanical, rote, or automatic procedure, but always involves selective borrowing. Cultures do not passively and indiscriminately take other elements from other groups with which they are in contact. Instead, borrowing is always a highly selective, discriminating, and dynamic process in which elements which are mutually incompatible force the selection of one against the other or lead to the adoption of compromises between the two. (Of special relevance in this connection is what Carneiro refers to as "supersedence" [1962: 166]; this was discussed earlier in connection with scaling techniques.) In these terms, then, it can be maintained that one of the goals of large-scale comparisons is to examine many cultures with respect to one problem at a time in order to learn which elements of culture are in potential harmony with each other, which are sufficiently incongruous as to be mutually exclusive, and which lead to the adoption of functional alternatives. As Murdock has observed, though from a slightly different point of view and in somewhat different terms,

Where similarities do occur among the societies of a restricted region, analysis reveals the probability that they are the result either of fission and migration [of groups] or of independent adaptation to similar conditions rather than diffusion in the ordinary sense. Traits of social structure appear to be borrowed, in general, only under conditions in which the same traits would be independently elaborated even in the absence of culture contacts (Murdock 1949:196).

Lévi-Strauss, in an analysis of similarities in art styles in different cultures, has stated the problem in this way:

How shall we explain the recurrence of a far from natural method of [artistic] representation among cultures so widely separated in time and space? The simplest hypothesis is that of historical contact or independent development from a common civilization. But even if this hypothesis is refuted by facts, or if, as seems more likely, it should lack adequate evidence, attempts at interpretation are not necessarily doomed to failure. I shall go further: Even if the most ambitious reconstructions of the diffusionist school were to be confirmed, we should still be faced with an essential problem which has nothing to do with history. Why should a cultural trait that has been borrowed or diffused through a long historical period remain intact? Stability is no less mysterious than change. The discovery of a unique origin for split representation [for example] would leave unanswered the question of why this means of expression was preserved by cultures which, in other respects, evolved along very different lines. External connections can explain transmission, but only internal connections can account for persistence. Two entirely different kinds of problems are involved here, and the attempt to explain one in no way prejudges the solution that must be given to the other (Lévi-Strauss 1963:258).

Although sampling is very important in large-scale comparative studies, it should not be blown up out of proportion to the goals of such investigations. The goal of cross-cultural research is to learn about the dynamics of cultural processes; exquisitely designed samples might have aesthetic and other value, but they have little utility unless they can increase our understanding of cultural processes. And since, given the nature of anthropological materials — especially the fact that it is often difficult to find the needed information — it is usually out of the question to find perfectly designed samples of societies, this criterion is often expendable within limits in the service of answering important questions.

One of the ideal standards of sampling in large-scale comparative studies is to represent all the world's societies in random fashion. However, some of the most valuable cross-cultural studies conducted have been confined to one continent, such as Driver's comparative analysis of economic and social integration in North America (1956), or to a single culture area. As Lewis noted in this connection in his review of comparative studies in anthropology:

The studies in this category, through preponderantly library comparisons are, on the whole, of high quality, and capitalize upon the controls inherent in the study of continuous geographical areas which, though large, have usually been subject to common historical influences. It should be noted that most of the comparative studies of culture areas are found here (Lewis 1956:272).

Once a sample is selected, the cross-cultural investigator is faced with the problem of evaluating the materials from different ethnographic sources in determining whether his hypothesis has been verified. It appears that many people feel (incorrectly, I think) that the same ethnographic information can have widely different meanings to different investigators. I say I think this is incorrect because where independently conducted comparative studies of the same problem have yielded different results, the divergences in conclusions are not due to different readings of the same record, but rather to different definitions and criteria being used. Thus, for example, one reason Whiting and his collaborators and I reached different conclusions about the interpretation of initiation ceremonies is that we were using quite different definitions of initiation ceremonies, in addition to the fact that we were evaluating different hypotheses (Whiting, Kluckhohn, and Anthony 1958; Cohen 1964a, 1964b).

An investigator in cross-cultural research, or any other inquiry for that matter, can be sorely tempted to "find" or "interpret" materials to substantiate his own hypotheses. In published writings and in conversations among anthropologists and sociologists since the landmark comparative study by Whiting and Child (1953), the practice of having ethnographic information rated by a series of independent observers who do not know the hypotheses seems increasingly to be considered standard and desirable procedure. In this procedure, a set of coded ratings are established for the information needed to evaluate the hypothesis; the final rating for these materials is a composite score, usually an average, which is derived from all the independent ratings. On the surface, and perhaps under some conditions of research, this appears to be an ideal procedure.

Parallel with ideals, however, exists reality, and I would like to discuss some of my reservations about this procedure of large-scale comparative research. One of the inexorable facts of the reality of modern science — that is, a "given" of contemporary social organization — is that research costs money, often in large quantities. Some anthropologists (and others) who are unable to obtain financial support for their cross-cultural research have to conduct their own

investigations. If the use of independent raters — who have to be paid — is made one of the absolute standards of acceptable cross-cultural research, the net result will be that the only acceptable cross-cultural research is that which has received financial support from a grant-giving agency. And since it occasionally happens that some legitimate research is not supported because it is unpopular or challenges established truths or enters uncharted areas, then the net result will be that some social-scientific research that seeks to explore new ground — often the most difficult to find support for — is unacceptable. Here again we can observe the maladaptive, dysfunctional, and even antiscientific consequences of rigid adherence in anthropology to the standards of nonsocial sciences.

Another difficulty with the use of raters in large-scale comparative studies, which also involves financial considerations, though to a lesser extent than the first, is that these ratings are usually made by graduate students. Since these ratings take considerable time, it is usually prohibitively expensive to have them done by mature scholars, who normally have their own work to do. Since students constitute the lowest stratum of the academic hierarchy, they are paid the least and their services can be afforded.

However, with all due respect to them, graduate students are not always mature scholars; they often do not have the necessary experience in making the same evaluations of data as their professors. It is not only the threat of unemployment which leads some professors to feel that many graduate students are not yet mature scholars capable of making the same judgments as their teachers. I think it is very important to train graduate students by having them do cross-cultural ratings, if that is what their instructors want them to know — but only as exercises, not as finished scientific products by people who have not yet completed their training in the evaluation of anthropological materials. Since graduate students do not have the experience which would enable them to make the same judgments as their mentors, there is a possibility that the composite ratings of many cross-cultural studies are averages of errors or inadequate evaluations of materials. Of course, if it can be shown empirically that the judgments made by graduate students coincide with those of mature scholars, this would serve to lend added confirmation to a hypothesis. But these assumptions have to be based on concrete experiences, and cannot be taken as a priori valid procedure.

Since the danger of bias in the judgment of other people's published information is great, I feel that, in the absence of independent ratings by mature scholars, the most feasible procedure in reporting the results of large-scale comparative studies is to report the actual statements of the original ethnographers in such a way that the hypotheses would then stand or fall on these ethnographic statements; students can easily assist in this procedure. This is what I tried to do in presenting the results of my inquiry into beliefs about where the soul goes — the ethnographers' statements are there for anyone else to "repeat the experiment," using the materials I have used or evaluating my hypothesis using entirely different sets of materials.

To a very large extent, this procedure of reporting information obviates the problem of the interpretation by coding of the ethnographic materials. If hypotheses are stated with sufficient clarity and in explicit behavioral terms, the danger of misinterpreting other people's statements or of coming to the wrong conclusions are considerably reduced. In colloquial language, hypotheses should be formulated strictly in terms of "do societies act as I have suggested in my hypotheses or don't they?"

Furthermore, if large-scale comparative studies are designed to uncover the regularities which govern human culture, it should be noted that people do not live by ratings; if we want to learn from a cross-cultural study what people in different societies do, we will not learn it from reading a table of plusses, minuses, and asterisks.

At this point, I would like to discuss some of my own experiences with the Human Relations Area Files. My purpose here is not to deny or discredit the usefulness of these Files, but to point to apparent limitations in them. I am going to discuss this in the light of two of my cross-cultural investigations, the ones dealing with patterns of food distribution and with the relationship between initiation ceremonies and legal and value systems, although I have had much the same experience with other cross-cultural studies.

In the first, my original trial formulation of the hypothesis dealt only with the relationships between early feeding experiences and adult behavior in the distribution of food. At the time I formulated this hypothesis, I evaluated it in the Files. The materials substantiated the hypothesis, and the results were reported as part of my doctoral dissertation (Cohen 1953).

However, while doing that research, I noted that there seemed to be different degrees of food-sharing, that is, that people in some societies shared more than people in other groups. But there was nothing in my hypothesis to account for this difference in degrees of sharing, so I grouped all the "sharing" societies together, in the belief that "sharing" constituted a single generic cultural category, and that individual societies elaborated on this pattern for a variety of undetermined reasons. In other words, I had a hypothesis that contained a "one-to-one" relationship, and the ethnographic materials seemed to substantiate it. Now I have learned to regard such "one-to-one" relationships with considerable suspicion.

A short time later, I wanted to continue this research but, living in a different city, I did not have access to the Files. I did, however, have access to an excellent library, and resumed the research using complete ethnographic reports. During this phase of the investigation, I began to realize that the "variations" in degree of sharing were other than mere cultural elaborations of a generic pattern. They turned out to be discrete phenomena or patterns, representing separate and distinct principles of organization that had to be accounted for by factors not present in my original hypothesis. This realization led me to abandon the material I had already collected, and to begin the research again, using only complete ethnographic reports.

Along with my "hunch" that different degrees of sharing actually reflect different economic and social systems, another factor began to suggest itself repeatedly: that these different systems had some relationship to spatial distances between households. From this, other variables dealing with relationships between households, especially temporal, began to build into a pattern, until I felt that I could more adequately explain sharing and nonsharing in fairly complete terms. The important point here is that I am certain that these relationships would not have been uncovered had I confined my research to the Files. This, of course, may indicate a lack in my own theoretical equipment, but I doubt that this alone would account for the experience.

Another side of this problem is empirical, though no less an intuitive or subjective aspect of cross-cultural research. George Gaylord Simpson has observed that one

. . . feature that distinguishes science from other fields of thought and of activity is that it is self-testing by the same kinds of observations from which it arises and to which it ap-

plies. It is, to use a currently popular but perhaps overworked bit of jargon, a cybernetic system with a feedback that in spite of oscillations keeps its orientation as nearly as may be toward reality (Simpson 1963:82).

Hypotheses about cultural events or patterns have to be derived from the very materials by which they are to be tested. This can sometimes be accomplished by using the Files, depending, of course, upon the nature of the problem. But there are innumerable instances in which an investigator can search for a particular datum in a most obvious category in the Files and not find it. He may then assume that this custom is absent in the societies examined or that it missed the attention of the ethnographer — but neither of these may be so.

Before turning to an illustration of this, I would like to note that this is another source of objection to having ratings done by students in lieu of a mature investigator reading the ethnographic materials himself, especially when the raters do not know the hypotheses being tested. For a variety of reasons, students making ratings usually do not have the training or opportunity necessary for finding new variables for a cross-cultural hypothesis which is being evaluated. Additionally, since they are usually kept in ignorance of the hypothesis, apparently in the belief that if they knew the hypothesis they would skew the materials in one direction or the other, they would not know which additional variables to look for while reading the ethnographic materials bearing on the hypothesis. If it is felt by cross-cultural investigators that students are, indeed, sufficiently mature to conduct the legwork of comparative research, then they should most emphatically be allowed to know what the hypotheses are and they should be encouraged to contribute their own insights and hunches toward the elaboration and refinement of hypotheses.

When I began my research into initiation

ceremonies, I conducted a "test run" of my original hypotheses in the Files to learn whether there was any foundation in fact for some of my ideas. It turned out to be completely fruitless, and the results I obtained indicated I should abandon the inquiry. Fortunately, however, I obeyed an intuition that my hypotheses were nonetheless useful, and guided by earlier experiences, decided to do the research anyway, using complete ethnographic sources.

Had I used the Files for the latter research, I would naturally have sought some of my data under the categories having to do with "socialization," child-rearing customs, and kinship relationships. The hypothesis to which I am referring, and which I set out to evaluate in that research, is to be found on page 416 of this chapter. In about one-fifth of the societies in my sample, the information one would normally expect to find in these categories, but which were not always filed properly, actually came from sections in ethnographies labeled "material culture," from photographs, and from maps or diagrams of settlement patterns. In other instances, the information I needed was in sections that had almost nothing to do with the upbringing of children. One of the societies in the sample, for instance, is represented in the published literature by only one monograph and this is devoted almost exclusively to the ways in which children are brought up. In seeking to learn whether children were sent to sleep at night away from their parental homes after about the age of eight ("extrusion"), I found this information in a census presented in a brief introduction to the book. In another case, my data were found in a phrase within a sentence: "Since children leave their parents' home at about the age of ten to live elsewhere. . . ." Often, the role of kinsmen in rearing children was mentioned briefly in sections of reports that had nothing to do with kinship relationships or with the rearing of children.

The point I want to stress is that even though an attempt is made in the Files to present such "buried" information, this is not done successfully and consistently. Therefore, when one relies on the Files to conduct his research, he is actually relying on someone else for the crucial first stage, and he is using information that is edited for him in advance, often by someone who is not a trained anthropologist.

I have gone into some detail in this connection, instead of leaving this line of thought to be shared informally with colleagues, because they indicate a limitation in the use of the Files; and by the standards of modern technology, the Files are among our most efficient instruments for the conduct of large-scale comparisons. Hypotheses, or statements of relationships and correlations, as suggested earlier, must emerge from the very data by which these hypotheses are to be tested. Eventually, as the number of cultures represented in the Files are increased, such hypotheses can be tested in greater breadth than is now possible. Thus, for example, one could select a representative sample of sixty cultures from Murdock's *World Ethnographic Sample* (1957) in order to derive and formulate hypotheses. After this preliminary small sample has been exhausted in complete ethnographic reports, the investigator could then evaluate his hypotheses empirically by the remainder of the sample in the Files. But at the same time, it should always be borne in mind that the quality of the Files is as good as the information included in them.

The question of when one can leave off reading hundreds of books and articles several times over for a single investigation and turn to the Files for speedier results is legitimate, and I do not think there is any definite answer beyond that suggested in the previous paragraph. Perhaps others will be forthcoming from other cross-cultural investigators. As those who have been most intimately associated with the Files have cautioned: "The files are intended as an aid to research in the human sciences, not as a substitute for other types of research" (Murdock *et al.* 1950:xxiii). I think that it can also be cautioned that the Files cannot substitute for the *sine qua non* of research and the construction of hypotheses, namely, slow and careful reflection and the play of intuition and imagination while confronting the data of the science in their original contexts.

THE UNITS OF COMPARISON

The final problem with which I want to deal can be stated succinctly: what is it that we are comparing in large-scale comparative studies?

Some anthropologists, like Leach, who feel that cross-cultural research is a matter of butterfly collecting, assume that it is impossible to compare societies because anthropologists are often vague about what they mean by a society. This is not only akin to throwing out the baby with the bath water, but it also suggests that we avoid difficult problems.

There are several approaches to the problem of defining just what it is we are comparing in cross-cultural research; I will discuss two. The first will be phrased in terms which are analogous to those of dependent and independent variables in hypothesis construction. The central theme of this approach is that it is the community as a boundary system which can serve as the unit of comparison. (For an alternative approach, see Narroll 1964.) Basic to this approach is that every comparative study is made up of at least two sets of comparisons. One is the territorial units — communities, societies, and the like — which form the substratum of the comparative study. The second is the variables of culture which constitute the hypothesis of the study. The latter are explored in relation to the territorial units which comprise the sample of the study.

The second approach will be phrased in terms of the comparison of levels of sociocultural integration. The two approaches are not mutually exclusive; in fact, the first can be considered to be an important step in the comparison of levels of sociocultural integration. The latter approach has been developing in my thinking since the completion of this chapter, especially as a result of a consideration of the methodological implications of two recently completed (but as yet unpublished) large-scale cross-cultural studies. The first deals with the relationship between political organization and sexual controls; the second deals with political organization and educational institutions. I will turn to this approach at the end of this section.

Like many other people, anthropologists sometimes tend to attribute reality to a phenomenon because they have named it. Thus, we sometimes are trapped by our own linguistic devices into thinking that we are really dealing with a society because we have labeled a group of people "a society." Among the many problems in connection with this are two which are outstanding. First, anthropologists do not ordinarily study tribes or societies; to do so is usually physically impossible. They usually study individual communities, because almost all tribes or societies are too large for direct observation. But at the same time, when an anthropologist investigates a community, especially in a preliterate society, he is often proceeding on the assumption that this particular community is more or less representative of the total society, however "society" is defined or conceptualized. He knows no two communities are identical, but he assumes that the processes and principles underlying the pattern of living are pretty much the same — that is, within a limited range — in most communities of the society. In that sense, he is studying one segment as a sample of the total society.

This is not dissimilar to the description of the way of life within the community itself; for example, the anthropologist knows no two individuals within the community are identical in their behavior and feelings, but they are usually roughly similar within a limited range of variability. Furthermore, aside from his census of the community he is studying, most of an anthropologist's information about life in a community comes from a relatively small number of informants, in addition to his observations, which, he hopes, will provide a fairly accurate picture of the range of behavior and beliefs in the community.

Second, the concept of society is artificial, if not spurious, when applied to most peoples of the world. The *sense* of society is a relatively very late development in human history. The member of a foraging band has no sense of society beyond the small number of people with whom he is in sustained contact. Even at the more advanced levels of horticulture, most peoples do not have a sense of "society" beyond the maximal kin group and the local territorial unit. Generally speaking, it is only with the development of true agriculture that the concept of society develops and becomes meaningful in the lives of the people, although there are agricultural peoples among whom this did not happen, just as there are horticultural peoples among whom it did occur. In other words, we must remain aware at all times that most "societies" are the artificial constructs of anthropologists, colonial administrators, tax collectors, the lackeys of diplomats who carve up the world among themselves, and so forth. Most such "societies" are made up of people who speak a common language, or mutually intelligible dialects, who have similar customs, and who share a continuous territory.

But not only do the people in most of the "societies" fail to have a *sense* of society but a great many also feel that the supposed members of their "societies" (or even "tribes") are actually alien to them.

An example of this is Warner's discussion of his definition and designation of the Murngin, an aboriginal Australian "tribe." Warner observes that although he uses the term "tribe" for the Murngin,

the tribe can hardly be said to exist in this area, and of all the tribes studied, the Murngin is the weakest in form. The word Murngin was found as a designation only after much effort. The people do not think of themselves under this name or classification. The word has been used by me as a general term for all of the eight tribes in the area and for the groups of people located in the central part of the territory of the eight tribes. I have seized upon this name as a convenient and concise way of talking about this whole group of people; had any of the other tribes who possess the particular type of social organization found in this area been located in the center of the group, I should have used the name of that tribe rather than Murngin (Warner 1964:15).

Hence, if most people do not live in societies or tribes in any meaningful sense, and if societies do not truly exist in most of the world and at most levels of sociocultural development, what can we use as our population-territorial unit of comparison? One way, among others, of approaching this problem is to seek out the most inclusive common denominators shared by all, or almost all, peoples. We have seen that the "society" is not common to all, hence cannot be used as a standard of comparison. Linguistic units or groupings cannot serve as a basis for comparison, because we know that there can be considerable variability within a linguistic grouping, and the sizes of populations within them can range from a few thousand people to several million.

Economic units — whether of production, consumption, exchange, and the like — are too variable in their memberships to serve as a basis of comparison; further, they do not include the total range of social activities and institutions, and in many cases are not self-perpetuating. The latter criterion is important because self-perpetuating groups are the essential carriers of culture. The same difficulties are posed by attempts to use political, stratification, juridical, or religious systems as bases of comparison.

It is the community which appears to serve best (though I do not maintain that this is an ideal solution to the problem) as a basis for comparison, at least at the population-territorial level (see, in this connection, Arensberg 1954, 1955). While the *sense* of community might be extraordinarily weak among some peoples (see, for example, Cohen 1955; Landes 1961; Service 1962; Steward 1955), all people nevertheless live in communities of some kind, at least for part of the year. These communities might be sedentary and permanent settlements built around a core of unilineally related kinsmen, in which boundaries are relatively impermeable, or they might be atomistic and fluid seasonal congregations of nuclear families, each of which is largely isolated for almost half the year. In the latter instances, the boundaries of the community — however defined — are vague, shifting, highly permeable, and disintegrate easily, especially seasonally, but they exist nonetheless.

As long as we do not insist on inflexible definitions of the community, in which every atom and element is identified and tagged, and if we are willing to consider the community as a process rather than a physical or material thing, "the community" is ideally suited — at least for the present — to serve as a basis of large-scale comparative studies. There are several reasons. First,

one characteristic that makes communities comparable for cross-cultural research purposes is that all communities are self-perpetuating — by reproduction or by recruitment, or both — and have boundaries. (For a fuller treatment of what is meant here by boundary systems, see Cohen 1964b.) Some boundary systems are more distinct than others, while some are very vague and poorly defined, whether they be social or physical boundaries. We know very little as yet about the processes involved in social boundary systems, about how they are maintained, and about their deeper functions. But it is known that most social life takes place within community and other social boundary systems.

It is not mere coincidence that most social life takes place within such boundaries; nor is this only an elaborate way of restating the obvious truism that behavior must occur "somewhere." The boundary systems within which people participate not only encapsulate their behavior, these systems are also part of the subjective experience of any behavior, and they help to mold it. For example, one conclusion of my study of patterns of food distribution — which can now be taken as a "given" and as a basis for reevaluating the hypotheses — is that consistent early food gratification produces a sense of "trust." Similarly, it can be posited that each type of community system or boundary system produces its own emotional predispositions. One of the major contentions of the original study is that the sense of trust is maximized and minimized (and thus given its final shape) by the sociologically produced emotional predispositions with which this sense of trust combines.

However, and not unlike any other activity, neither sharing nor mutual assistance — nor even competition — takes place with just anyone. Instead, each such activity takes place within the confines of highly particularized boundary systems. While it would be an error to suggest that these boundary systems are always communities, or that they are always the same kind of community, it is nevertheless the case that every cultural activity abuts upon or otherwise touches the boundaries of the participants' community (or communities, if they are members of different groups). To reiterate, these communities need not be as clearly demarcated as Peoria, Illinois, or a village in southern India. They can be as amorphous, fragmented, and seasonal as the summer groupings of the Shoshoneans of western Nevada. Each has its own consequences and each encapsulates behavior in its own way.

What is important to bear in mind in this connection — and once again we can observe the relationship between method and theory — is that no society permits the random and promiscuous expression of emotions or behavior to just anyone. Rather, one may communicate these feelings, either verbally, physically, or materially, only to certain people.

These are social communications. Communication not only makes social life possible, but the principal communicative activities of human life are in turn made possible by existing institutional lines, specifically, along the lines of the community as a boundary system or of boundary systems within the community. It is for this reason that the community, at least in these terms, serves as the unit-basis of comparative studies.

Addressing himself to the problem of language and communication per se in cultural perspective, rather than to institutionalized behaviors as communications, Hymes has recently elaborated this point of view as follows.

It is . . . not linguistics, but ethnography — not language, but communication — which must provide the frame of reference within which the place of language in culture and society is to be described. The boundaries of the community within which communication is possible; the boundaries of the situations within which communication occurs; the means and purposes and patterns of selection, their structure and hierarchy, that constitute the communicative economy of a group, are conditioned, to be sure, by properties of the linguistic codes within the group, but are not controlled by them. . . . Facets of the cultural values and beliefs, social institutions and forms, roles and personalities, history and ecology of a community must be examined together in relation to communicative events and patterns as focus of study (just as every aspect of a community's life may be brought selectively to bear on the study of a focus such as kinship, sex, or conflict). When this is done, it will be found that much that has impinged upon linguistics as variation and deviation from the standpoint of a single linguistic code emerge as structure and pattern from the standpoint of the communicative economy of the group in whose habits the code exists (Hymes 1964b:3).

Thus, whenever we compare communities with respect to a particular problem — whether in the realm of kinship, eschatology, the sense of responsibility, sharing, friendship, or the like — we are basically comparing boundary systems. Of course, we can only compare boundary systems that are of the same order. We cannot compare a community to a family because, although both are groupings and both have boundaries, they are of entirely different orders: it can be assumed that the forces that maintain these two sets of boundaries are completely different from each other even though they are interrelated and interdependent; further, they serve entirely different, though related and interdependent, goals of the social system. And it can be further assumed that units with boundaries that are at the same order of abstraction are comparable. If a *community* as a boundary-maintaining system among midwestern

Americans, for example, is not comparable at some level with a *community* as a boundary-maintaining system among the Trobrianders, then we must also come to the conclusion that we cannot compare the family organization of the midwestern Americans with the family of the Trobrianders. I have italicized the word community here because of a widely held misconception about cross-cultural research among some anthropologists and nonanthropologists. People in both groups often feel — and say — that comparative research is invalid or misleading because anthropologists sometimes compare Americans with Eskimos or Englishmen with Tiwi. While it is true that some anthropologists are occasionally seduced by their own temptations to make such global comparisons, two facts must be borne in mind. First, the errors of a few scientists do not invalidate a method. Second, such critics of comparative studies often misunderstand what it is that anthropologists are trying to do in large-scale cross-cultural studies. *These investigations are not the comparisons of societies or whole cultures but rather of specific and limited boundary systems.* The units of analysis must thus be comparable boundary-maintaining systems in a territorial sense; later, I will turn to the role of boundaries in the comparison of cultural variables.

Boundary systems within society — such as communities — are not of the same order of abstraction as are discrete items of behavior; they are of an entirely different universe than the custom of distending ear lobes with plugs or of embroidering arrow quivers. This is an important issue which extends beyond pure theoretical speculation. Without this concept I would not have been able to conduct even the first studies of patterns of food distribution and friendship, nor would I have been able to understand the practice of extrusion *and* its absence, as a way in which parents in a society manipulate the children in relation to the boundaries of the family to inculcate values and a sense of identity (Cohen 1964a, 1964b).

This, of course, is not to say that everything is comparable. It would be in gross error to imagine that we can compare processes of life in New York City or London with the customary ways of doing things on a Pacific atoll, or in a central highland community in Jamaica. The error does not lie in the fact that we can never really know what goes on in all of New York or London, or that the sizes of these two cities are so much larger than atoll communities, or that the ways in which people earn their livelihoods in these separate worlds are so completely different. The error resides in the fact that the boundaries of London and New York City are so distant from the individual in social as well as physical space, and have such little immediate meaning for his daily life and activities, that they are of entirely different levels of abstraction than the community boundaries on a Pacific isle or in a Jamaican mountain group. But social scientists do compare the families of London and New York with those of a Pacific island people and a Jamaican mountain community, and they have been doing so very comfortably for many years. They have been able to do this because the boundary systems are sufficiently similar.

How do we know that boundary-maintaining systems — such as the community and the family — are cross-culturally comparable and that they can serve as a basis for comparative studies? To some extent, we have to assume this as an expedient, because we need some bases of comparison if we feel it is necessary and desirable to conduct large-scale comparisons. Furthermore, it appears that boundary systems are the most inclusive common denominators among social systems. But even more importantly, there is increasing evidence that people in all societies behave with reference to boundaries, even though they might not be fully conscious of these referents.

For example, as I have suggested earlier, familial, political, juridical, kinship, and other institutionalized relationships are essentially boundaries on the limits and proprieties of behavior in all societies: prescriptions concerning cooperation and reciprocity are cultures' statements about the boundaries within which certain types of relations can transpire because, among other factors, people do not cooperate with just anyone. Rules concerning exogamy and incest are cultures' statements about behavior with reference to boundaries. Political and juridical relationships, to cite one more illustration, always occur within limited social or geographical boundaries, or both.

The fact that people might not be conscious of the boundaries which serve as referents in their role relations does not detract from the reality of these boundaries and it does not necessarily mean they are artificial abstractions constructed by anthropologists. *Inter alia,* boundaries are cultural symbols and categories; people are not always conscious of the symbols to which they respond, just as the speakers of a language are not necessarily aware of their language's grammar.

This conceptualization of boundaries as a basis of large-scale comparative studies has another implication which deserves to be noted. I mentioned earlier that large-scale comparative studies can shed light on lacunae in our ethnographic information and can direct the attention of ethnographers to data they might otherwise overlook during their field investigations. One of the problems of growing concern among anthropologists has to do with the ways in which people in different social systems conceptualize their physical and social environments and the other settings in which different kinds of role relations take place. This problem is of special importance in connection with growing

urbanization throughout the world, though no less so in cultures which remain outside the mainstream of the spread of urbanization. Do different conceptualizations of physical and social settings impede or facilitate acculturation and other types of culture change? Do different conceptualizations of the settings in which people interact have any effect on social behavior, or do different types of behavior lead to different conceptualizations of environments, or both? While these questions do not exhaust the entire range of investigations which can be conducted in connection with the roles of boundary systems in social life, they do highlight the intimate relationship between questions of method and concerns of theory.

I would now like to turn to the second approach to the problem of what is being compared in large-scale cross-cultural studies, namely, the comparison of levels of sociocultural integration, rather than the comparison of societal or cultural units. To an extent, I had anticipated this approach in my reinterpretation of the study of food distribution, when I suggested that the patterns of meat distribution among hunters contained hints of recurrent exchanges of food among many horticulturists.

It was suggested above that every cross-cultural hypothesis is, in effect, at least partially a hypothesis about the processes of cultural evolution. There are many ways of viewing the evolution of culture, one of which is to regard a given culture as representative of a particular level of sociocultural integration (in this connection, see Sahlins and Service 1960:12–44; Steward 1955). Among its other connotations, the concept of a level of sociocultural integration refers to the notion that at each of the stages of development that man has reached in the growing complexity of culture — determined largely by the nature of his relationship to the environment — we can observe particular patterns and institutions which are integrated in particular ways. At each stage or level of sociocultural integration, there are particular forms of cooperation and interaction, social aggregates, political and legal forms, modes of stratification, and the like (Steward 1955).

The concept of levels of sociocultural integration is an abstraction or taxonomic device; it is not intended to suggest that all the societies or cultural units included within a given level will be identical. Furthermore, anthropologists are nowhere near agreement about these levels or which cultures are to be included in each. But cross-cutting their disagreements in this regard, there are several points of concurrence.

One of these is that we can now begin to write the ethnographies of stages or levels of cultural development, in addition to the ethnographies of individual cultures. Several attempts in this direction have been completed (see, for example, Adams 1966; Goldschmidt *et al.* 1965; Service 1966; Wolf 1966), and more are under way. As can be seen from their dates of publication, these are relatively new developments, though they did have earlier anticipations (for example, Steward 1955; 101–222; Wittfogel 1957).

Another important point of agreement in this connection is that the integrations of cultures at given stages of development represent particular types of adaptations. That is, they constitute ways of coming to terms with the natural environment; these, in turn, lead to the development of aggregates and institutions which are necessary to maintain these adaptive relationships; and the latter underlie adaptive mechanisms which arise in response to the first two. Thus, and I am simplifying this for heuristic purposes, not only does each type of relationship to the environment require its commensurate organization of family relationships, but the two in juxtaposition lead to parallel developments in political and legal organizations,

religious institutions, modes of upbringing, and the like. A corollary of this is that the integration of institutions will change if there is a fundamental alteration in the society's relationship with the environment; similarly, as Adams has recently shown (1966), the development of highly complex political institutions, as in states, can give rise to basic technological changes, such as large-scale irrigation networks.

My purpose here is not to explore and explicate the concept of levels of sociocultural development, but rather to consider its implications for large-scale cross-cultural investigation. If the notion of levels of sociocultural integration in any way reflects cultural reality, and I do not think that there can be much question about this, we are forced to question and re-evaluate some of the fundamental tenets of large-scale comparisons in anthropology. Can we select a given variable and compare 60 or 120 societies randomly with respect to it, disregarding the different levels of development achieved by them? Can we compare modes of impulse control, for example, among a randomly selected sample of societies and disregard the fact that cultures at different stages of development require different controls as aspects of their adaptations? Can we, to cite one more instance, compare political organization among the Shoshoneans of western Nevada, the Tikopia of Polynesia, and the ancient Mesopotamians?

Or must we, instead, adopt the following two-fold procedure? First, establish a taxonomic scheme based on levels of sociocultural integration. This, of course, must include a statement explaining why the particular taxonomy has been established. Different problems require different classificatory schemes; a clear example of this is to be seen in connection with the cross-cultural study of eschatological beliefs and patterns of food distribution, each of which required a different taxonomy. Once this taxonomy has been established, a comparison of societies within each level of integration is undertaken. That is, for example, the investigator would compare all the foraging groups as a unit; he would then compare all the horticultural societies among whom domesticates make up 10 per cent of the diet; he would then compare all those among whom domesticates make up 50 per cent of the diet, and so forth.

The basic unit of comparison in each of the levels of sociocultural integration could be the community, along the lines discussed above. One of the purposes of comparing societies within each level of development would be to learn the extent of commonality, and the range of variation possible within it.

The second step in this two-fold procedure is a comparison of the levels of sociocultural integration. The important point to bear in mind in this connection is that not all levels are equally comparable, just as not all societal or cultural units are equally comparable. Instead, what is necessary is to compare stages sequentially, that is, to compare those stages that are closest to each other in developmental terms. Thus, for example, one would not compare people who subsist almost entirely by foraging with those who live in complex states with large-scale irrigation networks. Instead, it would be necessary to compare the foragers with those people among whom domesticates make up 10 per cent of the diet; one would then compare the latter with those among whom domesticates make up, let us say, 30 per cent or 50 per cent of the diet, and so on up the ladder of cultural development.

One of the principal purposes of this step is not only to determine the differences between stages of sociocultural integration but, especially, to determine the ways in which they shade off into each other in their institutional integrations and in meeting their institutional aims. Thus, not only can large-scale comparisons contribute greatly to our understanding of the evolution of culture but also, for example, to our insights into what is required in the way of shifts in cognitive orientation in order for a society to move from one stage to another.

This is a complex procedure, if not slightly cumbersome, especially for the neophyte. One of the reasons for its complexity is that each cross-cultural study carried out by this method is actually made up of several comparative investigations. It also requires a considerable measure of theoretical sophistication on the part of the investigator, especially when he is trying to grapple with the problem of which taxonomy is most appropriate to the problem under study. But if anthropological method generally, and cross-cultural methodology in particular, is to meet the needs of the discipline — if it is to mesh with theory — it must grow out of theoretical advances in the science. The method of comparing randomly selected discrete cultural units was a great achievement in the early years of anthropological science. It was fully compatible with what was known at the time. But we now know much more about culture and its evolution than we did then, and it is necessary to keep pace with these advances by making commensurate changes in our methodological procedures. Just as method serves to further theory in science, theory contributes greatly to the shape of method.

I said at the beginning of this section that in addition to being made up of a comparison of territorial units, every comparative study is also made up of the cultural variables which constitute the hypotheses of the study. In this connection, I would like to discuss briefly the question of the perimeters of the cultural variables in a hypothesis.

One goal of anthropology is to establish taxonomies of the elements and systems in culture. Correlatively, culture itself is made up, in part, of taxonomic systems, and one of our tasks in anthropology is to determine the precise relationships among these systems. As Devons and Gluckman have noted,

. . . if one is to succeed in studying society, one must split up reality by isolating a particular aspect which presents certain regularities and is *relatively* autonomous and independent of the other aspects. Having chosen a particular aspect for study, the social or human scientist . . . confines himself to that aspect and ignores aspects, and complexities, studied by others. If the aspects which one thinks are relatively independent are in fact closely interrelated, then confining one's study to a particular aspect leads nowhere in terms of understanding reality; and if the social scientist concerned is under the illusion that it does, he may be misled in his whole analysis. In . . . other terms, it is fruitless to demarcate as a relatively autonomous and independent system, a set of regularities which depend essentially on events and relations between events outside that system (Devons and Gluckman 1964:161–162).

There is an ordering or an assignment of place in every culture to every type of experience. Some experiences are grouped together into large categories which are set off from each other; in some instances, individual experiences are clearly demarcated and are considered separate from all other experiences. For instance, it is abundantly clear that cultures do not make clear or sharp distinctions between the areas of cognition generally and categories of language in particular (see, for example, Brown 1958; Hanks 1954; Lee 1949, 1950; Whorf 1956). Thus, linguistic categories and cognition can, in some respects, be considered to lie within the boundaries of one taxonomic system. One implication of this categorization is that it is possible to generalize from one to the other, as from linguistic categories to cognitive processes in a culture (although this does not

mean we can necessarily generalize in the other direction with equal facility).

On the other hand, there are areas of experience which are clearly demarcated from each other very narrowly within a culture and which are bounded in highly particularistic fashion. For example, there is growing evidence that a culture's modes of plant classification make up a discrete taxonomic system; although related to other areas of thought and classification, the boundaries of this taxonomic system are sufficiently clear to rule out generalizations between this system and others, and it must be understood in terms of its own dynamics and structure.

This, of course, also bears directly on the question of the nature of a culture trait. The concept of the trait is important and there is no reason even to suggest that we discard it; if anything, we have to sharpen it.

But it is extraordinarily rare that we employ isolated and discrete traits in the construction of cross-cultural hypotheses; instead, most such hypotheses consist of clusters of traits. But it is not possible to join just any traits within one analysis; any comparative exploration, and many other kinds of investigation, for that matter, must remain within the perimeters of explicitly demarcated boundary systems of cultural taxonomies.

This is not the place to go into the question of how the boundaries of any cultural taxonomic system or subsystem are determined. Comparative studies, such as the investigation of beliefs of where the soul goes, are one such procedure. In a general sense, of course, and as just mentioned, all of social and cultural anthropology is concerned with just this question, but not always consciously and systematically. In either event, however, this problem has special relevance and applicability to the conduct of large-scale comparative investigations. The boundaries of the taxonomic system or subsystem under investigation must be stated as clearly and as explicitly as possible, and the cross-cultural researcher must remain within those boundaries; if he should leave them, he must make it explicit that he is doing so. But we still have a long way to go before this problem is resolved.

It can be assumed, at least as a starting axiom, that every taxonomic system within a culture, or within culture generally, has its own boundaries or perimeters. A kinship system is one such taxonomic system, but there are several taxonomic subsystems within it. The rules of descent and inheritance are subsystems within the overall system of kinship, as are the rules of residence, kinship terminology, the organization of kin groupings, rules of exogamy and of incest, and the like. But despite the vast amount of research which has been conducted in connection with kinship, we are still unclear about the exact ranges and dimensions of these taxonomic subsystems and about the boundaries of kinship generally as a taxonomic system of culture.

This is more than a matter of definition; rather, it goes to the heart of the nature of these subsystems. What, for example, are the boundaries of kinship terminology as a taxonomic subsystem or of different types of terminology (e.g., cousin terminology)? Is kinship terminology merely a reflection of behavior and of expectations among kinsmen, or is the subsystem of terminology also a property or aspect of language generally? There are growing indications that the latter is indeed the case.

This is also more than merely interesting speculation, for it is central to the question of what it is we are comparing in cross-cultural research. To continue with the latter query concerning kinship terminology and language, is it valid to compare 100 or more societies with respect to the correlates of bifurcate-merging terminology when no variables regarding language — and perhaps cog-

nitive processes in addition — are included in the hypothesis? In other words, is it not possible that the exclusion of relevant variables from a hypothesis — that is, an erroneous or incomplete conceptualization of the boundaries of the system being investigated — makes the comparison a spurious one?

Let us take another example. What are the boundaries of eschatological beliefs? From the standpoint of Western culture, the outer limits of a culture's notion of where the soul goes are to be sought in the ideational aspects of the culture's religion. The results of the cross-cultural study presented in this chapter suggest that, while this might be true in Western culture (at least those with Christian religions), it is not necessarily true of all cultures. If there are no necessary relationships between eschatology and religion, we can then assert, among other things — and this is one of the consequences of the separateness of the boundaries of these systems — that we cannot generalize from one to the other.

The requirement in cross-cultural research that the boundaries of taxonomic systems of culture be kept clearly delineated does not, of course, mean that it is not legitimate to investigate relationships between such systems. Although there appears to be no necessary relationship between religion and eschatology, it would be perfectly legitimate to explore cross-culturally the conditions under which eschatological beliefs are made part of the society's religious ideation. To cite another example, we know there are specific relationships between the nature of exploitative economic activities (a taxonomic system which, in this case, is an independent variable) and political organization (a second taxonomic system, the dependent variable). Although one is dependent on the other, it is not possible to generalize from one to the other or to draw conclusions about one from the other. To cite still another example from material discussed earlier, if an anthropologist is investigating the correlates of the rules of marriage, he must not assume that he is also thereby investigating the cultural patterning of relationships and feelings between spouses; these are two taxonomic systems, but it would certainly be legitimate, if the data were available, to explore the relationships between the two.

CONCLUSION

Anthropology is often called the science of man, not the science of primitive or preliterate man or peasant man alone. It is the study of modern society as well as of preliterate or folk society. Very shortly, when there are no more primitive societies left to study first hand, anthropology will become increasingly concerned with developing and evaluating hypotheses about the dynamics and structure of industrialized societies and those societies which are on the way to an industrial socio-economic organization. One of the means by which these hypotheses are best evaluated is in the cultural laboratory, that is, through the investigation of nature's experiments in cultural growth and organization. Thus it is imperative that we come to grips with our methodological problems at the earliest time.

The problems and difficulties in the methods of large-scale comparisons are many and formidable; I have stressed these more than I have the significant accomplishments in cross-cultural research of Aberle, Banks and Textor, Ford, Goode, Murdock, Whiting and his collaborators, and many others. I have chosen this alternative because, even though anthropology has a way to go before it fully realizes the potentials of cross-cultural research, I believe the horizons of this branch of anthropology are vaster than we realize. These potentials can be increased to a maximum by resolving some of the problems raised in this chapter, especially in the development of anthropologically specific methodologies.

Suggested Readings

The following selected readings exclude works mentioned in the foregoing chapter. It includes some representative approaches to large-scale cross-cultural studies not mentioned, but it does not purport to be a comprehensive bibliography of cross-cultural research. Included also are a few salient and recent methodological works which are especially pertinent.

Arensberg and Kimball's 1965 volume is particularly relevant to the problem of employing the community as a geographical basis for comparative studies. Brown's thought on the problem of "explanation" is essential for those who would grapple with the nature of correlations and cause in the social sciences (Robert Brown 1963), while Judith Brown's work is an illuminating large-scale comparative study of initiation rites for women, who are usually neglected in this area (Judith Brown 1963). Elizabeth Colson's 1954 chapter is a discourse on the relationship between comparative and ethnographic field research. Eisenstadt's 1956 volume contains many testable hypotheses about the mechanisms by which societies maintain cultural continuity. Ember's 1962 article is a provocative large-scale comparative study. Irvin L. Child *et al.* (1965) reports on a five-part study of the consumption of alcoholic beverages. Gouldner and Peterson (1962) consists of a cross-cultural study based on factor analysis using electronic data processing. Hsu (1952) is a source of many hypotheses which can be tested in large-scale comparative research. Two important correlational studies by one of the pioneers in the method of large-scale comparison are George P. Murdock's 1950 and 1964 reports. Also see Murdock's 1966 paper on cross-cultural sampling. Naroll's 1962 book presents an important methodological point of view, one which rests on natural science models. The currently definitive work on matrilineality, which also includes examples of most types of cross-cultural research, among them a very instructive large-scale study by David Aberle, is the 1961 volume edited by Schneider and Gough. Spiro (1958) and Swanson (1960) both contain provocative and challenging cross-cultural inquiries. George Polya's 1954 book is an important methodological work dealing with problems of plausibility and credibility in scientific research, while the volume edited by Phillip Hammond (1964) contains accounts by researchers about how they really do their research, including one by Udy about the research mentioned in this chapter. One of the very early and influential large-scale comparative studies is that by Whiting (1950). Finally, a recent contribution to the cross-cultural literature has been made by Young (1965) in his study of initiation ceremonies. Also see Cohen's (1966) review of this book.

CHAPTER 17 discusses the cultural anthropologist at work as a special kind of historian. Readers who up to this point were convinced that cultural anthropology was simply a subbranch of American sociology will not find confirmation of their stereotype here. For, in its research methods and in attitude, cultural anthropology has always maintained, as one emphasis of recognized importance, a distinct historical viewpoint. In these pages Dr. Sturtevant asks, how is the discipline of cultural anthropology like and unlike that of history, and, what are the special distinguishing characteristics of the convergent field of ethnohistory? Part of his answer lies in the catholic, world-embracing scope of anthropology, and another part, in a discussion of the kinds of data anthropologists (unlike historians) are willing to use. Dr. Sturtevant points out that ideas and methods shared by these disciplines are as interesting as those features which render them distinct, and cultural anthropologists have much to learn from, as well as much to teach to historians. In this chapter the particularizing, humanistic emphasis of cultural anthropology, an emphasis which loomed large in Professor Berreman's assessment of the nature of ethnography, again comes to the fore. History, or rather, ethnohistory, whether documented or the product of nonwritten sources, adds to our knowledge of man and culture something ethnography and ethnology cannot. For example, ethnohistorical reports can provide one means of testing the kinds of propositions which are derived by the techniques discussed in the two preceding chapters. Moreover, although the anthropologist as historian rarely fails to take heed of or to draw upon the synchronic, structural-functional styles of explanations used by others to supplement his own methods and logic, he adds quite an alternate means of generating knowledge of man and culture. He adds time-depth, but with a humanistic flair, and with a specific historic focus quite unlike the generalizations teased from the facts of ethnography by ethnological techniques.

THE AUTHOR took his B.A. at the University of California (Berkeley) and his Ph.D. at Yale, both in anthropology. After teaching for two years at Yale, he joined the staff of the Smithsonian Institution in 1956. There he has been Ethnologist, then General Anthropologist in the Bureau of American Ethnology until its demise in 1965, and since then in its successor, the Office of Anthropology. He has conducted field work among the Florida Seminole, the Iroquois, and other eastern North American Indians, and in Burma. His ethnohistorical research has dealt principally with the Seminole, and with sixteenth-century Florida and Antillean Indians. His publications include articles on the significance of ethnological similarities between southeastern North America and the Antilles, Spanish-Indian relations in southeastern North America, and studies in ethnoscience.

17

Anthropology, History, and Ethnohistory[1]

WILLIAM C. STURTEVANT

Smithsonian Institution

This chapter discusses the intersection of anthropology with history. These two fields are sharply distinct as courses of training and in the social and political organization of their academic practitioners, yet their subject matters are sufficiently similar so that distinctions by definition are difficult, and specialists in each occasionally define the boundaries of their own field so that the other is included as a subdivision, or even, more rarely, characterize their own field as essentially the other. Nevertheless, when historians and anthropologists read each others' writings it is usually in search of specific data on a culture of mutual concern rather than through interest in the theory and method of the other field. However, there are some shared interests which draw them together under the relatively new label "ethnohistory," and other topics and methods of research in each field which have not yet been included under this rubric might well be.

[1] For suggestions and criticism used in preparing this chapter, the author acknowledges the assistance of Dell Hymes, Deward E. Walker, Jr., and Wilcomb E. Washburn.

Most generally, the word "history" refers to what is past, both static phenomena or stages, and changes over time; at the same time, it refers to the study, or the field of study, of the past. These meanings are clear in such expressions as "historical geology," "historical linguistics," "the history of the universe." In a narrower sense preferred by historians, "history" refers to the past which produced written records, and to the study of the past as reflected in written records. Thus, "prehistory" means the period, or the study of the period, before writing appeared, and cultures lacking writing are sometimes said to lack history. The traditional definition of history as a field of scholarship insists that it is based on the study of written documents. "Historiography" refers to the product of historians, to the writing of histories. "Historical documents" usually means written records only, and is so used here, although for some authors it includes nonwritten materials such as artifacts or even oral traditions which can be used as evidence for historiography.

So the importance of written records is one

central defining feature of history as a field of study. Another feature, one more difficult to characterize fairly, involves the feeling of many historians that their field is one of the humanities rather than a science, that in its pursuit literary techniques are of great importance, and, further, that historians may legitimately make ethical judgments about the past acts and policies they study. The usual anthropological view, in contrast, is that although ethical values are open to objective study, anthropologists themselves are qualified to apply them only as citizens and members of their own cultures, not as scientists.

Historians recognize that historiography involves the selection of some facts over others, and the attribution of meaning or significance to the facts selected. In this sense historians are concerned with generalization, theory, and comparison. But there still remains an emphasis on what was formerly crudely described as the description of "unique events" and the reconstruction of a picture of the past "as it really was." Anthropologists, on the other hand, are much more explicitly concerned with classifying, typologizing, and generalizing; they tend to select a different set of facts, and to see the events with which they deal as instances of more general types. Historians are much more cautious than anthropologists in erecting general theories or "laws." Historians such as Toynbee who do venture into these areas are likely to be accused of not really writing history, but rather philosophy or something else. This does not happen to the generalizers and theoreticians among anthropologists.

Historians, archeologists, and some ethnologists share an interest in diachronic, historical explanations, while other ethnologists and (descriptive) linguists favor synchronic, structural explanations. These are two different but complementary ways of understanding any cultural or social phenom-

enon. It is possible to concentrate on one type, ignoring the other nearly completely, without affecting the validity of that explanation; but more complete understanding results from the use of both synchronic and diachronic explanations. Ethnohistory is one of the means for bringing the two together, and the emergence of the term in recent decades — although some of the methods were used by Herodotus — is a symptom of movements in both anthropology and history tending towards integration of the structural and historical approaches to understanding culture.

As part of the controversy over whether history is or should be "scientific," some historians welcome the influence of anthropology, including its more structural approaches. These historians are not often involved with what is becoming known as ethnohistory, but they might accept a broadened meaning for that label. Other historians are now fighting the intrusion of concepts and methods from the social sciences by maintaining that structural, synchronic explanations are not explanatory at all, or are somehow less reliable than diachronic ones, less firmly grounded on "facts," and only to be used, if at all, as icing on the diachronic cake. There is a close parallel, with the opposite evaluation, in the supposed distinction drawn by social anthropologists between their own field and what they disparagingly refer to as "cultural anthropology." In the 1920's and 1930's when A. R. Radcliffe-Brown and Bronislaw Malinowski were establishing social anthropology as a distinct school, Radcliffe-Brown emphasized the difference of their approach by taking the extreme position that there is no value to "conjectural history," by which he meant the sorts of historical hypotheses produced by many anthropologists not in his circle. Some of the "historical" methods and theories in favor among some (but by no means all) anthropologists in the 1920's were indeed extremely conjectural, even ridiculous in the perspective of present knowledge; but Radcliffe-Brown's denigration of the historical methods of anthropologists is a classic case of throwing out the baby with the bath water.

Social anthropologists are still, as a matter of convention, repeating the old canard when they draw boundaries around their school. Thus, E. R. Leach maintains that the social anthropologist, in contrast to the cultural anthropologist, "concerns himself with history only at an empirical level. If historical evidence is available he uses it, but he refuses to speculate" (Leach 1965:29). Most historians, and many cultural anthropologists, argue that one cannot thus sharply distinguish "empirical" from "speculative" history — all historiography is speculative to a degree, and historical evidence is varyingly empirical. Of the many sorts of historical evidence, some are inherently more reliable than others, while most vary in reliability from case to case. Historians and anthropologists have long recognized, although under somewhat different labels, the necessity to "criticize the sources," to weigh the data, to test and compare all the available evidence. In essence this is nothing more than the core of the scientific method. It is the job of the historian to distinguish better evidence from worse, and construct a description or theory which best fits all available data.

Lowie long ago pointed out that despite his programmatic statements disavowing history, Radcliffe-Brown himself engaged in highly speculative historical reconstruction on occasion (Lowie 1933:293–294). Leach in 1960 published a paper on "The Frontiers of Burma" (1960a) in which he distinguished two distinct cultural types, "hill" and "valley," in northern Southeast Asia. His characterization is essentially social anthropological, and in its main outlines, it is a convincing typology of many of the cultures in the area now and for the last few centuries. But Leach felt obliged to add a quite conjectural historical hypothesis, deriving the hill type from China and the valley type from India. While his comments in this connection on the unreliability of the conventional historians' views on prehistoric migrations into the area are well taken and would be accepted by most anthropologists, he adds a curious denial of all relevance for linguistic data as historical evidence on the question. In a comment following Leach's paper, Isidore Dyen, a historical linguist, shows that evidence from historical linguistics is in fact highly relevant. Not all cultural anthropologists would be able to evaluate the linguistic evidence as successfully as Dyen, and many would not be so sophisticated as Leach in structural typology, but it is difficult to imagine anyone other than a social anthropologist excluding linguistic evidence *ab initio* as Leach did. There is still an average difference between social anthropologists and other cultural anthropologists in the degree of interest in history, and a sometimes corresponding difference in expertise in the handling of historical evidence.

But despite Leach and other recent examples, in actual practice and frequently also in programmatic statements the difference between "social" and "cultural" anthropologists has been steadily narrowing over the past few years, as social anthropologists become more concerned with change and process while other cultural anthropologists become more structuralist in outlook. Anthropologists are farther than historians along the path towards recognizing that historical and structural explanations are complementary rather than incompatible, and towards being able to integrate the two types.

ETHNOHISTORY

Ethnohistory has been defined, explicitly and implicitly, in several ways. Many of these definitions can be paraphrased to read, "ethnohistory is (the study of) the history of the peoples normally studied by anthropologists." Attending to the two meanings of "history," we find a reversal of the normal usage: anthropologists defining ethnohistory tend to specify that it relies on written documents (the narrow definition of history), whereas historians tend to use the label only for studies of the past of societies wherein written records are lacking or scanty (the broad definition of history). Anthropologists view the field as, essentially, the use of nonanthropological evidence (that is, historical documents) for anthropologists' purposes, whereas historians see it as the use of nonhistorical evidence (that is, anthropological data) for historians' purposes. History and anthropology as established disciplines lay claim to wide areas of subject matter; practitioners of each are more sensitive to these traditions in their own field than in the other. Thus, where historians apply the term broadly to the past of nonliterate societies, but not to any aspect of the past of fully literate Western societies, anthropologists hesitate to include under the label many of their studies of the past of nonliterate societies which are not primarily based on written records, but they may extend the term to include anthropological studies of the past of Western societies based on written records.

Three dimensions are thus most important for characterizing ethnohistory, even though they alone are not sufficient to delimit the field: concentration on the past or the present; the use of written or nonwritten "documents"; and a diachronic or a synchronic emphasis. Among additional dimensions are: concern with history as we understand it, or with the characterization of other, "folk," views of history; whether the society studied is a Western or Oriental civilization or a more exotic one; the value placed on typologizing cultural or social phenomena and their changes, that is, on generalizing or abstracting principles or theories from concrete data as opposed to emphasis on the

uniqueness of events, on the study of a specific period or sequence for its own sake rather than as an example of general processes.

Ethnohistory has two principal interests which may be labeled historical ethnography and the historiography of nonliterate cultures. Historical ethnography is the reconstruction of a synchronic, ethnographic description of a past stage of a culture, especially a description based on written documents contemporary with that stage. Historians have produced many such ethnographic statements — of the medieval European city, of the culture of the Renaissance, and so on — but the genre is a particular favorite of anthropologists, who tend to be more explicit in their efforts in this direction and more concerned with well-rounded descriptions of all aspects of the culture studied. The aim is to produce a description paralleling as closely as possible what would be possible in field ethnography, even though the evidence is not what the anthropologist has himself observed, overheard, and been told, but rather what others, nonanthropologists, have learned and written down. He must ask the documents, rather than informants — and there are often things the documents cannot tell him that he could find out in a living society. Also, these documents, usually written by nonnatives of the society under study, contain biases and errors not present in the statements and the responses of informants. These biases must be watched for, taken account of, and corrected where possible. The gaps can sometimes be partly filled, with a remnant of uncertainty, by deduction from comparative knowledge: other cultures of this same general type normally have such and such characteristics, hence this one probably does also.

Anthropologists are more likely than historians to describe a non-Western culture, but when topics of particular ethnological interest are involved they may turn to Western societies: historical sources have been used for an anthropological study of Anglo-Saxon kinship (Lancaster 1958), for a structural and diachronic study of the changes between 1842 and 1921 in the British laws governing marriage between relatives (Wolfram 1961), and to discover the regular cyclical changes in measurements and shapes characteristic of the style of European women's formal dress between 1605 and 1936 (Richardson and Kroeber 1940).

Diachronic ethnohistorical studies are not entirely restricted to nonliterate societies, as the last two examples show, but they usually are. In such studies the written documents are useful where they exist, but being the products of foreigners, they are inevitably scanty and biased. Other evidence must also be used: oral tradition, comparative ethnology, archeology, and so forth. Historians are beginning to appreciate the relevance of such evidence, even to illuminate aspects of literate cultures poorly reflected by the written records (as with colonial archeology, or the archiving of tape-recorded autobiographical reminiscences in "oral history" projects). Similarly, anthropologists are realizing how many written records are likely to be relevant to the past of a nonliterate culture, and also that their analytical techniques may usefully be applied to the documents of a literate society.

The sources of the present growth of ethnohistory are various. Historical ethnography becomes more necessary as culture change, particularly in the direction of Westernization, speeds up everywhere in the world, just when anthropological comparative interests require good data on the entire range of possibilities in human culture. Increasing communications and the spread of state control over isolated tribal groups mean that ethnohistorical methods are necessary to provide a wide range of ethnographic accounts of such interesting phenomena as cannibalism, human sacrifice, non-Western warfare, kingship and law and other aspects of small-scale independent political systems, economic specialization and trade in societies untouched by the "revolution of rising expectations," or the value systems of peoples almost entirely ignorant of the rest of the world. Theories of acculturation, culture change, and cultural evolution may initially be based on field ethnography, broad-scale typology, and general archeology, but it is plain that their testing, refining, and elaboration require the use of all available evidence, including the details of specific sequences provided by documentary materials. One of the roots of ethnohistory is the so-called "direct historical approach" of North American archeologists, which uses historical evidence to identify archeological sites with known tribal groups, thus tying the upper ends of archeological sequences to historical and ethnographic data, and which combines historical, archeological, and ethnographic data to produce historical ethnographies for these recent archeological periods, from which changes can be traced backward through earlier sites.

There are also more practical reasons for the development of the field. With the recent emergence of many former colonies as independent nations, considerations of national pride require the correction of the bias of colonial history. But for many such nations, a true history must be ethnohistory: the documents are scanty and written by foreigners, so the reconstruction must be based to a large extent on anthropological evidence. In the United States, the Indian Claims Commission Act of 1946 resulted in the employment (still continuing) of many anthropologists as expert witnesses by both the claimant Indian tribes and the defendant U.S. Department of Justice. On the witness stand under lawyers' cross-examination, and preparing evidence in cooperation and competition with historians, these anthropological consultants were pushed to consider documentary evidence in more detail than had previously been their custom, and they rapidly discovered the riches of the National Archives and other repositories of manuscripts. The result has been a marked increase in the use of documentary materials in the study of North American Indian cultures, and a noticeably greater sophistication in the criticism of written sources.

WRITTEN SOURCES

Conventional historiography is based almost exclusively on written documents. A consequence is that until very recent times historians have been largely concerned with those cultures which produced such documents: principally, the Western cultures whose roots extend back to ancient Mesopotamia and Egypt where writing was invented, and, secondarily, the great Oriental civilizations of India, Southeast Asia, China, and Japan, whose writing systems are partly a divergent branch of the Near Eastern systems and partly independent in origin. The extent of literacy in these cultures and the differential survival of their documents have also affected modern historiography. The classical Mediterranean civilizations left scanty written remains, and the historiography of these periods thus shades into archeology, which uses nonwritten "documents" as evidence. More recent Western cultures have left more documents, but until quite modern times literacy among their populations was limited to a small educated class and the uses of writing were correspondingly restricted; the nature of the written evidence has been one cause of historians' emphasis on political, dynastic, and military history, at the expense of cultural and economic history.

Because historians have normally treated Western civilization, they have been able to eschew generalizations and descriptive theories about culture and about causation. They have concentrated on the description of the "unique events" in a broad cultural tradition in which both historians and their readers are also participants. These unique events are minor variations against the background of cultural categories implicitly understood by writers and readers as bearers of that culture or of a very closely related one. A truly unique event would be incomprehensible and undescribable, since to be unique it would have to be unclassifiable, fitting no category of our language and culture. In the historian's selection and arrangement of events from the mass of written evidence available, he makes use of the implicit culturally-determined generalizations and theories about classificatory categories and about causal relations. It is not surprising that, among historians, those most given to explicit generalization and to the discussion of their assumptions are precisely those who deal with cultures most divergent from their own: historians of the Ancient Mediterranean and of the Orient.

Conventional anthropology, on the other hand, has dealt with the most exotic cultures — that is, those whose categories and assumptions are very different from those of the writer and his readers. In fact, one origin of anthropology as a field of study was the need to understand and explain the strange customs and beliefs of the peoples Europeans had to deal with during the Age of Discovery and the subsequent period of European imperialism and colonialism. Anthropology is a "science," in contrast to ordinary history, because the understanding of these exotic cultures required explicit generalization, typology, and theory. The progress of the field has been in increasing sophistication and accuracy in this understanding, in gradually developing methods for eliminating the bias due to the observer's own native cultural categories, so that any culture may be understood in its own terms.

An early assumption was that exotic cultures could be understood as surviving examples of cultural stages through which European culture had passed; the classical theory of cultural evolution attempted to assimilate all cultures to the then-current European model of European history. Particularly in nineteenth-century England, Germany, and France, these evolutionary anthropologists acted like historians in using descriptions written by others — travelers, traders, missionaries, soldiers — for their own purposes. None of these European founders of anthropology conducted their own field work (exceptions such as Adolf Bastian were secondary figures). The field-work tradition in the United States is older, because of the proximity of Indian societies. Lewis Henry Morgan's evolutionary theory grew partly from his own field work among the Iroquois in the 1840's. His foundation of the study of kinship — evolutionary then, but important now precisely in its explicit recognition of cultural variation in classification — was based on his own field work among the Iroquois and Western Indians, and on his direction (through questionnaires and letters) of field investigation by several hundred correspondents scattered all over the world. The field-work tradition he founded persisted, especially among anthropologists employed by the Bureau of American Ethnology (James Mooney, F. H. Cushing, J. Owen Dorsey, Alice C. Fletcher, and others), but these were essentially natural-historical collectors of data, and what theorizing they attempted was largely insignificant for subsequent anthropology (partly because they did not teach students).

Beginning shortly before 1900, the leading figures in anthropology realized that evolutionary and other theory was based on inadequate evidence and that it was not necessary to rely on descriptions written by anthropologically-naïve observers. Field work rapidly became the *sine qua non* of ethnology, under the leadership especially of Franz Boas and his early students in the United States, and W. H. R. Rivers, Bronislaw Malinowski, and A. R. Radcliffe-Brown in England. The quality of the basic ethnological documents quickly improved, and, concurrently, distrust of older sources written by nonanthropologists increased.

Ethnohistory in its reliance on descriptions of exotic cultures written by nonanthropologists is a partial return to the pre-field-work style of armchair ethnology. But it is distinguished by the greater sophistication acquired from field work. We are now quite aware of the sorts of bias due to the ethnocentrism of the naïve observer. We are sensitized to such bias by our training as anthropologists (which is largely a process of loss of ethnocentrism through learning of the great range possible in human cultures), by our difficulties in gaining understanding during our own field work (especially its initial stages), and by comparisons of our own field observations of an exotic culture, or those of another anthropologist, with those of untrained members of our own society (even those with many years of association with the foreign culture).

To the modern ethnologist, the data from ethnographic field work are primary, whereas written evidence by nonanthropologists is decidedly secondary, if indeed it is utilized at all. Most anthropological ethnohistorians have done field work among the modern descendants of the peoples whose earlier situation they reconstruct from documentary evidence; when they have not, they still examine the documents from perspectives gained by their own and others' ethnographic field work in other societies. From this, ethnohistorians add another criterion for estimating reliability and bias to the battery of tests historians have developed for the criticism of sources, especially when (as is usually the case) the documents were written by nonmembers of the society described: does this writer correctly understand cultural features we can presume to have existed, from our anthropological knowledge of this and other cultures? Even when such understanding is missing, we may be able to deduce the actual situation distorted by the ethnocentric bias or the ignorance of the old observer.

The use of ethnographic data on a modern culture to criticize and reinterpret old accounts of its ancestral culture has been called "upstreaming." The technique may require a careful balancing of the likelihood of culture change against the probabilities of ignorance and bias of the original observer (Fenton 1949). A historian writing of the famous escape in 1837 of the Seminole leader, Coacoochee (or Wildcat), through a small window high up in his cell in the fort in St. Augustine doubts a report that Wildcat used "medicinal roots" to reduce his weight so that he could squeeze through the narrow opening (Porter 1944:117, 131); but acquaintance with modern Seminole magical beliefs and practices leads one to accept this detail as a reliable report. Another historian has referred to a curious book by Andrew Welch (*A narrative of the early days and remembrances of Oceola Nikkanochee, prince of Econchatti, a young Seminole Indian . . . ,* London, 1841), as "a fabrication of fiction rather than a presentation of fact" (Boyd 1955:260). But this book contains (pp. 119–122) the only published description of an obsolete Seminole ceremony, the "Old-man Dance," recognizable as such from the accounts of modern Seminole informants and from a related Creek ceremony reported in the modern literature; further, most of the supposed Indian words quoted by Welch are recognizably Creek. The book is *not* entirely a fabrication. An English rendering of a French translation of a Russian translation of a passage from a fourteenth-century Persian history of the Mongols reads: "The Mongol custom has it that when young boys take part in hunting for the first time, their large digit (*grand doigt*) is annointed, that is to say smeared with grease

and meat" (Vladimirtsov 1948:72n.5). Since *grand doigt* is poor French, referring to no specific finger or toe, an obscurity has probably been introduced by translation and retranslation. Tracing back through the various languages to the original Persian or perhaps the ultimate Mongol (as proper historical method requires us to do), would doubtless show that "thumb" is meant. This seems more likely, and the significance of the Mongol custom becomes clear, when we apply ethnological knowledge of the presence in Central Asia in later periods of a technique of arrow release in which the bowstring is drawn back with the thumb, often with the aid of a special thumb ring.

As this last example shows, ethnographic data useful for interpreting early accounts need not be limited to that which refers to the direct modern descendant of the earlier culture. When a sixteenth-century Spanish missionary states that the high chief of the (now extinct) Calusa Indians of South Florida was required to marry his own full sister, the modern anthropologist thinks of examples elsewhere of the same exception to the usual incest rules of a society. A compilation of such cases strengthens the deduction from other evidence that Calusa society was sedentary, highly stratified, and with advanced political integration — all other known examples of "royal sibling marriage" occur in societies with these characteristics (Goggin and Sturtevant 1964). Contemporary accounts of the sixteenth-century Taino Indians of the West Indies (also now extinct) do not include the details which would allow their form of agriculture to be characterized as shifting or swidden; but even though there is no mention of the abandonment of fields for a fallow period longer than the period of cultivation, comparative evidence on swidden agriculture elsewhere in the world, taken with a few indirect hints in the documents, allows us to be almost certain that this was in fact the type of agriculture the Taino practiced (Sturtevant 1961). When John White draws Carolina Algonkian Indians of the 1580's in postures unknown in Europe, but known among modern Western United States Indians, we conclude that his depictions are correct; when he draws their rush mats of dimensions corresponding to those of modern Midwestern Indian mats, but with the rushes running longitudinally, rather than transversely as in all modern examples, we conclude that his observations in this instance were faulty (Hulton and Quinn 1964:40–41, 95, 100–101, 109). Historical evidence alone is too fragmentary to provide an understanding of Roman social organization prior to 400 A.D. But the application of structural and analytic principles derived from the study of many other kinship systems yields a reconstruction, contradicted by none of the historical evidence, which places Roman kinship among those of Omaha Type III; and the very incomplete evidence on early Roman law is consistent with comparative ethnological evidence on the family structure and family law expectably associated with kinship systems of this type (Lounsbury 1964).

Historians' methods for the criticism of sources are also relevant to ethnohistory. Anthropologists persist in citing Herman Melville's *Typee* as a primary source on Marquesan culture, despite the fact that historical detective work has shown that Melville was in the Marquesas for four weeks rather than the four months he claimed, and that the ethnographic detail he presents was drawn from earlier published sources (Anderson 1939). A less obvious but more flagrant case has been discovered by S. H. Riesenberg (1959): a Spanish description of Ponape Island in 1841, cited by anthropologists as an important eyewitness account, turned out to be directly copied, with a few omissions and distortions, from an article published in a Sydney newspaper in 1836. In another case, a minor controversy on the

significance for culture history of "platform beds" among the West Indian Taino, when traced back through the writings of anthropologists (amusingly contradicting their own previous statements as well as each other's) and early Spanish chroniclers, led ultimately to the discovery that the basic original account plainly referred to a dais for a stool, thus eliminating the platform bed as a Taino cultural trait (Sturtevant 1960:23–25).

Both the historian and the anthropologist contribute techniques for finding, evaluating, and using the written records which deal with almost every culture of the world. Such records are much rarer, and in some ways more difficult to use, when they are the product of foreign observers of nonliterate cultures. Here the anthropologist's insights from comparative ethnology are particularly valuable. But only recently have anthropologists begun to learn some of the historians' skills in dealing with such evidence, and still more lessons are needed. If historians can be made aware of the evidential value of artifacts by inventing the term "manufacts" to partake of the aura the word "manuscripts" has for them (Washburn 1964), then perhaps anthropologists could be encouraged to pay as much attention to "artiscripts" as they do to "artifacts." Anthropological ethnohistorians are still too prone to use printed sources uncritically, without comparing editions and searching for the manuscripts which may lie behind them. Historians have long emphasized the necessity to search for all available records, and have particularly valued the primary sources, the written materials which lie closest to the original eyewitness observations. Ethnologists can learn from this.

Even in ethnographic field work there are likely to be useful, more or less contemporary documents, often kept in the files of local governmental, religious, medical, and other organizations. Certainly there are vast quantities of relevant manuscript as well as printed documents relating to any modern Indian community in the United States, and ethnographers are only beginning to realize what a useful adjunct to their own field observations these can be. They are of course full of errors and omissions — especially since they normally represent records prepared by members of the dominant society on the affairs of a subordinate and culturally distinct group. But much of the bias can be corrected, or at least made explicit, from ethnographic field work, and a great deal of statistical, genealogical, and recent historical data remains which cannot otherwise be recovered, as well as the material they contain on intercultural relations.

The historian's point of view should make it clear that field ethnographers are engaged in assembling primary historical documents. It is becoming more common for ethnologists to reanalyze and reinterpret earlier ethnographers' published descriptions. Those interested in a particular type of structure — usually some sort of social structure — make restatements of earlier descriptions in order to place further societies in their typology and to elucidate the principles involved in the models with which they are working. Those inclined to statistical cross-cultural comparisons must first classify the cultures they sample according to their standard system, which normally involves significant features not explicitly recognized by the original ethnographers. In both cases the use of earlier anthropological accounts ideally should involve procedures for the comparison and criticism of sources quite analogous to those used by historians. So far most such reanalysis starts with the published literature (and often not even all of that), but one can anticipate that eventually the usefulness of a more historical approach will be recognized and searches will be made for the primary sources, which are here the original manuscript ethnographic field notes.

As ethnological theory develops, the re-analysis of earlier ethnographic sources will increase. As culture change proceeds and ethnographic descriptions grow older and less representative of present situations, ethnographers will increasingly refer to earlier descriptions as a background for their own field work in the same culture. The ethnography of the present is providing materials for the historical ethnography of the future. Yet, no archive, no museum, no library is making a strong effort to collect and preserve ethnographic field notes, and very few ethnographers think of their field notes as primary documents of any use to other workers either in the immediate or far distant future. In connection with my own ethnographic field work on the Florida Seminole I have attempted to trace the field notes of previous anthropological visitors to the tribe. I was fortunate in being able to borrow the notes of two of my predecessors — one had kept them forty-five years, another twelve — but in another case, I obtained some partial copies by correspondence, only to find, a year or two later, that the collector had burned the originals of these and all the rest of his Seminole notes, having decided that he would never use them himself. The field notes of another Seminole ethnographer were included in the files of the Cross Cultural Survey at Yale (now the Human Relations Area Files) — most fortunately, for the Survey ordinarily did not incorporate raw field notes. But the papers of two of the most important ethnographers of the Seminole, both deceased, dating from 1881 and 1910, have completely disappeared. Both published on their work, but it is plain from the publications that their field notes must have contained additional data which I could use in conjunction with my own field notes.

Even in their published reports, ethnographers are too often vague on some of the details required for the evaluation of their materials — sometimes, no doubt, because to be explicit would be damaging to their credibility. If field work is the production of primary ethnographic documents, the author should feel an obligation to assist those who will apply the historian's canons of criticism of sources. Yet, very often, inadequate information is provided on such crucial aspects as the precise dates and locations of field work, the number, names, and sociological characteristics of the principal informants, and the degree of the field worker's facility in the local language, or the quality of the interpreters he used.

The publications, field notes, and personal papers of anthropologists are also primary documents for another field, the history of anthropology. As part of the history of science, this is not ordinarily considered ethnohistory. But it is another area of research in which a combination of historical and anthropological knowledge and method is required. An evaluation of the significance of past work in the field requires familiarity with current anthropology. But a great deal of the history of their discipline as known to anthropologists turns out, on close examination by historical techniques, to be traditional or folk history rather than strict history (cf. Stocking 1963); much of it is carried by oral tradition, passed on to each succeeding generation of anthropologists by their elders, in classrooms and in conversation.

Appreciation of the history of anthropology is significant for the evaluation of earlier anthropological writings as historical documents. There is a tendency, in the absence of such appreciation, to evaluate past writings as though they were modern, not considering the state of the field at the time they were produced (an example of this fault is White's [1963] critique of Boas as a field worker and comparativist). Plainly, also, knowledge of the theory and method current at the time is required for adequate understanding and modern use of the ethnographies resulting from the application of this theory and method. Thus, Hickerson (1967)

has shown how the theoretical position of American anthropology in the 1920's and 1930's, with its strong opposition to notions of social evolution and historical materialism, was responsible for the formulation and wide acceptance of the idea that the northern Algonkian Indians' individual or family ownership of hunting territories, discovered by modern ethnography, represents a survival of aboriginal private ownership of land. This theory of aboriginal "socio-economic particularism," put forward about 1914, was finally disproved in 1954 by ethnohistorical research which showed that Indian ownership of hunting territories was a result of the European fur trade. But meanwhile, as Hickerson shows, it had strongly affected the formulation and acceptance of a theory of northern Algonkian "psychological particularism" as an aboriginal characteristic which has persisted to the present despite marked socio-economic changes. It is clear that evaluation of previous field descriptions of these Indians, and of theories of their culture history, is considerably aided by attention to the relation of such descriptions and theories to the history of general anthropological theory.

Ethnography and ethnological theory are affected by the state of anthropology as a science, and by the general intellectual milieu, at the time they are produced. So also, as historians are fond of saying, "each generation writes its own history." No historiography is final for all time. The documentary evidence in large part persists — indeed, increases with new discoveries and the opening for research of previously restricted collections — while historical methods and interests develop and change. There are no permanently fixed criteria of what is relevant in the mass of avilable evidence. One of the ways in which historiography is a literary art is precisely that the selection of interesting topics, and of the evidence to support the description and analysis, depends upon the imagination of the historian, the current fashions in academic history, and the cultural climate surrounding the historian as he writes.

The relativity of history is nicely illustrated by histories of Southern and Southeast Asia and of Africa written in the colonial period, as compared to those written after independence. There is a considerable difference — in the moral evaluations of colonialism, in the degree of emphasis on the colonial as compared with the precolonial periods, and in the stress laid on non-European documents. The extremes contrast most strikingly: the defenders of colonialism who were citizens of the colonial powers and often present or former colonial officials themselves, versus those citizens of the ex-colonies who are now erecting new nationalist historical mythologies. But even if one takes neither of these sorts seriously as historians, the general tenor of the interpretation of the colonial and precolonial periods has changed, be the modern historians citizens of the "new" nations, citizens of the former colonial powers, or citizens of other countries — all sharing the "modern" historical methodology and attitude (which is itself historically of Western origin, of course, but now widely diffused). As is the case with ethnography, citizens of ex-colonial countries have an advantage over the usual outside scholar in that they start with a knowledge of the language and culture, and are close to the local sources; they have the corresponding disadvantage of an initial nonobjectivity and of being more subject to the pressures of the historical mythologies, new or old, of the cultures they are studying.

FOLK HISTORY

If this relativity in historiography is true in one historical tradition over a rather short period of time, it is more strikingly obvious when one examines the attitudes toward the past and the uses of history in different societies. Here not only the criteria of relevance and the ethical evaluations differ, but also the canons of historical truth. The study of folk history, of the systematic and unsystematic knowledge of the past and the functions of historical tradition in a particular culture, is a form of ethnography. One of the principal ways in which the past influences the present is that ideas about the past — whether they are true or false is irrelevant in this context — are part of the present ideational system affecting present behavior. Studies of folk history need not involve evaluation of the validity of tradition as historical evidence in the academic sense, although in fact most such studies have mixed these two approaches and have not clearly distinguished the description of folk history as a system of knowledge and belief from comparison of it with academic historiography.

Examination of the primary sources and the works of scholarly historiography quickly makes one realize what distorted views of its past are customary in our own society. It can be quite a shock to read a contemporary Tory's description of the activities of the Patriots during the American Revolution, or to discover the responsibilities for Indian Removal of that great democrat, Andrew Jackson. The West of movies and television is clearly a historical myth. Folk history of course is important in our own society: consider its political use, in the assigning of credit or blame for complex historical events to the party which happened then to be in power, or the suggestion that a good measure of the assimilation into American society of immigrants is their acceptance as their own of the general American folk history. The lack of this last is particularly noticeable among many of the most acculturated Indian communities in the United States. The Lumbee Indians of North Carolina maintain their social isolation from the neighboring Whites and Negroes (especially the latter) largely by insisting on a historical myth (invented in the 1880's) which derives them from the supposed intermarriage with Indians of Raleigh's "Lost Colony" of Roanoke; but the lack of any firm historical evidence for this tale, coupled with the lack of any other known historical Indian ancestry, is used by their neighbors as a weapon against the Lumbee claim to Indian status. Many Lumbee are obviously Indian in physical appearance, but their lack of an acceptable history is crucial: many other Indian communities are fully as assimilated, culturally and physically, but easily maintain social status as Indians because of their accepted historical derivation.

Historical ideas are very important to these Indian communities. Their resistance to full incorporation into general American society, unique among minority groups in the United States, becomes more understandable when one finds how vivid and important are the Indian traditions of conquest and mistreatment by the larger society. The Seminole in Florida have not been fought by the federal or state governments since the 1850's, yet one Seminole faction still maintains its isolation partly through distrust of government intentions based on traditions of the broken promises and the deportations to Oklahoma of more than a century ago. The Iroquois and many other tribes place great emphasis on the immutability of their treaties with the government; they attempt to maintain their special rights and a small degree of independent control over their internal affairs by quoting old treaty promises of the federal government, although the latter has long held that Congress has a legal right to overthrow any Indian treaty unilaterally without Indian consent. And yet it is not only the Indians who feel that we all are somehow morally if not legally bound by the acts and words of our ancestors. The recitation of ancient wrongs is an effective Indian po-litical technique for gaining present concessions from the larger society.

Thus, folk history, the common view of the past, is often an important aspect of world view and of intergroup relations. It also very frequently serves as a charter and justification for aspects of present culture. It is plainly a topic of ethnographic interest.

When he looks at his own culture, a historian may well see the social function of his research as the substitution of the truth for the "irrational popular prejudices," the "illusions" and "myths" about the past held by other members of his society (e.g., Dovring 1960:89–93). He may look at such beliefs more objectively and systematically when he studies the history of history. Many analyses of the beliefs, methods, and principles of historical schools can also be termed studies in the ethnography of history, specifically, the historical ethnography of history. This is particularly true when the historian studies historical schools far removed from his own in cultural distance (temporal or spatial). Thus there are studies by historians of the nature of Classical Greek and Roman, Ancient Mesopotamian, Muslim, Indian, Japanese, Chinese, or Medieval European historiography. Often these are all the more ethnographic in being stated in general cultural terms, rather than focusing on the writings of a particular historian. Wright (1963), for example, identified three basic components of the self-image of the Chinese literati, and described their effects on the generalizations produced by traditional Chinese historians. One of these generalizations involved the notion of a repetitive dynastic cycle, which was more than a mere historian's theory: "when Chinese statesmen thought they discerned the classic symptoms of dynastic decline, they began to qualify the support they gave to the ruling house and thus contributed to its ultimate collapse" (Wright 1963:42). Chinese civilization is unique in the quantity and time-span of its historical documents and its formal historiography, and in the importance attached for so long to the study of the past, although traditional Chinese historiography differs in its assumptions and methods from modern Western historiography.

The ethnographic study of traditional or folk history is also possible in "ahistorical" cultures at the opposite pole from the Chinese. The nonliterate Gola of Liberia are described as a highly history-conscious people, among whom, as among the Chinese, history is "referred to as a guide in conduct and as an assurance of the continuity of their values" (d'Azevedo 1962:23). The Gola make a clear distinction between historical fact and nonhistorical myth. But their criteria for judging what is historically true are different from those of Western historiography. For example, one very important criterion is the age and social status of the recounter; and there are other striking differences between the Gola and Western views of and uses of the past (d'Azevedo 1962). A more complete account of the folk history of groups along the Luapala River on the eastern border of the Congo (Kinshasa) shows some striking resemblances to history among the distant Gola, but also some interesting differences (Cunnison 1951). For example, the Gola have a more detailed general history (although not an extensive one) distinct from the histories of specific social groups; there are occasions on which the separate Gola family histories are compared and reconciled, whereas the different Luapala histories are not so compared.

ORAL TRADITION

There are all too few ethnographic studies of folk history as a self-contained system of knowledge and belief. However, there are a great many instances of the use of fragments of folk history by historians and anthropologists as evidence for their own historiography. Nowadays one rarely meets the old uncritical radical disavowals of any evidential value of oral tradition, or the opposite naïve belief in its literal and complete historical validity. It is clear from the rapidly developing sophistication in the treatment of oral tradition as historical sources that the ethnography of history will increase. A great deal of the evaluation — "criticism," in historians' terms — of oral tradition as historical evidence depends upon detailed ethnographic knowledge of the social functions of folk history, of its manner of transmission, its variability within any one society, the local criteria for historical truth, and other features of folk history as a system within the culture under study (cf. Vansina 1965), rather than as isolated scraps of ideas.

A vivid example of the need to consider the cultural setting of historical traditions, and to compare versions, is provided by Mohave Indian "historical epics." These were very long, exceedingly detailed, circumstantial, sober, and concrete accounts of Mohave migrations, cast in a form which appears flatly historical. Yet by examining the manner in which these tales originated — by "dreaming" — by a comparison of different versions, and from a few improbable or impossible motifs contained in the tales, Kroeber (1951) concluded that these stories were "pseudohistory," products of imagination, literary efforts, and not in the slightest historical by our own criteria, although they were plainly historical by the criteria of Mohave folk history.

The Barundi of East Africa have criteria of truth and falsehood not different from our own, and techniques and occasions for applying them. But truth values are not here involved in historical tradition, which is conceived of as a literary genre in which esthetic elaboration is required. "It is taken for granted that each narrator will invent his own way of telling a story and, if he can, a new way for each telling. Multiple versions of historical events are common." Here, and presumably in some other cultures, "different versions of origin tales or so-called mythopoeic history . . . [are] the product of conscious art and effort, not signs of confusion about facts" (Albert 1964:52, 54).

The Tiv of Nigeria place great importance on genealogies, which in the absence of writing are transmitted orally. These genealogies serve as charters for Tiv social and political organization. But they are not systematically taught, being learned piecemeal as they are cited as precedent or justification for present affairs. Contradictory versions of the same genealogy exist, and may even be cited by the same authority on different occasions. The validity of any version is judged and determined by its fit with present social and political facts. The cultural function of genealogies among the Tiv results in their distortion, lessening their value as sources for our historiography, but at the same time ensuring their preservation as elements of Tiv folk history (Bohannan 1952). Bohannan suggests it is probable that

a lineage system can survive only in an illiterate society like that of the Tiv. . . . To place on record the genealogy which upholds the status quo is to strike a blow at the possibility of change without the accusation of forgery. To prefer one genealogy throughout time is to make rigid a charter which, if it is to work, must remain fluid — and to a certain extent is also to make rigid a fluid social system (Bohannan 1952:314).

Lewis (1962) picks up this point and shows that it is oversimplified, for the northern Somali have lineages of the Tiv type, yet their genealogies are not subject to the same sort of manipulation to reflect the current political relations between social groups. Somali genealogies are however somewhat shortened, and this loss of generations is correlated with the political functions of the genealogies. Further, the upper ends of these genealogies seem to be largely ahistorical mythological charters. As Lewis points out,

even in the same society a particular type of oral tradition — in this case the genealogy — does not necessarily have a uniform social function or a uniform historical validity. Not only in different tribal societies is oral tradition a medium of varying historical accuracy but even in a particular tribal society one type of oral tradition may vary in its authenticity, according to the structural level at which it occurs. This may perhaps serve to emphasize the complexity of the problem of deciding the historical content of tribal tradition and point to the necessity of evaluating oral tradition always in relation to its functions in the social matrix in which it occurs (Lewis 1962:47–48).

Different evaluations of the effects of function on the historical validity of oral tradition depend not only upon variation between cultures, but also upon differences in the degree of commitment of ethnologists to functionalism. An example of an extreme position is that of Zuidema (1962, 1964) with regard to the genealogies of the Inca royal house which were recorded from Inca oral tradition by the early Spanish chroniclers. Zuidema believes that the remarkable coincidence between the social organization of Cuzco, the Inca capital, and the traditions which make the various kings the ancestors of an equal number of Inca descent groups, casts much doubt on the historical validity of these traditions. He treats them as purely symbolic of Inca social structure at the time of the Spanish conquest, unworthy of credence as historical sources. These views are not accepted by all specialists on the Inca; part of the difficulty is that, since we have only fragmentary evidence on sixteenth-century Inca society, Zuidema's decisions as to the precise nature of Inca social structure depend largely upon typological hypotheses derived from comparisons with other societies and from abstract theories of social structure and its symbolization. Others (e.g., Hammel

1965) maintain that the evidence can be interpreted in other ways which result in greater confidence in the historical reliability of the royal genealogies.

The New Zealand Maori preserved very extensive genealogies which were carefully learned by specialists for whom word-perfect recitation was important. Many of these were written down during the nineteenth century, and some persist today in oral tradition. There has been some controversy over the historical reliability of these genealogies, but recent critical comparison of genealogies recorded at different times from different specialists and from different local Maori tribes shows that in general they are highly accurate over periods up to at least 500 years. The same comparisons have developed techniques by which occasional genealogies are shown to be distorted (Roberton 1956, 1962).

Genealogies are particularly important as historical sources since they provide a chronology (and one which can sometimes be supplied with approximate absolute dates, as in the Maori case), and since the usual existence of multiple versions permits the application of critical methods through detailed comparison. In societies in which extensive traditional genealogies are not remembered, ethnographic collection of recent genealogical information can still provide a chronological framework for remembered happenings of the recent past. As Rowe (1955) points out, "With patience and care a chronology built up in this way can be brought to a point where any event which an informant can recall as associated with any other event can be dated at least to the year for some time into the past." He believes, with reason, that ethnographers' failure to inquire about the recent past, within the memory span of living informants, is one source of the probably erroneous, often implicit, assumption that "cultures other than ours change slowly or not at all."

Traditions such as genealogies which tend to have important social and cultural functions are likely to survive for long periods, even though these very functions may result in systematic distortion. Other knowledge of the past is more subject to random errors and to disappearance through the vagaries of memory and unsystematic oral transmission. But in the ordinary situation one should be able to recover relatively reliable information going back at least two long lifetimes: aged informants with good memories and an interest in the past may well remember in considerable detail reminiscences they heard in their youth from other elderly people with similar talents. It is often useful to question such informants about information derived from documentary sources. Modern anthropologists and historians thought that the last survivors of the aboriginal South Florida Calusa Indians were the "Spanish Indians" mentioned in many written materials of the late eighteenth and early nineteenth centuries. By asking about specific individuals and incidents mentioned in the documents, I was able to elicit Seminole traditional accounts of the same and other occurrences involving Spanish Indians. These checked relatively well with the documentary accounts. However, my informants insisted that the Spanish Indians — whom they did not know by that name — were Seminole, not Calusa. When I reexamined the documentary evidence I failed to confirm this, although I did note that there was no good evidence for the usual identification of the Spanish Indians with the Calusa (Sturtevant 1953). But subsequently two other investigators located documentary evidence which supports the Seminole tradition (Covington 1954; Neill 1955). Consequently we no longer think there were any Calusa survivors in Florida after 1763. Seminole tradition also identified the site in the Everglades where United States troops killed Chakaika, the most famous Spanish Indian leader, in 1840. Contemporary maps are not accurate enough to locate this spot. I am convinced by the degree to which the rest of Seminole tradition about Chakaika checks with the documentary evidence that the place modern Seminole informants pointed out to me is the correct one, and I am quite sure that archeological investigation of this spot would recover information on Seminole culture in 1840.

Comparison with documentary evidence is a useful method for evaluating the reliability of oral tradition. Where the tradition and the documents derive from different cultures, the combination of the two points of view will often give a more rounded picture of historical events. This is true in the case of Chakaika already mentioned, in the case of the Eastern Cherokee hero Tsali (Kutsche 1963), in a colorful instance of a Tlingit tradition collected in 1886 of their first meeting with Europeans exactly one century earlier (Emmons 1911), and in many other examples.

However, it is well to remember that historical traditions may be borrowed and influence one another, so that the oral tradition of a nonliterate group may be affected by the traditions and, directly or indirectly, the written historiography of a literate people with whom they are in contact. This is especially probable with historical incidents and persons well known to members of the literate society and thus quite likely to be discussed in contacts between members of the two groups. General American history has in this way contaminated Seminole traditions of Osceola (Sturtevant 1955); African examples are mentioned by d'Azevedo (1962:29–30) and New Zealand ones by Roberton (1956:46). With increasing literacy, and increasing publication in ethnohistory, such influences are bound to become more important.

Similarly, the effects of increased travel and modern contacts must not be overlooked, as happened in a recent description of modern Southern Paiute traditions about the culture of the Pueblo people who occupied sites in their territory more than 800 years ago (Pendergast and Meighan 1959). This evaluation of oral tradition does not consider the probable influence of Paiute knowledge of the culture of the Hopi gained through modern intertribal contacts, even though the Hopi are not far to the south in terms of modern transportation, and plainly are known to the Paiute and equated with the inhabitants of the prehistoric Puebloid ruins, since both peoples are referred to by the same Paiute term.

The collection of specifically historical data from informants resembles the "memory ethnography" formerly very common in studies of North American Indians, and still engaged in on occasion. This is not usually termed ethnohistory, but it might well be. In essence it is a sort of historical ethnography, a description of a now-past stage of a culture (often conceived of as a rather static "traditional" stage preceding rapid modern changes) derived from the memories and oral traditions carried by aged informants. In the best examples the data from informants are cross-checked and supplemented with documentary and sometimes archeological evidence.

TRAIT COMPARISON

One of the methods for evaluating historical traditions is to consider them as culture traits, and compare them with the traditions of neighboring societies. If close correspondences are found, one may sometimes assume that these are due to borrowing, so that less credence may be placed in a tradition as reflecting the past of the society in which it occurs. This brings us to the use of trait comparison for deducing history. It is particularly these methods — relatively old ones in ethnology — which the social anthropologists attack as "conjectural history."

It is certainly true that they have often been used uncritically. But they are still useful, especially when taken in conjunction with other sorts of evidence.

The most commonly used techniques for deducing history from trait comparison are those involved in the reconstruction of culture history from geographical distributions. Here there are two types of criteria, one involving the nature of the similarity between the traits compared, and the other, the significance of their distributions. Similarity between culture traits in different societies may be purely analogous, that is, historically irrelevant or accidental, being due to independent inventions or independent series of inventions and modifications resulting in convergent developments. On the other hand, similarities may be homologous, the traits being historically related, sharing a common origin. The common origin may be in a culture ancestral to both or all of those in which the traits are found (in which case migration is involved in the resulting occurrence in different societies), or else it may lie in one culture, from which the trait diffused by borrowing to the other (or others). The difficulty is that there are no rigorous methods for distinguishing among these various alternatives. The evaluation depends ultimately upon an analysis of the complexity of the trait, in an attempt to gauge the probability of its independent invention. Estimates of the likelihood of homology are balanced with distributional evidence. A highly complex trait occurring in two adjacent cultures represents a borrowing or a common inheritance; a simple trait occurring in two cultures remote from each other and otherwise distinct represents convergence. But these are the obvious and uninteresting extreme cases; the interpretation of instances intermediate in nature involves many complexities and difficulties (see Sturtevant 1960 for a more detailed discussion, with examples).

Another use of trait comparison may be termed internal reconstruction. Here traits present at the same time in one culture are compared in an attempt to distinguish their relative ages. One measure sometimes used is pattern incongruity or the degree of functional integration of traits, which involves two contradictory criteria: an incongruous trait may be an anachronistic survival, or it may be an innovation or borrowing too recent to have become well integrated with the rest of the culture (Sapir 1949:405–406, 409–410).

Typological seriation is a method which may be used in internal reconstruction and in connection with trait distributions. It is particularly often applied to material culture. Older forms are assumed to have survived along with their later derivatives, and a direction of development is also assumed — usually from simple to complex, but sometimes the reverse. This is a risky procedure without other evidence, particularly from archeology. Many supposed cases — for example, Buck's simple-to-complex seriation of Hawaiian featherwork (1944) — are open to other interpretations. Variation at one time level may be due to varying techniques, materials, skills, or functions, and the historical relation of the different forms may be very complex rather than unilinear with survival of earlier stages.

The comparison of cultures known to be related is another method for historical reconstruction. Spoehr's (1942) work in Florida and Oklahoma Seminole kinship is an example. But such a comparison of more and less conservative descendants of an ancestral society assumes knowledge of post-separation changes in the more conservative group, which is not always easy to obtain.

Evidence from trait comparisons is thus not worth much by itself. But given a historical framework based on better evidence — documentary, archeological, linguistic, biological, traditional — trait comparison may be used with more confidence to fill in some of the details not derivable from these other lines of evidence.

BIOLOGY AND LINGUISTICS

Other sorts of indirect evidence can be used with considerably more confidence to yield historical hypotheses. The problems of distinguishing homology from analogy are much less severe with two sorts of evidence: biological, and linguistic. There is an unfortunate tendency for historians and culture historians to forget their principles of critical examination and adopt as firm conclusions of biology or linguistics what specialists in these areas consider only as hypotheses of varying degrees of probability. But it is true that in these two fields there are rigorous techniques for distinguishing analogy from homology, so that continuing research can test hypotheses, whereas this is not the case with the evaluation of most instances of similarity between culture traits.

Biology is relevant to culture history in two main areas: physical anthropology, and the study of plant and animal domesticates. The latter are culture traits, but biological evidence is useful in establishing identities (complete convergence being here impossible) and in identifying origins. There are some points the nonspecialist should bear in mind in evaluating biological evidence:

(1) One should look for the degree to which the evidence is genetic rather than morphological (in general, the more reliance is placed on phenotypic resemblances as opposed to genotypic ones, the less reliable the conclusions).

(2) There are many difficulties in estimating rates of evolution or the time required for varieties or species to differentiate.

(3) Except in the simplest cases, the criteria for determining centers of origin or places of original domestication are not well established.

(4) There are problems in distinguishing true wild forms from secondarily wild escapes and feral forms (errors here may profoundly affect judgments as to the place of origin of domesticates).

(5) In identifying archeological specimens it is often difficult to distinguish wild forms from domesticated ones, especially in the initial stages of domestication.

(6) There may be serious ethnographic (or archeological) faults in the methods by which biological specimens were collected and documented.

(7) Biologists' theories on the history of domesticates may be unduly influenced by nonbiological hypotheses, such as anthropological ones.

Some of these criteria are also important in evaluating evidence from physical anthropology. The best evidence here also is genetic. Human genetics is advancing very rapidly, but the evidence required for historical applications has not yet been collected from most human societies. The anthropometric data which have been widely collected for many years are of very doubtful use for most historical purposes. Unfortunately hardly any of the findings of human genetics can yet be applied to the skeletal remains recovered by archeologists. Where genetic data have been collected from living populations, proper attention has sometimes not been paid to ethnographic procedures for identifying the group, studying its recent breeding history, and so on. Finally, physical anthropologists and human geneticists have sometimes uncritically incorporated historical hypotheses from other fields, particularly in efforts to simplify the number of alternatives which must be considered in interpreting their frequently very complex statistical data.

There are situations in which the non-physical anthropologist can collect usable data. Hospital records in south Florida contain data on the ABO blood types of their patients: by searching under Seminole surnames, I collected a large enough sample for comparison of the Seminole frequencies with Caucasoid and Negro frequencies. The comparison showed that the Florida Seminole can have but very little White or Negro ancestry, even though documentary evidence would indicate the probability of considerable Seminole-Negro interbreeding during the early nineteenth century. The discrepancy has yet to be resolved, but it must come by reinterpretation of the documentary evidence, for the genetic evidence seems conclusive.

On the other hand, recent ethnological, archeological, and especially linguistic work tends ever more strongly towards the conclusion that the origins of the Polynesians and most of the Micronesians must be sought in southern Melanesia, rather than in Indonesia, Malaysia, or Southeast Asia, as had previously been assumed on the basis of anthropometric evidence. The striking physical differences between Melanesians and Polynesians-Micronesians must now be accounted for, but in this case it seems quite clear that the cultural evidence takes precedence.

Linguistics, like biology, can ordinarily (given sufficient evidence) distinguish accidental from historically significant resemblances, and often can distinguish resemblances due to borrowing from those due to inheritance from a common ancestral language. Historical linguistics has developed rigorous techniques for reconstructing past stages of a language or language family, and for specifying the precise degree and kind of relationship between languages (see Chapter 2). Evidence from this field is of great

utility in many connections in history, ethnohistory, and historical anthropology. Only a few examples can be given here (a useful source for more detail and for bibliographic guidance to the literature is Hymes 1964c:449–663).

People who speak the same language also hold most of the rest of their culture in common (the converse is usually but not always true). When a society divides, through migration or other interruption of communication, the linguistic as well as nonlinguistic aspects of the culture change in the new groups independently. But, long after other cultural resemblances between the new societies have become so dilute as to be problematical or entirely unidentifiable, the linguistic relationship can still be determined. Only after many millennia of complete separation do the linguistic resemblances become so tenuous that there is any doubt whether they may be due to chance analogies or to borrowings subsequent to the division, rather than to inheritance from a common ancestral language. Thus evidence from historical linguistics is of great utility for demonstrating that distinct cultures derive from a common ancestor (despite later changes and accretions from other sources, which are of course also of great importance).

Historical linguistics can sometimes indicate the location of an ancestral language. To simplify somewhat: if there are more than two descendant languages whose degree of relationship is equivalent, then the probable homeland can be deduced from the "principle of least moves"; with only two such languages, some possibilities are more probable than others but no one can be selected as the most probable without other evidence (Dyen 1956; Diebold 1960). There are some difficulties: the degree of relationship of the various languages is often not yet certain; frequently their present distribution is such that the indicated area of origin is so broad as to be relatively uninteresting as a historical hypothesis; and there are some documented exceptions to the principle.

Another technique for determining the homeland of a proto-language uses the meanings of items in the reconstructed vocabulary. Thus the series of plants and animals for which names exist in reconstructed Proto-Indoeuropean consistently points to the area of the Vistula, Oder, and Elbe Rivers as the homeland of the speakers of that language (Thieme, pp. 596–597, in Hymes 1964c). Reconstructed vocabularies are also useful for indicating other culture traits reflected by the proto-language, including kinship terminology, material culture (often useful for correlation with archeological evidence), and so on (see references in Hymes 1964c:597). But these reconstructions are best examined as systems. The presence of any individual item is not highly significant, since parallel semantic changes in different languages can give spurious results such as the fact that words for "gun" and "whisky" are reconstructed for Proto-Central-Algonkian which was spoken long before these items were introduced (Hockett, in Hymes 1964c:606–607).

Similarly, it is sometimes possible to distinguish older and more recent vocabulary items within one language, with the implication of corresponding relative ages for the associated culture traits. The basic assumption here is that "unanalyzable forms are older than those which are analyzable into several constituents" (Chafe 1964b). As Chafe points out, there are several sources of unreliability: borrowed forms are usually unanalyzable in the borrowing language; meanings may change; an old meaning may come to be expressed by a new form. Two examples of the latter two processes may be cited from the Mikasuki Seminole language — both cases are clear (as with the Proto-Central-Algonkian examples) only because we have documentary evidence that the his-

torical facts are the reverse of what the linguistic evidence would lead us to expect. In Mikasuki the word for "opossum" is *soki-hátkî*. which analyzes into the three unanalyzable items *soki-* "pig," *hátk-* "white," and *-î.* (a grammatical suffix); yet contrary to the principle, the pig, referred to with an unanalyzable term (*sokî.* in isolation), is a recent introduction, whereas the opposum, referred to with an analyzable term, is a native wild animal. The other Mikasuki example is *cosiwilî.* "moccasin(s)," which analyzes as *cosi-* "buckskin," *wil-* "shoe(s)," *-î.* (the same suffix), whereas commercially made "shoes" are termed simply *wilî..* In both these instances it is fairly clear that an introduced item was labeled with the term for a native item thought to resemble it, and with increasing frequency of use the qualifier which probably existed was dropped, whereas the native item, now less frequently mentioned than the introduced one, acquired a distinguishing qualifier.

Linguistic borrowings are another source of historical evidence. When the source language can be identified, direct or indirect contact between the speakers of the two languages is certain. Furthermore, since borrowing of a concept, technique, or artifact often involves the adoption also of its name in the source culture, linguistic borrowings are frequently indicative of the existence and the effects of contact between cultures. Examples are legion. But here again it is safer to deal with whole sets rather than isolated items, since it is not uncommon for a language to borrow a term for a trait already present, or to provide a name out of the native linguistic resources for a borrowed trait. The usual procedure is to examine sets of borrowings in one language. Conklin (1963) has recently demonstrated that historical conclusions may also be reached by an examination of the equivalents for a single term in a great many languages. By searching vocabularies of some 500 languages of Africa,

Madagascar, and Malaysia for names of the sweet potato he showed that, contrary to several recent hypotheses, this plant was almost certainly introduced into these areas by the Spanish and Portuguese after the discovery of America. In all these regions there are only four widespread terms for the plant, all of Spanish or Portuguese origin, and two of them originally borrowed by Spanish from American Indian languages.

Historical linguistics may also provide chronological information. Absolute dates are derivable from purely linguistic evidence only insofar as the techniques of glottochronology are reliable, and this is the most doubtful aspect of this method, which counts cognates on a standard list of "basic vocabulary" recorded from the two languages compared, and converts these statistics into centuries of separation with a formula derived from such counts between languages whose separation date is known from other evidence (see Gudschinsky in Hymes 1964c:612–622, and the references cited by Hymes on p. 622). But this technique as well as others can provide a *relative* chronology — which divisions of language communities preceded and followed which others, sometimes which borrowings preceded or followed which others, and the like.

ARCHEOLOGY

A major difficulty with almost every kind of nondocumentary historical evidence discussed so far is that it provides no absolute chronology, and rarely directly provides any relative chronology. Where documents are lacking, the best chronological evidence is provided by archeology. This is not the place for a detailed discussion of the various archeological techniques for determining both absolute and relative dates, but it must be emphasized that the main concern of archeology is culture history, and that almost any historical research in anthropology can benefit from the use of archeological evidence.

Like other fields of cultural anthropology, archeology makes both diachronic and synchronic analyses. There is an "archeological ethnography" (although it is not so named) which is concerned with the description of a culture at a given point in time. Dependent for their research upon material remains, which are themselves affected by varying conditions of preservation, archeologists have no direct evidence for many important aspects of culture; but there are some methods for filling some of these gaps with hypotheses based on ethnological data. However, archeological evidence on material objects, and the close chronological control often possible, sometimes provide data not otherwise available even on historically documented cultures. This is clearly the case with Classical Archeology, which studies the (partially) literate cultures of the ancient Mediterranean and Near East. It is also the reason for increasing interest in what is termed "colonial" or "historic" archeology in the United States (excavations at Jamestown and Williamsburg are well-known examples, and there are many others, such as investigations of Western frontier forts), and industrial archeology in Great Britain (which is beginning to provide new information even on the heavily documented nineteenth century, and will become more important as truly archeological methods are applied).

In its diachronic aspect archeology is concerned with a much greater time span than any other field dealing with the history of culture or aspects of culture. By far the greatest part of human history, considered areally as well as temporally, is accessible only through archeology. The study of large-scale and long-term historical phenomena such as cultural evolution must be based largely on archeological evidence; valid generalizations cannot be derived solely from the very few cultural traditions which have documentary evidence extending over several millennia.

Where there is no evidence from documents or ethnography, historical studies are purely archeological. Where other evidence exists, then we can consider archeology as one of the ancillary fields of ethnohistory. Tracing the route of De Soto and his men through southern North America in 1539–1543 requires the interpretation of the scanty documentary evidence on the expedition. Among the factors involved are the identification in modern terms of the geographical features mentioned, estimates of the rate of travel on this basis and from the hints in the original accounts, and particularly the identification of the Indian towns and tribes which are described with names difficult to recognize and with cultural details partly different from those indicated when adequate documents on the area first begin some 200 years later. Archeological evidence is crucial; when the documents suggest a specific location to the historian or ethnologist, the archeologist can often tell him whether in fact that site was occupied during the mid-sixteenth century, and in several instances archeological evidence has shown in this way that a suggested portion of the route was not probable. Once the route is fairly well established, the cultural details given in the narratives can in turn be associated with archeological cultures, filling in some of the information not archeologically preserved and providing the earliest linkages in the area between archeological sequences and historic tribes.

An example of the coordination of archeological and documentary data to provide chronological detail is Goggin's (1967) study of Spanish majolica pottery in the New World. Here sherds were sorted into types established by normal archeological methods, and these were arranged into a temporal sequence by a combination of (1) the usual archeological techniques for the seriation of pottery types, with (2) recording the occurrence of the sherd types at sites whose occupation dates are known from documentary evidence, plus (3) noting the types of majolica wares depicted in dated Spanish portraits and still lifes. The result is a much more precise and well-documented dating of types than was previously available from art-historical sources. Spanish majolica sherds can now be used to date any archeological manifestation — Indian or European —in which they occur. This combination of archeological and historical methods will certainly be increasingly applied.

Archeology may also provide useful conceptual models for history. Both fields are independently concerned with the periodization of the past. Archeologists are particularly interested in cultural typology, and in tracing the distribution of the types in both space and time. It is possible to adapt their techniques to ethnohistorical problems, for example, by establishing several distinct types of relations between Indians and Europeans, and diagramming their occurrence in space and time on a map and a time-space chart of an archeological sort (Sturtevant 1962). One advantage of this procedure is that it forces the historian to be explicit about the areas and periods his description covers, and about the criteria on which his periodization is based.

CONCLUSION

In a recent presidential address to the American Historical Association Carl Bridenbaugh warned his fellow historians that the rapid changes in Western culture over the last fifty years threaten to cut them off from a proper appreciation and understanding of the cultural and natural environment of even the relatively recent past of their own society (Bridenbaugh 1962). At almost the same time the historian H. Stuart Hughes (1963) spoke to the American Anthropological Association on the relation between culture and the human physique, drawing his examples from early modern European history, without realizing that many in his audience were familiar with similar conditions through first-hand observation in field work, while the rest knew them through the anthropological literature, which is much more detailed and reliable in this area than is historical literature. Thus it may well be that anthropology can bridge for historians the chasm which Bridenbaugh fears the "great mutation" of the twentieth century has opened between the conditions of modern Euroamerican life and those of the recent and more remote past.

Historians chasing unique events and the study of the past "as it really was" get lost among the myriads of trees, the only limits to their detailed enumeration being set by the availability of documents. Those who realize the difficulty of seeing the whole woods from this perspective are beginning to ask anthropologists what they have seen. Anthropologists have long been building models of woods to explain the isolated fossilized trees which, lacking most documents, are all they can find. But, in turn, they are beginning to examine the detailed, close-up evidence of history in order to test and refine their models. The emergence of ethnohistory as a recognized field of research is part of the rapprochement between anthropology and history in aims as well as in methods and techniques.

Suggested Readings

The French historian Marc Bloch's influential essay (1953) on historical methods (written about 1941, before the rise of ethnohistory) does not mention anthropology, but its relevance to Bloch's ideas on the nature of historiography is evident. In two useful essays, first published in 1950 and 1961,

Evans-Pritchard (1964) provides an anthropologist's views on the relationships between history and anthropology, with a peculiarly low evaluation of the possibility of structural explanations of culture and society independent of historical explanations. Bock (1956), a sociologist, addressing himself to sociologists and anthropologists, argues for the use of documentary materials and historians' methods for the testing of hypotheses, especially regarding social evolution, and gives useful critiques of historians' positions as to the "uniqueness" of historical events. McCall (1964) writes as an anthropologist, urging historians to use anthropological evidence in the study of African history. An important discussion of the use of oral tradition as historical evidence, with careful attention to methods of criticism adapted from historians' methods of criticizing written documents and ethnographers' and folklorists' methods of treating oral materials, will be found in the book by Vansina (1965), most of whose examples are African. Probably the best of the very few ethnographic studies of folk history is by Cunnison (1951), again an African instance. Gibson (1964), a historian, has written a very thorough study of the Aztecs under Spanish rule, based on Spanish and Indian documents and emphasizing Indian society and culture throughout. Spicer (1962) presents the effects of European contact on the Indians of the American Southwest, based on ethnological, historical, and some archeological evidence, the whole balanced by the author's intensive ethnographic field-work experience among modern Southwestern Indians. De Laguna (1960) discusses the relation between evidence from archeology, ethnology (including oral tradition), and historical documents, in historical ethnography and culture history, and then illustrates in detail with the case of the Tlingit of Alaska. Ewers' (1955) work on Plains Indian horse culture is a fine example of historical ethnography, with some attention to culture history, based on evidence from memory ethnography, oral tradition, comparative ethnology, museum collections, early illustrations, and historical documents. Homans' volume (1942) is a classic historical ethnography of English villages in the thirteenth century, explicitly modelled on anthropological field ethnographies. Another excellent illustration of anthropological techniques applied to the history of a literate culture is Noël Hume's (1963) nontechnical account of the historic archeology of Colonial Virginia. Finally, two important journals publish ethnohistorical materials: historians and anthropologists often write on ethnohistorical topics for the *Journal of African History,* founded in 1960; anthropologists and an occasional historian publish on the ethnohistory of North American Indians (and sometimes of other peoples) in *Ethnohistory,* founded in 1954.

CHAPTER **18** surveys a field of study which has long interested anthropologists as well as representatives of other sciences. What are the points of connection and the relationships among the parts of sociocultural systems and features of the physical-biological environment? Traditionally, this line of inquiry has been divided into several rather separate approaches, with one line of attack upon the correlations between features of a culture and aspects of an environment, narrowly defined in terms of topography, climate, and soil. Other approaches have sought causal connections between pieces of culture and the flora and fauna of a habitat, or even between the biological characteristics of human populations and the form and functioning of their cultures. Vayda and Rappaport ask that we seriously consider putting these pieces together, and that we attempt to bring to bear upon this whole problem area the ideas and findings of the discipline of general ecology. To do so would require that we de-emphasize differences and distinctions between man and other species; and to do so assumes that there is more than a possibility that as a result we might achieve a larger, more inclusive, and more powerful framework of concepts and findings for interpreting and explaining the behavior of man and other species. This is neither the first time nor the only place anthropologists have tried to fit their thinking about man into a larger scheme of thought. Today, other anthropologists are attacking traditional anthropological problems with general systems theory, communications theory, and general behavior theory. The issues raised by the authors are therefore substantial ones, and this chapter makes a point which should not be missed, for it illustrates the fact that anthropological theorizing is neither static nor confined within impermeable disciplinary boundaries.

THE AUTHORS: Andrew P. Vayda was born in Budapest, Hungary, in 1931. For most of his life, he has lived in the United States. He took his A.B. and Ph.D. degrees at Columbia, where he is now an Associate Professor of Anthropology. He has taught also at the University of British Columbia and the University of Hawaii. His research has been concerned with ecology, evolution, economics, and warfare, and he has published a monograph and numerous articles on one or another of these subjects. He has had several field trips to the South Pacific, the most recent being expeditions to study the ecology of the New Guinea rain forest.

Roy A. Rappaport was born in New York City in 1926. He received his B.S. degree from Cornell and his Ph.D. from Columbia. He has done archeological field work in the Society Islands and ethnographic and ecological field work in New Guinea. At present, he is Assistant Professor of Anthropology at the University of Michigan. He has published articles on ecology, one of his main fields of interest. His other main fields are religion, political organization, and evolution.

18

Ecology, Cultural and Noncultural

ANDREW P. VAYDA

Columbia University

AND

ROY A. RAPPAPORT

University of Michigan

In this chapter our concern will be to indicate the contribution of ecology, or an ecological perspective, towards realization of two major goals of cultural anthropology. One goal is to explain why particular traits or congeries of traits exist at particular times and in particular places: why, for example, do some human groups grow crops and keep domesticated animals while others do not? The other goal is to elucidate how the traits or congeries of traits function or "behave": how, for example, do certain modes of keeping and ritually slaughtering pigs in the New Guinea highlands help to maintain a balance between human populations and their subsistence resources? The two goals are of general interest to cultural anthropologists of various theoretical persuasions, and numerous approaches other than an ecological one have been and can be used both in accounting for the presence and in describing the functioning of particular cultural features. But an ecological approach does have important contributions to make.

Ecology is defined by the animal ecologist, W. C. Allee, and his associates as "the science of the interrelation between living organisms and their environment, including both the physical and the biotic environments, and emphasizing interspecies as well as intraspecies relations" (Allee *et al.* 1949:1). Because it is concerned with the measurable biological effects of these interrelations, ecology has generally been regarded as a biological science, and, indeed, terms such as "relations physiology" have been applied to it. On the other hand, some writers, emphasizing the interactions among organisms rather than the effects of the interactions, have regarded ecology as a behavioral science. The subtitle of Allee's study of groupings among animals and the ecological factors producing them is "A Study in General Sociology" (Allee 1931), and Amos Hawley, a sociologist, wrote as follows over twenty years ago:

That ecology is basically a social science has long been clear to most serious students of the subject. It is apparent, moreover, in almost every aspect of the discipline: in the root of the term ecology; in the historical details of the subject's development; in the large place given to sociological concepts such as community, society, niche, commensalism, symbiosis, dominance, succession, etc.; and in the manner in which problems for investigation are stated (Hawley 1944:399f.).

"Biological science" and "behavioral science" are, of course, not mutually exclusive categories, and ecology belongs to both.

Although ecology as a self-conscious science is relatively young — the name was first used in print by Haeckel in 1870 — speculation on the interrelations among plants and animals is no doubt very ancient. By classical times, at the latest, more or less systematized natural histories were being produced, some of which — for example, those of Aristotle, Theophrastus, and Pliny the Elder — survive to this day. The tradition of natural history, that is, the tradition of describing events involving interacting animals or plants observed in their natural settings, is one of the many foundations upon which ecology rests. Obviously there are others. Development of the science would not have been possible without minimal developments in the earth sciences, for instance, for the physical environment must be specified with some precision in any ecological study. At the same time, it is similarly necessary to identify and describe the organisms that interact both with the physical environment and with other organisms. Developments in ecology therefore had to wait for some developments in physiology. Nevertheless, as early as the late seventeenth century, an "environmental physiology" was already developing: Robert

Boyle, in 1670, was already examining the effects of reduced atmospheric pressure on a variety of organisms (Allee et al. 1949:16). And by the mid-eighteenth century, work had begun on the amount of heat necessary to mature various grains (Allee 1949:18). Although some ecologists have been concerned with the relationships of single organisms to their biological and nonbiological surroundings, most have taken as their units of study aggregates of organisms organized into groupings of various kinds. Some of these groupings are susceptible to measurement with regard to size, density, and so on. This quality provides ecologists with a means for describing ecological systems and changes in them in precise, quantified terms. Ecology thus also rests heavily upon demography, the study of population. Demography was initially concerned with human groups. It is interesting to note, in light of later developments, that speculations concerned primarily with the growth rates of human populations were of seminal importance in the emergence of a general population ecology dealing with aggregates of other animals and plants (cf. Hutchinson and Deevey 1949).

Although there were many earlier statements (summarized in Cole 1957), the demographic work which had perhaps the greatest impact upon early developments in ecology was T. R. Malthus' *An Essay on the Principle of Population,* which first appeared in 1798. The mathematical model Malthus used for demonstrating that organisms outrun their food supply has generally been abandoned. Still, it was a description of possibilities cogent enough for Darwin to use for his theory of evolution. Furthermore, Malthus' was an ecological statement — that is, a statement concerning populations in their environments — which did not distinguish human beings from other animals in any fundamental way.

We are faced with the irony that animal ecology rests heavily upon an approach indicated in an eighteenth-century ecological statement about human beings, while most later anthropological studies concerned with the ecology of human groups have had their roots elsewhere. The promising theoretical and methodological lead provided by the attempts of Malthus and his predecessors to treat human beings within a conceptual frame that could also accommodate other animals has not been generally followed by anthropologists. Their statements on ecological processes have generally been formulated not in terms of the relations among groups of organisms — that is, *populations* and their environments — but in terms of the relations among *cultures* and their environments. This theoretical direction has been chosen partly in reaction to unsupportable racist interpretations of differences in custom among human groups, and other reasons for the choice lie in the history of anthropology. But this is not the place to examine all the relevant developments. Suffice it to say that ecological work in anthropology has for more than a half-century had a predominantly cultural orientation. There is little indication that anthropologists during this period have been aware of ongoing developments in animal ecology. Indeed, communication between the two fields has been extremely tenuous.

It is our belief that, while ecological work in anthropology has had some successes, it has suffered from its isolation from developments in the field of general ecology. Later in this chapter, we shall offer some reasons for bringing ecological studies in anthropology within the theoretical framework of general ecology and some suggestions as to how this might be accomplished. However, our first task will be to examine some of the formulations of the past sixty years. We will not attempt a history of the field, nor will we try to be exhaustive. We will discuss a limited number of approaches and positions which have been and, with the possible ex-

ception of environmental determinism, continue to be influential within anthropology.

DETERMINISTS AND POSSIBILISTS

In the first two decades of this century, two views on environmental influences were distinguished, one labelled "determinism" (or, in some discussions, "environmentalism"), the other, "possibilism." The first, which has antecedents in antiquity (Tatham 1957), held in its most extreme statements that environmental forms dictate cultural ones and therefore cultural phenomena can be explained and should be predictable to a large extent by reference to their contemporary environments. This was denied by adherents of possibilism, some of whom argued that, consistent with what is described as a limiting rather than determining effect of the environment, only the absence of traits (for instance, "the absence of pineapple plantations in Greenland") could be predicted from characteristics of the environment. With regard to the cultural phenomena the environment permits or makes possible, there are, in the possibilist view, always alternatives, and there is no guarantee that any particular possibility (for instance, food storage rather than seasonal migration as an adjustment to seasonal changes in the amount of food yielded by the local environment) will be the one to materialize. Among some students, including the distinguished American anthropologist, A. L. Kroeber (1923:182), the rejection of environmental determinism led to the attribution of primacy to "historical or cultural influences" as determinants of cultural phenomena. Thus, concerning pre-Columbian agriculture among the Indians of the southwestern United States Kroeber wrote as follows:

. . . the Southwestern Indians did not farm because nature induced them to make the invention. They did not make the invention at all. A far away people made it, and from them it was transmitted to the Southwest through a series of successive tribal contacts. These contacts, which then are the specific cause of Southwestern agriculture, constitute a human social factor; a cultural or civilizational factor. Climactic or physical environment did not enter into the matter at all except to render agriculture somewhat difficult in the arid Southwest, though not difficult enough to prevent it. Had the Southwest been thoroughly desert, agriculture could not have got a foothold there. But this would be only a limiting condition; the active or positive causes that brought about the Southwestern agriculture are its invention farther South, the spread of the invention to the North, and its acceptance there (1923: 185f.).

The contending points of view are similar to those which long agitated biological science, wherein some students argued for external environmental factors as the determinants of biological traits and other students argued for factors within the organisms themselves as the determinants. The resolution in biology has been the recognition that both classes of factors and the interplay between them are determining (Simpson 1949: 142–143), and today a parallel resolution, emphasizing the interaction of cultural and environmental factors, is possible in cultural anthropology. However, before we discuss this, it is appropriate to note some of the work and the thinking that have led to current views.

Actually, even scholars whose names are closely associated with the position of environmental determinism did not completely reject nonenvironmental factors. Ellsworth Huntington (1945:8), for example, specified "the interaction of biological inheritance, physical environment, and cultural endowment" as influencing human actions and the march of civilization. However, climate was the factor that received the most conspicuous emphasis in Huntington's work. He saw the influence of climate upon cultural phenomena not only in its effects upon land forms

and vegetation but also in its alleged effects upon human physiology and psychology. Thus, hot climates were held to be conducive to a dulling of the mind and a disinclination to work and therefore to be antithetical to the development of civilization. Unanalyzed impressions and casual observations — for example, booksellers' remarks to the effect that no one touches "serious books" in Virginia during the long summer months (Huntington 1915:32f.) — were cited as evidence of the alleged effects of high temperatures. The lack of methodological rigor in the early work of Huntington and his associates no doubt contributed to the strength of the reaction against environmental determinism.

However, around the turn of the century, there also were somewhat more sophisticated attempts to use the environment for explanations of cultural phenomena. Otis T. Mason noted in two papers, published in 1896 and in 1905, that the North American climatic zones distinguished by the geographer C. Hart Merriam in a map prepared for the U.S. Department of Agriculture corresponded in large measure to the areas occupied by the linguistic families earlier delimited by J. W. Powell (1891). Powell's areas, in turn, were noted to be characterized by relative homogeneity in cultural traits in addition to language.

The twelve regions distinguished by Mason in North America north of Mexico were designated as "ethnic environments" by him, and he attempted, within the limited scope of the two papers, to specify them in terms of physiography, vegetation, fauna, and possibilities for human movement, as well as in terms of climate. Although he made the general statement that nonhuman environmental factors (that is, "physical geography," "climate," and "predominant plants, animals, and minerals") "determine cultural development of various kinds and degrees" (1905:427), his more specific observations were of a possibilistic nature. For instance, the North Pacific Coast was said to permit "unfettered travel in dugout canoes, which provided opportunity for the full development of the dispersive clan system" (1905:428). The language of this quotation, it may be noted, suggests Mason's "classical evolutionist" orientation and the place of environment in such a conceptual framework: a "natural" developmental trend through a series of "stages" will unfold unless it is inhibited by the environment.

Mason was aware also of the importance of intergroup relations in explanations of the content of particular cultures. He wrote that "few impassable barriers separated the culture areas," and that "in some respects, indeed, the entire region [i.e., North America] formed one environment, having easy communication N. and S. and few barriers E. and W." (1905:427).

But Mason's work had severe limitations. He himself provided no maps and demarcated areas only vaguely. The cultural inventories he listed for each of the ethnic environments were extremely brief. There was, in other words, considerable imprecision in Mason's work. Nevertheless, his "ethnic environments" were initially serviceable units for investigating covariations of cultural and environmental traits.

Impetus for making such investigations was provided also by the culture-area classifications developed in conjunction with the preparation of museum displays of artifacts arranged according to their geographical provenience. In 1917 Clark Wissler of the American Museum of Natural History presented a classification distinguishing nine North American Indian culture areas, and this scheme was revised slightly by Kroeber in his 1923 textbook, which contained a map of North American culture areas. Noting that the distribution of cultural traits depicted on this map closely paralleled floral and climatic distributions indicated on a map of North America prepared by the Ecological

Society of America, Wissler in 1926 stated: ". . . we find such a consistent relation between the generalized culture areas on the one hand and environmental areas on the other, it may be that the form of the distribution [of cultural traits] is . . . in some way based upon ecological relations" (Wissler 1926:214). Wissler recognized that to show "certain correspondences between the distributions for human traits on the one hand and the distributions of environmental traits on the other" was a limited accomplishment, but he thought that it might be an "essential step" toward the discovery of the mechanism whereby one class of traits affected the other (Wissler 1926:212).

While it is certainly true that the discovery of correlations can be a step toward the discovery of the causal connections between phenomena, the utility of culture-area classifications for realization of the latter objective has been limited severely, first of all, by the grossness of culture-area categories. The North American continent, with its approximately 8,000,000 square miles, was divided by Kroeber (1923:336) into only ten culture areas. The totality of cultural phenomena within an area of subcontinental size can hardly be expected to comprise a single unit whose interactions with the totality of environmental phenomena within the same area can be systematically investigated. In practice, of course, what was recognized by students as the culture of a culture area was restricted to a rather small number of distinctive traits. The only necessary relation these traits had to one another was that their existence had been reported in the same place, that is, within an area characterized, presumably, by fairly effective internal cultural diffusion. A bundle of what often were quite disparate traits (for instance, among other things, boxes, hats, solstitial calendars, and matrilineal clans in the North Pacific culture area) cannot be regarded as necessarily constituting a unit in interaction with anything at all or with the environment specifically. To put it a little differently, a culture area is not an integrated cultural, social, or demographic unit. Its utility in investigating interactions between social or cultural phenomena, on the one hand, and environmental phenomena, on the other, is, accordingly, severely limited and the positive statements that can be made about culture and environment in culture areas tend to be trivial. An example is the following generalization by Wissler:

It is clear . . . that the environment is in some way a determiner, and a principle, or law, may be formulated as, when two sections of a continent differ in climate, florae, and faunae, or in their ecological complexes, the culture of the tribal groups in one section will differ from that in the other (1926:214).

Culture-area classifications may still lead to a fruitful examination of the relation between specific cultural and environmental variables, and students of culture areas have, in fact, made such examination. For example, the presence of maize cultivation and associated traits in some culture areas and their absence from adjacent culture areas in North America has resulted in Kroeber's demonstration that maize-growing was, for the most part, confined aboriginally to climates affording four-month growing seasons with sufficient rain and no killing frosts (Kroeber 1939:207–212). Is this, however, a demonstration of how the "environments" of culture areas affect their "cultures"? It makes more sense to regard it as a demonstration of an important relationship between such specific variables as rainfall, frost incidence, and the success of maize cultivation, the last being a variable upon which a host of distinctive cultural traits depended.

It is noteworthy that in Kroeber's discussion the environmental variables are regarded as limiting factors, responsible for the *absence* of traits. This agrees closely with Mason's position. But despite this agreement, and despite agreement that environmental variables are insufficient to explain the presence of particular traits, there was a covert but wide disparity between Kroeber's and Mason's views. For Mason, the presence of traits was explicable by reference to the unimpeded expression of a grand evolutionary process. For Kroeber, explanation lay primarily in the specific "historical or cultural influences" referred to earlier. A similar possibilism, thus, rested upon somewhat different assumptions.

Specific history was invoked also by the British anthropologist, C. Daryll Forde. In a well-known book presenting descriptions of the economic and social life of a number of human groups varying in their technology and environment, he wrote:

. . . the culture of every single human community has had a specific history. How far that history is known will make all the difference to the degree of our understanding; but unless there is realization of the existence of that specific history, both of internal change and external contact in one or several specific environments, understanding cannot begin (Forde 1934:466).

However, Forde is to be distinguished from the culture-area students, for he rejected their large-scale regional approach on the grounds that "broad general classifications . . . are quite inadequate for the analysis of cultural possibilities . . . " (Forde 1934:464). He recommended instead the analysis of possibilities for "particular societies" or "human communities." These were regarded as differing not only in their specific histories but also in their inexplicably unique culture patterns which, according to Forde, influence adaptation to the environment: "Between the physical environment and human activity there is always a middle term, a collection of specific objectives and values, a body of knowledge and belief: in other words, a cultural pattern" (Forde 1934:463). In support of the possibilist position, Forde added a greater emphasis on cultural uniqueness or "relativism" to the historical particularism of Wissler and Kroeber.

It may be said that the culture-area studies and comparative studies, such as Forde's, effectively refuted a crude environmental determinism, if such ever really existed as a serious position, and, further, they indicated one kind of effect environmental phenomena can have: the exclusion or limitation of certain cultural developments. That there are complex interactions with the environment was recognized, and diffusion, specific history, and cultural patterns were seen to be important influences quite apart from the environmental factors. But these other influences were allowed to constitute a dark middle region between man and his physical environment in which almost anything could happen. That is to say, while the complexity of the problems of analysis and explanation were discerned, no models or methods for resolving the problems were put forward. Instead, possibilistic conclusions were reached. Concerning possibilism, we may say that it is neither a theory nor a hypothesis lending itself to empirical test. It is simply a way of saying that causation is not simple.

Steward's Method of Cultural Ecology

To the emphasis placed by Kroeber, Forde, and others on unique culture histories and unique cultural patterns, the American anthropologist, Julian Steward, reacted with an emphasis on local environments. Focusing on cultural adjustments and adaptations was to be a way out of the impasse resulting from what Steward described as the "relativistic conception of culture history" and its "fruitless assumption that culture comes from culture" (1955:36). The ecological studies he initiated in the 1930's and his theoretical and methodological statements, which were brought together in a volume published in 1955, have had considerable influence in anthropology and must be considered in some detail. A review of some aspects of Steward's contributions will provide an opportunity to note some recent work by other students also.

Steward (1955) is explicit about his general objective. His is the "social science problem of explaining the origin of unlike behavior patterns found among different societies of the human species" (pp. 33f.). More specifically, the problem is "to ascertain whether the adjustments of human societies to their environment require particular modes of behavior or whether they permit latitude for a certain range of possible behavior patterns" (p. 36).

Steward sees difficulties in dealing with the relation between human societies and the environment when the latter is viewed as the "total web of life wherein all plant and animal species interact with each other and with the physical features in a particular unit of territory" (p. 30). Some of the difficulties are attributed by Steward to the fact that "man enters the ecological scene . . . not merely as another organism which is related to other organisms in terms of his physical characteristics . . . [but rather] introduces the super-organic factor of culture, which also affects and is affected by the total web of life" (p. 31). In an attempt to reduce the magnitude of the difficulties, Steward regards the relationship of man, the organism, to environment as separate from the relationship of culture, the "super-organism," to environment. He views the elucidation of biological and of cultural phenomena as different objectives of ecological research, each requiring its own concepts and methods, each to be kept, generally, distinct from the other. He justifies this segregation on the grounds that "cultural patterns are not genetically derived and, therefore, cannot be analyzed in the same way as organic features" (p. 32). He argues that explanations of the presence of cultural phenomena must rely, rather, on culture-historical methods and concepts augmented by the methods and concepts of what he calls cultural ecology. The elucidation of specific histories has, however, only a limited place in Steward's ecological approach despite the fact that he himself has made numerous culture-historical studies. The view is taken that "cultural ecological adaptations" are not merely permitted by the environment but "constitute creative processes" (p. 34), and that there is a "degree of inevitability in cultural adjustments" (p. 89). The implication is that the origins of some (even if not all) particular cultural features can be discovered through the study of relationships between culture and its contemporary environment. The de-emphasizing of the historical influences with which Kroeber and others were preoccupied is indicated clearly in Steward's assertion that the role of cultural diffusion "in explaining culture has been greatly overestimated" (p. 42).

"Three fundamental procedures of cultural ecology" are set forth by Steward. These are analyses of: (1) the relation between environment and exploitative or productive technology; (2) the "behavior patterns involved in the exploitation of a particular area by means of a particular technology"; and (3) the "extent to which the behavior patterns entailed in exploiting the environment affect other aspects of culture" (Steward 1955:40f.). Following these procedures, Steward has examined cultures ranging from those of primitive hunters and gatherers to great civilizations, both ancient and modern. Examples of the kinds of conclusions to which these studies have led Steward are these:

(1) Among the Shoshonean Indians, who were hunters and gatherers in the Great Basin of the United States, a fragmentation of society into nuclear family units foraging about the country was entailed by the "er-ratic and unpredictable occurrence of practically all principal foods," by the absence of technical skills for harvesting and storing sufficient foods for fairly large permanent populations, and by the fact that staple wild vegetable products such as seeds and roots could not be gathered efficiently by collective means (Steward 1955:105–107).

(2) Patrilineal, patrilocal, landowning bands are produced among hunters and gatherers by low population densities (one person or less per square mile), nonmigratory and scattered game as a principal food resource, and the restriction of transportation to human carriers. The operation of these factors is described by Steward as follows:

The scattered distribution of the game, the poor transportation, and the general sparsity of the population make it impossible for groups that average over 50 or 60 persons and that have a maximum of about 100 to 150 persons to associate with one another frequently enough and to carry out sufficient joint activities to maintain social cohesion. The band consists of persons who habitually exploit a certain territory over which its members can conveniently range. Customary use leads to the concept of ownership. Were individual families to wander at will, hunting the game in neighboring areas, competition would lead to conflict. Conflict would call for alliance with other families, allies being found in related families. As the men tend to remain more or less in the territory in which they have been reared and with which they are familiar, patrilineally related families would tend to band together to protect their game resources. The territory would therefore become divided among these patrilineal bands (1955:135).

(3) Among the Carrier Indians of interior British Columbia, a change from hunting bands to localized landowning matrilineal moieties was unaccompanied by change in either habitat or technology. This indicates that the environmental adjustments of these Indians allowed a "certain latitude" in the range of possible social types, which

could, accordingly, be determined by historical factors (Steward 1955:6f., 173–177).

With these examples in mind, we may now consider certain difficulties presented by Steward's "method of cultural ecology."

A major source of difficulties for the realization of Steward's objective of explaining the origin of particular culture features and patterns is his selection of variables, that is, features of culture and environment, for analysis. Steward clearly recognized the virtual impossibility of dealing with "whole cultures," and his method calls for paying "primary attention to those features which empirical analysis shows to be most closely involved in the utilization of environment in culturally prescribed ways" (Steward 1955:37). These are the features that Steward designates the "cultural core." Similarly, instead of dealing with "total environments," the method calls for a focusing upon those environmental features which are significant for particular adaptations. Examples given by Steward are the "spacing of water holes in the desert [which] may be vital to a nomadic seed-gathering people . . . and the kinds and seasons of fish runs [which] will determine the habits of riverine and coastal tribes" (1955:40).

As Clifford Geertz (1963:10) has recently observed, this discrimination and specification of variables permit a replacement of the gross questions about the influence of environment upon culture with more incisive queries about how specific variables, both cultural and environmental, interact; how their functioning is regulated; how stable a system they constitute; and so forth. But such questions are directed not so much towards explaining the origins of particular cultural features and patterns as towards explaining how they function or operate, irrespective of their origin. In order to make his discrimination of variables bear upon the problem of origins, Steward has had recourse to cross-cultural comparisons. These

have led to his conclusion that the recurrence of the same interrelations of cultural and environmental variables in cultures not in contact with one another is evidence of "a degree of inevitability" in the association between certain cultural traits (for instance, "essential features" of patrilineal bands) and certain ecological adaptations considered to be causative (Steward 1955:89, 122, and *passim*). This conclusion may be questioned in a number of ways.

First, we may question the very existence of significant correlations between the cultural traits and ecological adaptations considered by Steward. This is because Steward is, for the most part, not concerned with devising adequate cross-cultural samples for testing the significance of correlations. Instead, he follows the procedure of choosing for consideration some cases in which an association between particular cultural traits and ecological adaptations of interest to him does seem to obtain. The procedure does not indicate how many other cases there might be in which there obtain either the adaptations but not the cultural traits in question, or the cultural traits but not the adaptations.

Second, the basis for concluding that the ecological adaptations are "causative" may be questioned. Even if correlations between the adaptations and certain cultural traits were shown to be significant, the task of demonstrating what is cause and what is effect would remain. As a matter of fact, ecologically minded social scientists have at times had to regard certain "social" factors (for instance, the organization of labor) as determinants of particular ecological adaptations. For example, Owen Lattimore, writing of "agricultural foundations and social forms" in Chinese history, has stated that "irrigation and drainage could be originated on a primitive scale of family labor, but they could not change the agricultural character of wide regions except by collective labor"

(1963:102). Chi Ch'ao-Ting has discussed in a similar vein the absence of the *"social prerequisites* of large-scale water-control development" in classical feudal China (Chi 1936:61–63; italics ours). In such cases, there presumably are feedbacks operating between social factors and ecological adaptations, and it would be necessary to look for circular or reticulate relations between effects and causes rather than for simple one-way linear cause-to-effect sequences (cf. Vayda and Rappaport 1963:143).

Third, even if Steward's correlations were shown to be significant and also the cultural traits were shown to be the dependent variables, we might still question the "inevitability" of the traits. Any demonstration of their functional relationship to ecological adaptations is by itself insufficient to make them inevitable. Considerations relevant to this point have been stated by Ernest Nagel in a discussion of functionalism in social science:

. . . to show that a given type of . . . function can be performed only by a particular social organization . . . [e.g., the patrilineal band], it would be necessary to show not only that the given function is not in fact performed by any organization other than the stated one, but also that no other organization (whether already in existence or only envisaged) *could* perform that function. However, in view of the varying functions that the same or similar organizations have exercised in the past, and in view also of human capacity for creating new institutional forms, such a task is almost hopeless (1961:534).

In light of the questions raised above, it is perhaps not surprising that recent studies have cast some doubt on the existence of patrilineal bands among the Australian Aborigines (Hiatt 1962) and African Bushmen (Marshall 1960), two of the seven populations used by Steward as type-cases of groups with patrilineal bands. At the risk of seeming to digress from consideration of

Steward's contributions, we must, however, note that refutation of his more specific conclusions does not necessitate a return to the possibilist notion that the environment limits but does not determine and that the "causes" of cultural traits are to be sought only in culture itself and its history. Another alternative is to recognize, as biologists have done, that there are two kinds of influences at work in evolution: what A. J. Lotka (1945:187) has called generating influences and selecting influences. The former provide the material for selection, while the latter do the selecting. To recognize this is to recognize that similar selecting influences, which are "environmental" in the broad sense, may produce different results, depending upon the material provided for selection. Just as biologists have interpreted the differences between mammalian kidney types as the result of the exposure of different genetic materials to similar selecting influences (Simpson 1953:181), so it may be possible for anthropologists to interpret, for example, some differences in the social organization of hunting groups as the result of the exposure of different cultural materials, the products of dissimilar specific histories, to similar selecting influences. An interpretation along such lines has in fact been put forward by Symmes C. Oliver (1962) in an anthropological monograph on Plains Indian social organization. On the one hand, Oliver shows that hunting and food-gathering tribes from the west and horticultural tribes from the east moved into the American Plains after the post-Columbian introduction of horses and that convergent cultural changes related to the mounted hunting of buffalo and to intertribal competition took place among the tribes. On the other hand, he also shows that, in spite of the similarities resulting from the convergent changes, some important differences in the social organization of the tribes persisted, and he is able to relate these differences to the tribes' different cultural heritages.

The compatibility and complementarity of environmental or ecological explanations of cultural phenomena with historical or so-called cultural explanations are indicated not only by studies such as Oliver's but also by studies concerned with cases wherein the fission of human populations has resulted in the exposure of the same or similar cultural materials to different environmental influences. Cases of this nature have been studied among East African tribes by P. H. Gulliver (1955) and among Polynesian societies by Marshall Sahlins (1958). In these situations, both cultural similarity deriving from the common cultural heritage of the populations and cultural diversity produced by different environmental pressures (for instance, different rainfall regimes, soil fertilities, and the like) have been disclosed. Steward of course also uses factors of culture history as explanations, but he does so only when, as in the case of social change among the Carrier Indians (see above, p. 484), he is not satisfied with any explanation provided by his method of cultural ecology.

The foregoing questions have been concerned mainly with Steward's use of ethnographic materials for cross-cultural comparisons. But further questions may be raised concerning his implied suggestions or criteria of relevance for the collection of materials by anthropological field workers.

Steward makes the statement, referred to earlier, that "cultural ecology pays primary attention to those features which empirical analysis shows to be most closely involved in the utilization of environment in culturally prescribed ways" (1955:37). Apart from the difficulties arising from a lack of adequate explicit criteria for closeness of involvement in environmental exploitation, the statement might be regarded as a legitimate program for delimiting the field of in-

quiry. In practice, however, Steward concentrates on certain technological and social features without due empirical analysis of other traits. A kind of technological determinism seems to inhere in his three procedures of cultural ecology (above, p. 484) and to lead him to regard as mere epiphenomena such features as, for example, those conventionally regarded as "religious." Yet some social scientists, writing after the publication of Steward's book, have put forward hypotheses assigning a major role to religious or ceremonial features as adaptive factors in the interactions of human populations with their environments. Some examples are the following: Omar Khayyam Moore's (1957) hypothesis that the recourse to the ritual of shoulder-blade divination among certain North American Indian hunters of caribou served to randomize the choice of hunting sites and thereby to prevent unwitting behavioral regularities which the caribou could have taken advantage of; Homer Aschmann's hypothesis (1959:140) that sexual license during a limited ceremonial season among the Indians of the Central Desert of Baja California resulted in a "seasonal pattern of reproduction related to the seasonal fluctuation of the food supply"; Andrew Vayda, Anthony Leeds, and David Smith's (1961) hypothesis that massive ritual slaughter of pigs in the New Guinea highlands functioned to maintain a long-term balance between human populations and the crops and fauna from which they drew their sustenance; and D. H. Stott's hypothesis (1962:365f.) about the population-limiting functions of circumcision and subincision rituals among Aborigines in arid central regions of Australia which were subject to food shortages. Such hypotheses deserve empirical analysis also — rather than a priori rejection because they deal with religious or ceremonial features.

Just as Steward takes a restricted view of the cultural features that may be closely involved in environmental exploitation and therefore need to be investigated, he also takes a restricted view of the environmental features that are relevant to particular adaptations. In showing the importance of food resources as environmental features to be dealt with in ecological studies, Steward tends to slight other environmental phenomena that may influence the cultures of human groups. Among such phenomena are parasites and disease organisms (Alland 1963, 1966; Bates 1953:705) and, perhaps most important, the presence of other and possibly competing human groups (see the studies by Barth 1956, 1964; Sahlins 1961; Secoy 1953; Sopher 1964; Vayda 1961a). Thus, a cultural response to disease among certain New Guinea groups studied by us is a dispersion of settlements, while, in many parts of the primitive world, a nucleation of dwellings for defense is one of numerous cultural responses to the presence of human enemies.

Biological aspects of human populations also are given little consideration by Steward. The view stated in his 1955 book is that "culture, rather than genetic potential for adaptation, accommodation, and survival, explains the nature of human societies" (p. 32). But in contrast to this and in light of recent studies, it is possible to see culture and genetics interacting and working together to effect adaptation in human populations much as they do in populations of nonhuman land mammals and birds, which are now recognized to share with human beings a capacity for intra-species transmission of learned behavior (Hockett and Ascher 1964:136; Scott 1958). Studies carried out for the most part after publication of Steward's book have indicated that the processes of biological and cultural evolution may produce biological differences among human populations in body builds (Brues 1959; Newman 1953), in physiological adaptations to heat, cold, and nutri-

tional stress (Dobzhansky 1962:276–278; Newman 1962; Schreider 1963, 1964; Weiner 1964), in susceptibility to such diseases as malaria (Livingstone 1958), in the incidence of dental and ocular defects (Brace 1962; Post 1962), and possibly even in the neuro-endocrinological adaptations to high population densities and crowding (Coon 1963:106ff.). With regard to such biological differences, we can ask, for example, about their influence upon the development of particular working and eating habits, particular items of material culture (for instance, eyeglasses, false teeth, and distinctive kinds of apparel, furniture, and shelter), and particular philosophies. These are questions that can no longer be dismissed by fiat but need rather to be investigated empirically.

Moreover, Steward tends to treat the terms "genetic" and "biological" as if they were interchangeable. Having decided not to regard cultural traits as in any way *genetically* determined, he regards it unnecessary to consider any biological variables.

It need hardly be pointed out that the terms "genetic" and "biological" are not synonyms. "Genetic" refers to certain, but not all, aspects of biological phenomena. A biological aspect of human groups which may be considered without reference to genetic processes and which Steward himself, somewhat inconsistently, recognizes to be a possible determinant of cultural adjustments is population size. Other such biological characteristics, varying both between and within populations and having an effect upon adjustments to the environment, include metabolism and body size. To ignore these characteristics of human groups is to ignore variables that are critical to any assessment of the nutrition that groups of organisms require from their surroundings. Although human groups carry complex cultures, it must not be forgotten that they are composed of organisms making organic demands upon other organisms in their surroundings.

Despite the exceptions that have been taken to specific aspects of Steward's theory and method of cultural ecology, it must be emphasized that his work has been of signal importance in a number of respects. For one thing, it has made anthropologists realize that the usual textbook refutations of environmental determinism (for instance, that the Pueblo and Navaho Indians had different cultures in purportedly the same environment, or that Japanese culture changed radically in the latter part of the nineteenth century, ostensibly without environmental change) did not constitute an adequate consideration of the relation between cultural phenomena and their environmental settings. Furthermore, his work has pointed to the importance of basing ecological generalizations upon the close examination of particular local groups and their environments. It is interesting to speculate that Steward's perhaps most enduring contribution to ecological method and theory will be his monograph (1938) on the Great Basin Shoshoneans, a study based largely upon his own field work. While the results of his comparative efforts may remain unconvincing to us, his very difficulties in working with materials collected by anthropologists for other purposes than cross-cultural comparisons of ecological systems and variables constitute a significant challenge to field anthropologists to improve the quality of data on the relations between human populations and their environments.

ETHNO-ECOLOGY

Investigations different from Steward's are being advocated by some anthropologists with training in linguistics. Their approach is intended to disclose ecology as seen by the people being studied, and therefore, following Harold Conklin (1954), we will call it the ethno-ecological approach. It belongs to the important category of studies which William Sturtevant (1964) has recently designated as "studies in ethnoscience." Consonant with Sturtevant's usage, the prefix "ethno-" is to be understood here as referring to a people's own view or knowledge of some subject matter, whether it is science in general or ecology in particular.

The nature and purposes of the ethno-ecological approach have been set forth programmatically by Charles Frake (1962a). Stating that "a description of cultural behavior is attained by a formulation of what one must know in order to respond in a culturally appropriate manner in a given socio-ecological context," Frake proposes that a "successful strategy for writing productive ethnographies must tap the cognitive world of one's informants" (1962a:54). Accordingly, methods drawn mainly from linguistics and systematics are to be brought to bear on the problem of producing descriptions of how the people being studied construe their world. The methods are to be directed first toward the construction of taxonomies of native terms on the basis of the discovery of the criterial or distinguishing attributes of named categories of phenomena in the environment (for instance, the characteristics setting apart the category "dog" from the category "cat" among English-speakers). The assumption is made that taxonomies of native terms either comprise in themselves statements of ethno-ecology or provide the information necessary for inferring ethno-ecology. This is indicated in the following quotation: "By discovering what one must know in order to *classify* plants and other ecological components in Hanunóo fashion, one learns what the Hanunóo [a people of Mindoro Island in the Philippines] consider worth attending to when making decisions on how to behave within their ecosystem [ecological system]" (Frake 1962a:55; italics ours).

After the taxonomies of native terms have been constructed, the next step is the formulation of rules of what the native speakers themselves would regard as appropriate behavior towards the environmental phenomena placed by them in one or another category. Frake puts this as follows:

From a presentation of the rules by which people decide upon the category membership of objects in their experience, an ethnographic ecology can proceed to rules for more complex kinds of behavior: killing game, clearing fields, building houses, etc. Determining the requisite knowledge for such behavior shows the ethnographer the extent to which ecological considerations, in contrast, say to sociological ones, enter into a person's decision of what to do (1962a:55).

The methods and goals of this program are far different from Steward's. Where Steward's program is to a large extent comparative, Frake's is ethnographic. Where Steward's aim is to explain the origins of behavior patterns by reference to aspects of the environments in which the patterns are found, the aim of the ethno-ecological approach is simply to present a people's view of the environmental setting itself and their view of behavior appropriate to that setting.

The aim is an important one. Its relevance to ecological studies lies in the fact that it is reasonable to regard a people's cognition with respect to environmental phenomena as part of the mechanism producing the actual physical behavior through which the people directly effect alterations in their environment. While confining observations to the actual physical behavior may lead to some success in the explanation and prediction of states and processes in ecological systems (cf. Harris 1964:29–30, 169–170; Wagner 1960:26–28), greater success can be expected if a fuller understanding of the mechanism producing the behavior is obtained. With such understanding, the dark

"middle term" of Forde (see above, p. 483) might be transformed into specific, identifiable variables amenable to empirical investigation.

However, there are some problems in implementing Frake's program, and they must be considered. It should be noted first that his approach calls for inferences about people's knowledge from the terms they apply to things in the environment. By the use of formal procedures for the analysis of the meanings of such terms (see Chafe, Chapter 2 in this volume, on componential analysis), the linguist or ethnographer can arrive at a set of rules for using these terms as the people themselves use them. Such rules, stating a limited number of principles of contrast whereby things within a certain class or domain (for example, the "plant world") can be assigned to different linguistic categories, are claimed by Frake to provide the means not only for predicting the terms native speakers will apply to particular objects but also for understanding what the native speakers' own classificatory concepts are and how the people construe their world. This claim has recently been questioned by Robbins Burling (1964a, 1964b), who has argued that the rules tell us only about verbal behavior and not about what is going on "inside people."

This is not the place for an attempt to adjudicate the issues raised by Burling, although it should be noted that a response to them has been made by Dell Hymes (1964a) and by Frake himself (1964a). But it is very much the place for us to note that even if we grant the validity of Frake's method for disclosing the "rules by which people decide upon the category membership of objects in their experience," we are still a long way from knowing just what the people know about their environment and about procedures for dealing with it. To discover a people's classificatory terms and concepts is to discover what might be designated their "ethno-systematics" or "ethno-taxonomy," and this must be distinguished from ethno-ecology. Thus when Conklin (1954:140) tells us that the Hanunóo people frequently discuss and well understand the effects that erosion, exposure, and the Hanunóo's own farming activities have upon the quality of soils, he is telling us about what the Hanunóo say or know about the relation of environmental phenomena to one another and to the Hanunóo themselves. It is, then, a statement about Hanunóo ethno-ecology. On the other hand, when Conklin (1954:140) tells us also that the Hanunóo distinguish thirty soil and mineral categories, more than 450 animal types, and over 1600 plant types, he is making a statement about ethno-systematics, about the Hanunóo view of the classificatory terms to be applied to things, and not necessarily about the Hanunóo view of how the things behave and how they influence one another. Taxonomies may of course be based on behavioral characteristics, but they need not be. They may, for example, be based on morphological characteristics whose correlates in behavioral traits or in function are not apparent to the very people employing the particular taxonomies. This is as true of folk taxonomies as it is of Western scientific ones. Clearly, then, there are no universally applicable procedures for inferring either ethno-ecology or the actual relations within an ecological system from ethno-systematics. One must therefore demur when Frake makes statements such as: "By discovering what one must know in order to classify plants and other ecological components in Hanunóo fashion, one learns what the Hanunóo consider worth attending to when making decisions on how to behave within their ecosystem" (1962a:55). Whether or not this is so for the Hanunóo case is an empirical question, and it is an empirical question for every case. The point needs under-

scoring only because Frake's language may be construed to mean that there are adequate a priori grounds for inferring ethno-ecology from ethno-systematics. There are not.

In addition to calling attention to such methodological problems, we must note that the ethno-ecological approach has a fundamental limitation for providing understanding of relations within ecological systems. Along with any success of the ethno-ecological approach in describing what one of us (Rappaport 1963:159) has elsewhere designated as "cognized environments" (that is, environments as understood by those who act within them) could go a failure to describe ecological processes and environmental relations which affect the people *without* their being aware of them. Putting this in the language of sociologists (Merton 1957b:60ff.), we can say that the ethno-ecological approach is not a means for the elucidation of "latent functions," that is, functions or consequences of behavior which are not intended or recognized by the behaving people. Yet the discovery of such functions may be crucial for the understanding of many interactions between human populations and their environments. In the hypotheses noted earlier with reference to Steward's treatment of religious features (above, p. 487), the ecological functions attributed to rituals are latent ones, and numerous similar hypotheses could be cited (cf. Harris 1964:92). It is worth noting that long-term advantages may accrue to a people as a result of their using other than ecological considerations in deciding upon courses of action that have ecological functions or consequences. For example, studies have indicated that decisions to change residences are made by some African tribesmen not on the basis of what we would regard as ecological considerations but rather on the basis of the extent of witchcraft accusations and suspicions (Bohannan 1954:13,

15; Middleton and Winter 1963:*passim*). Yet the changes of residence in these cases may have important ecological functions or effects: in reducing the crowding that has generated the tensions expressed in witchcraft accusations and suspicions, the changes may reduce or prevent local overpopulation and an associated overexploitation and deterioration of resources. In other words, they may serve to maintain a long-term balance between the tribesmen and their resources. Would the same results obtain if ecological rather than supernatural considerations were made the bases for decisions about residence? The answer might well be "no," for people might then be persuaded to remain in their original settlements on account of short-term material advantages associated with *not* moving, for example, perhaps the greater ease of clearing ground and protecting it from animal pests in the original locations. The provision of long-term material advantages to populations through behavior induced by immediate, conventional, and not solely material rewards to individuals (for instance, social status or tension-release) appears to have developed in many species other than man (cf. Wynne-Edwards 1959, 1962, 1965), and it seems likely that a fair number of similar behavioral mechanisms in addition to the witchcraft-induced migrations just noted can be found to be operating in human populations also (for example, see from this standpoint the discussions of "social-climbing" feasts in Bascom 1948; Fürer-Haimendorf 1962:117f.; Piddocke 1965; Schneider 1957; Suttles 1960; Vayda 1961b; and Vayda, Leeds, and Smith 1961). Where such mechanisms are operating, studies in ethnoscience and cognition might indicate the "nonecological" considerations on which individuals base decisions to act, but for an understanding of the ecological functions and consequences of their actions, the methods of Western biological science are required.

ECOLOGY RATHER THAN CULTURAL ECOLOGY

At the beginning of this chapter, it was stated that ecological work in anthropology has suffered from its restricted cultural orientation and its isolation from general ecology. This statement was followed by criticisms of ecological studies by anthropologists whose emphasis has been on cultural factors as something apart from the kinds of factors influencing the relation of nonhuman organisms to their environments. It is now time to make explicit some considerations bearing upon both the possibility and the desirability of a single science of ecology with laws and principles that apply to man as they do to other species.

It must be made clear, first of all, that the development of a unified science of ecology does not require that culture or cultural factors be omitted from consideration. Instead, the culture of the human species may, as has been proposed recently by the biologist George Gaylord Simpson, be "studied as animal behavior and interpreted in the same way as the behavior [or part of the behavior] of any other species, for instance, in its adaptive aspects and consequent interaction with natural selection" (1962:106). In the introductory section of this chapter, some reasons for anthropologists' reluctance to follow this procedure were indicated. During the latter part of the nineteenth century and the early part of the twentieth, "culture" was becoming for them the distinctive concept of their discipline. By the middle of this century, as shown by a reading of the textbooks published at the time, "culture" was well established in a central place in the conceptual apparatus of anthropologists. At this time, the concept was generally understood to refer to patterns of and for behavior transmitted socially by means of symbols (cf. Kroeber and Kluckhohn 1952:181). The emphasis was to a considerable extent on the mode of transmission of culture, and Kroeber in 1948 even stated that "perhaps *how it comes to be* is really more distinctive of culture than what it *is*" (Kroeber 1948: 253).

While the concept of culture was achieving its status in anthropology, the attention of biologists, especially from about 1900 on, was to a considerable extent shifting from animal behavior to genetics (Simpson 1958: 7–9). This development doubtless contributed to the alienation of cultural anthropology from biology, for what could be the relevance of the work in genetics to anthropologists if the distinctiveness of cultural phenomena lay in their transmission by nongenetic means?

The point of this simplified account of developments in anthropology and biology is merely to indicate that the separation of cultural from biological studies may be a result not so much of the nature of the phenomena being investigated as of other influences on the particular courses of intellectual history in the two fields. A new foundation is now being laid for a more unified approach. For one thing, among biologists there has been a general renewal of interest in behavior (Simpson 1958:9, 21). Recognition of its importance for studies of biological evolution is indicated in the following quotation from an article contributed to a conference of biologists and psychologists in 1956:

. . . the behavior of animals is a major contributing factor for their survival and, consequently, through the mechanisms of heredity, for the course of evolution. Maintaining favorable relations with the environment is largely a function of behavior. Possessing efficient skeletal, circulatory, digestive, sense organ, and effector systems is not enough. All these must be used effectively in activities such as food getting, reproduction, and defense. Behavioral incompetence leads to extinction as surely as does morphological disproportion or deficiency in any vital organ. Behavior is subject to selection as much as bodily size or resistance to disease (Nissen 1958:185).

Application of this point of view to studies of human species is indicated in the following quotation from an article by a physical anthropologist:

From the short-term point of view, human structure makes human behavior possible. From the evolutionary point of view, behavior and structure form an interacting complex, with each change in one affecting the other. Man began when populations of apes, about a million years ago, started the bipedal, tool-using way of life that gave rise to the man-apes of the genus *Australopithecus*. . . . Selection produced new systems of child care, maturation and sex, just as it did alterations in the skull and the teeth (Washburn 1960:63).

The possibility of studying human and nonhuman behavior in similar ways cannot fail to be enhanced by a new (or renewed) awareness of the broad similarities between the two indicated in the quotations above, viz., that both function to effect adaptation to the environment and that both are subject to a kind of selection resulting, *inter alia,* from the fact that individuals or populations behaving in certain different ways have different degrees of success in survival and reproduction and, consequently, in the transmission of their ways of behaving from generation to generation.

There are of course some special problems in studying human behavior. Although it is increasingly appreciated that both human and nonhuman animal behavior are products of a combination of learning and genetically determined capabilities (Lindzey 1964; Scott 1958; Simpson 1962), it is still true that the degree to which behavior is a result of learning rather than genetics is greater in the human species than in other animal species. This contributes to making human behavior relatively complex, varied, variable, and population-specific (cf. Simpson 1962:106f.). Certainly anthropologists are confronted because of this with formidable tasks in observation and description. But the mere fact that there might be more for anthropologists than for students of infrahuman species to observe and describe does not mean that the principles, concepts, or approaches employed by anthropologists studying behavior in interaction with environmental phenomena must be *basically* different from those employed by the other students. And if common principles, concepts, and approaches can be used, then, by the criterion of parsimony, these are to be preferred.

An immediate methodological requirement for a more unified ecological approach is some measure of agreement about the kinds of units whose relations are to be studied. In addition to individual organisms, the units important to ecologists are populations (groups of organisms living within a given area and belonging to the same species or variety), communities (all of the populations within a given area), and ecosystems (either individual organisms, populations, or communities, together with their nonliving environments) (Evans 1956; Odum 1959:6–8). The way in which ecologists demarcate these units in space and time varies according to the nature of the particular problems being investigated and the convenience of study. The units are, however, bounded units, even if the boundaries are to some degree arbitrary. Consistent with usage in ecology, the focus of anthropologists engaged in ecological studies can be upon human populations and upon ecosystems and biotic communities in which human populations are included. To have units fitting into the ecologists' frame of reference is a procedure with clear advantages. Human populations as units are commensurable with the other units with which they interact to form food webs, biotic communities, and ecosystems. Their capture of energy from and exchanges of material with these other units

can be measured and then described in quantitative terms. No such advantage of commensurability obtains if cultures are made the units, for cultures, unlike human populations, are not fed upon by predators, limited by food supplies, or debilitated by disease.

But if we make human populations the units, and if we place our emphasis upon their interactions with other components of their ecosystems, do we not thereby sacrifice traditional anthropological concerns? Are we not thereby abandoning the goals stated at the beginning of this chapter, that is, elucidating how particular cultural traits function and why they exist?

The answer is "no." We have already noted that ecology has been regarded a social as well as biological science by such writers as Allee and Hawley (above, pp. 477–478) and we have indicated the new recognition of the importance of animal behavior (including man's "cultural" behavior) in the relation of organisms to their environment (above, pp. 492–493). The ecologist is perforce concerned with behavioral as well as morphological attributes of the organisms and populations under study, whether these attributes are the predatory habits of lions, the "troop" deployments of baboons, or the tool-making, tool-using, socio-political arrangements, and other cultural traits of human beings. Any number of examples could be given of cultural traits that may, much as any animal behavior, be studied in relation to environmental phenomena.

Traits already viewed within the ecologists' frame of reference include ways of defining both territorial rights (Barth 1959; Birdsell 1958; Hallowell 1949; Knight 1965) and social groups (Brookfield and Brown 1963:176f.; Meggitt 1965:Chap. 9; Vayda and Rappaport 1963:137f.); the establishment of intertribal buffer zones (Hickerson 1965); institutionalized raiding for camels or horses by mounted tribesmen (Sweet 1965a, 1965b; Vayda, Leeds, and Smith 1961:73);

ceremonial feasting (see the references above, p. 492); the sacralization of such animals as cows (Harris 1965); and the practice of human sacrifice (Cook 1946). All these are cultural traits that even the most traditional anthropologist would regard as being properly of concern to him. At the same time, as indicated in the works cited parenthetically, the functioning of all these traits may be made more intelligible through investigation of their role in maintaining within an adaptive range certain variables (such as size or dispersion) pertaining to either particular human populations or the faunal and floral populations upon which these depend. Thus, re-drawing of territorial boundaries or redefinition of landowning groups (for instance, as to degree of unilineality) may, in specific circumstances, have the effect of restoring man-land ratios within a certain range. Intertribal buffer zones may serve as refuge areas for game that might otherwise be overhunted. The institutionalized raiding for camels or horses may prevent local groups of human beings from having either too few animals for their needs or too many for the available local pasturage. Ceremonial feasting may effect a wide distribution of subsistence goods by providing an occasion for well-off people to receive prestige in return for giving their foodstuffs to those less well supplied. Religious restrictions on the use of animals for meat may help to maintain the animals as sources of traction, dairy products, and manure. And human sacrifice may be important in checking population pressure. Other examples of such regulating or *homeostatic* functions of cultural practices have already been suggested in our discussion of Steward's neglect of "religious" features in relation to environmental phenomena (above, p. 487) and Frake's neglect of latent functions (above, p. 491).

Some warnings are in order. Most of the examples we have given must at present be regarded as hypothesized rather than empirically validated functions. That is to say, additional quantitative data on the relevant variables are required to provide either confirmation or invalidation. These variables, moreover, may be numerous, and they may constitute part of the usual subject matter of not one or two but rather a considerable number of the conventionally defined sciences or academic disciplines. We may illustrate this by considering the hypothesis that massive ritual slaughters of pigs in the New Guinea highlands function to keep the land from being overrun with pigs and to maintain a long-term balance between people and their crops and fauna (Vayda, Leeds, and Smith 1961:71–72). For testing this hypothesis, here are a few of the relevant variables: natality, mortality, immigration, and emigration of pigs as well as people; agricultural productivity; soil fertility; rate of reforestation of farmed land; and energy consumption and expenditure by the people. There are ways of obtaining data on all these variables, although it may be beyond the capacity of any single investigator to obtain them. As long as approximately the present division of labor in the sciences prevails, the validation or invalidation of ecological hypotheses about human populations can perhaps be best provided through coordinated research by workers from a variety of disciplines, for example, zoology, botany, soil science, forestry, nutrition, human genetics, and medicine, in addition to anthropology and other social sciences.

Another necessary warning concerns judgments about the utility or adaptiveness of particular cultural phenomena or patterned human activities on the basis of the empirical validation of some particular functions for them. It must be understood that any trait in question may also have effects that are deleterious to human populations under given conditions. These effects too have to be taken into account when assessments of utility or adaptiveness are made. For example, the use of human excrement as a fertilizer may maintain not only a high level of soil fertility but also a high level of exposure of people to disease organisms and a concomitantly high rate of disease. In areas of land shortage, the advantages of using human excrement may outweigh the disadvantages, but there is, as Alexander Alland (1966:47) has pointed out, little to be said in favor of the practice for human populations that can move on to new land after the fertility of previously farmed land has been exhausted. This example underscores that demonstrating a behavioral or cultural trait to have some one or more functions — for instance, the maintenance of soil fertility — does not by itself constitute an adequate basis for a judgment about the overall utility or adaptiveness of the trait.

Moreover, showing how traits function is an enterprise not to be equated with accounting for their presence or origins. This is a warning as applicable to the study of cultural traits (Collins 1965; Durkheim 1938:89–97) as to the biologists' study of molecules, cells, and other organic structures (Caspari 1963:5; Mayr 1958:341 and 1961: 1502). As suggested in our discussion of Steward's cross-cultural comparisons (above, p. 486), the fact is that more than one cultural trait may fulfill a particular function; soil fertility may, for example, be maintained through the use of night soil, through land rotation, or through recourse to a variety of other cultural practices. The implication is that a demonstration of function provides by itself no adequate answer to the question of why some particular traits rather than others occur at particular times and places. For the student of functions, the characteristic question necessarily is "How does it work?" rather than "Why is it present?" or "How did it get this way?"

Yet not only the operation or functioning of cultural traits but also their origins or

their presence can be illuminated by ecological studies. For example, studies of the productivity or energetics of particular ecosystems that include human populations can show the extent to which those populations have access to energy that may be channelled into non-food-producing activities. Accordingly, the studies bear upon such problems of anthropological concern as the origins and evolution of social stratification (that is, the development of non-food-producing elites) (Harris 1959; Mason 1959; Sahlins 1958) and the origins and evolution of the elaborated cultural practices that we call civilization (Cottrell 1965:Chap. 2; Dumond 1961; Ferdon 1959; Meggers 1954; Palerm and Wolf 1957; Wilbert 1961). Moreover, the endeavors of archeologists, paleontologists, and geologists working together to reconstruct ancient ecosystems have already served as a basis for plausible speculations about the influences likely to have favored the origin and development of such traits as plant and animal domestication (Braidwood and Willey 1962; Downs 1960:44 and *passim;* Zeuner 1963), intensive agriculture (Dumond 1961:304), and the human use of language (Hockett and Ascher 1964). Of course there are severe limitations on what can be reconstructed of conditions and processes that occurred centuries and, in some cases, even millenia ago. But, it is noteworthy that students who do not make the error of trying to explain the origin or presence of traits by relating them only to their contemporary environments are striving to obtain as full evidence as possible of both the cultural or behavioral antecedents of particular traits and the environmental conditions under which they have developed. That is to say, there is attention to both kinds of influences referred to earlier (above, p. 486): generating cultural ones and selecting environmental ones. For example, Robert Braidwood and his associates, in dealing with the question of agricultural beginings in prehistoric southwestern Asia, are concerned not only with reconstructing environmental conditions and assessing their influence but also with obtaining evidence of the kinds of interactions between wild food plants and Mesolithic food-collecting people which could have provided the latter with the experience (that is, the cultural or behavioral antecedents) for initiating cultivation (Braidwood 1960; Braidwood and Howe 1962: 137–138, 142–143). In other words, there is, just as in the works of Oliver, Gulliver, and Sahlins cited earlier (above, p. 487), a recognition that determinants of cultural traits are to be sought in an *interplay* of factors that include environmental ones and behavioral or cultural ones. Whenever possible, the influence of human biological variations should of course also be considered.

It would seem then that a unified science of ecology has definite contributions to make towards the realization of anthropological goals and does not entail any appreciable sacrifice of traditional anthropological interests. It may, however, entail a somewhat different sacrifice, that is, of the notion of the autonomy of a science of culture, a notion that Leslie White (1949) and others have vigorously defended. But to give this up may be a sacrifice well worth making, for it may make possible generalizations of much broader scope and applicability than have so far been achieved by anthropologists.

Suggested Readings

For more extensive statements by authors whose positions have been discussed critically in this chapter, the following works should be consulted: Kroeber (1939); Forde (1934), available also in paperback edition published in 1963; Steward (1955); and Frake (1962). A good introduction to principles and concepts of general ecology is the 1959 edition of Odum's textbook. The interdisciplinary symposium edited by Fosberg (1963) indicates uses of ecology in studying ecosystems that include man. A number of studies focusing upon how particular cultural traits function in such ecosystems may be found in the volume edited by Leeds and Vayda (1965). Clark and Haswell's book (1964) presents useful data on food production and consumption from a wide range of nonindustrial societies, while Weiner's work (1964) reviews findings and indicates problems in research on the *biological* adaptations of human groups to environmental phenomena.

BIBLIOGRAPHY

ABERLE, DAVID F.
1961   Matrilineal descent in cross-cultural perspective. *In* Schneider and Gough 1961.

ABERLE, DAVID F. *et al.*
1950   The functional prerequisites of a society. Ethics 60:100–111.

ABRAHAM, K.
1927   Selected papers on psycho-analysis, Ernest Jones, ed. London, Hogarth Press.

ACKERKNECHT, ERWIN H.
1954   On the comparative method in anthropology. *In* Spencer 1954.

ADAMS, ROBERT McC.
1966   The evolution of urban society. Chicago, Aldine Publishing.

ADCOCK, C. J. AND J. E. RITCHIE
1958   Intercultural use of the Rorschach. American Anthropologist 60:881–892.

ADORNO, T. W. *et al.*
1950   The authoritarian personality. New York, Harper.

AIKEN, H. D.
1962   Reason and conduct: new bearings in moral philosophy, 1st ed. New York, Knopf.

ALBERT, ETHEL M.
1956   The classification of values: a method and illustration. American Anthropologist 58:221–248.

1964   "Rhetoric," "logic," and "poetics" in Burundi: culture patterning of speech behavior. *In* The ethnography of communication, John J. Gumperz and Dell Hymes, eds. American Anthropologist 66:35–54.

ALBINO, R. C. AND V. J. THOMPSON
1956   The effects of sudden weaning on Zulu children. British Journal of Medical Psychology 29:177–210.

ALEXANDRE, P. AND J. BINET
1954   Australia: aboriginal paintings —

Arnheim Land. UNESCO World Art Series, New York Graphic Society.

1958   Le Groupe dit Pahouin (Fang, Boulou, Beti). Presses Universitaires de France.

ALLAND, ALEXANDER, JR.
1963   Cultural and biological factors in the ecology of infectious diseases. Paper read at the 62nd annual meeting of the American Anthropological Association in San Francisco, November, 1963.

1966   Medical anthropology and the study of biological and cultural adaptation. American Anthropologist 68 (in press).

ALLEE, W. C.
1931   Animal aggregations. A study in general sociology. Chicago, University of Chicago Press.

ALLEE, W. C. *et al.*
1949   Principles of animal ecology. Philadelphia, W. B. Saunders.

ALLPORT, G. W.
1937   Personality: a psychological interpretation. London, Constable and Co., Ltd.

1942   The use of personal documents in psychological science. Social Science Research Council Bulletin No. 49.

1957   European and American theories of personality. *In* Perspectives in personality theory, H. P. David and H. von Bracked, eds. New York, Basic Books.

ALLPORT, G. W. AND T. F. PETTIGREW
1957   Cultural influence on the perception of movement: the trapezoidal illusion among Zulus. Journal of Abnormal and Social Psychology 55:104–113.

ANASTASI, A. AND J. P. FOLEY, JR.
1949   Differential psychology, rev. ed. New York, Macmillan.

ANDERSON, CHARLES ROBERTS
1939   Melville in the South Seas. New York, Columbia University Press.

ANGULO, JAIME DE
1950   Indians in overalls. *In* Hudson Review anthology, Frederick Morgan, ed. New York, Random House, Vintage Books, pp. 3–60. (Reprinted from Hudson Review, Vol. 3.)

1953   Indian tales. New York, Hill and Wang.

ANN ARBOR NEWS
1965   Ann Arbor News, May, Ann Arbor, Mich.

ARENSBERG, CONRAD
1954   The community study method. American Journal of Sociology 60:109–124.

1955   American communities. American Anthropologist 57:1143–1162.

1961   The community as object and sample. American Anthropologist 63:241–264.

ARENSBURG, CONRAD AND SOLON T. KIMBALL
1965   Culture and community. New York, Harcourt, Brace & World.

AREWA, E. OJO AND ALAN DUNDES
1964   Proverbs and the ethnography of speaking folklore. American Anthropologist 66:70–85.

ASCHMANN, HOMER
1959   The central desert of Baja California: demography and ecology. Ibero-Americana 42:316.

ASHTON, HUGH
1952   The Basuto. London, Oxford University Press.

ATKINSON, ALEX
1960   Escape with Mrs. Dyson, No. 4, At home with the aborigines. Punch 238:769–772.

BACH, EMMON
1964   An introduction to transformational grammars. New York, Holt, Rinehart and Winston.

BACHOFEN, J. J.
1861   Das Mutterrecht. Stuttgart.

BAIER, K. M.
1958   The moral point of view: a rational basis of ethics. Ithaca, Cornell University Press.

BAILEY, FLORA
1942   Navaho motor habits. American Anthropologist 44:210–234.

BANKS, ARTHUR AND ROBERT B. TEXTOR
1963   A cross-polity survey. Cambridge, M.I.T. Press.

BANTON, MICHAEL (ED.)
1966a   The social anthropology of complex societies. New York, Praeger.

1966b   Anthropological approaches to the study of religion. New York, Praeger.

BARBEAU, C. MARIUS
1953   Haida myths; illustrated in Argillite carvings. National Museum of Canada, Anthropological Series No. 32, Bulletin No. 127. Ottawa.

BARKER, E.
1927   National character and the factors in its formation. London, Harper.

BARNES, J. A.
1963   Some ethical problems in modern fieldwork. British Journal of Sociology 14:118–134.

BARNETT, HOMER G.
1940   Cultural processes. American Anthropologist 42:21–48.

1942   Invention and culture change. American Anthropologist 44:21–48.

1953   Innovation: the basis of culture change. New York, McGraw-Hill.

1960   Being a Palauan. New York, Henry Holt.

BARNETT, HOMER G., LEONARD BROOM *et al.*
1954   Acculturation: an exploratory formulation. The Social Science Research Council Summer Seminar on

Acculturation, 1953. American Anthropologist 56:973–1002.

BARNOUW, VICTOR
1963   Culture and personality. Homewood, Ill., Dorsey Press.

BARRETT, S. A.
1908   Pomo Indian basketry. University of California Publication in American Archaeology and Ethnology 7, No. 3.

BARTH, FREDRIK
1956   Ecologic relationships of ethnic groups in Swat, North Pakistan. American Anthropologist 58:1079–1089.

1959   The land use pattern of migratory tribes of South Persia. Norsk Geografisk Tidsskrift 17:1–11.

1964   Competition and symbiosis in North East Baluchistan. Folk 6:15–22.

BARTLETT, F. C.
1932   Remembering: a study in experimental and social psychology. New York, Macmillan.

BARTON, R. F.
1919   Ifugao Law. University of California Publications in American Archaeology and Ethnology 15:1–186.

BASCOM, WILLIAM
1946   Ponape: a Pacific economy in transition. Honolulu, U.S. Commercial Company (mimeographed).

1948   Ponapean prestige economy. Southwestern Journal of Anthropology 4:211–221.

1954   Four functions of folklore. Journal of American Folklore 67:333–349.

1955   Verbal art. Journal of American Folklore 68:245–252.

1965   The forms of folklore: prose narratives. Journal of American Folklore 78:3–20.

BATES, MARSTON
1953   Human ecology. *In* Anthropology today: an encyclopedic inventory,

A. L. Kroeber, ed. Chicago, University of Chicago Press.

BATESON, G. AND M. MEAN
1942   Balinese character: a photographic analysis. Special publications of the New York Academy of Sciences, Vol. II.

BEAGLEHOLE, ERNEST
1938   Ethnology of Pukapuka. Bulletin No. 150, Bernice P. Bishop Museum.

BEALS, ALAN R.
1962   Gopalpur: a South Indian village. New York, Holt, Rinehart and Winston, Case Studies in Cultural Anthropology Series.

BEALS, RALPH
1946   Cheran: a Sierra Tarascan village. Smithsonian Institution, Institute of Social Anthropology, Publication No. 2.

1957   Native terms and anthropological method. American Anthropologist 59:716–717.

BEATTIE, J. H. M.
1955   Contemporary trends in British social anthropology. Sociologus 5:1–14.

BEATTIE, JOHN
1960   Bunyoro; an African kingdom. New York, Holt, Rinehart and Winston.

BECKER, HOWARD S.
1958   Problems of inference and proof in participant observation. American Sociological Review 23:652–660.

BELSHAW, C. S.
1955   In search of wealth. American Anthropological Association Memoir No. 80.

BENEDICT, RUTH
1932   Configurations of culture in North America. American Anthropologist 34:1–27.

1934   Patterns of culture. Boston, Houghton Mifflin.

1943   Two patterns of Indian acculturation. American Anthropologist
45:207–212.

1955   Continuities and discontinuities in
cultural conditioning. *In* Child-
hood in contemporary cultures,
M. Mead and M. Wolfenstein, eds.
Chicago, University of Chicago
Press.

BENNETT, JOHN W.
1944   The development of ethnological
theory as illustrated by studies of
the Plains Sun Dance. American
Anthropologist 46:162–181.

1946   The interpretation of Pueblo culture: a question of values. Southwestern Journal of Anthropology
2:361–374.

1948   The study of cultures: a survey of
techniques and methodology in
field work. American Sociological
Review 13:672–689.

1964   Myth, theory and value in cultural
anthropology. *In* Fact and theory
in social science, E. W. Count and
G. T. Bowles, eds. Syracuse, Syracuse University Press.

BERGER, PETER L.
1961   The noise of solemn assemblies:
Christian commitment and the religious establishment in America.
Garden City, Doubleday.

1963   Invitation to sociology, a humanistic perspective. Garden City, Doubleday.

BERNDT, RONALD M.
1962   Excess and restraint. Social control
among a New Guinea mountain
people. Chicago, University of
Chicago Press.

BERREMAN, GERALD D.
1962   Behind many masks: ethnography
and impression management in a
Himalayan village. Ithaca, Society
for Applied Anthropology, Monograph no. 4.

1963   Hindus of the Himalayas. Berkeley, University of California Press.

1965   Anemic and emetic analyses in social anthropology. American Anthropologist 68:346–354.

BEVAN, EDWIN
1957   Symbolism and belief. Boston,
Beacon Press.

BEVERIDGE, W. M.
1939   Racial differences in phenomenal
regression. British Journal of Psychology 24:59–62.

BHARATI, AGEHANANDA
1963   Pilgrimage in the Indian tradition.
History of Religions 3:135–167.

BIERCE, AMBROSE
1958   The devil's dictionary. New York,
Dover.

BIESHEUVEL, S.
1949   Psychological tests and their application to non-European peoples.
In The yearbook of education,
G. B. Jeffrey, ed. London, Evans.

1952a   The study of African ability. Part
I: the intellectual potentialities of
Africans. African Studies 11:45–
57.

1952b   The study of African ability. Part
II: a study of some research problems. African Studies 11:105–117.

BIRDSELL, JOSEPH B.
1958   On population structure in generalized hunting and collecting populations. Evolution 12:189–205.

BLACKWOOD, BEATRICE
1935   Both sides of Buka Passage: an
ethnographic study of social, sexual, and economic questions in the
North Western Solomon Islands.
Oxford, Clarendon Press.

BLOCH, BERNARD AND GEORGE L. TRAGER
1942   Outline of linguistic analysis. Baltimore, Linguistic Society of America.

BLOCH, MARC
1953   The historian's craft, translated by
Peter Putnam. New York, Knopf.

BLOOMFIELD, LEONARD
1933   Language. New York, Holt, Rinehart and Winston.

BOAS, FRANZ

1896   The growth of American Indian mythologies. Journal of American Folklore 9:1–11.

1911   Introduction to handbook of American Indian languages, Part 1. Bureau of American Ethnology Bulletin 40, Part 1. Washington, D.C.

1916   Tsimshian mythology. Annual Report of the Bureau of American Ethnology 31. Washington, D.C., Government Printing Office.

1927   Primitive art. New York, Dover (Reprinted 1955.)

1940a   The aims of anthropological research. *In* Mead and Bunzel, 1960: 577–591. (Reprinted from Race, Language and Culture.

1940b   Race, Language and Culture. New York, Macmillan.

BOCK, KENNETH E.

1956   The acceptance of histories; toward a perspective for social science. University of California Publications in Sociology and Social Institutions 3:1–132.

BOGORAZ, VLADIMIR G.

1904/9   The Chukchee. New York, G. E. Stechert. (Memoir of the American Museum of Natural History 11: Publications of the Jesup North Pacific Expedition 7.) 3 vols.

BOHANNAN, LAURA

1952   A genealogical charter. Africa 22:310–315.

BOHANNAN, PAUL

1954   The migration and expansion of the Tiv. Africa 24:2–16.

1956   On the use of native language categories in ethnology. American Anthropologist 58:557.

1957   Justice and judgment among the Tiv. New York, Oxford University Press.

1958   On anthropologists' use of language. American Anthropologist 60:161–162.

1963   Social anthropology. New York, Holt, Rinehart and Winston.

BOHANNAN, PAUL J. AND GEORGE DALTON (EDS.)

1962   Markets in Africa. Evanston, Ill., Northwestern University Press.

BOWEN, ELENORE S.

1954   Return to laughter. New York, Harcourt, Brace.

BOWERS, ALFRED W.

1950   Mandan social and ceremonial organization. Chicago, University of Chicago Press.

BOYCE, B.

1947   The theophrastian character in England to 1642. Cambridge, Harvard University Press.

BOYD, MARK F.

1955   Asi-yaholo or Osceola. Florida Historical Quarterly 33:249–305.

BRACE, C. LORING

1962   Cultural factors in the evolution of the human dentition. *In* Culture and the evolution of man, M. F. Ashley Montagu, ed. New York, Oxford University Press (Galaxy Book).

BRAIDWOOD, ROBERT J.

1960   The agricultural revolution. Scientific American 203:130–148.

BRAIDWOOD, ROBERT J. AND BRUCE HOWE

1962   Southwestern Asia beyond the lands of the Mediterranean littoral. *In* Braidwood and Wiley 1962.

BRAIDWOOD, ROBERT J. AND GORDON R. WILEY (EDS.)

1962   Courses toward urban life: archeological considerations of some cultural alternates. Viking Fund Publications in Anthropology No. 32.

BREER, PAUL E. AND EDWIN A. LOCKE

1965   Task experience as a source of attitudes. Homewood, Ill., Dorsey Press.

BRENNER, CHARLES

1955   An elementary textbook of psychoanalysis. Garden City, Doubleday (Anchor book).

BRIDENBAUGH, CARL
1962   The great mutation. American Historical Review 68:315–331.

BROOKFIELD, H. C. AND PAULA BROWN
1963   Struggle for land. Agriculture and group territories among the Chimbu of the New Guinea highlands. Melbourne, Oxford University Press.

BROWN, JUDITH
1963   A cross-cultural study of female initiation rites. American Anthropologist 65:837–853.

BROWN, ROBERT
1963   Explanation in social science. Chicago, Aldine Publishing.

BROWN, ROGER W.
1959   Words and things. Glencoe, Free Press.

BRUES, ALICE
1959   The spearman and the archer — an essay on selection in body build. American Anthropologist 61:457–469.

BRUNER, J. S.
1951   Personality dynamics and the process of perceiving. In Perception: an approach to personality, R. R. Blake and G. V. Ramsey, eds. New York, Ronald Press.

BRUNER, J. S. et al.
1966   Studies in cognitive growth. New York, Wiley.

BUCK, PETER H.
1944   The local evolution of Hawaiïan feather capes and cloaks. Journal of the Polynesian Society 53:1–16.

BUNZEL, RUTH
1929   The Pueblo potter. Columbia University Contributions to Anthropology No. 7. New York, Columbia University Press.

BURLING, ROBBINS
1962   Maximization theories and the study of economic anthropology. American Anthropologist 64:802–821.

1964a   Cognition and componential analysis: God's truth or hocus-pocus? American Anthropologist 66:20–28.

1964b   Burling's rejoinder [to Hymes and Frake]. American Anthropologist 66:120–122.

BURRIDGE, K. O. L.
1960   Mambu: a Melanesian millennium. London, Methuen.

CALENDER, CHARLES
1962   Social organization of the central Algonkian Indians. Milwaukee Public Museum Publications in Anthropology No. 8.

CAMPBELL, D. T.
1961   The mutual methodological relevance of anthropology and psychology. In Psychological anthropology: approaches to culture and personality, F. L. K. Hsu, ed. Homewood, Ill., Dorsey Press.

1964   Distinguishing differences of perception from failures of communication in cross-cultural studies. In Cross-cultural understanding: epistemology in anthropology, F. S. C. Northrop and H. H. Livingston, eds. New York and London, Harper and Row.

CARNEIRO, ROBERT L.
1962   Scale analysis as an instrument for the study of cultural evolution. Southwestern Journal of Anthropology 18:149–169.

CAROTHERS, M. C.
1953   The African mind in health and disease. Geneva, World Health Organization.

CASPARI, ERNST
1963   Selective forces in the evolution of man. American Naturalist 97:5–14.

CATTELL, R. B.
1946   Description and measurement of personality. New York, Harcourt, Brace & World.

1965   The scientific analysis of personality. Pelican Books.

CHADWICK, H. MUNRO AND N.
1940   The growth of literature. 3 vols. New York, Macmillan.

CHAFE, WALLACE L.
1964a   Another look at Siouan and Iroquoian. American Anthropologist 66:852–862.

1964b   Linguistic evidence for the relative age of Iroquois religious practices. Southwestern Journal of Anthropology 20:278–285.

CHI, CH'AO-TING
1936   Key economic areas in Chinese history, as revealed in the development of public works for water-control. London, G. Allen & Unwin.

CHILD, IRVIN L.
1954   Socialization. *In* Handbook of social psychology, Vol. II., G. Lindzey, ed. Cambridge, Addison-Wesley.

1965   A cross-cultural study of drinking. Quarterly Journal of Studies on Alcohol, Supplement 3.

CHILDE, V. GORDON
1946   What happened in history. New York, Penguin Books.

CHING, LIN HSIA, JAMES L. E. CHOW, AND LIU CHIEH YUKON CHANG
1931   The civil code of the Republic of China. Shanghai, Kelly and Walsh.

CHOMSKY, NOAM
1957   Syntatic structures. The Hague, Mouton and Co.

1965   Aspects of the theory of syntax. Cambridge, M.I.T. Press.

CHOWDHURY, U.
1960   An Indian modification of the Thematic Apperception Test. Journal of Social Psychology 51:245–263.

CICERO, MARCUS TULLIUS
1928   De Legibus, translated by Clinton Walker Keyes. New York, Putnam's.

CICOUREL, AARON V.
1964   Method and measurement in sociology. New York, Free Press of Glencoe.

CLARK, COLIN AND MARGARET HASWELL
1964   The economics of subsistence agriculture. London, Macmillan.

CLIFTON, JAMES A.
1959   On the intercultural use of the Rorschach. American Anthropologist 61:1087–1090.

1965a   The Southern Ute tribe as a fixed membership group. Human Organization 24:319–327.

1965b   Culture change, structural stability and factionalism in the Prairie Potawatomi Reservation community. Midcontinent American Studies Journal 6:101–123.

CLIFTON, JAMES A. AND BARRY ISAAC
1964   The Kansas Prairie Potawatomi: on the nature of a contemporary Indian community. Transactions of the Kansas Academy of Science 67:1–24.

COHEN, YEHUDI A.
1953   A study of interpersonal relationships in a Jamaican community. Doctoral dissertation, Yale University.

1955   Character formation and social structure in a Jamaican community. Psychiatry 18:275–296.

1961a   Food and its vicissitudes: a cross-cultural study of sharing and non-sharing. *In* Social structure and personality: a casebook, Y. A. Cohen, ed. New York, Holt, Rinehart and Winston.

1961b   Patterns of friendship. *In* Social structure and personality: a casebook, Y. A. Cohen, ed. New York, Holt, Rinehart and Winston.

1962a   Matrilineal descent, matrilocal residence, and political leadership. Paper presented at the 61st annual meeting of the American Anthropological Association, Chicago.

1962b   Review of Moore 1961. American Anthropologist 64:853–855.

1964a   The establishments of identity in a social nexus: the special case of initiation ceremonies and their relation to value and legal systems. American Anthropologist 66:529–552.

1964b   The transition from childhood to adolescence: cross-cultural studies of initiation ceremonies, legal systems, and incest taboos. Chicago, Aldine.

1966   Review of Initiation ceremonies, by Frank W. Young. American Anthropologist 68:776–778.

COLE, LAMONT C.
1957   Sketches of general and comparative demography. Cold Spring Harbor Symposia on Quantitative Biology 22:1–15.

COLLINS, PAUL W.
1965   Functional analyses in the symposium "Man, Culture, and Animals." In Leeds and Vayda 1965.

COLSON, ELIZABETH
1954   The intensive study of small sample communities. In Spencer 1954.

COMMITTEE OF THE ROYAL ANTHROPOLOGICAL INSTITUTE OF GREAT BRITAIN AND IRELAND
1951   Notes and queries on anthropology, revised and rewritten. London, Routledge and Kegan Paul.

COMMONER, BARRY AND RICHARD DALY
1964   What is the harm of nuclear testing to human inheritance? Scientist and Citizen 6:9–10, 18–24.

CONKLIN, HAROLD C.
1954   An ethnoecological approach to shifting agriculture. Transactions of the New York Academy of Sciences, 2nd series 17:133–142.

1963   The Oceanian-African hypotheses and the sweet potato. In Plants and the migrations of Pacific peoples, Jacques Barrau, ed. Honolulu, Bishop Museum Press.

1964   Ethnogenealogical method. In Explorations in cultural anthropology: essays in honor of George Peter Murdock, Ward H. Goodenough, ed. New York, McGraw-Hill.

COOK, EDWIN A.
1965   Manga social organization. Unpublished doctoral dissertation. New Haven, Yale University, Dept. of Anthropology.

COOK, S. F.
1946   Human sacrifice and warfare as factors in the demography of pre-colonial Mexico. Human Biology 18:81–100.

COON, CARLETON S.
1963   The origin of races. New York, Knopf.

COTTRELL, FRED
1965   Energy and society. The relation between energy, social change, and economic development. New York, McGraw-Hill.

COVARRUBIAS, MIQUEL
1947   Island of Bali. New York, Knopf.

COVINGTON, JAMES W.
1954   A petition from some Latin-American fishermen: 1838. Tequesta 14:61–65.

CRYNS, A.
1962   African intelligence: a critical survey of cross-cultural intelligence research in Africa south of the Sahara. Journal of Social Psychology 57:283–301.

CULWICK, A. T. AND G. M.
1935   Ubena of the rivers. London, Allen and Unwin.

CUNNISON, IAN
1951   History of the Luapula; an essay on the historical notions of a central African tribe. Rhodes-Livingstone Papers No. 21.

DALTON, GEORGE
1961   Economic theory and primitive society. American Anthropologist 63:1–25.

1965   Primitive money. American Anthropologist 67:44–65.

DANZIGER, K.
1960   Parental demands and social class in Java, Indonesia. Journal of Social Psychology 51:75–86. Independence training and social class in Java, Indonesia. Journal of Social Psychology 51:65–74.

DARK, PHILIP
1962   The art of Benin. Catalogue of an exhibition. Chicago Natural History Museum.

DARK, ROBERT TYLER
1949   Native arts of the Pacific Northwest. Stanford, Stanford University Press.

DAVIDSON, D. S.
1937   Snowshoes. Philadelphia, American Philosophical Society, Memoirs 6.

DAVIS, F. JAMES; HENRY H. FOSTER *et al.*
1962   Society and the law. New York, Free Press of Glencoe.

D'AZEVEDO, WARREN L.
1962   Uses of the past in Gola discourse. Journal of African History 3:11–34.

DEACON, A. BERNARD
1934   Malekula: a vanishing people in the New Hebrides. London, Routledge.

DEAN, JOHN P.
1954   Participant observation and interviewing. *In* An introduction to social research, J. T. Doby, ed. Harrisburg, Stackpole Company.

DEAN, JOHN P. AND W. F. WHYTE
1958   How do you know if the informant is telling the truth? Human Organization 17:34–38.

DENNIS, W.
1951   Cultural and developmental factors in perception. *In* Perception: an approach to personality, R. R. Blake and G. V. Ramsey, eds. New York, Ronald Press.

DENTON, ROBERT C. (ED.)
1955   The idea of history in the ancient Near East. New Haven, Yale University Press.

DEVONS, ELY AND MAX GLUCKMAN
1964   Modes and consequences of limiting a field of study. *In* Closed systems and open minds: the limits of naivety in social anthropology, Max Gluckman, ed. Chicago, Aldine.

DEVOS, GEORGE
1961   Symbolic analysis in the cross-cultural study of personality. *In* Kaplan 1961.

DIAMOND, STANLEY
1963   The search for the primitive. *In* Man's image in medicine and anthropology, Iago Galdston, ed. New York, International Universities Press.

DIAMOND, STANLEY (ED.)
1964   Primitive views of the world. New York, Columbia University Press.

DIEBOLD, A. RICHARD, JR.
1960   Determining the centers of dispersal of language groups. International Journal of American Linguistics 26:1–10.

DIXON, R. B.
1928   The building of cultures. New York, Scribner.

DOBZHANSKY, THEODOSIUS
1962   Mankind evolving. The evolution of the human species. New Haven, Yale University Press.

DOKE, CLEMENT M.
1931   The Lambas of Northern Rhodesia: a study of their customs and beliefs. London, George C. Harrap and Co.

DOLLARD, JOHN
1936   Criteria for the life history. New Haven, Yale University Press.

DONALDSON, BESS ALLEN
1938   The wild rue, a study of Muhammadan magic and folklore in Iran. London.

DONNER, ETTA (Becker-Donner)
1940   Kunst und Handwerk in Nordost
        Liberia. Baessler Archiv, Berlin,
        Vol. 23, Parts 2–3.

DOOB, L. W.
1957   An introduction to the psychology
        of acculturation. Journal of Social
        Psychology 45:143–160.

1957/8 The use of different test items in
        nonliterate societies. Public Opin-
        ion Quarterly 21:499–504.

1960   Becoming more civilized: a psy-
        chological exploration. New
        Haven, Yale University Press.

DORSON, RICHARD M.
1963   Current folklore theories. Current
        Anthropology 4:93–112.

DOVRING, FOLKE
1960   History as a social science; an es-
        say on the nature and purpose of
        historical studies. The Hague,
        Martinus Nijhoff.

DOWNS, JAMES F.
1960   Domestication: an examination of
        the changing social relationships
        between man and animals. Kroe-
        ber Anthropological Society Pa-
        pers 22:18–67.

DRIVER, HAROLD E.
1956   An integration of functional, evo-
        lutionary, and historical theory by
        means of correlations. Indiana
        University Publications in Anthro-
        pology and Linguistics 12:1–37.
        (Supplement to International Jour-
        nal of American Linguistics 22.)

DU BOIS, CORA
1944   The people of Alor: a socio-psy-
        chological study of an East Indian
        island. Minneapolis, University of
        Minnesota Press.

1960   The people of Alor. Cambridge,
        Harvard University Press.

DUMOND, D. E.
1961   Swidden agriculture and the rise
        of Maya civilization. Southwest-
        ern Journal of Anthropology
        17:301–316.

DUNDES, ALAN
1962a   Earthdiver: creation of the myth-
        opoeic male. American Anthro-
        pologist 64:1032–1051.

1962b   From etic to emic units in the
        structural study of folktales.
        Journal of American Folklore
        75:95–105.

1964   The morphology of North Ameri-
        can Indian folktales. Helsinki,
        Suomalainen Tiedeakatemia.

1965   The study of folklore. Englewood
        Cliffs, Prentice-Hall.

DURKHEIM, ÉMILE
1938   The rules of sociological method.
        Glencoe, Free Press.

1947a   The division of labor in society.
        Glencoe, Free Press.

1947b   The elementary forms of the reli-
        gious life, translated by Joseph
        Ward Swain. Glencoe, Free Press.

DURKHEIM, É. AND M. MAUSS
1963   Primitive classification, Rodney
        Needham, ed. London, Cohen and
        West.

DYEN, ISIDORE
1956   Language distribution and migra-
        tion theory. Language 32:611–
        626.

ECKHARDT, A. ROY
1961   The contribution of nomothesis in
        the science of man. The American
        Scientist 49:76–87.

EDEL, ABRAHAM
1963   Method in ethical theory. New
        York, Bobbs-Merrill.

EDEL, MAY M.
1944   Stability in Tillamook folklore.
        Journal of American Folklore
        57:116–127.

EELLS, K., A. DAVIS, R. J. HAVINGHURST et al.
1950   Intelligence and cultural differ-
        ences. Chicago, University of Chi-
        cago Press.

EGGAN, DOROTHY
1961   Dream analysis. In Kaplan 1961.

EGGAN, FRED

1950   Social organization of the western pueblos. Chicago, University of Chicago Press.

1954   Social anthropology and the method of controlled comparison. American Anthropologist 56:743–763.

1955a   The Cheyenne and Arapaho kinship system. *In* Social anthropology of North American tribes, Fred Eggan, ed. Chicago, University of Chicago Press.

1955b   Social anthropology: methods and results. *In* Social anthropology of North American tribes, Fred Eggan, ed. Chicago, University of Chicago Press.

EHRLICH, EUGEN

1936   Fundamental principles of the sociology of law, translated by Walter E. Mell. Cambridge, Harvard University Press.

EISENSTADT, S. N.

1956   From generation to generation: age groups and social structure. Glencoe, Free Press.

1961   Anthropological studies of complex societies. Current Anthropology 2:201–222.

ELKINS, S.

1961   Slavery and personality. *In* Kaplan 1961.

EMBER, MELVIN

1962   The relationship between economic and political development in non-industrialized societies. Ethnology 2:228–248.

EMBREE, J.

1946   Suye Mura: a Japanese village. London, Kegan Paul.

EMMONS, G. T.

1911   Native account of the meeting between La Perouse and the Tlingit. American Anthropologist n.s. 11:294–298.

ENGELS, FRIEDRICH

1926   The peasant war in Germany, translated by Moissaye J. Olgin. New York, International Publishers. (Originally published 1850.)

ESCARRA, JEAN

1936   Le Droit Chinois. Peking, Edition Henri Vetch.

EVANS, FRANCIS C.

1956   Ecosystem as the basic unit in ecology. Science 123:1127–1128.

EVANS-PRITCHARD, E. E.

1936   Witchcraft, oracles and magic among the Azande. Oxford, Clarendon Press.

1940   The Nuer. New York, Oxford University Press.

1964   Social anthropology and other essays. Glencoe, Free Press.

EVANS-PRITCHARD, E. E. *et al.*

1954   The institutions of primitive society. Glencoe, Free Press.

EWERS, JOHN C.

1955   The horse in Blackfoot Indian culture, with comparative material from other western tribes. Bureau of American Ethnology Bulletin 159.

EYSENCK, H.

1953   The structure of human personality. London, Methuen.

FALLDING, HAROLD

1965   A proposal for the empirical study of values. American Sociological Review 30:223–233.

FENTON, WILLIAM N.

1949   Collecting materials for a political history of the Six Nations. Proceedings of the American Philosophical Society 93:233–238.

FERDON, EDWIN N.

1959   Agricultural potential and the development of culture. Southwestern Journal of Anthropology 15:1–19.

FIELD, M. M.
1937   Religion and medicine of the Ga people. Oxford, Oxford University Press.

FIRTH, RAYMOND
1936   We, the Tikopia. London, Allen and Unwin.

1939   Primitive Polynesian economy. London, Routledge.

1946   Malay fishermen: their peasant economy. London.

1956a   Elements of social organization. London, Watts and Co.

1956b   Man and culture: an evaluation of
1964   the work of Bronislaw Malinowski. New ‑York, Harper, Torchbook TB1133.

1959   Economics of the New Zealand Maori. Wellington, New Zealand, R. E. Owen, Government Printer.

FIRTH, RAYMOND AND B. S. YAMEY (EDS.)
1964   Capital, saving and credit in peasant societies. Chicago, Aldine.

FISCHER, ANN
1965   History and current status of the Hauma Indians. Midcontinent American Studies Journal, Vol. 6, No. 2.

FISCHER, J. L.
1955   Language and folktale in Truk and Ponape: a study in cultural integration. Doctoral thesis (typed), Department of Social Relations (Social Anthropology). Cambridge, Harvard University.

1956   The position of men and women in Truk and Ponape. Journal of American Folklore 69:55-62.

1957   Totemism on Truk and Ponape. American Anthropologist 59:250-265.

1958a   The classification of residence in censuses. American Anthropologist 60:508-517.

1958b   Social influences on the choice of a linguistic variant. Word 14:47-56.

1959   Reply to Raulet. American Anthropologist 61:679-681.

1960   Sequence and structure in folktales. Selected papers, 5th International Congress of Anthropological and Ethnological Sciences: 442-446.

1963   The sociopsychological analysis of folktales. Current Anthropology 4:235-295.

FISCHER, J. L., ANN FISCHER, AND FRANK MAHONY
1959   Totemism and allergy. International Journal of Social Psychiatry 5:33-40.

FISCHER, J. L. AND MARC SWARTZ
1960   Sociopsychological aspects of some Trukese and Ponapean love songs. Journal of American Folklore 73:218-224.

FLAVELL, H. H.
1963   The developmental psychology of Jean Piaget. Princeton, Van Nostrand.

FLETCHER, ALICE C.
1885   Indian home building. Publications of the Women's National Indian Association.

FLETCHER, ALICE C. AND FRANCIS LA FLESCHE
1911   The Omaha tribe. 27th Annual Report of the Bureau of American Ethnology: 17-654.

FODOR, JERRY A. AND JERROLD J. KATZ
1964   The structure of language: readings in the philosophy of language. Englewood Cliffs, Prentice-Hall.

FORBES, R J.
1958   Man the maker. London and New York, Abelard-Schuman.

FORD, CLELLAN S. AND FRANK A. BEACH
1952   Patterns of sexual behavior. New York, Harper.

FORDE, C. DARYLL
1934   Habitat, economy and society: a geographical introduction to ethnology. London, Methuen.

1948   Habitat, economy and society. London, Methuen.

1963   Habitat, economy and society. New York, Dutton.

FORMAN, W. B. AND PHILIP DARK
1960   Benin art. London.

FORTES, MEYER
1949   The web of kinship among the Tallensi. London, Oxford University Press.

FORTES, MEYER AND E. E. EVANS-PRITCHARD (EDS.)
1940   African political systems. London, Oxford University Press.

FOSBERG, F. R. (ED.)
1963   Man's place in the island ecosystem. Honolulu, Bishop Museum Press.

FOSTER, GEORGE M.
1942   A primitive Mexican economy. Monographs of the American Ethnological Society, No. 5.

1948a   Empire's children: the people of Tzintzuntzan. Smithsonian Institution, Institute of Social Anthropology Publication No. 6.

1948b   Some implications of modern Mexican mold-made pottery. Southwestern Journal of Anthropology 4:356–370.

1960/61 Inter-personal relations in peasant society. Human Organization, Winter No. 4.

1962   Traditional cultures and the impact of technological change. New York, Harper.

FRAKE, CHARLES O.
1962a   Cultural ecology and ethnography. American Anthropologist 64:53–59.

1962b   The ethnographic study of cognitive systems. *In* Anthropology and human behavior, T. Gladwin and

W. C. Sturtevant, eds. Washington, D.C., Anthropological Society of Washington.

1964a   Further discussion of Burling. American Anthropologist 66:119.

1964b   Notes on queries in ethnography. American Anthropologist 66:99–131 (No. 3, Part II, Special Publication).

FRAENKEL, GERD
1961   Constructed languages in fiction. Indiana University.

FRANKFORT, H. AND H. A., JOHN A. WILSON et al.
1946   The intellectual adventure of ancient man: an essay on speculative thought in the ancient Near East. Chicago, University of Chicago Press.

FRAZER, JAMES GEORGE
1922   The golden bough. London, Macmillan.

FREEMAN, LINTON C. AND ROBERT F. WINCH
1957   Societal complexity: an empirical test of a typology of societies. American Journal of Sociology 62:461–466.

FRENCH, DAVID
1962   Ambiguity and irrelevance in factional leadership. *In* Intergroup relations and leadership, M. Sherif, ed. New York, Wiley.

1963   The relationship of anthropology to studies in perception and cognition. *In* Psychology: a study of a science, S. Koch, ed., Vol. 6. New York, McGraw-Hill.

FREUD, ANNA
1946   The ego and the mechanisms of defense. New York, International Universities Press.

FREUD, SIGMUND
1925   Some character-types met with in psycho-analytic work. *In* Collected papers, Vol. 4. London, Hogarth Press.

1939   Civilization and its discontents, translated by Joan Riviere. London, Hogarth Press. (Originally published 1929.)

1949a   The future of an illusion, translated by W. D. Robson-Scott. New York, Liveright. (Originally published 1928.)

1949b   Moses and monotheism, translated by Katherine Jones. New York, Knopf. (Originally published 1939.)

1950   Totem and taboo: some points of agreement between the mental lives of savages and neurotics, translated by James Strachey. London, Routledge and Kegan Paul. (Originally published 1912–1913.)

FRIEDL, ERNESTINE
1956   Persistence in Chippewa culture and personality. American Anthropologist 58:814–825.

1962   Vasilika: a village in modern Greece. New York, Holt, Rinehart and Winston, Case Studies in Cultural Anthropology Series.

1964   Lagging emulation in post-peasant society. American Anthropologist 66:569–586.

FROMM, ERICH
1951   The forgotten language. New York, Rinehart.

FÜRER-HAIMENDORF, CHRISTOPH VON
1943   The Chenchus: jungle folk of the Deccan. London, Macmillan.

1962   The Apa Tanis and their neighbours. A primitive civilization of the eastern Himalayas. London, Routledge.

GEARING, FRED
1962   Priests and warriors: social structures for Cherokee politics in the eighteenth century. American Anthropological Association Memoir No. 93.

1963   Idioms of human interaction: moral and technical orders. In Proceedings of the American Ethnological Society 1963. University of Washington Press.

GEERTZ, CLIFFORD
1963   Agricultural involution. The process of ecological change in Indonesia. Berkeley, University of California Press.

GEERTZ, CLIFFORD (ED.)
1963   Old societies and new states. Glencoe, Free Press.

GERTH, H. AND C. W. MILLS
1953   Character and social character: the psychology of social institutions. London, Routledge and Kegan Paul.

GIBSON, CHARLES
1964   The Aztecs under Spanish rule: a history of the Indians of the Valley of Mexico, 1519–1810. Stanford, Stanford University Press.

GILBERT, WILLIAM H., JR.
1955   Eastern Cherokee social organization. In Social anthropology of North American tribes, Fred Eggan, ed. Chicago, University of Chicago Press.

GILLIN, JOHN PAUL
1934   Crime and punishment among the Barama River Carib of British Guiana. American Anthropologist 36:331–344.

1942   Acquired drives in culture contact. American Anthropologist 44:545–554.

GINSBERG, M.
1956   National character and national sentiments. In Essays in sociology and social philosophy, Vol. 1. London, Heinemann.

GLADWIN, THOMAS
1955   Personal communication.

GLADWIN, THOMAS AND SEYMOUR B. SARASON
1953   Truk: man in Paradise. Viking Fund Publications in Anthropology No. 20.

GLAZER, NATHAN AND DANIEL PATRICK MOYNIHAN
1963   Beyond the melting pot. Cambridge, M.I.T. Press and Harvard University Press.

GLEASON, H. A., JR.

1961   An introduction to descriptive linguistics, rev. ed. New York, Holt, Rinehart and Winston.

GLUCKMAN, MAX

1944   The logic of African science and witchcraft: an appreciation of Evans-Pritchard's "Witchcraft, oracles and magic among the Azande" of the Sudan. Bobbs-Merrill Reprint Series, A-87. (Reprinted from the Rhodes-Livingstone Institute Journal.)

1955   The judicial process amongst the Barotse of Northern Rhodesia. Manchester, Manchester University Press.

GLUCKMAN, MAX AND FRED EGGAN (EDS.)

1965   Introduction. *In* The relevance of models for social anthropology. New York, Praeger.

GOFFMAN, ERVING

1959   The presentation of self in everyday life. Garden City, Doubleday.

GOGGIN, JOHN M.

1967   Spanish majolica in the New World. Yale University Publications in Anthropology No. 72.

GOGGIN, JOHN M. AND WILLIAM C. STURTEVANT

1964   The Calusa: a stratified, nonagricultural society (with notes on sibling marriage). *In* Explorations in cultural anthropology: essays in honor of George Peter Murdock, Ward H. Goodenough, ed. New York, McGraw-Hill.

GOLDENWEISER, ALEXANDER

1916   Religion and society: a critique of Émile Durkheim's theory of the origin and nature of religion. Journal of Philosophy. (Reprinted in Early civilization, New York, 1922.)

1933   History, psychology, and culture. New York, Knopf.

GOLDMAN, IRVING

1955   Status rivalry and cultural evolution in Polynesia. American Anthropologist 57:680–697.

GOLDSCHMIDT, WALTER (ED.)

1959   The anthropology of Franz Boas. American Anthropological Association Memoir No. 89.

1965   Theory and strategy in the study of cultural adaptability. American Anthropologist 67:402–408.

GOLDSTEIN, KENNETH S.

1964   A guide for field workers in folklore. Hatboro, Folklore Associates.

GOODE, WILLIAM J.

1963   World revolution and family patterns. New York, Free Press of Glencoe.

GOODENOUGH, WARD H.

1951   Property, kin and community on Truk. Yale Publications in Anthropology No. 46.

1955   Personal communication.

1956a   Componential analysis and the study of meaning. Language 32:195–216.

1956b   Residence rules. Southwestern Journal of Anthropology 12:22–37.

1957   Cultural anthropology and linguistics. *In* Report of the seventh annual round table meeting on linguistics and language study, Paul L. Garvin, ed. Georgetown University Monograph Series on Language and Linguistics 9:167–173.

1963a   Cooperation in change. New York, Russell Sage Foundation.

1963b   Some applications of Gutmann scale analysis to ethnography and culture theory. Southwestern Journal of Anthropology 19:235–250.

GOODNOW, JACQUELINE J.

1962   A test of milieu effects with some of Piaget's tasks. Psychological monographs: general and applied. Whole No. 555, Vol. 76, No. 36.

GOODY, JACK
1961   Religion and ritual: the definitional problem. British Journal of Sociology 12:42–164.

GORER, GEOFFREY
1938   Himalayan village: an account of the Lepchas of Sikkim. London, M. Joseph, Ind.

1943   Themes in Japanese culture. Transactions of the New York Academy of Sciences, Series II, Vol. 5.

GORER, G. AND J. RICKMAN
1950   The people of great Russia: a psychological study. New York, Chanticleer Press.

GOTTSCHALK, L., C. KLUCKHOHN, AND R. ANGELL
1945   The use of personal documents in history, anthropology, and sociology. Social Science Research Council Bulletin, No. 53.

GOULD, J. AND W. L. KALB (EDS.)
1964   A dictionary of the social sciences. London, Tavistock.

GOULDNER, ALVIN W. AND RICHARD A. PETERSON
1962   Technology and the moral order. Indianapolis, Bobbs-Merrill.

GRAEBNER, FRITZ
1931   Causality and culture. *In* The making of man, V. F. Calverton, ed. New York, Random House, Modern Library.

GRAZIOSI, PAOLO
1960   Paleolithic art. London, Faber and Faber.

GREENBERG, JOSEPH H.
1954   Concerning inferences from linguistic to nonlinguistic data. *In* Language and culture: proceedings of a conference on the interrelations of language and other aspects of culture, Harry Hoijer, ed. American Anthropological Association Memoir No. 79:3–19.

GREENOUGH, C. N.
1940   Characters of nations. Massachusetts Historical Society Proceedings, October 1932–May 1936, Vol. LXV.

GREGOR, A. J. AND D. A. McPHERSON
1965   A study of susceptibility to geometric illusions among cultural subgroups of Australian aborigines. Psychologia Africana 11:1–13.

GUILDFORD, J. P.
1959   Personality. New York, McGraw-Hill.

GULLIVER, P. H.
1955   The family herds. A study of two pastoral tribes in East Africa: the Jie and Turkana. London, Routledge and Kegan Paul.

GUNTHER, ERNA
1962   Northwest Coast Indian art. Seattle World's Fair Catalogue.

HADDON, A. C. (ED.)
1901   Reports of the Cambridge anthropological expedition to the Torres Straits, Vols. 1–2. Cambridge, The University Press.

HALL, C. S. AND G. LINDZEY
1957   Theories of personality. New York, Wiley.

HALL, EDWARD T.
1959   The silent language. Garden City, Doubleday.

HALLOWELL, A. IRVING
1949   The size of Algonkian hunting territories: a function of ecological adjustment. American Anthropologist 51:35–45.

1954   Psychology and anthropology. *In* For a science of social man: convergences in anthropology, psychology and sociology, J. Gillin, ed. New York, Macmillan.

1955   Culture and experience. Philadelphia, University of Pennsylvania Press.

HAMBRUCH, PAUL
1932   Ponape. *In* Ergebnisse der Sudsee-Expedition 1908–1910, ed. G. Thi-

lenius. Series II B, v. 7, subv. 2. Hamburg, Friedrichsen, De Gruyter.

HAMBRUCH, PAUL AND A. EILERS
1936   Ponape. *In* Ergebnisse der Sudsee-Expedition 1908–1910, ed. G. Thilenius. Series II B, v. 7, subv. 3. Hamburg, Friedrichsen, De Gruyter.

HAMMEL, E. A.
1965   Review of the ceque system of Cuzco, by R. T. Zuidema. American Anthropologist 67:780–785.

HAMMOND, PHILIP (ED.)
1964   Sociologists at work. New York, Basic Books.

HANDY, E. S. CRAIGHILL
1923   The native culture in the Marquesas. Bernice P. Bishop Museum Bulletin No. 9.

HANDY, ROLLO AND PAUL KURTZ
1963   A current appraisal of the behavioral sciences. Great Barrington, Mass., Behavior Research Council.

HANKS, LUCIEN M.
1954   A psychological exploration in the Blackfoot language. International Journal of American Linguistics 20:195–205.

HARE, R. M.
1963   Freedom and reason. Oxford, Clarendon Press.

HARING, DOUGLAS
1956   Comment on field techniques in ethnology: illustrated by a survey in the Ryukyu Islands. *In* Personal character and cultural milieu, D. Haring, ed. Syracuse, Syracuse University Press.

HARLEY, GEORGE W.
1950   Masks as agents of social control. Peabody Museum of American Archaeology and Ethnology Papers, Vol. 32, No. 2.

HARRIS, MARVIN
1959   The economy has no surplus? American Anthropologist 61:185–199.

1964   The nature of cultural things. New York, Random House.

1965   The myth of the sacred cow. *In* Leeds and Vayda 1965.

HART, C. W. M. AND ARNOLD R. PILLING
1960   The Tiwi of North Australia. New York, Holt, Rinehart and Winston.

HART, DONN V.
1964   Riddles in Filipino folklore: an anthropological analysis. Syracuse, Syracuse University Press.

HARTLAND, E. SIDNEY
1924   Primitive law. London, Methuen and Co.

HATT, GUDMUND
1949   Asiatic influences in American folklore. Copenhagen, I Komission Hos Munksgaard.

HAWLEY, AMOS H.
1944   Ecology and human ecology. Social Forces 22:398–405.

HEIZER, ROBERT AND MARTIN BAUMHOFF
1962   Prehistoric rock art of Nevada and eastern California. Berkeley, University of California Press.

HENRY, JULES
1963   Culture against man. New York, Random House.

HENRY, J. AND M. E. SPIRO
1953   Psychological techniques: projective tests in field work. *In* Anthropology today, A. L. Kroeber, ed. Chicago, University of Chicago Press.

HENRY, WILLIAM E.
1961   Projective tests in cross cultural research. *In* Kaplan 1961.

HERSKOVITS, MELVILLE J.
1938a   Acculturation. Gloucester, Mass., Peter Smith.

1938b   Dahomey: an ancient West African kingdom, Vol. 1. New York, J. J. Augustine.

1950   Man and his works. New York, Knopf.

1951   Tender- and tough-minded anthropology and the study of values in culture. Southwestern Journal of Anthropology 7:22–32.

1952   Economic anthropology. New York, Knopf.

1959   Past developments and present currents in ethnology. American Anthropologist 61:389–397.

HERSKOVITS, MELVILLE J. AND FRANCES S.
1958   Dahomean narrative. Evanston, Ill., Northwestern University Press.

HEWES, GORDON W.
1955   World distribution of certain postural traits. American Anthropologist 57:231–244.

HIATT, L. R.
1962   Local organization among the Australian Aborigines. Oceania 32:267–286.

HICKERSON, HAROLD
1963   The genesis of the theory of the particularity of northern Algonkian hunters. Manuscript.

1965   The Virginia deer and inter-tribal buffer zones in the Upper Mississippi Valley. *In* Leeds and Vayda 1965.

1967   Some implications of the theory of the particularity, or "atomism," of the Northern Algonkians. Current Anthropology (in press).

HIMMELHEBER, HANS
1963   Personality and technique of African sculptors. *In* Technique and personality, Margaret Mead, Junius B. Bird and Hans Himmelheber. New York Museum of Primitive Art; distributed by the New York Graphic Society.

HITCHCOCK, JOHN T. AND PATRICIA J.
1960   Some considerations for the prospective ethnographic cinematographer. American Anthropologist 62:656–674.

HJELMSLEV, LOUIS
1961   Prolegomena to a theory of language, translated by Francis J. Whitfield, rev. ed. Madison, University of Wisconsin Press.

HOBHOUSE, L. T.
1906   Morals in evolution. London, Chapman and Hall Ltd.

HOCKETT, CHARLES F.
1958   A course in modern linguistics. New York, Macmillan.

HOCKETT, CHARLES F. AND ROBERT ASCHER
1964   The human revolution. Current Anthropology 5:135–168.

HOEBEL, E. ADAMSON
1940   The political organization and lawways of the Comanche Indians. Memoirs of the American Anthropological Association No. 54.

1960   The Cheyennes: Indians of the Great Plains. New York, Holt, Rinehart and Winston, Case Studies in Cultural Anthropology Series.

1961   Three studies in African law. Stanford University Law Review 13: 418–442.

HOENIGSWALD, HENRY M.
1960   Language change and linguistic reconstruction. Chicago, University of Chicago Press.

HOGBIN, IAN
1964   A Guadalcanal society: the Kaoka Speakers. New York, Holt, Rinehart and Winston, Case Studies in Cultural Anthropology Series.

HOLLEMAN, J. F.
1952   Shona customary law. London, Oxford University Press.

HOLMBERG, ALLAN R.
1950   Nomads of the Long Bow. Washington, Smithsonian Institution, Institute of Social Anthropology Publication No. 10.

HOLMBERG, ALLAN R. AND HENRY F. DOBYNS
1962   The process of accelerating community change. Human Organization 21:107–124.

HOLMES, O. W., JR.
1881   The common law. Boston, Little, Brown.

1886   The law as a profession. American Law Review 20:741–742.

1897   The path of law. Harvard Law Review 10:457–478.

HOMANS, GEORGE CASPAR
1942   English villagers of the thirteenth century. Cambridge, Harvard University Press.

HOUGH, WALTER
1926   Fire as an agent in human culture. Washington, Smithsonian Institution, United States National Museum Bulletin 139.

HOWELL, P. P.
1954   A manual of Nuer law. London, Oxford University Press.

HSU, FRANCIS L. K.
1952   Religion, science, and human crises: a study on China in transition and its implications for the West. London, Routledge and Kegan Paul.

1961   Psychological anthropology in the behavioral sciences. *In* Psychological anthropology: approaches to culture and personality, F. L. K. Hsu, ed. Homewood, Ill., Dorsey Press.

1963   Clan, caste, and club. Princeton, Van Nostrand.

1964   Rethinking the concept primitive. Current Anthropology 5:169–178.

HUDSON, W.
1960   Pictorial depth perception in subcultural groups in Africa. Journal of Social Psychology 52:183.

HUGHES, H. STUART
1963   History, the humanities, and anthropological change. Current Anthropology 4:140–145. (Reprinted in pp. 22–41 of his History as art and as science: twin vistas on the past, World Prespectives Vol. 32. New York, Harper and Row, 1964.)

HULTON, PAUL, AND DAVID BEERS QUINN (EDS.)
1964   The American drawings of John White, 1577–1590, with drawings of European and Oriental subjects, 2 vols. London, The Trustees of the British Museum, and Chapel Hill, University of North Carolina Press.

HUNTINGTON, ELLSWORTH
1915   Civilization and climate. New Haven, Yale University Press.

1945   Mainsprings of civilization. New York, Wiley.

HUTCHINSON, G. E. AND E. S. DEEVEY, JR.
1949   Ecological studies on populations. *In* Survey of biological progress, Vol. I, George S. Avery, Jr., ed. New York, Academic Press.

HYMAN, HERBERT H.
1953   The values systems of different classes: a social psychological contribution to the analysis of stratification. *In* Class, status and power, R. Bendix and S. M. Lipset, eds. Glencoe, Free Press.

HYMES, DELL H.
1964a   Discussion of Burling's paper. American Anthropologist 66:116–119.

1964b   Introduction: toward ethnographies of communication. American Anthropologist 66:1–34.

1964c   Language in culture and society: a reader in linguistics and anthropology. New York, Harper and Row.

HYMES, DELL AND JOHN GUMPERZ (EDS.)
1964   The ethnography of communication. American Anthropologist 66; No. 6, Part 2.

INKELES, A. AND D. J. LEVINSON
1954   National character: the study of modal personality and sociocultural systems. In Handbook of social psychology, Vol. 2, G. Lindzey, ed. Cambridge, Addison-Wesley.

JACOBS, MELVILLE
1959   The content and style of an oral literature. Chicago, University of Chicago Press.

1960   The people are coming soon. Seattle, University of Washington Press.

1964   Pattern in cultural anthropology. Homewood, Ill., Dorsey Press.

JAHODA, G.
1956   Assessment of abstract behavior in a non-western culture. Journal of Abnormal and Social Psychology 53:237–243.

1965/
1966   Geometric illusions and environment: a study in Ghana. British Journal of Psychology (in press).

JOOS, MARTIN
1957   Readings in linguistics: the development of descriptive linguistics in America since 1925. New York, American Council of Learned Societies.

JUNG, C. G.
1923   Psychological types of the psychology of individuation. London, Kegan Paul, Trench, Trubner & Co.

JUNKER, BUFORD
1960   Field work. Chicago, University of Chicago Press.

JUNOD, HENRI
1927   The life of a South African tribe, Vol. 1. London, David Nutt.

KAPLAN, ABRAHAM
1964   The conduct of inquiry. San Francisco, Chandler Publishing.

KAPLAN, BERT
1961   Cross-cultural use of projective techniques. In Psychological anthropology: approaches to culture and personality, F. L. K. Hsu, ed. Homewood, Ill., Dorsey Press.

1962   Psychological themes in Zuni mythology and Zuni TAT's. The Psychoanalytic Study of Society 2:255–262.

KAPLAN, BERT (ED.)
1961   Studying personality cross-culturally. Evanston, Ill., Row, Peterson and Co.

KARDINER, A.
1939   The individual and society. New York, Columbia University Press.

KARDINER, A. et al.
1945   The psychological frontiers of society. New York, Columbia University Press.

KEESING, FELIX M.
1953   Culture change. An analysis and bibliography of anthropological sources to 1952. Stanford, Stanford University Press.

1958   Cultural anthropology: the science of custom. New York, Rinehart.

KERNER, GEORGE C.
1966   The revolution in ethical theory. Oxford, Clarendon Press.

KLUCKHOHN, CLYDE
1945   Field techniques and methods. In The use of personal documents in history, anthropology and sociology, Gottschalk, Kluckhohn, and Angell, eds. New York, Social Science Research Council.

1949a   Mirror for man. New York, McGraw-Hill.

1949b   The philosophy of the Navaho Indians. In Ideological differences and world order, F. S. C. Northrop, ed. New Haven, Yale University Press.

1951   Values and value orientations in the theory of action. In Toward a general theory of action, Talcott Parsons and Edward A. Shils, eds. Cambridge, Harvard University Press.

1954   Culture and behavior. In Handbook of social psychology, G. Lindzey, ed. Vol. II. Cambridge, Mass., Addison-Wesley.

1955   Anthropology. In What is science, James R. Newman, ed. New York, Simon and Schuster.

KLUCKHOHN, CLYDE AND DOROTHEA LEIGHTON
1946   The Navaho. Cambridge, Harvard University Press.

KLUCKHOHN, FLORENCE R.
1940   The participant-observer technique in small communities. American Journal of Sociology 46:331–343.

1956a   Dominant and variant value orientations. *In* Personaliity in nature, society and culture, Clyde Kluckhohn, Henry A. Murray and David M. Schneider, eds. New York, Knopf.

1956b   Value orientations. *In* Towards a unified theory of human behavior, R. R. Grinker, ed. New York, Basic Books.

KLUCKHOHN, F. AND F. L. STRODTBECK
1961   Variations in value orientations. Evanston, Ill., Row, Peterson and Co.

KNIGHT, ROLF
1965   A re-examination of hunting, trapping, and territoriality among the Algonkian Indians. *In* Leeds and Vayda 1965.

KRÄMER, A.
1932   Truk; Südsee expedition 1908–1910, Ser. II B5. Hamburg, Friedrichsen de Gruyter.

KROEBER, ALFRED L.
1917   The superorganic. American Anthropologist 19:41–54.

1923   Anthropology. New York, Harcourt, Brace.

1925   Handbook of the Indians of California. Bureau of American Ethnology Bulletin 78. Washington.

1939   Cultural and natural areas of native North America. University of California Publications in American Archaeology and Ethnology, Vol. 38.

1948   Anthropology. New York, Harcourt, Brace.

1951   A Mohave historical epic. University of California, Anthropological Records 11:71–176.

1959   The history and personality of anthropology. American Anthropologist 61:398–404.

KROEBER, A. L. AND CLYDE KLUCKHOHN
1952 &   Culture: a critical review of concepts and definitions. Papers of the Peabody Museum of American
1963

Archaeology and Ethnology, Harvard University, Vol. 47, No. 1. Also available in 1963 ed., Vintage Books, New York, Random House.

KROEBER, THEODORA
1961   Ishi in two worlds. Berkeley, University of California Press.

KUTSCHE, PAUL
1963   The Tsali legend: culture heroes and historiography. Ethnohistory 10:329–357.

LAGUNA, FREDERICA DE
1960   The story of a Tligit community: a problem in the relationship between archeological, ethnological and historical methods. Bureau of American Ethnology Bulletin 172.

LANCASTER, LORRAINE
1958   Kinship in Anglo-Saxon society. British Journal of Sociology 9:230–250, 359–377.

LANDES, RUTH
1961   The Ojibwa of Canada. *In* Mead 1961.

LATTIMORE, OWEN
1963   Studies in frontier history: collected papers, 1928–1958. London, Oxford University Press.

LAZARUS, M. AND H. STEINTHAL
1860   Einleitende gedanken uber volkerpsychologie. Zeitschrift fur Volkerpsychologie 1.

LEACH, EDMUND R.
1960a   The frontiers of "Burma," with comment by Isidore Dyen. Comparative Studies in Society and History 3:49–73.

1960b   Review of Udy 1959. American Sociological Review 25:136–138.

1961   Rethinking anthropology. London School of Economics. Monographs on Social Anthropology 22. The Athone Press, University of London.

1965   Culture and social cohesion: an anthropologist's view. *In* Science and culture, Gerlad Holton, ed. Daedalus 95.

LEE, DOROTHY
1949   Being and value in a primitive culture. Journal of Philosophy 46:401–415.

1950   Notes on the conception of self among the Wintu Indians. Journal of Abnormal and Social Psychology 45:538–543.

LEEDS, ANTHONY AND ANDREW VAYDA (EDS.)
1965   Man, culture and animals: the role of animals in human ecological adjustments. Washington, American Association for the Advancement of Science.

LEHMANN, WINFRED P.
1962   Historical linguistics: and introduction. New York, Holt, Rinehart and Winston.

LEIGHTON, A. H. AND D. C.
1949   Gregorio, the hand trembler: a psychobiological personality study of a Navaho Indian. Papers of the Peabody Museum of American Archaeology and Ethnology, Vol. XL, No. 1.

LESLIE, CHARLES (ED.)
1960   The anthropology of folk religion. New York, Random House, Vintage Books (C105).

LESSA, WILLIAM A. AND EVON Z. VOGT (EDS.)
1962   Reader in comparative religion: an anthropological approach. Evanston, Ill., Row, Peterson and Co.

LeVINE, R. A.
1960   The role of the family in authority systems: a cross-cultural application of stimulus-generalization theory. Behavioral Science 5:291–296.

LEVINE, MORTON
1957   Prehistoric art and ideology. American Anthropologist 59:949–964.

LEVI-STRAUSS, CLAUDE
1955   The structural study of myth. Journal of American Folklore 68:428–444.

1962   Social structure. In Anthropology today: selections, Sol Tax, ed.

Chicago, University of Chicago Press.

1963   Structural anthropology, translated by Claire Jacobson and Brooke Grundfest Schoepf. New York, Basic Books.

LEVY, MARION
1949   The family revolution in modern China. Cambridge, Harvard University Press.

LEVY-BRUHL, L.
1923   Primitive mentality. New York, Macmillan.

1926   How natives think. London, Allen and Unwin.

LEWIS, I. M.
1962   Historical aspects of genealogies in northern Somali social structure. Journal of African History 3:35–48.

LEWIS, OSCAR
1951   Life in a Mexican village: Tepoztlan restudied. Urbana, University of Illinois Press.

1953   Controls and experiments in field work. In Anthropology today, A. L. Kroeber, ed. Chicago, University of Chicago Press.

1956   Comparisons in cultural anthropology. In Current anthropology, W. L. Thomas, Jr., ed. Chicago, University of Chicago Press. (Reprinted in Moore 1961.)

1959   Five families: Mexican case studies in the culture of poverty. New York, Basic Books.

1960   Tepoztlan: village in Mexico. New York, Holt, Rinehart and Winston.

LHOTE, HENRI
1959   The search for the Tassili frescoes. New York, Dutton.

LI, AN-CHE
1937   Zuni: some observations and queries. American Anthropologist 39:62–76.

LINDGREN, E. J.
1938   An example of culture contact without conflict: reindeer tungus and Cossacks of northwestern Manchuria. American Anthropologist 40:605–662.

LINDZEY, GARDNER
1961   Projective techniques and cross-cultural research. New York, Appleton-Century-Crofts.

1964   Genetics and the social sciences. Items (Social Science Research Council) 18:29–35.

LINTON, RALPH
1933   The Tanala: a hill tribe in Madagascar. Anthropological Series, Field Museum of Natural History, Vol. 22.

1936   The study of man. New York, D. Appleton-Century Co.

1937   One hundred per cent American. The American Mercury 40:427–429.

1939   Marquesan culture. *In* Kardiner 1939.

1945   The cultural background of personality. New York, Appleton-Century-Crofts.

LIPS, JULIUS E.
1947   Naskapi law. Transactions of the American Philosophical Society 37:379–492.

LIVINGSTONE, FRANK B.
1958   Anthropological implications of sickle cell gene distribution in West Africa. American Anthropologist 60:533–562.

LLEWELLYN, KARL N. AND E. ADAMSON HOEBEL
1941   The Cheyenne way. Norman, University of Oklahoma Press.

LORD, ALBERT B.
1960   The singer of tales. Cambridge, Harvard University Press.

LOTKA, ALFRED J.
1945   The law of evolution as a maximal principle. Human Biology 17:167–194.

LOUNSBURY, FLOYD G.
1956   A semantic analysis of the Pawnee kinship usage. Language 32:158–194.

1964   The Latin kinship system and its relationship to Roman social organization. Proceedings of the 7th International Congress of Anthropological and Ethnological Sciences, Moscow.

LOWIE, ROBERT H.
1917   Culture and ethnology. New York, Douglas C. McMurtrie.

1933   Queries. American Anthropologist 35:288–296.

1937   The history of ethnological theory. New York, Rinehart and Company.

1940   Native languages as ethnographic tools. American Anthropologist 42:81–89.

1948   Primitive religion. New York, The Universal Library (UL-35), Grosset & Dunlap. (Originally published 1924.)

1956   The Crow Indians. New York, Holt, Rinehart, and Winston (paperback reissue of 1935 edition).

1959   The development of ethnography as a science. *In* Men and moments in the history of science, H. M. Evans, ed. Seattle, University of Washington Press.

LURIE, NANCY OESTREICH
1959   Indian cultural adjustment to European civilization. *In* Seventeenth century America, essays in colonial history, James M. Smith, ed. Chapel Hill, University of North Carolina Press.

n.d.   Alice Fletcher. New York, Encyclopedia of the Social Sciences (in press).

MACRAE, D. G.
1961   Psychology and culture in race relations. *In* Ideology and society: papers in sociology and politics. New York, Free Press of Glencoe.

MAHONY, FRANK
1955   Personal communication.

MAINE, SIR HENRY SUMNER
1950   Ancient law: its connection with
(1861)   the early history of society and its
relation to modern ideas. Oxford.
(Reprint of 1861 edition.)

1963   Ancient law. Boston, Beacon Press.
(Reprint of 1861 edition.)

MALINOWSKI, BRONISLAW
1922   Argonauts of the western Pacific.
London, Routledge.

1927   Sex and repression in savage society. London, Kegan Paul,
Trench, Trubner and Co., Ltd.

1930   The rationalization of anthropology and administration. Africa
3:405–429.

1932   Argonauts of the western Pacific.
New York, Dutton (U.S. edition).

1935   Coral gardens and their magic.
London, Allen and Unwin.

1944   A scientific theory of culture.
Chapel Hill, University of North
Carolina Press.

1945   The dynamics of culture change.
New Haven, Yale University Press.

1948   Magic, science and religion.
Glencoe, Free Press.

1955   Magic, science and religion. In
Magic, science and religion and
other essays. Garden City, Doubleday, Anchor Book (A23).

1959   Crime and custom in savage society. Patterson, N.J., Littlefield,
Adams and Co.

1961   Introduction. In Law and order
in Polynesia by H. Ian Hogbin.
Hamden, Conn., Shoe String Press,
Inc.

MANDELBAUM, DAVID G.
1956   The study of complex civilizations.
In Current anthropology, W. L.
Thomas, ed. Chicago, University
of Chicago Press.

MANDELBAUM, DAVID G. (ED.)
1957   The selected writings of Edward
Sapir in Culture, language and
personality. Berkeley, University
of California Press.

MANNHEIM, KARL
1964   Ideology and utopia: an introduction to the sociology of knowledge.
New York, Harcourt, Brace and
Company, Harvest Book (HB3).
(Originally published 1929 and
1936.)

MAQUET, JAQUES J.
1964   Objectivity in anthropology. Current Anthropology 5:47–55.

MARETT, R. R.
1914   The threshold of religion. New
York, Macmillan.

MARRIOTT, MCKIM
1957   Technological change in overdeveloped rural areas. In Underdeveloped areas, Lyle W. Shannon,
ed. New York, Harper.

MARRIOTT, MCKIM (ED.)
1955   Village India: studies in the little
community. Chicago, University
of Chicago Press. (Also printed
as Memoir 83, American Anthropological Association.)

MARSHALL, LORNA
1960   !Kung Bushman bands. Africa
30:325–355.

MARTINDALE, DON
1962   Social life and cultural change.
Princeton, Van Nostrand.

MARTINET, ANDRE
1955   Economie des changements pho-
netiques. Berne, A. Francke S.A.

MARX, KARL
1959   Excerpts from capital. In Marx
(1899)   and Engels: basic writings on politics and philosophy, Lewis S.
Feuer, ed. Garden City, Doubleday, Anchor Book.

MARX, KARL AND FRIEDRICH ENGELS
1964   Marx and Engels on religion. New
York, Schocken Books (SB67).

MASON, LEONARD
1959   Suprafamilial authority and economic process in Micronesian atolls. Cahiers de l'Institut de Science Economique Appliquee, Serie V, No. 1:87–118.

MASON, OTIS T.
1896   Influence of environment upon human industries or arts. Smithsonian Institution, Annual Report for 1895: 639–665.

1904   Aboriginal American basketry. Washington, Smithsonian Institution, United States National Museum, Report for 1902: 171–548.

1905   Environment. *In* Handbook of American Indians north of Mexico, F. W. Hodge, ed. Smithsonian Institution, Bureau of American Ethnology, Bulletin 30.

MAYBURY-LEWIS, DAVID
1965   The savage and the innocent. London, Evans Brothers, Ltd.

MAYR, ERNST
1958   Behavior and systematics. *In* Behavior and evolution, Anne Roe and George Gaylord Simpson, eds. New Haven, Yale University Press.

1961   Cause and effect in biology. Science 134:1501–1506.

McCALL, DANIEL F.
1964   Africa in time-perspective; a discussion of historical reconstruction from unwritten sources. Boston, Boston University Press, and Legon, Ghana University Press.

McCLELLAND, DAVID
1961   The achieving society. Princeton, Van Nostrand.

McCONNELL, J.
1954   Abstract behavior among the Tepehuan. Journal of Abnormal and Social Psychology 49:109–110.

McEWEN, WILLIAM J.
1963   Forms and problems of validation in social anthropology. Current Anthropology 4:155–183.

McHALE, THOMAS R.
1962   Econocological analysis. Human Organization 21:30–35.

McLENNAN, J. F.
1885   Studies in ancient history. London.

MEAD, MARGARET
1928   Coming of age in Samoa. New York, Wm. Morrow and Co.

1930   Growing up in New Guinea. New York, Wm. Morrow and Co.

1932   The changing culture of an Indian tribe. New York, Columbia University Press.

1938   Native languages as field work tools. American Anthropologist 41:181–205.

1956   Photography in field research. *In* Personal character and cultural milieu, D. Haring, ed. Syracuse, Syracuse University Press.

1961   Anthropology among the sciences. American Anthropologist 63:475–482.

MEAD, MARGARET (ED.)
1955   Cultural patterns and technical change. New York, Mentor.

1961   Cooperation and competition among primitive peoples, rev. ed. Boston, Beacon Press.

MEAD, MARGARET AND RUTH L. BUNZEL (EDS.)
1960   The golden age of American anthropology. New York, George Braziller.

MEAD, MARGARET AND THODA METRAUX
1953   The study of culture at a distance. Chicago, University of Chicago Press.

MEGGERS, BETTY J.
1954   Environmental limitation on the development of culture. American Anthropologist 56:801–824.

MEGGITT, M. J.
1962   Desert people. A study of the Walbiri aborigines of central Australia. Sydney, Angus and Robertson.

1965   The lineage system of the Mae-Enga of New Guinea. Edinburgh, Oliver & Boyd.

MERCADO, S. J., ROGELIO DIAZ GUERRERO, AND R. W. GARDNER
1963   Cognitive control in children of Mexico and the United States. Journal of Social Psychology 59:199–208.

MELIKIAN, L.
1959   Preference for delayed reinforcement: an experimental study among Palestinian Arab refugee children. Journal of Social Psychology 50:81–86.

MERTON, ROBERT K.
1957a   The bearing of sociological theory on empirical research, and The bearing of empirical research on sociological theory. In Social theory and social structure. Glencoe, Free Press.

1957b   Social theory and social structure, rev. ed. Glencoe, Free Press.

MICHAEL, D. N.
1953   A cross-cultural investigation of closure. Journal of Abnormal and Social Psychology 48:225–230.

MIDDLETON, J. AND E. WINTER (EDS.)
1963   Witchcraft and sorcery in East Africa. London, Routledge, Kegan Paul; and New York, Praeger.

MILLER, EDGAR G., JR.
1949   Scientific method and social problems. Science 109:290–291.

MILLS, C. WRIGHT
1959   The sociological imagination. New York, Oxford University Press.

1963a   On knowledge and power. In Power, politics and people, I. Horowitz, ed. New York, Oxford University Press.

1963b   The social role of the intellectual. In Power, politics and people, I. Horowitz, ed. New York, Oxford University Press.

MISCHEL, W.
1958   Preference for delayed reinforcement: an experimental study of a cultural observation. Journal of Abnormal and Social Psychology 56:57–61.

MITFORD, JESSICA
1963   The American way of death. New York, Simon and Schuster.

MOONEY, JAMES
1896   The Ghost Dance religion. Bureau of American Ethnology Annual Reports 14. Washington, D.C., Smithsonian Institution.

MOORE, FRANK W. (ED.)
1961   Readings in cross-cultural methodology. New Haven Human Relations Area File Press.

MOORE, OMAR KHAYYAM
1957   Divination — a new perspective. American Anthropologist 59:69–74.

MORGAN, LEWIS HENRY
1870   Systems of consanguinity and affinity of the human family. Washington, D.C., Smithsonian Institution Contributions to Knowledge.

1963   Ancient society. Cleveland and New York, World Publishing Company, Meridian Books. (Originally published in 1877.)

MORRISON, A.
1946   A child of the Jago. Baltimore, Penguin Books.

MUNDY-CASTLE, A. C. AND G. K. NELSON
1962   A neuropsychological study of the Knysna forest workers. Psychologia Africana 9:240–272.

MURDOCK, GEORGE P.
1940   The cross-cultural survey. American Sociological Review 5:361–370.

1949   Social structure. New York, Macmillan.

1950   Family stability in non-European cultures. Annals of the American Academy of Political and Social Science 270:195–201.

1957   World ethnographic sample. American Anthropologist 59:664–687.

1964   Cultural correlates of the regulation of premarital sex behavior. *In* Process and pattern in culture: essays in honor of Julian Steward, Robert Manners, ed. Chicago, Aldine.

1966   Cross-cultural sampling. Ethnology 5:97–114.

MURDOCK, GEORGE P. (ED.)
1950   Outline of cultural materials. New Haven, Human Relations Area File.

MURPHY, G.
1947   Personality: a biosocial approach to origins and structure. New York, Harper.

MYRDAL, GUNNAR
1953   The relation between social theory and social policy. British Journal of Sociology 4:210–242.

NADEL, S. F.
1937a   A field experiment in racial psychology. British Journal of Psychology 28:195–211.

1937b   Experiments on cultural psychology. Africa 10:421–435.

1951   The foundations of social anthropology. Glencoe, Free Press.

1952   Witchcraft in four African societies: an essay in comparison. American Anthropologist 54:18–29.

NADER, LAURA
1964   An analysis of Zapotec law cases. Ethnology 3:404–419.

NADER, LAURA AND DUANE METZGER
1963   Conflict resolution in two Mexican communities. American Anthropologist 65:584–592.

NAGEL, ERNEST
1961   The structure of science. Problems in the logic of scientific explanation. New York, Harcourt, Brace & World.

NAROLL, RAOUL
1962   Data quality control: a new research technique. New York: Free Press of Glencoe.

1964   On ethnic unit classification. Current Anthropology 5:283–312.

NAROLL, RAOUL AND FREDA
1963   On bias of exotic data. Man 63:24–26.

NASH, DENNISON
1963   The ethnologist as stranger: an essay in the sociology of knowledge. Southwestern Journal of Anthropology 19:149–167.

NASH, MANNING
1958   Machine-age Maya. American Anthropological Association Memoir No. 87.

1964   The organization of economic life. *In* Horizons of anthropology, Sol Tax, ed. Chicago, Aldine.

NEEDHAM, JOSEPH
1956   Science and civilization in China, Vol. 2. Cambridge, Cambridge University Press.

NEILL, WILFRED T.
1955   The identity of Florida's "Spanish Indians." Florida Anthropologist 8:43–57.

NEILSON, W. A. *et al.*
1940   Webster's New International Dictionary of the English Language. Springfield, Mass., G. & C. Merriam Company.

NEWMAN, MARSHALL T.
1953   The application of ecological rules to the racial anthropology of the aboriginal New World. American Anthropologist 55:311–327.

1962   Ecology and nutritional stress in man. American Anthropologist 64:22–34.

NEWMAN, STANLEY
1954   Semantic problems in grammatical system and lexemes: a search for method. *In* Language and culture: proceedings of a conference on the interrelations of language and oth-

er aspects of culture, Harry Hoijer, ed. American Anthropological Association Memoir 79:82–91.

NEWSWEEK
1965   Newsweek Magazine, August 16th, p. 1.

NISSEN, HENRY W.
1958   Axes of behavioral comparison. *In* Behavior and evolution, Anne Roe and G. G. Simpson, eds. New Haven, Yale University Press.

NOËL HUME, IVOR
1963   Here lies Virginia: an archaeologist's view of colonial life and history. New York, Knopf.

NORTHROP, F. S. C.
1947   The logic of the sciences and the humanities. New York, Macmillan.

1951   Philosophical anthropology and world law. Transactions of the New York Academy of Sciences Series II, 14:109–112.

NUNEZ, THERON A., JR.
1963   Tourism, tradition, and acculturation: weekendismo in a Mexican village. Ethnology 2:347–352.

ODUM, EUGENE P.
1959   Fundamentals of ecology, 2nd ed. Philadelphia, W. B. Saunders.

OLIVER, DOUGLAS L.
1955   A Soloman Island society: kinship and leadership among the Siuai of Bougainville. Cambridge, Harvard University Press.

OLIVER, SYMMES C.
1962   Ecology and cultural continuity as contributing factors in the social organization of the Plains Indians. University of California Publications in American Archaeology and Ethnology, Vol. 48, No. 1.

O'NEALE, L. M.
1932   Yurok-Karok basket weavers. Berkeley, University of California Publications in American Archaeology and Ethnology 32:1–182.

1963   Technology and personality. New York, Museum of Primitive Art, Lecture Series No. 2.

OPLER, MORRIS E.
1941   An Apache life-way: the economic, social and religious institutions of the Chiricahua Indians. Chicago, University of Chicago Press.

1945   Themes as dynamic forces in culture. American Journal of Sociology 51.

ORLANSKY, H.
1949   Infant care and personality. Psychological Bulletin 461:1–48.

OSGOOD, CORNELIUS
1940   Informants. *In* Ingalik material culture. London, Oxford University Press.

OVIDIUS NASO, PUBLIUS
1719   Metamorphoses, Daniel Crespin, ed. London, R. Knaplock.

1815   Metamorphoses, translated by John Dryden. New York, R. M'Dermut and D. D. Arden.

PALERM, ANGEL AND ERIC R. WOLF
1957   Ecological potential and cultural development in Meso-America. *In* Studies in human ecology. Pan American Union Social Science Monograph No. 3.

PARRY, N. E.
1932   The Lakhers. London, Macmillan.

PARSONS, ELSIE CLEWS
1936   Mitla, town of the souls. Chicago, University of Chicago Publications in Anthropology.

PARSONS, TALCOTT
1942   The theoretical development of the sociology of religion. Journal of the History of Ideas 5:176–190.

PARSONS, T. AND E. A. SHILS
1951   Values, motives and systems of action. *In* Toward a general theory of action, Talcott Parsons and Edward A. Shils, eds. Cambridge, Harvard University Press.

PASSIN, HERBERT
  1942   Tarahumara prevarication: a prob-
          lem in field method. American An-
          thropologist 44:235–247.

PAUL, BENJAMIN D.
  1953   Interview techniques and field re-
          lationships. *In* Anthropology to-
          day, A. L. Kroeber, ed. Chicago,
          University of Chicago Press.

  1955   Health, culture and community.
          New York, Russell Sage Founda-
          tion.

PEARSON, C. H.
  1896   National life and character. Lon-
          don.

PEDERSEN, HOLGER
  1962   The discovery of language, trans-
          lated by John Webster Spargo.
          Bloomington, Indiana, Indiana Uni-
          versity Press. Originally published
          in 1931 as Linguistic science in the
          nineteenth century, Harvard Uni-
          versity Press.

PELUFFO, N.
  1962   Les notions de conservation et de
          causalite chex les enfants prove-
          nant de differents mileux physiques
          et socioculturels. Archives de psy-
          chologie 38:275–291.

PENDERGAST, DAVID M. AND CLEMENT W.
MEIGHAN
  1959   Folk traditions as historical fact:
          a Paiute example. Journal of
          American Folklore 72:128–133.

PHILLIPS, HERBERT P.
  1960   Problems of translation and mean-
          ing in field work. *In* Human or-
          ganization research, R. N. Adams
          and J. J. Preiss, eds. Homewood,
          Ill., Dorsey Press.

PIAGET, J.
  1962   The child's conception of number.
          London, Routledge and Kegan
          Paul.

PIDDINGTON, RALPH
  1957   Methods of field work. *In* An in-
          troduction to social anthropology.
          Edinburgh, Oliver and Boyd.

PIDDOCKE, STUART
  1965   The potlatch system of the South-
          ern Kwakiutl: a new perspective.
          Southwestern Journal of Anthro-
          pology 21:244–264.

PITTENGER, ROBERT E., EVERETT HOCKETT,
AND J. J. DANELY
  1960   The first five minutes: a sample of
          microscopic intensive analysis.
          Ithaca, Martineau.

POLANYI, KARL
  1959   Anthropology and economic the-
          ory. *In* Readings in anthropology
          II, Norton H. Fried, ed. New
          York, Crowell.

POLANYI, KARL, CONRAD M. ARENSBERG, AND
HARRY W. PEARSON (EDS.)
  1957   Trade and market in the early em-
          pires. Glencoe, Free Press.

POLYA, GEORGE
  1954   Mathematics and plausible reason-
          ing. Princeton, Princeton Univer-
          sity Press.

POPE, SAXTON T.
  1923   A study of bows and arrows.
          Berkeley, University of California
          Press (reprinted 1962).

PORTER, KENNETH W.
  1944   Seminole flight from Fort Marion.
          Florida   Historical   Quarterly
          22:112–133.

POSPISIL, LEOPOLD
  1956   The nature of law. Transactions
          of the New York Academy of Sci-
          ences Series II 18:746–755.

  1958a   Kapauku Papuans and their law.
          Yale University Publications in
          Anthropology No. 54. New
          Haven, Department of Anthropol-
          ogy, Yale University.

  1958b   Social change and primitive law:
          consequences of a Papuan legal
          case. American Anthropologist
          60:832–837.

  1958c   Kapauku Papuan political struc-
          ture. *In* Systems of political con-
          trol and bureaucracy in human so-

cieties, Verne F. Ray, ed. Seattle, American Ethnological Society.

1965   A formal analysis of substantive law: Kapauku Papuan laws of inheritance. American Anthropologist 67:166–185.

POST, RICHARD H.
1962   Population differences in vision acuity: a review, with speculative notes on selection relaxation. Eugenics Quarterly 9:189–212.

POWDERMAKER, HORTENSE
1966   Stranger and friend: the way of an anthropologist. New York, Norton.

POWELL, J. W.
1891   Indian linguistic families north of Mexico. Bureau of American Ethnology. Annual Report No. 7.

PRICE-WILLIAMS, D. R.
1961   A study concerning concepts of conservation of quantities among primitive children. Acta Psychologia 18:297–305.

PROPP, VLADIMIR
1958   Morphology of the folktale. International Journal of American Linguistics 24: No. 4, Part 3.

PUTNAM, PATRICK
1948   The Pygmies of the Ituri Forest. *In* A reader in general anthropology, Carleton Coon, ed. New York, Henry Holt and Co.

RADCLIFFE-BROWN, A. R.
1930   Applied anthropology. Reports. Australian and New Zealand and Society for the Advancement of Science: 1–14.

1935   On the concept of function in social science. American Anthropologist 37:394–402.

1940   On social structure. Journal of the Royal Anthropological Institute 70:1–12.

1950   Introduction. *In* African systems of kinship and marriage, A. R. Radcliffe-Brown and Daryll Forde,

eds. New York, Oxford University Press.

1952   Structure and function in primitive society: essays and addresses. Glencoe, Free Press.

RADIN, M.
1938   A restatement of Hohfeld. Harvard Law Review 51:1141–1164.

RADIN, PAUL
1915/16   The Winnebago tribe. Bureau of American Ethnology Annual Report 37, Smithsonian Institution.

1933   The method and theory of ethnology. New York, McGraw-Hill.

1954/56   The evolution of an American Indian prose epic: a study in comparative literature. Parts I and II. Basel, Ethnographical Museum.

RAGLAN, LORD
1956   The hero. New York, Random House, Vintage Books.

RANK, OTTO
1959   The myth of the birth of the hero. New York, Random House, Vintage Books.

RAPPAPORT, ROY A.
1963   Aspects of man's influence upon island ecosystems: alteration and control. *In* Man's place in the island ecosystem, F. R. Fosberg, ed. Honolulu, Bishop Museum Press.

RASMUSSEN, KNUD
1929   Report of the fifth Thul expedition, 1921–24, Vol. 7, no. 1. Intellectual culture of the Igluik Eskimos. Gyldendalske Boghandel, Nordisk Forlag.

RATTRAY, R. S.
1927   Religion and art in Ashanti. Oxford, Oxford University Press.

READ, KENNETH
1965   The high valley. New York: Scribner.

REDFIELD, ROBERT
1930   Tepoztlan: a Mexican village. Chicago, University of Chicago Press.

1936   Tepoztlan: a Mexican village. Chicago, University of Chicago Publications in Anthropology.

1941   The folk culture of Yucatan. Chicago, University of Chicago Press.

1953   The primitive world and its transformations. Ithaca, Cornell University Press.

1955   A combination of opposites, *and* Whole and parts. *In* The little community. Chicago, University of Chicago Press.

1956   Peasant society and culture. Chicago, University of Chicago Press, Phoenix Books (P53).

1960   The little community. Chicago, University of Chicago Press, Phoenix Books (P53).

REDFIELD, ROBERT, MELVILLE HERSKOVITS, AND GORDON EKHOLM
1959   Aspects of primitive art. New York, Museum of Primitive Art Lecture Series No. 1.

REDFIELD, ROBERT, RALPH LINTON, AND M. J. HERSKOVITS
1936   A memorandum on acculturation. American Anthropologist 38:149–152.

REICHARD, GLADYS A.
1947   An analysis of Coeur d'Alene myths. Philadelphia, American Folklore Society.

REINING, CONRAD C.
1962   A lost period of applied anthropology. American Anthropologist 64:593–600.

RICHARDS, AUDREY I.
1938   The village census in the study of culture contact. *In* Methods of study of culture contact in Africa, B. Malinowski, ed. New York, Oxford University Press.

RICHARDSON, JANE AND A. L. KROEBER
1940   Three centuries of women's dress fashions: a quantitative analysis. University of California, Anthropological Records 5:111–153.

RIESENBERG, S. H.
1948   Magic and medicine in Ponape. Southwestern Journal of Anthropology 4:406–429.

1949   Ponapean political and social organization. Washington, D.C., Pacific Science Board (typed).

1959   A Pacific voyager's hoax. Ethnohistory 6:238–264.

RITZENTHALER, ROBERT E. AND FREDERICK A. PETERSON
1956   The Mexican Kickapoo Indians. Milwaukee Public Museum Publications in Anthropology No. 2.

RIVERS, W. H. R.
1905   Observations on the senses of the Todas. British Journal of Psychology 1:321–396.

1910   The genealogical method of anthropological inquiry. The Sociological Review 3:1–12.

1924   Social organization. New York, Knopf.

ROBERTSON, J. B. W.
1956   Genealogies as a basis for Maori chronology. Journal of the Polynesian Society 65:45–54.

1962   The evaluation of Maori tribal tradition as history. Journal of the Polynesian Society 71:293–309.

ROGERS, EVERETT M.
1962   Diffusion of innovations. Glencoe, Free Press.

ROHEIM, GÉZA
1952   The gates of the dream. New York, International Universities Press.

ROMNEY, A. KIMBALL AND R. G. D'ANDRADE (EDS.)
1964   Transcultural studies in cognition. American Anthropologist 66:No. 3, Pt. 2. Special Publication.

ROWE, JOHN H.
1953   Technical aids in anthropology: a historical survey. *In* Anthropology today, A. L. Kroeber, ed. Chicago, University of Chicago Press.

1955   Time perspective in ethnography. Kroeber Anthropological Society Papers 12:55–61.

1965   The renaissance foundations of anthropology. American Anthropologist 67:1–20.

ROYAL ANTHROPOLOGICAL INSTITUTE OF GREAT BRITAIN AND IRELAND
1951   Notes and queries on anthropology, 6th ed. London, Routledge and Kegan Paul.

RUTTER, OWEN
1929   The pagans of North Borneo. London, Hutchinson.

RYCROFF, W. STANLEY
1946   Indians of the High Andes. New York, Committee on Cooperation in Latin America.

SAHLINS, MARSHALL D.
1958   Social stratification in Polynesia. Seattle, University of Washington Press.

1961   The segmentary lineage: an organization of predatory expansion. American Anthropologist 63:322–345.

1964   Culture and environment: the study of cultural ecology. *In* Tax 1964.

1965   On the sociology of primitive exchange. *In* The relevance of models for social anthropology, A. S. A. Monographs 1. New York, Praeger.

SAHLINS, MARSHALL D. AND ELMAN R. SERVICE (EDS.)
1960   Evolution and culture. Ann Arbor, University of Michigan Press.

SALISBURY, R. F.
1962   From stone to steel. Cambridge, Cambridge University Press.

SAPIR, EDWARD
1921   Language: an introduction to the study of speech. New York, Harcourt, Brace and Co.

1931   Custom. *In* Encyclopedia of the social sciences, Vol. 5. (Reprinted in Mandelbaum 1957.)

1933   The psychological reality of phonemes. *In* Mandelbaum 1957.

1949   Time perspective in aboriginal American culture: a study in method. *In* Mandelbaum 1957.

SAUSSURE, FERDINAND DE
1959   Course in general linguistics, translated by Wade Baskin. New York, Philosophical Library.

SAYCE, R. U.
1963   Primitive arts and crafts. New York: Biblo and Tannen.

SCHNEIDER, DAVID M. AND KATHLEEN GOUGH
1961   Matrilineal kinship. Berkeley and Los Angeles, University of California Press.

SCHNEIDER, HAROLD K.
1957   The subsistence role of cattle among the Pakot and in East Africa. American Anthropologist 59:278–299.

SCHNEIDER, LOUIS (ED.)
1964   Religion, culture and society. New York, Wiley.

SCHREIDER, EUGÈNE
1963   Physiological anthropology and climatic variations. *In* Environmental physiology and psychology in arid conditions. Proceedings of the Lucknow Symposium (1962), UNESCO, Paris.

1964   Ecological rules, body-heat regulation, and human evolution. Evolution 18:1–9.

SCHWARTZ, MORRIS AND CHARLOTTE
1955   Problems in participant observation. American Journal of Sociology 60:343–353.

SCHWARTZ, RICHARD D. AND JAMES C. MILLER
1964   Legal evolution and societal complexity. American Journal of Sociology 69:159–169.

SCOTT, JOHN PAUL
1958   Animal behavior. Chicago, University of Chicago Press.

SEARS, R.
1961   Transcultural variables and conceptual equivalence. *In* Kaplan 1961.

SECOY, FRANK RAYMOND
1953   Changing military patterns on the Great Plains (seventeenth century through early nineteenth century). Monographs of the American Ethnological Society 21.

SEGALL, M. H.
1963   Acquiescence and "identification with the aggressor" among acculturating Africans. Journal of Social Psychology 61:247–262.

SEGALL, M. H., D. T. CAMPBELL, AND M. J. HERSKOVITS
1963   Cultural differences in the perception of geometric illusions. Science 139:769–771.

1965   The influence of culture on visual perception. Indianapolis, Bobbs-Merrill.

SELIGMAN, C. G.
1932   Anthropological perspective and psychological theory. Journal of the Royal Anthropological Institute 62:193–228.

SELLERS, W.
1941   The production of films for primitive people. Oversea Education 13:221.

SELLTIZ, CLAIRE *et al.*
1960   Research methods in social relations. New York, Henry Holt.

SERVICE, ELMAN R.
1962   Primitive social organization: an evolutionary perspective. New York, Random House.

1966   The hunters. Englewood Cliffs, Prentice-Hall.

SHELDON, WALT
1965   The blue kimono. New York, Fawcett Publications.

SHILS, EDWARD A.
1959   Social inquiry and the autonomy of the individual. *In* The human meaning of the social sciences, D. Lerner, ed. New York, Meridian Books.

SIMMONS, L.
1942   Sun Chief: the autobiography of a Hopi Indian. New Haven, Yale University Press.

SIMPSON, GEORGE GAYLORD
1949   The meaning of evolution. A study of the history of life and of its significance for man. New Haven, Yale University Press.

1953   The major features of evolution. New York, Columbia University Press.

1958   The study of evolution: methods and present status of the theory. *In* Behavior and evolution, A. Roe and G. G. Simpson, eds. New Haven, Yale University Press.

1962   Comments on cultural evolution. *In* Evolution and man's progress, Hudson Hoagland and Ralph W. Burhoe, eds. New York, Columbia University Press.

1963   Biology and the nature of science. Science 139:81–88.

SINGER, CHARLES *et al.*
1954/58   A history of technology. New York, Oxford University Press.

SINGER, MILTON
1960   The great tradition of Hinduism in the city of Madras. *In* Leslie 1960. (Reprinted from Journal of American Folklore 71:347–388.)

1961   A survey of culture and personality theory and research. *In* Kaplan 1961.

SINGER, M. G.
1961   Generalization in ethics: an essay in the logic of ethics, with the rudiments of a system of moral philosophy, 1st. ed. New York, Knopf.

SLEDD, JAMES AND WILMA R. EBBITT
1962   Dictionaries and *that* dictionary. Chicago, Scott, Foresman and Co.

SLOTKIN, J. S. (ED.)
1965   Readings in early anthropology. Viking Fund Publications in Anthropology 40.

SMELSER, NEIL J.
1963   The sociology of economic life. Englewood Cliffs, Prentice-Hall.

SMITH, ALFRED G.
1964   The Dionysian innovation. American Anthropologist 66:251–265.

SMITH, M. BREWSTER
1954   Anthropology and psychology. *In* For a science of social man: convergences in anthropology, psychology and sociology, J. Gillin, ed. New York, Macmillan.

SMITH, MARIAN W. (ED.)
1961   The artist in tribal society. New York, Free Press of Glencoe.

SMITH, WATSON AND JOHN M. ROBERTS
1954   Zuni law. A field of values. Papers of the Peabody Museum of American Archaeology and Ethnology, Harvard University, Vol. 43, No. 1. Cambridge, Peabody Museum.

SMITH, WILLIAM ROBERTSON
1957   The religion of the Semites: the fundamental institutions. New York, World Publishing, Meridian Books (M14). (Originally published 1889.)

SNOW, JOEL ALAN AND ALVIN W. WOLFE
1964   Radioactivity in Arctic peoples. Scientist and Citizen 6:9–10, 26–33.

SOMMER, OTAKAR
1932   Prameny Soukremého Pràvo Rimského. Praha, Melantrich.
1933   Ucebnice Soukromèho Práva Rimskèho. Vol. I. Nákladem Vlastnim.

SONNENFELD, J.
1960   Changes in an Eskimo hunting technology, an introduction to implement geography. Association of American Geographers Annals, 50:172–186.

SOPHER, DAVID E.
1964   The swidden/wet-rice transition zone in the Chittagong Hills. Annals of the Association of American Geographers 54:107–126.

SPENCER, ROBERT F. (ED.)
1954   Method and perspective in anthropology. Minneapolis, University of Minnesota Press.

SPICER, EDWARD H.
1962   Cycles of conquest: the impact of Spain, Mexico and the United States on the Indians of the Southwest, 1533–1960. Tucson, University of Arizona Press.

SPICER, EDWARD H. (ED.)
1952   Human problems in technological change. New York, Russell Sage Foundation.

SPIER, ROBERT F. G.
1958   Tool acculturation among nineteenth-century California Chinese. Ethnohistory 5:97–117.

SPINDLER, GEORGE AND W. GOLDSCHMIDT
1952   Experimental design in the study of culture change. Southwestern Journal of Anthropology 8:68–82.

SPINDLER, GEORGE D. (ED.)
1963   Education and culture: anthropological approaches. New York, Holt, Rinehart and Winston.

SPIRO, MELFORD
1951   Culture and personality: the natural history of a false dichotomy. Psychiatry 13:189–204.
1961   Social systems, personality, and functional analysis. *In* Kaplan 1961.

SPOEHR, ALEXANDER
1942   Kinship system of the Seminole. Anthropological Series, Field Museum of Natural History, Vol. 33, No. 2.

SPRANGER, E.
1928   Types of men, P. J. W. Pigors, ed. Halle M. Niemeyer.

STEENHOVEN, GEERT VAN DEN
1962   Leadership and law among the Eskimos of the Keewatin District, Northwest Territories. The Hague, Uitgeverij Excelsior.

STEIN, MAURICE AND ARTHUR VIDICH (EDS.)
1963   Sociology on trial. Englewood Cliffs, Prentice-Hall.

STEPHENS, W. N.
1962   The oedipus complex: cross-cultural evidence. New York, Free Press of Glencoe.

STERN, THEODORE
1963   Ideal and expected behavior as seen in Klamath mythology. Journal of American Folklore 76:21–30.

STEWARD, JULIAN
1938   Basin-Plateau aboriginal sociopolitical groups. Bureau of American Ethnology Bulletin No. 120.

1949   Cultural causality and law: a trial formulation of the development of early civilizations. American Anthropologist 51:1–27.

1955   Theory of culture change. Urbana, University of Illinois Press.

STOCKING, GEORGE W., JR.
1963   Matthew Arnold, E. B. Tylor, and the uses of invention. American Anthropologist 65:783–799.

STONE, JULIUS
1950   The province and function of law. Cambridge, Harvard University Press.

STOTT, D. H.
1962   Cultural and natural checks on population growth. *In* Culture and the evolution of man, M. F. Ashley Montagu, ed. New York, Oxford University Press (Galaxy Books).

STREHLOW, THEODOR G. H.
1947   Aranda traditions. Carlton, Melbourne University Press.

STURTEVANT, EDGAR H.
1947   An introduction to linguistic science. New Haven, Yale University Press.

STURTEVANT, WILLIAM C.
1953   Chakaika and the "Spanish Indians": documentary sources compared with Seminole tradition. Tequesta 13:35–73.

1955   Notes on modern Seminole traditions of Osceola. Florida Historical Quarterly 33:206–217.

1960   The significance of ethnological similarities between southeastern North America and the Antilles. Yale University Publications in Anthropology 64.

1961   Taino agriculture. *In* The evolution of horticultural systems in native South America: causes and consequences; a symposium, Johannes Wilbert, ed. Anthropological Supplement Publication No. 2. Caracas.

1962   Spanish-Indian relations in southeastern North America. Ethnohistory 9:41–94.

1964   Studies in ethnoscience. *In* Transcultural studies in cognition, A. Kimball Romney and Roy Goodwin D'Andrade, eds. American Anthropologist 66, No. 3, Pt. 2.

SUTTLES, WAYNE
1960   Affinal ties, subsistence, and prestige among the Coast Salish. American Anthropologist 62:296–305.

SWANSON, GUY E.
1960   The birth of the gods: the origin of primitive beliefs. Ann Arbor, University of Michigan Press.

SWEET, LOUISE E.
1965a   Camel pastoralism in North Arabia and the minimal camping unit. *In* Leeds and Vayda 1965.

1965b   Camel raiding of North Arabian Bedouin: a mechanism of ecological adaptation. American Anthropologist 67:1132–1150.

TATHAM, GEORGE
1957   Environmentalism and possibilism. *In* Geography in the twentieth cen-

tury, 3rd ed., Griffith Taylor, ed. New York, Philosophical Library.

TAWNEY, R. H.
1962   Religion and the rise of capitalism. New York, Harcourt, Brace and Co.

TAX, SOL
1953   Penny capitalism: a Guatemalan Indian economy. Washington, Smithsonian Institution, Institute of Social Anthropology Publication 16.

1955a   Some problems of social organization. *In* Social anthropology of North American tribes, Fred Eggan, ed. Chicago, University of Chicago Press.

1955b   The social organization of the Fox Indians. *In* Social anthropology of North American tribes, Fred Eggan, ed. Chicago, University of Chicago Press.

1955c   From Lafitau to Radcliffe-Brown: a short history of the study of social organization. *In* Social organization of North American tribes, Fred Eggan, ed. Chicago, University of Chicago Press.

TAX, SOL (ED.)
1964   Horizons in anthropology. Chicago, Aldine.

TAYLOR, P. S.
1961   Normative discourse. Englewood Cliffs, Prentice-Hall.

TEMPELS, (Rev. Father) PLACIDE
1959   Bantu philosophy, translated by Colin King. Paris, Presence Africaine.

THOMAS, WILLIAM I. AND FLORIAN ZNANIECKI
1918   Methodological note. *In* The Polish peasant in Europe and America. New York, Knopf.

THOMPSON, LAURA
1941   Guam and its people: a study of culture change and colonial education. New York, Institute of Pacific Relations.

THOMPSON, STITH
1951   The folktale. New York, Dryden Press.

1955/58 Motif-index of folk-literature. 6 vols. Bloomington, Indiana University Press.

1961   The types of the folktale. Helsinki, Suomalainen Tiedeakatemia.

THOULESS, R. H.
1931   Phenomenal regression to the real object. British Journal of Psychology 21:339–359 and 22:1–30.

1933   A racial difference in perception. Journal of Social Psychology 4: 330–339.

THURNWALD, RICHARD C.
1932   Economics in primitive communities. London, Oxford University Press.

TIMASHEFF, N. S.
1938   Law as a social phenomenon. *In* Readings in jurisprudence, J. Hall, ed. Indianapolis, Bobbs-Merrill.

TITIEV, MISCHA
1944   Old Oraibi: a study of the Hopi Indians of Third Mesa. Papers of the Peabody Museum of American Archaeology and Ethnology, Harvard University Vol. 22, No. 1.

TOULMIN, STEPHEN
1960   Reason in ethics. New York, Cambridge University Press.

TRIANDIS, H. C.
1964   Cultural influences upon cognitive processes. *In* Advances in experimental social psychology, L. Berkowitz, ed. New York, Academic Press, Vol. 1, pp. 1–47.

TSCHOPIK, HARRY, JR.
1941   Navaho pottery making. Cambridge, Peabody Museum papers 17, Pt. 1.

TURNBULL, COLIN M.
1962   The forest people: a study of the pygmies of the Congo. Garden City, Doubleday.

TYLOR, EDWARD B.
1889   On a method of investigating the development of institutions. Journal of the Royal Anthropological Institute 18:245–69. (Reprinted in Moore 1961.)
1958   Primitive culture. 2 vols. New York, Harpers, Torchbook (TB33–4). (Originally published 1871.)

UDY, STANLEY
1959   Organization of work: a comparative analysis of production among non-industrial peoples. New Haven, Human Relations Area Files Press.

UNDERHILL, RUTH M.
1939   Social organization of the Papago Indians. Columbia University Contributions in Anthropology 30.

UNIVERSITY OF NOTTINGHAM
1954   The social background of delinquency. Nottingham, University of Nottingham.

USEEM, JOHN, JOHN D. DONOGUE, AND RUTH HILL USEEM
1963   Men in the middle of the Third Culture. Human Organization 22:169–179.

UTLEY, FRANCIS LEE
1961   Folk literature: an operational definition. Journal of American Folklore 74:193–206.

VALENTINE, C. A.
1963   Men of anger and men of shame: Lakalai ethnopsychology and its implications for sociopsychological theory. Ethnology 2(4):441–477.

VALK, MARK VAN DER
1939   An outline of modern Chinese law. Monuments Serica, Monograph II.

VAN NIEUWENHUIJZE, C. A. O.
1962   Society as process. The Hague, Mouton and Co.

VANSINA, JAN
1965   Oral tradition: a study in historical methodolgy, translated by H. M. Wright. Chicago, Aldine.

VAYDA, ANDREW P.
1961a   Expansion and warfare among swidden agriculturalists. American Anthropologist 63:345–358.
1961b   A re-examination of Northwest Coast economic systems. Transactions of the New York Academy of Sciences, 2d ser. 23:618–624.

VAYDA, A. P., A. LEEDS, AND D. B. SMITH
1961   The place of pigs in Melanesian subsistence. Proceedings of the 1961 Annual Spring Meeting of the American Ethnological Society, Viola E. Garfield, ed. Seattle, University of Washington Press.

VAYDA, ANDREW P. AND ROY A. RAPPAPORT
1963   Island cultures. *In* Man's place in the island ecosystem, F. R. Fosberg, ed. Honolulu, Bishop Museum Press.

VEBLEN, THORSTEIN
1957   Theory of the leisure class. New
(1899) York, Mentor Books. (Originally published 1899.)

VIDICH, ARTHUR J.
1955   Participant observation and the collection and interpretation of data. American Journal of Sociology 60:354–360.

VIDICH, ARTHUR J. AND J. BENSMAN
1960   The validity of field data. *In* Human organization research, R. N. Adams and J. J. Preiss, eds. Homewood, Ill., Dorsey Press.

VLADIMIRTSOV, B.
1948   Le régime social des Mongols; le féodalisme namade. Translated by Michel Carsow from the 1934 Russian original. Publications du Musée Guimet, Bibliothèque d'Études 52.

VOGET, FRED W.
1960   Man and culture: an essay in changing anthropological interpretation. American Anthropologist 62:943–65.

VOGT, EVON Z. AND THOMAS F. O'DEA
1953   A comparative study of the role of values in social action in two southwestern communities. American Sociological Review 18:645–654.

VON MERING, OTTO
1961   A grammar of human values. Pittsburgh, University of Pittsburgh Press.

WADDINGTON, C. H.
1960   The ethical animal. London, Allen and Unwin.

WAGLEY, CHARLES
1949   The social and religious life of a Guatemalan village. American Anthropological Association Memoir 71.

WAGNER, GUNTER
1949   The Bantu of North Kavirondo, Vol. 1. London, Oxford University Press.

WAGNER, PHILIP L.
1960   The human use of the earth. Glencoe, Free Press.

WALLACE, ANTHONY F. C.
1952   The modal personality of the Tuscarora Indians as revealed by the Rorschach test. Smithsonian Institution, Bureau of American Ethnology, Bulletin 150.

1956   Revitalization movements. American Anthropologist 58:264–281.

1961   Culture and personality. New York, Random House, Studies in Anthropology Series, No. 1

WALLACE, ANTHONY F. C. AND JOHN ATKINS
1960   The meaning of kinship terms. American Anthropologist 62.

WARNER, WILLIAM LLOYD
1959   The living and the dead: a study of the symbolic life of Americans. New Haven, Yale University Press.

1964   A black civilization: a social study of an Australian tribe, rev. ed. New York, Harper and Row, Harper Torchbooks.

WASHBURN, SHERWOOD L.
1960   Tools and human evolution. Scientific American 203:63–75.

WASHBURN, WILCOMB E.
1964   Manuscripts and manufacts. American Archivist 27:245–250.

WAX, MURRAY L. AND ROSALIE H.
1962   The magical world view. Journal for the Scientific Study of Religion 1:179–188.

1963   The notion of magic. Current Anthropology 4:495–518.

1964   Magic and monotheism. In New approaches to the study of religion, M. Spiro, ed. Annual Proceedings, American Ethnological Society.

WEBER, MAX
1930   The Protestant ethic and the spirit of capitalism. London.

1954   Law in economy and society, Max Rheinstein, ed. Cambridge, Harvard University Press.

1958a   From Max Weber: essays in sociology, translated by H. H. Gerth and C. W. Mills. New York, Oxford University Press.

1958b   The Protestant ethic and the spirit of capitalism, translated by T. Parsons. New York, The Scribner Library (SL21).

WEINER, J. S.
1964   Human ecology. In Human biology: an introduction to human evolution, variation and growth, G. A. Harrison et al. New York, Oxford University Press.

WEINREICH, URIEL
1963   Languages in contact: findings and problems. The Hague, Mouton and Co. (Originally published, 1953, by the Linguistic Circle of New York.)

WELLS, RULON S.
1947   Immediate constituents. Language 23:81–117. (Reprinted in Readings in linguistics, Martin Joos, (ed.) New York, American Council of Learned Societies.

WERNER, H.
1948   Comparative psychology of mental development. New York, International Universities Press.

1961   Comparative psychology of mental development, rev. ed. Chicago, Follett Publishing.

WHIFFEN, THOMAS
1915   The North-West Amazons: notes of some months spent among a cannibal tribe. London, Constable.

WHITE, LESLIE A.
1945   History, evolutionism, and functionalism: three types of interpretation of culture. Southwestern Journal of Anthropology 1:221–248.

1949   The science of culture. New York, Farrar, Straus. Also, Grove Press, Inc.

1959a   The evolution of culture. New York, McGraw-Hill.

1959b   The concept of culture. American Anthropologist 61:227–251.

1963   The ethnography and ethnology of Franz Boas. Bulletin of the Texas Memorial Museum No. 6.

1965   Anthropology 1964: retrospect and prospect. American Anthropologist 67:629–637.

WHITING, BEATRICE B.
1950   A cross-cultural study of sorcery and social control. *In* Paiute sorcery, B. B. Whiting. Viking Fund Publications in Anthropology 15: 82–91.

WHITING, BEATRICE B. (ED.)
1963   Six cultures: studies of child rearing. New York and London, Wiley.

WHITING, JOHN W. M.
1954   The cross-cultural method. *In* Handbook of social psychology, Gardner Lindzey, ed., vol. 1. Cambridge, Addison-Wesley. (Reprinted in Moore 1961.)

1961   Socialization process and personality. *In* Psychological anthropology: approaches to culture and personality, F. L. K. Hsu, ed. Homewood, Ill., Dorsey Press.

WHITING, J. W. M. AND I. L. CHILD
1953   Child training and personality. New Haven, Yale University Press.

WHITING, J. W. M., RICHARD KLUCKHOHN, AND ALBERT ANTHONY
1958   The function of male initiation ceremonies at puberty. *In* Readings in social psychology, E. Maccoby, T. M. Newcomb, and E. L. Hartley, eds. New York, Holt, Rinehart and Winston.

WHORF, BENJAMIN LEE
1956a   Language, thought, and reality. Selected writings of Benjamin Lee Whorf, John B. Carroll, ed. Cambridge and New York, The Technology Press of Massachusetts Institute of Technology and John Wiley.

1956b   Science and linguistics. *In* Whorf 1956a.

WHYTE, WILLIAM F.
1955   Appendix. *In* Street corner society, 2nd ed. Chicago, University of Chicago Press.

WHYTE, WILLIAM F. *et al.*
1958/59 Freedom and responsibility in research: the 'Springdale Case.' Human Organization 17 (Summer) 1–2; 17 (Winter) 2–7; 18 (Summer) 49–52. Cf. A. J. Vidich and J. Bensman, Small town in mass society. Garden City, Doubleday, 1960.

WILBERT, JOHANNES (ED.)
1961   The evolution of horticultural systems in native South America: causes and consequences. Anthropologica Supplement Publication No. 2. Caracas.

WILLIAMS, ROBIN M., JR.
1963   American society, a sociological interpretation, 2nd ed. New York, Knopf.

WINANS, EDGAR V. AND ROBERT B. EDGERTON
1964   Hehe magical justice. American Anthropologist 66:745–746.

WINDELS, FERNAND
1950   The Lascaux Cave paintings. New York, Viking.

WINGERT, PAUL S.
1950   The sculpture of Negro Africa. New York, Columbia University Press.

1962   Primitive art. New York, Oxford University Press.

WINTRINGER, G.
1955   Considérations sur l'intelligence du noir africain. Revue de psychologie des peuples 10:37–55.

WISSLER, CLARK
1917   The American Indian. New York, Douglas C. McMurtrie.

1926   The relation of man to nature in aboriginal North America. New York, D. Appleton.

WITTFOGEL, KARL A.
1957   Oriental despotism: a comparative study of total power. New Haven, Yale University Press.

WITTKOWER, E. E., H. B. MURPHY, J. FRIED, AND H. ELLENBERGER
1960   Cross-cultural enquiry into the symptomatology of schizophrenia. Annals of the New York Academy of Sciences 84:854–863.

WOLF, ERIC R.
1964   The study of evolution. In Horizons of anthropology, Sol Tax, ed. Chicago, Aldine Publishing.

1966   Peasants Englewood Cliffs. Prentice-Hall.

WOLFRAM, SYBIL
1961   Le mariage entre alliés dans l'Angleterre contemporaine. l'Homme 1:47–71.

WRIGHT, ARTHUR F.
1963   On the uses of generalization in the study of Chinese history. In Generalization in the writing of history, a report of the Committee on Historical Analysis of the Social Science Research Council, Louis Gottschalk, ed. Chicago, University of Chicago Press.

WUNDT, W.
1900/20 Volkerpsychologie: eine untersuchung der entwicklungs gesetze von sprache, mythus und sitte. Vols. 1–10. Leipzig, Engelmann. Trans. (vols. 1–3) Elements of folk psychology. New York, Macmillan, 1916.

WYNNE-EDWARDS, V. C.
1959   The control of population-density through social behavior: a hypothesis. Ibis 101:436–441.

1962   Animal dispersion in relation to social behavior. Edinburgh, Oliver and Boyd.

1965   Self-regulating systems in populations of animals. Science 147:1543–1548.

YOUNG, FRANK W.
1965   Initiation ceremonies: a cross-cultural study of status dramatization. Indianapolis, Bobbs-Merrill.

ZAKE, S. J. L.
1962   Approaches to the study of legal systems in nonliterate societies. Doctoral dissertation. Evanston, Ill., Northwestern University.

ZEUNER, FREDERICK E.
1963   A history of domesticated animals. New York, Harper and Row.

ZINK, S.
1962   The concepts of ethics. London, Macmillan; New York, St. Martin's Press.

ZUIDEMA, R. T.
1962   Reflections on Inca historical conceptions. Akten des 34. Internationalen Amerikanistenkongresses: 718–721. Vienna.

1964   The ceque system of Cuzco: the social organization of the capital of the Inca. International Archives of Ethnography Supplement to Vol. 50.

Index

A

Aarne, Antti, 124
Aberle, David F., 447, 448, 499
Abraham, K., 323, 499
Abstract behavior, non-Western, 314, 518, 523. *See also* Primitive mentality
Acculturation, 292–294, 303, 500–502, 508, 515, 529; and aggression, 333–334; defined, 292; early use of the term, 282; tools, 155–156, 532. *See also* Culture change; Culture contact
Ackerknecht, Erwin H., 404, 499
Action, theory of, 518, 526
Adams, 424, 443
Adaptation. *See* Cultural adaptation; Ecological adaptation; Environmental adaptation
Adcock, C. J., 310, 499
Adorno, T. W., 325, 499
Africa: acculturation, 334, 531; Apartheid, 22; ethnohistory, 474–475; gene distribution in, 521; health and disease, 504; historical reconstruction, 523; histories of, 462; intelligence in, 502, 506, 538; kinship and marriage, 528; law, 516; markets in, 503; metallurgy, 93, 94, 97–99, 101; migrations, 491–492; national level culture, 47; neuropsychological study in, 524; political systems, 511; sculpture, 91–101, 516, 538; tales, 120; tribal life, 518; utilitarian art, 99–101; witchcraft, 387, 491–492, 509, 513, 524, 525
Age categories, 171–172, 509
Aggression: evidence in acculturation, 333–334; transcultural indices of, 309
Agriculture, 140–142, 190, 503, 509, 512; Chimbu, 54; intensive, 496; shifting, 141, 506; Southwestern Indian, 479–480; subsistence, 136–143, 159, 190, 505, 530, 535; swidden, 458–459, 508, 532, 535. *See also* Horticultural systems; Horticulture
Aiken, H. D., 257n, 499
Albert, Ethel M., 259–261, 265n, 465, 499
Albino, R. C., 320, 499
Alcohol consumption, studies of, 447, 505

Alexandre, P., 499
Algonkian Indians: ecological adaptation, 514; historical evidence on, 459; hunting territories, 514, 519; particularism, 461, 516; reconstructed vocabulary, 471; social organization, 504. *See also* Indians, North American
Alland, Alexander, Jr., 499
Allee, W. C., 477–478, 494, 499
Allport, Gordon, 306, 307, 322, 330, 341, 499
Alor, 508; eschatological beliefs, 408, 413; modal personality, 324, 327
Altamira cave paintings, 107, 110
Amazon Indians, 537
American culture, 500, 521, 537; equality premise, 253–254, 255; folk history, 462; folklore, Asiatic influences on, 515; kinship system, 167–168, 180; religion in, 502
Anastasi, A., 309, 500
Anderson, Charles Roberts, 459, 500
Angell, R., 330, 514
Angulo, Jaime de, 237–238, 500
Animals: aggregations, 499; behavior, 530; dispersion, 538; domestication, 469, 496, 508, 538; ecology, 478–479, 499; husbandry, 142–143; role in human ecological adjustments, 520; sacralization, 495; sacred cow myth, 515; transport, 147–148
Anthony, Albert, 437
Anthropologists, 370, 528; solidarity of, 4, 43
Anthropology, 518, 519, 523; applied, 7–10, 301–302, 528, 529; changing interpretation, 535; history of, 47, 461; method and perspective, 532; natural history approach, 13, 447, 478; objectivity in, 522; psychological (*see* Psychological anthropology); scientific versus humanistic approach to, 10, 368–369; social (*see* Social anthropology)
Antilles, ethnological comparison, 533
Apa Tanis, 512
Apache: eschatological beliefs, 408, 412; lifeway, 338, 526
Arabia: black tent, 145; child study, 524
Aranda traditions, 533

V

Valentine, C. A., 308, 535

Valk, Mark van der, 212–213, 535

Value orientations, 257–259, 264, 332, 518–519; and behavior, 261–262; causal relation to economic behavior, 188; contrasted to value system, 260–261; Mormon and Texan compared, 261–262; time, 333; as value premises, 259

Value premises, 259–260, 264

Value system, 259–261; validation of, 269

Valued and disvalued entities, 260, 265

Value-free social science, 270–271

Values, 509, 515–516, 518; through acts of selection, 246; and attitudes, primitive, 188, 198; analytical study of, 256–257; basic, 259; and behavior, 261–264; and choice, 248–249, 267; in class structure, 262–263; classification of, 499; and concepts of directives and character, 260; cultural identification of, 256; and disvalue, 260, 265; existence in actions, 255–256; fatalistic attitude, 188, 198; focal, 260; grammar of, 536; hierarchical ordering of, 259–260; in an industrial boom-town, 198; justification of judgments of, 257; negative, 265–266; objectivity in investigation of, 270–271; as penultimate ends, 267; and personality, 326; philosophical study of, 256–257; problems of definition, 264–267; and the recurrent theme, 326–327; role in social action, 536; social psychological, 332–333; sociological study of, 256–257, 261–264; and striving towards consistency, 249, 253–254; study of, defined, 250; result of task experience, 188, 503; use of the word, 246, 255

Van Nieuwenhuijze, C. A. O., 13, 39, 535

Vansina, Jan, 128, 464, 474, 535

Vasilika, 512

Vayda, Andrew, 9, 486–488, 492, 494, 495, 497, 520, 535

Veblen, Thorstein, 162, 535

"Venuses," 107–108

Verstehen, 231, 235

Vidich, A., 272, 372, 533, 535

Virginia deer, 516

Vision acuity, 528

Vision Quest, Plains Indian, 230, 282

Visual illusions, 306, 311–313, 499, 514, 518, 531

Vladimirtsov, B., 458, 535

Voget, Fred W., 38, 535

Vogt, Evon Z., 242, 261–263, 520, 536

von Mering, Otto, 265, 536

W

Waddington, C. H., 257n, 272, 536

Wagley, Charles, 409, 413, 536

Wagner, Gunter, 408, 536

Wagner, Philip L., 490, 536

Wakashan tribal art. *See* Indian art, Northwest Coast

Walbiri, 202, 523

Walker, Deward E., Jr., 451n

Wallace, Anthony F. C., 23, 35, 180n, 282, 328, 335, 536

Warner, William Lloyd, 230, 438, 536

Washburn, Sherwood L., 493, 536

Washburn, Wilcomb E., 451n, 459, 536

Watercraft, 148–150

Wax, Murray L. and Rosalie H., 235, 236, 239, 242, 536

"Way of life," 247

Wealth, 501

Weapons: hunting, 137–139; interchangeability with the tool, 134

Weaving, 101

Weber, Max, 188, 225, 227, 228, 235, 239, 242, 261, 536

Weiner, J. S., 488, 497, 536

Weinreich, Uriel, 75, 536

Welch, Andrew, 458

Wells, Rulon S., 536

Werner, H., 305, 537

Wheelbarrow, Chinese, 147

Wheeled transportation, 148

Whiffen, Thomas, 412, 537

White, John, 459, 517

White, Leslie A., 10, 38, 39, 46, 132, 279, 284, 303, 461, 497, 537

Whiting, B., 308, 448, 537

Whiting, J. W. M., 16, 308, 331, 377, 388n, 400, 404, 406, 416, 447, 537

Whorf, Benjamin Lee 52, 366, 445, 537

Whyte, W. F., 340, 372, 373, 507, 537

Wilbert, Johannes, 496, 537

Wildcat escape, 458